GOVERNMENT INTERVENTION IN AGRICULTURE

IAAE Occasional Paper No. 5

Government Intervention in Agriculture

Cause and Effect

Edited by
Bruce Greenshields
and Margot Bellamy

Published by
Dartmouth Publishing Company Limited
Gower House
Croft Road
Aldershot
Hants GU11 3HR
UK

Gower Publishing Company
Old Post Road
Brookfield
Vermont 05036
USA

British Library Cataloguing in Publication Data
Government intervention in agriculture; cause and effect
(IAAE Occasional Paper No. 5)
1. Agricultural economics.
I. Greenshields, Bruce L. II. Bellamy, Margot A. III. International Association of Agricultural Economists.
IV. Series.
338.1

ISBN 1 85521 004 5

Printed and Bound in Great Britain by
Athenaeum Press Ltd., Newcastle upon Tyne.

Contents

Foreword

This book is the fifth in the IAAE *Occasional Paper* series. It contains the 45 contributed papers—together with the discussion opening and summary of the general discussion of each—presented at the Twentieth International Conference of Agricultural Economists, Buenos Aires, Argentina, 24–31 August 1988. A companion publication from that conference—*Agriculture and Governments in an Interdependent World*—contains the invited papers presented at the conference.

The contributed papers were refereed using a blind review process, and the acceptance rate for presentation in contributed paper sessions and publication in full in this series was 15 percent. The referees, representing 11 countries and 6 continents, were Ian Behrmann (RSA), André Brun (France), David Colman (UK), Murray Hawkins (Canada), Wilhelm Henrichsmeyer (FRG), Nurul Islam (Bangladesh), Arne Larsen (Denmark), Nora Lustig (Mexico), William Martin (Australia), Marc Nerlove (USA), Hiroyuki Nishimura (Japan), George Ryland (Australia), Bernard Stanton (USA), Stephen Thompson (Canada), and Kelley White (USA).

The International Association of Agricultural Economists is grateful to these referees for their efforts in reviewing the papers, to Bruce Greenshields for organizing the review process and the contributed paper sessions, to Bruce Greenshields and Margot Bellamy for editing this volume, to Patty Beavers and Verla Rape for their production and editorial assistance, and to the Economic Research Service of the US Department of Agriculture for its support of this part of the Association's activities.

The views expressed herein are not necessarily those of the IAAE or of the institutions with which the contributors or editors are connected.

Allen Maunder
Editor, IAAE

IAAE Occasional Paper Series

No. 1—*Papers on Current Agricultural Economic Issues*

No. 2—*Rural Challenge*

No. 3—*Rural Development: Growth and Inequity*

No. 4—*Agriculture and Economic Instability*

No. 5—*Government Intervention in Agriculture: Cause and Effect*

Argentine Agricultural Structure and Policy Implications

Lilyan E. Fulginiti and Richard K. Perrin[1]

Abstract: This paper uses 1940-80 time-series data and a multiproduct, multiinput aggregate translog profit function to estimate the structure of Argentine agricultural technology. Estimates of own-price supply elasticity ranged between 0 and 1.5, and derived demand elasticities were between -1 and -2. Given the authors' estimates of price wedges due to currency overvaluation, trade restrictions, and domestic taxes, the implications of eliminating any one of these policy-induced wedges would be to increase production of the various agricultural commodities from as little as 5 percent to as much as 100 percent.

Introduction

Argentine agricultural output grew at a rate of about 1.4 percent per year between 1940 and 1972 (Cavallo and Mundlak, 1982), which is sluggish, given earlier rates of 1.8 percent during 1908-20 and 2.2 percent during 1920-40 (Schultz, 1956). It is also sluggish relative to growth in US agricultural output of 2.0 percent during the same period. Adjusting for factor use, total factor productivity in Argentine agriculture grew at a rate of only 0.6 percent during 1940-72, compared to 2.0 percent for the USA and 1.2 percent in the rest of the Argentine economy during the same period. Other studies have suggested that price and tax policies contributed to this sluggish growth. The purpose of this study is to provide further information on the effects of these policies on the production of various agricultural commodities.

The approach of this study is to specify and estimate a multiinput, multioutput model of the Argentine agricultural sector, so that the results can be used to examine the effects of price and tax policies in a comparative static framework. This model is developed using applied duality theory in a manner similar to previous studies of aggregate agricultural technology by Antle (1984), Lopez (1984), Shumway (1983), and Weaver (1983).

Estimation of the Structure

Model

The producer's variable profit function may be defined as:

$$(1)\ \pi(p, r; z) \equiv \max_{xy}\{py-rx; (y, x; z) \in T\},$$

where p is a vector of m output prices, r is a vector of n input prices, y is a vector of m output quantities, x is a vector of n input quantities, z is a vector of l fixed factors, and T is a closed, bounded, smooth, and strictly convex set of all feasible combinations of inputs and outputs; i.e., a production possibility set. In addition, technology is assumed to exhibit constant returns to scale. The profit function *(1)* is assumed to be convex, linearly homogeneous, and monotonic in prices. For this study of Argentine agriculture, a translog specification is used, which is a flexible functional form in the sense that it provides a local second-order approximation to any arbitrary functional form:

$$(2)\ \tilde{\pi} = \alpha_0 + \alpha\tilde{d} + \{(\tilde{d}'\beta\tilde{d})/2\}, \text{ where } \tilde{\pi} = \ln\pi, \text{ and } \tilde{d} = \begin{bmatrix}\tilde{p}\\ \tilde{r}\\ \tilde{z}\end{bmatrix} = \begin{bmatrix}\ln p\\ \ln r\\ \ln z\end{bmatrix}.$$

Differentiating the profit function and invoking Hotelling's lemma yields a system of share equations:

$$(3)\quad \begin{aligned} M_i^* &= \alpha_i + \sum_{j=1}^{m} \beta_{ij}\, \tilde{p}_j + \sum_{k=1}^{n} \beta_{ik}\, \tilde{r}_k + \sum_{r=1}^{l} \beta_{ir}\, \tilde{z}_r;\ \forall\ i=1, ..., m; \\ -M_h^* &= \alpha_h + \sum_{j=1}^{m} \beta_{hj}\, \tilde{p}_j + \sum_{k=1}^{n} \beta_{hk}\, \tilde{r}_k + \sum_{r=1}^{l} \beta_{hr}\, \tilde{z}_r;\ \forall\ h=1, ..., n; \end{aligned}$$

where M_i^* is the share of profit accounted for by revenues for the *i*th output and M_h^* is the share of profit accounted for by expenses for the *h*th input. In more compact notation, *(3)* can be expressed as:

$$(4)\quad M = \alpha + \beta\tilde{d},$$

where M is a column vector consisting of output shares and the negative of input shares.

Data

Parameters of the Argentine agricultural supply and factor demand structure *(4)* are estimated using time series data for 1940-80. The seven aggregate output categories used are wheat, maize, grain sorghum, sunflower, linseed, soyabeans, and beef. The three variable input aggregates are labour (number in the labour force), capital (current value times imputed rate of return to capital), and an aggregate index of fertilizers, seeds, and chemicals. The inputs considered fixed within the annual observation interval are land and precipitation in the crop-producing region of the Pampas. A time trend was included as an index of technical change. All prices and values were deflated to 1960 pesos.[2] The six crops in this study used 93.5 percent of nonforage crop acreage planted in the first five years of the data period and 89.3 percent in the final five years. Including fruits and vegetables plus industrial commodities such as sugar, cotton, and tobacco in the value of agricultural production, the seven commodities here constitute about 60 percent of the value of all output.

Estimation

In order to estimate the parameters of the profit function, a stochastic structure must be assumed for the equation system *(4)*. Any deviations of the observed output supply and input demand quantities from their profit maximizing levels are hypothesized to be caused by random errors in optimization. The disturbances are assumed to be additive and normally distributed with zero means and a positive semidefinite variance-covariance matrix.

The estimation procedure used is Zellner's seemingly unrelated regression technique. Contemporaneous correlation of the residuals in different equations is plausible and can therefore be exploited by the technique. Given the large number of parameters, the system of equations was not estimated using the iterative seemingly unrelated regression method because the likelihood function tends to be unstable. The equations were restricted to satisfy the symmetry and homogeneity conditions. Of the 85 independent parameter estimates (Table 1), 13 are significant at the 1-percent level, and 26 at the 5-percent level. A check of the regularity conditions shows that monotonicity does not hold; i.e., not all predicted shares are positive. Tests also failed to support the hypotheses of symmetry, homogeneity, and homotheticity.

Table 1-Parameter Estimates Restricted for Symmetry and Homogeneity*

Dependent Variable	Intercept	Price of: Beef	Wheat	Maize	Sunflower	Linseed	Soyabean	Sorghum	Capital	Labour	Others	Land	Rain	Time
Beef	6.432	1.165	-0.837	-0.410	-0.136	-0.099	-0.012	-0.133	0.099	0.266	0.098	0.0658	-0.0093	-0.057
	(2.51)	(0.344)	(0.217)	(0.115)	(0.093)	(0.068)	(0.040)	(0.069)	(0.291)	(0.171)	(0.086)	(0.122)	(0.179)	(0.089)
Wheat	0.466		1.307	-0.477	-0.034	-0.119	0.028	-0.179	0.174	-0.034	0.171	0.208	-0.202	0.006
	(1.97)		(0.206)	(0.087)	(0.066)	(0.040)	(0.037)	(0.043)	(0.223)	(0.130)	(0.069)	(0.094)	(0.140)	(0.071)
Maize	-1.446			0.884	-0.108	-0.038	0.004	0.012	0.093	0.002	0.038	-0.015	0.297	-0.282
	(0.958)			(0.077)	(0.043)	(0.029)	(0.022)	(0.030)	(0.102)	(.058)	(0.035)	(0.041)	(0.063)	(0.035)
Sunflower	-0.983				0.279	0.038	-0.009	0.006	-0.091	0.037	0.016	0.033	-0.045	0.012
	(0.656)				(0.044)	(0.024)	(0.015)	(0.025)	(0.074)	(0.048)	(0.024)	(0.031)	(0.046)	(0.024)
Linseed	-0.338					0.089	0.013	0.007	0.045	0.062	0.002	0.016	0.066	-0.094
Soyabean	-0.359						0.050	0.010	-0.059	-0.009	-0.017	0.021	-0.045	0.024
	(0.326)						(0.012)	(0.011)	(.036)	(0.021)	(0.013)	(0.016)	(0.023)	(0.013)
Sorghum	-0.153							0.240	-0.007	0.004	0.041	-0.046	0.030	0.016
	(0.373)							(0.034)	(0.038)	(0.033)	(0.017)	(0.018)	(0.024)	(0.014)
Capital	-1.050								-0.099	0.001	-0.155	-0.164	-0.108	0.272
	(2.967)								(0.346)	(0.192)	(0.096)	(0.140)	(0.211)	(0.104)
Labour	0.380									-0.224	-0.105	-0.095	-0.030	0.125
	(1.65)									(0.115)	(0.054)	(0.079)	(0.118)	(0.059)
Others	-1.949										-0.089	-0.024	0.046	-0.022
	(0.856)										(0.034)	(0.040)	(0.061)	(0.031)

*Standard errors in parentheses.

Elasticity Estimates

While the structure of equation *(4)*, as estimated above, can be used to evaluate the effects of prices and fixed factors on the *mix* (shares) of outputs and inputs, elasticities must be derived to evaluate their effects on the levels of outputs and inputs. The elasticities can be obtained by differentiation of the share equations.[3] Table 2 shows the own- and cross-price elasticities calculated in this manner from the Table 1 parameter estimates, using the mean value of shares.

Table 2-Estimated Own- and Cross-Price Elasticities

Quantity of:	Price of: Beef	Wheat	Maize	Sunflower	Linseed	Soyabean	Sorghum	Capital	Labour	Others
Beef	1.17	0.10	0.08	0.03	0.02	0.02	-0.02	-0.95	-0.26	-0.20
Wheat	0.15	1.42	-0.15	0.10	-0.04	0.07	-0.12	-0.82	-0.53	-0.07
Maize	0.22	-0.29	1.48	-0.11	0.02	0.04	0.12	-0.82	-0.48	-0.19
Sunflower	0.22	0.58	-0.33	1.10	0.38	-0.03	0.14	-1.67	-0.23	-0.17
Linseed	0.27	-0.26	0.08	0.49	-0.08	0.15	0.16	-0.62	0.08	-0.27
Soyabean	0.78	1.75	0.57	-0.14	0.54	0.66	0.42	-2.96	-0.78	-0.85
Sorghum	-0.19	-1.03	0.55	0.21	0.18	0.13	1.56	-1.11	-0.44	0.14
Capital	1.08	0.65	0.34	0.23	0.07	0.09	0.10	-1.94	-0.49	-0.13
Labour	0.63	0.89	0.43	0.07	-0.02	0.05	0.09	-1.03	-1.03	-0.07
Others	0.83	0.21	0.29	0.08	0.10	0.09	-0.05	-0.48	-0.12	-0.97

On the supply side, own-price elasticities fall between 0.7 and 1.5 except for linseed, implying a high degree of responsiveness to price. Outputs exhibit a substantial degree of complementarity, with 15 of the 21 cross-supply elasticities being positive. This result is intuitively plausible, as in this model a price increase for one commodity can stimulate additional purchases of variable inputs used jointly in the production of other commodities. Overall, the elasticities of output supply with respect to output prices indicate a considerable degree of flexibility exists in the choice of the output mix, even in the short run. The production of the various commodities is most responsive to the price of capital services (elasticities of -0.6 to -3.0), next most responsive to wages (elasticities of -0.1 to -0.8), and least responsive to the price of other inputs (elasticities of -0.1 to -0.8). These results support the hypothesis that the agricultural sector would be substantially affected by policies such as credit subsidies and wage controls.

In general, own-price elasticities are higher than results obtained by Weaver (1983) for the Dakotas, Antle (1984) for the USA, and Shumway (1983) for Texas. Antle's multiproduct model for Egypt produced higher supply and input demand elasticities than the ones presented in this study, but it was based on a cross section of firms rather than the aggregate economy. Weaver's results implied complementarity among all outputs and among all inputs. Results are not as conclusive for the studies of Texas and the USA. Antle's estimates for Egypt indicate complementarity in input and output space.

Own-price elasticities for input choice are about -1 for labour and "other inputs," and -2 for capital. Negative cross elasticities were obtained in all cases, as in Weaver. From the perspective of a multioutput, multiinput technology, these results are consistent with limited substitution possibilities among inputs. Elasticities of virtually all variable inputs with respect to output prices are positive.

Implications for Policy Effects on Argentine Agriculture

In this section, prices are assumed to be exogenous to the agricultural sector.[4] Therefore, the price wedges created by various policies can be characterized as simply exogenous price changes within the structure estimated above. Given an estimate of the price effect of a policy, equation *(4)* is then used with the coefficients of Table 1 to evaluate the effects of the policy on the mix (shares) of inputs and outputs. To evaluate effects on the levels of inputs and outputs, a similar linear elasticity model is used:

$$(5)\quad \delta \begin{bmatrix} \ln y \\ \ln x \end{bmatrix} = \Sigma\, \delta \begin{bmatrix} \ln p \\ \ln r \end{bmatrix},$$

where Σ is the 10×10 matrix of price elasticities from Table 2. The use of this linear elasticity model introduces a considerable approximation error with large price shifts if the true model is one of constant elasticity supply and derived demand equations. However, since only crude estimates of the sizes of the price changes can be obtained, the approximation seems appropriate.

Estimates of Policy Price Wedges

Previous studies by Reca (1980), Cavallo and Mundlak (1982), and Mielke (1984) identify relevant policies and provide information about their price effects. The general effect of these policies has been to tax agriculture very heavily, but the types and sizes of the interventions have tended to be erratic, as the various political factions in the country have wrested control from one another over the past four decades. Hence, for this study, the nature of the interventions are summarized and price wedges that seem to be representative of the period are rather arbitrarily specified (Table 3).

The most significant interventions have been those related to trade, in the form of exchange rate controls, export taxes and restrictions on imports of agricultural inputs. A recent unpublished World Bank study estimated that overvaluation averaged 18 percent during 1960-80, which is lower than the estimates by Reca and Cavallo and Mundlak. Export taxes on the commodities included here have varied from no tax to 56 percent for grains and 30 percent for beef. Cavallo and Mundlak's study shows an average export tax on all agriculture of 29 percent during 1940-73. Examination of the time path of these taxes (Mielke, p. 19) suggests that figures of 10 percent for beef, 15 percent for soyabeans, and 25 percent for other commodities are representative but still low estimates of the increases in prices if these export taxes were repealed. Finally, from discussions in Mielke and Reca, elimination of import taxes and import restrictions would decrease prices of

Table 3—Estimated Changes in Prices Faced by Farmers Due to Elimination of Policies

Commodity	Export Tax	Import Restrictions	Overvalued Currency	Domestic Taxes	Minimum Wages
	Percent				
Beef	10	0	18	0	0
Wheat	25	0	18	0	0
Maize	25	0	18	0	0
Sunflower	25	0	18	0	0
Linseed	25	0	18	0	0
Soyabean	15	0	18	0	0
Sorghum	25	0	18	0	0
Capital	0	-26	18	-18	0
Labour	0	0	0	-13	-10
Others	0	-26	18	-18	0

capital goods and other inputs (fertilizer, seed, and chemicals) by 26 percent.

Domestic policies of significance include the social security tax on labour, which raised wages by 13 percent (Reca indicates that this figure had risen to 40 percent by 1980); the minimum wage, which raised wages by 10 percent; and value-added taxes on capital and other inputs (Mielke, p. 9), estimated to be 18 percent.

Effects of Policies on Inputs and Outputs

The estimated price wedges associated with each of the policies identified above are summarized in Table 3. Not all of them were in effect in a given year, but most of the policies were in effect for much of the historical period. To obtain an estimate of their net impact on agriculture, the impact of eliminating all these wedges simultaneously is estimated by the use of equations *(4)* and *(5)*, using the average values of the variables during 1940-80 as a base.

The use of equation *(4)* yields changes in profit shares. Profit shares can be easily converted to the more useful concepts of revenue shares (outputs) and cost shares (inputs). The changes in these shares associated with the price policy wedges are reported in Table 4. Elimination of the wedges would reduce the relative size of the beef industry. Although these policies have held beef prices lower than world levels, grain prices were even more severely reduced (beef producers were apparently more successful in influencing the government than crop producers). As a result, elimination of all price wedges would reduce the relative size of the beef industry and increase that of each of the crops.

Table 4—Effects of Combined Interventions on Average Shares

	Profit Shares		Revenue/Cost Shares	
	Actual	without Intervention	Actual	without Intervention
Outputs:				
Beef	1.17	0.69	0.42	0.31
Wheat	0.82	0.73	0.29	0.33
Maize	0.43	0.40	0.15	0.18
Sunflower	0.14	0.19	0.05	0.09
Linseed	0.11	0.05	0.04	0.02
Soyabean	0.03	0.09	0.01	0.04
Sorghum	0.10	0.09	0.03	0.04
Inputs:				
Capital	-1.03	-0.87	0.57	0.70
Labour	-0.49	-0.31	0.27	0.25
Others	-0.28	-0.06	0.16	0.05

Elimination of all these wedges would decrease the price of capital and "other inputs" by 26 percent and labour by 23 percent. However, given the high elasticity of demand for capital (about -2), capital would rise in its share of costs. The interventions have also increased the prices of labour and other inputs, but, given their lower elasticities of demand, the elimination of the wedges would result in a relative decrease in their share of costs.

The elasticities of Table 2 are used with equation *(5)* to estimate the quantity effects of selected policies. The effect of currency devaluation (elimination of the exchange rate controls in Table 3) would have been to increase beef production by 5 percent, soyabean production by 14 percent, and other crops by similar amounts. Variable input use would have risen similarly (Table 5). The elimination of both export taxes and import restrictions would have had more dramatic effects, with increases in output ranging from about 47 percent for beef to a tripling of soyabean output. The use of capital would have doubled, and labour and others would have increased more than 50 percent. The estimated effects of eliminating the value-added tax on capital and chemicals and the social security tax on labour are shown in column 4, Table 5. The effects on output and input use are more modest, but still dramatic, with increases ranging from 15 percent to 80 percent. Elimination of minimum wages in agriculture would have had relatively minor effects (column 5).

Table 5–Estimated Effects of Policy Changes on Quantities

	Policy Set				
Commodity	Export Tax	Import Restriction	Overvalued Currency	Domestic Taxes	Minimum Wages
	Percent				
Beef	17	30	5	24	3
Wheat	33	23	10	23	5
Maize	34	26	9	24	5
Sunflower	49	48	4	36	2
Linseed	15	23	-2	15	-1
Soyabean	96	99	14	79	8
Sorghum	37	25	8	23	4
Weighted output	27	29	7	25	4
Capital	47	54	9	44	5
Labour	43	29	18	33	10
Others	26	38	2	28	1
Weighted input	43	44	10	38	6

These estimates of *mutatis mutandis* effects of interventions are in some cases quite large. The assumptions of the basic model, and therefore of these calculations, are that input supplies and product demands are perfectly elastic. To the extent that expansion would drive up input prices or drive down product prices, the effects of eliminating interventions *would be smaller* than those shown in Table 5. Furthermore, the use of Table 3 elasticities to calculate the shifts in Table 5 involves a linear approximation of the supply functions implied by the translog technology of Table 1, and this also exaggerates the output effects presented in Table 5. Because of these approximation errors in predicting large changes from current equilibrium levels, the results in Table 5 should be considered to be *upper bound estimates* of the effects of completely eliminating any one of the three wedges shown. For a partial reduction in the wedges, the responses shown may be quite accurate. Effects of the magnitude shown could certainly not be expected from the elimination of more than one wedge simultaneously. In any case, the results demonstrate that the various policies have certainly had dramatic effects in holding back agricultural output in Argentina.

Conclusions

The results of this study have confirmed the influence of relative output prices, relative variable input prices, and quantities of fixed inputs on production decisions. The findings imply that Argentina's agricultural price policies have had substantial adverse effects on productivity. Evidence on the distortion of resource allocation as a result of government intervention in markets is offered by the analysis. Agricultural output in Argentina has been implicitly and explicitly taxed—the static effect being lower agricultural output.

Notes

[1]World Bank; and Department of Economics and Business, North Carolina State University; respectively. With the usual disclaimers, the authors are grateful for valuable help and comments provided by Professors Antonio Besil, Domingo Cavallo, John Dutton, Paul Johnson, Luis Pellegrino, A.R. Gallant, and M.K. Wohlgenant.

[2]For additional descriptions and sources of the data, see Fulginiti (1986).

[3]See Sidhu and Baanante (1981) for details. The own-price elasticity of supply for crop *i*, for example, is $n_{ii} = (\beta_{ii}/M_i) + M_i - 1$.

[4]Argentina is a small country in the world market for these commodities, and, since agriculture represents only 8-10 percent of GNP, that sector is a reasonably small user of capital, labour, and "other inputs."

References

Antle, J.M. (1984) "Structure of US Agricultural Technology, 1910-78," *American Journal of Agricultural Economics*, Vol. 66, No. 4, pp. 414-421.

Cavallo, D., and Mundlak, Y. (1982) *Agriculture and Economic Growth in an Open Economy: Case of Argentina*, Research Report No. 36, International Food Policy Institute, Washington, D.C., USA.

Fulginiti, L.E. (1986) "Argentine Agricultural Policies in a Multiple Output, Multiple Input Framework," PhD dissertation, North Carolina State University, Raleigh, N.C., USA.

Lopez, R.E. (1984) "Estimating Substitution and Expansion Effects Using a Profit Function Framework," *American Journal of Agricultural Economics*, Vol. 66, No. 3, pp. 359-367.

Mielke, M.J. (1984) *Argentine Agricultural Policies in the Grain and Oilseed Sectors*, Foreign Agricultural Economic Report No. 206, Economic Research Service, US Department of Agriculture, Washington, D.C., USA.

Reca, L.G. (1980) *Argentina: Country Case Study of Agricultural Prices and Subsidies*, Staff Working Paper No. 386, World Bank, Washington, D.C., USA.

Schultz, T.W. (1956) "Reflections on Agricultural Production, Output and Supply," *Journal of Farm Economics*, Vol. 38, No. 3, pp. 748-762.

Shumway, C.R. (1983) "Supply, Demand, and Technology in a Multiproduct Industry: Texas Field Crops," *American Journal of Agricultural Economics*, Vol. 65, No. 4, pp. 748-760.

Sidhu, S.S., and Baanante, C.A. (1981) "Estimating Farm-level Input Demand and Wheat Supply in the Indian Punjab Using a Translog Profit Function," *American Journal of Agricultural Economics*, Vol. 63, No. 2, pp. 237-246.

Weaver, R.D. (1983) "Multiple Input, Multiple Output Production Choices and Technology in the U.S. Wheat Region," *American Journal of Agricultural Economics*, Vol. 65, No. 1, pp. 45-56.

DISCUSSION OPENING—*Urs Egger* (Department of Agricultural Economics, Swiss Federal Institute of Technology)

The authors present a model that permits simulation of the impacts of government intervention in markets in Argentina from 1940 to 1980. They conclude that agricultural policy had a dramatic effect in holding back agricultural output in Argentina. Considering how many agricultural policies discriminate against the agricultural sector in many countries, the result is not surprising. What is surprising are the positive cross-supply elasticities for most of the output categories, given the model's assumption of fixed input of land in production. Also, if the analysis had been continued into the 1980s, policy changes that diminish or remove some export taxes would have allowed a test of the model's qualities.

The paper should stimulate us to go a step further by asking what would happen if Argentine agricultural policy were changed in the way suggested by the paper. Increased prices would effect an increase in agricultural production. With limited time, only three major problem fields arising from such a change can be proposed for discussion: income distribution in agriculture, consumer prices and inflation, and export-oriented agriculture.

The impact of additional income as a consequence of increased output should be discussed. The structure of land tenure is not as unequal in Argentina as in other Latin American countries that have a relatively large share of medium-sized family farms. Nevertheless, 40 percent of the rural population have to live on 5 percent of the agricultural area. Considering the inflationary tendency, this large group will not have the necessary financial means for investment. Therefore, additional output would hardly improve income distribution in rural areas.

In 1985, about 80 percent of the population lived in urban areas. For several years, high rates of inflation were the daily reality in Argentina. The 1986 level of 82 percent per year marked the first time in the 1980s that the rate fell below 100 percent. Considering the importance of expenditures on food, the paper's proposed change of policy by raising food prices would affect the majority of the Argentine population in a negative way.

Another question is whether increased output would contribute to export performance. Fluctuating prices and effects of protectionist agricultural policies in industrial countries are major features of agricultural world markets. The export performance of Argentina's major export commodities—cereals and meat—strongly depends on the agricultural policies in the USA and EC. Therefore, increased output of those commodities can only be exported if import restrictions in those countries are removed or at least diminished. Also, the low price level on world markets caused by surpluses from industrial countries must be raised in order to be of interest for exports.

These remarks are intended to show the necessity of interpreting agricultural policy measures in their overall economic context, including foreign trade. An exclusive sectoral model involves the danger of evaluating certain policy measures differently than if their impacts were assessed as part of an overall economic strategy.

GENERAL DISCUSSION—*Ralph D. Christy, Rapporteur* (Department of Agricultural Economics and Agribusiness, Louisiana State University)

A series of questions focused on the importance of nonprice policy in Argentine agriculture. How does the duality model account for credit policy? Since the time period of this study was lengthy (1940-80), how was land reform policy treated? How has price stabilization policy (as opposed to price support policy) been accounted for in the model?

One participant commented that the elasticity values were relatively high and speculated that perhaps the constraints imposed in the model pushed up the coefficients, which would provide erroneous policy prescriptions. The participant suggested that rather than imposing constraints, hypotheses should be tested.

In reply, Fulginiti stated that the model did not account for interest rates explicitly; the price of capital was used as an exogenous variable. Therefore, credit policy was not addressed directly. With respect to land reform, the same response applies. The data were annual observations, which should capture quality adjustments in land; however, distributional questions may not be reflected.

Fulginiti also noted that the elasticities were admittedly high. The homogeneity restriction was respected. The model was not designed to examine price theory, but it is a translog function (profit/production model). Therefore, the model does not allow for oversupply of factors. Introduction of instrumental variables may be possible. Although income distribution is an important issue, the objective of the paper does not necessarily include such questions.

Participants in the general discussion included V. Beker, G. Flichman, and O. Knudsen.

Sector-Specific and Economywide Policies and Agricultural Incentives in LDCs

Maurice Schiff[1]

Abstract: The concept of sector-specific and economy-wide policies on incentives for agriculture is defined. A methodology is described for measuring the impact of those policies and results are given for a sample of commodities for 18 developing countries for 1975-84. On average, sector-specific policies tax agricultural exports and protect agricultural imports. Economywide policies tax agricultural products. The impacts of the economywide policies dominate those of the sector-specific policies both for agricultural exports (where they are negative) and imports (where the impact of the specific policy to agriculture is positive).

Introduction

Most developing countries have attempted to encourage the growth of industry by: (1) erecting high walls of protection against imports that would compete with domestic production; (2) maintaining overvalued exchange rates through exchange-control régimes and import licencing mechanisms even more restrictive than those adopted in connection with import substitution; and (3) often attempting to suppress producer prices of agricultural commodities through government procurement policies (especially agricultural marketing boards), export taxation, and/or export quotas. Some governments have attempted to offset, at least in part, these latter disincentive effects on producers by subsidizing input prices and investing in irrigation and other capital inputs.

The third of these sets of policies has been extensively studied. But attempts have been made to estimate the combined impacts on incentives and returns to agricultural producers of those direct government policies and the indirect effects of exchange rate policy and protection to industry. Moreover, those few studies that have attempted to estimate those indirect effects have been undertaken with widely varying methodologies; e.g., Valdés (1973) on Chile, Schuh (1981) on the USA, Oliveira (1981) on Brazil, Garcia Garcia (1981) on Colombia, Cavallo and Mundlak (1982) on Argentina, Oyejide (1986) on Nigeria, and Bautista (1987) on the Philippines. These studies, therefore, do not permit systematic comparative analysis across countries of the effects of differing degrees of discrimination against agriculture.

In this paper, however, such estimates are provided on a comparable basis for 18 developing countries.[2] These estimates are some of the results of the World Bank's research project on the political economy of agricultural pricing policies. The first section gives background information on the way the estimates were made in order to permit appropriate interpretation of the data. The second section provides estimates of the direct, indirect, and total intervention affecting incentives for agricultural output for the 18 countries, for 1975-84 and presents some preliminary analysis of the findings. The final section draws some conclusions.

Estimates

In this paper, the focus is on quantification of the magnitude of the impacts of direct and indirect policies on agricultural prices. For all countries, the impacts are measured relative to what prices would have been had there been no interventions and a régime of free trade. For all tradeable commodities, the reference prices used were the border prices that would have prevailed under an intervention-free régime (adjusted for transport, marketing margins, quality difference, etc.).[3] The results presented here are limited to one exported and one imported product per country. In the project, the concentration was on four to six commodities for most countries, and that coverage typically represented about half to three quarters of net agricultural product.

A second step was to obtain estimates of domestic producer and consumer prices as well as border prices (adjusted for transport costs to or from producer and consumer locations, storage costs, quality difference, etc.) of these commodities. For instance, in the case of wheat in Chile, adjustments were made for domestic transport costs from the main port of entry for wheat to the mills, for customs duties and custom agent fees, for unloading costs and losses in transit, for the annual average quality difference between domestic and imported wheat, and for seasonality (storage).

Estimation of the effects of direct interventions (i.e., those aimed directly at agricultural inputs or outputs) was relatively simple contrasted with the procedures needed to estimate indirect effects. Here the focus was on the real exchange rate and on the tax on agricultural production implicit in the protection of industry. A full account of the procedures used to obtain these estimates may be found in Krueger, Schiff, and Valdés (forthcoming, b, Vol. 1). Here, only the economic rationale behind the estimates is conveyed.

First, estimates were made of the degree of divergence between the actual real exchange rate and the real exchange rate that would have kept the current account at a sustainable level—taking into account normal capital flows—if all quantitative and tariff protection to imports as well as the interventions affecting exports had been removed. This involved estimation of the equivalent tariff of import protection, use of foreign exchange demand and supply elasticity estimates, and use of the resultant numbers to estimate the amount of real exchange rate change that would have had to be undertaken to yield the sustainable current account level.

Taking the border price at the equilibrium exchange rate gave an estimate of the border price that would have prevailed in the absence of interventions. Measuring the nonagricultural price index at the equilibrium exchange rate and in the absence of tariffs and quantitative restrictions on imports and interventions on nonagricultural exports (by adjusting the tradeable part of the price index) gave an estimate of the value of that price index in the absence of interventions. Using these estimates, the indirect effects of the interventions on the prices (and value added) of agricultural products (relative to the nonagricultural price index) were obtained.

Calculations of the indirect effects are less sensitive to the choice of elasticity values for supply and demand for foreign exchange and to the choice of a sustainable level of current account deficit than they might first appear. The indirect effects have three components. First, elimination of the nonsustainable part of the current account deficit requires an increase in the real exchange rate. Second, removal of trade policy interventions (mainly industrial protection policies) also leads to an increase in the real exchange rate. Both the first and second components raise the price of agricultural products relative to the nontradeable part of the nonagricultural price index. Third, removal of trade policy interventions raises the price of agricultural products relative to the tradeable part of the nonagricultural price index. In many cases, the third component was as important as or more important than the first two components.

Empirically, the assumptions about the current account imbalance turned out to be less influential for the indirect effects than industrial protection because the former only affects the first component while the latter affects both the second and the third components. The indirect effects also turned out to be less sensitive to the selected value of elasticities than expected because a proportional change in the elasticities of demand and supply for foreign exchange only affects the first component of the indirect effects. It has no effect on the second or third component.[4]

For those countries where reliable estimates of supply and demand elasticities for foreign exchange were not available, elasticity values of 1 for supply and 2 (in absolute value) for demand were used, based on estimated elasticities from other studies.

Changing the real exchange rate to close the nonsustainable part of the current account deficit might imply changing the underlying macroeconomic policies, and this may affect the location of the supply and demand curves for foreign exchange and may thus affect the results. However, this problem is part of a more general claim that simulations of policy changes alter the constraints agents face and thus affect the parameter values of the model.

In the case of Ghana, calculation of the equilibrium real exchange rate involved an additional complication. The increase or depreciation of the real exchange rate to its equilibrium value for a given world price of cocoa implies an increase in Ghana's cocoa output and therefore a reduction in cocoa's world price. The equilibrium real exchange rate was therefore determined in a simultaneous system where the world price of cocoa is determined endogenously as a function of Ghana's real exchange rate. This methodology resulted in a higher equilibrium real exchange rate than the one based on calculations that ignore the impact of Ghana's real exchange rate on the world price of cocoa.

The total effect of the interventions was taken to be simply the sum of the direct and indirect effects.

Degrees of Intervention

Table 1 presents estimates of the degree of direct and indirect intervention in representative key exportable and importable products for the 18 countries for 1975-84. The impacts of "direct" pricing policies are given in columns (3) and (6). These numbers provide an estimate of the percentage by which domestic producer prices diverged from those that would have prevailed in a well-functioning market at free trade (but at the exchange rate and with the degree of protection that actually prevailed). The measure is equivalent to the nominal protection accorded to the product in question.

Table 1—Direct, Indirect, and Total Nominal Protection Rates for Exported and Imported Products, 1975-84 (in percent)

		Exportables			Importables		
Country	Indirect (1)	Product (2)	Direct (3)	Total (4)	Product (5)	Direct (6)	Total (7)
Argentina	-27	Wheat	-19	-46	*		
Brazil	-23	Soyabeans	-14	-37	Wheat	14	-9
Chile	7	Grapes	1	8	Wheat	10	17
Colombia	-30	Coffee	-6	-36	Wheat	7	-23
Dominican Rep.	-19	Coffee	-23	-42	Rice	23	4
Egypt	-16	Cotton	-29	-45	Wheat	-20	-36
Ghana	-78	Cocoa	30	-48	Rice	99	21
Ivory Coast	-30	Cocoa	-26	-56	Rice	12	-18
Korea	-15	†			Rice	89	74
Malaysia	-7	Rubber	-22	-29	Rice	53	46
Morocco	-10	†			Wheat	-4	-14
Pakistan	-42	Cotton	-9	-51	Wheat	-17	-59
Philippines	-28	Copra	-18	-46	Maize	22	-6
Portugal	-9	Tomatoes	17	8	Wheat	21	12
Sri Lanka	-33	Rubber	-30	-63	Rice	15	-18
Thailand	-17	Rice	-22	-39	*		
Turkey	-38	Tobacco	-13	-51	Wheat	13	-25
Zambia	-50	Tobacco	4	-46	Maize	-11	-61
Average	-27		-11	-38		21	-6

*Argentina and Thailand's main agricultural products are all exported.
†Korea and Morocco's main agricultural products are all imported.

Although government policies differ significantly among individual agricultural commodities, commodities were selected for analysis that were deemed fairly representative of government policy towards agricultural exportables. Thus, the group of commodities shown here can be used as a rough indicator of the incentives provided for agricultural products in general. As can be seen in column (2), most countries adopted policies that resulted in the equivalent of export taxes for the exportable commodities covered here. The exceptions were Ghana (where a highly unrealistic exchange rate resulted in such strong disincentives that some compensatory action was politically essential), Portugal, Chile, and Zambia. The average taxation rate for the products selected was 11 percent.

The more surprising finding is that the impact of indirect interventions on producer incentives was even stronger than the direct ones.[5] Indirect effects include both the effects of trade and macroeconomic policies on the real exchange rate and the extent of protection afforded to nonagricultural commodities. As can be seen from column (1), exchange rate policy, protection to industry, and other policies that were not aimed at agricultural exports often had larger impacts than the direct policies. For Argentina, Brazil, Colombia, Ghana, Ivory Coast, Pakistan, Philippines, Sri Lanka, Turkey, and Zambia, the discrimination against the agricultural exportable crops inherent in policies external to agriculture had larger impacts on agricultural incentives than did policies aimed directly at agriculture. As already noted, indirect negative protection in Ghana was so large that direct agricultural policy provided something of an offset.

For most countries, indirect negative protection intensified the negative direct protection, often resulting in extremely large total negative protection equivalents. The resulting total nominal protection rates are given in column (4) for exportables. As can be seen, the magnitude of disprotection was in many cases large indeed. In the Ivory Coast, for example, cocoa producers received less than half the price they would have received under a free-trade régime at realistic exchange rates and no direct intervention. Sri Lankan rubber producer prices were close to two thirds less than the nonintervention prices. Producer prices were also less than half of the nonintervention price in Pakistan and Turkey. Overall, a simple unweighted average rate of total nominal protection was -38 percent.

People have long recognized that agriculture has been discriminated against. What Table 1 brings out is the degree. As is analyzed in the individual country studies, the negative protection accorded to producers of agricultural export commodities was a significant factor in depressing export earnings in many countries. Even those countries regarded as successful exporters of agricultural commodities, such as Thailand and Malaysia, adhered to this pattern. Of the 18 countries covered in the project, only Chile and Portugal maintained régimes that provided positive total protection to producers. The dominant pattern has been one of systematic and sizeable discrimination.

As for importable products, the impact of direct interventions is shown in column (6). Several findings are noteworthy. First and foremost, in contrast with the negative direct protection accorded to exportable crops, the countries covered here (with few exceptions) provided positive direct protection to import-competing crops. Indeed, the degree of discrimination in policy against exportables and in favour of import-competing crops is remarkable: contrast Malaysian rice, receiving the equivalent of 53 percent nominal protection, with Malaysian rubber, taxed at the equivalent of 22 percent. Direct pricing policy led to an increase in the relative price of rice of 96 percent (relative to rubber).

By definition, those policies that indirectly affect agriculture have the same net impact on import-competing commodities as on exportable commodities. Taking the effects of both direct and indirect policies into account, the effects of direct price policies were in many cases reversed. In Brazil, Colombia, Ivory Coast, Philippines, Sri Lanka, and Turkey,[6] positive direct effects were more than offset by negative indirect effects.

In this regard, one remarkable developing country is South Korea, where direct protection of agricultural commodities (no exportables exist) is very high, and the impact of policies towards the rest of the economy is not large by comparison. However, even with the strong Korean protection and sizeable total protection of rice in Malaysia, the average level of total protection for all the import-competing commodities covered here was negative, although not large (6 percent). If the numbers for Korea and Malaysia are excluded, the average negative total protection for import-competing crops changes to -17 percent.

Summary and Conclusions

The above discussion deals only with the measures of price intervention and reports only for a subset of the products and of the subperiods included in the country studies. The results are striking. A first observation is how differently imported food products and exported products are affected by the direct, sector-specific pricing policies, with the imported products being subsidized on average and exported products being taxed. Why this difference? A number of reasons emerge from the individual country studies, including a desire for self-sufficiency for the basic staples (and in some cases a reversal of policy from subsidy to tax once self-sufficiency is attained and the product becomes exported) and the need for government revenue form the taxation of exported products.

The taxation of foods *exports*, such as wheat and beef in Argentina and rice in Thailand, generates revenues and reduces the cost of food, and thus results in a subsidy to consumers. However, subsidizing consumption of a food *import*, such as wheat in Egypt, results in a fiscal expenditure. This may also help explain why imported food products tend to be protected rather than taxed. The direct protection granted to the production of food in about 70 percent of the countries included suggests that the wage-good argument for cheap food policies would seem to operate mainly through the overvaluation of the exchange rate rather than through explicit price policies.

Perhaps even more striking is the magnitude of the effects of the indirect, economywide interventions, which generally dominate the direct effects, whether the latter are positive or negative. Thus, if indirect price interventions are ignored, the results indicate that on average imported food products were protected (at a rate of 21 percent) and exports were taxed (11 percent). However, the results for total price interventions show that both activities were taxed, at a rate of 6 percent for imported food products and 38 percent for exports.

Notes

[1]World Bank. The views expressed in this paper are those of the author and should not be construed as representing those of the World Bank.

[2]A more detailed presentation and analysis of results and methodology are found in Krueger, Schiff, and Valdés (forthcoming, a). The countries covered in the project are listed in Table 1. Summaries of the results of the individual country studies are found in Krueger, Schiff, and Valdés (forthcoming, b). Chapter 1 and the Appendices of Volumes 1 and 2 provide information on the concepts and methods used to ensure comparability across countries. A third (synthesis) volume, containing an analysis of the comparative results, will cover quantification of the direct and indirect effects on incentives in much greater depth than can be undertaken in this paper, analysis of the effects of these policies, and analysis of the political economy of agricultural price policy and its evolution over time.

[3]Several authors have also calculated the deviations from the domestic price that would have prevailed if optimal export taxes were applied. These results are not presented here but may be found in Krueger, Schiff, and Valdés (forthcoming, b).

[4]This should be clear from examining the model of exchange rate determination used, which is presented in Krueger, Schiff, and Valdés (forthcoming, b, Appendices to Vols. 1 and 2).

[5]In most studies, relatively large elasticities were used to ensure that calculations of the indirect effects were not biased upwards, and the values obtained thus tend to represent a lower bound of the indirect effects.

[6]Wheat is exported in some years and imported in other years in Turkey.

References

Bautista, R.M. (1987) *Production Incentives in Philippine Agriculture: Effects of Trade and Exchange Rate Policies*, Research Report No. 59, International Food Policy Research Institute, Washington, D.C., USA.

Cavallo, D., and Mundlak, Y. (1982) *Agriculture and Economic Growth in an Open Economy: Case of Argentina*, Research Report No. 36, International Food Policy Research Institute, Washington, D.C., USA.

Garcia Garcia, J. (1981) *Effects of Exchange Rates and Commercial Policy on Agricultural Incentives in Colombia: 1953-78*, Research Report No. 24, International Food Policy Research Institute, Washington, D.C., USA.

Krueger, A.O., Schiff, M., and Valdés, A. (forthcoming, a) "Measuring the Impact of Sector-Specific and Economy-Wide Policies on Agricultural Incentives in LDCs," *World Bank Economic Review*.

Krueger, A.O., Schiff, M., and Valdés, A. (forthcoming, b) *Political Economy of Agriculture Pricing Policies: Country Studies*, Vols. 1 and 2, Johns Hopkins University Press, Baltimore, Md., USA.

Oliveira, J. do C. (1981) "Analysis of Transfers from Agricultural Sector and Brazilian Development, 1950-1974," PhD dissertation, University of Cambridge, Cambridge, UK.

Oyejide, T.A. (1986) *Effects of Trade and Exchange Rate Policies on Agriculture in Nigeria*, Research Report No. 55, International Food Policy Research Institute, Washington, D.C., USA.

Schuh, G.E. (1981) "Floating Exchange Rates, International Interdependence, and Agricultural Policy," in Johnson, G., and Maunder, A., *Rural Change: Challenge for Agricultural Economists*, Gower Publishing Co., Aldershot, UK, pp. 416-423.

Valdés, A. (1973) "Trade Policy and Its Effect on the External Agricultural Trade of Chile, 1945-1965," *American Journal of Agricultural Economics*, Vol. 55, No. 2, pp. 154-164.

DISCUSSION OPENING—*John Strasma* (Department of Agricultural Economics, University of Wisconsin)

Schiff and his colleagues have made a brilliant contribution to the measurement of the effects of government policies. This is truly an impressive and extraordinarily useful project. To open the discussion, however, I want to suggest two areas in which the method used leads to bias in interpretation of the results—taxation and use of border prices to measure domestic intervention.

Taxation. Exports are taxed because governments need revenue and not just because they want to repress prices. Schiff and his colleagues call this intervention, and implicitly they compare these taxes with a no-tax situation. That is not reality. Someone has to pay for at least minimum government services—the lights in the presidential palace and at least some roads and bridges. Agriculture's share is not zero. The intervention should thus be measured by the amount by which the export and other taxes on the sector exceed agriculture's fair share and not by the entire amount of the tax.

Agriculture in many countries is practically exempt from income tax. In Chile, fruit growers pay on a presumptive income related to the tax on land (without the value of the fruit trees). The result is a higher rate of after-tax return on investment in fruit for export than in domestic commerce or other activities. This tax preference is also an intervention, but it apparently has not been included in the Schiff calculations.

Use of border prices to measure domestic intervention. European and US producers receive double and triple the prices charged to importing countries, and the resulting surpluses depress world market prices. The imported commodities shown by Schiff are wheat, rice, and maize. None of their border prices are free of intervention, and they are not valid measures of an intervention-free price.

To correct this enormous bias, the Krueger-Schiff-Valdés project could estimate what the prices of these commodities would be in the absence of intervention by exporting countries and then use those prices to estimate protection in the developing countries. The result would be very different from that shown in this paper.

Finally, where the papers resulting from this study now say "free trade régime," they should say "régime of one-way free trade" and where they say "intervention-free régime," they should say "a régime in which the developing country does not intervene but its trading partners do."

GENERAL DISCUSSION—*Ralph D. Christy, Rapporteur* (Department of Agricultural Economics and Agribusiness, Louisiana State University)

A comment was made that this paper was excellent and provided some useful information on the nature of protectionism in LDCs. The use of the real exchange rate is correct, in theory, but the questioner wondered if the author had considered a simpler measure of purchasing power.

In reply, Schiff essentially agreed with the concerns regarding border price assumptions; border prices are interventionist prices. However, the border prices are still of some use because they are an opportunity cost and, if the intervention were removed, border prices would increase.

What matters for the farmer in his decision process is not always the current prices but the expected prices. And to the extent prices are largely shaped by policy, the farmer is also interested in expected policy and changes in policy.

Participants in the general discussion included V. Beker, G. Flichman, and O. Knudsen.

Agricultural Credit Cooperatives and Supply Restructuring in Portugal: Healthy Innovation or Institutional Collapse?

Ezequiel de Almeida Pinho and Douglas H. Graham[1]

Abstract: This paper documents the radical restructuring of the supply of agricultural credit in Portugal in the 1980s. In the previous decade, commercial banks and Ministry of Agriculture programmes dominated the supply of agricultural finance. By 1986, however, the national network of agricultural credit cooperatives (Caixas de Crédito Agrícola Mútuo) had emerged as the major supplier of agricultural credit in the country. Controversies such as portfolio concentration, a high incidence of rescheduled loans, high equity multipliers, low capital-asset ratios, and unstable and ambiguous rates of return on equity (net worth) have led to the creation of a second-tier institution to intermediate excess liquidity in the network and act as a lender of last resort. Statutory limitations on CCAM lending activity and controversies surrounding a new national bank-type role for the second-tier institution currently create uncertainty about the future of the CCAM system in Portugal.

Introduction

The institutional framework and supply of agricultural credit in Portugal experienced dramatic changes during the 1980s. In the previous decade, government credit channels through the Ministry of Agriculture or through the recently nationalized commercial bank network dominated the institutional supply of credit to agricultural producers in the country. Yet within five years, this scenario changed. This paper documents that change and underlines the pattern of decentralization of agricultural credit supply in the 1980s through the extensive network of small agricultural credit cooperatives in the country, Caixas de Crédito Agrícola Mútuo (CCAMs). To highlight these changes, we look not only at the profile of change in the country's rural financial markets but also at the changes within the structure of assets and liabilities for the CCAMs in a key growth region of Portugal, the Algarve. The results indicate that this decentralized pattern of growth of agricultural credit carries both promise and potential danger for the future of agricultural finance in Portugal.

Evolution of Agricultural Credit Markets in Portugal in the 1980s

Table 1 sets forth the major indicators of credit activity in the financial markets of Portugal in the first half of the 1980s. Not surprisingly, the world recession affected the performance of the country's credit markets. The index of real credit underlines the rapid decline in both agricultural and nonagricultural credit from 1980 to 1985; however, the decline in the real value of new loans to agriculture was more striking than for nonagricultural credit. In general, the decline in nonagricultural credit was less severe than the decline in nonagricultural GDP; hence the ratio by 1984 and 1985 had risen in comparison to 1979 or 1980. The agricultural sector was much less serviced with credit throughout this period, with credit-to-GDP ratios far lower than those registered by the nonagricultural sector. Nevertheless, these ratios compare favourably to those for other middle income LDCs but unfavourably for other lower income European countries. By the end of the period, the ratio was roughly the same as in the beginning.

The surprising finding is that the relative role of the small-scale agricultural credit cooperatives in the total supply of agricultural credit grew appreciably during this period (from roughly one-fifth to two-thirds). The balance of this paper is concerned with why this happened, how it changed the financial structure of these cooperatives, and the current controversies surrounding their future role as a major supplier of credit to Portuguese farmers.

Despite the gradual liberalization of economic policies in Portugal in the 1980s, price controls constrained the rate of return for many agricultural products for most of this period. At the same time, declining market demand induced by the recession of the early 1980s

Table 1—Financial Market Indicators for Agricultural and Nonagricultural Credit in Portugal

	1979	1980	1981	1982	1983	1984	1985	1986
Index of real credit (1980=100):								
Agricultural credit (new loans)	--	100	71.4	72.6	64.2	50.5	29.1	--
Nonagricultural credit (new loans)	--	100	71.2	65.6	67.2	61.6	56.2	--
Share of volume of credit (end-of-period balance):								
Agricultural credit/total credit	0.04	0.03	0.04	0.04	0.03	0.03	0.03	--
Agricultural credit/agricultural GDP	0.24	0.26	0.41	0.39	0.38	0.32	0.28	--
Nonagricultural credit/nonagricultural GDP	0.82	0.82	0.96	0.96	0.97	0.97	0.98	--
CCAM credit activity (percent):								
CCAM loans/total agricultural credit balance	--	--	0.21	0.32	0.39	0.45	0.50	0.67

Source: Banco do Portugal.

added to the risk of agricultural investments. As a result, the commercial bank network began to ration out this risky and low-rate-of-return agricultural clientele from their portfolios. The agricultural credit cooperatives, on the other hand, were prohibited from engaging in similar behaviour. By statute, they are only allowed to make loans to agriculture, since they are limited to making loans to their members who by law can only be farmers. Hence the CCAMs by default began to inherit a proportionately larger share of the agricultural portfolio in the Portuguese economy.

Another development during 1980-86 was the creation of the Agricultural and Fisheries Investment Finance System (SIFAP), in which government rediscount funds were made available at subsidized interest rates largely for medium- and long-term investment loans in agriculture. This tended to lengthen the portfolio of the CCAMs. The peak years of this financing were 1980-82, which accounts for the rise in the agricultural credit to GDP ratio in 1981-82 (Table 1). However, by 1984-85 this financing had declined in importance. Still, this alternative source of financing did allow the CCAMs to break away from the rigid control and supervision of the Caixa Geral de Depósitos (CGD). This large government savings bank had directed the operation of the several hundred CCAMs scattered throughout the country in their respective municipalities (*conselhos*) where they were to service the loan needs of their farmer members. This connection with the CGD was gradually removed from 1979 onwards when the network of CCAMs was allowed to mobilize its own deposits and secure longer term loan financing from SIFAP. The growing financial autonomy of the CCAMs from 1979 onwards forms the basis of the rest of the paper, with progress evaluated through a case study of the CCAMs in the country's important southern region, the Algarve.

Organizational Restructuring of Rural Finance in Portugal: Case of the Algarve CCAMs

The Algarve is a dynamic agricultural region in southernmost Portugal in which the growth of horticultural products in intensive greenhouse operations marks the 1980s. Seventeen CCAMs operate in their respective county-sized *conselhos*. Five of these credit cooperatives are quite large in assets and liabilities (those located in the *conselhos* of Monchique, Portimão, Faro, Silves, and Lagoa). The other 13 are of more modest or smaller sizes, serving a lower income and less dynamic agricultural clientele. This split also reflects the heterogeneous nature of the national network of CCAMs, in which roughly 18-20 credit cooperatives are quite large while the remaining 180 or so active CCAMs are smaller in size. Finally, the experience of the Algarve CCAMs offers a valuable insight into the changing structure of assets and liabilities for the more dynamic cooperatives of the national network; i.e., the Algarve network grew more rapidly than the national network as a whole, increasing its share of total deposits throughout the system from 8.6 percent in 1981 to 10.9 percent in 1986, and of loans from 7.9 percent in 1981 to 11.2 percent in 1986.

Tables 2 and 3 summarize the experience of the CCAMs in the Algarve in the first half of the 1980s. Table 2 shows a distinct shift in the structure of assets and liabilities for these 17 credit cooperatives. The source of funding (i.e., liabilities) has shifted from largely outside borrowing (i.e., CGD funds) in 1980 to own deposits by 1986. This reflects the growing financial autonomy of the CCAMs as they have come to rely more on local depositors for loan resources.

Table 2—Relative Distribution of the Structure of Aggregate Assets and Liabilities for the 17 CCAMs in the Algarve

	1980	1981	1982	1983	1984	1985	1986
	Percent						
Assets:							
Vault cash	1.2	1.6	2.4	2.0	2.1	1.2	0.8
Deposits	15.9	18.6	20.9	19.2	21.7	26.4	28.5
Loans	82.2	78.8	73.8	69.7	64.2	60.4	60.4
Fixed assets	0.5	0.7	1.8	2.7	3.7	3.9	3.6
Other assets	0.2	0.3	1.1	6.4	8.3	8.1	6.7
Liabilities:							
Sight deposits	27.2	24.1	30.2	25.2	18.3	17.8	19.8
Time deposits	16.4	22.4	30.1	42.4	45.8	52.2	56.6
Borrowing	51.2	49.3	33.4	24.7	26.6	20.0	14.1
Other liabilities	0.2	0.2	2.5	4.6	6.9	6.7	4.7
Net worth	5.0	4.0	3.8	3.1	2.4	3.3	4.8

Source: Financial statements of CCAMs in the Algarve.

Table 2 also shows a shift in the structure of assets as loans have declined from 82 percent of total assets in 1980 to 60 percent in 1986. On the other hand, deposits in other CCAMs, in branches of commercial banks, and in the recently created Central Liquidity Fund for the national network (the Caixa Central) have grown from 15.9 percent of total assets in 1980 to 28.5 percent in 1986. Thus, as these Algarve CCAMS gained greater autonomy through local deposit mobilization strategies, they became more conservative in their lending practices. Instead of lending out all their resources, they hedged by increasing the share of their risk-free assets (i.e., deposits in other institutions).

The net worth (or capital) base, except for a brief rise in 1986, has generally been declining during this period as a share of total liabilities. The implications of this small capital base can be seen in Table 3 where unusually high rates of return on equity are recorded for the Algarve group of CCAMs. This in turn grows out of unusually high equity multipliers and commensurately low capital-asset ratios. Banks in developed countries rarely record equity multipliers beyond 20 to 1 or capital-asset ratios below 6 percent. The CCAM results in Table 3 are usually above or below these two thresholds. In short, the CCAMs have leveraged their meagre capital base into unusually high asset positions. On the one hand, this potentially vulnerable situation is partially offset or minimized by having a good portion of their assets held in risk-free deposits. On the other hand, these high rates of return are clearly overstated in that the net income used for this measure includes accrued (but uncollected) loan interest payments as income received (from delinquent or rescheduled loans). Thus higher capital-asset ratios are clearly advisable to cover potential default risks.

An additional feature of this slim capital base is the highly unstable fluctuation in the rates of return on capital or equity. Table 3 illustrates this profile with two measures of dispersion. This instability is in part associated with greater earnings fluctuations for the smaller units in the network. A negative correlation (-0.56) existed between the coefficient of variation for the rates of return on equity during 1978-86 and the size of the CCAMs (in total assets) in 1986. Similarly, a negative tendency existed (though not statistically significant) between the rank order of rates of return in 1985 and 1986 and the size of the CCAMs of -0.18 and -0.22, respectively.

A final feature of the evolution of the Algarve CCAMs merits comment. Personal interviews with CCAM managers in the spring of 1987 documented fairly high portfolio concentration with a large part of the portfolio concentrated in a few large-sized loans in

Table 3—Financial Indicators for the 17 CCAMs in the Algarve

	1978	1979	1980	1981	1982	1983	1984	1985	1986
Return on equity (percent)	21.3	21.2	29.4	27.3	35.7	28.3	50.9	47.4	42.5
Coefficient of variation	0.9	0.7	2.8	1.0	-3.8	2.2	1.4	1.9	0.5
Range over mean	16.5	2.8	11.9	3.4	-15.6	9.8	2.8	6.5	2.1
Equity multiplier (assets/net worth)	15.2	16.6	19.9	25.2	26.1	32.8	41.4	30.2	21.0
Capital-asset ratio (net worth/assets)	6.6	6.0	5.0	4.0	3.8	3.1	2.4	3.3	4.8

Source: Derived from financial statements of the 17 CCAMs in the Algarve.

some of the credit cooperatives. Also, the common practice of rescheduling loans falling due could be hiding a potential growing loan arrears problem in some CCAMs. Both of these fears have led to the creation of a Central Liquidity Fund to draw off excess liquidity, intermediate between surplus and deficit units, and act as a lender of last resort to the national network of CCAMs. This last function will shortly be reinforced by a guarantee fund to be set up through contributions from the Central Bank of Portugal and the CCAMs themselves.

Conclusions: Emergence of a New System of Rural Finance in Portugal

The rapid growth of the agricultural credit cooperatives in Portugal illustrates several important lessons about the creation and expansion of financial institutions in rural financial markets of LDCs. First, given the proper incentives, credit cooperatives can mobilize savings successfully. By the mid-1980s, this local resource mobilization allowed the CCAMs to gain financial autonomy and become the major supplier of agricultural credit in the country. The CCAMs in the Algarve still experienced growing excess liquidity with declining loan-deposit ratios in the face of the decline in demand for agricultural loans during the recession years of the early to mid-1980s. To loan out all these resources was no doubt unwise, hence contingency reserves were held in commercial banks until a Central Liquidity Fund was established in 1985 to intermediate the redistribution of these excess funds within and outside the network for the benefit of the CCAMs.

A second lesson from the CCAM experience is that depositors could be placed at risk (i.e., moral hazard) in a widely dispersed network of relatively autonomous credit cooperatives operating in a weak regulatory environment. Thus the authorities view the recently created Central Liquidity Fund (Caixa Central) as not only serving as an intermediary between surplus and deficit units and check-clearing functions, but also acting as an implicit deposit insurance mechanism (i.e., lender of last resort to cover deposit runs) for the system as a whole. These functions, taken together, presumably justify the reserves that the CCAMs are required to hold in the Central Liquidity Fund.

The third lesson from the CCAM experience highlights both the heterogeneity and uneven performance that can emerge in a dispersed system of agricultural credit cooperatives. Field data from the Algarve documented several large, solid CCAMs with relatively stable returns, and many smaller units with more problematic performances in their statutory areas of operation. Portfolio concentration, a high incidence of rescheduled loans, and high equity or capital multipliers are evident in a number of these cooperatives. While this in part grows out of inexperienced management, it also results from the statutory constraints that prevent mergers of cooperatives across geographical lines to gain scale economies and that limit lending activity to agriculture, thereby preventing diversification or scope economies in the loan portfolio.

The CCAM movement is currently at a crossroads in Portugal. Should the roughly 220 CCAMs remain locked into their current set of statutory rules limiting scale and scope economies? If they do, the Central Liquidity Fund, established to act as a minicentral bank on their behalf will have to be given the opportunity to gain the scale economies and diversified portfolio denied to the member cooperatives. Or should the current statutory limitations on CCAM lending and mergers be relaxed to allow these field-level institutions to acquire more widespread services and financial products? If the latter path is followed, the cooperative movement will have to abandon its special tax exempt status and become subject to the same competitive rules governing commercial banks in Portugal. The correct decision is still an open question. This issue merits more detailed field studies and research on the financial viability of the credit cooperatives and the potential scale and scope economies in the CCAM network in Portugal.

Note

[1]Department of Agricultural Economics and Rural Sociology, Ohio State University.

DISCUSSION OPENING—*Anna Burger* (József Attila University of Szeged)

Agricultural credit systems are generally important parts of agricultural support systems. Institutions in both well- and less-developed countries have been founded or endorsed and supported by governments to provide agricultural loans under more favourable conditions than those under which loans are provided for the rest of the economy. Lending terms are usually longer, and interest rates lower, than would otherwise be the case.

Apart from the objective of supporting agriculture, agricultural credit, like any other means of subsidization, has an important role in transmitting definite aims to agriculture. These aims concern mostly the viability of farming, reshaping of the production structure according to market demand and business prospects, promotion of development of some prospering farm sectors, and reduction of some other ailing ones.

Accordingly, the provision of preferential loans in some countries is tied to farm plans approved by the banks; in others, to investment (in particular in the farm sector) or the restriction of production (e.g., the participation in the set-aside programme in the USA). First, the well-defined aims and tasks should be clarified in connection with any agricultural credit system. These aims may vary from country to country, particularly between well- and less-developed countries. Second, the fulfilment of targets has to observed.

Agricultural credit may have two side effects. The first is undersupply of loans if lending resources are meagre. In this case, credit targets cannot be met. The second is connected with the oversupply of loans leading to indebtedness of farmers. Both effects are particularly dangerous in less-developed countries where poor farmers cannot even repay small loans.

The paper commented on the organizational and financial techniques of Portugal's agricultural credit institutions rather than on the economic motives and impacts of their activities. The paper fails to give a broader view on the Portugal economy and agriculture. The motives of credit policy are only briefly mentioned in connection with the institutional setup. Some credit policy impacts on farming can be guessed rather than learned from hints about the meagre capital base of credit cooperatives, the decline in demand for agricultural loans, and the practice of rescheduling loans.

Of utmost interest would be to learn something about the agricultural credit policy and its motives and effects in Portugal, where the political changeover, land reform, and radical peasant and cooperative movements have been quite recent.

[No general discussion of this paper was reported.]

Wheat Production in Semiarid Areas and the Role of Drought Compensation: Israeli Experience in Northern Negev

David Bigman, Nir Becker, and Hector Barak[1]

Abstract: Moral hazard, a mostly inevitable byproduct of all insurance programmes, creates special difficulties in crop insurance programmes. In this study of drought compensation programmes in Israel's Northern Negev, moral hazard was reflected mostly by the transition from the least extensive crop rotation (which fallows some 50 percent of the land under cultivation) to the most extensive crop rotation (which fallows only 20 percent of the land). This transition caused a considerable waste in the budget and losses to the national economy. Nevertheless, drastic measures to abolish the programme in its entirety—as has sometimes been suggested—may be even less desirable and more wasteful because the high risks involved in dryland farming may deter farmers from cultivating these lands at all. This dilemma, which is well known in many crop insurance programmes, may be resolved, at least for selected field crops, with use of aerial photography to monitor crop rotation and soil tillage practices. This study indicates that, by imposing appropriate restrictions on participating farmers with respect to their crop rotation, a large portion of the moral hazard can be eliminated, and the fiscal budget required for the programme can be drastically reduced.

Introduction

The objective of this paper is to summarize an extensive, two-year study on alternative methods of wheat production in Israel's Northern Negev and on the desirability of a drought compensation programme that the government administers in this area.

An important conclusion that came out of this study is that technological innovations in the field of satellite and aerial photography in agriculture have the potential of providing an extremely efficient and inexpensive instrument to monitor implementation of the drought compensation programme and, possibly also, other forms of crop insurance programmes. In a number of field crops, these technologies may permit a drastic reduction of the moral hazard that all too often undermines crop insurance programmes, thereby making them a much more attractive policy instrument.

In recent years, economists have seemingly reached a consensus that governments should, as much as possible, stay out of the financing and implementation of crop insurance programmes (e.g., see the collection of studies in Hazell and Valdés, 1986); and international agencies such as the World Bank have turned down requests for any support for these programmes. With new technologies of aerial photography in agriculture that permit more accurate crop estimates, this consensus should be reconsidered, and governments may object less to becoming involved, especially as government involvement is often pivotal in semiarid areas.

Background

Northern Negev is the largest agricultural land area in Israel. It contains 2.7 million *dunams* of cultivated land, of which 1.2 million are used for grazing, 1.2 million for nonirrigated field crops (mostly wheat), and 0.3 million for irrigated crops (almost half for wheat, although this may vary from year to year). The climate in the area is typical semiarid, characterized by a low and variable level of precipitation—both from year to year and within each year. Also, considerable differences exist in the climate among subregions in the area, as illustrated in Table 1.

Most of the nonirrigated lands are cultivated by *Kibbutzim* (communal farms), and, until the mid-1970s, a large portion of their income came from agriculture—especially wheat. Over the last decade, the share of industry on *Kibbutzim* has increased continuously, and, with the expansion of the irrigated lands, the *Kibbutzim* have also diversified their crops. Since 1964, the government has implemented a drought compensation programme centred on this region. Even earlier, however, the government had supported local settlers during years of severe drought, its major objective being to solidify settlements in this region, which at that time was very sparsely populated.

The drought compensation programme covers about 85 percent of the cultivated land in Northern Negev (north of Beer Sheva, south of Kiryat Gat). The remaining 15 percent, situated south of what is known locally as the "drought line," is not covered by the programme but still cultivated by local settlers. The cultivation practices in these latter lands will serve as a reference to evaluate the practices in the lands covered by the programme—albeit with some reservations that will be mentioned later on.

Table 1—Distribution of Precipitation in the Three Subregions of Northern Negev

	Dorot (North)	Lahav (Central)	Gilat (South)
	Millimetres		
Annual average	330	306	218
Maximum	608	562	569
Minimum	92	137	42
Standard deviation	147	115	89
Coefficient of variation	0.45	0.38	0.41

The programme compensates wheat growers up to 100 percent of their production costs whenever the yield falls below the break-even level.[2] The break-even level (and thus the calculated production cost) is determined by a joint committee consisting of government representatives, representatives of local settlers, and field experts.

Until the early 1980s, this committee was also in charge of determining actual yields in a drought year to determine the actual amount of compensations. To assess actual yields, members of the committee visited the affected fields to inspect their state first-hand and take various samples. This process was necessarily very tedious and clumsy and often resulted in arduous disputes. In the early 1980s, this system was replaced by another method, involving evaluations on the basis of a biological model of wheat growing, which estimates output on the basis of climatic, geographical, and managerial data. This model is also used here. The model was fed actual climatic data (collected at a number of observation points throughout the region) and produced yield estimates. These estimates were compared with samples and, on the basis of these two sources, final estimates were determined. Over the years, the model proved to be accurate and highly efficient in minimizing haggling, disputes, and estimation costs. Furthermore, the model was continually revised, its parameters reestimated with accumulated data, and, from time to time, new variables were added to take into account new technologies, etc.

Practices of Wheat Growing in Northern Negev

This study focuses on the following managerial decisions that have been found to be pivotal in farming drylands in Northern Negev.

From year to year: Crop rotation that is primarily a decision on the percentage of land idled.

Within the year: Sowing data and the decision whether or not to sow that year, and harvest date and the decision whether or not to harvest that year.

The decision on crop rotation is especially crucial in dry farming. By idling part of their lands, farmers prevent escalation in losses due to pest activity and allow an accumulation of water in lower layers of the soil. Furthermore, the practices of soil tillage during the years in which the land is fallowed may play an important role in allowing accumulation of water. The model used was not constructed, however, to detect the effects of soil tillage practices; they require further research.

The decision on the sowing date is designed to guarantee that the seed has at least the minimum level of moisture necessary for successful budding. The period suitable for sowing in Northern Negev is from early November to mid-December. An early sowing ensures relatively warm temperatures that are ideal for budding and growth of the plant in its early stages. In mid-November, however, the amount of rainfall may not suffice to provide the minimum level of moisture necessary for budding.[3] The later the sowing date, the higher the probability of having sufficient moisture but the lower the temperatures. Studies in the area have shown that for every single day sowing of wheat is postponed beyond mid-November, a loss in yield occurs that is equal to, on average, 0.5-1.5 percent of the total yield, depending on the region.

In the authors' visits to the area, striking differences in the farming practices between the two sides of the drought line were found. North of the line, in the area covered by the drought compensation programme, farmers invariably had sown their land in early November, irrespective of the amount of rainfall. South of the line, in the area not covered by the programme, sowing was postponed as much as possible to assure the minimum level of moisture. The operating rule in lands south of the line was the following: If, at any date prior to mid-December, the soil had more than the minimum level of moisture (the equivalent of 80 mm of rain), they would start sowing at that date. If the soil had insufficient moisture, even by mid-December, they would not sow these lands at all in that year.[4]

These differences in practices north and south of the drought line are but one manifestation of the moral hazard that accompanies the compensation programme.

The decision whether or not to harvest in a given year depends primarily on the yield (of both grain and hay). It may also depend on the possibility of using the fields for grazing.

To analyze the crop rotation decisions, the authors inquired first about the actual farming practices in the various subregions. Many *Kibbutzim* included fodder in their crop rotations for two reasons: first, they need fodder to feed their animals, and they found it cheaper to grow the fodder themselves; and second, inclusion of fodder in the crop rotation prevented the spread of pests that are typical to wheat, and added important nutrients to the soil. On the other hand, though, fodder extracts water from the deeper layers of the soil and, as a result, the yield of wheat in that field the following year is lower than the yield in a field that was fallowed in the previous year.

As a conclusion of the inquiry, the following alternative crop rotations were examined:

I—wheat and fallow (i.e., every year half the land is fallowed);

II—wheat and wheat and fallow (i.e., every year one-third of the land is fallowed);

III—wheat and fodder and wheat and fallow (i.e., every year a quarter of the land is fallowed; and

IV—wheat and wheat and fodder and wheat and fallow (i.e., every year one-fifth of the land is fallowed).

In all these alternatives, sowing takes place in early November. A fifth alternative considered is the practice south of the drought line whereby the sowing decision is reexamined every day from early November to mid-December on the basis of the moisture level at the three top layers of soil. This alternative is denoted "dynamic."

Finally, the possibility was examined of adding supplementary irrigation in mid-November to secure optimal moisture level during budding. This possibility only applies to 20 percent of the lands that have the appropriate infrastructure for irrigation. Until recent years, farmers used to irrigate wheat in these fields twice during the season: in mid-November and in mid-February. With these irrigations, they have obviously eliminated the risk of a drought. In the last three years, following a succession of droughts countrywide, water for irrigation has been in short supply. This forced farmers to choose between irrigating all their irrigated fields only once a year (i.e., in mid-November) or irrigating only part of their irrigated fields twice a year, as before. Having only one irrigation exposed them to the risk of drought. It did, however, allow a more efficient use of the water. This study considered the alternative of supplementary irrigation in mid-November for the above four crop rotations and the effects of the drought compensation programme on these methods.[5] Nine methods were examined: four dry farming rotations, four with supplementary irrigations, and one with a dynamic decision process with respect to the sowing date.

Methodology

To evaluate the effects of the drought compensation programme, the yield and net profit were calculated over a period of 20 years for each of the above methods with and without the compensation programme. Daily climatic data on temperatures and precipitation were collected in each of the three subregions that comprise Northern Negev (Dorot, the northern subregion; Lahav, the central subregion; and Gilat, the southern subregion). The yield was calculated by the biological model mentioned earlier.[6] The model estimates the daily growth of wheat on the basis of daily climatic data on temperature, precipitation, and evaporation, as well as on the basis of agronomic characteristics such as soil composition at different layers (up to a depth of 210 cm), soil salinity, etc., and managerial decisions such as sowing date, crop rotation, level of fertilization, pesticide use, etc. Revenue over the 20-year period for the nine production methods was calculated from the yield assuming the price of wheat to be $180 per ton, the average price for imported wheat in Israel (including freight, insurance, etc.) over the previous three years (not including premia for quality). The revenue estimate also included revenue from hay and fodder. To estimate the cost, total costs were divided into eight categories and each category estimated for each of the three subregions. The cost estimates were based on calculations made by the drought compensation committee (which calculates the cost for the central region only), estimates made by the farmers themselves, and estimates made by field experts in the regional extension services.

Nine distributions of net profit for the nine methods of farming over a period of 20 years were thus obtained. From these distributions, the efficient methods could be determined and the inefficient ones eliminated. The main efficiency criterion was second stochastic dominance (SSD), but a number of other criteria were also examined. By comparing the efficiency frontier without the drought compensation programme to that with the programme, the effects of the programme on the choice of the farming method could be determined. Also estimated were the net benefit (or loss) to the overall economy and the dollars saved under each of the farming methods to determine the overall desirability of the programme.

Economic Evaluation of the Present and Alternative Compensation Programmes

The moral hazard induced by the drought compensation programme is a common problem in practically all insurance programmes.[7] In this case, the moral hazard was manifest in two ways: first, farmers were induced to switch to more extensive crop rotations; and second, the programme eliminated the incentive to take precautionary measures before sowing so as to secure a minimum level of moisture in the soil. In this study, the authors were able to assess the financial losses that can be attributed to these effects of the moral hazard. These effects of the programme have raised considerable criticism in Israel over the years and brought forth repeated calls, both from within the government and from field experts, to abolish the programme in its entirety or replace it by direct income transfers. The intention of the latter proposal was to provide financial support to local settlers in a form of lump-sum payments that would not have any effect on their farming practices. In a longer version of this paper, the authors objected to that proposal on the grounds that, by abolishing the drought compensation programme, the government would eliminate not only the moral hazard induced by the programme but also its positive effects. The authors' concern was that, without some form of insurance, farmers would not be able or willing to bear the risks; and they may choose either not to cultivate these lands at all or to select farming methods that are much *less* extensive than the desirable ones for the national economy.

Table 2 summarizes the economic gains or losses from the programme. It shows the net gains for the national economy due to the transition from any one of the methods on the efficiency frontier without compensation to the efficient method with compensation. Without precise knowledge of the farmers' utility functions, one could not determine which of the efficient methods they would have chosen had they not received the drought compensation. All the possible methods on the efficiency frontier were thus examined. Their choice of crop rotation with the programme was easier to determine both because the more extensive rotations clearly dominate the less extensive ones and because the present results have been substantiated by an extensive field inquiry among the farmers in the various subregions.

Table 2–Economic Gain or Loss from Drought Compensation: Present Programme

	Without Compensation Method	Without Compensation Net Gain	With Compensation Method	With Compensation Net Gain	Net Gain from Compensation
		Dollars per dunam			
Dorot:					
	I	2.09			0.69
	II	2.96			-0.16
	IV	2.78	IV	2.78	0.00
	Dynamic	3.36			-0.58
	0	0.00			2.78
Lahav:					
	Dynamic	3.06			-5.04
			IV	-1.98	
	0	0.00			-1.98
Gilat:					
	0	0.00	IV	-9.47	-9.47

As Table 2 clearly indicates, if farmers in Dorot had chosen method II without the programme, the programme would have yielded a loss as a result of the switch to the more extensive method IV. If, however, the more risk averse farmers in that subregion had chosen not to cultivate the land at all without compensation, then the programme would have yielded a substantial gain of $2.78 per *dunam.* In Lahav and Gilat, the programme yields only losses by inducing farmers to abandon the more cautious and less extensive dynamic method or by changing their decision not to cultivate the land at all without compensation in favour of the most extensive and, hence, most risky crop rotation when the programme is in effect.

Recent technological developments in the area of aerial photography made possible an alternative approach. Under the proposed scheme, participation in the drought compensation programme will be conditioned on an agreement to follow a *predetermined* crop rotation that will set clear limits on farming practices. Field experts and government officials will determine the desirable crop rotation that can best meet national goals—broadly defined—for each geographical subregion. Aerial photography will be used to monitor farmers to see that they comply with these constraints. It will allow experts to determine not only what crop has been grown in each field or whether the land has been laid idle, but also the tillage practices of the soil, particularly in years when the field is fallowed.

Table 3 illustrates the overall economic gains that can be expected from the constrained compensation programme. Under this programme, farmers in the Dorot subregion would have to observe crop rotation method II, and farmers in the Lahav subregion would have to follow the dynamic sowing method. The Gilat subregion was not included in these calculations because, at the price of $180 per ton, wheat growing in that subregion would not be desirable for the national economy unless objectives other than substituting for imported wheat are taken into account.

Perhaps more meaningful than the latter figures is the calculation of the net gain that can be expected from constraining the present compensation programme (Table 4, with constraints on the programme slightly different from those in Table 3). In the Dorot subregion, farmers must observe crop rotation method II. This would result in net economic gains of $0.16 per *dunam* and a saving of $1.26 per *dunam* in the average compensation; i.e., a reduction of 20 percent in the budget for compensation. In Lahav, three different constraints were examined. If farmers were required to observe crop rotation method II, the net economic gain would total $0.94 per *dunam*, and the budgetary savings would be $1.92 per *dunam* or 18 percent. The savings would be much higher if more severe restrictions were enforced.

Table 3—Economic Gain or Loss from Constrained Compensation

	Without Compensation		With Constrained Compensation		Net Gain from Constrained Compensation
	Method	Net Gain	Method	Net Gain	
	Dollars per dunam				
Dorot:					
	I	2.09			0.87
	II	2.96	II	2.96	0.00
	IV	2.78			0.16
	Dynamic	3.36			-0.40
	0	0.00			2.96
Lahav:					
	Dynamic	3.06	Dynamic	3.06	0.00
	0	0.00			3.06

Table 4—Economic and Fiscal Gain from the Constraints on Drought Compensation

	Present Programme			Constrained Programme			Change in	Change in
	Method	Compensation	Net Gain	Method	Compensation	Net Gain	Compensation	Net Gain
		Dollars per dunam				*Dollars per dunam*		
Dorot:								
	IV	6.24	2.78	II	4.98	2.96	-1.26	0.16
Lahav:								
	IV	10.65	-1.98	II	8.73	-1.04	-1.92	0.94
				I	6.09	-0.38	-4.56	1.60
				Dynamic	2.01	3.06	-8.64	5.04
Gilat:								
	IV	15.26	-9.47	II	12.78	-8.30	-2.48	1.17
				I	9.57	-6.59	-5.69	2.88
				Dynamic	3.31	-2.78	-11.95	6.69

Most dramatic are the gains in the Gilat subregion. Indeed, as a result of the authors' recommendations, the Ministry of Finance, which is in charge of the programme, has already decided to constrain the programme as of 1988 to crop rotation method II (i.e., to fallow one-third of these lands each year instead of one-fifth, as before). Even with this mild restriction, the Ministry is likely to save $2.48 per *dunam* or some 16 percent of the total compensation budget for that subregion. These savings would allow the Ministry to expand the programme at no extra cost to the 150,000 *dunams* of lands south of the drought line, which are at present not covered.

Notes

[1]Department of Agricultural and Resource Economics, University of California, Berkeley; Department of Agricultural Economics, University of Minnesota; and Department of Agricultural Economics, Hebrew University of Jerusalem; respectively. This research was supported by a grant from the USA-Israel Binational Agricultural Research and Development Fund.

[2]Wheat growers north of Kiryat Gat (i.e., in the central and northern regions of the country) are compensated only up to 60 percent of their costs.

[3]To lower that risk, the seeds are sown 8 cm deep.

[4]In 1985, the early rains came only on December 20. In one *Kibbutz*, farmers decided to sow all their land; in a neighbouring *Kibbutz*, they decided not to sow at all.

[5]Until 1987, fields under irrigation—even once a year—were not included in the compensation programme. As a result of the authors' recommendation, this restriction has been cancelled.

[6]The model was constructed and estimated by Tzaban (1979). It was later further developed by the Tahal Company on behalf of the government ministry in charge of the programme.

[7]The other problem that often undermines crop insurance programmes (viz., adverse selection) creates no difficulty here.

References

Hazell, P., and Valdés, A. (Eds.) (1986) *Crop Insurance for Agricultural Development*, Johns Hopkins University Press, Baltimore, Md., USA.

Tzaban, H. (1979) "A Biological Model of Wheat Growing in Northern Negev," PhD thesis, Hebrew University of Jerusalem, Rehovot, Israel.

DISCUSSION OPENING—*Robert R. Deuson and Edna T. Loehman* (Purdue University)

The paper by Bigman, Becker, and Barak describes a new type of moral hazard relevant to agriculture in semiarid areas: in response to drought compensation, crop rotation periods are different and planting dates are earlier with insurance than without it. A "dynamic" aspect is thus introduced into moral hazard.

Nine sets of rotation/irrigation/planting decisions were examined in terms of the resulting distribution of net profit. Historical data and a biological yield model were used to generate the distribution. A fixed price of wheat was assumed; i.e., price effects of alternative decisions were ignored. Such price effects may be large if large increases occur in production as a result of the programme.

Farmer decisions with and without insurance were first modelled using stochastic dominance as the choice criterion. With the compensation programme, all farmers would switch to a rotation in which every year one-fifth of the land is fallowed. The effects on production are evaluated in terms of net gain for the national economy—evidently the value of increased grain production minus the cost of compensation. However, the meaning of the two "net gain" columns in Table 2 is not clear, and the paper lacks sufficient detail for one to be able to assess the analysis.

The paper looks at the effects of constraining rotation decisions as a necessary condition for farmers to obtain compensation. The effect of the constraint is to increase the amount of fallow land, thus reducing the compensation that must be paid. Again, following the numerical results is difficult because of the lack of explanation. The authors argue that such constraints are possible to enforce because of the technology of aerial photography. However, the costs of use of this technology are not compared to its benefits.

The problem studied by the paper is thus very interesting, but the paper is unsatisfactory because of the lack of detail and some serious omissions. The paper also does not draw any general conclusions from the analysis other than the specific application to constrained compensation in the Negev.

[No general discussion of this paper was reported.]

Dynamic Model of Capital Structure for the Noncorporate Firm

Larry S. Karp and Robert A. Collins[1]

Abstract: A dynamic model of capital structure for the noncorporate farm is developed and analyzed. In this model, the probability of bankruptcy increases as the farmer's debt/asset ratio increases. Funds invested outside agriculture earn a riskless rate of return. The farmer/proprietor is also able to obtain a riskless wage from off-farm employment; this wage may differ from the implicit wage received as a farmer. The expected return to equity on the farm depends on the leverage. The model examines the effects on optimal capital structure of (1) bankruptcy risk, (2) the difference between the riskless rate and the expected return in agriculture, and (3) the difference between the off-farm wage and the implicit on-farm wage. The third element introduces an incentive for the proprietor to change leverage over the proprietor's lifetime; this occurs if the difference between the wages is nonzero but constant. If the difference between the wages is zero, a constant leverage is optimal under reasonable circumstances. The model predicts that older farmers require more leverage to induce them to remain in farming and that they tend to reduce their leverage as retirement approaches. The model is tested with cross-sectional data.

Introduction

Current financial difficulties in commercial agriculture highlight the importance of the capital structure of agricultural firms. This paper develops a theory to explain the noncorporate firm's choice of capital structure at a point in time and the evolution of capital structure over the lifetime of the proprietor.

The Modigliani-Miller theorem (Modigliani and Miller, 1958) provides conditions under which the value of a publicly traded firm is independent of its capital structure. Hellwig (1981) reexamines the theorem and concludes, "From a practical point of view, it seems reasonable to suppose that the Modigliani-Miller principle fails when there is a chance of bankruptcy" (p. 167). Myers (1984) reviews the various explanations that have been advanced to explain the capital structure of publicly traded firms. In answer to the question, "How do firms choose their capital structures?," he replies, "We don't know" (p. 575).

The theory of the capital structure of public forms is, at best, unresolved; theories about the capital structure of noncorporate firms are virtually nonexistent. The incompleteness of markets for noncorporate equity means that one cannot appeal to market arbitrage forces, which form the basis for models in the Modigliani-Miller tradition. The market value of proprietary equity is the liquidating value of the firm (the market value of assets minus liabilities). The value of proprietary equity is determined in the asset markets and does not necessarily reflect the management of the individual firm. Rather than attempting to maximize the market value of equity, the proprietor is likely to concentrate on the stream of income that can be withdrawn from the firm or on the expected liquidation value of the firm at retirement. The choice of capital structure affects these goals.

The farmer's only source of external financing is assumed to be debt; given a level of equity, the farmer decides whether to remain in farming and, if so, how much debt to acquire. Since debt is, by an overwhelming margin, the most significant source of external finance for US farms, the assumption is reasonable. Innes (1987) models the debt/external equity option for firms as an agency problem; his model provides conditions under which an all-debt contract results in equilibrium.

By assumption, bankruptcy occurs when debt equals assets. Bulow and Shoven (1978) demonstrate that in a variety of circumstances this assumption does not provide the optimal foreclosure rule. Their model describes the publicly held firm, but similar arguments hold for the proprietary firm. For the purposes of the present model, foreclosures must occur under prescribed conditions; for simplicity, this is taken to be where assets net of debt are less than or equal to zero.

The chief concern here is with the dynamics of capital structure. In order to keep the model tractable, a simple description of the stochastics is used and the farmer is assumed to be risk neutral. This permits identification on the effects on capital structure of the:

underlying riskiness of the enterprise, constraints on the reinvestment of income, level of equity, time until retirement, and opportunity cost of managing the enterprise.

The next section assumes that the opportunity cost of managing the enterprise is zero. This results in a very simple problem for which a closed-form solution can be obtained. The optimal leverage is independent of equity; under plausible circumstances, the optimal leverage is a constant that balances risks and returns.

In the subsequent section, the opportunity cost of managing the firm is assumed to be positive; an approximate solution for this problem is obtained. Young farmers who go bankrupt have greater possibilities of starting a second career than do old farmers, so the opportunity cost of managing the firm decreases over time. The optimal leverage depends on the level of equity and the time until retirement. This model provides two explanations for why young farmers would be expected to be more highly leveraged than old farmers: they tend to have less equity, and their opportunities outside farming are greater. In neither model is it optimal to plan to retire free of debt.

The model abstracts from small variations in income in order to concentrate on a single catastrophic event, bankruptcy. The probability that bankruptcy occurs over a unit of time depends on the leverage. For example, a firm with a debt/asset ratio of 0.8 will not survive a 25-percent loss in assets; the same loss with a debt/asset ratio of 0.7 is tolerable. If the firm does not go bankrupt, it earns a nonstochastic rate of return on assets. The evolution of the equity in continuous time is modelled using a jump process. This model is consistent with Bulow and Shoven's description of a financial crisis. They compare such a crisis with an earthquake. "The important assumption is that the expected future productivity of the firm's plant decreased discontinuously" (note 12, p. 442). This corresponds in the present model to a discontinuous decrease in the value of assets due, for example, to a fall in land prices.

The following two sections elaborate the versions of the present model with and without opportunity cost of managing the firm. Proofs are contained in a longer version of this paper available upon request. The subsequent section provides an empirical test of the hypotheses implied by the theory. A conclusion follows.

Simple Model with Bankruptcy Risk

The farmer's equity at a point in time is $E(t)$ and his debt/asset ratio is δ. The probability of bankruptcy occurring over an interval of time dt is proportional to the increasing convex function $\gamma(\delta)$.

The rate of return on equity net of borrowing costs is the concave function $I(\delta)$ that first increases and then decreases. If the rate of return on assets exceeds the cost of borrowing, an increase in financial leverage increases the rate of return on equity since more assets work for each dollar of equity; this is the leverage multiplier effect. The expected net rate of return on assets declines, however, because of the higher borrowing costs associated with the firm's increased probability of bankruptcy. As long as the multiplier effect exceeds the increased borrowing costs, $I(\ )$ increases; at some value of δ less than 1, $I(\ )$ reaches a maximum and thereafter decreases.

The proportion of income withdrawn from the firm is w. With these definitions, the stochastic differential for equity is:

$$(1)\ dE = (1 - w)\, I[\delta(t)]\, E(t)\, dt + E d\pi,$$

where:

$$Pr(d\pi=-1) = \gamma[\delta(t)]\, dt + o(dt), \text{ and } Pr(d\pi=0) = 1 - \gamma[\delta(t)]\, dt + o(dt),$$

where $o(dt)$ denotes terms of order dt. The deterministic portion of dE is $(1-w)IEdt$, which is the retained portion of earnings over an interval dt; when $d\pi = 0$, equity increases at the expected rate; $(d\pi = -1)$ means that the firm is bankrupt. Equation *(1)* is a jump process.

The manager is assumed to maximize the expectation of the present value of withdrawals plus the liquidation value at retirement. At time t, given equity $E(t)$, his problem is:

$$(2)\quad J(E, t) = \max_{\substack{\delta\in[0,\,1] \\ w\in[\underline{w},\,\infty]}} \xi_t\{\textstyle\int_t^T e^{-\rho s} wIEds + e^{-\rho T}E(T)\},$$

subject to *(1)*. The value function $J(\ )$ gives the farmer's expectation of the present value of the firm. Provided that this is greater than the liquidation value, $e^{-\rho t}E$, the farmer wishes to remain in business.

The optimization problem in *(2)* can be reinterpreted as one of maximizing the expected value of a retirement portfolio consisting of equity in the firm and riskless bonds. With this interpretation, a withdrawal of $wIEdt$ implies an investment of the same amount at the riskless rate ρ.

The withdrawal rate w is unbounded above, so that at any point the farmer can liquidate the firm and receive equity $E(t)$. The lower bound on w is $\underline{w}$. In many cases, one can reasonably assume that $\underline{w} = 0$; i.e., the farmer is capable of retaining all earnings of equity but has no source of outside funds other than debt. A positive value of $\underline{w}$ is appropriate if the proprietor is required to consume more as the proprietor's equity increases, or if the proprietor is committed to a particular balance in the retirement fund consisting of riskless bonds and equity in the firm. A negative value of $\underline{w}$ implies that the proprietor is able to obtain funds at the riskless rate (e.g., by drawing on the proprietor's retirement fund). The additional equity the proprietor can obtain in this manner is proportional to the proprietor's earnings, $I(\ )E$. $\underline{w}$ is assumed to be given, although in a more general model it might be regarded as a control variable.

The important assumptions implicit in *(1)* and *(2)* are:

(i) The farmer is risk neutral.

(ii) The world has two states: either bankruptcy occurs or the farmer earns a nonstochastic return.

(iii) Bankruptcy occurs whenever $E(t) \leq 0$.

(iv) Functions $I(\ )$ and $\gamma(\ )$ do not depend on time.

For the remainder of this section, the following is also assumed:

(v) The value of the programme without equity is zero: $J(0, t) = 0$.

Assumption *(v)* is not innocuous. It implies that the opportunity cost of the farmer's labour equals the (implicit) wage received as a proprietor. More typically, the wage under alternative employment may be greater than the implicit wage. The effect of relaxing assumption *(v)* is considered in the next section. The assumption is useful because it clarifies the effect of the functions $I(\ )$ and $\gamma(\ )$ and the parameter $\underline{w}$ on the choice of δ.

The quantity $\hat{\delta}$ is defined as the leverage that maximizes $I(\delta) - \gamma(\delta)$. At $\hat{\delta}$, the marginal risk and the marginal expected return of increasing the leverage are equal. The quantity $I(\hat{\delta}) - \gamma(\hat{\delta})$ gives the maximized risk-adjusted expected rate of return to equity. The optimal leverage equals $\hat{\delta}$ at retirement, provided that the firm is still in operation. The optimal leverage and withdrawal policy is described in the following proposition.

PROPOSITION 1.

(i) If $\rho = I(\hat{\delta}) - \gamma(\hat{\delta})$, setting $\delta = \hat{\delta}$ is optimal; withdrawal policy is irrelevant.

(ii) If $\rho > I(\hat{\delta}) - \gamma(\hat{\delta})$, liquidating immediately is optimal.

(iii) If $\rho < I(\hat{\delta}) - \gamma(\hat{\delta})$, setting $w = \underline{w}$ is optimal. (a) For $\underline{w} > 0$, the optimal δ increases over time; (b) for $\underline{w} = 0$, maintaining $\delta = \hat{\delta}$ is optimal; and (c) for $\underline{w} < 0$, the optimal δ decreases over time.

This proposition has an intuitive interpretation. If the discount rate ρ equals the risk adjusted rate $I - \gamma$, where the latter is maximized, then the farmer is indifferent between liquidation and staying in business. If asset markets were perfect and management ability homogenous, competitive pressure would cause the liquidation value of the firm to equal its value as a going concern. If the discount rate is greater than the maximized value of the risk-adjusted expected return, the farmer does better to liquidate immediately.

In the case where the discount rate is less than the maximized risk-adjusted expected rate, the value of the firm as a going concern exceeds the liquidation value. The optimal leverage depends on the lower bound of the proportion of withdrawals. If $\underline{w} = 0$, the farmer chooses the leverage that maximizes the risk-adjusted expected return on equity and holds it constant.

Bankruptcy Risk with Positive Opportunity Cost

This section replaces assumption *(v)* with

(v′) $J(0, t) = e^{-\rho t}(c/\rho)(1-e^{-\rho\tau})$,

which uses the definition $\tau = T - t$, the time to retirement. This assumption can be interpreted as the statement that either the wage in the alternative employment exceeds the implicit wage by the amount c or that, in the alternative employment, the farmer accumulates a pension fund at the rate c. Replacing the constant c by a function $c(\tau)$ would complicate the solution without adding insight. The following assumptions are also made:

(vi) $I(\hat{\delta}) > \rho + \gamma(\hat{\delta}) \equiv \alpha$.

(vii) $\underline{w} = 0$.

An appropriate solution to this problem is obtained, which is valid for small c. This solution implies the following two results:

PROPOSITION 2. Older farmers require higher levels of equity to induce them to remain in farming.

PROPOSITION 3.

(i) Farmers with high equity are less highly leveraged than farmers with low equity.

(ii) Given the same level of equity, old farmers are less highly leveraged than middle-aged farmers; the latter may be more highly leveraged than very young farmers.

(iii) An individual farmer tends to decrease leverage over time, conditional on not going bankrupt.

Empirical Test of Model

The principle implications of the model are stated in Propositions 2 and 3. Survey data from Arkansas farmers in 1986 (Collins, 1987) was used to test the model. The survey consisted of a stratified random sample of 2,500 farms selected from the nine crop and livestock reporting districts in Arkansas; the survey resulted in 989 usable survey forms. The average annual earnings of farm labourers in each county of Arkansas (Bureau of the Census, 1982) was used as a proxy for the individual farmer's opportunity cost (the constant c in the previous section).

Since the data did not include time series, one could not determine the extent to which the probability of future financial difficulty depends on current capital structure. That is, the function $\gamma(\delta)$ could not be estimated.

The model assumes constant returns to scale. Previous empirical tests of this hypothesis have been ambiguous. Using OLS, we regressed the rate of return on equity, defined as net cash flows divided by equity, against δ (debt/assets), δ^2, assets, and age. The results strongly support the hypotheses that the return to equity is increasing in leverage and is independent of scale. Weak evidence exists that $I(\delta)$ is concave. The F statistic for the null hypothesis that all coefficients are insignificant exceeds 30, so that hypothesis is strongly rejected.

The data suggest that younger farmers have a higher expected rate of return on equity than older farmers; this may be due to different levels of education. This does not contradict the model, which allows the function $I(\delta)$ to vary across individuals; it does, however, suggest an additional reason why older farmers may be less highly leveraged.

Proposition 2 states that older farmers require more equity to keep them from retiring than do younger farmers. The minimum equity level $\bar{E}$ is directly observable for those who choose to leave farming voluntarily. A sample of farmers who leave farming voluntarily was created by taking farmers who leave because of financial problems, better alternative occupation, or other nonhealth related reasons and who had positive equity. Farmers who indicated they were leaving because of health problems or retirement or those who had nonpositive equity were eliminated from the sample. The results are shown in Table 1. The coefficient on age has the expected sign and is significant at the 3.5-percent level for a one-tailed test. This provides a moderate level of support for Proposition 2.

Proposition 3 states that older farmers and farmers with higher levels of equity tend to be less highly leveraged. In addition, a higher opportunity cost implies higher optimal leverage. The observed leverage was regressed against age, equity, and opportunity cost. All coefficients were highly significant and had the expected sign. Since equity is an explanatory variable and also appears in the denominator of the independent variable, the potential exists for spurious correlation. Proposition 3 was therefore interpreted in terms of debt rather than debt/assets. The proposition implies that the elasticity of debt with respect to equity is less than 1, that the derivative of debt with respect to age is negative, and that the derivative with respect to opportunity cost is positive. Debt was regressed against age, equity, and opportunity cost; we used Tobit analysis since debt is constrained to be nonnegative. The results, shown in Table 2, are consistent with the theory. The derivatives of debt with respect to age and opportunity cost have the expected sign and are significant. The elasticity of debt with respect to equity was calculated using Thraen, Hammond, and Buxton (1978). The elasticity at the sample mean was 0.0526 and was less than 0.2 at all data points.

Table 1—Dependent Variable: Equity

Independent Variable	$\hat{\beta}$	Standard Error	t
Intercept	-176,403	--	--
Age	7,307.6	3,910.69	1.87

[R^2 = 0.0907; $\bar{R}^2$ = 0.0647; Equity = $\beta_0 + \beta_1 AGE + \varepsilon$; N = 36.]

Table 2—Dependent Variable: Debt

Independent Variable	Estimated Coefficient	T-Ratio
Constant	12.5256	2.570
Opportunity cost ($1,000)	3.12345	5.263
Age (years)	-0.384612	-4.427
Equity ($10,000)	0.048492	10.974

Conclusion

This paper has provided a model to explain the evolution of the capital structure of a noncorporate firm over the lifetime of the proprietor. Even if the expected rate of return and probability of failure are stationary, optimal capital structure is likely to change as retirement approaches. The cost of failure is likely to be greater for older farmers, because their opportunities for alternative employment are less attractive; to the extent that they have more equity, they also have more to loose.

The theory is consistent with cross-sectional data of Arkansas farmers. A more comprehensive test will require time series data.

Note

[1]University of California, Berkeley; and University of Arkansas; respectively.

References

Bulow, J.I., and Shoven, J.B. (1978) "Bankruptcy Decision," *Bell Journal of Economics*, Vol. 9.

Collins, R. (1987) "Financial Condition of Arkansas Farm Survey Respondents by Farm Type and Location: 1986," Arkansas Agricultural Experiment Station Bulletin No. 910, Fayetteville, Ark., USA.

Bureau of the Census (1982) "Geographic Area Series Part 4," Vol. 1, Arkansas State and County Data, US Department of Commerce, Washington, D.C., USA.

Hellwig, M. (1981) "Bankruptcy, Limited Liability, and the Modigliani-Miller Theorem," *American Economic Review*, Vol. 71, pp. 155-170.

Innes, R. (1987) "Agency Cost, Farm Debt and Foreclosure: Positive and Policy Issues," Working Paper, Department of Agricultural Economics, University of California, Davis, Calif., USA.

Modigliani, F., and Miller, M. (1958) "Cost of Capital, Corporation Finance, and the Theory of Investment," *American Economic Review*, Vol. 48, No. 3, pp. 261-297.

Myers, S.C. (1984) "Capital Structure Puzzle," *Journal of Finance*, Vol. 39.

Thraen, C.S., Hammond, J.W., and Buxton, B.M. (1978) "Estimating Components of Demand Elasticities from Cross-Sectional Data," *American Journal of Agricultural Economics*, Vol. 60, No. 4, pp. 674-677.

DISCUSSION OPENING—*Shankar Narayanan* (Agriculture Canada)

Karp and Collins' model of optimal capital structure for the noncorporate farm firm is conceptually sound in terms of investment and finance theory and encompasses key capital and investment variables; i.e., net cash flow, debt/equity, rate of return to equity, opportunity costs of the absence of market arbitrage for noncorporate assets, and risk of bankruptcy. The assumptions and limiting conditions also appear quite relevant. The prepositions that follow validate traditional theories and observations relating to business and capital investment. Specifically, propositions 2 and 3 follow from the analysis of optimal leverage under bankruptcy risk with positive opportunity cost to the owner, and the dynamic relationship between current financial leverage and future financial condition present very useful and interesting policy and programme implications.

Including a well-defined net revenue function that incorporates unrealized capital appreciation in the rate of return to equity component of the value function *J( )* is suggested for consideration. Such explicit representation of the production environment will not only help to enhance the model's analytical ability but also facilitate obtaining determinate measurements of expected future values of prices (inputs and outputs) and capital gains and losses from available medium and long-term forecasts of the market situation and macroeconomic environment.

By the same token, a discount rate function can also be endogenized to reduce the dependence on exogenous expected discount rate values used for present value purposes. This function will generally depend on financial leverage and therefore could be linked to the bankruptcy risk function under a simultaneous system.

Consideration of liquidation value of equity at the time of retirement in the model implies allowing for liquidation losses due to sale under duress (losses varying according to type of assets—more for some and less for others). Expected future market value seems more logical in this regard.

Some of my professional colleagues are of the view that experimental simulations using this dynamic model could be tried for representative farm situations. Hypothetical or probable values for changing equity levels, withdrawal rates, rates of returns to equity, or, in the case of endogenized revenue function, the corresponding production coefficients, costs, and prices, discount rates or discount rate function parameters, expected time path to retirement, etc., will have to be assumed in this regard. In this way, the impacts on maximizing the value function for alternative leverage situations for representative farm firms could be evaluated. The results from these experiments can be used to determine the probability of future financial difficulty based on the current capital structure for typical farm situations. The estimation of the probability at the aggregate level is reportedly not feasible due to lack of time series data with adequate degrees of freedom. In this regard, in Canada, data from three farm credit surveys (6,000 sample farms) conducted in 1981, 1984, and 1986 supplemented with the census and national farm survey data for 1980, 1982, 1983, 1985, and 1987 provide a good eight-year series of matched time series/cross section farm finance data for such estimation.

Defining the rate of return to equity as net cash flow divided by equity (as shown in the empirical analysis) precludes noncash expenses (depreciation) in a conventional accounting sense. Strictly speaking, total return to equity is the residual from farm cash income plus real capital gains on assets and debts after depreciation and interest charges.

The effect of inflation on real interest rates in determining the optimal capital structure in this model is not clear and needs clarification. This is important because, as observed in the 1980s, real interest rates were lowest (negative) when the land value and nominal capital gains were at the peak, followed by a rapid slide in land values in the early to mid-1980s when real interest rates rose sharply.

Government policy and programmes (credit and income policy) impact directly and indirectly on the firm's behaviour with respect to acquisitions, income generation, and liquidation of assets over time. This has taken a special significance after the 1980s financial crisis of the industry in the USA and Canada, resulting in new credit and debt review programmes to facilitate restructuring. How to allow for the impact of government policy and programmes in the model warrants consideration.

This model is clearly relevant to large noncorporate commercial farms in the developed economies (North America, EC, and some Latin American countries). Its applicability to commercial farm situations in developing country agriculture is perhaps questionable.

GENERAL DISCUSSION—*Manuel Cabanes, Rapporteur* (Escuela Superior de Técnica Empresarial Agrícola, Universidad de Córdoba)

Karp was asked about the time horizon considered in his dynamic model of capital structure for the noncorporate farm. In his answer, he stated that the time horizon used was the farmer's life expectancy. Karp was asked whether the constant consumption hypothesis contemplated in the model implied the reinvestment of the surplus obtained. In his reply, Karp stated that reinvestment was not a significant aspect in his model.

Participants in the general discussion included C. Alves, G. Corazza, G.T. Jones, E. Soliman, and H. von Witzke.

Export Elasticities for US and Brazilian Soyabeans: Weighted-Market-Share Approach

Cecil W. Davison and Carlos A. Arnade[1]

Abstract: Price and income elasticities for imports of US and Brazilian soyabeans by each of the eight major world soyabean importers and the rest of the world were weighted by their shares of the respective soyabean markets and summed to approximate total price and income elasticities for US and Brazilian soyabean exports. This weighted-market-share technique was applied to elasticity estimates derived from two different procedures: Sirhan and Johnson's market-share approach and direct estimation. Estimates from both procedures indicated that, in the short run (1 year) during 1972-85, soyabean exports from the USA were inelastic with respect to price; from Brazil they were elastic with respect to price; and from both countries they were elastic with respect to income.

Introduction

The price elasticity of demand is important to policy makers interested in expanding agricultural exports and increasing revenues to farmers. If the demand for agricultural exports is elastic, then lowering the export price will increase exports and sales revenue. Consequently, both policy makers and researchers are interested in elasticity estimates that most accurately reflect price and quantity responses in the market. Published estimates of US soyabean export elasticities range from inelastic to elastic, with no consensus on the appropriate range. This paper presents a new approach for estimating such elasticities, and gives the results for US and Brazilian soyabean exports.

Background

Gardiner and Dixit (1987) reviewed 16 estimates of the short-run price elasticity of demand for US soyabean exports, ranging from -0.14 to -2.00 and published during 1971-84. The price elasticity is expected to differ among commodities and change with time. Typically, estimates for a particular commodity vary because of differences in estimation methods, assumptions in the analysis, time period of estimation, type of data (quarterly or annual), and quality of data available to researchers. Variations in assumptions, time periods, and data are expected among published elasticity estimates, and can obscure variations due to the methods employed and data aggregation. The research summarized by Gardiner and Dixit includes the estimation methods of direct estimation, calculation, and simulation.

Direct estimation and other approaches that use aggregate data (commodity-specific export demand data added across country-specific markets) in one or a few equations to estimate export demand equations and elasticities are subject to inherent problems that include the following:

1. Elasticities vary across countries. An aggregate response estimate does not reveal the different responses in individual markets. This becomes important as markets and market shares change over time.

2. Simultaneous-equation bias is likely when a producer's exports are aggregated. Imports of US soyabeans by one or two countries may not influence US prices, but aggregate US exports may.

These problems associated with aggregate data in estimation and the inconclusive range of published elasticity estimates for US soyabean exports highlight the need for a better estimation approach with credible results.

New Estimation Approach

Sirhan and Johnson (1971) used a market-share approach to estimate price elasticities in two US cotton markets. Their approach is extended in this study by identifying all the world's major soyabean importers, which collectively took over 85 percent of all US and Brazilian soyabean exports during the estimation period, and using market-specific (disaggregated) data in estimating elasticities for US and Brazilian soyabeans in each of those markets. A single rest-of-the-world equation, estimated for the remainder of the US and Brazilian market, is subject to aggregate-data problems, but they have now been confined to an estimate associated with less than 15 percent of the exports.

Elasticity estimates from each of these markets are then weighted by their respective share of the US and Brazilian export market and totalled to approximate an export demand elasticity for the USA and Brazil across all markets. For comparison, this weighted-market-share method is also applied to elasticity estimates from direct estimation of imports of US and Brazilian soyabeans by these major world markets.

Method

World soyabean importers were ranked for 1980-85 to identify current markets. The top eight (EC-9, Japan, Spain, China, Mexico, USSR, South Korea, and Portugal) imported 83 percent of all soyabean exports during that period. Following previous research (Davison and Arnade, 1987), the estimating equations were specified two ways, as linear and log-linear (Cobb-Douglas) combinations of the independent variables. Since the fits of the linear functions were generally not better than the logarithmic ones, the latter were used for this analysis. The equations were specified as:

$$(1)\ Y = a_0 X_1^{a_1} X_2^{a_2}, \ldots, X_n^{a_n} e^{u},$$

and estimated in the form:

$$(2)\ \log Y_i = \log a_{0i} + a_{1i} \log X_{1i} + a_{2i} \log X_{2i}, \ldots, + a_{5i} \log X_{5i} + u_1, \text{ and}$$

$$(3)\ \log Z_i = \log b_{0i} + b_{1i} \log X_{1i} + b_{2i} \log X_{2i}, \ldots, + b_{5i} \log X_{5i} + u_2,$$

where:

Y_i = total soyabean imports by a country-specific (*i*th) market;
Z_i = exporter's share of that market (e.g., imports of US soyabeans/total soyabean imports in the *i*th country);
X_{1i} = exporter's soyabean price ($i = 1$ for the US gulf and $i = 2$ for Brazil, Jan.-Dec. average, \$/t, in Table 1);
X_{2i} = per capita real GNP in the *i*th country and, for the rest of the world, per capita total reserves minus gold divided by industrial country CPI;
X_{3i} = pigmeat production in the *i*th country (1,000 t);
X_{4i} = real exchange rate (foreign currency units divided by foreign CPI per US dollar divided by the US CPI), and, for the rest of the world, Special Drawing Rights divided by industrial country CPI per dollar divided by the US CPI;
X_{5i} = freight rate ratio (rate from US gulf to *i*th market divided by the rate from Argentina), or, for the EC-9 and South Korea, soyabean supply in the *i*th country (beginning stocks plus production);
a_{ji}, b_{ji} = fixed parameters; and
u_i = normally distributed random errors.

To expand the degrees of freedom and reflect the influence of floating exchange rates, data were selected for 1972-85. Macroeconomic data (GNP, exchange rates, and CPI indexes) came from the International Monetary Fund (1986); population, price, soyabean stocks and production, and livestock data came from the US Department of Agriculture (1986); soyabean exports (imports) from United Nations trade data tapes; and freight rates from the International Wheat Council (1981-85 and 1986). Zellner's (1962) unrestricted seemingly unrelated regression, using annual data, provided individual estimates of the parameters on the exogenous variables (X's).

In the market-share approach used by Sirhan and Johnson, the price elasticity of an exporter in a specific market equals the sum of the price elasticities from the total import equation and the market-share equation. Since the parameters estimated in this specification are elasticity estimates, the price elasticity of demand for an exporter to the ith country is a_{1i} plus b_{1i}, from equations *(2)* and *(3)*. The elasticity estimate from the ith country is then weighted by its share of the exporter's 1972-85 market, and added to other similarly weighted elasticity estimates from the rest of the exporter's markets to a total price elasticity approximation for that exporter.

The price elasticity of demand for imports of US and Brazilian soyabeans was also estimated directly, using:

$$(4)\ \log W_i = \log c_{0i} + c_{1i} \log X_{1i} + c_{2i} \log X_{2i}, \ldots, + c_{5i} \log X_{5i} + u_3,$$

where W_i represents imports of US and Brazilian soyabeans by the ith country.

Results

Estimators and t-values from the regression estimations of the total-soyabean-import and the exporter-share equations are presented in Table 1. Elasticity estimates, added from the estimators in Table 1, are presented in Table 2, where they are weighted by market shares and totalled to get aggregate elasticity approximations for the USA and Brazil, the two leading soyabean exporters for 1972-85. Space constraints do not allow presentation of all the estimators and t-values from equations where US and Brazilian elasticities were estimated directly, but the price and income elasticities are presented, weighted, and totalled in Table 3.

The weighted elasticities were summed two ways: first by totalling all that had the expected sign and then adding the wrong-sign estimates. Adding the wrong-sign estimates to the expected-sign totals changed the price and income elasticity approximations but did not change them from elastic to inelastic or vice versa. The market-share approach and the direct estimation approach produced similar aggregate elasticity approximations: US soyabean exports were inelastic with respect to price, while Brazil's were elastic. Exports from both countries were elastic with respect to income.

Implications

Results of this study contain implications for researchers who estimate elasticities by various methods and for policy makers who are confronted by numerous elasticity estimates that are not always consistent.

For Researchers

Elasticity estimates from Sirhan and Johnson's market-share approach (Table 2) and from direct estimation (Table 3) are so similar that they appear fairly robust across these two methods.

Table 1–Estimation Results for Soyabean Import Equations, 1972-85†

	a_{01}	X_{11}	X_{12}	X_{21}	X_{31}	X_{41}	X_{51}	R^2	D-W	F
EC-9:										
Total	7.235	-0.2524	0.3140	1.663	--	-0.4269	-0.0093	0.91	2.273	405**
	(11.72)**	(-3.03)**	(3.97)**	(7.39)**		(-7.38)**	(-0.72)			
USA	0.8057	-0.2040	0.1340	0.2905	--	-0.3153	-0.0364	-0.16	0.921	8.40**
	(0.72)	(1.14)	(0.82)	(0.70)		(-3.27)**	(-0.63)			
Brazil	-31.12	1.400	-0.7445	-12.46	--	2.878	0.4885	0.16	1.213	20**
	(-3.25)	(0.92)	(-0.52)	(-3.48)		(3.84)	(1.00)			
Japan:										
Total	3.083	0.1527	-0.2927	0.0985	0.8218	0.0154	--	0.74	1.927	126**
	(1.61)	(0.66)	(-1.39)	(0.36)	(4.33)**	(0.14)				
USA	1.274	-0.1276	0.0164	0.1722	--	-0.1569	-0.0329	0.70	2.210	93**
	(5.97)**	(-2.39)**	(0.33)	(4.99)**		(-6.69)	(-1.89)			
Brazil	-57.40	28.86	-19.71	-13.93	--	1.643	-1.050	0.58	2.201	60**
	(-3.01)	(4.67)	(-3.38)	(-3.73)		(0.84)	(-0.52)			
Spain:										
Total	-1.858	0.3505	0.5926	-1.536	0.4085	0.0279	--	0.38	1.204	39**
	(-0.48)	(0.35)	(0.66)	(-0.95)	(1.25)	(0.20)				
USA	-1.708	-0.3836	0.4126	-1.388	--	-0.0084	0.0389	-0.07	1.690	11**
	(-0.64)	(-0.60)	(0.76)	(-1.19)		(-0.10)	(0.22)			
Brazil	14.03	1.276	-2.417	6.818	--	-0.4764	1.338	-0.36	1.959	4.13**
	(0.94)	(0.30)	(-0.64)	(1.07)		(-0.86)	(1.09)			
China:										
Total	4.165	-0.1600	-0.1695	1.406	-0.2256	-0.0335	--	0.80	1.953	170**
	(2.21)*	(-0.32)	(-0.37)	(5.36)**	(-0.78)	(-0.09)				
Mexico:										
Total	-10.78	3.419	-1.064	1.378	1.852	0.0509	--	0.37	2.189	39**
	(-0.85)	(0.93)	(-0.31)	(0.63)	(1.79)*	(0.06)				
USA	-5.774	0.2627	-0.1105	-1.755	--	0.0719	0.7569	0.62	2.336	68**
	(-3.92)**	(0.45)	(-0.20)	(-6.65)		(0.67)	(4.23)			
Brazil	47.15	5.176	-8.215	14.79	--	0.8278	-6.797	0.07	1.998	16**
	(1.73)*	(0.51)	(-0.87)	(2.91)**		(0.42)	(-2.16)			
USSR:										
Total	312.02	5.316	-10.05	26.33	-14.30	2.061	--	0.14	2.073	23**
	(4.93)**	(0.75)	(-1.50)	(2.58)**	(-3.94)	(1.05)				
USA	386.01	-18.22	11.13	59.52	--	-13.10	0.4341	0.30	2.245	28**
	(5.88)**	(-2.17)*	(1.39)	(6.07)**		(-7.34)**	(0.16)			
Brazil	297.19	3.799	-1.497	53.37	--	-17.86	2.290	0.16	1.558	20**
	(2.10)*	(0.39)	(-0.16)	(2.43)**		(-4.30)**	(0.72)			
South Korea:										
Total	11.45	-1.508	0.9246	3.436	0.4929	-1.017	0.3648	0.95	2.579	705**
	(3.37)**	(-1.99)*	(1.29)	(5.65)**	(1.98)*	(-2.96)**	(1.66)			
Portugal:										
Total	4.129	0.2256	-0.0239	3.901	2.691	0.2256	--	0.67	1.646	95**
	(0.43)	(0.34)	(-0.01)	(2.57)**	(3.45)**	(0.34)				
USA	-4.775	0.5797	-0.3310	-0.7759	--	0.3635	-0.1368	-0.40	2.657	3.38**
	(-1.37)	(0.64)	(-0.41)	(-1.34)		(1.29)	(-0.48)			
Brazil	34.95	-2.722	0.7739	4.378	--	-4.437	1.123	-0.54	2.499	1.19
	(0.62)	(-0.21)	(0.07)	(0.47)		(-0.93)	(0.26)			
Rest of the world:‡										
Total	8.418	0.4698	-0.6899	-0.1044	--	-2.521	--	0.77	1.993	156**
	(6.74)**	(0.79)	(-1.23)	(-0.66)		(-4.02)**				
USA	0.7318	0.2470	-0.3555	0.0693	--	0.069	0.0758	-0.02	1.712	12**
	(1.71)*	(1.20)	(-1.85)	(0.23)		(0.23)	(1.00)			
Brazil	-15.61	3.358	0.0430	1.609	--	13.00	-0.2989	0.36	1.550	33**
	(-2.39)**	(1.18)	(0.02)	(1.31)		(2.33)	(-0.25)			

†For explanation of variables, see text; *D-W* = Durbin-Watson statistic; *F* = test of significance of the model (see Chow, 1983, pp. 58-60); *t*-values in parentheses (significance levels for one-tail test: * = 5 percent and ** = 1 percent); and -- = insufficient data for estimation or variable not used.

‡Excludes the USA, Brazil, and Argentina, which are major soyabean exporters, not major soyabean importers.

The multiple-equation weighted-market-share approach substantially reduces the aggregated data problems, including the spectre of simultaneous equation bias intrinsic to a single rest-of-the-world equation.

The multiple-equation approach requires more data but has the advantage of providing market-specific elasticity estimates that can be evaluated individually. Questionable equations or estimators can be identified and isolated. Results from the equations for the USSR and Spain, plus some of the share equations, illustrate this point with their poor fits. Researchers can then re-estimate weak equations or use market-specific elasticities judged more appropriate.

Table 2–Price and Income Elasticities, US and Brazilian Soyabean Exports, 1972-85: Market-Share Method†

	Elasticities						Weighted Elasticities			
	Price		Income		Market Share		Price		Income	
	US	Brazil	US	Brazil	US	Brazil	US	Brazil	US	Brazil
EC-9	-0.456	-0.430	1.95	-10.80	0.427	0.507	-0.195	-0.218	0.834	-5.474
	(-3.03)**	(-0.52)	(7.39)**	(-3.48)						
Japan	0.025	-20.00	0.271	-13.83	0.213	0.031	0.005	-0.620	0.058	-0.429
	(0.66)	(-3.38)**	(4.99)**	(-3.73)						
Spain	-0.033	-1.82	-2.92	5.28	0.092	0.198	-0.003	-0.361	-0.269	1.046
	(-0.60)	(-0.64)	(-0.95)	(1.07)						
China	-0.160	-0.170	1.41	1.41	0.054	0.005	-0.009	-0.001	0.076	0.076
	(-0.32)	(-0.37)	(5.36)**	(5.36)**						
Mexico	3.68	-9.28	-0.377	16.17	0.027	0.030	0.099	-0.278	-0.010	0.485
	(0.93)	(-0.87)	(-6.65)	(2.91)**						
USSR	-12.90	-11.55	85.85	79.70	0.025	0.142	-0.323	-1.640	2.146	11.32
	(-2.17)*	(-1.50)	(6.07)**	(2.43)**						
South Korea	-1.51	0.92	3.44	3.44	0.020	0.004	-0.030	0.004	0.069	0.014
	(-1.99)*	(1.29)	(5.65)**	(5.65)**						
Portugal	0.805	0.750	3.13	8.28	0.013	0.023	0.010	0.017	0.041	0.190
	(0.64)	(0.07)	(2.57)**	(0.47)						
Rest of the world‡	0.717	-0.647	-0.035	1.50	0.127	0.060	0.091	-0.039	-0.004	0.090
	(0.79)	(-1.23)	(-0.66)	(1.31)						
World total					0.998	1.000				
Right sign							-0.56	-3.16	3.22	13.22
All							-0.35	-3.14	2.94	7.32

†Market shares are averages for 1972-85; weighted elasticities are elasticities times the market shares, computed from unrounded data; *t*-values in parentheses, from the largest of the two estimators (Table 1) totaled to obtain these estimates; and significance levels (one-tail test), * = 5 percent and ** = 1 percent.
‡Excludes the USA, Brazil, and Argentina.

Table 3–Price and Income Elasticities, US and Brazilian Soyabean Exports, 1972-85: Direct Estimation†

	Elasticities						Weighted Elasticities			
	Price		Income		Market Share		Price		Income	
	US	Brazil	US	Brazil	US	Brazil	US	Brazil	US	Brazil
EC-9	-0.478	-0.519	2.69	-14.01	0.427	0.507	-0.204*	-0.263	1.148**	-7.101
	(-2.00)*	(-0.35)	(4.71)**	(-2.50)						
Japan	0.104	-20.37	0.149	-22.15	0.213	0.031	0.022	-0.631**	0.032	-0.687
	(0.46)	(-3.51)**	(0.78)	(-2.55)						
Spain	-0.457	5.97	-1.53	3.69	0.092	0.198	-0.042	1.182	-0.140	0.731
	(-0.44)	(0.96)	(-2.07)	(0.27)						
China	-0.309	--	1.27	--	0.054	0.005	-0.017	--	0.069**	--
	(-0.64)		(5.89)**							
Mexico	3.78	-8.00	-3.10	52.80	0.027	0.030	0.102	-0.240	-0.084	1.584**
	(1.06)	(-0.81)	(-1.76)	(4.86)**						
USSR	-13.18	-12.90	86.58	74.69	0.025	0.142	-0.330	-1.832	2.165**	10.607**
	(-1.64)	(-1.36)	(7.67)**	(3.27)**						
South Korea	-1.51	--	4.79	--	0.020	0.004	-0.030*	--	0.096**	--
	(-1.91)*		(7.17)**							
Portugal	-0.566	12.84	3.22	38.79	0.013	0.023	-0.007	0.295	0.042	0.892**
	(-0.22)	(1.09)	(1.65)	(3.27)**						
Rest of the world‡	0.565	-0.751	-0.259	2.44	0.127	0.060	0.072	-0.045	-0.033	0.146**
	(0.79)	(-0.31)	(-1.34)	(2.84)**						
World total					0.998	1.000				
Right sign							-0.63	-3.01	3.55	13.98
All							-0.43	-1.53	3.30	6.17

†Market shares are averages for 1972-85; weighted elasticities are elasticities times the market shares, computed from unrounded data; *t*-values in parentheses; significance levels (one-tail test), * = 5 percent and ** = 1 percent; and -- = insufficient data for estimation.
‡Excludes the USA, Brazil, and Argentina.

For Policy Makers

This multiple-equation approach provides information, including price and income elasticity estimates, that could help policy makers tailor export marketing strategies to fit specific markets. This approach, with elasticities weighted by market shares, also allows export programme planners to adjust for changes in customer elasticities and shares of the US and Brazilian soyabean market, whereas elasticity estimates from the single-equation approach must presume that individual customer elasticities and market shares will remain unchanged from the estimation period.

The inelastic price elasticity estimates for US soyabean exports indicate that revenues would be decreased in the short run by lowering US export prices, while the elastic estimates for Brazilian soyabean exports indicate that revenues could be increased in the short run by lowering prices. The elastic income elasticity estimates suggest that increased income in the importing countries would increase US and Brazilian export revenues.

Note

[1]Economic Research Service, US Department of Agriculture.

References

Chow, G.C. (1983) *Econometrics*, McGraw-Hill Book Co., New York, N.Y., USA.

Davison, C.W., and Arnade, C.A. (1987) *Export Demand for U.S. Corn and Soybeans*, Staff Report No. AGES870723, Economic Research Service, US Department of Agriculture, Washington, D.C., USA.

Gardiner, W.H., and Dixit, P.M. (1987) *Price Elasticity of Demand: Concepts and Estimates*, Foreign Agricultural Economic Report No. 228, Economic Research Service, US Department of Agriculture, Washington, D.C., USA.

International Monetary Fund (1986) *International Financial Statistics: 1986 Yearbook*, Washington, D.C., USA.

International Wheat Council (1981-85) *World Wheat Statistics*, London, UK.

International Wheat Council (1986) *Market Report*, London, UK, Jan.-Aug.

Sirhan, G.A., and Johnson, P.R. (1971) "Market-Share Approach to the Foreign Demand for US Cotton," *American Journal of Agricultural Economics*, Vol. 53, No. 4, pp. 593-599.

US Department of Agriculture (1986) "Commodity and Livestock Production, Supply, and Disposition Database," unpublished computer data, Foreign Agricultural Service, US Department of Agriculture, Washington, D.C., USA.

Zellner, A. (1962) "Efficient Method of Estimating Seemingly Unrelated Regressions and Tests for Aggregation Bias," *Journal of the American Statistical Association*, Vol. 57, No. 298, pp. 348-368.

DISCUSSION OPENING—*Jack E. Houston* (University of Georgia)

Alfred North Whitehead was quoted as saying, "A theory is an unguarded statement of a partial truth.... Criticism of a theory does not start from the question, True or False? It consists in noting its scope of useful application, and its failure beyond that scope." In an extension of a Sirhan and Johnson approach, Davison and Arnade have presented a "new" disaggregated weighted-market-share approach for estimating soyabean export and import elasticities. The intended users of these elasticity estimates are policy makers in the major exporting countries, the USA and Brazil.

Disaggregation of the total, US, and Brazilian exports by importing countries appears to offer potentially valuable information not available in more aggregated world trade models.

Variables included in the theoretically and historically based model clearly affected importing countries differently, but, in many cases, insignificantly. Brazilian soyabean prices were significant only in EC total import elasticity estimates. Several factors discussed later may have some bearing on this finding, but US Gulf port prices, which are closely linked to world commodity futures trading markets in the USA were little better in price elasticity measures. Other structural and supply-related variables not considered in this approach may also be responsible within this particular 1972-85 time period, not least of which may be Brazil's changes in export policies from beans and products to soyabean meal only.

Perhaps due to the brevity of the paper, several aspects of the estimation procedure were not discussed. The shortness of the time series (14 annual observations) and the number of parameters being estimated may not be entirely overcome by employing the seemingly unrelated regressions technique. Multicolinearity was not explicitly addressed and likely influenced the incidence of theoretically incorrect signs and/or insignificance of some variables and thus their elasticities. This was particularly evident in estimates of the market shares, which were assumed to have constant elasticities in the log-log specification. Weather and politically motivated soyabean supply volatility during the period estimated subverted any meaningful relationship between the US and Brazilian market shares and variables included in the model.

Serial correlation problems in many of the country-specific elasticity and market-share equations diminish confidence in the efficiency of the estimated parameters and their significance, but could have been overcome in a Parks two-step procedure. Market-share weights used multiplicatively with price elasticity estimates, however, were simple averages over the 1972-85 period. Combined with Brazil's entry into the world soyabean export market and early circumstance-specific gains in share, these multipliers are only examples of information potentially available from a more completely developed model of weighted-market-share elasticities.

The exploratory use of the disaggregated weighted-market-share approach was referred to in the authors' concluding remarks, including suggestions for further analysis. While raising the possibility of country-specific market policy information, effects of admittedly "questionable estimates, for individual markets, on the estimate of aggregate elasticities" remain in this approach. Whether the approach has the potential to overcome soyabean supply volatility, structural change, and export market structure factors not presently included in the approach remains to be seen. Credible implications depend on satisfying these and other remaining questions.

GENERAL DISCUSSION—*Manuel Cabanes, Rapporteur* (Escuela Superior de Técnica Empresarial Agrícola, Universidad de Córdoba)

Questions were asked about the fact that soyabeans are not a single product, but several products (e.g., meal and oil), and how this could affect the authors' analysis. In reply, Arnade stated that as far as exports were concerned, only soyabeans were considered. With respect to the possibility that different importing countries may use the product derived from soyabeans in different proportions, he answered that perhaps the different set of equations formulated for each market would take care of that.

One participant commented that the consumption of pigmeat was included as an explanatory variable but not consumption of chicken or milk. Arnade explained that pigmeat consumption was the only data available for all the markets considered and for the whole period of time. He added that perhaps in the future the quality of the model could be improved.

Participants in the general discussion included C. Alves, G. Corazza, G.T. Jones, E. Soliman, and H. von Witzke.

EC Enlargement and US Agricultural Exports

Tassos Haniotis and Glenn C.W. Ames[1]

Abstract: The impact of the EC enlargement on US agricultural exports to the EC is analyzed using a model differentiating products by origin. Simulation of the enlargement, based on average 1983-85 trade flows, indicates that the integration of Spanish and Portuguese agriculture into the EC variable import levy régime results, *ceteris paribus*, in an 8-percent drop in maize imports by the new EC members. Soyabean exports to the EC increase by 11 percent, benefiting from the combination of increased maize tariffs and duty free entry of oilseeds into the EC. Changes in US maize and soyabean exports to the EC are comparable to total changes in trade flows. The above developments could generate further strains in US-EC agricultural trade relations by increasing the pressure within the EC to balance the CAP reform with the imposition of some form of protection against EC oilseed imports. Simulating the recent EC Commission proposal for an oilseed tax indicates that its imposition would result in a moderate decrease of 3.8 percent in soyabean imports into the enlarged EC because of offsetting changes in maize and soyabean exports into the EC.

Introduction

The 1986 enlargement of the EC to include Spain and Portugal was viewed by the USA as a positive step in the process of European integration. As indicated by previous experience, however, agricultural interests in the USA are not always in harmony with the often reaffirmed US commitment to the ideal of European unity. Only two months after the Spanish and Portuguese accession, the USA and the EC were disputing the impact of the enlargement on US agricultural exports to the new EC members.

Against a background of declining US agricultural exports in the 1980s, the accession of Spain and Portugal to the EC complicated the already strained US-EC agricultural trade relations, and their conflict over the enlargement brought the two sides to the brink of a trade war. Despite their agreement on compensation for US losses of grain exports to Spain, the underlying causes of the US-EC trade conflict are still unresolved and the future of their agricultural trade relations is uncertain. The process of reform that the Common Agricultural Policy is undergoing and its interaction with the new US farm policy objectives, outlined in the Food Security Act of 1985, account for this uncertainty. The concurrence of such developments with the new round of the multilateral trade negotiations of the General Agreement on Tariffs and Trade, in which the two sides entered with apparently different objectives, will probably generate conditions for a further deterioration in US-EC trade relations precisely when their improvement is necessary for the success of the new GATT round.

In the last two decades, US-EC trade conflicts have shifted from US objections to the EC variable import levies to US reaction to the negative impact of EC export subsidies on world markets (Petit, 1985). Yet the recent US-EC trade dispute shifted attention back to the access of US exports to EC markets and to the complexity of the issues involved. The combination of a highly protectionist grain import régime and free entry of oilseeds (and grain substitutes) into the EC has led to the severe dependence of the latter on the USA for nongrain feed imports (Buchholz, 1984). As a result, the process of CAP reform is directly linked, at least in EC priorities, to the issue of the completion of the CAP; i.e., of balancing any liberalization of the CAP grain régime with the introduction of some form of protection for the EC oilseed and grain substitute markets. The recent EC Commission proposal for the imposition of a tax on the consumption of oilseeds, which is still under consideration despite its withdrawal from the 1987 price package, is just an example of possible EC reforms that can adversely affect US-EC trade relations.

US concerns raised by the enlargement were thus directly related to the CAP reform issue because of the integration of the new EC members into the CAP structures. However, import tariff changes in soyabeans and maize, two products that together accounted for 78 percent of US agricultural exports to Spain and Portugal before the enlargement, were implemented in opposite directions. Grain exports from the USA to Spain and Portugal fell under the variable import levy régime, thus resulting in significantly higher import tariffs, while the moderate Spanish and Portuguese soyabean import tariffs were abolished because of the zero tariff binding for EC oilseed imports.

Hence, assessing the impact of the enlargement on US farm exports to the enlarged EC is important in terms of the changes it generated in trade flows to the EC and also in terms of its impact on US-EC agricultural trade relations. The objective of this analysis is to assess this impact on US soyabean and maize exports by simulating alternative policy scenarios concerning policy changes in the enlarged EC.

Methodological Framework

The objective of the present study requires the adoption of a theoretical framework to combine: (a) product differentiation by region of origin and destination, (b) incorporation of trade policies into its structure, and (c) projection of trade flows under alternative assumptions concerning policy changes in the importing regions. Product differentiation by origin and destination is justified by the variability in harvesting seasons among major exporters to the European Community. In addition, the impact of the enlargement requires that the import behaviour of the new EC members is treated separately from that of the EC-10.

A model for differentiated products was first developed by Armington (1969), and was based on the recognition that the perfect substitutability assumption used in world trade models is unrealistic. Consumers do not distinguish commodities only by their kind but also by their place of production. Henceforth, commodities differentiated by *kind* are denoted as "goods" (e.g., soyabeans vs. maize), and those differentiated by *origin* are denoted as "products" (e.g., US vs. Brazilian soyabeans). Three assumptions underlie Armington's model: (1) weak separability of the utility function (which is also assumed to be linearly homogeneous), (2) constant elasticity of substitution between a pair of products in a given market, and (3) equality of the elasticity of substitution between any pair of products in a given market.

Given these assumptions, the methodology developed by Armington treats an importing region's purchasing decision as a two-stage process. In the first stage, expenditure allocation among n imported goods is determined by maximizing importers' utility subject to their income constraint, with resulting import demand functions of the form $X_h = X_h(P_1, P_2, \ldots, P_n, Y)$, where X_h and P_h are quantity and price indexes for good h, and Y is total expenditure. In the second stage, total expenditure on each good (Y_h) is allocated among the m products of that good that are differentiated by origin. This allocation is determined as a solution to the problem of minimizing the cost of purchasing total imports of good h, with resulting import demand functions of the form $X_{hi} = X_{hi}\ (P_{h1}, P_{h2}, \ldots, P_{hm}, Y_h)$. Minimizing the cost of procuring the quantity index X_{hk} subject to X_k and solving for the first order conditions yields the following import demand function for product X_{ik} imported from region i into region k (Armington, 1969; and Sarris, 1980):

$$(1)\ X_{ik}/X_k = a_{ik}^{\sigma_k}(P_{ik}/P_k)^{-\sigma_k},$$

where the subscript h of the good is dropped for reasons of notational simplicity, σ_k is the absolute value of the elasticity of substitution between imports from different origins in region k, P_{ik} is the price of X_{ik}, and P_k is the price index of X_k in region k.

The core of Armington's model is an expression that links changes in the demand for product X_{ik} to changes in its explanatory variables. This expression decomposes the growth in the demand for X_{ik} into an income effect, an own-price effect, the effect of price changes in all related products of the good in question, and the cross-price effect of related goods. In the most general form, percentage changes in the demand for X_{ik} are given by:

$$(2)\ \tilde{X}_{ik} = \theta_k\tilde{Y}_k + \varepsilon_{iik}\tilde{P}_{ik} + \sum_{\substack{j=1\\ j\neq i}}^{m} \varepsilon_{jik}\tilde{P}_{jk} + \sum_{\substack{g=1\\ g\neq h}}^{n} \eta_{gh}\tilde{P}_g,$$

where ε_{jik} is found as (Alston and Scobie, 1987):

$$(3a)\ \varepsilon_{iik} = -(1-S_{ik})\sigma_k + S_{ik}\varepsilon_k,$$

$$(3b)\ \varepsilon_{jik} = S_{jk}(\sigma_k+\varepsilon_k).$$

Equation *(2)* expresses the demand side of the model used in the present analysis. The tilde (˜) denotes percentage changes ($\tilde{x} = dx/x_0$), X_{ik} and P_{ik} are the quantity and price of the product imported from region i into region k, Y_k represents total expenditure for the good in question (h) in region k, P_g is the price of competing good g in region k, and S_{ik} is the value share of imports of the product exported from region i to region k. Parameters σ_k, ε_k, and θ_k are the elasticity of substitution, the import demand elasticity, and the income elasticity for good h respectively, and subscript j corresponds to products of the imported good competing with product i in region k. Finally, η_{gh} is the cross-price elasticity of good h with respect to good g in region k.

Following Sarris (1983), export supply flows of the ith exporting region, expressed in terms of percentage changes, are assumed here to be given by:

$$(4)\ \tilde{X}_i = \beta_i\tilde{p}_i + \phi_i\Delta t,$$

where p_i is the internal export price (excluding all export subsidies or taxes), β_i is the export supply elasticity, and ϕ_i is a trend constant.

Import and export prices are linked by identities of the form:

$$(5)\ \tilde{\tau}_{ik} = \tilde{P}_{ik} - E_{ik}\tilde{p}_i,$$

where E_{ik} is the price transmission elasticity and τ_{ik} is an exogenous shifter through which changes in policy variables, such as tariff changes or exchange rate fluctuations, can be introduced into the model. Finally, the model is closed by the following clearing condition that restricts export supply from region i to equal the summation, across all regions k, of import demand from region i:

$$(6)\ 0 = \tilde{X}_i - \sum_{k=1}^{m} H_{ik}\tilde{X}_{ik}.$$

H_{ik} is the base period quantity share of exports from the ith exporting region to the kth market. Equations *(2)*, *(4)*, *(5)*, and *(6)* form a system of N equations, where $N = 2m^2 + 2m$, that yields percentage changes in its endogenous variables that result from exogenous variable changes. Trade policy changes and their impacts on trade flows can be evaluated by varying the value of the τ_{ik} parameters, while different assumptions concerning the exogenously determined variables (Y_k, ϕ_i) could shed light on the importance of these variables in determining trade flows.

Data and Empirical Specification

Since the focus of this analysis is US exports into the EC and its new member states, the world is divided into five regions: the USA (US), the EC-10 (EC), Spain and Portugal (SP), other major exporters (OE), and the residual rest of the world (RW). Trade data were obtained from the EC *Analytical Tables of Foreign Trade*, UN *Commodity Trade Statistics*, and USDA supply and use tables. Prices used are per-unit values in real terms and adjusted for exchange rate fluctuations. Average trade shares (S_{ik}, H_{ik}) for maize and soyabeans, in volume terms for exports and value terms for imports, were calculated from trade flow matrices constructed for the 1983-85 period.

First-stage import demand equations were estimated using time-series annual data for the 1966-85 period and were specified as:

$$(7)\ lnM = b_0 + b_1 lnPC + b_2 lnPS + b_3 lnY + b_4 lnS + b_5 T + b_6 D.$$

M is the quantity of imports for soyabeans or maize, PC and PS are import prices of maize and soyabeans respectively, Y and S represent real income and domestic supply in the importing region, T is time, and D is a dummy variable for the period after the first EC enlargement. Due to the log-linear form of the import demand equations, estimated coefficients were the elasticities of the corresponding variables ($b_2 = \varepsilon_k$, $b_3 = \eta_k$, and $b_4 = \theta_k$).

The elasticities of substitution σ_k were estimated from equation *(1)* by transforming it into a logarithmic form and then pooling cross-section, time-series data on imports from all origins into an importing region (Figueroa, 1986). Export supply elasticities were derived from simultaneously estimating the demand for and supply of exports of a region by using the methodology proposed by Goldstein and Khan (1978). The structural form of the estimated system is given by:

$$(8a)\ lnX_t = c_0 + c_1 ln(PX/PXW)_t + c_2 lnYW_t + c_3 lnX_{t-1},\ \text{and}$$

$$(8b)\ lnPX_t = d_0 + d_1 lnX_t + d_2 lnP_t + d_3 lnY_t + d_4 lnPX_{t-1}.$$

X and PX are quantity and price indices of exports, PXW and YW are trade-weighted indices of the world export price and the importers' real income, P is the domestic price index, and Y is an index of export capacity. The export supply elasticities were recovered from the estimated structural equations as $\beta_i = (1-d_4)/d_1$. Elasticity values used in model simulations are reported in Table 1. Except for the assumed values of the σ_k and β_i parameters for *RW*, all other reported elasticities are based on estimated equations whose results were generally very robust.

Table 1–Estimated Elasticity Values Used in Model Simulations

*	Maize					Soyabeans				
	US	EC	SP	OE	RW	US	EC	SP	OE	RW
ε_k	--	-0.80	-0.25	--	-0.45	--	-0.29	-1.24	--	-0.60
η_k	--	0.16	0.40	--	0.57	--	0.21	0.45	--	0.18
θ_k	--	2.80	1.69	--	3.33	--	3.70	1.57	--	1.04
σ_k	--	1.59	6.43	--	2.50	--	2.78	4.80	--	2.50
β_i	1.11	0.88	--	0.69	1.00	0.29	--	--	2.84	1.00
E_{ik}	--	0.25	0.75	--	0.50	--	0.90	0.85	--	0.50

*ε_k is the own-price elasticity of import demand, η_k is the cross-price elasticity of import demand between maize and soyabeans, θ_k is the income elasticity of import demand, σ_k is the elasticity of substitution, β_i is the export supply elasticity, and E_{ik} is the price transmission elasticity.

Export growth rates (ϕ_i) were obtained by applying the detrending technique, while real income growth rates (Y_k) of the importing regions were obtained from the IMF *Financial Statistics*. Changes in trade policy variables implied by the EC enlargement were simulated by changing the value of the τ_{ik} parameters that correspond to the price differential between the export price in the *i*th exporting region and the import price in the *k*th importing region. Post-enlargement levels of tariff changes for SP were estimated by weighting tariff changes in each country by its import market share. Finally, values of the price transmission elasticities (E_{ik}) were obtained from Meyers, Devadoss, and Helmar (1966).

Results and Policy Implications

Results of the four alternative scenarios used in model simulations are reported in Table 2. Scenario A simulates the impact of the enlargement including the quota imposed under the US-EC agreement on maize exports to Spain, while the oilseed tax proposal of the EC Commission was simulated by scenario B. Both scenarios A and B incorporate the assumption that past export and income growth trends would continue. In order to isolate the impact of the enlargement from the interaction of export and income growth effects, scenarios A and B were also simulated by setting ϕ_i and Y_k equal to zero (scenarios C and D, respectively).

Table 2—Simulated Impact of the EC Enlargement on Maize and Soyabean Trade Flows*

Trade Flow	Maize Scenarios A	B	C	D	Soyabean Scenarios A	B	C	D
	Percentage changes							
EC imports:								
From US	-0.23	0.40	0.19	0.82	-0.12	-2.20	-0.91	-3.00
From OE	-2.07	-1.44	0.21	0.83	-0.01	-7.81	1.33	-6.40
Total	0.44	1.05	0.21	0.82	-0.12	-3.54	-0.42	-3.84
SP imports:								
From US	0.40	4.30	-8.37	-4.47	3.25	-10.79	11.25	-2.79
From OE	-21.62	-17.75	-7.90	-4.04	3.23	-20.03	14.92	-8.34
Total	-2.40	1.45	-8.17	-4.32	3.00	-12.00	11.20	-3.80
Total exports:								
Of US	9.37	9.63	-0.67	-0.41	0.95	-0.43	0.53	-0.85
Of OE	2.78	2.94	-0.44	-0.27	0.80	-6.37	2.65	-4.53

*Percentage changes are based on average 1983-85 trade flows. Scenario A corresponds to the impact of the enlargement and scenario B to the oilseed tax under the assumption that past export and real income growth trends would continue, while scenarios C and D simulate A and B by ignoring the above trends.

As a result of the adoption of the variable import levy régime by SP, total maize exports to SP decrease by 2.4 percent, while US maize exports increase by 0.4 percent because of the positive impact of their past trend. The significant drop in OE exports to SP (21.6 percent) is also attributed to the influence of past trends, since isolating export and income effects results in a 7.9 percent decline of OE exports to SP. Under the same scenario (D), total and US maize exports to SP decline by 8.2 percent and 8.4 percent, respectively. Finally, due to the small share of the SP market in total US and OE maize exports, the drop in total exports of both the USA and OE is under 1 percent.

The combination of the developments in the SP maize market with those in the SP soyabean market, where import tariffs were abolished, results in a significant shift of soyabean exports to SP. As a result of the enlargement, total and US soyabean exports to SP increase by 3.0 percent and 3.3 percent, respectively. In fact, isolation of the enlargement from other factors indicates that its impact causes corresponding increases of

11.2 percent and 11.3 percent in the above exports. Total US and OE soyabean exports increase by 0.5 percent and 2.6 percent, respectively, under the same scenario (C).

Changes in EC trade flows under scenarios A and C are residual effects of tariff changes in the SP market and are thus insignificant. However, the impact of the imposition of the oilseed tax would be more significant. Under scenario B, total soyabean exports to the EC decline by 3.5 percent, while US exports drop by 2.2 percent. Under scenario D, respective declines are 3.8 percent and 3.0 percent, while maize exports to the EC increase by 0.8 percent, *ceteris paribus*. In SP, the impact of the tax outweighs the impact of the increase in maize tariffs, resulting in a drop of 12.0 percent in soyabean imports and an increase of 1.5 percent in maize imports. Scenario D, however, indicates that the oilseed tax alone causes postenlargement decreases of 4.3 percent and 3.8 percent in SP maize and soyabean imports respectively, while US maize and soyabean exports fall by 4.5 percent and 2.8 percent.

The impact of the oilseed tax on US exports is smaller than US concerns would seem to indicate. This is due to several factors. First, because of the low value of the US export supply elasticity, US exports drop less than OE exports. Second, the low own- and cross-price import demand and price transmission elasticities minimize import substitution possibilities between maize and soyabeans in the EC. Finally, the adverse impact of the enlargement on maize exports into SP limits the substitution impact in the SP, thus resulting in parallel and significant, instead of opposing and significant, impacts on both maize and soyabean markets.

In terms of annual trade flows and based on 1983-85 averages, the enlargement results, *ceteris paribus*, in a decline of 450,000 tons of maize imports and an increase of 380,000 tons of soyabean imports into SP. US maize exports drop by 360,000 tons, while US soyabean exports increase by 250,000 tons. The oilseed tax results in a total decline of 390,000 and 130,000 tons of soyabean exports to EC and SP, while combined maize exports to both the EC and SP drop by 280,000 tons.

The above results provide quantitative evidence of the fact that the EC enlargement might result in the development of trends similar to those observed in the past in the EC. The combination of a highly protectionist EC grain régime with the free entry of oilseeds distorts trade flows to the EC. As a result of the generated imbalances, which derive from the inconsistencies of the CAP, potential moves towards a lower level of protection for EC agriculture generate the possibility for some level of protection in the oilseed and grain substitute markets, and put further strains on US-EC trade relations.

Note

[1]Wye College and University of Georgia, respectively.

References

Alston, J.M., and Scobie, G.M. (1987) "Differentiated Goods Model of the Effects of European Policies in International Poultry Markets," *Southern Journal of Agricultural Economics*, Vol. 19, No. 1, pp. 59-68.

Armington, P.S. (1969) "Theory of Demand for Products Distinguished by Place of Production," *IMF Staff Papers*, Vol. 16, No. 1, pp. 159-178.

Buchholz, H.E. (1984) "Feed Imports as a Problem of the CAP," in Johnson, K.J., and Warren, R.M. (Eds.) *Price and Market Policies in European Agriculture*, University of Newcastle upon Tyne, Newcastle, UK.

Figueroa, E. (1986) "Implications of Changes in the U.S. Exchange Rate for Commodity Trade Patterns and Composition," PhD dissertation, University of California, Davis, Calif., USA.

Goldstein, M., and Khan, M.S. (1978) "Supply and Demand for Exports: Simultaneous Approach," *Review of Economics and Statistics*, Vol. 60, No. 2, pp. 275-286.

Meyers, W.H., Devadoss, S., and Helmar, M.D. (1986) "U.S. Export Response to Price and the Impact of Trade Liberalization: Regional Trade Model Analysis," paper presented at the International Agricultural Trade Research Consortium conference on Modeling for Analysis of International Trade, Reno, Nev., USA, July.

Petit, M. (1985) *Determinants of Agricultural Policies in the United States and the European Community*, Research Report No. 51, International Food Policy Research Institute, Washington, D.C., USA.

Sarris, A.H. (1980) "Geographical Substitution Possibilities in the European Community's Imports of Fruit and Vegetable Products in View of the Next Enlargement," Working Paper No. 111, Giannini Foundation, University of California, Berkeley, Calif., USA.

Sarris, A.H. (1983) "European Community Enlargement and World Trade in Fruits and Vegetables," *American Journal of Agricultural Economics*, Vol. 65, No. 2, pp. 235-246.

DISCUSSION OPENING—*Folkhard Isermeyer* (Institut für Agrarökonomie, Universität Göttingen)

Estimating how the EC-enlargement will affect international trade flows is certainly a complex problem. The authors have tried as far as possible to consider the interdependent nature of supply and demand in different product markets, and they have presented a fairly comprehensive and highly sophisticated world trade model that is able to explain both supply and demand of soyabeans and maize. This attempt is very commendable.

One serious problem that often arises with such models is that testing the quality of the model empirically is almost impossible. Therefore, the following questions are designed to give a little assistance for a discussion of possible shortcomings in the construction of the model.

In the first stage, the importer's expenditures for different goods are estimated using time series data from 1966 to 1985. Two questions arise: first, given the tremendous structural change in the EC since 1966, do figures for the late 1960s and the early 1970s contain any useful information for today's problems?; and, second, should one include other prices than those of maize and soyabeans in the analysis, especially the prices of small grains, grain substitutes, and important animal products, since they clearly have an impact on the import demand of soyabeans and maize?

In the second stage, the import demand for one good is allocated to different exporting countries. This is the core of the model, and we will have to discuss whether it is also the core of the problem. In other words, are consumer preferences, differences in product quality, or different harvesting seasons among major exporters really the important factors that determine, for example, whether the USA or Brazil obtains a greater share of an increased European import demand for soyabeans? A second set of questions touches on the measurement of elasticities of substitution. Imagine the "true" long-term elasticity of substitution to be infinite. Are top-quality statistics available on cif prices that make equation *(1)* calculate this "true" result? If not, the authors may be measuring the quality of price statistics. What are they trying to measure after all: long-, medium-, or short-term elasticities of substitution? How do they explain the considerable differences in the results between Spain/Portugal and the EC-10? And then, if the "true" long-term elasticity of substitution is really less than infinite, are the authors still justified in regarding the two products as one good? Where should the fine line be drawn between products and goods in a world in which almost everything is substitutable?

The way the model is built, it should be able to tell us how world prices will develop as a consequence of the EC-enlargement. A presentation of price results would have been of great help in assessing the quality of the model. For example, we would have learned whether internal agricultural supply in Spain and Portugal is considered, whether it will increase when these countries join the Common Market, and what the impact on world prices will be. I would also be very interested in seeing which price developments are responsible for the remarkable result that due to the EC-enlargement the EC-10 will import fewer soyabeans from the USA and more soyabeans from other exporters.

An advantage of the model is that policies such as the oilseed tax can be incorporated. Yet the model would be more valuable if products other than maize and soyabeans, particularly grain substitutes, were included. Consider, for example, the case if the EC were to erect strong political barriers against a further expansion of grain substitute imports (e.g., by strengthening the voluntary export restrictions). In this case, Spanish farmers might find it more profitable to feed European grain instead of a soyabean/grain substitute mixture. Even in Spain, pigs cannot be kept profitably on a pure soyabean diet. In contrast to the model results, the world price of soyabeans might thus fall and the world price for cereals might rise as a consequence of the EC enlargement.

GENERAL DISCUSSION—*Ming-Ming Wu, Rapporteur* (Department of Agricultural Marketing, National Chung-Hsing University)

The authors were asked whether they obtained statistically reliable results on supply elasticities. In reply, they stated that several other products were included in the estimation of first-stage import demand. Reported elasticities are those for which empirical estimates were statistically significant. Sensitivity analysis, which could not be included due to space limitations, focused on testing the validity of the results by using various parameter values. The obtained results were not qualitatively different from those of the reported results.

Furthermore, the authors said, the study has several limitations related to the exclusion of domestic change in the Spanish and Portuguese grain market as a result of the enlargement and to the impact of other cross-product effects. These, however, do not directly affect the conclusions, which focus on the immediate impact of the enlargement on US agricultural exports.

Participants in the discussion included S. Tarditi.

Institutional Agreements and Evolution of the Spanish Maize Sector

Fernando Andrada and Felisa Ceña[1]

Abstract: Spain's accession to the EC in 1986 turned out to prove soon enough, in practical terms, the logic of the Customs Union Theory. Substantial reductions in maize imports by Spain, mainly from the USA and, to a lesser extent, from Argentina, fuelled the world agricultural trade conflict. Under GATT Article 24/6, the USA and EC agreed on a quota of 2 million tons to be purchased by Spain from non-EC sources at lower prices. This institutional agreement, together with regulations contained in the Accession Treaty, were considered in the analysis of expected trends of the Spanish maize sector during the transition period. Although only crop producers, livestock producers, and taxpayers were considered, the analysis seems to support the view that the last two groups will suffer welfare losses whereas crop producers will obtain welfare gains. However, differences between positive benefits (crop producers) and negative benefits (livestock producers) due to the gap between world prices and Spanish policy prices will become gradually smaller as the transition period (1986-92) comes to an end.

Introduction

The main purpose of this paper is to project the evolution of the maize sector in Spain during its transition period of accession to the European Community; i.e., from 1986/87 to 1992/93. The projection takes into account both economic and institutional, domestic and international factors that are likely to contribute to the shaping and performance of this sector. Analysis of internal conditions of supply and demand (in terms of elasticities and structural changes) and the expected evolution of Spanish farm support (i.e., prices and subsidies to be aligned to those in the EC) are thus complemented with some assumptions involving world prices, rates of exchange, and EAGGF[2] decisions on guarantee measures.

The issue has implications that go beyond domestic or even European borders, as it constitutes an interesting example of one of the various areas of conflict between the two main agricultural trade powers, the USA and EC, during the last few years. This issue can be placed in a context of recent disputes concerning international trends on agricultural trade shares.

US export sales declined dramatically in a number of agricultural markets over recent years. Analysis of the reasons behind this situation lies beyond the scope of this paper. However, the integration of Spain into the EC has meant for the USA a further loss of its market shares abroad. Thus, invoking Article 24/6 of GATT, the latter forced an agreement with the EC, whereby the new members, Spain and Portugal, would benefit from a reduction in the CAP's variable levies on cereal imports from third countries. In the case of Spain, the agreement was established for the 1987-90 period on the basis of 2 million tons of maize and 300,000 tons of sorghum, although these quotas allow for other feed substitutes.

Future developments in the Spanish maize sector will be strongly influenced by two different sets of forces: operation of the market system, and institutional agreement (i.e., Spanish agricultural policies aligned to those of the EC's CAP, and the US-EC agreement under the GATT Article 24/6). The model is an attempt to integrate those conflicting forces into a coherent set of relationships, so that the evolution of the sector and its effects on the main agricultural groups involved can be assessed.

Model

The economic analysis of the maize sector is based on a framework of quantitative relationships in which the main characteristics of the sector are reflected through a set of dependent variables: production, consumption, trade, prices, costs and benefits to consumers, producers, and taxpayers, and intervention costs. The time scenario goes from 1981 to 1992: a period of five years prior to accession (1981-86) and a transition period of seven years, as established in the Accession Treaty by Spain and the EC. The analysis of the first period has two objectives: to serve as a basis for and to make comparisons with projections of the second period, and to test the model. During the second period, however, the aim is to phase in the alignment of Spanish agricultural policies to CAP regulations. Projections to 1992 are intended to show the economic effects on the maize sector induced by the new set of agricultural policies adopted by Spain.

The complete model is run in a spreadsheet generated in Lotus 1-2-3 and contains a set of five tables in descending order (Josling, 1988).[3] The first table is a block of parametric assumptions and actual data intended to "feed" the rest of the model: policy and world prices, rates of inflation, elasticities of supply and demand, population, real income, feed demand, and trade shares with the EC and third countries. The data are either expressed in growth rates or fixed parameters for the whole period.

Operative CAP price. Intervention prices were chosen as the operative price. Threshold prices are much closer to market prices than intervention prices when the country is a net importer, as in the case of Spain. Moreover, although threshold prices are somewhat higher than market prices, the difference could be ignored, bearing in mind that Spain will benefit during the first four years of the transition period from some reductions in the variable levies applied to world prices. However, intervention prices are much more stable and represent the worst possible situation for crop producer income.

World price. International maize prices are very much influenced by internal levels of US farm support. Loan rate fluctuations in that country can thus be taken as a proxy for those in world prices. Assumed rates of growth during the transition period equal the 1986 loan rate.

Exogenous supply shift. This is a comprehensive term, accounting for a variety of factors that influence production; i.e., opening of new lands to irrigation, new hybrid varieties, and substitution of wheat by maize in some areas of Spain. An increase of 15 percent in production is expected in the next five years, although the average annual rate of increase during the last decade was 8 percent. However, an annual rate of growth of only 4 percent has been adopted because Spanish maize yields are already close to EC's yields (Josling and Andrada, 1987). The likely upwards trends will thus become increasingly harder to attain.

Elasticities. Values for elasticities were taken either from other studies, when available, as in the case of supply elasticity (Wesley *et al.*, 1980), or were estimated (income elasticity of food demand)[4] or were assumed by reference to neighbouring countries (price elasticity of food demand). Consumption increases due to population growth were projected by assuming stability in per capita consumption levels.

Trade shares. In the case of a country like Spain, which is a net importer, percentages included in the assumptions (Table 1) will mainly affect EAGGF earnings through collection of variable levies. The 98 percent from third countries is actually the "Extra-Community Trade Share" during the last marketing year, which is not expected to experience significant changes through the transition period, as the USA is sure to try to maintain its export shares in international markets.

Feed demand. The value of this parameter was estimated by considering expected trends in Spanish livestock production, given current levels of self-sufficien-

Table 1—Assumptions and Data

Country	Spain
Commodity	Maize
Operative CAP price	Intervention
1986 per capita national income (market prices)	$5,198
1981 population	37,616,947
Annual rate of change (percent after 1981)	0.500
Annual rates of inflation (1987-89)	5.000
(1990-92)	4.500
World price growth (percent, in current dollars)*	1.800
CAP price growth (percent in current ECUs)*	0.000
Price elasticity of supply	0.600
Exogenous supply shift	4.000
Price elasticity of food demand	-0.300
Income elasticity of food demand	0.250
Real per capita income growth (percent per year)	2.000
Demand shift due to population growth (percent per year)	0.500
Intracommunity trade share (percent)	2.000
Extracommunity trade share (percent)	98.000
Annual feed demand growth (percent)	0.766

*Annual rates after 1985.

cy and the alignment of prices (they are now lower in Spain) during the transition period. Maize feeding patterns were also taken into account.

Table 2 is the physical balance of the commodity: supply, demand (food and feed), net imports, and self-sufficiency ratios. Projections for production are based on an average of past performance, while production is linked straightforwardly to changes in net producer prices through its supply elasticity and to the term labelled "exogenous supply shift." Food consumption is also projected according to its corresponding prices and elasticities. Feed demand, however, is based on a fixed rate of growth. Closing stocks are assumed to be a certain share of production, following similar trends to those in the past. They are included in the amount of maize supplied the following year as opening stocks. Finally, net imports are the difference between supply and demand. Self-sufficiency ratios are also included for illustrative purposes.

Table 2—Physical Commodity Balance (Maize)

Year	Production	Stocks Carryin	Consumption Nonfeed	Consumption Feed	Consumption Total	Stocks Carryout	Net Exports	Self-Sufficiency Ratio
	Tons							Percent
1981	2,156,800	832,000	544,000	7,000,000	7,544,000	1,041,800	(5,597,000)	29
1982	2,330,100	1,042,000	520,000	6,980,000	7,500,000	700,100	(4,828,000)	31
1983	1,803,400	700,000	506,000	5,478,000	5,984,000	112,400	(3,593,000)	30
1984	2,529,000	112,000	670,000	4,620,000	5,290,000	404,000	(3,053,000)	48
1985	3,300,000	380,000	700,000	5,207,000	5,907,000	471,000	(2,698,000)	56
1986	3,200,000	471,000	726,110	4,300,000	5,026,110	344,890	(1,700,000)	64
1987	3,254,281	344,890	741,735	4,332,938	5,074,673	439,679	(1,915,181)	64
1988	3,278,845	439,679	761,187	4,366,128	5,127,315	422,053	(1,830,843)	64
1989	3,303,508	422,053	781,160	4,399,573	5,180,733	409,538	(1,864,710)	64
1990	3,337,238	409,538	800,607	4,433,274	5,233,890	431,299	(1,918,404)	64
1991	3,371,220	431,299	820,549	4,467,232	5,297,781	429,199	(1,914,461)	64
1992	3,405,455	429,199	840,999	4,501,451	5,342,450	431,988	(1,939,785)	64

In Tables 3 and 4, prices and welfare changes, respectively, lie at the heart of the model. Defined relationships among prices and between prices and policy instruments allow for empirical estimation of the dependent variables included in the benefit distribution table (Table 5). Table 3 is structured into several sets of prices, subsidies, and marketing margins. Table 4 is just a reflection of Table 3. It shows prices in Table 3 in terms of year-to-year changes, in local currency and dollars. Finally, Table 5 contains some relevant concepts for policy-making decisions. This table is mainly concerned with financial flows and welfare changes in the two main conflicting groups on the supply side: crop and livestock producers. Calculation of financial flows (i.e., farm receipts, feed expenditure, foreign exchange earnings, national budgets costs, and transfers to EAGGF) is straightforward. Welfare changes (i.e., producer and "consumer" surpluses) and implied costs and benefits from both the EC's and all policies were estimated using a Marshallian approach.

Results of Analysis

The *physical balance* of the Spanish maize sector under the base scenario can be seen in Table 2. Maize production in Spain would grow by 1992 up to 3.4 million tons, almost a 100-percent increase over 1981. On the other hand, global consumption could be approximately 5.3 million tons, also at the end of the transition period. Feed consumption represents some 84 percent of total consumption. It is mainly used to feed broilers and layers. Supply, then, has to meet utilization levels by importing large, though gradually smaller, quantities of maize. However, as net imports were calculated as a residual of

Table 3—Prices

Year	Crop Producer Receipts	Feed Expenditure	Foreign Exchange Earnings	Budget Costs: National	Budget Costs: EAGGF	Budget Costs: Total
	1,000,000 real local currency units					
1981	61,331	265,403	-117,813	-59,027	0	-59,027
1982	77,789	310,699	-101,265	-77,825	0	-77,825
1983	52,068	210,883	-83,132	-32,132	0	-32,132
1984	55,694	135,657	-62,514	-12,190	0	-12,190
1985	64,754	136,231	-50,975	-7,848	0	-7,848
1986	57,077	102,264	-33,692	0	-12,803	-12,803
1987	55,817	99,091	-36,499	0	-15,259	-15,259
1988	53,197	94,449	-33,004	0	-15,518	-15,518
1989	50,695	90,021	-31,795	0	-14,544	-14,544
1990	48,670	86,207	-31,087	0	-13,813	-13,813
1991	46,723	82,550	-29,481	0	-12,703	-12,703
1992	44,849	79,045	-28,385	0	-11,839	-11,839

Table 4—Welfare Changes (from previous year)

Year	Crop Producer Welfare	Livestock Producer Welfare	Budget Increase	Net	Crop Producer Welfare	Livestock Producer Welfare	Budget Increase	Net
	1,000,000 real local currency units				*Dollars per capita*			
1982	10,871	-45,829	-18,798	-53,755	31,749	-133,843	-54,899	-156,992
1983	-9,162	37,267	45,692	73,796	-23,301	94,771	116,195	187,665
1984	-14,492	45,847	19,942	51,298	-41,289	130,622	56,817	146,150
1985	-6,836	15,617	4,342	13,123	-20,596	47,053	13,081	-39,537
1986	-5,689	11,252	-4,955	608	-13,488	26,678	-11,748	1,443
1987	-2,166	3,916	-2,456	-705	-4,769	8,626	-5,409	-1,553
1988	-2,969	5,346	-259	2,117	-5,789	10,421	-505	4,128
1989	-2,832	5,100	974	3,241	-5,522	9,941	1,899	6,318
1990	-2,479	4,458	731	2,710	-4,833	8,691	1,425	5,284
1991	-2,382	4,273	1,110	3,001	-4,644	8,330	2,164	5,850
1992	-2,289	4,096	864	2,671	-4,462	7,984	1,685	5,207

Table 5—Benefit Distribution

Year	Produced by All Policies: Crop Producers	Livestock Producers	Spanish Taxpayers	Total	Produced by EC Support: Crop Producers	Livestock Producers	Community Taxpayers	Total
	1,000,000 real local currency units							
1981	28,419	-172,234	59,027	-84,788				
1982	42,118	-254,495	77,825	-134,552				
1983	21,387	-115,753	32,132	-62,234				
1984	15,192	-44,316	12,190	-16,934				
1985	14,922	-36,462	7,848	-13,692				
1986	19,558	-44,268	0	-24,710	19,558	-44,268	12,803	-11,906
1987	20,764	-47,683	0	-26,919	20,764	-47,683	15,259	-11,659
1988	21,849	-51,837	0	-29,988	21,849	-51,837	15,518	-14,470
1989	20,350	-47,903	0	-27,554	20,350	-47,903	14,544	-13,009
1990	19,066	-44,404	0	-25,338	19,066	-44,404	13,813	-11,525
1991	17,834	-41,084	0	-23,251	17,834	-41,084	12,703	-10,547
1992	16,651	-37,936	0	-21,286	16,651	-37,936	11,839	-9,447

internal supply and global demand, they show a great degree of stability through the whole transition period; they are consistently under 2 million tons. This is almost exactly the amount Spain can purchase from third countries at a reduced variable levy under the terms of the US-EC 24/6 agreement.

Some selected *financial effects* are expressed in Table 3. Crop producer revenue would fall by 30 percent between 1985 and 1992. This is because production increases cannot offset declining intervention prices. Livestock producers would benefit from a reduction of expenses of about 42 percent, also in the same period. This is due to lower wholesale prices, which largely compensate modest increases in feed consumption. Observed upward trend in the self-sufficiency ratio would allow for significant amounts of savings in foreign currency (in percent). Yet the CAP's variable levies applied to lower imports would mean a loss of revenues for the EAGGF. EAGGF would only collect $109 million in 1992, as compared with $136 million in 1987.

Annual changes in *welfare levels*, are included in Table 4. Crop producers would undergo decreasing rates of welfare losses during the transition period, whereas livestock producers would experience welfare gains, also at declining rates. The overall change of these two groups, plus the government, shows a positive change of welfare after 1988, with no clear patterns of change. If these changes are expressed in US dollars per capita, the overall average, after 1988, would be $5,300. Livestock producers obviously take the largest share in such a gain.

Benefits accruing to crop producers from differences between world prices and Spanish policy prices are expressed in Table 5, together with the negative effects of such gaps for livestock producers. The monetary value of positive benefits is lower than that of negative benefits. Both taxpayers and livestock producers thus are "in charge," as it were, of supporting internal prices at levels well above those for world prices.[5] Differences between positive benefits (crop producers) and negative benefits (livestock producers), however, become gradually smaller as the transition period is coming to an end.

This base scenario could be significantly altered by assuming different rates for growth for either world prices or CAP intervention prices.[6] For example, an annual reduction in world prices of 5 percent (the current loan rate for maize in the USA) would result, *ceteris paribus*, in a hypothetical increase in EC subsidies, i.e., (for a net exporting country) of about 146 percent. Subsequent lowering of welfare levels because of higher budget costs would accelerate. Induced rates of decrease would sink to 73 percent. This widening of differences between world prices and CAP prices would bring about a benefit increase for crop producers of nearly 40 percent, while negative effects for livestock producers would escalate up to 60 percent.

On the other hand, if CAP/Spanish prices grew at 2 percent, annual average in nominal terms, instead of the zero percent growth in the base scenario, the following effects would occur: production would increase more than 70 percent; imports would decline almost 14 percent; self-sufficiency levels would be 69 percent (64 percent in the base scenario); the proportion of EC subsidies would increase (in the case of a country being a net exporter) by 30 percent; crop producer receipts would increase 21 percent and livestock producer expenses would increase 13 percent; foreign currency savings would decrease 2.5 percent whereas EAGGF revenues would be 13 percent higher; crop producers would experience welfare gains, but only in terms of a slowing down of 28 percent in their annual rate of welfare losses; livestock producers would accordingly worsen their situation, by speeding up their annual rate of welfare reduction to approximately 32 percent; benefit differences between crop producers (positive) and livestock producers (negative) would widen (crop producer benefits would grow 36 percent in real terms, whereas livestock producers would lose 32 percent); taxpayers would have to increase their contribution to the budget by more than 12 percent; and overall costs for the groups concerned (crop producers, livestock producers, and taxpayers) would increase by 51 percent as the results of the assumed 2 percent growth of the CAP's intervention price, in nominal terms.

Conclusion

Spain will continue being a net importer of maize despite dramatic increases in self-sufficiency ratios during the 1980s. Net imports will likely fluctuate around 2 million tons. The agreement between the USA and the EC concerning a fixed quota of 2 million tons to be purchased by Spain thus should not pose any obstacles to the stability of the Spanish maize market.

However, Spanish crop producers have already started putting some pressure on the Spanish government to reduce that level of imports. Whether they can succeed or not on imposing their own views on this issue will largely depend on the outcome of forthcoming talks at the Uruguay Round.

Notes

[1]Department of Agricultural Economics and Sociology, Universidad de Córdoba.

[2]European Agricultural Guarantee and Guidance Fund.

[3]Only a reduced version of the model is presented here. Tables on nominal and deflated prices and subsidies are not included in this paper.

[4]Food demand is actually a simplification for all industrial uses of maize processing as well as food consumption proper.

[5]Final consumers are not considered in this analysis.

[6]According to regulations of the Accession Treaty between the EC and Spain, Spanish policy prices for maize will be aligned to CAP prices in 1988/89.

References

Josling, T.E. (1988) "European Community Evaluation Framework: Software Documentation," unpublished paper, Stanford University, Stanford, Calif., USA.

Josling, T.E., and Andrada, F. (1987) "La Política Agrícola Común y la Adhesión de España y Portugal," *Revista de Estudios Agrosociales*, No. 140, pp. 157-181.

Wesley, E., *et al.* (1980) *Spain's Entry into the European Community: Effects on the Feed Grain and Livestock Sectors*, Foreign Agricultural Economic Report No. 180, Economic Research Service, US Department of Agriculture, Washington, D.C., USA.

Discussion Opening—*Mark D. Newman* (Abt Associates, Inc.)

Andrada and Ceña indicate that Spanish market prices are expected to be closer to EC threshold prices than intervention prices, implying a significant increase in producer prices relative to those in pre-accession Spain. Nonetheless, the analysis appears to be based on intervention prices. Support prices in Spain were only 4.5 percent below EC intervention prices when Spain began its transition to EC membership in 1986, so a smaller impact on production incentives would be expected if Spain were no longer an importer, so prices remained closer to intervention levels. The issue here goes beyond Andrada and Ceña's paper. The literature examining impacts of Spanish accession exhibits considerable confusion on what price should be used in the analysis.

Since Spain has been a net maize importer, accession should raise internal prices to closer to the EC threshold price. The agreement to permit a reduced levy quota of up to 2.3 million tons of maize and sorghum from outside the EC should offset some of the gain to Spanish crop producers that might be expected to accompany accession and higher market prices. The increased imports should push prices closer to intervention levels (although keeping them well above world prices). In this context, the authors' conclusions are made more understandable. Higher prices resulting from the accession would have led to 20-percent production increases by 1992, but the predicted welfare losses by producers and welfare gains by livestock producers are relative to this increased price and production level, not relative to the absence of increased barriers to imports that accompanied accession to the EC.

As this is a single commodity, partial analysis, it does not consider the fact that accession permits imports of relatively cheap nongrain feed ingredients (called cereal substitutes by some) without the same levies faced by cereals. As the 24/6 agreement calls for the reduced levy quota to be cut by any increase in imports of certain nongrain feeds, an important component of the required calculus for examining welfare implications of the agreement for livestock producers is missing.

Enlarging the EC presumably offers a range of gains and losses to interest groups within and outside the EC. Spanish grain producers may get higher prices, but also a shift in competition towards higher cost EC sources of supply. To the extent that grain producers are also livestock producers, their input costs go up.

Interviews with feed and livestock producers in Spain in 1987 yielded two particularly striking observations. First, the market structure of the compound feed industry in Spain is such that technology shifted with amazing rapidity from the EC-10 to Spain on accession. Feed formulation is thus now using rations with a complex set of ingredients in response to the distortions in relative prices introduced by variable levies on maize and other grains, but zero or near zero levies on oilseeds and nongrain feed ingredients. The ability or inability to adjust will have striking impacts on certain participants and the overall structure of the Spanish feed industry. The aggregate analysis of welfare implications in the paper could not address these issues, but perhaps future analysis by others should.

Also meriting discussion are the international welfare effects of Spanish accession and the 24/6 agreement. Maize producers in the USA and Argentina obviously lose when their maize faces a levy of up to 200 percent of its world price to enter the Spanish market. The 24/6 agreement will offset some of the loss, as long as it is honoured. However, grain producers in France have complained bitterly that the agreement deprives them of market outlets that they gained in return for the increased competition that they will face from Spanish horticultural products as a result of accession. Negotiators for the USA and EC argue that the 24/6 agreement was the best achievable, while producers in Spain, France, and the USA complain bitterly. Perhaps this foreshadows some of what the MTN round holds in store. Do the political economics of accession and the 24/6 agreement provide insights useful in understanding what is possible in the Uruguay Round?

GENERAL DISCUSSION—*Ming-Ming Wu, Rapporteur* (Department of Agricultural Marketing, National Chung-Hsing University)

One participant underlined the importance of nongrain feeds and asked that new models account for shifts to nongrain feeds. In reply, the authors said that the issue has not been considered as far as building a parallel model is concerned. The usefulness of the model presented here lies in its ability to relate changes in the parameters with their impacts on producers' and consumers' welfare, so that the process of decision making can be assessed. Furthermore, even if *ad hoc* models could be designed, continuous changes in nongrain substitutes, together with significant changes in prices, would make the feed demand model of low workability.

Participants in the discussion included W. Gardiner.

Unbalancing Act: Strategies for Trade in Manufactures and Agricultural Trade Impacts

Nancy E. Schwartz and Barry Krissoff[1]

Abstract: Global trade tensions have risen due to bilateral trade imbalances, principally in manufactures. For example, recent US policy debate has emphasized methods to reduce US bilateral trade deficits with Japan and the EC. Changes in the level of bilateral protection of trade in manufactures can affect agricultural trade through exchange-rate, price, and income effects. This analysis focuses on how different policies on trade in manufactures would affect US agricultural exports. The analysis uses a static equilibrium world model, which includes endogenous exchange rates, income, sectoral prices, and traded quantities. The model contains disaggregated agriculture, aggregated Armington-type manufactures, and aggregated nontraded goods. Two different trade policies are analyzed: foreign liberalization of trade in manufactures and increased US protection of trade in manufactures. The results indicate that these strategies to reduce bilateral trade deficits have negative effects on US agriculture, with significantly worse effects occurring when US protection of trade in manufactures is raised. When foreign countries liberalize trade in manufactures, the dollar appreciates, but some of its negative effects on US agricultural trade are mitigated by a rise in foreign income. By contrast, when US protection of trade in manufactures is increased, the dollar appreciates and foreign income falls, exacerbating the negative effects on US agricultural trade.

Introduction

During the 1980s, bilateral trade conflicts have proliferated. Much of the global tension has been focused on bilateral trade surpluses in manufactures. During this time, the US trade deficit reached record levels, rising from a deficit of $35,000 million in 1982 to around $160,000 million in 1986. This increase has led to a major debate over the appropriateness and effectiveness of current US trade policies. Some argue that if foreign markets were more open or if foreign exports were less subsidized, US exports would expand and US imports would shrink. Supporters of this argument contend that the USA should adopt policies to put pressure on other countries to reduce their unfair trade practices.

Two trading areas are the most likely targets for aggressive US reactions towards perceived unfair practices: Japan and the EC. These areas have incurred the fastest growth in their bilateral trade surpluses with the USA (over $50,000 million and $25,000 million, respectively, in 1986). In addition, US exports to these areas have largely stagnated over the past five years, while their exports to the USA have risen sharply. The harbinger of future policies is sanctions against Japanese construction firms in new US budget legislation passed in December 1987.

The adoption of a tougher stance against foreign practices in the manufacturing sectors will not only affect manufactures but will also indirectly affect agriculture. If the USA takes such a posture on trade in manufactures, what are the likely effects on US agricultural trade? How are trade in agricultural and nonagricultural products related? This paper provides a framework in which to look at these questions and to provide some preliminary results. This study analyzes how US trade, and US agricultural trade in particular, would be affected under two different types of policy responses. Under the first type, Japan and the EC liberalize their trading practices on manufactures to avoid US retaliatory behaviour. Under the second type, the USA imposes retaliatory import restrictions on manufactures because these countries do not liberalize their trading practices. A key result is that agricultural exports are likely to be adversely affected by either type of policy, even in the absence of foreign retaliation specifically against agriculture.

Model and Methodology

A static world policy simulation framework (Roningen, 1986) is used to develop a multicountry, multicommodity model. It includes eight countries/regions: USA, EC, Japan, Canada, Argentina, Brazil, Mexico, and the rest of the world. Commodities for each country are disaggregated into individual agricultural goods (wheat, maize, soyabeans, rice, sugar, dairy, beef, and poultry), a composite "other" agricultural good, a composite nonagricultural manufactured traded good, and a composite nontraded good. A base level (1984) is established for consumption and production, consumer prices, producer prices, and world prices. For each country, producer and consumer prices (or the implicit per unit values) deviate from world price by the *ad valorem* rate of protection. For nonagricultural goods, *ad valorem* tariff and nontariff barrier tariff-equivalent rates are used for protection measures based on estimates by Deardorff and Stern (1986), Whalley (1985 and 1986), and Anjaria, Kirmani, and Petersen (1985). The model extends the analysis in Schwartz and Krissoff (1987) by introducing endogenous income effects in addition to trade, price, and exchange-rate effects. A brief description of the model is as follows.

For the *i*th country/region in the model, demand (*D*) and supply (*S*) functions depend on all prices (*P*) and income (*Y*):

$$(1)\ DA_i = DA_i(PA_i, PT_i, PH_i, Y_i),$$

$$(2)\ DT_i = DT_i(PA_i, PT_i, PH_i, Y_i),$$

$$(3)\ DH_i = DH_i(PA_i, PT_i, PH_i, Y_i),$$

$$(4)\ SA_i = SA_i(PA_i, PT_i, PH_i),$$

$$(5)\ ST_i = ST_i(PA_i, PT_i, PH_i), \text{ and}$$

$$(6)\ SH_i = SH_i(PA_i, PT_i, PH_i),$$

where *A* denotes agricultural goods, *T* represents the nonagricultural manufactured traded products (exported or imported), and *H* represents the nontraded (home) good. The model excludes wages and factor rental rates.

Income is defined as expenditures on all traded agricultural and manufactured goods (*j=1, ..., n*) and on the nontraded good:

$$(7)\ Y_i = \sum_{j=1}^{n} PT_{ij}DT_{ij} + PH_iDH_i.$$

Alternatively, income equals the value of production plus "net capital flows" (net foreign borrowing).

The domestic economy reaches an equilibrium when home goods have an excess supply (*ES*) equal to zero and when net traded goods (including agricultural goods) equal "net capital flows" (*F*). *F* is defined as including capital and service accounts and accommodating changes in international reserves. For country *i*,

$$(8)\ ESH_i = SH_i - DH_i = 0, \text{ and}$$

$$(9)\ \sum_{j=1}^{n} P_{ij}ES_{ij} = \sum_{j=1}^{n} P_{ij}S_{ij} - \sum_{j=1}^{n} P_{ij}D_{ij} = F_i,$$

for traded goods *j*. World markets clear when excess supply of a good across all countries is equal to zero. For agricultural commodities, this occurs when:

$$(10)\ \sum_{i=1}^{m} ESA_{ij} = \sum_{i=1}^{m} SA_{ij} - \sum_{i=1}^{m} DA_{ij} = 0,$$

for each j, $j = 1, ..., n - 1$. For the nonagricultural good that is traded, n, equilibrium occurs when:

$$(11)\ \sum_{i=1}^{m} EST_{in} = \sum_{i=1}^{m} ST_{in} - \sum_{i=1}^{m} DT_{in} = 0.$$

The traded price in each country's home currency is:

$$(12)\ P_{ij} = E_i\ PW_j\ (1+t_{ij}),$$

where E_i equals home currency per US dollar, PW_j is the world dollar price of the jth traded good and t_{ij} can be interpreted as an export subsidy or import tariff ($t_{ij}>0$), or export tax or import subsidy ($t_{ij}<0$), and is assumed to be exogenous.

A shock to the system—in terms of a change in protection of either sector of the economy in any country or commodity market—leads to changes in base values in quantities produced, consumed, and traded and world and domestic prices. The system also determines either (1) changes in each country's balance of trade under the assumption of fixed exchange rates and the availability of external financing or (2) changes in each country's exchange rate under the assumption of floating rates, which return all countries' trade balances to their initial equilibria:[2]

$$(13)\ (\Pi_1+\Pi_2)E^* + \Pi_1[PWA^*+(1+tA)^*] + \Pi_2[PWT^*+(1+tT)^*] = F^*,$$

where * indicates percentage changes in variables and Π is a parameter consisting of supply and demand elasticities and the shares of agricultural and nonagricultural goods in trade.[3]

Under fixed exchange rates, in the small country case, agricultural markets are affected by (1) changes in domestic prices of nonagricultural and nontraded goods resulting from changes in the country's nonagricultural protection and (2) changes in national incomes arising from changes in nonagricultural protection. In the large country case, the additional effects of changes in world prices feed back to domestic prices and affect domestic production and consumption, and, consequently, trade.

Under a floating exchange rate system, the country's currency would depreciate or appreciate following liberalization until the changes in the external trade imbalance are eliminated; i.e., until $F^* = 0$. Hence the exchange rate change causes a further feedback from world prices to domestic prices and subsequent adjustments to quantities. In the analysis reported here, exchange rates are assumed to be endogenous.

If the parameters of equation *(13)*, Π_1 and Π_2, are positive, then a reduction in protection leads to a depreciation of the exchange rate which offsets, to some extent, the negative effects on domestic prices of a reduction in protection levels. If the agricultural protection levels are initially negative and nonagricultural protection is initially positive, then a reduction of protection can lead to a depreciation, which would reinforce the positive effects of liberalization on domestic agricultural prices.

In order to permit the analysis of targeted trade policies, the model is modified so that the nonagricultural manufacture is treated as an Armington-type good. By treating the nonagricultural domestic and imported products as imperfect substitutes (Armington-type structure), the model can be specified in terms of bilateral trade flows (e.g., see Dixit and Roningen, 1986). This specification is particularly appropriate for a composite good where each country is not buying and selling a homogeneous commodity. Consumers distinguish, within the nonagricultural traded goods, between products which are produced domestically and those which are imported. Consumers, in the decision-making process, are assumed to determine their expenditures for the agricultural goods, for each nonagricultural traded product depending on country/region of origin (one product from each country), and the nontraded good.

Simulation Results

The essence of the current trade policy debate is that the USA should single out countries with unfair trading practices and put pressure on them to reduce their trade barriers. If they refuse, the USA should raise its trade barriers against those individual countries. This paper reports the simulation results of three basic scenarios, assuming that Japan and the EC would be major targets of such a trade policy. In the first scenario, Japan liberalizes protection of its trade in manufactures so that its level of external protection is identical to the US level of protection. In the second scenario, both Japan and the EC lower their rates of protection of trade in manufactures to the US level. The third scenario raises US protection against both Japanese and EC manufactures to their respective existing rates of protection. The simulations yield medium-term effects of policy changes. These results are reported in Tables 1 and 2.

Overall Trade-Balance and Exchange-Rate Effects

Although the change in the overall trade balance in each country is forced to zero in the simulations, changes in bilateral trade balances are not. Therefore, one can analyze how much of the bilateral trade deficits in manufactures with the EC and Japan would be eliminated under the three policy scenarios. Liberalization by Japan alone (scenario 1) has the smallest effect, improving the US bilateral trade deficit with Japan and the EC by about 3.0 percent each over the base level (Table 1). The effects of liberalization are offset slightly by small depreciations of the yen and ECU.

Table 1—Changes in US Exports, Bilateral Trade, and Exchange Rates

	Scenario* 1	Scenario* 2	Scenario* 3
	Percent change from base period		
US manufacturing exports†	0.5	1.5	-6.0
US manufacturing trade deficit:†			
With Japan	-3.2	-2.5	-14.2
With EC-10	1.7	-13.2	-18.3
Yen/US dollar exchange rate‡	0.5	0.7	3.2
ECU/US dollar exchange rate‡	0.1	0.7	2.0

*See text for description of scenarios.

†A negative entry indicates a fall in value from the base period (i.e., lower exports or lower trade deficit); a positive number indicates an increase in value.

‡A negative entry indicates a fall in the yen/dollar exchange rate or a depreciation of the dollar; a positive number indicates a rise in the yen/dollar exchange rate or an appreciation of the dollar. The same relationship holds for the ECU/dollar exchange rate.

When both the EC and Japan liberalize (scenario 2), the US-EC trade balance improves substantially, by 13.2 percent. But, the US-Japan deficit improves by only 2.5 percent, due mainly to a larger depreciation of the yen, which induces higher US imports and a lower increase in exports than in scenario 1. When the USA imposes retaliatory tariffs on Japan and the EC (scenario 3), the US bilateral trade deficits shrink by over 14 percent with Japan and by over 18 percent with the EC. However, unlike the first two scenarios in which total US exports of manufactures show small increases, US exports fall by nearly 6 percent. Whereas liberalizing trade causes both US imports and exports to increase, imposing tariffs causes both US imports and exports of manufactures to fall.

In each of the three cases, the improvements in the US bilateral trade deficits come about differently. When the EC and Japan liberalize their trade, the improvement occurs due to an increase in US exports over and above the increase in US imports from these countries. The rise in exports is stimulated largely by greater access to these foreign markets. The rise causes the dollar to appreciate, which, in turn, causes US imports from these countries to grow (by less than exports). By contrast, when the USA imposes retaliatory tariffs on foreign manufactures, both US imports and exports fall. Imports fall due to higher tariff/nontariff protection. The fall in imports causes the dollar to appreciate, which, in turn, causes US exports to fall.[4]

US Agricultural Trade-Balance Effects

Only protection of trade in manufactures changes in the simulations. Protection of trade in agricultural products remains fixed at its base-period levels in all countries. Changes in agricultural prices that occur due to changes in protection of trade in manufactures are transmitted across countries. Agricultural protection is assumed to be exogenous and does not respond to changes in agricultural prices. In addition, perfect price transmission is assumed to hold. Because cross-price effects, complementarity, substitution, and input effects tend to be small between agricultural and nonagricultural manufactured goods, the major effects on agriculture tend to come through exchange rate changes.

US agricultural exports fall when foreign countries liberalize their trade in manufactures due to a small appreciation of the dollar (Table 2). When only Japanese protection of trade in manufactures is reduced (scenario 1), the effect on agriculture is very small, about a 1-percent drop in the value of agricultural net trade. The drop is due mainly to changes in trade volumes; prices sustain small declines. Small reductions in exports of dairy and small increases in net imports of livestock and "other" agriculture account for the overall decline. Changes in grains/oilseed and sugar trade are insignificant.

Table 2—Changes in the Value of US Agricultural Trade

	- - Scenario* - -			Base period
	1	2	3	
	Percent change from base period†			*$1,000,000,000*
US total agricultural trade balance (net exports)‡	-1.2	-2.9	-11.2	15.5
Grain/oilseed net exports	-0.4	-0.9	-4.2	17.4
Sugar net imports	-0.2	-0.4	4.0	0.3
Dairy net exports	-1.6	-5.9	-7.5	0.2
Livestock net imports	4.3	11.7	40.5	1.3

*See text for description of scenarios.

†A negative entry indicates a fall in value from the base period (i.e., lower net imports or lower net exports); a positive number indicates an increase in value.

‡Total agricultural net exports equal the sum of net exports of grain and oilseeds, sugar, dairy, livestock, and "other" agriculture.

When the EC liberalizes trade of manufactures in addition to Japan (scenario 2), the effects are more pronounced. The US agricultural trade balance falls by almost 3 percent. Grain/oilseed trade drops by nearly 1 percent. As in scenario 1, reduced volumes of dairy exports and increased livestock imports account for most of the decline in total trade. Sugar imports are virtually unchanged.

When the USA raises protection of trade in Japanese and EC manufactures (scenario 3), the deterioration in the US agricultural trade balance is more than triple that under liberalization, falling by over 11 percent. The decline in grain/oilseed trade is also over three times scenario 2. Dairy and livestock balances are also significantly worse than under liberalization. Sugar import expenditures increase slightly (or sugar exporter quota rents increase slightly) for the same reason as in scenario 2. The principal cause for the general decline in agricultural exports and increase in imports is the increased appreciation of the dollar induced by higher protection (Table 1). The large difference in the results between scenario 2 and 3 is also due to divergent income effects. Foreign liberalization of trade in manufactures increases foreign income and foreign imports of agricultural products, thereby mitigating some of the appreciation of the dollar. By contrast, when the USA increases its protection of trade in manufactures, foreign income falls and the exchange-rate effect is compounded rather than offset.

Conclusions

US strategies to reduce bilateral trade deficits on manufactures through targeted trade policies are likely to have a negative effect on US agriculture. This tends to be the case whether foreign governments open up their markets to allow more imports of US manufactures or whether the USA imposes retaliatory restrictions on targeted manufactures coming into the USA. In either case, US bilateral trade deficits improve, but at the expense of agricultural trade. Either an increase in protection of trade in manufactures by the USA or foreign liberalization of trade in manufactures will tend to raise the value of the dollar and reduce the competitiveness of US agricultural products.

Foreign liberalization of trade in manufactures tends to produce small negative effects on US agriculture. By contrast, a retaliatory increase in US protection of trade in manufactures appears to create significantly worse effects on agriculture. The analysis does not consider the possibility that foreign governments may, in turn, also retaliate by increasing tariffs and restrictions on US exports, including agriculture. In that case, the effect on agriculture is likely to be more severe than the results found in this analysis.

The results suggest that a balanced approach towards reducing (or raising) protection of both agricultural and nonagricultural goods is necessary in order to avoid penalizing agriculture. Under a balanced approach, for example, foreign liberalization of trade in agricultural goods along with manufactures would tend to offset the bias against US agricultural exports introduced by foreign liberalization of trade in manufactures. An analogous argument can be made in the case where US protection is increased against imported manufactures.

Notes

[1]Economic Research Service, US Department of Agriculture.

[2]In the second case, changes in trade protection are assumed to affect currency values indirectly through the elasticities of demand and supply for traded and nontraded goods. Since the elasticities approach does not consider a world with capital flows, the shock is implicitly assumed to affect only the trade balance and does not induce changes in capital flows. Corden (1987) argues that since the capital account depends on savings and investment decisions, changes in protection have an ambiguous effect on capital flows. While one could have arbitrarily selected to limit the change in the trade balance so that it did not always equal zero, no rigorous criterion requires one to do so. Therefore, the standard convention was adopted.

[3]The entire system of equations, derivation of the reduced-form equations (for prices, income, and exchange rates) in terms of the exogenous variables, and details on protection of the agricultural and nonagricultural sectors are reported in Krissoff and Ballenger (1987b). Sources for the data and base values used in the model are reported in Krissoff and Ballenger (1987a).

[4]To see why an increase in protection causes the dollar to appreciate, consider the following. As protection increases, imports fall. As a result, fewer dollars enter the world currency markets to obtain foreign exchange needed to purchase foreign goods. As the supply of dollars in world currency markets falls, the price of dollars rises; i.e., the dollar appreciates.

References

Anjaria, S.J., Kirmani, N., and Petersen, A.B. (1985) *Trade Policy Issues and Developments*, Occasional Paper No. 38, International Monetary Fund, Washington, D.C., USA.

Corden, M. (1987) *Protection and Liberalization: Review of Analytical Issues*, Occasional Paper No. 54, International Monetary Fund, Washington, D.C., USA.

Deardorff, A.V., and Stern, R.M. (1986) *Michigan Model of World Production and Trade*, MIT Press, Cambridge, Mass., USA.

Dixit, P.M., and Roningen, V.O. (1986) *Modeling Bilateral Trade Flows with the Static World Policy Simulation (SWOPSIM) Modeling Framework*, Staff Report No. AGES-861124, Economic Research Service, US Department of Agriculture, Washington, D.C., USA.

Krissoff, B., and Ballenger, N. (1987a) *Effect of Protection and Exchange Rate Policies on Agricultural Trade: Implications for Argentina, Brazil, and Mexico*, Staff Report No. AGES-870825, Economic Research Service, US Department of Agriculture, Washington, D.C., USA.

Krissoff, B., and Ballenger, N. (1987b) "Agricultural Trade Liberalization in a Multi-Sector World Model," unpublished paper, Economic Research Service, US Department of Agriculture, Washington, D.C., USA.

Roningen, V.O. (1986) *Static World Policy Simulation (SWOPSIM) Modeling Framework*, Staff Report No. AGES-860625, Economic Research Service, US Department of Agriculture, Washington, D.C., USA.

Schwartz, N.E., and Krissoff, B. (1987) *How Strategies to Reduce U.S. Bilateral Trade Deficits in Manufactures Affect U.S. Agricultural Exports*, Staff Report No. AGES-871005, Economic Research Service, US Department of Agriculture, Washington, D.C., USA.

Whalley, J. (1985) *Trade Liberalization among Major World Trading Areas*, MIT Press, Cambridge, Mass., USA.

Whalley, J. (1986) "Impacts of 50% Tariff Reduction in an Eight-Region Global Trade Model," in Srinivasan, T.N., and Whalley, J. (Eds.) *General Equilibrium Trade Policy and Modeling*, MIT Press, Cambridge, Mass., USA.

DISCUSSION OPENING—*Eduardo Segarra* (Department of Agricultural Economics, Texas Tech University)

Given the conference theme of "Agriculture and Governments in an Interdependent World," this conference could not have been a better forum for discussing the topic addressed by Schwartz and Krissoff. International trade studies based on traditional comparative advantage concepts alone have become part of the history of economic thought rather than of contemporary analytical economic literature on methods that should be used in the analysis and evaluation of international trade issues. International trade economists have come to recognize the existence of the notion of competitive advantage, which refers to comparative advantage concepts once government intervention and interdependencies among economic sectors are taken into consideration. That is, by acknowledging the existence of competitive advantages among trading countries, economic as well as political interdependencies among governments are internalized in analyzing and evaluating international trade issues.

Current concerns over the increased intensity of protectionist policies have provided the impetus to move towards the elimination of some or all barriers to trade. The elimination of these distortive policies are viewed as a necessary condition for promoting free trade or trade liberalization. For this reason, I commend Schwartz and Krissoff's efforts in analyzing and evaluating the impacts on agriculture of liberalization of trade in manufactures among the USA, Japan, and the EC. Their analysis is important because tariffs and other measures that protect the manufacturing sector reduce the competitiveness of agriculture since they are equivalent to import taxes.

In evaluating the impacts on agriculture of liberalization of trade in manufactures, however, in addition to internalizing interdependencies between the manufacturing and agricultural sectors, one must recognize that if domestic production externalities exist in agriculture and are not internalized in production costs, then trade remains distorted. That is, trade and resource economists rarely analyze the implications of the linkages between natural resources and trade even though their analyses are generally centred on objectives of maximizing social welfare. This is important because if significant trade liberalization stems from the Uruguay Round, changes in the resource mix used in agricultural production could be quite significant. This implies that if externalities stemming from agricultural production are not considered in evaluating welfare losses due to trade losses, welfare losses due to decreases in exports could be overestimated. This is due to the fact that reduced exports would imply lower optimal production levels for the exporting country, which in turn would imply lower levels of natural resource use and/or lower rates of natural resource deterioration. In looking at the simulation results obtained by Schwartz and Krissoff and depending on the particular trade liberalization scenarios that they analyzed, one can find that the change in the total value of US agricultural exports could decrease anywhere from $200 million to $1,740 million. However, what they fail to recognize is the presence of production externalities in terms of natural resource degradation in agriculture in the USA. If agricultural exports were to be reduced as a result of trade liberalization, as they found, and if, in response to that, domestic production was to be reduced, then a decreased burden on natural resource use would arise that would tend to increase welfare due to the reduced levels of production externalities domestically, thus implying a lower loss than that pointed out above. Therefore, Schwartz and Krissoff's losses could be regarded as upper bounds on losses, which would have to be revised downwards to account for domestic production externalities abatement. Their analysis is in the right direction and I commend them for that, but some room exists for improvements.

GENERAL DISCUSSION—*Ming-Ming Wu, Rapporteur* (Department of Agricultural Marketing, National Chung-Hsing University)

The authors were asked how liberalization of policies on trade in manufactures abroad affects US farm income. In reply, they said that farm revenues had two components: those earned from domestic sales and those earned from export sales. Foreign liberalization of policies on trade in manufactures increases demand for US manufactures. This raises the value of the dollar, which in turn puts downward pressure on US tradeable prices (of both manufactures and agricultural products) relative to the rest of the world and to US nontraded goods. But the rise in foreign demand for US exports of manufactures means that prices of manufactures rise relative to agricultural prices. Therefore, in relative terms, domestic farm revenues fall. In addition, the rise in the dollar depresses export sales and export revenues. The combined effect is a decline in US farm income due to a change in foreign policies on trade in manufactures.

Participants in the discussion included F. Thoumi.

Agricultural Trade Liberalization in a Multisector World Model: Implications for Argentina, Brazil, and Mexico

Barry Krissoff and Nicole Ballenger[1]

Abstract: Impacts of agricultural and nonagricultural trade liberalization on agriculture are assessed in a multicommodity, multicountry framework. By modelling simultaneously all goods sectors of the economy, the importance of (1) relative price changes between sectors and (2) income and exchange rate adjustments that follow trade liberalization in a world of floating rates are evaluated. Specifically, four cases are compared using a static world policy simulation (SWOPSIM) model: industrial market economy agricultural liberalization, global agricultural liberalization, all-sector industrial market economy liberalization, and all sector global liberalization. Under all sector liberalization scenarios, exchange rates are allowed to float for all countries/regions. In all cases, agricultural commodity prices tend to increase, an effect that is more pronounced when currency values adjust but less pronounced under global relative to industrial market economy liberalization. Three Latin American countries are modelled individually: Argentina, Brazil, and Mexico. Argentina and Brazil have the most significant advances in agricultural trade with an all-sector global liberalization. The deterioration of the Mexican agricultural trade balance is reduced when exchange rates are allowed to vary.

Introduction

Most analyses of agricultural protectionism have been conducted in a partial equilibrium framework. OECD (1987) and World Bank studies (Tyers and Anderson, 1986; and World Bank, 1986) examine liberalization in an agricultural, multicommodity model but do not consider nonagricultural sectors, even though a reduction in protection for the nonagricultural sector can cause changes in nonagricultural and agricultural prices, changes in income, and changes in relative prices across countries via exchange rate movements. This would influence resource allocations across sectors and countries and thereby affect agricultural production, consumption, and trade. The nonagricultural component of the economy may have even more influence than sector-specific policies.

In view of the potential importance of a broad-based framework, a multicommodity, multicountry static model is developed and the effects assessed of all-sector (agricultural and nonagricultural) trade liberalization on the agricultural sector. By modelling all goods sectors of the economy, industrial market economy and global liberalization scenarios in which exchange rates are endogenous can be compared with scenarios in which only agricultural trade is liberalized and no exchange rate changes are assumed. The focus is on price, exchange rate, and trade effects in Argentina, Brazil, and Mexico.

To undertake the scenarios, a static world policy simulation model (SWOPSIM) is used (Roningen, 1986; and Dixit and Roningen, 1986), which includes eight countries/regions (USA, EC, Japan, Canada, Argentina, Brazil, Mexico, and the rest of the world), a breakdown of commodities for each country into agricultural goods (wheat, maize, soyabeans, rice, sugar, dairy, beef, and poultry), a composite "other agricultural" good, a composite nonagricultural traded good, and a nontraded good. A base level (1984) is established for demand and supply, consumer prices, producer prices, and world prices. For each country, producer and consumer prices (or the implicit per unit values) deviate from world price by an *ad valorem* rate of protection. The levels of government intervention in agriculture are measured by producer and consumer subsidy equivalents (USDA, 1987). For nonagricultural goods, *ad valorem* tariff and nontariff barrier tariff-equivalent rates are used for protection measures (Whalley, 1985 and 1986; Deardorff and Stern, 1986; and Anjaria, Kirmani, and Petersen, 1985).

Analytical Framework

The framework for this analysis has its origins in studies by Valdés (1986) and Deardorff and Stern (1986). A more complete partial equilibrium model is set up here, with all produced and consumed goods specified in demand and supply functions. The present model falls short of a general equilibrium characterization since factor markets are not explicitly described. This approach has the advantage over agricultural sector models of accounting for feedback from one sector to another as relative prices alter. Additionally, because all goods in the economy are accounted for (and hence, the total balance of trade), income and exchange rates can be modelled endogenously, and the effects of floating rates (or exchange rate liberalization) can be evaluated.

The model is developed for *m* countries/regions ($i=1$ *to* m), producing and trading *n* goods ($j=1$ *to* n) and a nontraded good, *k*. The traded goods include a breakdown of agricultural goods ($1, ..., n-2$), a composite "other agricultural" good ($j=n-1$), and a composite nonagricultural good ($j=n$).

The demand and supply functions, assumed to be derived from consumer and producer maximizing behaviour, depend on all prices and income as delineated below:

$$(1)\ DA_{ij} = DA_{ij}\ (PA_{ij}, PT_{in}, PH_{ik}, Y_i),$$

$$(2)\ DT_{in} = DT_{in}\ (PA_{ij}, PT_{in}, PH_{ik}, Y_i),$$

$$(3)\ DH_{ik} = DH_{ik}\ (PA_{ij}, PT_{in}, PH_{ik}, Y_i),$$

$$(4)\ SA_{ij} = SA_{ij}\ (PA_{ij}, PT_{in}, PH_{ik}),$$

$$(5)\ ST_{in} = ST_{in}\ (PA_{ij}, PT_{in}, PH_{ik}), \text{ and}$$

$$(6)\ SH_{ik} = SH_{ik}\ (PA_{ij}, PT_{in}, PH_{ik}),$$

where *D* and *S* are demand and supply equations, respectively, *P* is prices, *Y* is income, *A* denotes agricultural goods, *T* represents the nonagricultural traded products either exported or imported, and *H* represents the nontraded good. Farm input prices are included implicitly in the price of nonagricultural goods faced by agricultural producers; likewise, agricultural prices represent both prices of inputs and prices of alternative outputs to nonagricultural producers.

Expenditure is defined as:

$$(7)\ Y_i = \sum_{j=1}^{n} P_{ij}\, D_{ij} + P_{ik}\, D_{ik}.$$

Alternatively, expenditure equals the value of production plus (minus) the change in foreign borrowing.

The domestic economy reaches an equilibrium when domestic goods have an excess supply equal to zero and when net traded goods (including agricultural goods) equal "net capital flows" (*F*). *F* is defined as including capital and service accounts and accommodating changes in international reserves. For country *i*,

$$(8)\ ESH_{ik} = SH_{ik} - DH_{ik} = 0, \text{ and}$$

$$(9)\ \sum_{j=1}^{n} ES_{ij}\, P_{ij} = \sum_{j=1}^{n} S_{ij}\, P_{ij} - \sum_{j=1}^{n} D_{ij}\, P_{ij} = F_i.$$

World markets clear when excess supply of a good across all countries is equal to zero. For agricultural commodities, this occurs when:

$$(10)\ \sum_{i=1}^{m} ESA_{ij} = \sum_{i=1}^{m} SA_{ij} - \sum_{i=1}^{m} DA_{ij} = 0,$$

for each j, ($j=1, ..., n-1$). For the traded nonagricultural good n, equilibrium occurs when:

$$(11)\ \sum_{i=1}^{m} EST_{in} = \sum_{i=1}^{m} ST_{in} - \sum_{i=1}^{m} DT_{in} = 0.$$

The traded good price in each country's domestic currency is:

$$(12)\ P_{ij} = E_i\, PW_j(1+t_{ij}),$$

where E_i equals domestic currency per US dollar, PW_j is the world dollar price of good j for all traded js, and t_{ij} can be interpreted as an export subsidy or import tariff ($t_{ij}>0$), or export tax or import subsidy ($t_{ij}<0$) and is assumed to be exogenous.

A shock to the system—in terms of a change in protection in either sector of the economy in any country or commodity market—leads to changes from base values in quantities produced, consumed, and traded and world and domestic prices. The system also determines either (1) changes in each country's balance of trade under the assumption of fixed exchange rates and the availability of external financing or (2) changes in each country's exchange rate under the assumption of floating rates that return all countries' trade balances to their initial equilibria:[2]

$$(13)\ (\Gamma_1+\Gamma_2)Ei^* + \Gamma_1[PWA^*+(1+tA_i)^*] + \Gamma_2[PWT^*+(1+tT_i)^*] = F_i^*,$$

where * indicates percentage change in the variable and Γ is a parameter consisting of supply and demand elasticities, sector expenditure shares, and agricultural and nonagricultural trade shares.

Under a fixed exchange rate system, $E_i^* = 0$, the balance of trade changes in response to changes in protection in the agricultural and nonagricultural sectors and changes in the world prices of traded goods. External financing is assumed to be forthcoming to balance the change in the value of net trade.[3] In the small country case, agricultural markets would be affected (1) directly by changes in the country's agricultural protection, (2) indirectly by changes in prices of nonagricultural and nontraded goods resulting from changes in the country's nonagricultural protection, and (3) by gains in income resulting from liberalization. In the large country case, the additional effects of changes in world prices feed back to domestic prices and affect domestic production and consumption and, consequently, trade.

Under a floating exchange rate system, the country's currency would depreciate or appreciate following liberalization until the changes in the external imbalance are eliminated; i.e., until $F_i^* = 0$. Hence, the exchange rate change causes a further feedback from world prices to domestic prices and subsequent adjustments to quantities.

If the parameters of equation *(13)*, Γ_1 and Γ_2, are positive, then a reduction in protection leads to a depreciation of the exchange rate, which offsets, to some extent, the negative impacts on domestic prices of a reduction in protection levels. If the agricultural protection levels are initially negative (e.g., most agricultural commodities in Argentina) and nonagricultural protection is initially positive, then a reduction of protection can lead to a depreciation, which would reinforce the positive impacts of liberalization on domestic agricultural prices.

Simulation Results

Although many alternative scenarios could have been simulated, four cases were chosen: (1) a 100-percent industrial market economy (USA, EC, Canada, and Japan) liberalization of agriculture under the assumption of fixed exchange rates for all countries/regions; (2) a 100-percent industrial market economy liberalization of all sectors (total liberalization) under the assumption of floating exchange rates for all countries/regions; (3) a 100-percent global liberalization of agriculture for all countries under the assumption of fixed exchange rates; and (4) a 100-percent global liberalization of all sectors for all countries under the assumption of floating exchange rates. These scenarios were designed to explore the participation compared to nonparticipation of developing countries in trade negotiations and to explore the bias in agricultural trade liberalization analyses that do not account for cross-sector linkages, income, or exchange rate effects due to changes in protection (not to predict actual outcomes of trade negotiations).

Table 1—World Agricultural Prices

	Case 1	Case 2	Case 3	Case 4
	Percent change			
Wheat	2.9	7.0	1.6	5.0
Maize	1.3	5.1	0.2	2.7
Soyabeans	-0.1	2.9	-5.4	-4.9
Rice	6.7	13.6	6.6	13.2
Sugar	32.0	38.6	29.1	33.4
Dairy	18.7	24.4	20.0	25.5
Beef	13.8	17.2	12.9	14.7
Poultry	4.9	8.4	4.9	7.2

Table 1 shows that, in each scenario, world prices of all agricultural goods except soyabeans rise. Sugar prices increase the most, followed by dairy prices, reflecting the relatively high levels of industrial market economy protection in these commodity markets. All-sector liberalization (and the resulting exchange rate movements) tends to *reinforce* the price effects of liberalization confined to the agricultural sector (Case 2 compared to Case 1 and Case 4 compared to Case 3). The appreciation of the rest-of-the-world currency (and Argentine, Brazilian, and Mexican currencies in Case 2) relative to the industrial market economy currencies increases (reduces) its willingness to import (export) agricultural commodities, placing additional upward pressure on world prices. For example, consider the large differences in the world price of wheat in Case 2 compared to Case 1. The appreciation of the Argentine and Brazilian currencies reduces those countries' willingness to export wheat at the lower domestic price (in comparison to the fixed exchange rate Case 1).

Global liberalization tends to *dampen* the price effects relative to industrial market economy liberalization (Case 3 compared to Case 1 and Case 4 compared to Case 2), reflecting the tendency for the three Latin American countries to tax their producers. This is particularly illustrated in the soyabean market where Argentina and Brazil account for 25 percent of the export market. Soyabean prices decline mainly because of the increased Argentine and Brazilian exports following the removal of producer taxes and consumer subsidies in these countries.

In all four scenarios, substantial changes occur in foreign exchange earnings or costs in agricultural trade following liberalization (Table 2). If agricultural liberalization occurs in industrial market economies only (Case 1), then Argentina and Brazil improve their agricultural trade balances by about 20 percent, and Mexico is no longer a net agricultural importer, but a net exporter of beef, poultry, and sugar, while decreasing its imports of grains and dairy.

An industrial market economy all-sector liberalization (Case 2) reduces the gain in agricultural exports for Argentina and Brazil relative to Case 1, while Mexico incurs increases in net agricultural imports. The removal of nonagricultural import barriers and, to a lesser extent, the elimination of agricultural support contribute to a deterioration of the industrial market economies' overall trade balances. With endogenous exchange rates, industrial market economy currencies are pressured to depreciate relative to other nations in order to offset the decline in the trade balance. Argentine, Brazilian, and Mexican currencies, therefore, appreciate by approximately 5 percent relative to the US dollar The agricultural competitiveness of these countries is diminished.

Table 2-Changes in the Value of Trade and Exchange Rates*

	Argentina	Brazil	Mexico
	- - *Percent change* - -		
Case 1:			
Agriculture	21	22	252
Nonagriculture	-3	1	0
Total	33	16	5
Case 2:			
Agriculture	9	4	-79
Nonagriculture	-23	-8	1
Total	0	0	0
Exchange Rates	5	6	5
Case 3:			
Agriculture	70	28	-828
Nonagriculture	0	0	0
Total	121	21	-19
Case 4:			
Agriculture	74	66	-188
Nonagriculture	-186	-136	4
Total	0	0	0
Exchange Rates	-2	-9	-11

*A minus sign represents depreciation relative to the dollar.

Analysis of global liberalization in agricultural commodities (Case 3) reveals export revenue gains for Argentina and Brazil of 70 and 28 percent, while Mexico's agricultural costs rise by over 800 percent.[4] The removal of taxes on producers, especially in Argentina, combined with higher world prices (relative to the preliberalization base), spurs increases in soyabean, sugar, and beef exports. However, increases in production and exports modify the world price increases (Table 1), indicating that these two Latin American countries' agricultural policies have some influence on world markets. As for Mexico, where agricultural policies tend to subsidize producers, particularly in grains and dairy, the removal of support reduces the implied domestic price, and the demand for imports rises.

In the all-sector global liberalization scenario (Case 4), Argentina and Brazil post agricultural trade balance gains of 74 and 66 percent, respectively, as the volume of soyabeans, sugar, dairy, and beef exports expand by a minimum of 60 percent. Eradication of the high levels of nonagricultural import protection encourages new nonagricultural imports and leads to a decline in the trade balance; and currency values depreciate (in contrast to case 2). The lower valued Brazilian and Argentine currencies reinforce the export-stimulating effect of removing these countries' agricultural producer taxes. For Brazil, particularly, this gain in agricultural export revenues is significantly larger than in agricultural trade liberalization (Case 3), due to the 9-percent exchange rate depreciation. Protection of the nonagricultural sector has generally represented a strong bias against agricultural exports.

When currency values are allowed to vary (Case 4), the Mexican peso depreciates 11 percent and net expenditures on agricultural imports are much smaller than in the fixed exchange rate case (Case 3). Moreover, Mexico registers a 140-percent rise in foreign exchange earnings from "other agricultural" goods (such as tomatoes and fresh vegetables) over the base period and becomes a net exporter of sugar.

Finally, a word about the rest of the world. The rest of the world improves its net export position in all agricultural goods except soyabeans and "other agriculture." This is not surprising since the rest of the world, in net terms, is assumed to have no trade barriers. With agricultural prices generally rising and perfect price transmission assumed, the rest of the world increases its agricultural production and decreases its consumption. The improved net trade position of the rest of the world, which is biased because of the lack of protection measures, enhances any decline or diminishes any improvement in other countries' commodity trade balances. In the global liberalization case, appreciation of the rest of the world's currency causes its exports to be higher priced in dollar terms and therefore mitigates some of the bias.

Conclusion

This paper illustrates the value of a broader approach to analyzing agricultural trade liberalization issues. Substantial differences for individual countries arise when results of an industrial market economy liberalization scenario are compared with the results of a global liberalization scenario. Similarly, substantial differences arise when results of agricultural liberalization are compared with all-sector liberalization. The model indicates that these differences may be especially large for developing countries where the protection of the nonagricultural sector remains relatively high. Some of the main findings are:

1. Simultaneous reductions in agricultural and nonagricultural protection, allowing exchange rates to vary, tend to reinforce the upward pressure on agricultural prices that follows from agricultural liberalization.

2. For some countries—those that experience the largest exchange rate movements following all-sector trade liberalization, such as Brazil and Mexico—the two simulations produce significantly improved impacts on agricultural trade values relative to agricultural global liberalization.

3. Global liberalization relative to industrial market economy liberalization provides greater impetus to Argentine and Brazilian agricultural exports and Mexican imports. In general, developing countries that remove producer taxes (subsidies) could experience an expansion (contraction) of foreign exchange earnings from agricultural trade.

Notes

[1]Economic Research Service, US Department of Agriculture.

[2]In the second case, changes in trade protection are assumed to be able to change currency values depending on the elasticities of demand and supply for traded and nontraded goods. Since the elasticities approach does not consider a world with capital flows, the shock is implicitly assumed to have an impact only on the trade balance and not to induce changes in capital flows. Corden (1987) argues that the capital account depends on savings and investment decisions and he is ambiguous as to whether a capital-flows effect would obtain with implementation or removal of protection measures. While one could have arbitrarily selected to limit the *change* in the trade balance so that it did not always equal zero, no rigorous criterion to do so exists.

[3]Trade policy changes do not directly influence capital flows but do so indirectly in order to balance the trade account.

[4]Mexico's agricultural trade balance (net importer) is small, so even modest absolute changes in Mexican agricultural trade balance lead to large percentage changes.

References

Anjaria, S.J., Kirmani, N., and Petersen, A.B. (1985) *Trade Policy Issues and Developments*, Occasional Paper No. 38, International Monetary Fund, Washington, D.C., USA.

Corden, W.M. (1987) *Protection and Liberalization: Review of Analytical Issues*, Occasional Paper No. 54, International Monetary Fund, Washington D.C., USA.

Deardorff, A.V., and Stern, R.M. (1986) *Michigan Model of World Production and Trade*, MIT Press, Cambridge, Mass., USA.

Dixit, P.M., and Roningen, V.O. (1986) *Modeling Bilateral Trade Flows with the Static World Policy Simulation Model (SWOPSIM) Modeling Framework*, Staff Report No. AGES-861124, Economic Research Service, US Department of Agriculture, Washington, D.C., USA.

OECD (Organization for Economic Cooperation and Development) (1987) *National Policies and Agricultural Trade*, Paris, France.

Roningen, V.O. (1986) *Static World Policy Simulation (SWOPSIM) Modeling Framework*, Staff Report No. AGES-860625, Economic Research Service, US Department of Agriculture, Washington, D.C., USA.

Tyers, R., and Anderson, K. (1986) "Distortions in World Food Markets: Quantitative Assessment," Background Paper, World Bank, Washington, D.C., USA.

USDA (US Department of Agriculture) (1987) *Government Intervention in Agriculture: Measurement, Evaluation, and Implications for Trade Negotiations*, Foreign Agricultural Economic Report No. 229, Economic Research Service, Washington, D.C., USA.

Valdés, A. (1986) "Exchange Rates and Trade Policy: Help or Hindrance to Agricultural Growth?," in Maunder, A., and Renborg, U. (Eds.) *Agriculture in a Turbulent World Economy*, Gower Publishing Co., Aldershot, UK, pp. 624-637.

Whalley, J. (1985) *Trade Liberalization Among Major World Trading Areas*, MIT Press, Cambridge, Mass., USA.

Whalley, J. (1986) "Impacts of 50% Tariff Reduction in an Eight-Region Global Trade Model," in Srinivasan, T.N., and Whalley, J. (Eds.) *General Equilibrium Trade Policy and Modeling*, MIT Press, Cambridge, Mass., USA.

World Bank (1986) *World Development Report, 1986*, Washington D.C., USA.

DISCUSSION OPENING—*Thomas W. Hertel* (Purdue University)

The authors have extended previous studies of agricultural trade liberalization by developing a global trade model with both farm and nonfarm sectors and with endogenous exchange rates. Most of the previous work in this area has either focused solely on agriculture or has treated the farm sectors in insufficient detail to allow anything to be concluded about the effects of agricultural trade liberalization. Krissoff and Ballenger's research thus focuses on an important gap, particularly since the current GATT negotiations are not limited to agriculture and many opportunities exist for trading reductions in nonfarm protection in one country for farm support cuts in another.

Some good reasons exist to explain the limited amount of work of this sort in the past. To do an adequate job on agriculture is difficult enough, let alone attempting to treat nonagricultural trade as well. In this regard, the authors have benefited by building upon the SWOPSIM framework developed by Vernon Roningen and his associates at USDA for the analysis of global agricultural trade. This assures a certain degree of comparability between their results and those of a wide range of global agricultural models. This is very important, since, as a consumer of this research, I am particularly interested in obtaining some general rules of thumb for adjusting the results of those models that do not treat nonagricultural sector liberalization and that assume fixed exchange rates.

As a fellow modeller, I am all too aware of how easy it is to criticize specific aspects of any ambitious modelling effort. To be constructive is much more difficult. What I will try to do here is identify some of this model's limitations—which should be borne in mind when interpreting the results.

First of all, the model used here is an equilibrium model. As such, it is more useful in understanding the basic market forces set in motion by a given policy change. It is appropriate for medium-run policy analysis, but not for shorter run prediction. In the short run, observed changes may well be dominated by disequilibrium forces.

Consider, for example, exchange rates. That they have been persistently in disequilibrium in many countries is well known. Furthermore, overvaluation of exchange rates often serves as an indirect tax on the agricultural sector. A recent study by Brandão and Carvalho for selected crops in Brazil indicates that this indirect effect can dominate the direct effects of farm policies. They conclude that, in the early 1980s, cotton and maize were subsidized through direct agricultural policies, but taxed when both direct and indirect effects are taken into account.

Given that we start off in a disequilibrium position, to which adjustment is still occurring, when we overlay a trade liberalization scenario, the observed changes in the exchange rate may be quite different from that simulated by a static equilibrium model.

A second qualification stems from the treatment of public policies in the model. The appropriate methodology for quantifying the effects of agricultural policies on quantities produced and consumed is the focus of considerable research by agricultural economists and a number of papers at this conference. I believe we are making progress—and that the price wedges used for the industrial market economies in this paper are largely plausible in the direction and magnitude of their effects.

However, I am less comfortable with the treatment of policies in the rest of the world. In Brazil, for example, credit subsidies have historically been the dominant public expenditure on agriculture. But the evidence indicates that these subsidies have a relatively small impact on output, presumably because of the way in which they are administered. Treating the full amount of these subsidies as a marginal producer price enhancement thus considerably overstates their supply-inducing effects. A second example of such a limitation is the apparent absence of the Brazilian programme for encouraging the substitution of sugar-cane-derived alcohol for petrol. This has led to a massive increase in sugar cane acreage in Brazil—probably at the expense of other farm outputs.

A related concern has to do with the choices for aggregation across countries and commodities (which I recognize were largely dictated by limitations on length and research resources). The commodity aggregation scheme is motivated by industrial market economy production and public policies in agriculture. Thus, in the case of Mexico, for example, the residual "other agricultural" sector is three times as large as the remaining eight sectors. Similarly, when it comes to country aggregation, the residual "rest of the world" is a very large aggregate, which is assumed to be policy neutral with respect to world markets.

I do not have a problem with these research choices made by the authors. In fact, I think they have chosen quite wisely, given their constraints. However, all of this does lead me to prefer to focus on the industrial market economy liberalization experiments—cases 1 and 2 in their paper. Global liberalization exercises will become more credible as these authors and others in this field continue their research efforts.

These qualifications notwithstanding, the authors are to be congratulated for tackling a difficult but important problem. Furthermore, I believe they have succeeded in delivering a few handy rules of thumb for adjusting the results of existing agricultural trade liberalization studies. In particular, I conclude, after reading their paper, that those current studies that ignore nonfarm liberalization and exchange rate effects probably understate the upward farm price effects of industrial market economy trade liberalization. Since this upward movement in agricultural prices provides the main incentive for industrial market economies to include agriculture in future liberalization efforts, this is a conclusion that deserves further attention.

GENERAL DISCUSSION—*Terrence S. Veeman, Rapporteur* (Department of Rural Economy, University of Alberta)

The major concern raised in discussion from the floor was whether agricultural trade liberalization would be harmful to the less-developed countries. Given that world price levels for most agricultural commodities were predicted to rise with trade liberalization, fears were expressed that the import bill for the poor nations would rise initially or that several poor nations, especially net importers of food items, would have more difficulty in feeding their populations.

Discussion also focused on the particular conditions under which factor-biased (land-saving) technical change would lead to a lower factor share for a particular input—in this case, land; e.g., how output quantity or price changes were influencing the factor share going to land. Finally, interest was expressed in how policy reforms in the centrally planned economies, especially the USSR and China, might affect trade liberalization.

Participants in the discussion included D. Harvey, E. Liboreiro, S. Manzke, G. Peters, and I. Soliman.

Distribution of Domestic Policy Benefits and the Willingness to Support Trade Liberalization

Susan Offutt and Robbin Shoemaker[1]

Abstract: Agricultural trade liberalization for developed countries may mean elimination of existing domestic support programmes. The difficulty of achieving freer trade is directly related to the distribution of the pain of adjustment in domestic agricultural economies. A cost function is estimated for post-World War II US agriculture to examine the functional distribution of agricultural income in a consistent way, disentangling the separate effects of technological and policy influences on factor shares. Insight is thereby gained into the probable effects of removal of government support for agriculture. The analysis implies that landowners have the most to lose from removal of domestic support programmes as a prelude to trade liberalization. Application of this framework to the experience of other nations would provide a basis for the comparison of the size of prospective domestic losses affecting a country's willingness to negotiate trade liberalizing measures.

Introduction

As general economic growth has proceeded, developed countries have allocated a smaller portion of their aggregate resources to agricultural production. Many observers, among them Schultz (1951), and, more recently, Anderson (1987) have remarked upon the decline in economic importance of the farm sector in developed countries. Both the low income elasticity of demand for food and the productivity impacts of technological advance in agriculture have relieved societies of the need to devote an increasing part of their resources to growing food.

Beyond a comparison of the status of agriculture relative to other sectors of the economy, the question arises as to how the decline in agriculture's share has been apportioned among the factors of production. The functional distribution of income within the sector is largely determined by changes in factor use, as production possibilities expand with technological advance. Technological change in developed country agriculture has generally been labour and land saving and capital and materials using (see, for example, Antle, 1984, on the USA; Lopez, 1980, on Canada; and Behrens and de Haen, 1980, on the EC). Consequently, the impact of the decline in sectoral income is felt more acutely by some factors than others.

In spite of the decline in farming, or perhaps because of it, developed country agriculture is characterized by pervasive government intervention in factor and commodity markets. Were it not that high-income countries tend to overprice agricultural products, Anderson (1987) suggests that the "measured rates of decline in agriculture's importance would be even faster" (p. 197). To what extent can the policies of developed countries to maintain returns to agriculture overcome the structural tendency towards decline? And, how does government intervention affect the distribution of income to factors of agricultural production?

These questions about the sectoral effects of government intervention have particular relevance when multilateral trade talks may, for the first time, consider agricultural trade liberalization. Success in obtaining freer trade will be conditioned by the willingness of nations to reduce or eliminate domestic support. The distribution of the pain of adjustment to removing support can be an important determinant of the kinds of concessions a nation will make in multilateral negotiations. Here, linkages among factor returns, technological advance, and government intervention in developed country agriculture are considered. An analytical framework for quantifying these relationships is described and implemented for post-World War II US agriculture. Finally, the implications of the findings for the formulation of multilateral trade negotiating positions are examined.

Susan Offutt and Robbin Shoemaker

Technology, Policy, and Factor Shares

In discussing the consequences of the decline in the relative importance of farming, Schultz (1951) paid particular attention to the implications for the share of land in the value of production. Schultz noted that "because of technical advances, it has become economic to substitute to an increasing extent several classes of inputs for both land and labour, notably motor vehicles and fertilizer and lime" (p. 740). These technological improvements may result in a decrease in the share of land in the value of agricultural production, a reversal of the Malthusian prediction of ever increasing land rents. This possibility is known as Ricardo's paradox (Offer, 1980, p. 237). Whenever the relative importance of agriculture in the economy diminishes and other factors are substituted for land in farming, the fall of the importance of land in the aggregate and in agricultural production is accelerated.

This focus on land is appropriate, as it represents the major source of wealth in the farming community. In developed country agriculture, land and labour are supplied by the farming sector, while capital and intermediate inputs (materials such as fertilizers and pesticides) are supplied from outside its traditional boundaries. When farmers are also landowners, returns to both factors remain in production agriculture. However, to the extent that the bias in technological change is to save both land and labour, their shares in the value of production are diminished. As farming comes to rely more heavily on inputs supplied from the financial and manufacturing sectors, an increasing portion of returns flows out of agriculture.

To start, one may consider the effects of government policy intervention on factor shares, independently of the effects of technological advance. Floyd (1965) describes the implications of three stylized forms of intervention representative of developed country agricultural programmes. First, commodity prices may be supported without output controls, as in the EC. In that case, gross income will rise and so increase the demand for all factors. In the second form of intervention, prices are raised as a result of reducing production by restricting input use, usually land. This feature is characteristic of US support programmes for major grains. The third form of intervention involves controlling output directly through the issuance of marketing certificates that establish quotas. In that case, no specific directive is made as to how input use may be adjusted. The EC dairy programme most closely resembles this scheme, although it has not been widely applied in other developed country programmes. In all three cases, intervention raises the price of the factor in most inelastic supply by the greatest extent. This factor is land.

In considering the effects of alternative support policies on returns to land, recall the definition of share (i.e., input quantity multiplied by its own price divided by total costs or returns). Then, in Floyd's first case, comparable to EC policy, output price support causes the demand for land to shift outwards, increasing its price and use and so its share. To the extent that land supply is ultimately fixed, prices and the value of the share will rise even further. In the second case, more representative of US intervention, the acreage restriction shifts the supply curve for land inwards, thereby raising its price but reducing the quantity used. This sequence of events may or may not lead to an increase in land's share in the value of production. In either case, the price of land, as reflected in rents, will rise, but the direction of the change in its cost share is ambiguous in the US case.[2]

The net effect of technological advance and policy intervention on land share must be determined empirically. If Ricardo's paradox holds, then the share of land will be diminished by land-saving technological change. At the same time, if government intervention is successful in maintaining returns to resources in agriculture, then the effect of the programmes on land share would be positive. The question to be resolved is one of the relative strengths of the tendency of technological changed to diminish land share and the possibility that government support will increase or maintain it. These separate effects of technology and policy need to be disentangled to judge the impact on factor returns of removing domestic support programmes as part of trade liberalization. In the next section, a framework is proposed for evaluating these two effects simultaneously.

Empirical Analysis

The empirical analysis will focus on measurement of changes in land's share of the value of US agricultural production when support programmes restricting acreage as an input are in place. Acreage control programmes are hypothesized to have held the share of land in the value of production above the level that would prevail in their absence. In the case of the USA, total land in farms has remained fairly constant over the past three decades, implying that any change in the share is due to factor price movement. The portion of land in farms idled under government programmes varies, and these changes in programme participation affect the price of land remaining in production. As Floyd explains, the price of the factor in most inelastic supply (i.e., land) will rise when acreage restrictions are in place, and the right to receive government payments for acreage reduction may be capitalized into land values by raising expected income earnings capacity. Technological change is hypothesized to be land saving, thereby decreasing the share of land in the value of production.

These hypotheses are examined via the concept of duality that follows from a producer optimizing framework. A translog cost function and factor share equations, as suggested by Christensen and Greene (1976), are estimated using data on aggregate US agricultural production during 1948-84. The cost function is specified generally as $C = C(Y, W, T, D)$, where C represents total cost, W is a $n \times 1$ vector of input prices ($i=1, ..., n$), T represents the level of technology, and D represents a fixed factor, in this case total idled programme acres. The variable inputs are capital (K), labour (L), materials (M), and land remaining in production (A). All variables are expressed in logarithms except T and D. The system of factor demand equations were derived via the envelope theorem. Because the arguments are expressed in logarithms, the demands are expressed as cost shares, which makes the translog particularly appropriate due to the interest in how shares have changed with acreage control programmes.[3]

Land removed from the production of programme crops may be treated as a fixed factor because farmers must agree to participate in acreage control before any crops are planted. Once farmers have accepted programme requirements, decisions about input use on the remaining acreage can be made. In the aggregate, "slippage" may occur when acreage planted increases as nonparticipants attempt to take advantage of higher product markets prices that may result from output reduction as an effect of the acreage control programmes.

The variables are constructed as Divisia price indices. The capital service price is derived following Hall and Jorgenson (1967). Capital includes durable equipment, structures, and inventory. Labour includes hired and self-employed labour. Materials include all purchased inputs, such as feed, seed, breeding stock, fertilizer, agricultural services, energy, and other intermediate inputs. All data are found in US Departments of Agriculture and Commerce sources. The cost share of land is calculated as the product of the quantity of land in production net of idled acres and an implicit rental price divided by total cost. As in Hall and Jorgenson, the implicit rental price is defined to reflect the opportunity cost of capital. The quantity of output, including all crops and livestock, is represented by a Divisia quantity index. Because the value of D, the measure of acreage controlled by programmes, is zero in a few years, this variable is normalized to its 1972 value, which bounds its value between zero and slightly over one (Gollop and Karlson, 1978).

The full information maximum likelihood estimates of the model's coefficients in the system of input share equations were obtained using TROLL software. The cost share equations are expressed as:

$$(1)\ S_i = a_i + \sum_j b_{ij} \ln w_j + b_{iy} \ln y + b_{it} T + b_{id} D.$$

The cost function is linearly homogeneous in prices, which requires:

$$(2)\ \sum_i a_i = 1, \text{ and } \sum_i \sum_j b_{ij} = \sum_i b_{iy} = \sum_i b_{id} = \sum_i b_{it} = 0.$$

Only those coefficient estimates of immediate interest are reported here.

The direct effect (factor bias) of acreage control is examined by partially differentiating each factor cost share, S_i, with respect to D; i.e., $b_{id} = \delta S_i/\delta D$. If this derivative is greater than zero, then (holding other shares, prices, and output constant) the implication is that acreage control programmes have resulted in increasing the share of input i. The effects of technological change can be evaluated by differentiating each cost share with respect to T, the linear trend term representing technological advance. When the derivative with respect to a particular input i's cost share is positive, technological change is considered ith factor using. When negative, the change has been relatively ith factor saving; if zero, change has been neutral with respect to input i. Here, $b_{it} = \delta S_i/\delta T$ denotes the factor bias associated with technological change.

Table 1—Direct Factor Biases Associated with Technological Change (b_{it}) and Acreage Control Programmes (b_{id})

	Capital	Labour	Materials	Land
b_{it}	0.045 (0.002)	-0.100 (0.005)	0.096 (0.014)	-0.042 (0.013)
b_{id}	-0.011 (0.001)	-0.002 (0.005)	0.007 (0.006)	0.006 (0.002)

Note: Standard errors are in parentheses.

The importance of agricultural land is expected to decrease with technological advance in farming. In Table 1, the top row shows that the sign on the change in the land cost share with respect to technological change is negative, implying a fall in the share of land, as would be expected from the notion of Ricardo's paradox. The null hypothesis, that the value of b_{At} is positive or zero at the 95-percent confidence level, is rejected. The empirical results indicate that technological change has also been labour saving and capital and material using, consistent with the findings of other researchers.

While technological change has depressed land's share, acreage control programmes might increase it. When acres are idled, the shift inwards of the supply curve of land in production will put upward pressure on the land price. In addition, the diversion of land from production has often been associated with a transfer (deficiency) payment which accrues to landowners and is capitalized into the value of land. The transfer payment could be thought of as the economic rent going to the fixed factor, the diverted acreage, thereby increasing the value of all agricultural land (Floyd, 1965).

The change in land share's with respect to these programmes has indeed been positive. The null hypothesis, that the value of b_{Ad} is negative or zero at the 95-percent confidence level, is rejected. At the same time, the programmes have apparently decreased the shares of capital and labour, while that of materials has risen. This outcome is consistent with the supposition that the use of some nonland inputs, most likely the fertilizer component of materials, may increase with acreage controls.

Comparing the technology and programme effects on land share in Table 1, the technology effect is seen to be seven times larger in absolute value than the programme effect. One can infer, therefore, that government intervention can only hope at best to slow the decline in the share of land. When policy aims include maintenance of returns to the factor as well, programme costs will only rise with time, since the deficit to be made up increases as technological advance continues to drive land's share downwards. Moreover, when the concept of parity between farm and nonfarm income is based on some notion of costs of production, programmes that increase land values only create a further need for compensation. Additional empirical evidence (not reported here) suggests that by acting to buoy the value of land, government programmes may actually enhance the land-saving bias of technological change, since factors in relatively short supply are used the most sparingly.

The cost function has been employed in a novel way to try to disentangle the separate effects of policy and technology on factor shares. The advantages of this approach are that the influences can be dealt with simultaneously and in a consistent way and that effects are traced to their ultimate implications for resource allocation. The perspective adopted is long run, so the transitory effects of limited income transfers are diminished. The disadvantages of this approach are similar to any application of duality relations to aggregate, nonmicrolevel data. At the sectoral level, the assumptions of exogenous factor and commodity prices and of fixed output level are tenuous. Furthermore, in introducing policy into the neoclassical framework, all its effect is summarized in one instrument, acreage diversion. While this approach is convenient, it may overestimate policy's effect. Nonetheless, this attempt is one of only a few to inject realism into agricultural production studies employing duality concepts.

Domestic and International Policy Implications

An important determinant of agricultural support and trade policy is not just the level of income going to the sector but its distribution among the factors of production. This distribution is particularly important in developed country agriculture where a large portion of the value of production is captured by the providers of capital and intermediate inputs who are not part of the traditional farming community. Land and labour are the factors that remain largely in the control of the farm population that is the target of much policy intervention. Because political decisions often turn on distributional issues, knowledge of the effects on factor shares may ultimately be of more interest to policy makers than gross measures of changes in producer welfare, such as producer subsidy equivalents.

Conclusion

The implications of technological change and government support on factor shares for one developed country, the USA, have been investigated. Were the data available, one could apply this approach to other developed countries' experience and thereby gain a basis for international comparison. Agricultural trade liberalization for developed countries may mean elimination of existing domestic support programmes. The difficulty of achieving freer trade is directly related to the distribution of the pain of adjustment in domestic agricultural economies. The present analysis implies that landowners have the most to lose from removal of domestic support programmes as a prelude to trade liberalization. Unless trade reform substantially increases real demand for their agricultural output, landowners of the developed countries will suffer a loss of wealth as the share of land in the value of production falls.

The cost function approach permits examination of the functional distribution of agricultural income in a consistent way, disentangling the separate effects of structural and policy influences on factor shares. Insight is thereby gained into the probable effects of removal of government support for agriculture. Application of this framework to other nations would provide similar information. Developed country policies could probably be shown to have slowed the decline in the value of the share of land, but to not have overcome the land-saving bias of technological advance. If support is removed, the farming community will experience a decline in wealth. Ultimately, the size of this prospective loss is what affects a country's willingness to negotiate trade liberalizing measures.

Notes

[1]US Office of Management and Budget; and Economic Research Service, US Department of Agriculture; respectively.

[2]A body of literature on the effects of US support programmes on land values has failed to incorporate the crucial characteristics of acreage restriction (e.g., Herdt and Cochrane, 1966; Boehlje and Griffin, 1979; and Harris, 1977). Research on the EC experience (e.g., Traill, 1979) with price supports is not susceptible to this error.

[3]The function was estimated assuming nonhomothetic and Hicksian nonneutral technologies to allow maximum flexibility in establishing the effects of the acreage control programmes. A nonhomothetic function implies nonconstant returns to scale due to the presence of a fixed factor; in this case, idled acres. Estimated bias due to these factors and compensated price elasticities are available from the authors.

References

Anderson, K. (1987) "On Why Agriculture Declines with Economic Growth," *Agricultural Economics*, Vol. 1, No. 3, pp. 195-207.

Antle, J. (1984) "Structure of U.S. Agricultural Technology, 1910-78," *American Journal of Agricultural Economics*, Vol. 66, No. 4, pp. 414-421.

Behrens, R., and de Haen, H. (1980) "Aggregate Factor Input and Productivity in Agriculture: Comparison for the EC-Member Countries, 1963-76," *European Review of Agricultural Economics*, Vol. 7, No. 2, pp. 109-146.

Boehlje, M., and Griffin, S. (1979) "Financial Impacts of Government Price Support Programs," *American Journal of Agricultural Economics*, Vol. 61, No. 2, pp. 285-296.

Christensen, L.R., and Greene, W.H. (1976) "Economies of Scale in U.S. Electric Power Generation," *Journal of Political Economy*, Vol. 84, No. 4, pp. 655-676.

Floyd, J. (1965) "Effects of Farm Price Supports on the Returns to Land and Labor in Agriculture," *Journal of Political Economy*, Vol. 73, No. 2, pp. 148-158.

Gollop, F.M., and Karlson, S.H. (1978) "Impact of Fuel Adjustment Mechanism on Economic Efficiency," *Review of Economics and Statistics*, Vol. 60, No. 4, pp. 574-584.

Hall, R.E., and Jorgenson, D. (1967) "Tax Policy and Investment Behavior," *American Economic Review*, Vol. 57, No. 3, pp. 391-414.

Harris, D.G. (1977) "Inflation-Indexed Price Supports and Land Values," *American Journal of Agricultural Economics*, Vol. 59, No. 3, pp. 489-495.

Herdt, R.W., and Cochrane, W.W. (1966) "Farmland Prices and Technological Advance," *Journal of Farm Economics*, Vol. 48, No. 2, pp. 243-264.

Lopez, R.E. (1980) "Structure of Production and the Derived Demand for Inputs in Canadian Agriculture," *American Journal of Agricultural Economics*, Vol. 62, No. 1, pp. 38-45.

Offer, A. (1980) "Ricardo's Paradox and the Movement of Rents in England, c. 1870-1910," *Economic History Review*, Vol. 33, No. 2, pp. 236-252.

Schultz, T.W. (1951) "Declining Economic Importance of Agricultural Land," *Economic Journal*, Vol. 61, No. 2, pp. 725-740.

Traill, B. (1979) "Empirical Model of the U.K. Land Market and the Impact of Price Policy on Land Values and Rents," *European Review of Agricultural Economics*, Vol. 6, No. 2, pp. 209-232.

DISCUSSION OPENING—*R.G.F. Spitze* (University of Illinois)

The authors are commended for a professional performance on an important area of economic supply analysis of agricultural production. Their study design, theoretical foundation, and demonstration of a useful technique leave little to quibble about. However, their policy efforts deserve more scrutiny.

In a developing economy, the implications for any sector with a highly inelastic demand against income, such as agriculture, are generally understood. That is, factors of production in such sectors continually face relatively slower gains in returns compared to sectors producing less inelastic products and hence must continually adjust resources, usually involving an outmigration of human resources. Thus we have Ricardo's paradox and the dilemma of agricultural economies throughout a developing world.

This study gives us some additional corroboration, with the added bonus of an analytical technique for measuring the relative economic impacts among those agricultural factors using their comparative cost share in total production. The results generally bear out our theoretical expectations. A few, admittedly minor, questions trouble me about this part of the paper. First, we should be cautioned to speak of a decline in the *relative economic importance* of the farm sector, not just "decline in farming" or "decline in economic importance." Farming and agriculture surely remain economically important regardless of country.

Second, is it operationally logical to separate land capital from structures and durable equipment capital? Third, do we adequately understand that, in recent US policy, deficiency payments accrue to both landowners and most renters? Fourth, how useful is acreage control as a proxy for policy when programmes of both compulsory and voluntary controls over a 36-year period are lumped together, and this is only one of many varied provisions? Finally, how comfortable do we feel drawing inferences from technical results measured by differences between -0.002 and +0.007.

I am much more concerned about the authors' efforts to hook their empirical analysis to the policy area with such words as "multilateral trade talks" and distribution of domestic policy benefits." Their analysis has merit because we need reliable measurement of what happens to farm factor returns as an economy develops, not because it tells us much, if anything, about trade negotiations. Do they really ask the relevant policy question; i.e., Can policies to maintain returns overcome the structural tendency to decline? To imply that a major determinant of interventions, such as trade barriers, is the relative pain of owners of the farmland factor as contrasted to all other farm factors, much less nonfarm interests in food, is a formidable leap.

The owners of agricultural factors do suffer pain during development, and participatory governments intervene to ease that pain and smooth the necessary adjustments, as well as recognize the role of food in political and economic survival. Operators in most developed countries reap some returns from all the production factors of land, labour, management, and capital; their differentiation may be of more concern to economists than policy makers. Trade negotiation implies trade-offs among gainers and losers, among sectors, and among nations. Reliable knowledge helps negotiators. However, to recognize the limitations of economic analysis in policy is not to demean our product but to dignify it with creditability.

Additional knowledge exists about US agriculture: (1) the real total farm factor returns have generally declined for 40 years, but per-farm returns have increased slowly due to relentless outmigration of 1 to 4 percent per year, and to persistent evolving public policy; (2) these returns per operator are not significantly different between the participants and nonparticipants in our voluntary supply-demand balancing policies, and the benefits contribute to less inequality of incomes; (3) the productivity of the total farm labour factor has continuously outperformed that of the rest of the economy; (4) total federal government programme outlays as a proportion of all government costs has trended downwards; and (5) the adjustment of surplus farm labour is threatened by a slowing over three decades to a trickle of increases in off-farm incomes. This knowledge does not point directions of policy nor even of trade negotiations any more than that provided in this study, but we can respect both the value of our research to public policy, and its limitations.

[Refer to the general discussion following Krissoff and Ballenger's paper on page 72.]

Individual and Multilateral Trade Liberalization

Douglas L. Maxwell[1]

Abstract: This paper uses a general equilibrium model with nine agricultural sectors to project a reference scenario, five unilateral agricultural liberalizations by Oceania, Canada, the EC, Japan, and the USA, and a multilateral trade liberalization by all of the preceding countries together. The effects on prices and production are examined along with the interaction effects of a multilateral liberalization.

Introduction

In late spring 1987, the USA proposed a multilateral phasing out of agricultural protection over a period of 10 years. This proposal was based partly on the theory that a decrease in agricultural protection would reduce production and raise world prices. The multilateral reduction would thus cause less dislocation in the agricultural sectors of the liberalizing countries because producer prices would not need to fall all the way to current world prices but only to the higher postliberalization world price level. Such a multilateral reduction is simulated here. The possible interaction effects between countries and commodities in a multilateral liberalization are also investigated. Some extra space is devoted to the effects on the USA in order to ascertain the effects of the US proposal on US crop and livestock farmers.

A revised version of the IIASA model system was used to make seven projections: a reference projection with no change in policies, an OECD liberalization projection with complete agricultural liberalization in the more important OECD countries, and five unilateral agricultural liberalizations of these OECD countries. A comparison of the reference and OECD liberalization scenarios is presented first. It shows that real gross world agricultural product would rise 0.22 percent, with an overall increase in traded agricultural prices of 7 percent and price increases in each of the 9 agricultural (composite) traded commodities in the IIASA system. US agricultural exports would rise 16 percent in value. The five unilateral projections are then examined to determine the impact of each of the individual countries on the overall result and the strength of the interaction effects of a multilateral liberalization.

Overview of the IIASA System

The version of the IIASA world agricultural modelling system used here contains 34 models of countries, country groups, or regions, with a fixed international commodity list of nine agricultural commodities and one nonagricultural commodity; 20 full models of countries or country groups; and a set of 14 simple regional models based on exogenous trends and elasticities. This whole system is referred to as the basic linked system.

Each full model estimates production, inputs, stocks, and consumption consistent with that country's policy variables, especially tariffs, quotas, and price controls. These internal commodities are then aggregated into the ten internationally traded commodities, which are wheat, rice, coarse grains (other cereals), beef and sheep, dairy products, other animal products, protein feeds, other foods, nonfood agriculture, and a nonagricultural composite.

The full country models available in the present basic linked system are Argentina, Australia, Austria, Brazil, Canada, China, CMEA (USSR and Eastern Europe), Egypt, EC-10, India, Indonesia, Japan, Kenya, Mexico, New Zealand, Nigeria, Pakistan, Thailand, Turkey, and the USA.

Reference and OECD Liberalization Projections

Assumptions of the OECD Liberalization Projection

The IIASA system was run to the year 2000, with all agricultural protection measures, including US commodity programmes, removed for a set of six OECD countries over the 1984-93 period. These OECD countries are Australia, Canada, the EC-10, Japan, New Zealand, and the USA. For convenience, this set of countries and economic communities will be called the OECD-6.

For the USA, both the border measures and the federal government commodity policies were phased out over the transition period.[2] Although some tariffs were in effect, the most important border measures were the import quotas on beef, mutton, and dairy products. Sugar quotas are not in the model since sugar is combined in other foods. No dairy programmes are in the present US model; the import quota is the only measure protecting domestic prices from the world market.

The Canadian model has a ceiling on dairy production that keeps production just slightly less than Canadian consumption. In the OECD liberalization projection, the ceiling was doubled over the 1984-93 period, with the result that it stopped acting as a constraint.

The endogenous border protection is eliminated over the 1984-93 period for all agricultural commodities for Australia, Canada, EC, and Japan. In New Zealand, constant tariff equivalents were eliminated.

Overview of Results

This summary discusses the long-run results in the 1995-2000 period, after the system has settled down. The results of the liberalization runs are compared with a reference run in which no policy changes are made. The long-run result of full trade liberalization in the OECD-6 was to raise world prices for all nine agricultural commodity groups but especially for grains, dairy products, and protein feeds (Table 1). Ruminant (beef/sheep) prices rose more than prices for other animals, other foods, and nonfood agriculture.

Table 1–Change in World Results Due to OECD-6 Liberalization (1995-2000 Average)

	Price Change*	Production Change	
	Percent	*Percent*	*1,000 tons*
Wheat	12.1	-0.19	-1,143
Rice (milled)	20.2	0.97	3,481
Coarse grains	8.5	0.73	7,953
Beef/sheep (carcass weight)	6.6	-0.05	-36
Dairy products (fresh milk equivalent)	19.7	0.69	4,399
Other animal products (protein equivalent)	0.9	0.61	159
Protein feeds (protein equivalent)	15.6	1.16	708
Other food	4.1	-0.08	
Nonfood agriculture	1.7	-1.04	
Nonagriculture	0.0	0.09	

*Relative to nonagriculture.
Source: Runs of the IIASA/FAP system (August 1987 ERS version).

Overall, both world agricultural prices and production increased. All the agricultural price changes were increases, and some of them (grains, dairy products, and protein feeds) were quite large. During the 1995-2000 period, overall agricultural prices (relative to nonagricultural) are 7 percent higher in the liberalization projection than in the reference projection. On the other hand, production showed only slight changes, with an overall global increase of 0.22 percent in real world gross agricultural product. Slight declines occurred in the global production of wheat, ruminants, other foods, and nonfood agriculture. The global production decreases in wheat, ruminant, and other food (including sugar) production were smaller than the EC decreases. Production outside the EC actually increased. In the case of nonfood agriculture, the EC and USA accounted for the bulk of the global production decrease.

Effects on Gross Domestic Product

For 1995-2000, the gross world product (including nonagriculture) in the OECD liberalization projection was 0.099 percent larger than the reference projection, with world agricultural product about 0.22 percent larger (Table 2). Of the countries that liberalized, all gained in total GDP, but sharply mixed results obtained in agricultural GDP. On the other hand, except for the centrally planned countries, all the nonliberalizing countries showed an increase in agricultural GDP but had mixed results on total GDP. Except for the centrally planned economies and Indonesia and India, all nonliberalizing countries experienced an increase in agricultural GDP of more than 0.75 percent over the 1995-2000 period. China showed no change at all, while in the CMEA not only total GDP but also agricultural GDP declined as resources (including more fertilizer application) were shifted to the grain, ruminant, and dairy sectors from both nonagriculture and other agriculture.

Table 2—Percent Change in Gross Domestic Product Due to OECD Liberalization Relative to the Reference Run (1995-2000 Average)

	GDP	Agricultural GDP		GDP	Agricultural GDP
World	0.099	0.22			
Argentina	0.026	3.11	Indonesia	-0.019	0.17
Australia	0.008	-2.81	Japan	0.203	-5.49
Austria	-0.068	0.79	Kenya	0.554	1.61
Brazil	-0.292	0.91	Mexico	-0.916	1.86
Canada	0.137	2.76	New Zealand	0.235	1.59
China	0.000	0.00	Nigeria	0.463	2.12
CMEA	-0.096	-0.16	Pakistan	0.065	2.06
EC-10	0.312	-7.28	Thailand	0.083	1.28
Egypt	-0.309	1.57	Turkey	-0.087	2.64
India	0.106	0.12	USA	0.146	0.78

Source: Runs of the IIASA/FAP system (August 1987 ERS version).

Grain Price Relationships

The world price of wheat rose more than the world price of coarse grains. The protection for wheat was higher than the coarse grains in the EC model. This caused a shift in EC acreage to coarse grains as protection was eliminated, so that the EC produced somewhat more coarse grains and much less wheat.

The world price of rice rose due to a large increase in the use of rice in Japan. Rice use for feed (which includes rice bran) increased, which probably means that the increase in Japanese rice consumption is overstated.

Effects of the OECD-6 Liberalization on the USA

The effect of trade liberalization by the OECD-6 is to increase both prices and export values by the USA (Table 3). The effects differ sharply by commodity, with the export volume of grains, protein feeds, and other foods increasing, imports of beef and sheep decreasing, imports of other animals up slightly, and imports of dairy products up sharply. Nonfood agriculture is not affected much. The net result of the free importation of dairy products combined with the increase in the world price is that domestic dairy producer prices fall approximately 20 percent. This domestic price drop increases consumption significantly.

Table 3—Change in US Exports and World Prices Due to OECD Liberalization Relative to the Reference Run (1995-2000 Average)

	Change in Export Volume	Price
	1,000 tons	*Percent change*
Wheat	6,561	12.13
Rice	289	20.21
Coarse grains	12,724	8.52
Beef/sheep	414	6.58
Dairy products	-5,897	19.65
Other animals	-49	0.91
Protein feeds	463	15.64
Other foods	9*	4.13
Nonfood agriculture	-14*	1.71

*Millions of 1970 dollars.
Source: Runs of the IIASA/FAP system (August 1987 ERS version).

The reference or base value of US agricultural exports varies a great deal by commodity (Table 4). Grains, protein feeds, and other foods (which include fats and oils) together total more than all of net agricultural exports, with livestock products being a net drain on the agricultural balance of trade. The liberalization increases the agricultural balance of trade by 16.1 percent, but the disparity between the crop and livestock sectors is increased, with crop exports expanding but livestock imports increasing except for beef and sheep.

Table 4—Value of US Exports as a Percentage of Total Agricultural Exports in the Reference Projection (1995-2000 Average)

	Reference	Liberalization	OECD-6 Change
Wheat	26.86	33.02	6.16
Rice (milled)	5.92	7.46	1.54
Coarse grains	33.86	41.30	7.44
Beef/sheep (carcass weight)	-8.96	-7.33	1.64
Dairy products (fresh milk equivalent)	-0.85	-5.49	-4.63
Other animals (protein equivalent)	-1.93	-3.40	-1.47
Protein feeds (protein equivalent)	24.25	28.89	4.64
Other foods	20.82	21.74	0.92
Nonfood agriculture	0.04	-0.05	-0.09
Total agriculture	100.00	116.13	16.13

Source: Runs of the IIASA/FAP system (August 1987 ERS version).

Effects of the Unilateral Liberalizations

This section first examines the effects of the five different unilateral liberalizations[3] on the world prices of traded commodities, then on the quantities exported or imported by the USA, and finally on the change in export or import values by commodity in relation to the overall agricultural balance of trade of the USA.

The effects of a multilateral trade liberalization on world prices can, to a large extent, be decomposed into the sum of individual country liberalizations (Table 5). Few significant interactions occurred among the different unilateral liberalizations. The most significant interaction occurred with dairy products, with a 26.7-percent total increase obtained by summing the five different individual liberalizations, but only a 19.6-percent increase in the OECD-6 liberalization. This seems to be due to the fact that in a liberalization that includes both the USA and the EC, the increase in world prices due to the addition of the EC to the set of liberalizing countries causes consumption in the USA to fall partway back to the reference projection levels. The second largest interaction is not large—the individual protein meal price changes sum up to 15.6 percent, but the OECD-6 liberalization shows a price increase of only 14 percent.

Table 5—World Prices for Six Different Liberalization Scenarios Compared to the Reference Run (1995-2000 Average)

	OECD-6	Canada	EC-10	Japan	Oceania	USA
	Percent					
Wheat	12.15	3.09	6.26	1.19	1.96	0.17
Rice	20.21	0.37	2.36	15.97	0.35	0.62
Coarse grains	8.52	2.50	2.61	1.68	1.94	-0.13
Beef/sheep	6.58	0.38	4.20	0.16	-0.27	2.07
Dairy products	19.65	1.08	15.02	2.34	-1.24	9.46
Other animals	0.91	0.55	3.35	-3.59	1.05	0.00
Protein feeds	15.64	0.29	1.46	10.26	0.71	1.33
Other foods	4.13	0.11	2.42	0.86	0.32	0.64
Nonfood agriculture	1.71	0.18	1.45	1.27	-0.71	-0.45

Source: Runs of the IIASA/FAP system (August 1987 ERS version).

Next, the impact of the five different unilateral liberalizations on the physical export volume of the USA is examined (Table 6). For dairy products, protein feeds, and other foods, US domestic policies make more difference than foreign policies. Dairy policies obviously involve the quota on imports of dairy products, while the protein feeds and other foods (which include fats and oils) seem to involve a shift from oilseeds to coarse grain

Table 6—Change in US Exports for Six Different Liberalization Scenarios Compared to the Reference Run (1995–2000 Average)

	OECD-6	Canada	EC	Japan	Oceania	USA
	- - - - - - - 1,000 tons - - - - - - -					
Wheat	6,561	1,125	3,113	378	544	1,296
Rice	288	2	25	218	2	38
Coarse grains	12,724	3,896	-2,368	9,887	3,070	2,625
Beef/sheep	414	57	624	231	-106	-33
Dairy products	-5,897	-1	-24	1	3	-8,181
Other animals	-48	-2	37	-91	8	11
Protein feeds	463	-192	-90	1,058	-55	-255
	- - - $1,000,000 (1970) dollars - - -					
Other foods	9	-32	187	194	10	-287
Nonfood agriculture	-14	-1	0	0	-1	-15

Source: Runs of the IIASA/FAP system (August 1987 ERS version).

production. For each commodity, either the EC or Japan is the primary foreign influence on US farm exports. In each case, this influence is negative except for other animals and other foods. In the case of other animals, Japan would import more grains and protein feeds than it would produce domestically. Except for dairy products, the sum of the five individual liberalizations is approximately the same as the OECD-6 liberalization. In the case of dairy products, the addition of EC liberalization to US liberalization would raise world prices and reduce the impact on US production and consumption of an elimination of dairy quotas and programmes.

The impacts of changes in price and export or import volume combine to produce the effect of liberalization on the value of US agricultural exports and imports by commodity and overall. The effect of the five unilateral liberalizations sums to approximately the same amount as the OECD-6 liberalization for every commodity, with the largest discrepancy for dairy products, where the five liberalizations sum up to a negative impact equal to 5.91 percent of the overall reference balance of agricultural trade, contrasted with a negative 4.64 percent in the OECD-6 multilateral liberalization. The EC and Japan liberalizations each have a favourable effect on the US agricultural balance of trade of about half the total from OECD liberalization. Liberalizations by Canada and Oceania only serve to almost offset the negative influence of the US liberalization.

Conclusion

The change to free trade in the developed market economies would definitely help their overall economies as the OECD countries shifted production towards their comparative advantage, both among the agricultural commodities and between agriculture and nonagriculture. The effects on the various agricultural sectors in the different OECD countries, however, would vary sharply. In the LDCs, however, the overall effect would depend mainly on whether the country in question was a food exporter or importer. In almost all cases, production in the agricultural sector would increase due to higher world prices for agricultural commodities.

In the USA, the agricultural sector would gain as a whole, but dairy producers would lose significantly. The loss by dairy producers would be partly offset by the rise in world dairy prices that would result from liberalization by the EC and an increase in consumption in the USA. Even so, imports would be up sharply and domestic prices would be lower. These projections thus indicate that liberalization would create important losers as well as gainers in the USA. Since the opening up of the US dairy sectors would be one of the principal inducements for any EC participation in a multilateral agricultural trade liberalization, and since the dairy sector seems to have the most significant interactions, this subject will undoubtedly be revisited.

Notes

[1]Economic Research Service, US Department of Agriculture.

[2]In the liberalization studies done at IIASA, US crop commodity policies were left intact.

[3]Australia and New Zealand are treated together as Oceania.

DISCUSSION OPENING—*S. Kjeldsen-Kragh* (Royal Agricultural University, Copenhagen)

The quantitative estimates of the impact of agricultural trade liberalization vary substantially depending on the model used. We should therefore look at the importance of the different assumptions behind the different models.

The IIASA model is a general equilibrium model where the agricultural sector is linked with the rest of the economy. What are the transmission mechanisms between the two sectors, and how important are those links?

An understanding of those links could cast some light on the results in Table 2. The impacts of the trade liberalization on the GDP in total and in the agricultural sector have opposite signs in some countries but not in other countries.

Table 2 shows that the agricultural sector in Australia will suffer from a multilateral trade liberalization among the OECD countries.

When some important countries liberalize their agricultural trade, world market prices will change. One has to make some assumptions about how the world market changes are transmitted to the internal markets in the countries that are not liberalizing.

Table 1 shows that a multilateral trade liberalization will in most cases give a production increase. The consumer price level in the developed countries will decrease and Maxwell assumes that the consumer price level in developing countries will increase. The price elasticities should then be higher in the developed countries than in the developing countries; or what other reasons lie behind the production increase?

Are the expenditures associated with the US set-aside programme incorporated in the model? Is the set-aside programme abandoned when trade is liberalized?

Quite often, nominal rates of protection are used as an indicator of the level of protection. These calculations exaggerate the level of protection because cereals and protein feeds are used as inputs in the livestock sector. Instead, one should use the effective rate of protection.

The simulation runs are for the period 1995-2000, meaning that a long-run adjustment has been taken into consideration. The parameters in the model are not unaffected by the price changes. The productivity gains in the long run are not independent of the price policy.

The results from the simulation model also depend on macroeconomic policies in the developed and the developing countries. The foreign exchange rate is a decisive factor influencing the world price level and the trade pattern.

[Refer to the general discussion following Krissoff and Ballenger's paper on page 72.]

Sources of Growth in French Agriculture: Short-Run Supply and Input Demand Responses and Effects of Technological Change

Frederic Bouchet, David Orden, and George W. Norton[1]

Abstract: A disaggregated variable profit function model is estimated for French agriculture. Short-run results suggest price inelastic, positively sloped supply functions and that French agricultural production has benefited from important technological gains since the early 1960s. These gains are due both to domestic public agricultural research expenditures and international transfers of technology.

Introduction

Since the slowdown in the growth of world agricultural trade in 1980, the USA and the EC have engaged in a series of confrontations over their respective agricultural policies. High producer prices and the general absence of production controls in Europe have been of particular concern in the USA as world grain stocks have risen and the EC has emerged, with substantial subsidies, as a net cereals exporter. Levels of frustration have increased on both sides of the Atlantic as the USA has responded with its own export enhancement payments and other costly policies.

While the drought affecting US production in 1988 may lower budget costs temporarily, it will not lessen the long-run conflict about policy-induced excess supplies. With current adversarial positions difficult to sustain, the USA and some members of the EC continue to seek means to limit their conflict and obtain relief from the high costs of their agricultural programmes.

However, two fundamentally different views of the sources of growth in European agriculture remain. The US view emphasizes that growth has been created by artificially high prices. European agriculture is seen as cost noncompetitive, and some argue that rather dramatic price-support reductions to bring internal prices to world levels would have large effects on agricultural input use, investment, and output (Schmidt, Frohberg, and Maxwell, 1987). The European view emphasizes the political infeasibility of such large price reductions (Bergmann and Petit, 1987) and the effects on output growth of factors such as technological change, structural policies, investments in input supply, processing and marketing facilities, and substitution of capital for labour in the modernization process (Petit, 1987; and Stanton, 1986). From this perspective, reduced price supports can have only a limited impact on output, and European agriculture is becoming increasingly competitive over time.

This paper addresses the debate about sources of growth in European agriculture by evaluating the changes in French agriculture from 1960 to 1984. A multiproduct variable profit function model is used as the basis for the analysis.

Empirical Specification

French agricultural output, which accounts for almost 30 percent of the agricultural production within the EC, is disaggregated into four output categories. Quantities of French agricultural production of cereals (Q_C), noncereal crops (Q_V), milk (Q_M), and animal products (Q_N) were computed from output series published by the Institut National de la Statistique et des Études Économiques (INSEE, 1985).[2] Output price indices (P_C, P_M, P_V, *and* P_N) were derived from INSEE data provided by the French Ministry of Agriculture. One-year-lagged average market prices were used in the model as proxies for expected output prices.

On the input side, the variable inputs are feed, fertilizer-energy, and hired labour, while family labour and capital investments (buildings and machinery) are considered quasi-fixed, and cultivated acreage and pasture acreage are assumed to be fixed factors of production.[3] For the fertilizer-energy and feed inputs, INSEE quantity (I_F *and* I_D) and price (r_F *and* r_D) data are used. Employment of hired agricultural labour (I_H) and a series on family labour, adjusted for off-farm work, were obtained from the French Ministry of Planning. These series are the ones used in the Ministry of Agriculture's MAGALI short-run forecasting model (Albecker and Lefebvre, 1985) and are more complete than previously published agricultural labour series. INSEE also publishes data on the cost of hired labour (r_H), which includes wages and social charges paid by farm owners on behalf of farm workers. INSEE data are also available on the total value of farm buildings and machinery (*K*). Series on cultivated acreage (*CL*) and pasture acreage (*PL*) are published by the Ministry of Agriculture.

Sources of technological change are represented by two variables. First, French public expenditures on agricultural research (*RES*) enter the model with a lag structure (several structures were tested and the results are discussed). Public agricultural research expenditures by the Institut National de la Recherche Agronomique and three smaller research institutes were compiled from budgets of the Ministry of Agriculture. These budgets include total expenditures in six categories but not a breakdown of expenditures by commodity. Data on private agricultural research expenditure are not available, nor are consistent data series on expenditures for agricultural extension and the levels of education and training of French farmers. Omission of these variables may bias upwards the estimated coefficients of public agricultural research expenditures in the model, since private research may be complementary to public research and extension expenditures, and education and training levels of farmers are likely to be positively correlated with research expenditures.

The second technological change variable included in the model is the level of total agricultural productivity in the USA. This variable was used as a proxy for international availability of technology. In the choice of this proxy, the hypothesis is that the USA is a major source of new agricultural technologies applied in France (other sources of international technology transfer, such as among European countries, were not modelled) and changes in US agricultural productivity were assumed to reflect, to a large extent, the availability of these new technologies, whether produced by the public or private sector. A five-year moving average of US productivity was used to account for possible lags in technology transfers and to minimize the effect of random yearly fluctuations. Use of a productivity index rather than US research expenditures eliminated the need to measure the lag associated with the effects of US research on US productivity.

In terms of agricultural policies, three French policy variables related to structural change were also included in the model. These variables were the cumulative area of farmland consolidated under voluntary programmes (*REM*) (lagged one year), the annual value of farm sales handled by the SAFERs to accommodate farm consolidation (*SAF*), and the annual value of early and supplementary retirement payments made to exiting farmers (*IVD*). Each of these policies is designed to facilitate modernization of the agricultural sector through consolidation and enlargement of production units. A fourth policy variable (*CR*) measures credit subsidies by the ratio of the average loan rate given to farmers to the market rate. This variable was constructed from unpublished data on the amounts of loans given to farmers by the Crédit Agricole at market and preferred interest rates.[4]

Finally, the average yearly deviations from normal rainfall (*WEA*) were included in the model to control for weather variations. A dummy variable (*DUM*) with a value of one starting in 1976 and zero otherwise was also included. This variable proxied for the aftereffects of the world oil shock in the early 1970s and an extremely severe drought in France in 1976. These events caused enduring structural changes in the French agricultural production system (Bourgeois, 1983).

Short-Run Output Supplies and Input Demands

The short-run model includes the four output supply and three variable input demand equations derived from a restricted profit function specified as a normalized quadratic. Coefficients of these equations were estimated by normalizing on the feed price and treating the remaining six equations as seemingly unrelated regressions. The hypothesis that the six equations are derived from profit maximization implies fifteen cross-equation symmetry restrictions. These restrictions were tested jointly, and symmetry was not rejected at a 5-percent significance level. The cross-price coefficients in the missing (feed) equation were then obtained by imposing the symmetry conditions, and its own-price coefficient was derived by homogeneity. The remaining coefficients of the feed equation are not subject to theoretical constraints. After fixing the price terms, these remaining coefficients were estimated by OLS.

Estimated elasticities at the data sample means are reported in Table 1. The estimated own-price elasticities suggest upwards-sloping output supply functions and downwards-sloping variable input demand functions for French agriculture that are price inelastic in the short run. The estimated own-price elasticities for cereals, noncereal crops, milk, and animal products are 0.34, 0.66, 0.53, and -0.006, respectively. The estimated fertilizer-energy, hired labour, and feed own-price elasticities are -0.88, -0.68 and -1.90, respectively. The own-price elasticities are statistically significant at the 5-percent significance level, with the exception of the cereal price elasticity (p=0.22) and the animal products elasticity (p=0.95).

The estimated cross-price elasticities shown in Table 1 suggest complementarities between production of cereals and milk and cereals and animal products that are marginally significant (p=0.11 and 0.15, respectively) and substitutability between noncereal crops and milk (p=0.07). Substitutabilities between production of cereals and noncereal crops and milk and animal products that might be expected *a priori* are not statistically significant. Thus, cross-price elasticities among the outputs seem to be less well estimated than own-price elasticities. Among the variable inputs, hired labour and fertilizer-energy are estimated to be substitutes (p=0.0003), while feed does not show substitutability with the other inputs.

With respect to the quasi-fixed factors, family labour is estimated to have positive effects on production of cereals, milk, and animal products. The estimated elasticities are 1.40, 0.49, and 0.87, respectively, with p-values of 0.12, 0.09, and 0.04, respectively. Capital also has positive effects in the cereals, milk, and animal products equations, with elasticities of 0.72, 0.80, and 0.74, respectively. The statistical significance of the capital elasticity is low in the cereals equation (p=0.58) and higher in the equations for milk (p=0.09) and animal products (p=0.19). Capital has a positive and significant effect (p=0.07) on use of fertilizer-energy, while family labour has a positive and significant effect (p=0.003) on employment of hired labour.

The elasticities for public agricultural research expenditures reported in Table 1 are 1.27, 0.27, 0.10, and 0.12, respectively, in the cereals, noncereal crops, milk, and animal products equations. The associated p-values are 0.0001, 0.02, 0.07, and 0.09, respectively. In each case, research expenditures have a positive and significant impact on production, the estimated effect being particularly large for cereals. French public agricultural research expenditures are not significant in the short-run variable input demand equations.

Because of the importance of the research variable, some additional comments on its lag specification are warranted. The estimated effects of public agricultural research expenditures shown in Table 1 are based on inclusion of one lag of the research expenditures variable in each equation. Research expenditures were lagged five years in the cereals, milk, and fertilizer-energy equations and four years in the other equations.[5] These lag lengths were selected after a preliminary estimation in which current research expenditures and five years of lagged expenditures were included in each equation without constraints on the lag coefficients. Despite collinearity introduced by inclusion of multiple lags, one or more lagged research expenditure variables were statistically significant in three of the four output equations (the exception was noncereal crops). The final model was

Table 1–Estimated Elasticities of the Short-Run Output Supply and Variable Input Demand Functions for French Agriculture and Significance Levels of the Estimated Coefficients*

Explanatory Variable	Q_C	Q_V	Q_M	Q_A	I_F	I_H	I_O
P_C	**0.34**	**-0.05**	**0.16**	**0.11**	**0.18**	**0.17**	**0.58**
	0.22	0.62	0.11	0.15	0.44	0.25	0.30
P_V	**-0.16**	**0.66**	**-0.24**	**-0.13**	**0.03**	**0.02**	**0.86**
	0.63	0.02	0.07	0.32	0.93	0.87	0.30
P_M	**0.18**	**-0.09**	**0.53**	**-0.02**	**0.26**	**0.04**	**0.25**
	0.11	0.06	0.0008	0.56	0.06	0.65	0.30
P_A	**0.40**	**-0.16**	**-0.007**	**-0.006**	**-0.38**	**-0.19**	**0.19**
	0.12	0.27	0.54	0.95	0.21	0.19	0.70
r_F	**-0.12**	**-0.007**	**-0.15**	**0.07**	**-0.88**	**0.59**	**0.10**
	0.44	0.92	0.06	0.23	0.03	0.0003	0.90
r_H	**-0.15**	**-0.006**	**-0.03**	**0.04**	**0.73**	**-0.68**	**-0.05**
	0.29	0.88	0.68	0.26	0.001	0.005	0.70
r_O	**-0.42**	**-0.23**	**-0.16**	**-0.04**	**0.12**	**-0.06**	**-1.90**
	0.30	0.30	0.30	0.70	0.90	0.70	†
L	**1.40**	**0.73**	**0.49**	**0.87**	**1.47**	**0.18**	**-0.70**
	0.12	0.32	0.09	0.04	0.16	0.003	0.60
K	**0.72**	**-0.38**	**0.80**	**0.74**	**2.83**	**0.19**	**1.50**
	0.58	0.73	0.09	0.19	0.07	0.61	0.38
RES	**1.27**	**0.27**	**0.10**	**0.12**	**-0.02**	**0.16**	**-0.04**
	0.0001	0.02	0.07	0.09	0.88	0.11	0.92
USP	**0.31**	**1.92**	**0.99**	**0.20**	--	--	--
	0.65	0.004	0.02	0.66			
CR	**-0.32**	--	**-0.14**	**-0.05**	**0.48**	--	**0.66**
	0.05		0.05	0.45	0.02		0.08
REM	--	--	**-0.19**	**0.27**	--	--	--
			0.55	0.49			
CL	**2.27**	**-0.62**	--	--	**-0.87**	**1.28**	**2.04**
	0.04	0.43			0.54	0.03	0.02
PL	--	--	**0.75**	**0.37**	**-0.95**	**-0.52**	**1.19**
			0.002	0.12	0.13	0.07	0.21
R^2‡	0.9903	0.9279	0.9908	0.9865	0.9814	0.9988	0.9549

*Elasticities are given in bold typeface; significance levels (*p*-values) are reported below the respective elasticities. All variables are defined in the text.

†The *p*-value of the own-price coefficient of the feed input is not computed but is likely to be greater than 0.30 since the variances of the other coefficients in the feed input equation are high.

‡Obtained in first-stage of GLS estimation, except for I_O, which is obtained from separate OLS estimation fixing coefficients of output and input prices based on symmetry and homogeneity properties of the system of equations.

estimated with only one lag of research expenditures to reduce collinearity and save degrees of freedom.[6]

The second technological change measure, international technology transfers proxied by the five-year moving average of US agricultural productivity, is also estimated to have significant positive effects on French agricultural production. The estimated elasticities of noncereal crops and milk supplies with respect to this measure of international technology availability are 1.92 and 0.99, respectively, with *p*-values of .004 and .02, respectively. The international technology transfer variable is not significant in the cereals or animal products equations. It is not included in the variable input demand equations because of the limited number of degrees of freedom afforded by the data. When included, it is not statistically significant (the *p*-values of its coefficient in the fertilizer-energy, hired labour, and feed equations were 0.61, 0.98, and 0.36, respectively).

The limited degrees of freedom afforded by the data also explain why all the policy variables are not present in all the equations. Overall, the French policy variables related to structural change and credit policy are not very robust in the model. Collinearity among the policy variables led to a focus on the cumulative area of farmland consolidated (REM) and on the measure of credit subsidies (CR). These variables were dropped from the final equations when their *p*-values in initial models were greater than 0.3 unless their exclusion noticeably affected the estimates of other coefficients. With this procedure for model specification, the credit variable has statistically significant effects in four equations ($p \leq 0.08$), but its negative sign in the input demand equations is difficult to interpret.

Among the remaining fixed and exogenous factors, the allocation of land between crops and pasture has a significant effect on cereals ($p=0.04$) and milk ($p=0.002$) production. The estimated elasticity of cereal production with respect to crop acreage is 2.27, somewhat larger than expected and suggesting the possibility of measurement error with respect to changes in land quality over time. Yearly deviations from normal rainfall do not enter the final model. Coefficients of the rainfall variable were not statistically significant, and their inclusion caused rejection of the cross-price symmetry conditions. These problems are likely to be due to the inadequacy of total annual rainfall as a proxy for weather conditions affecting agricultural production. The coefficient of the dummy variable for structural changes induced by weather and other shocks in the mid-1970s was statistically significant in three of the output equations and one of the variable input demand equations ($p \leq 0.05$), and it was retained in these equations.

Conclusions

Conflicting US and European views about the sources of growth and competitiveness of European agriculture shape agricultural trade negotiating positions and will have much to do with accomplishments in discussions, such as the current GATT round, and with the character of international competition in agriculture that emerges.

This paper has presented short-run results from a variable profit function model in which French agriculture is aggregated into four outputs, three variable inputs, and two quasi-fixed inputs. Some of the estimated coefficients should be interpreted with caution due to lack of statistical significance and possible bias (especially in the long run). Nevertheless, various caveats are unlikely to change several of the major results of the analysis or their policy implications. On the issues at stake in the trade negotiations, the analysis of growth in French agriculture cuts in several directions.

Estimates of the short-run output supply functions for French agriculture suggest that agricultural output levels in France are price responsive. This provides support for the view that European price policies have been a source of high European output levels. Lower European prices for agricultural products would reduce European production.[7]

Moreover, the analysis suggests that French agricultural production has benefited from important technological gains since the early 1960s. Growth of French agricultural output can not be attributed solely or even primarily to high prices. Production has increased despite falling real output prices and rising labour costs.

The importance of technological change in French agriculture has several implications. First, gains from a one-time reduction in farm price levels are likely to prove illusory. If France continues to pursue a strong programme of public (and private) agricultural research and continues to adopt new technologies available internationally, then outward shifts of its agricultural supply functions will quickly offset any given downwards movement along these functions. The case for negotiating fixed lower prices is weak, from either the point of view of those who might anticipate large gains from such an agreement or from the point of view of those who would like to claim such an outcome would be a major concession.

A second implication of the importance of technological change is that France is achieving a favourable competitive position relative to other producers. If France finds itself in a situation of comparative advantage in agriculture, the French approach to trade negotiations should shift towards a freer market stance in which France's comparative advantage would reap the largest benefits. This may pave the way for unexpected progress in trade negotiations. A freer market also implies that competition will remain stiff.

The USA and the EC may compete for agricultural export markets in the future largely through the generation and adoption of new technology. On this issue, the results are, perhaps, the most interesting and the most preliminary, and additional research is needed. While the technology spillover variable used in the analysis is imprecise, the results suggest that international transfers of technology play an important role for some commodities but not others. Under these circumstances, competition in world markets will affect domestic perceptions of optimal allocations of research expenditures among commodities. From a global perspective, domestic allocation decisions of individual countries may not be optimal. Additional work on the allocation of public research expenditures in Europe by commodity, on appropriate proxies for international availability of technology, and on the mechanisms, incidence, and magnitude of international technology transfers are warranted. In the interim, the study suggests that development of a sensible international framework for agricultural research among industrial countries will become increasingly important as more explicit trade barriers fade.

Notes

[1]Fédération Nationale Porcine (Paris), Virginia Polytechnic Institute and State University, and Virginia Polytechnic Institute and State University, respectively. The authors gratefully acknowledge the International Agricultural Trade Research Consortium for partial financial support and thank Michel Petit, Maury Bredahl, Jean-Marc Boussard, Albert Hayem, and participants in seminars at OECD and the Economic Research Service, US Department of Agriculture, for constructive early suggestions and assistance.

[2]The data used in the study covers the 1959-84 period. Many statistical series were not reported prior to this period, and data quality is poor for those that are available. Cereals accounted for 17.4 percent and milk for 18.0 percent of the value of French agricultural production in 1980. Noncereal crops and animal products are aggregates among diverse products.

[3]In the short-run analysis, both quasi-fixed and fixed factors are held at historical levels. In the complete study, long-run output supply and variable input demand functions are estimated, assuming use of family labour and capital adjusted optimally to long-run equilibrium values. Only the short-run results are presented here. The long-run results and a comparative analysis of the short- and long-run models are reported in Bouchet (1987).

[4]See Bouchet (1987) for further discussion of each of the variables included in the model. Of 31 million hectares in agricultural use, over 12 million hectares have been consolidated under the voluntary programme (Tuppen, 1983). Funding levels have limited the effectiveness of the SAFERs and IVD (Chombart de Lauwe, 1979), while loans at preferential rates represent between 60 and 70 percent of the loans administered by the Crédit Agricole, which provides about 70 percent of all farm credit.

[5]The research expenditures data series was cast back to 1955-58 using a regression of the research series on a constant, a trend, and a dummy variable, capturing a faster rate of increase of expenditures before 1970. Lags of research expenditures of up to five years could then be included in the model without losing observations. Five years is a shorter lag length than reported in much of the research evaluation literature (Pardey and Craig, forthcoming). The sum of the coefficients is not likely to be affected too much by truncating the lag length, but individual coefficients are likely to be biased upwards due to specification error. Given the purpose of the current study (to assess sources of growth), the sum, not the individual coefficients, is important.

[6]Imposing specific lag distributions did not prove to be a satisfactory alternative. With an imposed linear distribution, the research expenditures coefficient was statistically significant only in the cereals equation, despite the significance of the coefficient of at least one unconstrained research lag in the cereals, milk, and animal products equations. The cross-price symmetry conditions on the output supply and input demand equations were also strongly rejected when the linear lag distribution was imposed on the research expenditures variables. Imposing a quadratic structure with five lags maintained acceptance of the symmetry conditions, but levels of significance of the coefficients of the research variables were poor (only one coefficient had an associated *p*-value smaller than 0.15). The number of lags (five) is probably not sufficient to impose a quadratic lag.

[7]The responses to price changes are estimated to be inelastic even in the long run when usage of quasi-fixed capital and family labour have fully adjusted to optimal levels (see Bouchet, 1987).

References

Albecker, C., and Lefebvre, C. (1985) "Modèle Économetrique de l'Agriculture Française (MAGALI)," *Économie Rurale*, No. 165, pp. 27-33.

Bergmann, D., and Petit, M. (1987) "Modernization of Agriculture in Western Europe after World War II: Result of Luck, Circumstances or Government Policies," paper presented at the International Symposium on Rural Development Strategy, Beijing, China (Oct.).

Bouchet, F.C. (1987) "Analysis of the Sources of Growth in French Agriculture, 1960-1984," PhD dissertation, Virginia Polytechnic Institute and State University, Blacksburg, Va., USA.

Bourgeois, L. (1983) "L'Expansion de la Production Agricole Française depuis 20 Ans," *Problèmes Économiques*, Vol. 18, No. 8, pp. 14-19.

Chombart de Lauwe, J. (1979) *L'Aventure Agricole de la France de 1945 a Nos Jours*, Presses Universitaires de France, Paris, France.

INSEE (Institut National de la Statistique et des Études Économiques) (1985) *Annuaire Statistique de la France*, various issues, Paris, France.

Pardey, P.G., and Craig, B. (forthcoming) "Causal Relationships between Public Sector Agricultural Research Expenditures and Output," *American Journal of Agricultural Economics*.

Petit, M. (1987) "Economics and Politics in the International Trade of Agricultural Products," paper presented at the International Agricultural Trade Research Consortium, Airlie, Va., USA (Dec.).

Schmidt, S.C., Frohberg, K.K., and Maxwell, D.L. (1987) *Implications of Grain Trade Liberalization in the European Community*, Agricultural Economics Research Report No. 202, University of Illinois, Urbana, Ill., USA.

Stanton, B.F. (1986) *Production Costs for Cereals in the European Community: Comparisons with the United States, 1977-1984*, Agricultural Economics Research No. 86-2, Cornell University, Ithaca, N.Y., USA.

Tuppen, J. (1983) *Economic Geography of France*, Croom Helm, London, UK.

DISCUSSION OPENING—*Robert Innes* (University of California, Davis)

The authors have sought to capture technological change with two variables: French government research expenditures and a measure of international technological progress. However, technological change in France could occur without either of these inducements. For example, over time, farmers may learn to make better use of a franc of capital stock or a unit input of another factor, even without government expenditures on research or international technology transfer. To test for this possibility, the authors might want to incorporate a time trend measure in their regression model.

In the short-run analysis, the authors include capital stock (measured with value of land and buildings) as a right-hand-side (exogenous) variable. This treatment gives rise to two problems: First, since capital stock changes are likely to be driven by both productivity and price indices, simultaneity exists that is not accounted for in the seemingly unrelated regressions approach employed in the paper. Secondly, the coefficient on capital stock is, to some extent, capturing output responses to price, which suggests that the "short-run" price elasticities understate medium-to-long run price effects.

In the long-run analysis, capital stock is assumed to be "chosen" optimally so that it can simply be excluded from the right-hand side. Here, the price variables would appear to pick up both their partial effects on output and their indirect effects via capital stock changes. And the own-price elasticities do increase as a result. Moreover, the model here can be viewed as a reduced form in which the simultaneity mentioned above is no longer a problem.

However, the authors' long-run treatment is subject to another criticism: capital stock choices follow a complex dynamic process. They are not simply a function of last period's prices, as is implicitly assumed in the regression model constructed here. Rather, they are likely to depend on a more extensive history of both prices and productivity changes. These dynamics, I believe, should be explicitly modelled.

Why might these dynamics be important to the results? The reason is that other variables in the model, such as government research expenditures and/or the US productivity index may be picking up the longer run effects of price changes, leading to overstatement of research effects on output and understatement of price effects.

A government's choice of research expenditures is likely to be related to the economic performance of affected agricultural markets. For example, rapid improvements in productivity may well spur a government on to invest more in research, perhaps because of the impression conveyed by agricultural economists that research has generated these terrific benefits! In any event, an important simultaneity problem may exist here.

To measure the effects of international technological developments on French agricultural productivity, the authors included a measure of total US agricultural productivity as a right-hand variable. Like French agricultural output, US agricultural output responds to prices, capital stock changes, etc.

This variable therefore picks up output expansion that results from economic as well as technological phenomena. This observation suggests that, at face value, the US productivity variable may be a poor proxy for international technology transfer. But, more importantly, it suggests a reinterpretation of the paper's results. Specifically, farmer prices received in the USA are correlated with farmer prices received in France. This variable is a good proxy for the dynamic capital stock adjustment mechanism discussed earlier. As a result, the large effects of this variable in the authors' long-run analysis may be price driven.

Suppose we believe that some asset fixity exists in the French agricultural sector. We would then expect to see an output supply function (in own price) that is increasingly inelastic as price rises. Given this expectation, how should we interpret the paper's price elasticity estimates in an effort to deduce the effects of EC removal of its agricultural support policies?

In recent times, EC supported cereals prices have been as much as two to three times world levels. Variation in real farmer prices received (over the past 20 years) has been relatively little vis-à-vis the decline that would be experienced with the removal of supports. These observations suggest that the price elasticity estimates emerging from this paper are associated with points high up the supply curvey vis-à-vis world prices. Therefore, if we are performing the thought experiment of eliminating supports (and thus reducing farmer prices received by a large amount), the price elasticity we should use is considerably higher than estimated here.

One of the main questions motivating this analysis is: if government price supports were removed, would the EC switch back from being a net exporter to being a net importer of cereals? As concluding food for thought, consider a little back-of-the-envelope calculation in answer to this question. The authors estimate a long-run cereal own-price supply elasticity of 0.45. Adjusting this estimate to, say, 0.5-0.8 for the reasons mentioned above, a 50-percent reduction in price would reduce output by 25-40 percent. If technological change is as important as the authors suggest, then this medium-to-long-run reduction would be accompanied and probably overshadowed by the effects of technological progress. However, if the technological change variables are picking up longer run capital stock responses to price change—and I do not believe that this possibility can be ruled out at this point—then this reduction is likely to return the EC to self-sufficiency in cereals.

GENERAL DISCUSSION—*Winfried Manig, Rapporteur* (Universität Göttingen)

This paper was discussed with regard to the general impact of research or of the generation of new technologies on labour input in general and hired labour input in particular; especially the long-run effects were questioned. In this respect, time as a variable becomes important. Other discussion points were the effects of research expenditures and the treatment of capital stock in the model used.

Participants in the discussion included G. Escobar, R. Evenson, F. Jarrett, T.P. Phillips, S. Setboonsarng, and S.C. Thompson.

Rates of Return on Agricultural Research Expenditures in Argentina

Manuel L. Cordomí[1]

Abstract: This paper surveys three papers that explored the topic of returns on agricultural research expenditures in Argentina. Two, Elías (1971) and del Rey (1975), studied this problem with data on sugarcane, and the third, Feijóo (1984), dealt with aggregate agricultural data. The main task was to recompute the reported findings so as to get two rates of return that have been widely used to present the results of studies of this type: the internal rate of return and the rate of return of benefits over costs using an external rate of 10 percent. The main finding is that annual rates of return on agricultural research expenditures in Argentina are of the same order of magnitude as the ones found in similar studies for other countries.

Introduction

The purpose of this paper is to collect and present empirical work done in Tucumán, Argentina, on the rate of return on public funds devoted to agricultural research and extension in Argentina. For this reason, the authors of the selected papers are members of or worked in close association with the Institute for Economic Research at the Universidad Nacional de Tucumán.

Since the studies surveyed here were done over a fairly long time span (more than 15 years), the approach as well as the way in which the authors reported their findings varied notably. This led to the idea of putting these studies as well as their results into a common, homogeneous framework.

For this purpose, the methodology used was adopted from Griliches' (1958) study on the returns of public funds devoted to the development of hybrid maize in the USA. In that study, Griliches considered the development of hybrid maize as an investment project with its costs and benefits. For evaluating it, he estimated two different rates of return that have been widely used ever since: the internal rate of return (*IRR*), which in his case turned out to be between 35 percent and 40 percent; and the rate of return of benefits over costs, which turned out to be in the neighbourhood of 700 percent when an external rate of 10 percent was used for computational purposes, hereafter referred to as *r(10%)*.

With this methodology in mind, the work done by the surveyed authors is inspected, placing special emphasis on their approach as well as their findings. Their results are then recomputed to obtain rates comparable with those obtained by Griliches in his pioneering work.

Elías Paper

The first paper to be examined here is a lecture delivered by Víctor J. Elías in 1971 in which he presented his findings on the rate of return on the funds used by the Estación Experimental Agrícola de Tucumán (EEAT) for the development and adoption of new varieties of sugarcane. He estimated Cobb-Douglas production functions using as the dependent variable tons of sugarcane processed by Tucumán sugar factories during 1943-63. The form of the production function is as follows:

$$(1)\ Q = AL^{\alpha}K^{\beta}T^{\gamma}.$$

Notice that, in addition to the usual independent variables labour *(L)* and capital *(K)*, a proxy for the stock of technology *(T)* was included to capture the effects in production of the research activities of the EEAT. The stock of technology available in any year T_t was estimated using the following equation:

$$(2)\ T_t = (1\text{-}\delta)T_{t-1} + I_{t-10},$$

where δ, the annual rate of depreciation, was assumed to be equal to 5 percent and I_{t-10} is the gross investment plus current expenses made 10 years before. For computational purposes, the stock of technology for 1935 was estimated, which was taken to be equal to I_{1925}/δ.

Two estimates of the parameter associated with the stock of technology, γ, were obtained: one using the stock of technology as the only independent variable, coupled with a trend to capture the effect of the omitted variables labour and capital; and the other using technology and labour as the independent variables and a trend to capture the effect of omitting capital. Once the statistical estimates of the parameter γ were obtained, two different rates of return of the stock of technology could be estimated using the following equation:

$$(3)\ r = \hat{\gamma}(\bar{Q}/\bar{T}),$$

Where $\bar{Q}$ and $\bar{T}$ are mean values.

As the result of this experiment, Elías obtained an upper and a lower value for r of 500 percent and 2 percent, respectively. Strictly speaking, these rates are not rates of return of outlays on agricultural research and extension but a measure of the marginal productivity of the stock of technology expressed as a percentage. Since the contemporary stock of technology is the result of a weighted sum of past investments, these rates are not the ones referred to by Griliches in his study of hybrid maize. To obtain magnitudes of this type, one must recompute the results of Elías in such a way that two important components can be explicitly considered: the gestation period, which is the lag that exists between the moment in which the investment is made and the moment in which the technology associated with this investment is adopted (i.e., 10 years later); and the assumption that technology, once adopted, declines at a compound rate of δ per year.

The rates of return estimated by Elías can be used to obtain good measures of the flows of benefits of investing in the EEAT "project." However, if the purpose is to pin down rates of return of the type referred to at the beginning of this paper, one must also have a well-defined profile of the costs of the project.

The annual flow of costs was estimated using Elías' data at constant 1960 pesos from 1909, the year in which the EEAT was created, to 1964. From 1964 to the year 2000, the annual costs were assumed to be equal to the costs incurred in 1964. To estimate the annual flow of benefits, one had to estimate the stocks of technology using equation *(2)* and multiply the stocks by 5 or 20, depending on the assumed rate of return. Once the flows of costs and benefits were obtained, one could compute the *IRR* and *r(10%)*. Hence, under the hypotheses of a 500 percent rate of return, the corresponding *IRR* was 33 percent and *r(10%)* was 141 percent. Under the hypothesis of a 2 percent rate, the *IRR* was 49 percent and *r(10%)* was 503 percent.

A theoretical approximation to the results presented above is obtained under the assumption of a uniform yearly investment. Under this assumption, one peso invested in year t means a stock of technology $T_{t+10} = 1$, $T_{t+11} = (1-\delta)^2$, etc., and a flow of benefits from the year $t+10$ onwards equals from 5 to 20 times those values. The present value of the flow of benefits in year t when a rate of 500 percent is assumed will be:

$$(4)\ B_t = \{5/[(1+i)^{10}]\}[(1+i)/(1+\delta)].$$

From the present value of the costs $(C_t=1)$ and the rate of depreciation of the stock of technology $(\delta=0.05)$, the *IRR* and *r(10%)* can easily be estimated. The values obtained turned out to be practically equal to the ones presented above.

del Rey Paper

The second paper reviewed here was presented by Eusebio C. del Rey in 1975 at the X Annual Meeting of the Asociación Argentina de Economía Política. This paper belongs to the same class as the one already discussed and uses the same statistical tool; i.e., the production-function approach. The novelty here is the high degree of disaggregation del Rey used to obtain parameters of a Cobb-Douglas production function. For this purpose, he constructed data series of production, labour, and capital for sugarcane plantations owned by sugar factories of Tucumán; a total of 22 for the 1943-64 period. This important effort concerning agricultural estimates allowed him to work with a total of 394 observations.

In addition to the usual independent variables already mentioned, del Rey assumed that production at the farm level is affected by the stock of technology. This variable plays the role of a "public good" because this stock in any year is the same for every farm. As in the previous case, this level of technology is assumed to increase with the funds allocated to the EEAT.

In the process of obtaining production function estimates, del Rey tried many alternative ways of computing the stock of technology. Here, special emphasis is placed on one that gave him more promising results, labelled as "T_{10}" in his experiments. Hence, for any year *t*, estimates of the contemporaneous stock of technology were obtained using the following equation:

$$(5)\quad T_t = \sum_{i=7}^{18} w_i\, I_{t-i},$$

where I_{t-i} are current expenditures plus net investment in year *t-i*. This equation assumes a gestation period of 6 years and a rate of adoption that increases gradually during the ensuing 12 years, according to a system of weights whose sum is 0.631 followed by a sudden death.

Del Rey has recently revised the statistical estimates he obtained in 1975, and these new findings are taken into account here. Regression analysis on the 394 observations using a Cobb-Douglas production function of the form presented in equation *(1)* gave plausible results for the shares of labour and capital. The estimate of the exponent of technology was also significant with a value $\hat{\gamma} = 0.21$. To estimate the marginal productivity of the stock of technology, equation *(3)* is applied:

$$r = \hat{\gamma}(\bar{Q}/\bar{T}) = 0.21(50.21/4.48) = 2.35,$$

where $\bar{Q}$ and $\bar{T}$ are expressed in millions of 1960 pesos. This result implies a marginal productivity of technology of 235 percent.

This percentage is not a unique measure of the marginal productivity of technology. Should the stock of technology be multiplied by an arbitrary constant Θ (which in the experiments of del Rey means inflating the system of weights w_i by this factor), the corresponding estimate of its rate of return would be automatically divided by the same number. Also, their product, which is a measure of the benefits of the stock of technology, is invariant to this arbitrary transformation.

The fact that the measure of the benefits of technology is unique opens the possibility of estimating rates of return on the investments in the EEAT by comparing, as was done before, the annual flows of costs and benefits. This measure of benefits corresponds to the average farm and thus should be expanded to cover the entire sugarcane agricultural sector of Tucumán. This factor turned out to be in the neighbourhood of 76. To estimate the *IRR*, one must take into account not only the existence of a gestation period of 6 years but also the fact that the accruing benefits increase during the next 12 years to collapse later on as a result of a sudden death. So, for the investment of one peso made in time 0, a corresponding benefit of $w_t(2.35)(76)$ is obtained in year t. To obtain the *IRR*, the following equation must be solved for the variable i:

$$(6)\ (2.35)(76) \sum_{t=7}^{18} [w_t/(1+i)^t] = 1$$

The solution of this equation resulted in an *IRR* = 40.9 percent. The rate of return of benefits over costs using an external rate of 10 percent was *r(10%)* = 254 percent.[2]

Alternative values for these rates were estimated using a value of γ obtained by del Rey in a regression analysis in which he used 21 dummy variables to capture a "plantation effect." The statistical estimates of the shares of labour and capital remained substantially similar, but the estimate of γ, which was also statistically significant, declined to 0.12. With this value and using the same methodology as before, what can be regarded as lower limits were obtained: an *IRR* = 34.8 percent and a *r(10%)* = 137 percent.

Feijóo Paper

The last paper to be examined here was presented by Victor M. Feijóo at the XIX Meeting of the Asociación Argentina de Economía Política in 1984. This paper differs from the previous ones in at least two important aspects. The first is that its purpose is to estimate rates of return on funds invested in research and extension in agriculture-at-large in Argentina. For this reason, this study places special emphasis on the funds allocated by the Federal Government to the Instituto Nacional de Tecnología Agropecuaria (INTA). The second feature of this study is that, due to the lack of information on labour and capital employed in the agricultural sector of Argentina, the traditional production function approach was dismissed. Instead, an aggregate supply function was used.

To study the aggregate supply of the agricultural sector of Argentina, Feijóo uses a Nerlove model of supply consisting of two equations: a supply function and an adjustment equation. The supply function is:

$$(7)\ Q^*_t = a_1 + a_2P^*_t + a_3X_t + e_t,$$

where Q^*_t is the long run equilibrium output, P^*_t is the expected price, and X_t are other variables relevant to the problem.

The adjustment equation is:

$$(8)\ Q_t - Q_{t-1} = \alpha(Q^*_t - Q_{t-1}),\ 0 \leq \alpha \leq 1.$$

For the simple case in which $P^*_t = P_{t-1}$, the model has the following reduced form:

$$(9)\ Q_t = \pi_0 + \pi_1P_{t-1} + \pi_2T_t + \pi_3D_t + \pi_4Q_{t-1},$$

where $\pi_0 = \alpha a_1$, $\pi_1 = \alpha a_2$, $\pi_2 = \alpha a_3$, $\pi_3 = \alpha a_4$, and $\pi_4 = 1 - \alpha$.

Among the independent variables, two are relevant to this problem: T_t, the stock of technology; and D_t, a dummy variable to capture the effects on supply of unusual weather conditions.

The stock of technology in any year t was computed using the following equation:

$$(10)\ T_t = \sum_{i \geq 6} NT_{t-i},$$

where NT_{t-1} represents government expenditures in agricultural research and extension in year $t-i$. The equation assumes a gestation period; i.e., a lag of 6 years between the moment in which the expenditure is made and the moment in which the technology that it generates is adopted. For the 1958-80 period, the values of *NT* were assumed to be equal to the funds appropriated by the national government to INTA, and, for the 1911-57 period, the *NT* values were estimated using related time series.

The parameters of the reduced form equation *(9)* were estimated for the 1950-80 period using ordinary least squares. All the parameters turned out to possess the right sign and were statistically significant except for π_4. The estimate of π_2 is particularly important because it is the marginal productivity of the stock of technology:

$$(11)\ \delta Q_t/\delta T_t = \hat{\pi}_2.$$

Since the dependent variable is measured in the same units as the stock of technology (1970 pesos), the marginal productivity has the dimension of a percentage. The statistical estimate of the marginal productivity turned out to be $\hat{\pi}_2 = 2.34$, which means a rate of 234 percent. To estimate the *IRR*, Feijóo proceeds in the same vein as in the previous papers. Knowing the value of this parameter and the fact that, after a gestation period of 6 years, the emerging technology lasts forever, he estimated the *IRR* by solving the following expression for the unknown variable *i* (see equation *(4)*:

$$(12)\ [(2.34)/(1+i)^6][(1+i)/i] = 1.$$

The solution of this equation gave an *IRR* of 41.5 percent. Finally, to complete Feijóo's experiments, *r(10%)* was found to be 145 percent.

Summary of Results

The main results of the task of recomputing results of the three research papers are presented in Table 1.

Table 1—Estimates of Rates of Return on Investment in Agricultural Research in Argentina

Author	Year	Product	Region	Period	*IRR* (%)	*r(10%)*
Elias	1971	Sugarcane	Tucumán	1943-63	33.0 49.0	141 lower limit 503 upper limit
del Rey	1975	Sugarcane	Tucumán	1943-64	34.8 40.9	137 lower limit 254 upper limit
Feijóo	1984	Aggregate	Argentina	1950-80	41.5	145

Notes

[1]Universidad Nacional de Tucumán. The author wishes to express his thanks to the members of the Institute of Economic Research at the University of Tucumán for their comments on an earlier version of the present paper. Computing assistance from Prof. Juan M. Jorrat is gratefully acknowledged.

[2]To carry del Rey's experiments a bit further, a Cobb-Douglas production function was estimated employing the same observations used by del Rey but replacing his stock of technology with an estimate obtained using equation *(2)*, which is the one used by Elías in his study. The shares of labour and capital turned out to be in line with del Rey's findings, and the coefficient of technology led to a value of r = 20.23 percent when

equation *(3)* was applied. Since the estimates were made at the farm level, in order to make the results comparable with the findings of Elías, this rate was expanded by a factor of 76 so as to cover the entire sugarcane sector of Tucumán. The resulting rate was 1.537 percent. When this result is plugged into equation *(4)*, an *IRR* = 46 percent and a *r(10%)* = 4.35 percent were obtained, values that fall somewhere in between the values of Elías.

References

del Rey, E.C. (1975) "Rentabilidad de la Estación Experimental Agrícola de Tucumán, 1943-64," *Xª Reunión Anual de la Asociación Argentina de Economía Política*, Tomo I., Mar del Plata, Argentina.

Elías, V.J. (1971) *Investigación y Desarrollo Económico*, Documento de Trabajo de Investigación y Desarrollo Nº 7, Universidad Nacional de Tucumán, Tucumán, Argentina.

Feijóo, V.M. (1984) "La Rentabilidad de la Inversión en Investigación Agrícola," *XIXª Reunión Anual de la Asociación Argentina de Economía Política*, Tomo 1, Misiones, Argentina.

Griliches, Z. (1958) "Research Costs and Social Returns: Hybrid Corn and Related Innovations," *Journal of Political Economy*, Vol. 66, No. 3, pp. 419-431.

DISCUSSION OPENING—*K.K. Klein* (University of Lethbridge)

This paper makes a further contribution to the rapidly growing literature on the economics of agricultural research. The author made a solid effort in recalculating rates of return in three separate studies so that they could be compared on a common basis.

The question begged in the paper is why this analysis was necessary. Without having had access to the three original papers, how can one judge the contribution made by Cordomí? He should have demonstrated the need for these recalculations by including some table or chart that could demonstrate the incomparability of the previous estimates. One would expect that all modern-day scholars would have calculated an internal rate of return, which has become the "industry standard" for comparison purposes.

The author used as a common denominator Griliches' original work in this area. Since many methodological developments have occurred in the three decades since the publication of Griliches' seminal article, one suspects that important information from the three studies may not have been used in this attempt at homogenization.

Two of the studies considered in this paper (Elías and del Rey) were on the same sector (sugarcane) and over essentially the same time period (1943-63). That the use of the same methodology to recalculate the original data sets should result in the same estimated returns should not be surprising (41 percent from del Rey's data is exactly midway between the lower and upper limits of 33 percent and 49 percent from Elías' data). The apparent richness of del Rey's data set is lost by the aggregation necessary for Griliches' methodology.

A pervading question that must strike everyone who reads this paper is what its purpose is. This effort appears to be part of a larger study, perhaps to assist in setting research priorities in Argentina. If this is the case, the author should have addressed such issues as why sugarcane was the subject of inquiry in two of the analyses that were recalculated. What is its relative contribution to per capita incomes or to exports from the region? Does evidence exist of a higher rate of return to research on sugarcane than on other agricultural products in the Tucumán region? And what is the purpose of comparing rates of return to aggregate research in the entire country to those to a single product in one region? Finally, the return to investment in all research in Argentina is reported to be the same as the return to investment in sugarcane research in Tucumán. Is that only a coincidence?

GENERAL DISCUSSION—*Winfried Manig, Rapporteur* (Universität Göttingen)

Cordomí's paper served as a basis for discussing the problems that arise when comparing the results found in studies of different origin and obtained by applying different methods, beginning with confusion over the methods used. The role of agricultural extension in the ascertained high rate of return on agricultural research expenditure was then debated. This high rate of return on research expenditure was due mainly to improvement in local sugarcane varieties, which produced a great impact.

Participants in the discussion included G. Escobar, R. Evenson, F. Jarrett, T.P. Phillips, S. Setboonsarng, and S.C. Thompson.

Uncertain Marriage of Price Policy and Agricultural Research: Case of Cassava in Latin America

John K. Lynam, Willem Janssen, and Luis R. Sanint[1]

Abstract: To foster agricultural development, a number of strategies are available. A well-known, long-run strategy is productivity-increasing research. Another familiar, short-run strategy is input and output price policy. This paper argues that effectiveness of price and research policies can only be obtained if they are defined interactively, with one complementing the other. This is illustrated by showing how cassava, a traditional crop in Latin America, has evolved with respect to research and price policy over the last few decades. Three main dimensions are distinguished. The first is appropriate timing of research and price policies in relation to changing structural features of the economy. The second is price policy to support diffusion of research-based technology. The third is definition of research policy in relation to the socioeconomic environment in order to maximize the impact of price policies. The historical development of Latin American agriculture and cassava's position within it over the last 10 years is used to illustrate these points. A major problem in obtaining more consistent and development-focused research and price policy is that the locus of decision making for these two policies is often in completely different institutions.

Introduction

Should price policy and investment in agricultural research[2] be more functionally integrated? Prices will influence the adoption of technologies and in turn the potential returns to research investment. Induced innovation theory would extend the relationship even further by suggesting a functional link between relative prices and selection of research lines (Binswanger and Ruttan, 1978). Conversely, widespread adoption of an improved technology can radically change relative prices in an agricultural economy, fundamentally altering consumption patterns, producer incentives, and income streams. How price policy should be more consistently integrated into decision making within agricultural research programmes is by no means clear. Do policy makers have a clear framework for incorporating agricultural research resource allocation into medium-to-long-term price policy objectives? To date, decision making in each area has usually been independent of the other area, often leading to significant inconsistencies and inefficient use of resources. This paper will argue for a better integration of the two, focusing on the case of cassava in Latin America.[3]

Subsector Approach to Linking Agricultural Research and Price Policy

Price policy principally influences relative commodity prices. Price supports, subsidies, and interventions by marketing boards have a commodity focus. Exchange rate policy, although having a more generalized effect, nevertheless has a significant impact on relative prices of tradeable versus nontradeable commodities. Moreover, many governments will intervene through import controls to further mediate the effect of exchange rates on relative commodity prices. Even input price policies have direct impacts on commodity prices by favouring crops where those inputs are intensively used; furthermore, rationed credit is usually linked to particular commodities. Thus, although price policy objectives in the agricultural sector may derive from broader development goals, the instrument is normally relative commodity prices.

Agricultural research is predominately organized along commodity lines. A natural congruence occurs, therefore, between price policy and resource allocation within agricultural research. That this congruence has not been exploited has in part to do with the short-to-medium-term planning frame of price policy compared to the medium-to-long-term planning frame of agricultural research, as well as with the weak institutional linkages between policy and agricultural research institutions. Nevertheless, the frequent complaint from scientists that economic incentives are limiting the diffusion of new technologies points to the need for a more consistent integration of decision making within the two areas.

Agricultural research, particularly within commodity programmes, focuses almost exclusively on production issues, usually on research to overcome yield constraints. Price policy, on the other hand, is principally formulated in terms of objectives that originate on the demand side; e.g., price of wage goods, nutrition and food costs for low-income consumers, and inflation control. Where producer income and/or commodity trade objectives are not consistent with price norms to meet demand objectives, usually subsidies rather than increased investment in commodity research are used to meet these multiple and otherwise inconsistent objectives. However, because of the increasing ease of substitution among commodities, such interventions give rise to a favouring of some commodities over others, often resulting in redistribution of income among regions and farm size strata.

Governments have not fully exploited either the cost reductions or the substitution possibilities arising from agricultural research in the planning of the agricultural sector. Like subsidies, agricultural research allows governments to reconcile otherwise inconsistent objectives, but, unlike subsidies, research investment does not introduce market inefficiencies. Medium-to-long-term changes in relative commodity prices induce real resource allocations in terms of shifts in farm investments, processing capacity, and marketing channels and can cause significant changes in consumer preferences. The link between investment in commodity research and impacts on production costs and market prices is more uncertain in terms of the size of the impact and the time frame, but the market, resource, and demand adjustments are economically efficient rather than dependent on the size and stability of fiscal budgets.

To begin to forge better links between price policy and agricultural research, the latter must integrate demand issues more effectively into research planning. The idea that commodity research should encompass postharvest and use aspects raises questions about how demand studies should influence what is essentially production-oriented research. The argument in this paper is that production, processing, marketing, demand, and policy studies can be integrated within a commodity subsector analysis. The approach, as shall be seen, broadens the scope of research and technology development and attempts to introduce a dynamic element in research planning, especially through attempting to forecast changing demand.

Major foods crops are a principal focus of agricultural research in developing countries. Nevertheless, as incomes increase and these economies urbanize, direct food demand for starchy staples becomes very inelastic. Since a principal objective of agricultural research is improved farmer income, often linked to increased labour productivity and employment, diffusion of new technology under inelastic demand conditions can lead (but only rarely does in LDCs) to immiserizing growth in rural areas. This has led to what may be termed the "diversification" problem (Schuh, 1987): how to achieve a balanced adjustment in commodity mix and resource use as the agricultural sector declines in relative importance in the economy, as growth in rural labour starts to decline absolutely, and as urban food markets start to supersede rural markets in relative importance. Crop diversification is the traditional solution; diversification of end markets for a particular commodity is an alternative solution. Agricultural research has an obvious role in facilitating these adjustments, but planning must employ a dynamic framework that explicitly incorporates demand issues.

Latin America: Structural Change and the Policy Framework

In the postwar period, tropical Latin American countries have been beset by a complex environment in which to administer food policy. Latin American economies underwent significant structural change, led by significant growth in the industrial and service sectors, relatively high rates of population growth, and what in many instances amounted to hyperurbanization. In the postwar period, these countries were transformed from essentially agrarian economies to urban, industrial economies, a process that created significant economic and social stresses. These stresses had their origin in the skewed distribution of land in the agricultural sector. Push factors, such as the rapid mechanization and intensification of large-scale farming—capital inputs increased from 20 to 48 percent of the value added in the agricultural sector in the period (CIDA, 1986)—and pull factors such as the disparity between industrial and agricultural wages, resulted in "excessive" rates of rural-urban migration. Unbalanced growth set up the food policy context; i.e., high rates of urban underemployment leading to growth in urban malnutrition, rising incomes and urbanization leading to changing food consumption patterns, and significant imbalances in availability and demand for key commodities leading to upward pressure on food prices. Policy makers were faced with the contradictory objectives of maintaining producer incentives in order to increase food supplies and control migration and of keeping the prices of key food staples in urban areas low.

Tropical Latin American countries have all intervened in their domestic agricultural markets. State marketing agencies were created as agents for administering price policy, usually with control over price supports and varying degrees of control over agricultural trade. Credit subsidies, often linked to other input subsidies, were used to stimulate priority commodities differentially. Governments often used consumer subsidies and programmed imports, usually under overvalued exchange rates, to maintain low, urban staple prices. Resulting fiscal deficits, nevertheless, either fuelled inflation or contributed to a growing external debt, a flexibility that was lost in the 1982 debt crisis.

Cereal grains were the logical focus of these interventions, due to the ease of controlling prices through stocks, import controls, and purchases, as well as their overall importance in the diet. However, the rising demand for animal products and the shifting of grain use to animal feeds created problems in the management of price policy due to unforeseen substitution effects; e.g., Mexico had to prohibit the use of maize in animal feeds, while in Brazil and Venezuela significant quantities of subsidized wheat went into feed rations. Moreover, substitution effects in basic foods as well were significant; in particular the rise of rice and wheat as urban staples came at the expense of the traditional staples, especially cassava and maize—apart from Mexico and parts of Central America. The latter resulted in a stagnation of income for producers of these commodities, mainly small-scale farmers, usually in poorer agricultural regions, and thus accentuated the dualism in the agricultural sector. Thus, while governments attempted to design programmes to address the problems of rural poverty and small-farm incomes, price policies indirectly undercut the economic basic of such programmes.

Cassava Subsector: Research Strategy within a Policy Context

Cassava, a tropical starchy staple, is a commodity that clearly demonstrates the value of the subsector approach to designing a research strategy. The crop's physiological characteristics result in high starch yields under a wide range of tropical conditions and with a comparative advantage over other crops in marginal agroclimatic zones. These factors, together with cassava's indeterminate harvest period, make it an ideal subsistence crop. Cassava's postharvest characteristics, on the other hand, define cassava's potential as a cash crop and are especially demanding in the provision of timely marketing services. The roots, once harvested, are highly perishable, bulky to transport, and normally contain about two-thirds water by weight. These characteristics, together with the hydrocyanic acid content, usually require cassava to be processed to develop extensive markets.

Because of perishability and bulkiness, processing should be well integrated with root supply in the production zones. Processing, however, is defined by the use characteristics of individual end markets; price signals and marketing channels should therefore be sufficiently flexible to convey and respond to the changing needs of diverse end markets, normally centred in urban areas. The difficulty is that in these end markets (i.e., starch, animal feed, traditional food products, and flours) cassava must usually compete with relatively dissimilar substitutes, resulting in demand and price being determined quite independently in each market. These supply and demand characteristics create the problem of defining an appropriate development strategy within a cassava subsector.

The issue then is how to link research strategy on cassava to development objectives and price policy in Latin American countries. Cassava provides a natural linkage to development of the small-farm sector, especially that portion that tends to be concentrated in more marginal agroclimatic regions such as Brazil's Northeast. Cassava is relatively difficult to mechanize, provides a significant return when the land resource is limited, and responds well to improved management. Cassava is almost exclusively grown by small-scale producers. One rarely finds a crop in Latin America where new techniques can be directed principally towards small-scale producers. Cassava research is virtually alone in being able to be targeted on small-scale farmers in marginal agricultural areas.

However, if increased small-farmer income is the objective of cassava research, efficient marketing channels and elastic market demand become complementary and in many cases necessary components of the strategy. In Latin America, cassava markets are still dominated by traditional food products: *farinha de mandioca* in Brazil, *casabe* in the Caribbean, and fresh roots in the rest of Latin America. Demand for both *farinha* and *casabe* is inelastic, and markets for fresh cassava are highly fragmented. However, unlike what has occurred in Asia, no diversification of cassava markets has occurred; extreme price variability in traditional markets and discriminatory price policies for grain substitutes have limited the development of a multiple market structure for cassava. Thus, for a research strategy in cassava to be successful, it must incorporate demand and price policy as well. Integrating production, marketing, use, and price policy is the hallmark of a subsector analysis.

The limited research history in cassava compared to that for grain crops also provides arguments for the integration of research on both production and use. Production research in this tropical root crop has been very scarce compared to the research on grains in temperate countries. What is often not noticed is that processing and use research is even more limited. Developed countries have done extensive research on technologies for processing rice, wheat, maize, and, to a lesser extent, sorghum, and significant manufacturing capacity has developed. Grain milling capacity in developing countries has been based on this imported technology and, in general, has captured economies of scale as urban centres have developed and processing capacity has concentrated there. Not only does cassava processing and use have a limited research history, but achieving economies of scale has been difficult because of the concentration of processing and use in production zones. When the setting up of large factories has been rushed, cassava projects have failed miserably. In Latin America, the limited investment in production research on cassava has achieved little because of the lack of investment in processing research and market development.

In the case of cassava in Latin America, the orientation of subsector studies should focus on evaluation of market diversification and/or improving market efficiency. In tropical Latin America, market diversification implies the capture of an increasing market share, which can be achieved by substitution for maize, sorghum, or wheat imports. However, this is the juncture where price, exchange rate, and grain import policy influence whether cassava can begin to compete in these alternative markets. Because of policy interventions, cassava's competitive ability can be independent of comparative costs of production, processing, and marketing. Cassava subsector studies must thus begin with a macro, country-level assessment of grain markets, existing cassava markets, and price policies. The dual side of the problem focuses on comparative costs—optimally within a DRC framework. By necessity, this is more disaggregated, requiring specification of principal production regions, production systems, and marketing and processing costs. The analysis leads optimally to a targeting of research; i.e., policy research, market development priorities, the mix of production and use research, and production region priorities. Small-farmer income generation provides the common thread that must run through the analysis, and the process necessarily leads to a better integration of price policy formation and research investment.

Strategies for Cassava Development in Latin America

Agricultural price has been a principal mechanism for achieving development objectives in Latin America. However, too often policy makers have resorted to subsidies in order to accommodate conflicting objectives, and when individual policy objectives have been matched with single commodities, substitution effects have often either undercut the effectiveness (or budgetary cost) of the policy or have had unanticipated negative impacts in other sectors of the agricultural economy. The 1982 debt crisis and the policy commitments to control inflation have severely curtailed traditional policy interventions by eliminating subsidies, correcting overvalued exchange rates, and reducing import capacity. Tropical Latin American countries have thus been forced to stimulate their domestic agricultural sectors with less flexibility in terms of traditional policy options. In this environment, well-focused agricultural research linked to market and agroindustrial development, exploitation of a larger range of crops, and policy interventions on the basis of sectors (e.g., the grain-livestock or oilseed sectors) rather than individual commodities, would all provide increased alternatives to meeting a range of difficult development objectives.

Within this "new" policy environment, cassava provides an unexploited means of having an impact on such objectives, particularly increased small-farm incomes in more marginal agricultural regions, increased rural employment and rural incomes in more marginal agricultural regions, increased rural employment and rural incomes through rural-based agroindustry, and improved domestic supplies of food and feed. With the changes in price policy, cassava is now competitive in a range of end markets. Thus, bringing cassava into the policy process and ensuring consistency across starch sources introduces new flexibility to policy makers in meeting difficult policy goals/objectives.

Cassava development in Latin America depends on a close integration of production and use research. Nevertheless, cassava development starts with use, by defining a market of sufficient size and in which the product can feasibly compete with substitutes. Once this market has been defined, marketing, processing, and production plans have to be designed and coordinated. Care has to be taken that the scale of operations is compatible at different market stages and appropriate for the target group of beneficiaries. These will be mainly small farmers, for whom developing appropriate credit schemes, organization forms, and marketing arrangements will be critical to cassava expansion.

Given the need to restructure marketing channels, cassava development can best be promoted through pilot projects and their subsequent multiplication. Pilot projects facilitate fine-tuning and integration of production, processing, and marketing components, as well as adaptive research at each of these stages. The flexible nature and low investment costs in a small-scale, pilot project allow stepwise improvements in production, processing, and marketing efficiency. Matching a target production region and target farmer population with end-market development is the key to attaining effective impacts in cassava development projects.

Research and development strategy in cassava has been conditioned by the vagaries of price policy in competing grains. A dynamic and interactive relationship exists between cassava research and grain price policy, best analyzed within a subsector framework. Cassava research becomes focused by concentrating on the commodity subsystem (i.e., the vertical set of functions from production to consumption of the commodity), while profitability and impacts are guaranteed by focusing on markets and price policy within the whole grain subsector. The dynamic and interactive nature of the process depends on the link between research and policy institutions. What binds them together is the analysis; where the analysis is done depends on the makeup of the respective institutions, but some analytical capacity within crop research institutions is necessary. Grain price policy and cassava development are integrally linked in Latin America; policy makers must realize this.

Notes

[1]Centro Internacional de Agricultura Tropical, Cali, Colombia.

[2]Agricultural research in this paper means principally commodity-based research, including those activities that extend from more basic research to adaptive research, including extension.

[3]Price policy can either promote or inhibit the adoption of improved technologies. Whether or not price policy and investment in agricultural research are institutionally linked, the efficiency of research investment is necessarily linked to relative prices in agricultural markets. Conversely, agricultural research can be an efficient means of achieving price policy objectives. A rational, economic argument thus exists for consistent integration of the two. This integration, however, necessarily leads to institutional capacity to further politicize agricultural research. This is a legitimate concern and should condition how the institutional linkage is made; however, that topic lies outside the scope of this paper.

References

Binswanger, H.P., and Ruttan, V.W. (1978) *Induced Innovation: Technology, Institutions, and Development*, Johns Hopkins University Press, Baltimore, Md., USA.

CIDA (Canadian International Development Agency) (1986) "Agriculture and Rural Development in Latin America," Ottawa, Ont., Canada.

Schuh, G.E. (1987) "Meeting the Challenge of Diversification Out of Rice Production in Asia: Towards a Research Agenda," paper presented at a CGIAR Group Meeting, Montpellier, France.

DISCUSSION OPENING—*J.S. Sarma* (International Food Policy Research Institute)

The results of a cassava study recently completed by the International Food Policy Research Institute, "Past Trends and Prospects for Cassava in the Third World," illustrate some of the conclusions in the paper by Lynam *et al.* While analysis at the subsector level to study the integration between the price policy and agricultural research is useful and necessary, decisions on price policy need to be taken at macro level. Subsector analysis sometimes leads to certain commodities being advocated, when their development may not otherwise be justified. The Delphi survey for assessment of potential yields of cassava and constraints on farmers achieving the yields confirmed that lack of incentives inhibited the diffusion of technology. However, the technology route to increased net returns through increased productivity is preferable to the price policy route, although remunerative prices are necessary to ensure the adoption of new technology.

Application of fertilizer alone would increase cassava yields by five tons per hectare even on ordinary soils, without irrigation; and with high-yielding varieties, the productivity would rise further, reducing the unit costs. This would facilitate end-use diversification. Experience in Thailand showed that crop diversification was difficult to achieve in marginal areas where cassava is grown.

The high priority to be given to cassava R&D is justified by considerations of equity and poverty alleviation in marginal areas, as in Northeast Brazil and Northeast Thailand, and by food security considerations in Sub-Saharan Africa, where food shortages are expected to continue for some time to come.

GENERAL DISCUSSION—*Winfried Manig, Rapporteur* (Universität Göttingen)

The discussion on this paper centred on the importance of the price policy for cassava. Price policy has become important because cassava has for a long time been excluded from the market system. Since cassava is regarded as an inferior food, the analysis should use different income strata, as the demand depends on income, and not a general model. Another aspect stressed was the importance of demand for animal feed, which should be included in the analysis. Cassava has for a long time been neglected in research activities; however, the impact of technological improvement has been very significant in recent times.

Participants in the discussion included G. Escobar, R. Evenson, F. Jarrett, T.P. Phillips, S. Setboonsarng, and S.C. Thompson.

Introduction of New Maize Technology in Zaire's Kasai Oriental: Application of Risk Analysis in Farming Systems Research

Glenn C.W. Ames, Donald W. Reid, and Tshidinda M. Lukusa[1]

Abstract: The risks associated with new maize technology and the impact of mandatory cotton production on traditional farmers in Zaire's Kasai Oriental Region were evaluated with stochastic dominance analysis. Net returns for four levels of maize technology were evaluated in combination with three staple food crops, for four cropping systems with and without mandatory cotton cultivation. Thus, net returns for 32 separate cropping systems were assessed for the primary and secondary rainy seasons, respectively. The results indicate that cropping systems including new maize technology are first-order stochastic dominant in both seasons over cropping systems using local maize. Although the variances for the different cropping systems indicate that using new maize with fertilizer has greater variance than with local maize, the increase in expected net returns for new maize technology appears to compensate farmers for this increased variability. Also, analysis of the mandatory cotton production revealed that it is not risk efficient at current price and yield levels. Cropping systems without cotton were first-order stochastic dominant over systems with cotton. As expected, the inclusion of fibre production reduced the coefficient of variation for the more diversified system. Nevertheless, reduction in the coefficient of variation is not sufficient to make cotton production risk efficient.

Introduction

Before independence in 1960, Zaire was self-sufficient in food production and exported substantial amounts of palm oil, cotton, timber, and other commodities to Western Europe. In subsequent years, production has not kept pace with population growth, increasing at nearly 4 percent per year (Boute and de Saint, 1978). Imports of maize, rice, wheat, and sugar have been necessary to meet domestic needs.

Maize is the staple food in Zaire's Kasai Oriental and Shaba Regions, where annual consumption is 100-120 kg per year (Département de l'Agriculture, 1982, p. 315). In order to meet growing demand and reduce imports, the Government of Zaire has promoted the use of improved maize seed, fertilizer, cultural practices, and appropriate cropping systems in its strategy to increase food production in the region.

At the same time, Zaire has changed some of its pricing policies for food crops but maintained price and production controls on cotton, an important commercial crop. Thus, progress in Zaire's maize production programme will depend on the yield advantages of improved varieties, which vary according to growing conditions, farmer economic circumstances and attitudes towards risk, and government support for local maize research.

The objectives of this study are to (1) investigate the economic feasibility of introducing new maize technology in the cropping system of Kasai Oriental, (2) estimate the variability in returns to different levels of maize technology under seasonal cropping systems, and (3) evaluate the impacts of agricultural policies, including mandatory cotton production, on the adoption of new technology. The results of the analysis should be applicable to other African countries with similar levels of technology and agricultural policies.

Historical Perspective on Maize Research in Zaire

In the early 1970s, three important agricultural research projects were started on maize production in Kasai Oriental. The projects were sponsored by the National Institute for Agronomic Study and Research, the National Maize Programme, and the FAO National Fertilizer Programme. In 1971, a CIMMYT team began a 10-year programme of maize research in Zaire. Its goals were the development of a maize breeding programme for new, higher yielding varieties, the diffusion and adoption of the higher yielding varieties by traditional farmers to increase food production, and the establishment of institutions to sustain the programme (Terman and Hart, 1977, p. 211).

Higher yielding, open-pollinated cultivars (HYVs) adapted to Shaba and Kasai Oriental were used to develop improved maize varieties from which seed could be selected and sold by farmers for the next season without declining yields. Progression to sophisticated hybrids was not recommended for the early stages of the programme. In the early 1970s, demonstration plots under heavy fertilization and higher plant populations yielded four times the average grain output of local varieties under traditional methods. In 1973-74, a supervised credit programme began on a limited scale to encourage fertilizer use on CIMMYT's new maize varieties. These recommendations have continued throughout the mid-1980s.

In 1980, the Kasai Oriental Maize Project was implemented in the rural areas to ensure extensive use of fertilizer and HYV maize. That project also encouraged the National Institute for Agronomic Study and Research and the National Maize Programme to continue research on rotations of maize, leguminous crops, cassava, and cotton (World Bank, 1980, p. 23).

In addition to technology recommendations, agricultural policy also influenced the cropping system. In Kasai Oriental, government regulations imposed on farmers the planting of a minimum acreage of cotton (Mwamufiya, 1977, p. 4; and Département de l'Agriculture, 1977, p. 37). In the setting of the National Food Production Programme, any adult person was obliged to plant a minimum area to crops such as maize, cassava, rice, groundnuts, soyabeans or beans, and cotton (0.5 ha) each growing season. Penalties and fines were imposed for noncompliance. This production/extraction system, held over from the colonial period, has certainly had an impact on the farming system and the risk associated with the adoption of new technology.

Farming Systems in the Survey Area of Kasai Oriental

The focus of this study is the Kasai Oriental Maize Project in the subregions of Tshilenge and Kabinda, in the southern part of Kasai Oriental, covering 26,300 km². Farming occurs in either forest or savannah environments. Annual precipitation averages between 1200 and 1600 mm. The heavy subtropical rains last from late August to late January or early February and are followed by a short dry season lasting 10 to 15 days. A second, light rainy season lasts from February to early May, followed by a longer dry season. Two crops of maize are grown: one in season *A* from August to January, another in season *B* from February to May. Shifting cultivation is commonly practised in the study area. Successive plantings of one or more crops take place until unacceptable yields are reached, then the site is abandoned to fallow.

The basic crops cultivated in the survey area are maize, cassava, beans, groundnuts, and cotton. Generally, cassava, maize, or cotton precede the main crop in the survey area. Maize-maize, maize-cassava, and cotton-maize-cotton are the most common crop rotation sequences. The Kasai Oriental Maize Project encourages farmers to rotate maize with maize when fertilizer is applied in the cropping sequence. Under this assumption, the current maize crop would benefit from the secondary effects of fertilizer used on previous maize plots if some residual nutrients remain in the soil after the first crop.

Intercropping maize with other crops is another prevalent practice in Kasai Oriental. Farmers consider intercropping to be an effective way of allocating scarce labour over time. They believe that the instability of their crop production increased with the adoption of improved maize seed and fertilizer in 1978. Input prices also started to increase at that time. Terman and Hart (1977, pp. 220-221) have succinctly described the traditional Zairian farmer risk aversion:

> *When the subsistence farmer considers a new innovation, he has two main questions: (1) Will the new method, considering costs, produce an expected yield appreciably higher than his old method?, and (2) Is it likely that something might go wrong and result in a net yield below his subsistence level? Even though the*

answer to 1 is "Yes," he will not change his method unless the answer to 2 is "No." Thus, the closer that his current output comes to his minimum subsistence level, the more conservative he is likely to be. The more unfamiliar he is with the proposed innovation the more cautious he will be.... Successful innovations tend to be adopted more rapidly for commercial crops not needed for the farmer's subsistence than for necessary food crops.

Both local, traditional, and new high-yielding varieties of maize are planted in the subregions, the former by nonsupervised farmers and the latter, named either "SALONGO II" or "KASAI I," by those who are supervised by the Kasai Oriental Maize Project. In general, maize is considered to be a crop of high but unstable yield and profitability with low cash outlay.

Other planting patterns of farmers in the eight rural zones of Kasai Oriental indicate that cotton comes at the beginning of the crop rotation sequence with maize. This is established by the authorities (i.e., La Cotonnière, a cotton ginning company) supervising the production of cotton under the government mandate. This crop is characterized by unstable yield, high cash outlay, and intertemporally declining profitability.

In the study area, farmer participation in the Kasai Oriental Maize Project ranged from a low of 40 percent in Kamiji to 70 percent in Gandajika. On average, 60 percent of the farmers participated in the maize improvement project; 58 percent of the farmers reported that they were growing HYVs of maize while 42 percent were growing traditional varieties. On average, 72 percent of the farmers were using fertilizer. Since fertilizer was part of the package of inputs, the ability to purchase it was important to the success of the project. Only 14 percent of the farmers were able to purchase fertilizer with cash. The balance of the farmers received their fertilizer allotment as a loan. Generally, the farmers had to deposit Z225 ($4) with the Kasai Oriental Maize Project to receive the minimum amount of fertilizer.

Analysis of Farm Plans in Kasai Oriental

Data used in this study were first collected from the available literature for 11 growing seasons between 1981 and 1985. Time-series yield data, taken from the Kasai Oriental Maize Project's annual reports, were available by technology type, local and improved maize, and fertilizer treatment (Project Maïs au Kasai Oriental, 1980-86). Secondly, field surveys were conducted in eight zones of Kasai Oriental in July 1986 to gather information about the local farming systems and farmer perceptions of risk; 140 small farmers were randomly interviewed by using a survey questionnaire focusing on the local farming system and participation in the Kasai Oriental Maize Project (Lukusa, 1988). Yields reported by farmers in the survey were consistent with those in the Kasai Oriental Maize Project's reports for previous years. Analysis of the survey data indicates that farms were small, averaging about 1.95 ha or less of cropland (Lukusa, 1988).

Expected net returns per crop and cropping system were calculated from data published in the Kasai Oriental Maize Project's annual reports and collected during the farm survey. Real net return per hectare for each crop was multiplied by the percentage of each crop in the eight cropping systems (Table 1). The weighted net return for each crop was summed to provide total net return per hectare for each system represented in the eight rural zones (Tables 2 and 3). Five years of data, 1981-85, were used to calculate the mean return and represent risk for each system. For season *A*, farm plans 5-8 correspond to net returns for local maize without fertilizer, local maize with fertilizer, new HYV maize without fertilizer, and HYV with fertilizer, respectively. Farm plans 1-4 are the same combinations except for the exclusion of the mandatory cotton crop. For each season, 32 separate farm plans were analyzed, four for each of the eight zones.

First-order stochastic dominance was used to analyze the relative risk and returns of the alternative farm plans (Calkins and DiPietre, 1983). The results indicate that new maize

Table 1—Distribution of Area Planted to Selected Crops in Eight Zones in Kasai Oriental, 1986

Crops	Rural Zone*							
	Gandajika	Mwene-Ditu	Kamiji	Miabi	Kabeya-Kamuanga	Lupatapata	Tshilenge	Katanda
	Percent							
Maize	29.82	31.11	35.00	37.03	32.68	38.71	33.33	30.44
Cassava	24.56	28.89	25.00	25.93	26.14	25.81	15.39	23.91
Groundnuts	14.04	15.56	20.00	18.52	18.30	16.13	20.51	17.39
Beans	17.54	13.33	20.00	18.52	22.88	19.35	20.51	13.04
Cotton	14.04	11.11	†	†	†	†	10.26	15.22
	100.00	100.00	100.00	100.00	100.00	100.00	100.00	100.00

*Number of farmers interviewed: Gandajika–25, Mwene-Ditu–20, Kamiji–8, Miabi–15, Kabeya-Kamuanga–20, Lupatapata–18, Tshilenge–20, and Katanda–14.
†Farmers in these four zones did not plant cotton.
Source: Survey data, 1986.

technology, in both seasons, is the preferred technology, given the existing cropping plans. When mandatory cotton cultivation was imposed in the cropping plans, M Plan 8 and T Plan 8 dominated other cropping plans for both seasons. The allocation of cropland in M Plan 8 consisted of 31.19 percent HYV maize, 28.89 percent cassava, 15.56 percent groundnuts, 13.33 percent beans, and 11.11 percent cotton. T Plan 8 is similar but with more maize, groundnuts, and beans, and less cassava and cotton. The coefficient of variation of 15.84 percent for M Plan 8 indicated that more variation relative to the expected return was associated with this cropping plan than other plans. However, using HYV maize reduces the probability of receiving net returns lower than those obtained with local maize. T Plan 8 provided net returns of Z340 per hectare, only 0.20 percent less than M Plan 8 and with about 1.7 percent less relative variation. Although T Plan 8 has a smaller amount of variation for a nearly identical expected net return, T Plan 8 is not stochastically dominant over M Plan 8 in either the first- or second-order sense.

When cotton was *not* specifically imposed on the cropping plan, the dominant plans were L Plan 4, I Plan 4, and K Plan 4, with expected net returns of Z383, Z379, and Z373, respectively (Table 3). This indicates that plans without cotton would be preferred to those with mandatory fibre production. However, more relative variation was associated with these cropping systems, as indicated by coefficients of variation of 17.82, 16.41, and 14.80 percent respectively.

In general, expected net returns in season *B* were substantially lower than net returns for season *A*. For example, expected net returns for the dominant plan M Plan 8 in season *B* were 73.7 percent less than in season *A*. Also, the coefficient of variation was larger for season *B* (19.74 vs. 15.84 percent), indicating more relative variation in the secondary season. This is consistent with the results of the National Maize Programme's rotational trials in the 1977-78 period (Programme National Maïs, 1978, p. 25).

Explaining cropping plans in the context of portfolio theory gives some insight into the importance of diversification and why some farm plans are dominant (Elton and Gruber, 1984). Dominant cropping plans, with and without cotton, have a higher percentage of land allocated to HYVs with fertilizer than the dominated plans. The dominance of these plans is partially explained by the fact that HYVs with fertilizer have the most negative or least positive covariance of any maize production alternative with beans, groundnuts, or cotton, both for seasons *A* and *B*. This also may help explain why land allocation responses from the land-use survey did not distinguish separate land allocation for each season—the same farm plan is dominant for both seasons, perhaps in large part because of the similar type of covariance effects in each season.

Table 2—Average Real Net Returns in the Primary Rainy Season (Season A) for Eight Cropping Systems in Kasai Oriental, 1981-85

Rural Zone	Plan	Mean (Zaires)	Standard Deviation (Zaires)	Coefficient of Variation (Percent)
With mandatory cotton cultivation:				
Gandajika	G Plan 5	234.80	4.50	1.92
	G Plan 6	260.73	24.70	9.48
	G Plan 7	248.41	7.09	2.85
	G Plan 8	325.79	49.58	15.22
Mwene-Ditu	M Plan 5	245.71	6.54	2.66
	M Plan 6	272.75	27.17	9.96
	M Plan 7	259.90	8.19	3.15
	M Plan 8	340.63	53.97	15.84
Tshilenge	T Plan 5	238.42	8.36	3.51
	T Plan 6	267.39	25.79	9.64
	T Plan 7	253.62	9.77	3.85
	T Plan 8	340.11	48.10	14.14
Katanda	A Plan 5	234.88	2.66	1.13
	A Plan 6	261.34	24.85	9.51
	A Plan 7	248.76	4.81	1.93
	A Plan 8	327.73	49.16	15.00
Without mandatory cotton cultivation:				
Kamiji	K Plan 1	265.80	4.43	1.67
	K Plan 2	296.22	27.37	9.24
	K Plan 3	281.76	7.19	2.55
	K Plan 4	372.59	55.14	14.80
Miabi	I Plan 1	266.20	6.55	2.46
	I Plan 2	298.40	31.42	10.53
	I Plan 3	283.10	9.37	3.31
	I Plan 4	279.22	62.22	16.41
Kabeya-Kamuanga	B Plan 1	264.89	4.55	1.72
	B Plan 2	293.30	24.48	8.35
	B Plan 3	279.80	7.29	2.61
	B Plan 4	364.60	50.64	13.89
Lupatapata	L Plan 1	264.71	9.84	3.72
	L Plan 2	298.36	35.07	11.75
	L Plan 3	282.37	12.69	4.49
	L Plan 4	382.83	68.22	17.82

Sources: Project Mais au Kasai Oriental (1980-86) and World Bank (1980).

Conclusions

Farmer risk aversion influences farmer decisions regarding the adoption of new maize technology. However, analysis of existing farm plans with new maize varieties with fertilizer shows these to be first-order stochastic dominant over those with no fertilizer or those containing local maize. Although new maize with fertilizer is more variable than new maize without fertilizer and either local maize with or without fertilizer, the increase in expected net returns for new maize with fertilizer appears to compensate farmers for the increased variation in expected returns.

The first-order stochastic dominance analysis also implies that mandatory cotton production is *not* risk efficient at current price and yield levels. The dominant cropping plan for season *A*, L Plan 4, provided 12.4 percent higher returns (Z383 versus Z341) than the dominant cropping plan, M Plan 8, which included an average 11.1 percent of its cultivated area devoted to fibre production. The coefficient of variation for the dominant plan with cotton production was 15.84 percent versus 17.82 percent for the plan without cotton, a small increase in relative variation for such a significant increase (12.4 percent) in absolute expected returns. Cropping plans including new maize technology with fertilizer dominated in both seasons. Thus, even the most risk averse farmers would prefer the new technology in season *B* relative to local maize if their perceptions were consistent with the historical outcomes analyzed in this study.

In conclusion, farmers must evaluate the risk associated with the new technology before adopting it completely. However, they probably will adopt the new technology if additional information continues to reflect the outcomes represented in the data analyzed. The general adoption of HYVs with fertilizer would be expected because the analysis implies that farmers would be better off (in terms of increased food production and revenue) with the improved technology even though the variance for HYVs is higher. Although the decline from the expected mean return would be greater for HYVs relative to the decline for local maize, farmers would be better off with improved varieties with fertilizer even in the most adverse environmental conditions.

Other implications of this study for the adoption of new technology in other African countries include intraregional differences in the yields of the new seed-fertilizer technology due to soil and rainfall patterns. Although cotton prices were fixed at the national level, food prices were also "controlled" at the regional level by the governor's office. Price risk enters the evaluation of portfolios of cropping systems because a system of managed prices may not adjust sufficiently to rapidly changing costs and thus increase farmer risk. This recognition of increased costs relative to managed prices led to the Executive Council's price liberalization decree of May 29, 1982 (Département de l'Agriculture et du Développement Rural, 1986, pp. 187-197). Results of price liberalization are not yet known since an element of managed prices still exists in Kasai Oriental and other regions of Zaire. Finally, institutional support is a vital component in the adoption and maintenance of new crop varieties at the farm and national level. Without the continual testing and evaluation of seed varieties, the yield of improved varieties may decline over time and expectations of increased food production may not be realized. Thus, farmers and policy makers must view the adoption of new technology as a continuous process in the farming systems of developing countries and adjust their decisions and policies accordingly.

Table 3—Average Real Net Returns in the Secondary Rainy Season (Season B) for Eight Cropping Systems in Kasai Oriental, 1981-86

Rural Zone	Plan	Mean (Zaires)	Standard Deviation (Zaires)	Coefficient of Variation (Percent)
	With mandatory cotton cultivation:			
Gandajika	G Plan 5	145.78	29.63	20.33
	G Plan 6	150.86	30.25	20.05
	G Plan 7	149.93	30.96	20.65
	G Plan 8	186.92	37.42	20.02
Mwene-Ditu	M Plan 5	153.21	29.90	19.51
	M Plan 6	158.52	30.54	19.27
	M Plan 7	157.54	31.29	19.86
	M Plan 8	196.14	38.72	19.74
Tshilenge	T Plan 5	147.86	33.21	22.47
	T Plan 6	153.54	33.29	21.69
	T Plan 7	152.49	34.44	22.58
	T Plan 8	193.84	39.33	20.29
Katanda	A Plan 5	146.96	30.43	20.71
	A Plan 6	152.15	30.84	20.27
	A Plan 7	151.19	31.70	20.97
	A Plan 8	188.94	37.76	19.98
	Without mandatory cotton cultivation:			
Kamiji	K Plan 1	164.43	32.98	20.06
	K Plan 2	170.41	33.12	19.44
	K Plan 3	169.31	34.31	20.27
	K Plan 4	212.73	41.09	19.31
Miabi	I Plan 1	164.48	32.60	19.82
	I Plan 2	170.80	33.28	19.48
	I Plan 3	169.63	34.19	20.15
	I Plan 4	215.59	43.03	19.96
Kabeya-Kamuanga	B Plan 1	163.47	32.30	19.76
	B Plan 2	169.04	32.29	19.10
	B Plan 3	168.01	33.51	19.94
	B Plan 4	208.56	39.34	18.86
Lupatapata	L Plan 1	162.89	32.26	19.80
	L Plan 2	169.50	33.53	19.78
	L Plan 3	168.28	34.11	20.27
	L Plan 4	216.31	44.83	20.72

Sources: Survey data (1986), Project Maïs au Kasai Oriental (1980-86), and World Bank (1980).

Note

[1]University of Georgia, Athens; University of Georgia, Athens; and Département de l'Agriculture et du Développement Rural, Zaire; respectively.

References

Boute, J., and de Saint, M. (1978) *Perspectives Démographiques Régionales, 1975-1985*, Kinshasa, Zaire.

Calkins, F.H., and DiPietre, D. (1983) *Farm Business Management: Successful Decisions in a Changing Environment*, Macmillan Publishing Co., New York, N.Y., USA.

Département de l'Agriculture (1977) *Les Nouvelles Structures de la Production Agricole: Arrête Départemental*, No. 00748/BCE/AGR 76, For. Info., Kinshasa, Zaire.

Département de l'Agriculture (1982) *Situation Actuelle de l'Agriculture Zaïroise*, Project 660-070 USAID, Division d'Études et Planification, Kinshasa, Zaire.

Département de l'Agriculture et du Développement Rural (1986) *Région du Kasai Oriental Étude Regionale pour la Planification Agricole*, Service d'Études et Planification, Kinshasa, Zaire.

Elton, E.J., and Gruber, M.J. (1984) *Modern Portfolio Theory and Investment Analysis*, John Wiley and Sons, New York, N.Y., USA.

Lukusa, T.M. (1988) "Introduction of New Maize Technology in the Farming Systems of the Kasai-Oriental Region of Zaire," MS thesis, University of Georgia, Athens, Ga., USA.

Mwamufiya, M. (1977) "Maize Production and Marketing in Four Districts of Zaire: An Introductory Economic Analysis," PhD dissertation, Oregon State University, Corvallis, Oreg., USA.

Programme National Maïs (1978) *Sixième Rapport Annuel, 1978*, Département de l'Agriculture, Kinshasa, Zaire.

Project Maïs au Kasai Oriental (1980-86) *Rapport Annuel*, Mbuji-Mayi, Zaire.

Terman, G.L., and Hart, T.G. (1977) "Improved Technology Replaces Traditional Agriculture," *World Crops and Livestock*, Vol. 29, pp. 217-221.

World Bank (1980) "Smallholder Maize Project," Staff Appraisal Report No. 2194-ZR, Implementation Volume, African Agriculture Division, Washington, D.C., USA.

DISCUSSION OPENING—*Robert B. Koopman* (Economic Research Service, US Department of Agriculture)

This paper applies stochastic dominance and mean variance analysis to evaluate the risk associated with the introduction of new maize technology in a province of Zaire. The results of the analysis suggest that farmers are more than adequately compensated for the increased risk associated with cropping patterns using high yielding maize varieties.

Stochastic dominance is a popular technique for analyzing risk and is widely applied in agricultural economics. What do the authors mean by a composite approach of mean-variance analysis and stochastic dominance?—this is not explained in the paper. Second, since first-order stochastic dominance is a conservative measure, and most other papers using stochastic dominance have to use less conservative, higher orders of dominance, the finding in this paper of dominant cropping patterns is rather strong. It would suggest that, in the absence of constraints and information problems, the dominant patterns would replace the dominated patterns rather quickly. The paper itself raises this point; I wonder if the dominated patterns are being dropped?

Further, assumptions about diversification are important in stochastic dominance analysis. The paper is unclear about the nature and extent of diversification allowed (probably due to the page limitations). Are the areas described in Table 1 assumed to hold across all types of maize grown within that province? If so, wouldn't that eliminate a large number of possible portfolios? Also, pairwise comparisons among maize alternatives (with the apparently fixed portfolios of other crops) may also be restrictive. Diversification, especially in the presence of covariation, has been shown to be an important factor among pairwise comparisons. Does a portfolio exist that considers the diversification among maize as well as other crops, and would such a portfolio dominate the ones considered? If so, that could explain any persistence of non-HYVs, if such persistence existed.

GENERAL DISCUSSION—*K. Sain, Rapporteur* (Bidhan Chandra Krishi Viswavidyalaya)

A comment was made that the sampling technique suffered from inadequate coverage. A question was raised about the procedure for estimating the relative efficiency of new maize technology only on the basis of relative per-hectare yields of HYV maize *vis-à-vis* controlled varieties. Another comment was made that the diversification of crops grown by the sample farmers was not fully representative of all farmers in the region.

Market Performance of Poultry Industries under Different North American and European Market Structures

Donald E. Farris and Doris von Dosky[1]

Abstract: The broiler chicken and egg industries are compared across the economies of the USA, Canada, FRG, and Switzerland to contrast the impacts on market performance of different market structures due to different government policies. The US industries approximate free market conditions whereas the other three countries use different methods to restrict entry or expansion or to set prices. Two different data sets show substantially higher retail prices for broilers and eggs in Canada and Western Europe than in the USA. Producer egg prices were 34 to 166 percent above and live broiler chicken prices 29 to 110 percent higher than those in the USA during 1980-85.

Introduction

Comparison of the market performance of poultry under four different market structures in four countries offers substantial insight into the role of different market structures in shaping market conduct and performance. The broiler chicken and egg industries are compared across the economies of the USA, Canada, FRG, and Switzerland to contrast market structure and performance due to government policies. The field of industrial organization is concerned with policies that produce good market performance; however, measures of different levels of market performance are often difficult to interpret unless appropriate comparisons can be made.

The advantages of using the poultry industries as examples are that reasonably good data are available, and the industries are not as resource specific as many other agricultural product industries. The poultry industries (broilers, eggs, and turkeys) have made substantial management and technological advances since World War II, and these advances have been generally adopted in most developed countries and many developing countries. Evidence will be provided that these the poultry industries have performed well in terms of efficiency, progressiveness, and innovation. Performance is not as good in equity and efficient resource allocation where market entry is limited.

Because of the lack of regulation or government subsidy in the USA, the benefits from this rapid progress have been passed on to domestic consumers and to some US trading partners, with relatively low returns to producing and marketing firms compared to other agricultural enterprises (Farris *et al.*, 1966). Innovators often had high returns for only a relatively short period in the USA because the innovations were generally easy for competitors to copy and adopt (Singleton, 1986). Comparison of the US industries with those in other countries could be considered similar to comparing alternative market structures where one approaching pure competition, while each of the other three countries provides different levels of protection and/or subsidies. Although elements of oligopoly/oligopsony exist in all four countries, this is expected to have little impact compared to government control of prices or entry.

Evaluation of market performance must consider the goals of society, and, in this cross-country comparison, the goals of each of the four countries. The primary objective of the study, however, is to demonstrate the impact of alternative policies on market performance and to contribute to more enlightened policy not only in the poultry industry but in other industries as well.

The hypotheses derived from economic theory that apply here are: (1) the USA, being a major exporter of poultry products and feed grains, would have the lowest producer and retail prices among the countries considered; and (2) general equilibrium theory can show that, without barriers, adjacent countries should have only small price differences at the producer and retail levels.

Market Structure

Barriers to entry are generally the market structure characteristic found to be the greatest deterrent to good market performance, and Brozen (1969) shows that government is the principal cause of barriers to entry resulting in lower market performance.

This study will show that trade barriers are the major (but not the only) method used by governments resulting in reduced market performance of the poultry industries of the countries selected.

The four countries studied are: (1) the USA, with no effective barriers to entry and no subsidies (except some recent retaliatory export subsidies); (2) Canada, whose market structure for broiler chickens and eggs controls entry and expansion by establishing (via marketing boards) national and regional marketing quotas and import quotas; (3) the FRG, a member of the EC, where the EC restricts entry from third countries by a high variable levy while maintaining a high domestic (EC) target price and subsidizing the export of surplus product; and (4) Switzerland, a high-cost producer that protects domestic producers by an import tariff and requires buyers to purchase a minimum percentage of their product from domestic production (a federal council sets domestic guide prices and, as a result of this system, imports are limited and high domestic prices are maintained).

The key market structure variable in these industries is barriers to entry; the market conduct variable is government setting the price level in the case of the EC and Switzerland; in the case of Canada, output and imports are limited. Efficiency and equity are the key market performance variables affected; however, full employment of societies' resources and progressiveness are also influenced.

Market Performance

Data on all aspects of efficiency were not readily available, but most of the developed countries have adopted much of the available technology, management, marketing, and financing innovations. The significant differences relate mostly to input costs. In other words, the sharp reduction in feed required per pound of bird, the low labour requirement per thousand birds, and the low-cost processing and distribution that have been generally achieved in the developed countries. The big differences are the costs of feed, housing, fuel, processing, and distribution. Advantages of economies of scale, risk management, and marketing from vertical and horizontal integration are also significant but difficult to measure.

The efficiency of poultry production and marketing compared to other important agricultural enterprises in the USA has been remarkable since 1940 when the broiler chicken industry was in its infancy. In 1980, the average deflated price that US farmers received for broilers was only 30 percent of the 1940 price, whereas the prices for beef, soyabeans, cotton, wheat, and maize were 141, 144, 115, 101, and 93 percent, respectively, of their 1940 deflated prices (Table 1).

Table 1—Index of Average Annual Deflated Prices Received by US Farmers for Selected Commodities as a Percent of 1940*

Year	Wheat	Maize	Cotton	Soyabeans	Beef	Poultry
1940	100	100	100	100	100	100
1950	173	147	206	160	179	94
1960	123	79	126	112	128	47
1970	72	80	70	114	129	30
1980	101	93	115	144	141	30

*Actual prices deflated by the CPI index to 1970 = 100, yet indexed to 1940 = 100.

Source: Calculated from Kohls, R.L., and Uhl, J.M. (1985) *Marketing of Agricultural Products*, 6th Ed.

This dramatic real price reduction was made possible by the feed required to produce a pound of live bird being cut from 100 to 49 percent from 1940 to 1978 and pounds of broiler production per hour of grow-out labour increasing from 12 to 776—or 6,467 percent (Table 2). At the same time, the industry shifted to areas with mild climates for lower cost housing and heating and lower labour and land costs.

Table 2–Feed Efficiency, Labour Efficiency, and Broiler Prices

Year	Feed Used per Pound of Broiler	Broiler Production per Hour of Grow-Out Labour	Market Value of Live Weight Broilers, 1967 Dollars
	- - - - *Pounds* - - - -		*Cents/lb*
1940	4.22	12	43.2
1950	3.27	31	26.6
1955	2.80	64	27.1
1960	2.41	98	17.8
1965	2.28	134	15.3
1970	2.15	258	12.4
1975	2.10	537	14.2
1978	2.05 (49%)*	776 (6,467%)*	12.5 (29%)*

*Percentage of 1940 values.
Source: Brooks, C.R. (1980) *Tar Heel Economist*, April.

Comparison of Prices and Price Spreads

The advantage of comparing the same industry across countries is that the price level at each stage in the production and marketing system can be related to market structure differences to identify market performance differences. Precise comparisons must depend on comparable quality at each point and comparable services and/or processing. This is somewhat easier in poultry than some other industries, but, with the rapid growth of further processing, it may also become more difficult. Other difficulties are fluctuations of currency exchange values and different price reporting procedures. Nevertheless, price levels indicate the degrees of efficiency and equity and the levels of market performance.

Chickens

Production and marketing charges for broilers and for eggs are compared for the 1980-85 period. Prices at both the producer and retail level were lower in the USA than in the three other countries that protect their markets from entry by outside competitors. Canada limits domestic production expansion by marketing quotas as well as imports. Producer prices there were 32 percent higher and retail prices 51 percent higher than in the USA. The result has also been a significantly higher retail price for Canadian broilers than for those in the FRG ($2.48/kg vs. $1.93/kg), where the EC has not limited Community production or intra-EC trade (Table 3a). Since 1960, the original EC-5 has increased broiler output about 500 percent (USDA). Switzerland manages price levels as well as import levels, resulting in producer prices being 110 percent and retail prices 79 percent above US levels. The marketing price spread in the USA was also the lowest at $.77/kg, while the FRG averaged only 4 cents per kg higher. Canada's, at $1.33/kg, was even higher than Switzerland's marketing charge (Table 3a).

Producer and retail prices would be expected to be lowest in the USA, as the leading exporting country. Switzerland would be expected to have the highest prices. With relatively free trade, however, the price difference among neighbouring countries such as the USA and Canada or the FRG and Switzerland would be small and probably not exceed 10 percent.

The existing market structure suggests that producers are being favoured in the three protected markets at the expense of consumers. Processor and/or marketing firms are also being favoured in the Canadian and Swiss methods of control. In the USA, on the other hand, producers have experienced some periods of low returns (Farris *et al.*, 1966).

Table 3a–Prices and Price Spreads for Broiler Chickens, 1980-85 Average

Country	Retail	Producer*	Producer-to-Retailer Price Spread	Producer's Share
	Dollars per kilogram, retail basis			*Percent*
USA	1.64	0.87	0.77	53
Canada	2.48	1.15	1.33	46
FRG	1.93	1.12	0.81	58
Switzerland	2.93	1.83	1.10	62

*Producer price multiplied by 1.333 to convert to a retail weight basis (except for Switzerland, where prices were quoted on retail weight).

Table 3b–Prices and Price Spreads for Eggs, 1980-85 Average

Country	Retail	Producer*	Producer-to-Retailer Price Spread	Producer's Share
	Dollars per kilogram, retail basis			*Percent*
USA	7.56	4.93	2.63	65
Canada	8.44	6.59	1.85	78
FRG	9.53	7.27	2.26	76
Switzerland	19.15	13.14	6.01	69

*1.03 times producer price for breakage, etc.

Sources: Calculated from USDA, *Livestock and Poultry Situation*; Agriculture Canada, *Market Commentary*; ZMP Bilanz 1983 and 1985; and Eiler and Gefluegel.

From these data, one cannot infer that processors and/or marketing firms in the FRG have been favoured substantially. Taxpayers, on the other hand, have had to support export subsidies from overproduction due to the domestic price support. On November 24, 1987, the intervention price for ready-to-cook broilers at the German border was $1,676 per ton, while the US broiler price was $954/ton. The EC import levy was $546/ton and EC export restitutions (subsidies) were $453/ton.

Eggs

As with broilers, the USA had the lowest egg prices for the 1980-85 period, as expected, while the producer and retail prices were significantly higher in the three protected markets. Producer prices were 34, 47, and 166 percent higher in Canada, the FRG, and Switzerland, respectively. Retail prices were not as high, at 12, 26, and 153 percent above the USA (Table 3b). With broilers and eggs in the FRG, however, producer and retail price premiums over the USA declined as the US dollar gained in value up to 1985.

Surprisingly, marketing margins for eggs were higher in the USA than in Canada and the FRG for the 6-year period, at $2.63 per 100 eggs. Whether this a measurement problem, where producer cooperatives in Canada and the FRG account for some of this difference with more marketing service, is not clear. The available data do not provide information on the cause of the higher US marketing margin.

The Swiss price levels are among the highest in the world for both eggs and broilers. In May 1987, retail prices of large eggs reported by the USDA in major capital cities were $3.84 per dozen in Bern, $3.37 in Stockholm, $1.36 in Bonn (the lowest of the five EC capitals listed), $0.74 in Ottawa, and $0.73 in Washington, D.C. Ottawa is generally one of the lower retail price markets for eggs in Canada, while this is not the case for Washington, D.C., with respect to the US egg market. Country average prices given previously show a

7-cent-per-dozen higher price in Canada, on average. The median for the 16 capital cities reported by the USDA was $1.27 or 74 percent above Washington, D.C., and Ottawa. The price pattern is clear. Switzerland and Sweden have the highest retail prices for eggs—even higher than Tokyo (because Japan has lower barriers on feed grain imports). The EC retail market is next highest among important poultry markets. These price levels relate directly to the degree of market protection.

Summary and Conclusions

International poultry market prices are badly distorted. Two different data sets were used to show this: (1) the standard country annual average time series of producer and retail prices for broiler chickens and eggs; and (2) the USDA's periodic survey of retail food prices in capital cities. Examination of government policies affecting market structure of four countries, namely the USA, Canada, FRG, and Switzerland, shows that market performance follows from the market structure as theory suggests. The US poultry industries represent purely competitive industries with open market structures that have no protection or subsidies (Table 4).

Table 4—Summary of Key Differences in Poultry Market Structure, Conduct, and Performance in Four Different Countries*

Country	Structure	Conduct	Performance
USA	No entry restrictions. No subsidies (except some retaliatory export subsidies). Processor oligopoly/ oligopsony. Demand increasing.	Price and output policies set by individual firms in response to national and international market prices.	Lower prices than most countries. Real poultry meat prices declined from 44 cents/lb in 1950 to 14 cents/lb in 1980 (in 1970 dollars).
Canada	National and regional marketing quotas. Import quotas.	Marketing boards set output policy and import quotas to protect domestic price.	Price of broilers 30-50 percent above USA prices. Egg prices higher by 34 percent at producer level and 12 percent at retail.
FRG	EC policy restricts non-EC imports with high variable levy. Grain costs high for same reason. Export subsidy disposes of surpluses.	Target price and import tariff maintain high domestic price. No output restrictions.	Broiler and egg prices at retail 18 and 26 percent above USA, at producer level 29 and 47 percent above.
Switzerland	High import tariff to protect high cost producers. Maximum of 12,000 head of poultry per farm.	Importer pays high tariff and must buy a certain percent of domestic supplies. Federal council sets guide prices.	Producer and retail prices two to three times USA.

*Other market structure variables such as industry concentration, rate of growth in demand, and degree of product differentiation are relatively minor in their impacts, compared to the differences in price levels caused by differences in government policy. Costs are influenced greatly by input prices and especially by policies that influence feed prices.

Producer prices for broilers in Canada, FRG, and Switzerland averaged 32, 29, and 110 percent higher, respectively, than those in the USA during 1980-85. At retail, they were 51, 18, and 79 percent higher, respectively. For eggs, producer prices were 34, 47, and 166 percent higher, and, at retail, they were 12, 26, and 153 percent higher, respectively.

Within-country market performance problems may exist, but these are generally small compared to those caused by restrictive trade policies. Most of the trade barriers have some elements of nontariff barriers that effectively limit imports. The EC problem is especially disruptive because not only is the EC a high-cost producer, but also protection has sharply increased output and resulted in export subsidies that generally depress the international market. As a result of widespread protection in high-cost markets, prices are enhanced in these markets and depressed in the lower cost markets. The reaction by the lower cost producers to the EC "dumping" has been to subsidize exports. The likelihood of multilateral trade improvements is slim, but even unilateral changes could improve market performance in poultry. The result would be improvement in equity and more efficient allocation of resource use. The market structure, conduct, and performance paradigm for each country is summarized in Table 4.

Note

[1]Department of Agricultural Economics and Department of Urban and Regional Planning, respectively, Texas A&M University.

References

Brozen, Y. (1969) "Is Government the Source of Monopoly?," *Intercollegiate Review*, Vol. 5, No. 2.

Farris, P.L., *et al.* (1966) *Organization and Competition in the Poultry and Egg Industries*, Technical Study No. 2, National Commission on Food Marketing, US Government Printing Office, Washington, D.C., USA.

Singleton, R.C. (1986) *Industrial Organization and Antitrust—Survey of Alternative Perspectives*, Publishing Horizons, Columbus, Ohio, USA.

USDA (US Department of Agriculture) (various issues) *Livestock and Poultry Situation*, Foreign Agricultural Circular, Foreign Agricultural Service, Washington, D.C., USA.

DISCUSSION OPENING—*Carol A. Goodloe* (Economic Research Service, US Department of Agriculture)

The basic question with which this paper is concerned is that public policy directly or indirectly influences market performance of an industry. The authors attempt to answer this question by comparing producer and retail prices across four countries for a six-year period. The conclusion of this comparison is that the more market-oriented policies of the USA have resulted in relatively lower producer and retail prices and that these lower prices are evidence of good market performance.

One cannot accept or reject this conclusion because the authors only define "market performance" in the context of US prices. The authors talk about "good" and "reduced" market performance, but these terms simply mean that prices in the other three countries are lower or higher than US prices. To equate low relative prices with a concept as broad as market performance is not justified by either economic theory or practice.

For example, producer prices for grains in Argentina are often below US and world prices, just as consumer prices for many basic staples in Romania are below comparable US and world prices. But would anyone want to cite the agricultural sectors of those two countries as evidence of good market performance? From whose perspective do low relative prices indicate good market performance? Canadian producers no doubt accept the relatively higher Canadian prices as evidence of good market performance, just as Canadian consumers reject the same evidence.

In several other respects, the paper promised more than it delivered. The authors state that they will provide evidence to "document that the poultry industries have performed well in efficiency, progressiveness, and innovation categories." They do provide data for the USA on prices received and feed and labour efficiency as evidence of efficiency gains. But no linkages are made between these data and progressiveness or innovation. Neither is progressiveness defined. Data are not provided for the other three countries, so one cannot draw conclusions about relative efficiency among the countries.

The authors also state that "performance is not as good in equity and efficient resource allocation where market entry is limited," but provide no empirical evidence for that statement. The authors say that "the goals of each of the four countries must be considered," but then fail to do so. An understanding of such public policy goals is crucial to understanding market performance of the three highly regulated poultry sectors of Canada, Switzerland, and the FRG. Assuming that the three countries did not leap from a free market system to a highly regulated system overnight, what were the reasons underlying the Government's action? Was the Government trying to correct for market failure in Canada? Did Switzerland adopt a system similar to the CAP to prevent its poultry farmers from moving to the FRG?

A last point concerns the authors' hypothesis that the USA, as a major exporter of poultry and feed grains, would have the lowest prices. This relationship simply does not hold because a country can achieve large exports through the use of subsidies; the EC is a good example of this for many commodities, including poultry.

In conclusion, this paper raises two basic questions: (1) how does one define market performance, and (2) how and from whose perspective—producers, consumers, or taxpayers—does one measure that performance? Although one can agree that US prices are lower than those in the other three countries, to draw conclusions about market performance based on price comparisons alone is not justified.

GENERAL DISCUSSION—*K. Sain, Rapporteur* (Bidhan Chandra Krishi Viswavidyalaya)

A comment was made that because of how different markets are affected by the existence of tariffs and producer quotas and the widely different extent of quality control, the performance of poultry industries in different situations are not strictly comparable. One participant stated that the extent of vertical integration and marketing efficiency was not adequately related to concentration and monopoly power. Another question was raised as to why the US poultry prices were taken as the basis for comparison to all other countries. One participant suggested that the extent of linkage between different market channels and production units might have been examined in more detail. Finally, a participant stated that the method adopted for ascertaining market performance was not optimal because of an inadequate database.

Participants in the discussion included U. Koester.

Normative Supply Response Analysis under Production Uncertainty: Irrigated Multicrop Farming Sector of Sudan

Rashid M. Hassan, B. D'Silva, and A. Hallam[1]

Abstract: Sudan's irrigated subsector is the largest in sub-Saharan Africa. Farming is practised under a scheme-mandated rotation with highly centralized decision making. Under this system, labour is the major input for which the tenant has allocation flexibility both during the season and across the three crops grown, sorghum, cotton, and groundnuts. This paper analyzes the risk attributes of the production technology and measures farmer's attitudes towards risk in the irrigation schemes of Sudan. Stochastic production functions are specified where risk increasing and risk reducing input effects are allowed. Single-equation and systems procedures are employed to estimate the parameters of the first two moments of the distribution of crop yields. The analysis supports the existence of aggregate indices for weeding and harvesting labour for cotton and sorghum, while the hypothesis of separability in hired and family labour is rejected. The form of labour contract for hired labour is found to have significant implications on its production risk effects. When hired labour is paid in cash, production risks increase, as is the case with cotton and sorghum. When sharecropping takes place, as in groundnuts, production risks decrease with increased labour use. Supply behaviour of the tenant farmers under production uncertainty is simulated using a farm programming model.

Introduction

In recent years, the main concern of policy makers in Sudan as well as in most developing countries has been the large external debt and food security. To enhance agricultural productivity and export earnings, emphasis has been placed on measures directed towards changing the structure of incentives to agricultural producers in order to promote adoption of new technologies and improved farming methods. While these methods and technologies raise yield levels, they also influence yield variability and production risks and hence have uncertain effects on the economic returns and welfare of the agricultural producers. Consequently, if farmers respond to risk, the rate of adoption and diffusion of new technologies in agriculture depends not only on their yield effects but also on their risk effects. Hence a comprehensive characterization of the risk attributes of the production technology and farmer attitudes towards risk is crucial to designing appropriate policy measures to bring about the desired adjustments in agricultural supply.

In this paper, a normative supply response model is developed to analyze supply decisions under production uncertainty in the multicrop farming system of the Rahad irrigation scheme in the Sudan. Stochastic production functions are specified where risk increasing as well as risk reducing input effects are allowed. Single equation methods as well as systems procedures are employed to estimate the parameters of the first two moments of the distribution of crop yields.

Various separability tests were performed on family, hired, weeding, and harvesting labour classes. The manner in which hired labour is paid is found to have significant implications on its risk effects. While hired labour increases production risks in cotton and sorghum (where cash wages are paid), it reduces production risk for groundnuts (where sharecropping prevails).

An average farm programming model is constructed to simulate supply behaviour of the Rahad tenants under production uncertainty. The generated response functions are found to be more elastic when factor inputs are allowed to influence production risks.

Production Uncertainty and Stochastic Technology

One way to represent random technology is by a conditional probability distribution function rather than a single function of output (Day, 1965; Anderson, 1973; Roumasset, 1976; and Antle, 1983):

(1) $F(Y/X, \beta)$.

Alternatively, a random disturbance term can be appended to a deterministic neoclassical production function to represent stochastic technology (the production function representation):

(2) $Y = f(X, \beta, \varepsilon)$.

Of major concern in incorporating error terms are the implications of alternative specifications of the stochastic component ε on econometric estimation of the mean function (Marschak and Andrews, 1944; Mundlak and Hock, 1965; and Zellner, Kmenta, and Dreze, 1966).

Part of the variability in crop yields is explained by controllable factors such as irrigation, fertilizers, improved seeds, cultivation methods, etc. (Day, 1965; Fuller, 1965; de Janvry, 1972; Just and Pope, 1978; and Pope and Kramer, 1979). If agricultural producers can influence production risks by varying the levels of input use, then factor demands under risk aversion are different from those under risk neutrality. A risk averter will use more (less) of the risk reducing (increasing) factor than the risk neutral firm (Pope and Kramer, 1979).

Various specifications have been used to represent stochastic technology. Just and Pope (1978) have shown that some popular formulations of stochastic production functions are very restrictive. The main deficiency of the common forms is the implication that all factors are risk increasing and thus are all used less under risk aversion (Ratti and Ullah, 1976; and Batra and Ullah, 1974). According to several reasonable risk considerations suggested by Just and Pope (1978), the log-linear and multiplicative disturbance forms are found lacking. An alternative, more flexible form is proposed by Just and Pope (1978):

(3) $Y = f(X, \beta) + h(x, \alpha)\varepsilon$.

Model *(3)* allows for separate effects of factor inputs (*X*) on the deterministic (*f*) and the stochastic (*h*) components of production. This formulation also allows for both risk increasing and risk reducing effects (e.g., $h' \gtreqless 0$). Model *(3)* is used in the present study.

A multistage nonlinear generalized least squares (MNGLS) procedure has been suggested to estimate the parameters β and α of model *(3)* (Just and Pope, 1978; and Griffiths and Anderson, 1982). The suggested procedure extends the error components approach of Hoch (1962), Wallace and Hussain (1969) and Fuller and Battese (1973) to nonlinear models with both firm and time disturbance components. The MNGLS is briefly outlined below.

For the model in *(3)*, let $E[\varepsilon] = 0$ and $V(\varepsilon) = \sigma$. Therefore, $E[Y] = f(x, \beta)$ and $V(Y) = h^2(x, \alpha)\sigma$. The MNGLS estimators of β and α are obtained with the following procedure:

(a) A consistent estimator for β is obtained in the first stage by nonlinear least squares (NLS) from the regression of Y on (x, β). A consistent estimator of $h(x,)$ is derived as:

(4) $\hat{U} = Y - f(x, \hat{\beta}) = h(x, \alpha)\varepsilon$.

(b) An NLS estimator of α is then obtained in the second stage from the regression of $\hat{U}^2$ on $\hat{h}^2(x, \alpha)$. The consistent estimator $\hat{\alpha}$ is then used to derive $h(x, \hat{\alpha})$.

(c) An NLS estimator of β is then obtained from the weighted regression of Y^* on $f^*(x, \beta)$, where:

(5) $(Y^*, f^*) = [\hat{h}(x, \hat{\alpha})]^{-1} [y, f(x, \beta)]$.

The estimator β obtained in (c) (the MNGLS) has been shown to be consistent, asymptotically efficient, and unbiased under a broad range of conditions (Just and Pope, 1978). The asymptotic efficiency of the MNGLS procedure has also been shown to hold when the disturbance term ε includes both cross-section as well as time-series components in Just and Pope (1978) and Griffiths and Anderson (1982).

While data generated by controlled experiments do not contain certain behavioural restrictions, survey data, on the other hand, represent optimal choices of the sampled firms. When working with survey data, input and output levels are assumed to be jointly determined in the first-order equations of the optimizing firm. According to Marshak and Andrews (1944), production function disturbances are transmitted to the system of first-order-condition equations of factor demands and output supply leading to endogeneity of input levels. Therefore, the application of the above described procedure could result in simultaneous equation bias in parameter estimates when survey data are employed. Hoch (1962), and Zellner, Kmenta, and Dreze (1966) have shown that production disturbances, which are unknown at the time of decision making, are not transmitted to factor-use equations when maximization of expected profits is assumed.

To allow for efficiency gains when known variance components are likely, the MNGLS procedure is modified to handle the simultaneity problem. The NLS estimator obtained in step (a) of the above procedure is replaced by an instrumental variable estimator. This is equivalent to the nonlinear two-stage least squares (N2SLS) procedure. The N2SLS yields consistent estimators of β, $f(x, \beta)$, and hence U in the step (a) (Amemiya, 1974; and Gallant and Jorgenson, 1979). In stage two (b), the heteroscedastic structure $h(x, \;)$ is estimated using the consistent N2SLS estimator of U obtained in (a). The consistent estimator of $h(x, \alpha)$ is then used in the third stage weighted N2SLS regression of Y^* on $f(x, \beta)$ to obtain the instrumental variable, multistage nonlinear GLS (IMNGLS) estimator of β.

With joint production assumed for the three crops modelled here, across-equation correlations are assumed to exist between the production disturbances in the three technology functions to be estimated. A system procedure is yet more efficient than the single-equation methods described above. A nonlinear simultaneous equation method that corrects for heteroscedasticity and cross-equation correlations is employed. This procedure is referred to here as the iterative nonlinear three-stage least squares (IN3SLS). The asymptotic properties of the nonlinear systems estimators are established in Barnett (1976), Amemiya (1977), Gallant (1977), Gallant and Jorgenson (1979), and Gallant (1987). Both the IMNGLS and the IN3SLS procedures are employed to estimate the technology parameters of the empirical model developed below.

Econometric Model

Cotton, groundnuts, and sorghum are grown in the Rahad scheme under regular irrigation and mechanical power. A fixed cropping pattern is imposed on the tenants. Levels of most of the production inputs are determined by the scheme administration (acreage, seed rates, and chemical and mechanical inputs). Thus, except for family and hired labour (working capital) allocations, other inputs are considered fixed for all farmers. Crop yields, however, are responsive to the quantity and quality of the labour and managerial resources under farmer control. Crop yield functions are thus specified to depend on labour allocations, managerial ability and skill, as well as sowing dates. Weeding and harvesting are identified to be the major activities that employ farmer resources.[2]

Three yield equations are specified to represent the multicrop production technology of the Rahad tenants. Flexible functional forms (the translog and the generalized power) are used in estimating the mean and variance of yield functions of model *(3)* and for testing for the technology structure. The unrestricted form of the functions has six factors: sowing date, years in farming, family and hired weeding labour, and family and hired harvesting labour. While sowing dates and years of farming are considered exogenous, weeding and harvesting family and hired labour are assumed endogenous. Sets of instrumental variables are constructed for each of the endogenous labour variables in each of the three yield equations. The set of instrumental variables include age, sex, farming years, education, distance between tenancies and homesteads, family size, average wage rates, sowing, weeding and harvesting dates overlap indices, labour recruitment methods, labour origin, etc.

Symmetry is imposed on the translog function ($\beta_{ij} = \beta_{ji}$). Other structural features are statistically tested using the unrestricted translog function proposed by Christensen *et al.* (1971):

$$(6)\ \ln Y_k = \ln \beta_{0k} + \sum_{i=1}^{N} \beta_{ik} \ln X_{ik} + \sum_{i=1}^{N} \sum_{j=1}^{N} \beta_{ij,k} \ln X_{ik} \ln X_{jk}.$$

Following Berndt and Christensen (1973), the following tests are performed on the translog function:

(a) **Homogeneity:** The function is homogeneous of degree r if and only if:

$$(7)\ \ln F(\lambda X_1, \ldots, \lambda X_n) = \ln F(X_1, \ldots, X_n) + r \ln \lambda.$$

Constant returns to scale ($r=1$), therefore, imply the following restrictions on the translog production function:

$$(8)\ \Sigma\, \beta_i = 1, \text{ and}$$

$$(9)\ \sum_i \beta_{ij} = \sum_j \beta_{ij} = 0 \text{ (zero row and column sums).}$$

(b) **Functional separability**: For inputs i and j to be separable from input k in the production function $F(X)$, the following must hold:

$$(10)\ F_j F_{jk} - F_j F_{ik} = 0,$$

where F_i and F_{ij} are the first and second derivatives of F.

The translog function condition *(10)* is satisfied with either of the following alternative restrictions (Berndt and Christensen, 1973):

(i) **Linear separability restrictions**: which reduces the translog to the logarithmic Cobb-Douglas function ($\delta_{ik}=\delta_{jk}=1$):

$$(11)\ \beta_{ij} = \beta_{jk} = 0.$$

(ii) **Nonlinear separability conditions**: which imply that $\delta_{ik} = \delta_{jk}$ but not necessarily equal to one:

$$(12)\ \beta_i = \beta_j - \beta_{ij} / \beta_{jj}, \text{ and}$$

$$(13)\ \beta_{ii} = \beta_{ij}^2 / \beta_{jj}.$$

The study tested for the existence of aggregate indices of the various labour services used by the production process.

(c) **Monotonicity and convexity**: These are tested for indirectly by evaluating F_i and the bordered Hessian at various data points.

The results of the various structural tests failed to support the hypothesis that family and hired labour provide homogeneous services in cotton and sorghum. Complete separability was accepted for groundnuts. The data supported the hypothesis that aggregate indices for weeding and harvesting labour services exist for cotton and sorghum. This result implies that wages paid to hired labour cannot be used as a proxy for the marginal value product of family labour.

Optimal sowing was found to reduce production risks significantly. Hired labour is risk increasing for cotton and sorghum. The reverse is true for groundnuts. A sound interpretation could be found in the form of labour contracts; e.g., the way hired labour is paid. While sharecropping arrangements dominate groundnuts production, cotton and sorghum hired labour are paid cash wages. Moreover, cotton and sorghum receive the highest attention and care from the farming family as they are the main food and cash crops for the household. Family labour is more skilful than hired labour in cotton and sorghum production.

Programming Model

An average farm programming model is constructed in this section to study the supply behaviour of agricultural producers in the scheme and estimate their risk preference parameters.

The two-moments (E-V) expected utility model is used to represent the risk preferences of producers (Markowitz, 1959). In this model, expected utility U is expressed as a quadratic function of the first two moments (mean $E[N]$ and variance $V(N)$) of the distribution of random economic returns N:

$$(14)\ U(N) = E[N] - [QV(N)]/2,$$

where Q is the Arrow-Pratt measure of *ARA*. Equation *(14)* is maximized subject to the technical, institutional and resource constraints defining the feasible set of the choice problem. The parameters of model *(3)* (β and α) represent the technology constraints of the system. Accordingly, expected net return $E[N]$ is a function of the parameters of the mean yield functions $f(x, \beta)$, crop areas A, and net returns per unit of output P:

$$(15)\ E[N] = A'R(x, \beta, P),$$

where A is a 3×1 vector of crop areas and R is a 3×1 vector of net returns per unit area. Similarly, the variance of net returns $V(N)$ is a function of the parameters of the variance of yield function $h(x, \alpha)$ for crop areas A and P:

$$(16)\ V(N) = A'V_R(X, \alpha, P)A,$$

where V is the 3×3 symmetric covariance matrix of net returns per unit of area. According to model *(3)*, the diagonal elements V_k (V_{ii}) are functions of the *X*s (variance of yield functions). The off-diagonals of V (the yield covariances V_{ij} for $i \neq j$) are, on the other hand, considered constants. The residual covariances of the IN3SLS econometric estimation of model *(3)* are used as consistent estimates for the yield covariances V_{ij} of V_k. The restricted forms of the generalized power yield functions are estimated for the three crops under study to be used in the programming model. Other resource constraints include labour and land constraints. Construction of the model parameters is discussed in detail in Hassan, D'Silva, and Hallam (1987).

The general interactive optimizer (GINO) is used to solve the model. Different solutions to the model are generated by varying the coefficient of *ARA (Q)*. Simulated solutions are compared to the actual farm plans. The value of Q that best simulates observed choices of the farmers was found to be 0.001. The same coefficient (0.001) was estimated by Hassan, D'Silva, and Hallam (forthcoming) for the dryland traditional farmers. *This implies that risk preferences of agricultural producers in the irrigated commercial agriculture and dryland subsistence farming are not significantly different.* Response functions are estimated for different behavioural and structural specifications to analyze the risk effects of factor inputs. The following scenarios are employed to represent different specifications of the model:

(a) **Risk Neutrality:** Q is assumed to be zero and thus the effects of factor inputs on the second moment of the distribution of returns do not affect farmer decisions.

(b) **Risk Aversion and Zero Risk Effects:** In this formulation of the model, Q is positive but farmer actions cannot influence production risks. In other words, the diagonal elements as well as the off-diagonals in the covariance matrix of net returns V are constant.

(c) **Risk Aversion and Nonzero Risk Effect:** Q is positive and factor inputs have nonzero risk effects. This implies that farmers are allowed to alter production risks by optimally choosing input levels; e.g., the diagonal elements of the V_k are functions of input levels X.

The risk averse firm was found to use more of the marginally risk-reducing factor (family labour in cotton and hired labour in groundnuts) than the risk neutral firm. The reverse is true for the risk-increasing factor (hired labour in cotton and family labour in groundnuts). Risk neutral firms, on the other hand, produce more and thus use more of all inputs than risk averters when zero risk effects are assumed. Demand for factor inputs is more elastic when their risk effects are taken into consideration.

Summary and Conclusions

The uncertain nature of farming and the important role of risk in supply decisions necessitate comprehensive characterization and measurement of the structure and risk attributes of the production technology as well as farmer risk attitudes. A normative supply response model was developed to study the supply behaviour of agricultural producers in the irrigated farms of Sudan under production uncertainty. Stochastic production functions were specified for the three crops grown. Risk-increasing as well as risk-reducing input effects were allowed in the stochastic representation. Single equation methods (IMNGLS) as well as systems procedures (IN3SLS) were employed to estimate the parameters of the first two moments of the distribution of crop yields. Significant efficiency gains were realized in parameter estimation when the heteroscedastic structure and the cross-equation correlation of production disturbances were taken into consideration.

Separability tests showed that family and hired labour perform distinct tasks and did not support their aggregation. The existence of aggregate indices for weeding and harvesting labour is supported. The way hired labour was paid influences its risk effects. Hired labour was found to increase production risks when sharecropping prevails in groundnut production. Family labour was found to be risk reducing in cotton and sorghum production.

An average farm programming model was constructed. The estimated mean and variance of yield functions were employed in the two-moment model of expected utility maximization. An average coefficient of ARA was estimated by the model to be 0.001. The same degree of risk aversion was estimated for Sudanese farmers using traditional production methods in rainfed areas (Hassan, D'Silva, and Hallam, 1988).

Supply responses of the average farmer are simulated under different behavioural and structural assumptions. As expected, risk averse farmers were found to demand more of the risk-decreasing factor than the risk-neutral firm. This fact, that the rate of adoption and diffusion of improved production technologies and farming methods is dependent not only on their effects on average yield levels but also on their risk effects, has policy implications. This points out the importance of studying the risk attributes of production technology to designing successful and effective agricultural development policies.

Notes

[1]Department of Economics, Iowa State University; Economic Research Service, US Department of Agriculture; and Department of Economics, Iowa State University; respectively.

[2]A detailed discussion of the Rahad farming system is found in D'Silva and Hassan (1987).

References

Amemiya, T. (1974) "Nonlinear Two-Stage Least-Squares Estimator," *Journal of Econometrics*, Vol. 2, No. 2, pp. 105-110.

Amemiya, T. (1977) "Maximum Likelihood and Non-Linear Three Stage Least Squares Estimator in the General Non-Linear Simultaneous Equations Model," *Econometrica*, Vol. 45, No. 4, pp. 955-968.

Anderson, J.R. (1973) "Sparse Data, Climatic Variability, and Yield Uncertainty in Response Analysis," *American Journal of Agricultural Economics*, Vol. 55, No. 1, pp. 77-82.

Antle, J. (1983) "Testing the Stochastic Structure of Production: Flexible Moment-Based Approach," *Journal of Business and Economic Statistics*, Vol. 1, No. 3, pp. 192-201.

Barnett, W.A. (1976) "Maximum Likelihood and the Iterative Aitken Estimation of Non-Linear Systems of Equations," *Journal of the American Statistical Association*, Vol. 71, No. 354, pp. 354-360.

Batra, R.N., and Ullah, A. (1974) "Competitive Firm and the Theory of Input Demand under Price Uncertainty," *Journal of Political Economy*, Vol. 82, No. 3, pp. 537-548.

Berndt, E.R., and Christensen, L.R. (1973) "Translog Function and the Substitution of Equipment, Structures, and Labor in U.S. Manufacturing, 1929-68," *Journal of Econometrics*, Vol. 1, No. 1, pp. 81-114.

Christensen, L.R., *et al.* (1971) "Conjugate Duality and the Transcendental Logarithmic Production Function," *Econometrica*, Vol. 39, No. 4, pp. 255-256.

Day, R.H. (1965) "Probability Distribution of Field Crops," *Journal of Farm Economics*, Vol. 47, No. 3, pp. 713-741.

de Janvry, A. (1972) "Generalized Power Production Function," *American Journal of Agricultural Economics*, Vol. 54, No. 2, pp. 234-237.

D'Silva, B., and Hassan, K. (1987) *Institutional Change, Incentive Effects, and Choice of Technology in Sudan's Irrigated Subsector*, Staff Report No. AGES-870922, Economic Research Service, US Department of Agriculture, Washington, D.C., USA.

Fuller, W.A. (1965) "Stochastic Fertilizer Production Functions for Continuous Corn," *Journal of Farm Economics*, Vol. 47, No. 1, pp. 105-119.

Fuller, W.A., and Battese, G.E. (1973) "Transformations for Estimation of Linear Models with Nested Error Structure," *Journal of the American Statistical Association*, Vol. 68, No. 343, pp. 626-636.

Gallant, A.R. (1977) "Three-Stage Least-Squares Estimation for a System of Simultaneous, Non-Linear, Implicit Equations," *Journal of Econometrics*, Vol. 5, No. 1, pp. 71-88.

Gallant, A.R. (1987) *Non-Linear Statistical Models*, John Wiley and Sons, New York, N.Y., USA.

Gallant, A.R., and Jorgenson, D.W. (1979) "Statistical Inference for a System of Simultaneous, Non-Linear, Implicit Equations," *Journal of Econometrics*, Vol. 11, Nos. 2-3, pp. 71-88.

Griffiths, W.E., and Anderson, J.R. (1982) "Using Time Series and Cross Section Data to Estimate a Function with Positive and Negative Marginal Risks," *Journal of the American Statistical Association*, Vol. 77, No. 379, pp. 529-536.

Hassan, R.M., D'Silva, B., and Hallam, A. (1987) *Supply Response Analysis under Production Uncertainty: Irrigated Multi-Crop Farming System of Sudan*, Policy Analysis of Sudan's Irrigated Sector Discussion Paper Series, No. 4, US Agency for International Development, Washington, D.C., USA.

Hassan, R.M., D'Silva, B., and Hallam, A. (forthcoming) "Testing for Decreasing Risk Aversion in Traditional Farming: Case of Sudan," *Cambridge Journal of Economics*.

Hoch, I. (1962) "Estimation of Production Function Parameters Combining Time-Series and Cross-Section Data," *Econometrica*, Vol. 30, No. 1, pp. 34-53.

Just, R.E., and Pope, R. (1978) "Stochastic Specification of Production Functions and Econometric Implications," *Journal of Econometrics*, Vol. 7, No. 1, pp. 67-86.

Markowitz, H.M. (1959) *Portfolio Selection: Efficient Diversification of Investments*, Cowels-Wiley, New York, N.Y., USA.

Marschak, J., and Andrews, W.H. (1944) "Random Simultaneous Equations and the Theory of Production," *Econometrica*, Vol. 12, Nos. 3-4, pp. 143-205.

Mundlak, Y., and Hoch, I. (1965) "Consequences of Alternative Specifications in Estimation of Cobb-Douglas Production Functions," *Econometrica*, Vol. 33, No. 4, pp. 814-828.

Pope, R., and Kramer, R. (1979) "Production Uncertainty and Factor Demands for the Competitive Firm," *Southern Economic Journal*, Vol. 46, No. 2, pp. 489-501.

Ratti, R., and Ullah, A. (1976) "Uncertainty in Production and the Competitive Firm." *Southern Economic Journal*, Vol. 42, No. 4, pp. 703-710.

Roumasset, J.A. (1976) *Rice and Risk: Decision Making among the Low Income Farmers*, North Holland, Amsterdam, Netherlands.

Wallace, T.D., and Hussain, A. (1969) "Use of Error Components Models in Combining Cross-Section with Time-Series Data," *Econometrica*, Vol. 37, No. 1, pp. 55-72.

Zellner, A., Kmenta, J., and Dreze, J. (1966) "Specification and Estimation of Cobb-Douglas Production Function Models," *Econometrica*, Vol. 34, No. 4, pp. 784-795.

DISCUSSION OPENING—*Joachim von Braun* (International Food Policy Research Institute)

Hassan, D'Silva, and Hallam examine the important issue of risk attributes of new production technology and farmer attitudes towards risk in the context of a scheme in Sudan's irrigated multicrop farming sector. Yield variability in three crops—sorghum, cotton, groundnuts—is the focus of the risk-related analysis. Special emphasis is placed on labour as much of other variable input use is considered predetermined, given the scheme production regulations for land use, water, seed, and fertilizer. Farmer deviations from production prescriptions, quite common under such conditions, are not evaluated.

The skillfully applied approach to evaluate some causes and farmer responses to yield variability deals with a subset of the risk issue. The role of new production technology as a (potential) cause of risk is, however, not isolated, because all sample farmers are inside the scheme and basically face the same technology options. A with/without new technology situation is not depicted. A descriptive account of the change from what to what technology that may have induced a shift in the production function would be desirable. According to the analysis, different skills, size of enterprise (degree of labour use), and level and timeliness of cropping practices determine yield variability in the expected way. One would like to know the length of the time period (crop seasons) of observation to which "variability" refers. Cross-sectional assessment of yield differences is certainly inappropriate if risk and risk response are to be evaluated.

The paper raises a number of interesting methodological issues. One relates to the yield functions: latent unobserved variables such as soil conditions (probably not so important in this case) and irrigation water/drainage conditions (probably important here) tend to determine factor use (labour) and yield levels. Detailed technical information is required to account for such relationships. If available, it should be used in the yield functions. Otherwise, labour productivity tends to be overestimated. If not available in the data set used, the results are to be interpreted with caution. I suggest two broader policy research issues related to *supply response* and to *risk* in irrigated agriculture for further discussion.

1. Supply response in irrigated agriculture cannot be assessed in isolation. Intra- and intersectoral relationships come into play. If irrigation schemes are surrounded by rainfed agriculture, the opportunity cost of labour changes with rainfall and supply of hired labour may accordingly change dramatically. In other environments, nonagricultural sector

employment may fluctuate and impinge on labour allocation to irrigated agriculture and thus yields.

2. Much of the production risk in irrigation schemes relates not to farm level technology problems but to management of schemes and to policy.

Year-to-year and seasonal labour use in irrigation schemes is much determined by labour's alternative employment opportunities. Where labour has the short-term option to move between irrigated and rainfed agriculture, good rains are bad for yields in irrigation schemes and vice versa. An irrigation scheme in West Africa observed through drought years and good years shows labour-input-related yield fluctuations between 6 t of paddy (drought years) and 3.5 t (years of good rainfall pulling labour into the upland crops). Obviously this yield variability is *not* reflecting a *risk* of the irrigation technology but is the result of efficient short-term factor reallocation. It is also relevant in drought-prone Sudan. The point is: supply response in a subset of agriculture—e.g., the irrigated sector—cannot be evaluated in isolation without considering the factor movements (i.e., labour) between the subsectors of agriculture and the rest of the rural economy.

Yield risk and production risk in irrigation schemes are induced by management problems (water and cultivation services) and input supply problems (fertilizer and seed). The individual farmers may be affected by such risks differently within supervised schemes. Location of fields and status of farmers impinge on the outcome of, for instance, who gets ploughing services on time, who gets fertilizer in sufficient quantities, or which pumps are operated if fuel is in short supply.

In the Sudanese schemes with area allotment by crop, an additional factor comes into play: the area allotment may change due to changing policy priorities. Foreign exchange needs and international competitiveness (cotton) and domestic food needs (sorghum) do change the area allotments. The irrigated food crop area, for instance, was substantially expanded as a consequence of the drought in Sudan in 1983-84. Thus the drought and policy in response to drought were transmitted into the irrigated subsector. Production patterns changed. Therefore, risk in the irrigation subsector is not only risk in yields of crops actually grown but also entails the risk of policy changes.

We have an interesting and stimulating paper here, but one would like to know more about the technical change actually assessed. Yield variability as such is not a measure of production risk and uncertainty. We need to know more about the nature of the data set we are looking at here (time series and seasons). Yield measures for changing cotton varieties in the state-ordered variety choices pose a problem of comparison.

Two broader policy research issues certainly deserve more attention. *Supply response* in irrigated agriculture cannot be comprehensively assessed in isolation. Relationships to other agricultural subsectors and nonagricultural sectors—where relevant—have to be explicitly included in the analysis. Production *risk* in irrigated agriculture relates closely to management failures of schemes and to policy changes in supervised agriculture as is the case in Sudanese irrigation schemes. Yield risk is only a subset of the risk story under these conditions.

GENERAL DISCUSSION—*K. Sain, Rapporteur* (Bidhan Chandra Krishi Viswavidyalaya)

Questions were raised about the coverage of different types of risk and uncertainty and the efficacy of the production-function analysis. Several types of functions related risk to different independent variables, both deterministic and stochastic, using rigid and unrealistic underlying assumptions.

Asked whether nonuse of hired labour was a problem in estimating the production function, the author replied that all farmers had to use hired labour.

Another question related to the possible inefficiency of the estimates of supply response due to the nonuse of time-series data.

Participants in the discussion included G.D. Thompson.

Intraregional Trade in West Africa

Mary E. Burfisher and Margaret B. Missiaen[1]

Abstract: Interest in intraregional trade within West Africa has been stimulated by debate on its potential to support broad economic growth and to enhance food security. This paper documents intraregional trade during 1970-82 among 18 West African countries, including estimated unrecorded trade. Analysis of trends in the size, composition, and flow of this trade indicate its continued importance and its vitality, as it changed rapidly in response to changing regional market conditions. Policies to promote intraregional trade need to consider product choice carefully. Efforts to achieve food security are not promising, since little complementarity exists in grain production. Some important sectors (in particular, cattle) cannot easily expand output. New industries, such as Ivorian processed foods, have the potential to achieve economies of scale and to supplant non-African suppliers due to lower transport costs. In general, any efforts to exploit the identifiable benefits of intraregional trade need to deal with the existing barriers to this trade, including tariff barriers, weak regional institutions, and nonconvertible currencies.

Introduction

Interest in intraregional trade within West Africa has been stimulated by debate on the potential for trade among LDCs to meet various political and economic objectives. Such trade may be more effective than world trade in general in stimulating broad economic growth. Trade among LDCs can be beneficial because: a wider array of export markets can help a developing country's comparative advantage evolve; product demand may be similar among the trading countries so that small countries can achieve economies of scale; export markets and products can be diversified; and alternative export markets among LDCs can be developed as economic growth and import demand in developed countries slows down (Belassa, 1979; Lewis, 1980; and Linder, 1961). Increased trade among LDCs is politically desirable, as evidenced by its prominence among the objectives of many regional groupings of LDCs, including the Economic Community of West African States (ECOWAS). Finally, intra-LDC trade has been explored as a means for achieving food security within regional groupings of LDCs (Koester, 1986).

Assessing the potential of West African trade to meet these objectives has been hampered by the sketchiness of information on trade patterns within the region. One purpose of this paper is to document intraregional trade during 1970-82 among the 18 developing countries of West Africa. Unrecorded trade, which accounts for about 40 percent of intraregional trade, is also estimated. Trends in the size of this trade and in its composition and flow, which changed rapidly during this period in response to changing supply and demand conditions in the region, are analyzed. Whether West African governments can or should direct policy towards promotion of intraregional trade is considered in the "Conclusions" section below.

Recorded and Unrecorded Intraregional Trade

A study of West African intraregional trade immediately confronts the problem of how to document it accurately, because a sizeable proportion is unrecorded by customs. Unrecorded trade is partly composed of smuggled, underinvoiced, and overinvoiced goods. But, in West Africa, it also results from the traditional nature of production and marketing systems for some of the region's most important traded commodities, notably live cattle. The limited administrative and statistical capabilities of some countries also result in poor or unavailable trade data.

Most of this study is based on officially recorded trade, using exporter data from UN trade tapes, supplemented with country trade statistics and various issues of FAO's *Trade Yearbook*. Two methods were used to estimate unrecorded trade. One source of information was *L'Économie Ouest Africaine*, published by the Banque Centrale des États de l'Afrique de l'Ouest (BCEAO), the central bank serving the monetary union among seven West African states and France. The BCEAO estimates unrecorded trade within the

BCEAO community based on assessments and, if necessary, a revaluation of officially reported export unit prices. The BCEAO also reconciles customs trade data with the distribution of Communauté Financière Africaine (CFA) currency within member countries. All CFA notes are tagged with member-country designations. For example, foreign CFA notes in circulation in excess of the amount reasonably warranted by official trade statistics would cause the BCEAO to revise upwards its estimates of that member's exports to other BCEAO countries (Haggblade, 1984).

A second basis for estimating unrecorded trade is to examine country trade data discrepancies between exporters and importers. The difference between the value of trade as reported by exporters and importers can occur for many reasons, but such a discrepancy is widely viewed as indicating illegal trade (e.g., Bhagwati, 1974).

Estimates of unrecorded trade cover only 10 of the 18 countries in West Africa. These countries, however, accounted for 95 percent of the recorded trade within the region during 1970-80. Some countries have an especially high proportion of unrecorded trade. For example, Benin's unrecorded exports accounted for nearly 80 percent of its total exports in the late 1970s. In contrast, unrecorded trade accounted for an average of only four percent of Ivory Coast's exports.

Intraregional trade among these West African countries was valued at $1,600 million in 1981, a more than sevenfold increase in nominal value since 1970. Unrecorded trade accounted for an average of 40 percent of the intraregional trade during 1970-82 and was valued at nearly $500 million annually in recent years (Table 1).

Table 1–Unrecorded and Recorded Regional Trade of Major West African Countries*

Year	Unrecorded Trade						Recorded Trade	Total Trade	Share of Trade Unrecorded
	Mali	Cameroon	Ghana	BCEAO†	Nigeria	Total			
	$1,000								Percent
1970	1,802	54	3,603	86,355	10,369	102,183	111,930	214,113	48
1971	1,780	153	2,559	128,820	12,678	145,990	142,228	288,218	51
1972	78	2,497	2,735	135,405	20,373	161,088	174,801	335,889	48
1973	5,369	624	3,712	140,118	18,240	168,063	229,070	397,133	42
1974	4,218	1,738	3,363	202,709	21,489	233,517	418,347	651,864	36
1975	1,449	846	2,174	268,200	21,447	294,116	555,828	849,944	35
1976	80	6,204	4,973	304,009	2,973	318,239	489,375	807,614	39
1977	17	3,121	7,365	506,329	11,924	528,756	682,800	1,211,556	44
1978	2,069	2,663	10,679	434,960	39,105	489,476	667,943	1,157,419	42
1979	--	10,006	6,906	472,800	53,481	543,193	755,205	1,298,398	42
1980	2,996	17,945	10,365	252,423	49,057	332,786	1,268,660	1,601,446	21
1981	--	--	8,652	446,160	72,973	527,785	1,113,739	1,641,524	32
1982	--	--	2,815	410,246	13,785	426,846	788,526	1,215,372	35

*Includes Benin, Burkina Faso, Cameroon, Ghana, Mali, Niger, Nigeria, Senegal, and Togo, accounting for 95 percent of regional trade during 1970-80.

†BCEAO members are Benin, Burkina Faso, Ivory Coast, Niger, Senegal, and Togo. Mali became a full member in 1984.

-- = not available.

Sources: BCEAO and UN trade tapes.

Major Intraregional Traders

Based on recorded trade data, intraregional trade is concentrated among less than half of the countries and became more concentrated during 1970-82. Nigeria, Ivory Coast, and Senegal are by far the top exporters in the region, accounting for about 50 percent of recorded intraregional exports in the early 1970s and 75 percent by the late 1970s. The livestock-exporting countries of Mali, Niger, and Burkina Faso also accounted for a large proportion of recorded intraregional trade. Togo held a brief role as a major exporter to other West African countries in the late 1970s when projects in its industrial development programme began production; by the early 1980s, many of Togo's projects had proved inefficient and began to fail. The leading regional exporters are also the region's major importers, for the most part.

Agricultural Trade

The region's five major agricultural exporters (Mali, Niger, Ivory Coast, Burkina Faso, and Senegal) accounted for about 90 percent of recorded intraregional agricultural trade during the 1970s. Burkina Faso, Mali, and Niger depended heavily on live cattle exports to the more affluent coastal countries. Ivory Coast and Senegal supplied a variety of agricultural products, including processed agricultural items, to a number of countries in the region. Ivory Coast, the region's leading agricultural exporter during most of the study period, doubled its market share from 15 percent to 30 percent during the 1970s. In the early 1970s, cola nuts and coffee accounted for 75 percent of its agricultural exports. Expansion of its market share was based on development of its agricultural processing industries, which enabled it to meet regional demand for food products such as bread, pasta, instant coffee, and dried soup. Ivory Coast replaced European or other suppliers for these products.

Ivory Coast's market expansion also rested on increased regional demand for its palm oil, as neighbouring countries changed from being exporters to importers of vegetable oil. In addition, Ivorian palm oil benefited from the region's substitution of more expensive oils, such as Senegal's groundnut oil, for cheaper palm oil.

Like Ivory Coast, Senegal has traditionally exported processed agricultural goods to other West African countries, but its share of intraregional agricultural trade declined slightly during 1970-82. In the early 1970s, its most valuable agricultural exports to neighbouring countries were cigarettes, groundnut oil, and wheat flour. Cigarette exports declined in importance, and wheat flour exports became insignificant as most West African countries built their own flour mills. Senegal's groundnut oil exports became uncompetitive with Ivorian palm oil exports to the region. As with Ivory Coast, Senegal's agricultural exports to the region became more diversified by the 1980s, to include animal feedstuffs, groundnut oil, fruits and vegetables, and cereal preparations (mostly pasta and bakery products).

Commodity Composition of Intraregional Trade

The role of agricultural commodities in intraregional trade fell sharply in the early 1970s, from 45 percent in 1970 to 22 percent in 1974. It remained at about 20 percent up to 1979 before declining slightly again in 1980-82. That trend is mostly explained by developments in the world petroleum market. Petroleum is the leading nonagricultural commodity in intraregional trade. Nigeria and Cameroon are producers and regional exporters of crude petroleum. Several West African coastal countries refine imported crude for reexport to neighbouring countries. The increase in quantity and unit price of intraregional trade in petroleum caused the relative importance of all other intraregionally traded commodities to decline. In absolute terms, intraregional agricultural trade performed well in West Africa during 1970-81. West Africa's intraregional trade grew faster than its trade with the rest of the world throughout 1970-81. Annual growth in intraregional exports during 1970-75 was only slightly higher than growth in West Africa's other markets, but, when Nigeria is excluded, the annual growth rate of West Africa's intraregional trade was 21 percent, nearly double the growth rate of West Africa's other trade. West Africa's export growth in both markets began to slow during 1976-81, but intraregional trade retained its edge.

Intraregional Livestock Trade

Livestock is the highest valued agricultural commodity in intraregional trade. In terms of cattle trade, West Africa can be characterized as an insular region, within which two groups exist. The Sahelian countries are the major producers and exporters, primarily because their vast land areas are marginal or unsuitable for crop production and because of the absence of the tsetse fly. The southward flow of cattle from the Sahel states is accounted for by the generally higher incomes in coastal countries.

Two factors have been particularly important in accounting for changed cattle trade patterns during 1970-82: drought and changing economic conditions, which shifted the distribution of import demand among the coastal consumption points. In addition, national policies (such as changes in export and import taxes) caused some apparent change in trade patterns as trade shifted between legal and illegal markets.

One way that prolonged drought has affected supply patterns is by causing changes in the areas suitable for traditional livestock rearing. In Mauritania, for example, export availability has fallen as meat production has declined. A second consequence of regional drought has been its effect in opening up the formerly secure Sahelian export markets to non-African suppliers. Volatile prices and disruption of Sahelian meat supplies to the coastal states following the 1973 drought prompted them to find new suppliers from outside the region and induced the development of infrastructure to handle chilled and frozen meat imports from Latin America and Europe. Despite the recovery of Sahelian meat exports, their market position is now more affected by their price competitiveness with non-African suppliers.

The most notable change in intraregional trade flows is the shift away from Ghana and towards Ivory Coast and Nigeria. Because its economy began to flounder and trade barriers were erected, Ghana's cattle imports were by 1984 only 2 percent of the 1970 level. Increased cattle imports by Ivory Coast reflect its relative prosperity within the region. However, since the 1973 Sahel drought, not much of its increased meat demand has been met from within the region. In 1970, live cattle imports, mainly from the Sahel, provided 84 percent of its beef supply. Imports from Europe and Latin America accounted for only about 3 percent of beef intake but jumped to 38 percent by 1976. In 1981, Ivory Coast imported prepared meats valued at $25 million, mainly from France, other EC members and Argentina. This dwarfed its Sahelian live animal imports, valued at $81,000.

Growth in Nigerian cattle imports during 1970-80 was driven by boom conditions in its economy, which raised the demand for meat. Unlike Ivory Coast, however, Nigerian meat import requirements were met mainly by Sahelian suppliers.

Intraregional Grain Trade

Recorded intraregional trade in maize, rice, and sorghum among the West African countries more than quadrupled to 18,000 tons during 1970-82. Nevertheless, it remained less than 1 percent of total imports of these commodities, which more than tripled to 2.6 million tons during the same period.

Although several West African countries exported small quantities of grain during the 1970s, all countries are net importers. A few countries are self-sufficient in a commodity and can export the surplus. These exports, however, are often financed by donors and not by the importing countries. Complementarity is difficult to achieve, since most of these countries are affected by drought in the same year. Rice is by far the most important imported grain in West Africa. Even though many West African countries produce rice, their high production costs make their rice noncompetitive with Asian suppliers.

Inefficient transport systems also increase West African grain prices. Transport networks are poorly developed and not set up to move grain from surplus to deficit regions. Also, most roads connect with ports, restricting grain movement in other directions.

Most West African countries attempt to restrict food exports to keep available supplies within the country. Information on production, stocks, and trade is so poor that most governments have no way of knowing whether domestic supplies are adequate. Differing tariff structures, quantitative import restrictions, and exchange controls discourage official transactions but may encourage unrecorded trade. Imports from suppliers outside the region are easier to arrange because of traditional ties and reliability of supplies.

Estimates of unrecorded grain trade do not exist. Grain is expected to move to high priced, hard currency countries from lower priced, soft currency countries. The situation is, however, much more complicated (see Map 1, below, where the arrows show grain movement under normal conditions). In the 1970s, despite a weak Ghanaian currency, little grain was sold in neighbouring countries because of high food prices in Ghana. Southern Nigeria imported rice and maize from Benin and Cameroon, while northern Nigeria exported sorghum to Niger. The Nigerian nairas earned in these exchanges were then used to purchase imported consumer goods and petroleum products that were subsidized by the overvalued naira.

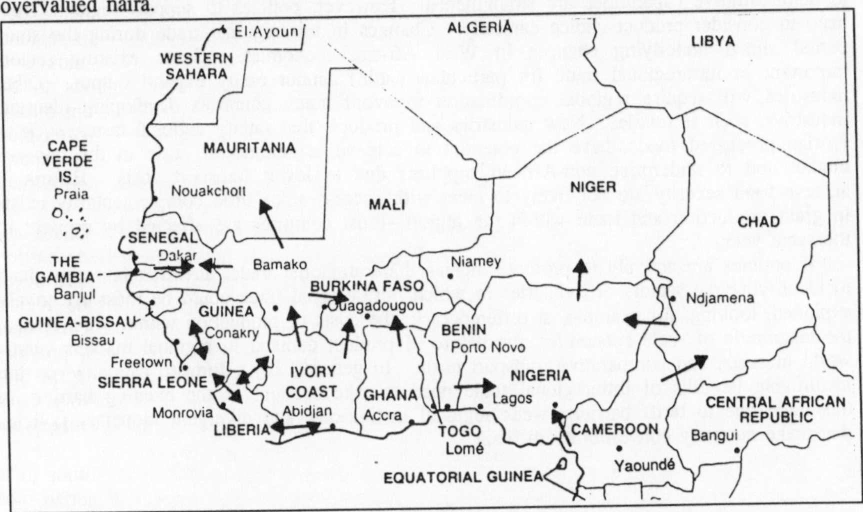

Map 1—Direction of Grain Flows among West African Countries

An analysis of producer grain prices converted to dollars at both the official and unofficial exchange rates gives an indication of the direction of grain flows. Even though sorghum prices were relatively high in Nigeria, converting sorghum prices to dollars at unofficial rates brings the prices below those in Niger in most years, helping to explain Nigerian sorghum exports to Niger. In the early 1980s, the high producer price for rice in Liberia combined with the attractiveness of its currency pegged to the US dollar, generated an inflow of rice from neighbouring Sierra Leone and Guinea and created severe financial problems for Liberia's swamped cereal purchasing agency.

Other agricultural commodities that are presently traded within the region, and which hold potential for expanded trade, are palm oil, raw cotton, and cotton textiles. Most countries in the region import palm oil. West African producers should be able to compete with other palm oil suppliers to the regional market because of lower transport costs, although production and processing costs tend to be higher.

Intraregional trade in textile yarn and fabric showed a growing complementarity among some West African countries. In particular, Ivory Coast's textile production is based on imported cotton yarns from Burkina Faso, Nigeria, and Senegal. In turn, Ivory Coast exports fabrics and other textile goods to Mali, Benin, Niger, Senegal, and Togo. Further development of the textile industry within the region is inhibited by the high producer prices for cotton, which increase the costs of local inputs for textile mills.

Conclusions

Trade among West African countries continues to be important, with recorded and unrecorded trade accounting for seven percent of their world exports in 1981. The favourable growth rate of West Africa's intraregional trade relative to other world trade is an indication that the intraregional trade can be an important economic stimulus. The changing composition and direction of intraregional agricultural trade during the study period show it to be quickly responsive to changing market conditions in West Africa.

Trade contributes to growth through its dynamic role in promoting the development and modernization of productive capacity. Policies may be used to promote intraregional trade as administrative capabilities are strengthened. However, policies to support regional trade need to consider product choice carefully. Changes in intraregional trade during the study period signal underlying changes in West African economies. Some existing sectors important in intraregional trade (in particular, cattle) cannot easily expand output. Other industries will require regional coordination to avoid many countries developing identical industries, such as textiles. New industries and products that satisfy regional tastes, such as Ivorian processed foods, have the potential to achieve economies of scale in the regional market and to underprice non-African suppliers due to lower transport costs. Efforts to achieve food security are not likely to meet with success since little complementarity exists in grain production and trade within the region—most countries are affected by drought in the same year.

If policies are actively to promote increased intraregional trade, attention must be given to identifying the sectors or industries in which intraregional trade could be most effectively exploited, looking, for example, at differences in the costs of production within West Africa, the magnitude of scale economies, the nature of product demand in regional markets versus world markets, and comparative transport costs. In general, any efforts to capitalize on the identifiable benefits of intraregional trade need to take account of the existing barriers to this trade due to tariff barriers, weak regional institutions, and divergent monetary policies that make currency convertibility difficult.

Note

[1]Economic Research Service, US Department of Agriculture.

References

Belassa, B. (1979) "Changing Pattern of Comparative Advantage in Manufactured Goods," *Review of Economics and Statistics*, Vol. 61, No. 2, pp. 259-266.

Bhagwati, J.N. (Ed.) (1974) *Illegal Transactions in International Trade*, North Holland, Amsterdam, Netherlands.

Haggblade, S. (1984) "Overview of Food Security in Upper Volta," report prepared for USAID/Upper Volta.

Koester, U. (1986) *Regional Cooperation to Improve Food Security in Southern and Eastern African Countries*, Research Report No. 53, International Food Policy Research Institute, Washington D.C., USA.

Lewis, W.A. (1980) "Slowing Down of the Engine of Growth," *American Economic Review*, Vol. 70, No. 4, pp. 555-564.

Linder, S.B. (1961) *Essay on Trade and Transformation*, Almquist and Wikesell, Stockholm, Sweden.

DISCUSSION OPENING—*Timothy J. Bembridge* (University of Fort Hare)

Intraregional trade is nearly always more important than "world trade in general." For example, EC and Canada-US trade are intraregional. Even the vast so-called "world trade" carried on in the newly industrialized countries in Southeast Asia is intraregional. Thus, the West Africa case is not unique.

Government policy should be restricted to encouraging cross-border trade by eliminating many of the artificial barriers to such trade. Many barriers were created in the postcolonial period and, with the exception of the market-oriented Ivory Coast, have discouraged economic development. Active government policy should be to provide information and promote a common market along the lines of the EC. A common currency could be an important foundation stone.

The authors are correct in emphasizing the unreliability of trade statistics. One only has to look at the errors and omissions in balance-of-payments statements in many countries. The paper provided an interesting method of estimating unrecorded trade data. However, the authors do not explain how trade data discrepancies relate to unrecorded trade. Exporters and importers are different economic agents, and any equality in values would be coincidental.

Figures on unrecorded trade for Benin and Ivory Coast are *prima facie* evidence of the free market of the latter country and the socialist policies of the former. When trade is unfettered and free, trade is recorded. It tends to go "underground" when tampered with by restrictions and/or higher taxes.

Nigeria, being the largest country in the region, is obviously going to be the largest exporter and importer, and its inclusion in any group of countries will substantially swell that group's trade figures. Any trade statistics of this nature should be on a ratio basis; e.g., exports as a percentage of GDP.

The low shares of recorded trade given in Table 1 are somewhat surprising. Clearly, no "value" or "currency" measurements are going to reveal bilateral or bartering deals.

The authors could have strengthened their interesting paper by including a discussion on the reasons for Ivory Coast's prosperous processing industries. They state that its market expansion was assisted by the demand for palm oil. Why didn't countries respond?

The authors have made a sound economic analysis of the composition of traded commodities. Whatever the disturbing implications for agriculture of that composition, I would point out that, if a poor country can sell oil and buy food, it may be economically better off. Kuwait is an example of this. Likewise, Japan imports food and sells high-technology products.

The section on livestock trade is a fascinating piece of applied economic theory. One major supplier dries up and new suppliers fill the vacuum. Can the Sahel recover those markets if conditions improve? As Ivory Coast's industries shift from primary to secondary production (processing), the relative affluence accompanying such change allows them to import such primary products as meat. Ghana's plight appears to be politically induced.

With regard to trade in grain, a commodity is not necessarily exported because of a surplus of that commodity. As with any transaction, more is gained from its sale than its value for internal consumption. The likelihood of a grain surplus in Africa is remote. The authors aptly describe the massive economic disruptions caused by government mismanagement and shifting practices. This situation is already well documented.

Policies to support regional trade should not be concerned with choice of products. The question arises as to who will make the choice. The track record of governments in West Africa in this regard is not a good one. The decision should rather be left to the people themselves. One has only to compare the history of cocoa production in Ivory Coast and Ghana, which clearly suggests the direction government policy should take. If we must have an active government policy, it should be directed at dismantling marketing boards, import licences, export controls, and other trade restrictions. In LDCs, according to some estimates, almost half of customs duties go into the hands of officials.

Finally, I do not believe one can plan the affairs of millions of heterogeneous individuals in a developing country context. One should rather get on with the task of assisting them to manage their own affairs by promoting unfettered free trade.

GENERAL DISCUSSION—*Jacques Brossier, Rapporteur* (Institut National de la Recherche Agronomique, Dijon)

The authors were asked if potential existed to increase intraregional trade. They replied that potential does exist, but the countries must reduce or eliminate customs barriers. During the drought, all the countries closed their frontiers. Also, the economies of the countries are not complementary.

One participant asked about the consequences of the end of the petrol boom in Nigeria. The authors replied that Nigeria has never been an agricultural exporter in West Africa, but, before and after the petrol boom, many commodities (e.g., sorghum and livestock) have been exported to Nigeria, where the prices are always the highest in the region.

A question was asked about how currency issues, including devaluations and the impact of the Communauté Financière Africaine, affected the countries in the region. The authors replied that the CFA countries should have more intracountry trade, but their economies are too similar. World prices probably have more of an impact on trade than currency devaluations in the region.

One participant commented that because the data were mainly in terms of volume, one could not see the influence of prices.

Participants in the discussion included S.K. Ehui, K. El-Kheshen, U. Koester, E. Tollens, and J.C. Wells.

Agricultural Competitiveness in an Interdependent World

Thomas L. Vollrath and De Huu Vo[1]

Abstract: The concept of competitiveness and its measurement are cast within a general equilibrium interdependent framework that juxtaposes home country with rest-of-the-world trade behaviour. The quantitative index constructed here, called "revealed competitiveness," is a useful indicator that can be readily applied to any aggregate commodity or specific sector. Here it is applied to total agriculture. Econometric analysis is used to identify the importance of government intervention and real economic factors affecting global agricultural competitiveness. Time-series and cross-section data covering 78 countries during 16- to 26-year periods provided the empirical basis for this study.

Introduction

Expansion of world trade beginning in the early 1970s dramatically increased both real economic welfare and economic interdependence among sovereign nations. However, many governments are currently under increasing pressure to erect protective trade barriers because of contraction in world demand. As a consequence, many individual exporters are confronted with potential market losses. More importantly, global prosperity is threatened because of the possibility that specialization in production and commodity exchange among countries will be reduced.

Given this global environment, considerable attention is understandably being focused on international competitiveness, a complex issue with many dimensions (Davis, 1987). In the present paper, the concept of competitiveness and its measurement are cast within a general equilibrium framework.[2] The measure, called "revealed competitiveness," is a useful indicator that can be readily applied to any aggregate commodity or specific sector.

Statistical measures of revealed competitiveness are applied to total agriculture. In addition, the underlying components of global competitiveness in agriculture are examined using econometric analyses that isolate important causal relationships among key factors affecting trade flows. This is helpful in ascertaining the relative importance of real economic factors and government intervention.

Competitiveness Index and Its Components

The following revealed agricultural competitiveness index (*RAC*) is posited:[3]

$$(1)\ RAC = \ln(RACS) - \ln(RACD),$$

where revealed agricultural comparative supply (*RACS*) is the ratio of the relative (home country to rest-of-the-world) agricultural export share ratio (*RAX*) to the relative nonagricultural export share (*RNX*); and revealed agricultural comparative demand (*RACD*) is the ratio of the relative agricultural import share ratio (*RAM*) to the relative nonagricultural import share (*RNM*).

The revealed competitiveness index is analogous to the concepts of comparative advantage and comparative disadvantage because both the statistical measure and the theoretical concepts embody a comparison between two trading entities (i.e., any home country and the rest of the world) as well as a comparison between two commodities (i.e., any traded commodity and all other traded goods and nonfactor services).

Equation *(1)* can be rewritten as a triple trade relative:

$$(2)\ RAC = \ln[(RAX/RNX)/(RAM/RNM)].$$

A positive value means that the home country reveals a competitive advantage in agriculture; a negative value means that the home country reveals a competitive disadvantage in agriculture.

Time series *RAC* estimates for the USA, Argentina, Japan, and South Korea are shown in Figure 1. Argentina and the USA are characterized by positive *RAC* coefficients, indicating that both countries have a competitive advantage in agriculture. By contrast, Japan and South Korea, two countries with relatively unfavourable factor endowments for agriculture, show negative and declining *RAC* trends. This shows that Japan and South Korea possess competitive disadvantages in agriculture that are intensifying with time.

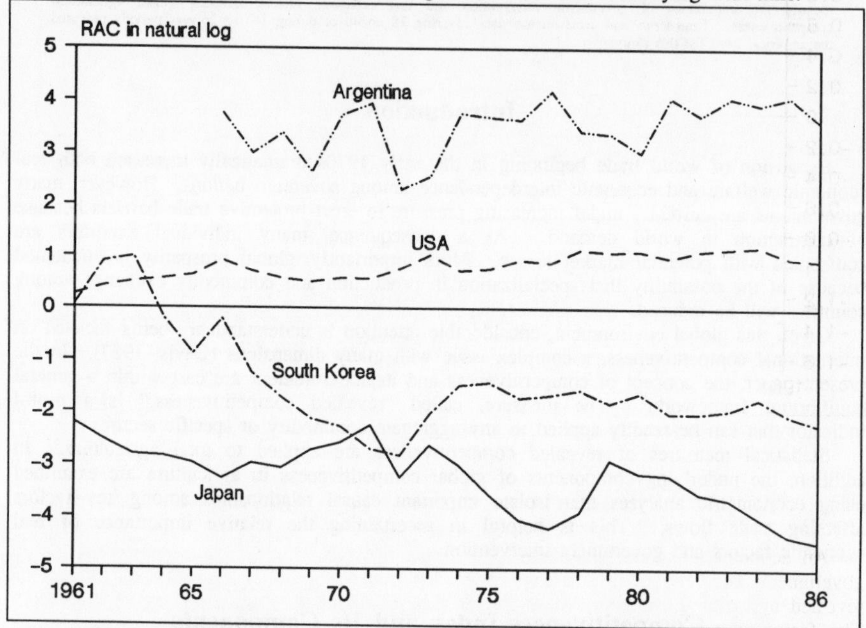

Figure 1—Revealed Agricultural Competitiveness: Argentina, Japan, South Korea, and the USA

RAC estimates for high-, middle-, and low-income country groupings show that between 1961 and 1986, the developing world has been more competitive in agriculture than the developed world (Figure 2).[4] But, the *RAC* gap between the developed and developing countries is narrowing. Since the late 1970s, the high-income countries have markedly increased their competitiveness in agriculture. By contrast, the developing world and the low income countries in particular have seen their agricultural competitive position severely eroded. The middle-income-country category displays a slight long-run decline in agricultural competitiveness. This is not surprising given the success of middle-income countries in exports of manufactured goods. Some might argue that deteriorating agricultural competitiveness in the low-income group is disturbing because agriculture is a leading growth sector in countries at this level of development and these developing countries should maintain both a comparative and competitive advantage in agriculture.

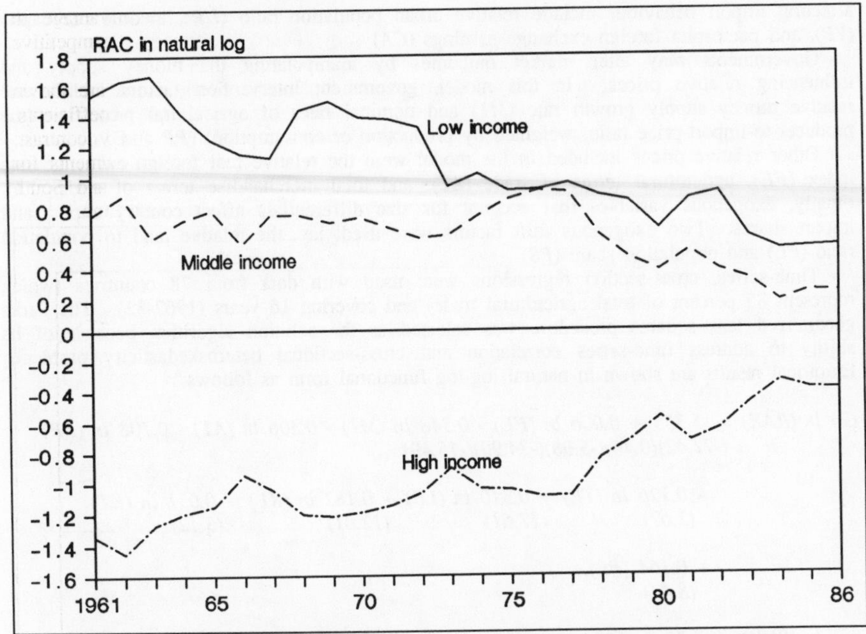

Figure 2—Revealed Agricultural Competitiveness: High-, Middle-, and Low-Income Countries

Structural Model and Its Elements

An econometric model was developed to identify the importance of real economic (*e*), government intervention (*g*), relative price (*p*), and exogenous (*z*) elements influencing revealed agricultural competitiveness and its four components, *RAX*, *RNX*, *RAM*, and *RNM*. The factors directly affecting these four components were independently regressed rather than regressing all the related determinants of agricultural competitiveness on *RAC* to mitigate simultaneity problems. The structural equations, using variables expressed in relative terms (i.e., home country with respect to the rest of the world), are specified as follows:[5]

$$(3)\ RAX = f[e(TP, LP, KL, KT); g(M1, PP); p(FE, AT); z(PL)],$$

$$(4)\ RNX = h[e(EP); g(M1); p(FE, TT); z(PS)],$$

$$(5)\ RAM = k[e(YP, CA, UR); g(M1, PC); p(FE, AT); z(PS)], \text{ and}$$

$$(6)\ RNM = l[e(YP, CA); g(M1); p(FE, TT); z(PS)].$$

Land and labour are primary economic determinants of agricultural trade because they are essential to the agricultural production process. Capital, a manufactured element, is not necessarily, however, a required input. It is, therefore, considered to "augment" the land and labour endowment. Real economic factors affecting export behaviour include relative land productivity (*TP*), agricultural labour productivity (*LP*), nonagricultural labour productivity (*EP*), agricultural labour-augmenting capital (tractor/labour ratio in agriculture) (*KL*), and land-augmenting capital (irrigation/cropland) (*KT*). Real economic factors affecting import behaviour include relative urban population ratio (*UR*), income per capita (*YP*), and per capita foreign exchange earnings (*CA*).

Governments may alter market outcomes by manipulating the money supply and influencing relative prices. In this model, government intervention factors include the relative money supply growth rate (*M1*) and nominal rates of agricultural protection (the producer-to-import-price ratio, weighted by production or consumption) (*PP* and *PC*).

Other relative prices included in the model were the relative real foreign exchange rate index (*FE*), agricultural terms of trade (*AT*), and total merchandise terms of trade (*TT*). Finally, exogenous variables that account for size differentials affect country export and import shares. Two exogenous shift factors were used; i.e., the relative land to population ratio (*PL*) and population share (*PS*).

Time-series, cross-section regressions were used with data from 78 countries (which represent 85 percent of total agricultural trade) and covering 16 years (1967-82). The Parks generalized least-squares procedure was selected as the solution algorithm because of its ability to address time-series correlation and cross-sectional heteroskedasticity problems. Empirical results are shown in natural log-log functional form as follows:[6]

$$(7)\ \ln(RAX) = \underset{(-72.42)}{-5.355} + \underset{(0.46)}{0.006}\ln(FE) - \underset{(-5.08)}{0.348}\ln(M1) - \underset{(-34.90)}{0.306}\ln(AT) - \underset{(-15.49)}{0.108}\ln(PP)$$

$$+ \underset{(2.67)}{0.126}\ln(TP) + \underset{(7.61)}{0.310}\ln(LP) + \underset{(12.01)}{0.182}\ln(KL) + \underset{(3.12)}{0.031}\ln(KT)$$

$$+ \underset{(8.44)}{0.164}(PL),$$

$$(8)\ \ln(RNX) = \underset{(-254.99)}{-5.32} + \underset{(1.68)}{0.033}\ln(FE) + \underset{(12.32)}{0.896}\ln(M1) - \underset{(-28.24)}{5.04}\ln(TT) + \underset{(76.23)}{1.726}\ln(EP)$$

$$+ \underset{(35.39)}{27.426}(PS),$$

$$(9)\ \ln(RAM) = \underset{(-271.93)}{-5.780} - \underset{(-9.05)}{0.105}\ln(FE) - \underset{(-15.58)}{1.300}\ln(M1) + \underset{(55.27)}{0.451}\ln(AT) + \underset{(4.01)}{0.025}\ln(PC)$$

$$+ \underset{(23.78)}{0.481}\ln(YP) + \underset{(6.33)}{0.098}\ln(CA) + \underset{(8.87)}{0.480}\ln(UR) + \underset{(11.92)}{30.763}(PS), \text{ and}$$

$$(10)\ \ln(RNM) = \underset{(-852.01)}{-5.318} - \underset{(-165.51)}{0.157}\ln(FE) - \underset{(-156.35)}{1.649}\ln(M1) + \underset{(181.09)}{0.377}\ln(TT)$$

$$+ \underset{(171.19)}{0.644}\ln(YP) + \underset{(230.56)}{0.296}\ln(CA) + \underset{(23.87)}{24.687}(PS).$$

Discussion about the economic implications of the empirical results are presented in three behaviourial categories: real economic factors, government intervention, and relative prices.

Real Economic Factors

The empirical results show that real economic factors explain trade behaviour in a manner consistent with trade theory. The relevance of Ricardo's concept of comparative costs is evident, given that relative labour and land productivity (*LP*, *TP*, and *EP*) are directly related to country export shares (*RAX* and *RNX*).

Positive *KL* and *KT* coefficients lend support to the Heckscher-Ohlin explanation of trade. The direct relationship between the intensity of capital usage and competitiveness in agriculture is consistent with the Heckscher-Ohlin factor proportion theorem.

In the *RAX* equation, the productivity of agricultural labour (*LP*) was found to be a more influential factor than land productivity (*TP*) in explaining agricultural export behaviour.[7] The differential in the *LP* and *TP* coefficients show that country agricultural export share was 2.5 times more responsive to changes in agricultural labour productivity than to changes in land productivity.

The responsiveness of *RAX* to increases in agricultural labour and land productivity are greater than its responsiveness to increases in capital-augmenting investments of tractors and irrigation.[8] This finding suggests that inputs other than machinery and irrigation (such as human capital, research and development, and infrastructure, which were not included in empirical model because of inadequate data) contribute significantly to export performance and, hence, to agricultural competitiveness.

The empirical estimates indicate that targeting capital to agricultural labour is more effective than targeting capital to land.[9] In other words, capital investments that substitute for agricultural labour generate higher agricultural export returns than do capital investments that substitute for land. This suggests that human capital is likely to enhance agricultural competitiveness more than infrastructural capital.

The significant import response to income growth underlines the limitation of supply-oriented explanations of trade. In both the *RAM* and *RNM* equations, per capita income (*YP*), a demand factor, was more responsive than all other independent variables, with the exception of changes in the money supply.[10] These findings indicate that consumers spend more of each additional dollar earned on nonagricultural imports than on agricultural imports.

The high *RAM* elasticity with respect to the relative urban population ratio (*UR*)—a proxy measure for development within the context of cross-sectional analysis—provides additional evidence that demand considerations influence trade patterns.[11] This indicates that rural-to-urban migration, which lowers domestic agricultural production because of a decline in the agricultural labour force, increases the demand for agricultural imports and reduces *RAC*.

Agricultural and nonagricultural import shares were relatively unresponsive to per capita foreign exchange earnings.[12] The estimated *CA* coefficients do, however, suggest that agricultural imports are "necessities" in comparison with nonagricultural imports, while nonagricultural imports are "luxuries" relative to agricultural imports.[13]

Government Intervention

An inverse relationship was hypothesized between agricultural export share (*RAX*) and the relative domestic-to-import-price ratio (*PP*) because the higher producer prices are relative to traded prices, the less internationally competitive countries are likely to be. Further, agricultural price protection policy (i.e., *PC*) was hypothesized to be positively related to agricultural import share (*RAM*) because consumers generally purchase commodities with lower prices, irrespective of their production origin. The empirical results confirmed both of these hypotheses.

Changes in the money supply growth rates affect exchange rates values. Unanticipated increases in the money supply induce a rise in the price of home country exchange rates; i.e., the home country's exchange rate decreases in value on the international market. Initially, domestic traders respond by increasing exports and decreasing imports of goods and services.

The initial exchange rate effects of changes in the money supply on current account transactions can, however, be offset by responses occurring on capital accounts. Increases in monetary supply growth lowers home country interest rates, inducing an outward flow of domestic capital and a smaller inward flow of foreign capital. The upshot of these capital movements is that the home country's currency increases in value in the international market. As a result, exports (imports) of goods and services become more (less) expensive to foreign (domestic) consumers, inducing a decrease (increase) of exports (imports) of real goods.

Parameter estimates for *M1* were, for the most part, consistent with the initial current-account-induced effects of unanticipated changes in domestic monetary growth.[14] The *RAX* elasticity with respect to *M1* was, however, negative. The capital-account-induced exchange rate effect of changes in the money supply may explain the asymmetrical *RAX* response with respect to *M1*. Other possible explanations include: (1) the fixed and quasiflexible exchange rate régimes in developing countries: (2) the relative importance of agricultural exports as a source of foreign exchange in developing countries; and (3) intervention policies in developed countries' agriculture.

The explanation that exports increase in response to unanticipated increases in the domestic money supply assumes that exchange rates are permitted to fluctuate. In the actual world, not all real-world exchange rates float freely. Exchange rates in many developing countries are either fixed or are tied to a basket of currencies, becoming only quasiflexible. When *nominal* exchange rates are not allowed to freely fluctuate, increases in the domestic money supply lower *real* exchange rates, increasing domestic prices relative to rest of the world prices. Commodity trade responds little at first because *nominal* exchange rates are fixed. However, a failure to devalue in response to domestic inflation causes *real* exchange rates to become overvalued. Overvalued rates discriminate against exports, encourage imports, and foster home country trade deficits and rest-of-the-world trade surpluses.

Another possible reason for the asymmetrical response is that agriculture is a relatively more (less) important source of foreign exchange earnings than nonagriculture in developing (developed) countries. The inelasticity of agricultural exports regarding the value of the home country exchange rate could cause a dominance of the inverse-versus-direct relationship between *M1* and *RAX* in the sample where the majority of observations are of developing countries.

Government intervention may provide yet another explanation for the negative *M1* coefficient in the *RAX* equation. Developed countries insulate their agricultural producers from income losses attributable to declining world commodity prices. Seldom do farm-gate prices move downwards because of official support prices. For example, export restitutions (subsidies) in the EC provide export outlet guarantees. The negative *M1*-induced exchange rate response in the *RAX* equation could, therefore, have been muted because of these income support policies.

The magnitude of the four estimated *M1* coefficients suggest that importers are more responsive to growth in the domestic money supply and, hence, to short-run price changes than are exporters.[15] This is not surprising since domestic changes in money supply growth rates has a more direct effect on domestic consumers (i.e., home country importers) than foreign consumers (i.e., importers of home country exports). Furthermore, domestic exporters are less price sensitive in the short run because of the long-run nature of establishing a market niche. For instance, customers need to be identified, contracts signed, goods transported, etc. By the time exporters are ready to respond, the capital-account-induced exchange rate effect becomes operative.

In addition, the estimated *M1* coefficients suggest that exporters of nonagricultural commodities respond more quickly to price changes than do exporters of agricultural commodities.[16] This is reasonable given the comparatively long-run nature of the agricultural production process. In addition, the decomposition analysis of *M1* on trade shares reinforces an earlier finding that agricultural imports are "necessities" in comparison with nonagricultural imports and that nonagricultural imports are "luxuries" in comparison with agricultural imports.[17]

Finally, the net effect of monetary growth on agricultural competitiveness was found to be negative. Taking the derivative of *RAC* with respect to *M1* indicates that a 1-percent increase in relative monetary growth decreases the home country's competitiveness in agriculture by 1.58.

Relative Prices

Negative relationships were expected between terms of trade (*AT* and *TT*) and export shares because a country's competitiveness ranking is believed to be low when export prices are high relative to import prices. In addition, positive relationships were envisioned between terms of trade and import shares because of the inverse relationship between import prices and import levels. The empirical results confirmed these two hypotheses and showed that the trade-share responsiveness to changes in the terms of trade is inelastic.

In the long run, money is neutral. Foreign exchange rates merely provide the means through which trade takes place as one currency is valued in terms of another. Movements in the long-run real foreign exchange rate should not, therefore, affect international trade behaviour.[18]

Indeed, the empirical results demonstrate that fluctuations in the relative (trade-weighted) real foreign exchange rate index (*FE*) do not affect changes in either agricultural or nonagricultural export shares (*RAX* and RNX). Furthermore, *FE* is a relatively unimportant determinant of agricultural and nonagricultural import shares.[19] This suggests that movements of real exchange rates do not significantly affect market shares because money eventually becomes neutral. Also, other determinants, most notably unanticipated growth in the relative money supply (*M1*), which affects foreign exchange rates in the short run, capture much of the variation in trade shares.

The *FE* coefficients show that importer behaviour, unlike export behaviour, was somewhat more sensitive to fluctuations in relative real foreign exchange rates.[20] In the event of adverse movements in the home country's *FE* (appreciation), exporters were, evidently, willing to cut profit margins in order to retain market share and to stay in business. Importers, on the other hand, tended to purchase commodities from the least costly supplier, be they foreign or domestic. In other words, when the home country's *FE* appreciates (depreciates), its consumers prefer foreign to domestic goods.

Conclusion

The analysis suggests that countries tend to export goods for which an underlying comparative advantage really exists. Country agricultural and nonagricultural export specialization patterns exhibit a certain inevitability. Real economic fundamentals are important. Relative productivity and factor endowments affect export behaviour more than policy instruments such as changes in the money supply or protectionist price policies.

On the other hand, the analysis shows that the real economic fundamentals underlying demand, such as relative per capita income, foreign exchange availability, and the structure of urbanization, are not as important as government intervention in shaping import behaviour.

An important implication for policy makers is that rather than become overly preoccupied with unfair trading practices of competitors, they should put more emphasis on opening up markets for their exportable commodities. International trade rewards the efficient producer. And the consumer also benefits through lower commodity prices. More attention and resources therefore need to be devoted to eliminating policies that prevent consumers from importing low-priced commodities.

Notes

[1]Economic Research Service, US Department of Agriculture.

[2]A relative measure of competitiveness was developed using the two-good, two-country neoclassical model of comparative advantage.

[3]The use of logarithms has the advantage of rendering estimates of relative trade shares symmetrical through the origin.

[4]High-, middle-, and low-income countries are defined, respectively, as having annual per capita incomes greater than $4,500, between $4,500 and $2,000, and less than $2,000 (using 1980-82 averages of GDP expressed in 1980 US dollars that were adjusted by purchasing power parities). The high-income countries include the following 18 countries: Australia, Austria, Belgium-Luxembourg, Canada, Denmark, Finland, France, Italy, Japan, Netherlands, New Zealand, Norway, Saudi Arabia, Sweden, Switzerland, UK, USA, and FRG. The following 21 countries comprise the middle income category: Algeria, Argentina, Brazil, Chile, Costa Rica, Greece, Republic of Ireland, Israel, Malaysia, Mexico, Panama, Portugal, RSA, South Korea, Spain, Syria, China (Taiwan only), Turkey, Uruguay, Venezuela, and Yugoslavia. The low income category includes the following 39 countries: Bangladesh, Bolivia, Burkina Faso, Cameroon, Colombia, Benin, Dominican Republic, Ecuador, Egypt, Ghana, Guyana, India, Indonesia, Ivory Coast, Jamaica, Kenya, Madagascar, Malawi, Mali, Mauritius, Morocco, Nicaragua, Niger, Nigeria, Pakistan, Paraguay, Peru, Philippines, Rwanda, Senegal, Sierra Leone, Sri Lanka, Sudan, Tanzania, Thailand, Togo, Tunisia, Zaire, and Zambia.

[5]All variables, except population share (*PS*), are expressed in relative terms.

[6]Figures in parentheses are *t*-values.

[7]Witness the 0.31 elasticity for relative agricultural labour efficiency and the 0.12 elasticity for relative agricultural land efficiency.

[8]The sum of the *RAX* elasticities with respect to *LP* and *TP* (0.44) was over twice the sum of the *RAX* elasticities with respect to *KL* and *KT* (0.21).

[9]Agricultural export share (*RAX*) was not only more responsive to changes in agricultural labour efficiency (*LP*) than to changes in land efficiency (*TP*), but it was also more responsive to changes in agricultural-labour-augmenting investment (*KL*) than to land-augmenting investment (*KT*).

[10]A 1-percent increase in the real per capita income ratio between the home country and the rest of the world induced a 0.48- and 0.64-percent increase in relative agricultural imports and relative nonagricultural imports, respectively.

[11]A strong positive relationship exists between urbanization and development level.

[12]The elasticities of *CA* with respect to *RAM* and *RNM* were 0.10 and 0.30 respectively, smaller than anticipated. A more complete measure for *CA* is likely to generate larger coefficients. The capacity to pay for imports depends not only on exports of goods and services in the current account but also on debt service payments. Unfortunately, information on country debt is often confidential. As debt service payment data were not readily available for all countries, they could not be used in this analysis.

[13]Nonagricultural import share (*RNM*) was found to be more responsive to fluctuations in per capita foreign exchange earnings (*CA*) than was agricultural imports (*RAM*). Given a decline in the availability of foreign exchange, country imports of nonagricultural commodities decrease more than agricultural imports.

[14]This is the case for the *RNX*, *RAM*, and *RNM* equations.

[15]Both the *RAM* and *RNM* elasticities with respect to *M1* were elastic, while the corresponding *RAX* and *RNX* elasticities were inelastic.

[16]Note that the *M1* elasticity for nonagricultural exports is greater than the *M1* elasticity for agricultural exports.

[17]Note also that the *M1* elasticity for nonagricultural imports is greater than the corresponding elasticity for agricultural imports.

[18]Dervis, de Melo, and Robinson (1982) argue that the real exchange rate has no role to play in traditional two-good models of exchange.

[19]The elasticity of *RAX* with respect to *FE* was not statistically significant. In other words, the null hypothesis that the foreign exchange rate coefficient is equal to zero could not be rejected. The *RNX* elasticity with respect to *FE* was, however, significant at the 90-percent level. But the estimated coefficient was 0.03, which is close to zero. The *FE* coefficients for *RAM* and *RNM*, though statistically significant, were small relative to the elasticity magnitudes of the other exogenous determinants.

[20]Even though the *FE* coefficients in the *RAM* and *RNM* import equations are small, they are greater in magnitude than those in the *RAX* and *RNX* export equations.

References

Davis, V. (Ed.) (1987) *U.S. Competitiveness in the World Wheat Market: Proceedings of a Research Conference, June 1986*, Staff Report No. AGES-860903, Economic Research Service, US Department of Agriculture, Washington, D.C., USA.

Dervis, K., de Melo, J., and Robinson, S. (1982) *General Equilibrium Models for Development Policy*, Cambridge University Press, Cambridge, UK.

DISCUSSION OPENING—*Shun-yi Shei* (Academia Sinica)

Vollrath and Vo's paper is an important piece of work. Conceptually, they developed a useful indicator, called "revealed competitiveness," which can be easily applied to measure a country's competitiveness in agricultural production and trade. Empirically, they examined the underlying determinants of competitiveness in agriculture using time-series and cross-section data and covering 78 countries during a 16-year period. The paper thus provides both theoretical and empirical contributions for the understanding of the sources of international agricultural competitiveness. I read their paper with great respect and congratulate the authors on their success in obtaining satisfactory quantitative results that are, in general, consistent with their prior expectations. However, since their paper involved many explanatory variables, they also produced several conflicting and unanswered questions.

The revealed comparative advantage index, initially developed by Belassa, has some undesirable properties. It may fail to serve either as a reliable cardinal or ordinal measure of a country's revealed comparative advantage. Key properties of the *RAC* concept developed in Vollrath and Vo's paper may also suffer from similar undesirable properties.

Figure 1 shows that the developing countries have been more competitive in agriculture than developed countries in the past 20 years. This does not agree with recent findings by Hayami.

The empirical study focused on measuring the accuracy of the *RAC* model. If it were shown that the model is accurate, then one could claim that the model is also useful in studies relating to structural adjustment or trade and development issues. In that limited sense, the hypothesis that the *RAC* is useful can be and is tested. Unfortunately the accuracy of the model, usually expressed by the R^2 or $\bar{R}^2$ and F test statistics, was not shown in their paper.

The more-developed countries, the developing countries, and the LDCs may reveal different patterns of comparative advantage. Their underlying determinants may not be the same. This is especially true in agriculture. We might thus gain some useful information if these three groups of countries were treated differently by using dummy variables and subjected to statistical tests.

The change in the market share on which the *RAC* is based depends both on changes in competitiveness of the exporting countries and on changes in the demand of the importing countries. The *RAX* equation included only the supply side of the comparative advantage and ignored the demand side by assuming that consumer preferences were internationally identical and homothetic. This implicit assumption seems too strong for agricultural products, especially if the stages of economic development among countries differ greatly.

The empirical results are informative and useful. However, the validity of these results is questionable due to a lack of theoretical foundation. For example, in the *RAX* equation, the authors claimed that positive coefficients for *KL* and *KT* lend support to the Hecksher-Ohlin explanation of trade. However, the empirical test of the theory should involve net exports, factor intensity, and factor abundance. One cannot, therefore, appropriately regress export share on factor intensity and infer factor abundance. A rigorous test would be the comparison of factor ratios in production, consumption, and trade.

The finding that fluctuations in the relative real foreign exchange rate index do not affect change in *RAX* is surprising. The real world would indicate the opposite result. I would rather explain this undesirable outcome as a consequence of bad luck or lack of patience to get the right sign.

The finding that country agricultural export shares were 2.5 times more responsive to changes in agricultural labour productivity than to changes in land productivity is interesting. Does this finding agree with prior thinking?

Why was the nominal variable (changes in the money supply) more responsive than the real variable (per capita income) in the *RAM* and *RNM* equations?

An important question before we seriously discuss the meaning and statistical and economic significance of the estimates is the sensitivity tests of the coefficients. How sensitive do these coefficients respond to model specification? Traditional regression techniques are not enough to deal with this estimation problem. A useful approach to the reliability and robustness issues of these coefficients should be based on Bayesian econometrics.

These are some of the minor points. Once again, I applaud the authors' success in identifying the sources of international comparative advantage in agriculture. This paper serves as a useful reference in studies relating to policy recommendations for the farm sector.

GENERAL DISCUSSION—*Jacques Brossier, Rapporteur* (Institut National de la Recherche Agronomique, Dijon)

A participant commented that LDCs have lost competitiveness. Do LDCs still have some comparative advantage? Another commented that the "revealed competitiveness" index was too aggregated and that he would like to see indices by sector and product.

Vollrath replied that the index is only for the agricultural sector. LDCs always have a comparative advantage for at least one product, but they tend to not want to exploit it when its in agriculture because that would imply that they are not developing their industrial sectors. The index is not a measure of comparative advantage but competitiveness with respect to supply and exports. The theoretical background of the index is not developed here. Nor are the tests used very accurate or rigorous.

Participants in the discussion included T. Takavarasha and J.C. Wells.

Everything You Ever Wanted to Know about Food Aid But Were Afraid to Ask

Truman P. Phillips and Daphne S. Taylor[1]

Abstract: Three food aid delivery systems are discussed. They illustrate the possible benefits and costs related to food aid activities. Case one is an example of anticipated food aid obligations, where commitments to food aid relief increase domestic production in the donor nation. Case two illustrates the situation where potential export markets are curtailed by a lack of foreign exchange, thereby leading to balance-of-payments support by the donor nation. Case three illustrates how food surpluses can be disposed of through food aid programmes. The Consultative Subcommittee on Surplus Disposal (CSSD) was established to ensure that normal commercial trade and recipient agricultural production were not adversely affected by food assistance programmes. The analysis reported on here reveals that the CSSD is clearly hampered in its attempts to fulfil its mandate, although it is still a necessary watchdog of food aid activities. The CSSD could be better used if the impact of food aid activities were better understood.

What Constitutes Food Aid

Most would agree that food aid should be defined as either the provision of food during time of emergencies or the planned and budgeted provision of food to overcome foreseen problems. Agricultural trade, on the other hand, implies the provision of food on a commercial basis. Concessional trade, which is often used by exporters to increase market shares or to dispose of agricultural surpluses, is not as easy to define and often lies in the "grey area" between food aid and agricultural trade. Exporters may, therefore, classify concessional trade as food aid, which may be disruptive to agricultural production and trade. This paper is an attempt to clarify some of the issues surrounding food aid and trade.

The provision of food aid to deficit countries is monitored by the Consultative Subcommittee on Surplus Disposal (CSSD),[2] while trade is governed by the provisions of GATT. According to CSSD principles, food shipments can be defined as food aid if the delivery mechanism corresponds to one of the 13 methods listed in the CSSD's Catalogue of Transactions, if the food aid does not diminish usual marketing requirements (UMRs), and if no formal complaints are made by recipient or third party nation(s).

UMRs, if specified, represent a level of imports that must be maintained by the recipient country while receiving food aid shipments. The UMR limit, which must be agreed to by the CSSD, is usually calculated by the supplying country. Normally, UMRs are based on the imports of the commodities to be covered by food aid for the preceding five years, adjusted to reflect the recipient nation's balance-of-payments position and general economic situation. Table 1 illustrates the amount and number of countries that had UMR commitments for the split years 1983/84 to 1986/87.

Table 1–UMRs by Commodity, Year, Number of Countries, and Amount*

Commodity	1983/84		1984/85		1985/86		1986/87	
	No.	*Tons*	*No.*	*Tons*	*No.*	*Tons*	*No.*	*Tons*
Wheat and flour	41	9,533,739	37	10,344,150	32	11,041,166	35	12,997,646
Rice	34	1,966,370	23	1,659,790	12	477,300	24	981,100
Coarse grains	12	581,200	12	1,812,700	9	585,530	4	298,800
Vegetable oil	10	1,485,000	12	1,779,606	15	1,730,494	11	1,924,948
Butter oil	18	37,659	16	45,007	13	35,787	20	55,865
Skim milk powder	35	274,283	31	267,878	27	251,538	31	301,875
Fish and fish products	3	16,600	4	17,600	3	15,800	2	21,300
Pulses			1	670				
Sugar					1	538,000		

*Source: FAO (1982, 1983, 1984, 1985a, and 1986a).

Although UMRs were established to protect commercial trade, they may act as an upper limit on commercial export markets because additional food requirements can be received as food aid. Any rational consumer would prefer to receive free food as opposed to purchasing food; UMRs thus do little to safeguard the potential increases of export markets to developing countries.

Since the CSSD is responsible for safeguarding the interests of both exporters and importers, it is the forum in which complaints of detrimental aid practices can be made and dealt with. This provision is, however, seldom used, since recipient countries generally do not complain and very few exporting countries wish to enter a round of disputes over the validity of their aid policies in developing countries.

As noted above, for food shipments to qualify as food aid they must correspond to one of the 13 methods outlined in the Catalogue of Transactions. Of the 13 methods, the least contentious are those that provide food for emergency relief or provide food aid to nongovernment and multilateral food organizations such as the World Food Programme. Likewise, targeted food aid (the provision of food to selected groups of people within the recipient country free or at subsidized prices) is normally not seen as interfering with commercial trade. These transactions clearly correspond to the simple definition of food aid presented at the outset of this paper.

However, the distinction between food aid and concessional trade becomes less clear for transactions that involve the provision of food or cash grants for general distribution in the recipient country. As can be seen in Figure 1, nonproject food aid is clearly the largest category in which food aid is transferred. In most instances this aid is "tied," requiring the recipient country to purchase food from the donor country. This aid can be further tied to a specific commodity or commodities.

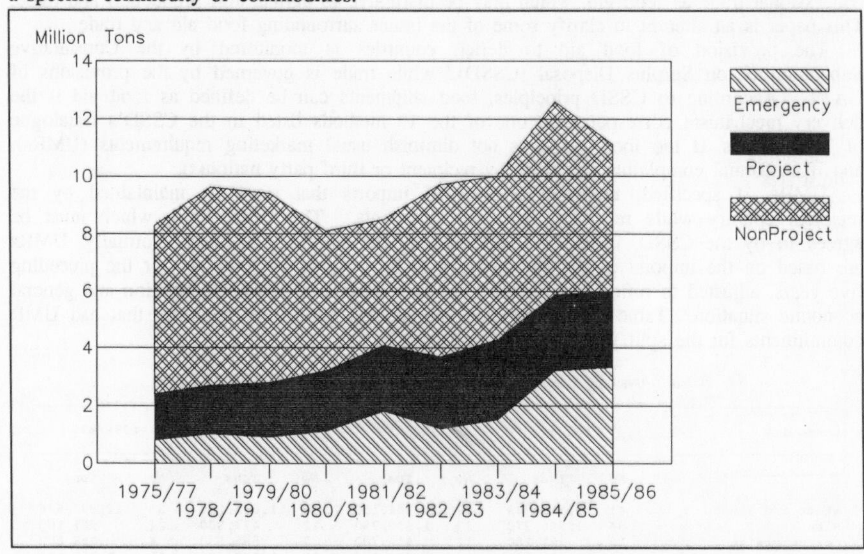

Figure 1—Cereal Food Aid Receipts by Main Categories of Use (Source: FAO, 1987, p. 100)

Nonproject food aid can be grouped into four general delivery systems. The first system[3] entails the gift of food, which is then sold through normal marketing channels in the recipient country. The recipient country is usually required to take all necessary measures to avoid reexportation of the gift commodity, its by-products, or similar products. Revenue generated from the sale of the gift commodity in the recipient nation must be used to assist its economic development. The second system entails the sale of food to the recipient country on concessional terms of credit. To comply with CSSD regulations, the repayment period must be greater than three years. The third delivery system entails giving the recipient country a cash grant, in the name of balance-of-payments support, which is then used to import food. Similar to the first system, the revenue from these food sales is often earmarked for development projects. The third system allows the recipient country to purchase food with nonconvertible currency. In all these cases, "normal" patterns of trade must not be altered; i.e., UMRs must be maintained.

Food shipments not complying to the CSSD's Catalogue of Transactions do not qualify as food aid and, therefore, fall under the purview of the GATT and may be subject to international retaliation. While the role of the CSSD is to safeguard normal commercial trade patterns and agricultural production, one cannot easily prove that concessional trade has disrupted normal trade conditions, given the relative magnitudes of commercial agricultural imports by developing countries to food aid ($683,000 million versus $2,900 million in 1984) (FAO, 1985b and 1986b). In addition, food can be provided on concessional terms with greater than three-year repayment periods but with the unwritten expectation that the recipient country will pay for the food in less than three years.

Thus, in spite of the CSSD's activities to define what constitutes food aid and how it may be delivered, numerous opportunities exist to use food aid as a means of enhancing markets and disposing of surplus food supplies while ignoring GATT regulations.

Impacts of Aid

To think of food aid as a generic concept that benefits only the recipient nation is simplistic and incorrect. Food aid can benefit producers in the donor countries as well as handicap producers in the recipient countries. The impacts of food aid depend on the relative supply and demand elasticities of each nation, the mechanism used to deliver food aid, and the ability of the recipient to absorb additional food supplies. Three food aid delivery systems are discussed below, illustrating the possible benefits and costs related to food aid activities. Case one is an example of anticipated food aid obligations, where commitments to food aid relief increase domestic production in the donor nation. Case two illustrates the situation where potential export markets are curtailed by a lack of foreign exchange, thereby leading to balance-of-payments support by the donor nation. Case three illustrates how food surpluses can be disposed of through food aid programmes.

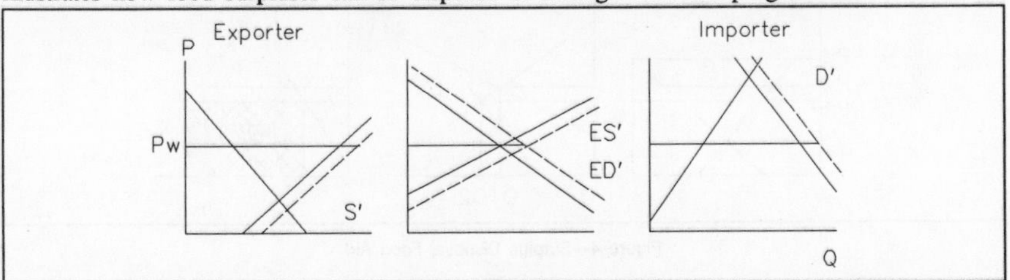

Figure 2—Humanitarian Food Aid

Figure 2 illustrates case 1, where food aid is provided to food deficit nations. In the long run, the donating countries shift their supply curve and hence the excess supply curve to *ES'* to the right (for example, by relaxing production restrictions) in response to anticipated food aid needs by an amount sufficient to allow the recipient countries to shift their demand curves to the right (excess demand curve to *ED'*) so that they are no longer consuming below an acceptable nutritional level. Assuming that both excess curves shift the same amount, world prices will not change. The government of the exporting country purchases the additional food that is produced and provides it to the recipient country as food aid. Producers in the donor country gain from the shift in their supply curves, while the consumers in the recipient country gain by the shift in their demand curves. The cost of these benefits is borne by the government of the donor country.

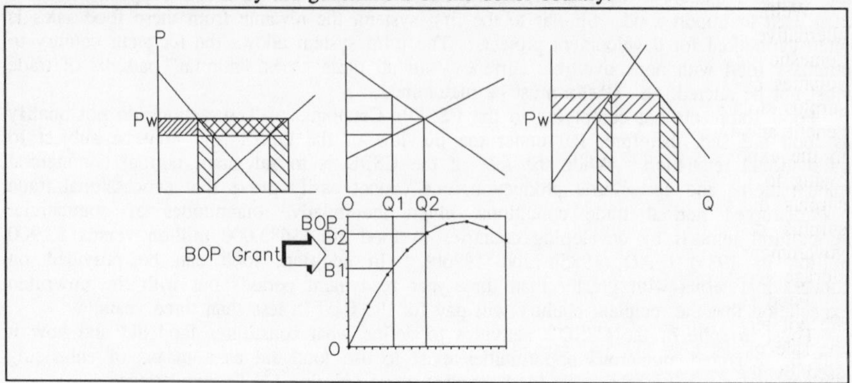

Figure 3—Balance-of-Payments Food Aid

Case 2, illustrated in Figure 3, represents the impact of balance-of-payments (BOP) support to a developing country. Prior to the BOP grant the importing country can only import *OQ1*, owing to the BOP constraint on food imports *OB1*, assuming a fixed exchange rate. After the provision of the BOP grant *B2-B1*, the importing country will be able to import *OQ2*. When this occurs, the consumers in the donor country and the producers in the recipient country will lose, while the producers in the exporting country and consumers in the recipient country will gain. The impacts on producers and consumers will depend on the relative supply and demand elasticities in both countries. If the donor country is large and the excess supply curve is elastic, the net welfare effects in the donor country will be small. If the recipient country is small, the net welfare effects may be relatively large, favouring either the producers or the consumers, depending on their relative elasticities. Again, the cost of food aid is borne by the donor country.

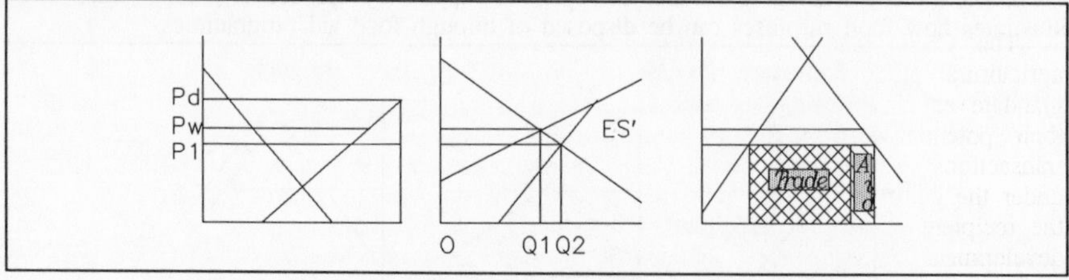

Figure 4—Surplus Disposal Food Aid

Case 3, illustrated in Figure 4, depicts how a donor country might dispose of surpluses through food aid programmes. The donor country is assumed to support a domestic price P_d above the world price P_w. This produces the kinked excess supply curve *ES'*. Theoretically, this reduces world price to *P1* and expands trade by *Q2-Q1*. If, however, the market will not clear at *P1* because of a lack of foreign exchange or unwillingness on the part of the importing country to absorb the surplus, the price in the exporting country will have to be further reduced for market clearing to take place at a volume acceptable to the importing country, creating a wedge similar to that created by import quotas. If this were to occur, the cost of the agricultural price support programmes in the exporting country would increase substantially to compensate producers for the difference between P_d and the low export clearing price. Faced with this situation, the exporter may chose to trade *OQ1* at the reduced world price *P1* and provide the amount *Q2-Q1* as aid. These food shipments may then be considered food aid if UMRs are maintained, even though the world price has been reduced.

Welfare effects from this type of surplus disposal programme can be compared in two alternative scenarios. The first scenario is the case described above, which allowed the domestic price in the exporting country to drop to a level that maintained previous trade volumes *OQ1*. The second scenario is a government storage programme where storage of surplus stocks would maintain a world price at P_w. In both of these instances, consumers benefit and producers lose in the recipient country, owing to a surplus disposal programme in the exporting country. Producer welfare in the exporting country remains unchanged, owing to the domestic support price P_d. Consumers in the exporting country gain if the surplus disposal programme replaces a government storage programme and lose if the surplus disposal programme replaces a lower export clearing price. The saving to government revenues from a surplus disposal programme depends on the relative costs of storage versus the costs of the deficiency payments.

Food shipments outlined in these three cases would qualify as food aid because UMRs are not reduced. In all three cases, the returns generated within the recipient country from the sale of the food aid may be collected as counterpart funds. These funds may then be used by the recipient governments to develop indigenous agriculture, with the intention of reducing food aid and imports. Alternatively, these funds could be invested in nonagricultural development, with the intention of reducing future food aid needs through increased food imports.

The preceding discussion illustrates the influence that food aid delivery systems can have on the welfare of producers and consumers in donor and recipient countries, reinforcing the conclusion that food aid cannot be treated as a generic concept. The preceding discussion also reveals that, in principle, food aid distorts natural marketing conditions. Even though these distortions may be difficult to measure, owing to the relatively small size of food aid donations, donor countries can benefit from the provision of food aid. The question that still remains is, "How does one prevent donor countries from seeking these benefits at the expense of recipient or competing exporting countries?"

Conclusions

The CSSD was established to ensure that normal commercial trade and recipient agricultural production were not adversely affected by food assistance programmes. This mandate entails safeguarding current levels of commercial agricultural exports as well as their potential growth in the future. The mandate also entails monitoring food aid transactions so that concessional trading arrangements do not undermine fair trade practices under the guise of food aid programmes. Finally, the CSSD's mandate requires monitoring the recipient country's agriculture to determine if food aid has been a disincentive to the development of indigenous commodity markets. This is often the most difficult task because it usually involves the estimation of the trade-offs between the possible development of indigenous products and markets and the use of food aid in existing markets.

The CSSD is clearly hampered in its attempts to fulfil its mandate. The current definition of UMRs is useful for maintaining historical commercial import levels but does little to promote export expansion.[4] The Catalogue of Transactions leaves numerous opportunities for exporting nations to practise concessional trading, which may undermine normal trading practices. Finally, the forum mechanism, which is used to check complaints of harmful disruption caused by food aid activities, is seldom used by exporters or recipient countries. Even if exporters do complain, the principles set out by the CSSD are not binding and represent only a commitment by signatory countries to consider the interests of recipient and other signatory countries when designing their food aid programmes.[5]

Although the CSSD may be limited in its ability to fulfil its mandate, the CSSD is still a necessary watchdog of food aid activities and could be better used if the impact of food aid activities were better understood. Further investigation by agricultural economists into the complexities surrounding food aid transactions could result in new mechanisms to safeguard recipient production and commercial trading patterns.

Notes

[1]Department of Agricultural Economics and Business, University of Guelph.

[2]The CSSD was established in 1954 as a subcommittee of the FAO Committee on Commodity Problems. CSSD's function is to examine, and regulate if necessary, the impact surplus disposal programmes have on commercial export patterns, world prices, and agricultural production and economic development within recipient countries.

[3]Note that the following descriptions capture the essence of permissible food aid transactions. For a detailed description of CSSD provisions, see FAO (1980, pp. 7-9).

[4]UMRs might be more useful if they were per-capita based and adjusted to reflect population growth and income changes.

[5]For example, the issue of whether "tied usual marketing requirements" (the obligation to continue usual commercial imports from the country supplying the commodities in the concessional transactions) can be considered food aid is still unresolved.

References

FAO (1980) *FAO Principles of Surplus Disposal and Consultative Obligations of Member Nations*, Rome, Italy.
FAO (1982) *Food Aid Bulletin*, No. 4, Rome, Italy.
FAO (1983) *Food Aid Bulletin*, No. 5, Rome, Italy.
FAO (1984) *Food Aid Bulletin*, No. 6, Rome, Italy.
FAO (1985a) *Food Aid Bulletin*, No. 7, Rome, Italy.
FAO (1985b) *Trade Yearbook 1985*, Rome, Italy.
FAO (1986a) *Food Aid Bulletin*, No. 8, Rome, Italy.
FAO (1986b) *Trade Yearbook 1986*, Rome, Italy.
FAO (1987) *Food Aid in Figures 1987*, No. 5, Rome, Italy.

DISCUSSION OPENING—*Robert D. Stevens* (Michigan State University)

Increasing our ability to analyze the impacts of food aid on different affected groups is important, as the authors point out, because food aid can have wider impacts than benefits to consumers in recipient nations. As the authors propose, better analysis tools could aid FAO's Consultative Subcommittee on Surplus Disposal to carry out its watchdog role to attempt to ensure that food aid does not have negative effects on other groups, including producers in recipient nations, food producers in donor nations, and producers and exporters in other nations.

Does the paper increase our analytical ability for these purposes? The analysis is weakened by two mistaken assumptions about food aid: first, that food aid is available from donor nations to fill any additional requirements of recipient nations not specified by UMRs; and, second, that food aid flows are of sufficient volume in the world market to influence world prices (Figures 2 and 3). Food aid represents about 5 percent of world trade in cereals and a much smaller proportion of world agricultural trade.

Three specific questions relating to the analysis follow. First, in case one, why will food aid shift the demand curve to the right in the recipient nation as indicated instead of decreasing prices? Additional supplies of food in a nation would usually depress prices unless the food were sold by the government and the funds from government sale of the food were used to pay wage labourers, whose increased food demand would maintain the prices. This is unlikely, however, as less than 100 percent of additional income will be spent for food.

Second, case two appears analytically the same as case one but is not sufficiently specified. In the recipient country, greater supplies of food could either benefit consumers through lower prices or benefit producers if internal prices could be maintained and the proceeds of government food sales channelled to development projects that increase farm income.

Third, in case three, concerned with what food disposal activities might benefit a donor nation, the conclusion was drawn that food disposal activities lead to consumer benefits in a donor country. Missing in the discussion was the cost of the disposal activities to consumers. The authors thus fail to prove that donor countries benefit financially from food aid.

In conclusion, three points: (1) the paper should have focused on the small-country case and assumed no appreciable effect on world market prices; (2) as the positive impact on consumers in the recipient country is clear, focus should have been placed on the effects on different groups of producers; and (3) a real issue is possible third-country market displacement by donor food aid. Finally, we should recognize that as aid always increases total world trade by increasing foreign exchange availability in recipient countries, third countries will usually obtain some benefit from food aid.

GENERAL DISCUSSION—*Jacques Brossier, Rapporteur* (Institut National de la Recherche Agronomique, Dijon)

One participant stated that the countries that give food aid seek a political advantage. The recipient countries, being LDCs, are in a difficult position in commercial transactions. Another participant commented that India had become dependent on food aid, and only with great difficulty did it get out of that situation. It is now a net exporter of food. A question was raised about the impact of 50 percent of total food not being for projects or emergencies. What are the implications of such a large amount of food aid (5 million tons) on output prices in the recipient countries, especially the small ones? A comment was made that all economic activities produce distortions, but food aid has positive as well as negative distortions.

The author agreed that food aid has negative effects, especially when it is in fact an implicit case of dumping (case three); i.e., why buy or produce if you can receive the food free? But, in this case, food aid limits the UMRs, so that one should follow up on the distribution of the aid in the country. The influence of changes in exchange rates was not studied.

Participants in the discussion included R. Deuson, H.S. Kehal, K. Korayem, and M. Schiff.

1988 Japanese Beef Market Access Agreement: Forecast Simulation Analysis

Thomas I. Wahl, Gary W. Williams, and Dermot J. Hayes[1]

Abstract: This paper uses dynamic simulation analysis to consider the likely consequences of the 1988 Japanese Beef Market Access Agreement (BMAA) on the Japanese livestock industry and beef imports. Using a simultaneous equations, econometric model of Japanese livestock markets, a forecast baseline up to 1997 was first established, assuming that the Japanese beef import quota continues to increase by 9,000 tons annually as under the 1984 agreement. The restrictions of the new agreement were then imposed on the model. The results lead to a number of conclusions. Beef imports will increase to the new quota level in the first three years and continue increasing at about the same rate thereafter. The shift from the import quota to the import tariff in 1991 will have little effect on imports or prices. The US share of increasing Japanese beef imports will increase at the expense of Australia and New Zealand. The effects of the BMAA on the Japanese beef industry will be significant but less than devastating. The pigmeat industry will also be affected. The chicken and fish industries will be little affected. Finally, the degree of responsiveness of Japanese cattle producers to the expected beef price decline will significantly affect the outcome.

Introduction

Following years of often heated negotiations with the USA and Australia, Japan recently agreed to a phased reduction of its longstanding restrictions on beef imports. The new agreement requires a substantial increase in the Japanese beef import quota for three years, followed by a switch to a declining import tariff over the subsequent three-year period. Japan has historically rejected calls for greater access to its beef market, allowing only relatively small increases in the import quota in an attempt both to appease US interests and to minimize the opposition of the politically powerful domestic cattle producers. This recent agreement, however, will significantly curtail Japanese intervention in its beef market over a number of years and force the Japanese cattle industry to adjust slowly to greater market determination of the supply of, demand for, and prices of beef.

The previous agreement, implemented in 1984, only required the Japanese to expand the import quota by 9,000 tons per year for four years, which would have brought the total import quota to 177,000 tons by early 1988. Despite a quota increase of 46,000 tons (37,000 tons above the negotiated level) in the last year of the agreement, the Japanese refused to consider additional increases when the agreement expired on March 31, 1988. Consequently, the USA, along with Australia and New Zealand, filed a complaint with the GATT on the Japanese beef import restrictions. Before GATT could take action, however, bilateral negotiations between the USA and Japan resulted in the signing of a new agreement in June 1988. Under the new agreement, the Japanese import quota will increase by 60,000 tons per year up to 1990 (the transition period), after which the quota system will be replaced with a temporary import tariff to be reduced from 70 percent in 1991 to 60 percent in 1992 and 50 percent in 1993 (the post-transition period). Additional safeguards for the Japanese allow for an additional 25-percent tariff in any year of the post-transition period in which beef imports increase by 20 percent over the previous year. Beginning in 1994, border measures on Japanese beef imports will be limited to those yet to be agreed upon in the ongoing Uruguay round of the multilateral trade negotiations.

Throughout the negotiations with Japan, US policy makers have implicitly assumed that an elimination of the quota will lead to increased imports of US beef. No guarantee exists, however, that imports will increase during the transition period or, at least, increase enough to reach the higher quota levels. During the post-transition period, the behaviour of imports will depend crucially on the price effects of the import tariff and the relative responsiveness of the domestic demand and supply of meat.

The Japanese, on the other hand, have assumed that beef import liberalization would devastate the domestic cattle industry. Although elimination of the restrictions on beef imports could be expected to put pressure on the domestic Japanese cattle industry as well as the domestic pig, poultry, and fish industries, the extent of the impact depends crucially on the degree to which imports increase, the response of cattle producers to the expected price effects, and the degree of substitutability among meats (including fish) in Japanese consumption.

The likely dynamic effects of the 1988 Japanese Beef Market Access Agreement (BMAA) on the Japanese meat industry and imports of beef over the agreement period up to 1997 are measured in this study using an annual, simultaneous equations, econometric simulation model of the Japanese livestock industry. First, some discussion of Japanese beef policy is provided as background. Next, the econometric model and analytical techniques used are briefly described, followed by a forecast simulation analysis of the effects of the new agreement. Finally, the paper concludes with some policy implications.

Japanese Beef Policy

A restrictive import quota has been the main tool of the Japanese government to support the domestic cattle industry and encourage beef production. Through the complicated import quota structure, the government attempts to maintain the established domestic beef target prices. Then, through a fine-tuning mechanism of purchasing and storing or releasing beef from stocks (the beef price stabilization scheme), the government stabilizes the domestic prices of beef around the targets within a politically and socially acceptable range (the upper and lower stabilization prices). As a consequence, Japanese domestic beef prices have tended to be higher and more stable than otherwise might have been the case. The rapidly increasing demand for beef in Japan has required the government to allow imports to increase at least in line with demand increases over time in order to keep prices from increasing significantly above the established price stabilization range. Under the new agreement, if the annual increases in the quota during the transition period are large enough compared to the annual growth in beef demand in Japan over that period, imports might not increase to the higher quota levels, and prices in Japan would fall towards world levels. As illustrated in Figure 1, an increase in the quota from OQ_m^* to OQ_m^1 would lead to a decline in the internal price of beef to P^1 and an increase in imports to the new quota level. An increase in the quota to OQ_m^2, however, would allow an increase in imports to only OQ_m^w, which is below the established quota level. The interaction of Japanese excess demand (*ED*) and the world net excess supply facing Japanese consumers (*ES*) would then determine the internal beef price level (P^w).[2] When the quota is dismantled and the import tariff is implemented in the post-transition period of the BMAA, beef imports could decline from the level attained by the end of the previous three-year period. If the tariff to be

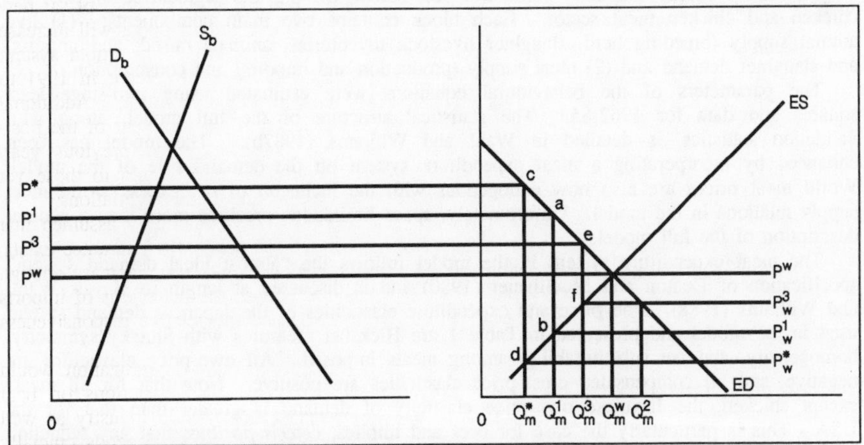

Figure 1—BMAA and Japanese Beef Imports

implemented is greater than the tariff equivalent of the quota (i.e., the percentage difference between the internal and world prices of beef), then imports will decline when the tariff is imposed. On the other hand, if the tariff is less than the tariff equivalent of the quota, imports will increase. Suppose, for example, that the quota has risen to OQ_m^1 (Figure 1) just before it is replaced by an *ad valorem* tariff of cd/dQ_m^*, which is greater than the tariff equivalent of the quota (ab/bQ_m^1). Imports would then decline from the quota level (OQ_m^1) to OQ_m^*. But if the tariff were less than the tariff equivalent of the quota at ef/fQ_m^3, for example, imports would increase to OQ_m^3. Thus, whether Japanese beef imports will increase or decrease in 1991 from the level achieved in the first three years of the BMAA depends largely on the tariff equivalent of the quota in 1990; i.e., the divergence of the internal and world prices of beef in that year. If the internal price is more than 70 percent above the world price of beef in 1990, then Japanese beef imports will increase in 1991. Otherwise, the imposition of the 70-percent tariff in 1991 could actually lead to a decline in imports.

Because the Japanese government has consistently intervened in the past to stabilize prices, price changes within the established range have not been considered by cattle producers to be signals of future price movements. Consequently, Japanese cattle inventories historically have been relatively unresponsive to price changes. If the price of cattle were lower than expected in any given year and producers believed that this was the result of an announced change in policy to reduce support to beef producers, however, producers would likely become more price responsive than was the case historically. This suggests that, given a change in policy, producer price expectations would be more affected by current price movements than would normally be the case. At the same time, the responsiveness of producers to the change in expectations would increase. Consequently, a realistic measure of Japanese cattle producer and, therefore, domestic beef supply response to a reduction in government support of domestic beef production over the agreement period must account for the likelihood of increased producer responsiveness to price movements in a changed policy environment.

Japanese Livestock Industry Model

The dynamic effects of the BMAA (1988-97) on the Japanese livestock industry are measured in this study using an annual, simultaneous equations, econometric model of the Japanese livestock industry. The 70-equation model contains three simultaneous blocks: the Wagyu (native breed) and dairy cattle and beef sector, the pig and pigmeat sector, and the chicken and chicken meat sector. Each block contains two main components: (1) live animal supply (breeding herd, slaughter livestock inventories, animals raised, and imports) and slaughter demand and (2) meat supply (production and imports) and consumption.

The parameters of the behavioural equations were estimated using two-stage least squares and data for 1962-85. The statistical structure of the full model, along with validation statistics, is detailed in Wahl and Williams (1987b). The model has been enhanced by incorporating a meat expenditure system on the demand side of the model. World meat prices are also now endogenous with the inclusion of net excess world meat supply relations in the model. Unfortunately, space limitations preclude more than a general description of the full model.

The meat expenditure system in the model follows the "almost ideal demand system" specification of Deaton and Muellbauer (1980) and is discussed at length in Hayes, Wahl, and Williams (1988). The price and expenditure elasticities of the Japanese demand system used in the model and presented in Table 1 are Hicksian measures with Slutsky symmetry, homogeneity, and net substitutability among meats imposed. All own-price elasticities are negative, and all compensated cross-price elasticities are positive. Note that for all meats except chicken, the Japanese own-price elasticity of demand is greater than that for the USA. This is particularly the case for beef and implies, *ceteris paribus*, that any reduction in the Japanese beef import barrier would lead to a large increase in the quantity demanded of import-quality beef.[3] The estimated expenditure elasticities indicate that both Wagyu and import-quality beef are luxury goods in Japan (Table 1). The expenditure elasticity of demand for import-quality beef is also slightly greater than that for Wagyu beef. This result is somewhat surprising because Wagyu beef is much more expensive than import-quality beef. Japanese consumers reportedly consider Wagyu beef to be a higher quality and more desirable commodity than imported beef (Miyazaki, 1986). Nevertheless, the share of consumer meat expenditures accounted for by import-quality beef more than doubled between the early 1960s and the mid-1980s while that of Wagyu beef was virtually constant over the same period (Wahl, Hayes, and Williams, 1987).

Table 1–Japanese and US Meat Demand and Expenditure Elasticities*

Price or	Wagyu	Beef†		Pigmeat		Chicken		Fish	
Expenditure	Japan	Japan	USA	Japan	USA	Japan	USA	Japan	USA
Wagyu	-2.06	0.32	--	0.23	--	0.05	--	0.06	--
Beef†	0.49	-1.00	-0.37	0.13	0.52	0.06	0.34	0.04	0.19
Pigmeat	0.95	0.36	0.27	-0.81	-0.67	0.06	0.24	0.20	0.16
Chicken	0.16	0.11	0.08	0.05	0.10	-0.21	-0.51	0.17	-0.12
Fish	0.47	0.20	0.02	0.39	0.04	0.04	-0.07	-0.31	-0.23
Expenditure	1.42	1.47	1.28	0.34	0.99	1.07	0.21	1.16	0.15

*US elasticities are from Chalfant (1987); all elasticities are Hicksian measures with Slutsky symmetry and homogeneity imposed; and net substitutability is also imposed for Japan.

†Import quality.

The estimated compensated cross-price elasticities suggest that Wagyu and import-quality beef are not highly substitutable. Hayes, Wahl, and Williams (1988) test and reject the hypothesis that Wagyu and import-quality beef are perfect substitutes. This result is of particular relevance for this analysis. The Japanese government has restricted beef imports in the past in order to protect the Wagyu beef industry. The implicit assumption underlying that policy has been that Wagyu and imported beef are near-perfect substitutes. This does not appear to be the case, however, so that any change in the level of beef imports will influence Wagyu beef demand only through the import-quality beef cross-price elasticity.

The expenditure elasticities for both poultry and fish are greater than the pigmeat expenditure elasticity for Japan, whereas the opposite is the case for the USA. The implication is that pigmeat occupies the same position in Japanese spending priorities as does poultry in the USA. Increased pigmeat consumption is not an automatic consequence of income growth, as is the case for beef. Increased pigmeat consumption in Japan is thus only likely to occur if pigmeat prices fall, regardless of changes in real income. The estimated elasticities of the fish expenditure share with respect to the prices of other meats are not significantly different from zero, suggesting little substitutability between fish and other meats in consumption.

Dynamic Forecast Simulation Analysis of the BMAA

To forecast the likely dynamic effects of the BMAA on Japanese beef imports and the Japanese livestock and meat industry, a forecast baseline was first established for 1988-97. The baseline assumes no change in Japanese beef policy over the forecast period; i.e., a continuing annual increase in the Japanese beef import quota of 9,000 tons as under the 1984-88 agreement up to the end of the forecast period.[4] Forecasts of the exogenous agricultural and macroeconomic variables in the model were based on the long-term international projections of the Food and Agricultural Policy Research Institute (1988) and the WEFA Group (1988).[5]

Producer Behaviour under the New Policy

The primary objective of the simulation analysis is to determine the likely effects of the new agreement on Japanese beef imports, the import shares of the USA and competing exporters, and domestic meat supplies, consumption, and prices in Japan over the next decade. What is likely to happen, however, depends crucially on how domestic beef producers will respond to the reduction in government price support. The typical analytical procedure would be simply to simulate the model over the forecast period, given the restrictions of the new agreement. The changes in the model variables from their baseline forecast values in the simultaneous system would be taken as a measure of the impact of the new agreement on the Japanese livestock industry. Lucas (1981), among others, however, has questioned this procedure because a policy change alters the underlying structure of a market. Thus, such a permanent shift in beef import policy would result in permanent changes in Japanese beef prices so that the price responsiveness of Japanese breeding herds, as estimated from historical data, would be inappropriate to use for the forecast simulation analysis. This is because producers would probably be more responsive to price changes under the changed policy environment than would otherwise be the case. As a consequence, the typical simulation analysis would tend to underestimate the effects of the new policy.

Based on a procedure suggested by Wahl and Williams (1987a), the estimated coefficients in the Wagyu and dairy cattle breeding inventory equations were altered to reflect an increase in both the coefficient of price expectations (θ) and the parameter for breeding herd size responsiveness to changes in price expectations (b), before simulating the implementation of the new policy.[6] The result is a more representative measure of cattle producers and, therefore, of domestic beef supply response to reduced support from the government. Unfortunately, the extent to which θ and b should be increased is unknown, so that any particular choice is arbitrary. The historically estimated values of θ and b represent the minimum likely responsiveness. The maximum feasible values of each are those that are consistent with the biological restrictions on the year-to-year growth in the Wagyu and dairy breeding herd sizes, given the price changes under the new policy. Given the extreme nature of the shift in policy in Japan from a slowly increasing import quota to a substantially liberalized beef market, the maximum levels of both θ and b would probably most nearly approximate the price responsiveness of domestic beef producers under the new policy. For purposes of comparison, two sets of simulations representing the historical producer price responsiveness (HIST) and the maximum feasible producer price responsiveness (MAX) are compared to the baseline forecast. The simulated changes in the values of the model variables in each scenario from their baseline values approximate the range of likely effects of the new agreement.

Simulation Results

The beef import quota was increased by 60,000 tons in each year of the transition period (1988-90), becoming the upper limit on beef imports in each year. If imports are below the quota level in any year of the transition period, the interaction of the domestic and world beef markets in the model determines the simulated internal price of beef as the world price plus a 25-percent tariff. Otherwise, the quota is binding, cutting the link between internal and world beef prices. In accordance with the agreement, the quota was replaced in 1991 by a 70-percent import tariff that declined to 60 percent in 1992 and 50 percent in 1993. If necessary, an additional 25-percent tariff is imposed in any year of the post-transition period in which imports increase by more than 20 percent, as stipulated in the agreement. The 50-percent tariff was assumed to hold for the 1994-97 period. Beef in government inventories at the end of 1987 as part of the price stabilization programme was assumed to be sold in 1988. Other Japanese farm programmes, such as milk price supports, were assumed to remain in effect over the simulation period.

Despite the significant increase in the level of the import quota under the BMAA during the transition period, the demand for beef is strong enough to push imports to the quota in each year during that period. When the tariff is implemented in 1991 and the quota eliminated, imports continue to increase to a peak of nearly 590,000 tons in 1993, about 50 percent above the last quota level in 1990 and over 100 percent above the baseline level under the MAX assumption. Even under the assumption of minimum producer price response (HIST), however, imports increase significantly as a result of the new policy. Imports from the USA and Australia both increase from 85,000 tons and 121,000 tons (carcass weight basis), respectively, to 264,000 tons and 324,000 tons. The USA gains slightly in import share from 39 percent in 1987 to 43 percent in 1997, while the Australian and New Zealand shares drop from 55 percent and 3 percent, respectively, to 53 percent and 1 percent.

The BMAA leads to a sharp reduction in beef prices in Japan. At the retail level, the price of beef drops by nearly 20 percent in the first year of the new policy. This occurs because not only do imports increase but also domestic beef supply increases to some extent as producers send Wagyu and dairy breeding stock to slaughter. Internal beef prices subsequently rebound to some extent, because the liquidation of breeding herds leads to a tighter supply situation in later years. The shift in 1991 to the 70-percent tariff has little effect on internal beef prices and, therefore, on the domestic supply and demand for beef. The tariff equivalent of the quota drops gradually from about 240 percent in 1987 to 137 percent in 1988, 97 percent in 1989, and 63 percent in 1990, under the MAX assumption. Consequently, the switch to a 70-percent import tariff in 1991 from the quota forces only a relatively mild increase in domestic prices.

In the baseline, the dairy industry continues in the liquidation phase of the dairy cattle cycle up to 1988. The dairy breeding herd begins to build again in 1989 and hits a peak in 1992, about 12 percent above the previous peak in 1985. The profitability of milk production continues to rise as the highly protective Japanese milk producer support policy maintains milk prices at a relatively high and increasing level. With the implementation of the BMAA, however, the drop in the domestic price of beef forces an immediate reduction of the dairy breeding herd, which has long-run implications. In essence, Japanese dairy beef producers recognize that beef prices will decline significantly in the future when the new policy is implemented and react accordingly. Consequently, dairy steer fatteners bear the burden of the reduction in the price of beef. Nevertheless, even under the assumption of maximum dairy producer responsiveness to the price drop, the dairy breeding herd declines by only about 22 percent between 1987 and 1990 before rebounding to some extent. Because 90 percent of the revenues of dairy calf producers come from milk production, the predicted increase in the profitability of milk production forestalls any larger impact from the reduction in the profitability of dairy steer fattening. By the end of the forecast period, the dairy herd is about 27 percent below the baseline as a result of the new policy. The effects of the new policy on the dairy industry are greatly underestimated if the change in the behaviour of dairy cattle producers to the changed policy environment is ignored. For example, the simulation of the policy effects using the historically estimated producer responsiveness to changes in expected prices (HIST) differs little from the baseline, underestimating the effects of the new policy on the Japanese dairy breeding herd by nearly 80 percent by the end of the agreement. The additional beef imports under the new policy would be unlikely to displace feed grain imports to any great extent, as the Japanese milk price support remains unaffected. As a corollary, a reduction in the very high protection afforded Japanese milk producers would probably do more to reduce domestic production of beef than is estimated to occur under the BMAA.

The BMAA affects the Wagyu industry in the model only through the estimated cross-price elasticity between import-quality and Wagyu beef. Because this elasticity is significantly larger than zero (Table 1), the simulated decline in the import-quality beef price as a result of the new policy has a significant impact on the Wagyu industry. Under the MAX assumption, the Wagyu steer carcass price drops by 15 percent in 1988 and is over 16 percent lower than the baseline, inducing a decline in the Wagyu breeding herd of about 23 percent in 1988. Consequently, Wagyu beef output initially increases as farmers reduce the size of their breeding herds, placing further downward pressure on Wagyu prices. After the initial declines, both the Wagyu breeding herd and the carcass price tend to rebound to some extent. A continuing consumer preference for Wagyu beef combined with declining supplies puts some upward pressure on prices and arrests the decline in Wagyu inventories and beef output. By the end of the forecast period, the Wagyu breeding herd is about 16 percent lower and Wagyu prices only 2 percent below what would otherwise have been the case. Again, the reductions in the Wagyu carcass price and, hence, in the Wagyu breeding herd are quite small if producers are assumed to be fairly unresponsive to price changes (i.e., the HIST assumption).

The effects of the change in Japanese beef import policy on the pig and chicken sectors are significant. Sow inventories under the MAX assumption, for example, drop to nearly 8 percent below the baseline by the end of the forecast period. Pigmeat prices drop by 14 percent in 1988 and are 5 percent below the baseline at the end of the period. Pigmeat consumption also drops over the period to about 8 percent below the baseline despite the drop in price because of the reduction in the production of pigmeat from the lower prices. Chicken and fish consumption are little affected by the new policy. Consequently, their shares of total meat expenditures increase along with that of import-quality beef, as the shares of both Wagyu beef and pigmeat decline.

Implications for Policy

Beef imports under the new agreement will increase to the quota level in each year of the transition period and continue increasing at about the same rate in the post-transition period. The internal demand for beef at the reduced price implied by the increasing quota is thus strong enough to absorb the additional beef output from a reduction in Japanese breeding herds and still push imports to the levels allowed by the quota.

The shift from the import quota to the tariff in 1991 will have little impact on imports, prices, or the domestic Japanese livestock industry. The tariff equivalent of the quota (i.e., the percentage difference between the internal and world prices of beef) drops gradually from about 240 percent in 1987 to 137 percent in 1988, 97 percent in 1989, and 63 percent in 1990. Consequently, the switch to a 70-percent import tariff in 1991 results in only a relatively mild increase in the domestic price of beef. This conclusion could be affected by any number of unanticipated exogenous events, including, for example, changes in US or Japanese macroeconomic policies affecting exchange rates, income growth rates, or the rate of inflation.

Exports of beef to Japan by both the USA and Australia will increase, with the USA gaining slightly in market share as a result of the BMAA. US exports are estimated to increase on average by about 26,000 tons or $132 million a year over the six years of the agreement. Gross revenues of the US beef industry are estimated to increase by about $795 million over the life of the agreement.

The effects of the new agreement on the domestic Japanese livestock industry will be significant but less than devastating. The dairy breeding herd could decline by as much as 22 percent as a result of the decline in profitability of dairy steer fattening. Any larger effect is unlikely because of the high level of price support provided to milk producers and the relatively small proportion of average dairy producer income that depends on dairy steer fattening. An agreement to reduce the milk price supports in Japan would probably have a greater impact on Japanese beef production than would any agreement simply to reduce support for beef producers. Wagyu beef is not highly substitutable for import-quality beef in Japan. Consequently, increased imports of beef under the new agreement will have a more limited impact on the Wagyu industry than on the dairy industry. By the end of the forecast period, for example, Wagyu beef output is only about 18 percent below the baseline, whereas that of dairy beef is nearly 30 percent below. Note that treating Wagyu and dairy beef as close substitutes would lead to an overestimation of the impact of the new agreement. Considering them as completely unrelated commodities, however, would lead to the equally erroneous conclusion that the new beef import agreement would have no impact on the Wagyu industry.

The degree of responsiveness of Japanese cattle producers to the expected beef price decline in the changed policy environment will significantly affect the outcome of the new agreement for the Japanese livestock industry. If Wagyu and dairy cattle producers are assumed to be no more responsive to expected price changes under the new agreement than they have been historically under a stable price environment, the BMAA would be expected to have little effect on the domestic cattle industry. Given the extreme nature of the shift in policy from a slowly increasing import quota to a substantially liberalized beef market in Japan, however, producers are likely to be quite responsive to the shift in policy. If producers are assumed to respond to price changes according to historical standards, the effects of the new policy on the dairy breeding herd, for example, could be underestimated by as much as 80 percent.

The new agreement will have a significant effect not only on the beef but also on the pigmeat industry in Japan. Pigmeat production, for example, could be as much as 8 percent lower than the baseline by 1993 as a result of the agreement. The chicken and fish industries will be little affected.

Finally, what happens after the agreement expires in 1993 will depend on the outcome of the current GATT negotiations. If negotiators agree to a further reduction in the Japanese import tariff, Japanese beef demand should be strong enough to cause further increases in Japanese beef imports.

Notes

[1]Department of Economics and Meat Export Research Center, Iowa State University.

[2]The BMAA allows for the continuation of the 25-percent import tariff in this case. Note that the upward sloping excess supply curve in Figure 1 implies the usual "large country" assumption in which the behaviour of Japanese beef producers and consumers affects world beef prices and markets.

[3]The term "import-quality beef" is used to refer to the aggregate of imported and domestic dairy beef.

[4]This assumes that the 37,000-ton increase in the quota above the negotiated level in 1987 was a one-off occurrence.

[5]The average annual growth rate of Japanese household income, a particularly important exogenous variable for this analysis, is about 3 percent above the forecast period.

[6]Space limitations preclude a detailed discussion of the procedure. See Wahl and Williams (1987a) for details.

References

Chalfant, J.A. (1987) "Globally Flexible, Almost Ideal Demand System," *Journal of Business and Economic Statistics*, Vol. 5, pp. 233-242.

Deaton, A., and Muellbauer, J. (1980) "Almost Ideal Demand System," *American Economic Review*, Vol. 70, pp. 312-326.

Food and Agricultural Policy Research Institute (1988) *Ten-Year International Agricultural Outlook*, Iowa State University, Ames, Iowa, USA.

Hayes, D.J., Wahl, T.I., and Williams, G.W. (1988) "Testing Restrictions on a Model of Japanese Meat Demand," selected paper presented at the annual meeting of the American Agricultural Economics Association, Knoxville, Tenn., USA, 31 July–3 August.

Lucas, R.E., Jr. (1981) *Studies in Business-Cycle Theory*, MIT Press, Cambridge, Mass., USA.

Miyazaki, A. (1986) "Production and Consumption of Beef in Japan," in *Research Opportunities in Beef Export Markets: United States and Pacific Rim Countries*, Proceedings of an International Symposium Sponsored by the W-177 Western Regional Beef Research Project and the Farm Foundation, Tucson, Ariz., USA, 19-20 Nov.

Wahl, T.I., Hayes, D.J., and Williams, G.W. (1987) *Japanese Beef Policy and GATT Negotiations: Analysis of Reducing Assistance to Beef Producers*, Staff Report No. 6-87, Meat Export Research Center, Iowa State University, Ames, Iowa, USA.

Wahl, T.I., and Williams, G.W. (1987a) *Consequences of the Japanese Beef Import Quota Concessions: Implications for Current Negotiations*, Staff Report No. 3-87, Meat Export Research Center, Iowa State University, Ames, Iowa, USA.

Wahl, T.I., and Williams, G.W. (1987b) *Japanese Livestock Industry Model: Second Generation*, Working Paper No. WP1-87, Meat Export Research Center, Iowa State University, Ames, Iowa, USA.

WEFA Group (1988) *World Economic Outlook*, Bala Cynwyd, Pa., USA.

DISCUSSION OPENING—*Toshio Kuroyanagi* (Hokkaido University)

In June 1988, the negotiations over Japan's programme for beef import liberalization were concluded between the USA and Japan. The agreement on the programme is as follows: (1) Japan shall increase beef imports by 85,714 t of dressed carcass every year from 1988 to 1990; (2) after 1991, Japan will liberalize beef imports; and (3) the rate of duties on imported beef prices will be gradually decreased; i.e., 70 percent in 1991, 60 percent in 1992, and 50 percent in 1993.

In Japan, results of simulation analyses on import beef liberalization were made by Keiji Ohga and Shigemasa Matsubara of the Ministry of Agriculture, Forestry and Fishery. The simulation analysis by Ohga is based on the Japan-USA agreement on beef import liberalization mentioned above. Other assumptions are as follows: case 1 is without deficiency payments for calves; in case 2, the deficiency payment is the difference between ¥300,000 and the average market price per Wagyu calf, and the difference between ¥160,000 and the average market price per dairy calf. The exchange rate is ¥125/$1. The rate of increase in population is 0.7 percent and that in annual expenditure on personal consumption is 2.7 percent. The beef import price is $3.20/kg of dressed carcass f.o.b., and the freight is $0.40/kg. The study by Wahl *et al.* differs from that by Ohga in terms of assumptions for simulation methods. However, the two studies agree roughly concerning the assumption that the PSE will be reduced to zero by 1997.

Japan's situation on consumption of beef is as follows: (1) consumption of beef per capita in 1985 was 4.4 kg, about one-sixth of the level in Europe and America; (2) in 1985, the ratio of demand for beef to total meat was 18 percent, being expected to increase, while that for pigmeat was 42 percent and for chicken 34 percent; (3) beef production costs for Wagyu steers in 1983 were about three times those for US steers, and those for dairy steers were about double.

A point of the simulation analysis on import beef liberalization common to Wahl and Ohga is that their assumptions for simulation agree roughly. Namely, reduction of producer price support results in an increase in beef imports, substitution of dairy beef for Wagyu beef, and lower prices of both types of beef. The Ohga model shows that the deficiency payment for beef increases the production of both Wagyu and dairy beef, and this fact further increases the deficiency payment. On the other hand, Wahl's paper shows that dairy beef production increases due to the government support to dairy farming, while Wagyu beef decreases. Accordingly, abolition of this support leads to a great decrease in total beef production compared with reduction of support for beef production, except dairy farming, because dairy beef is mainly produced in Japan.

In this way, the reduction of support to beef cattle producers has a great influence on dairy farming, because dairy beef forms 70 percent of Japan's beef production. Even among dairy farmers, the decrease in newborn calf prices results in an economic loss to stock feeders and a gain to growing and finishing farmers.

Following the beef import liberalization, bipolarization on Japan's market occurs between the increase in calf prices of high-quality Wagyu steers and the decrease in calf prices of middle-class Wagyu steers and dairy steers. Moreover, consumers will react to the standard to prevent agricultural chemical pollution of import beef in the future.

I have some specific questions about Wahl's paper: (1) exogenous variables do not include input prices (i.e., why were wages and feed prices not used?); (2) is the level of statistical significance of the cross-elasticity of meat satisfactory?; and (3) PSE is effective in terms of CSE or free trade, but is PSE, regardless of input prices, a reasonable index to show degree of government support for agriculture.

GENERAL DISCUSSION—*Mathew Shane* (Economic Research Service, US Department of Agriculture)

A participant asked which elements of the Japanese livestock model were based on trend extrapolations and which were based on income and price effects. The author replied that income and population growth rates were taken from WEFA. Wholesale prices were also assumed exogenously. Quantities were then assumed to respond through income and price effects.

Another participant asked what retail prices were used in the calculations and if the retail margin was allowed to vary. The author replied that dairy and Wagyu beef were assumed to have separate prices, while the retail margin was assumed to be constant throughout the projection period.

A question was raised about whether the variables chosen biased the outcome towards increasing US market share over Australia. The author replied that the USA gained market share because of the assumptions about relative demands for high quality versus lower quality beef and the relative initial positions of the two suppliers.

Participants in the discussion included I. Jarratt, G.T. Jones, and K. Terfertiller.

Tariff and Nontariff Barrier Impacts on Illegal Migration: US Fresh Winter Tomato Market

Gary D. Thompson[1]

Abstract: A partial equilibrium, duality-based empirical model is used to measure the tariff and nontariff barrier effects on fresh tomato prices, quantities, and labour demand in Florida, USA, and Sinaloa, Mexico. Reduced-form estimates indicate that the US unit tariff has increased agricultural labour demand in Florida while reducing field labour demand in Mexico. Nontariff barriers have had a less significant impact on labour demand. Product heterogeneity may account for varying nontariff barrier impacts on fresh tomato supplies and derived labour demand. Linkages between Mexican agricultural labour supply and Florida agricultural labour demand require further analysis.

Introduction

The Immigration Reform and Control Act (IRCA) of 1986 is designed to stem the flow of illegal aliens into the USA by means of domestically oriented amnesty and employer sanctions. The economic migration "push" factors in the countries of origin such as Mexico are not covered by the IRCA. Both Mexican and US officials have argued that reduction of US-Mexican trade barriers for labour-intensive commodities would allow Mexico to export commodities rather than workers.

The factor price equalization theorem suggests that, in a general equilibrium setting, trade in commodities can substitute for labour migration (Mundell, 1957). Some partial equilibrium studies have attempted to test the proposition that liberalized trade in the US fresh winter tomato market, for which Florida and Mexico are almost the exclusive producers, could reduce illegal migration from Mexico to the USA (Emerson, 1982; Huffman, 1982; and Torok and Huffman, 1986). None of these studies, however, has attempted to quantify the effects of both tariff and nontariff barriers on labour migration for the US fresh winter tomato market. This paper examines the effects of tariff and nontariff barriers on tomato production and labour use in Florida and Mexico.

The fresh winter tomato industry in southern Florida and Sinaloa began flourishing during the 1940s and 1950s, as US per capita incomes increased and demand for fresh vegetables during winter months grew. Infrastructure investment in Mexico, access to US working capital, and low labour costs allowed Mexican growers to become more competitive. Following the US embargo on all trade from Cuba in 1962, Mexico and Florida became sole competitors during the January to May winter season.

Both producing regions have implemented measures to protect their US market shares. Florida growers have approved a federal marketing order, which establishes minimum quality standards for all imported fresh tomatoes, and Mexican producers have adopted quality control restrictions, which are administered by the Unión Nacional de Productores de Hortalizas (UNPH). Trade disputes over the US fresh winter tomato market culminated in the dumping controversy of the 1970s, which was finally resolved in favour of Mexican producers. During the last two decades, nontariff quality restrictions on both sides of the border and the US unit tariff have affected tomato production and labour use in Florida and Mexico (Bredahl, Schmitz, and Hillman, 1987).

This paper first develops a partial equilibrium empirical model of the US fresh winter tomato market and Florida and Mexico labour demand using duality theory. Structural and reduced-form estimates of the empirical model are analyzed for policy implications.

Model of Commodity Trade and Labour Demand

The empirical model is derived from a translog variable profit function (Diewert, 1984). The translog profit function in theoretically reasonable (Lopez, 1985) and performs relatively well in Monte Carlo studies (Dixon, Garcia, and Anderson, 1987). Aggregate output supply and labour demand equations are derived from the profit function using Hotelling's lemma.

When producers in each region face the same output prices, the aggregate variable profit function displays the same homogeneity, monotonicity, and convexity properties as the individual producer's profit function (Bliss, 1978). Derivation of the output supply and labour demand functions from the aggregate profit function is attractive because both derivative functions consistently embody the underlying technology through duality mapping.

In the aggregate US tomato market, output quantity and price are assumed to be determined uniquely. Equilibrium tomato price and quantity levels are determined by the two regional product supply share equations *(1)* and *(2)* and an aggregate demand function *(3)*, as follows:

$$(1)\ (P_{ft}Y^*_{ft})/\Pi_{ft} = \alpha_{f1} + \beta_{f1}\, ln\, q_{ft} + \gamma_{f1}\, ln\, P_{ft} + \delta_{f1}\, ln\, A_{ft} + \omega_{f1} DUNPH_t + \theta^J_{f1} DJAN + \theta^F_{f1} DFEB$$

$$+ \theta^M_{f1} DMAR + \theta^A_{f1} DAPR + \phi_{f1} FF_t + \tau_{f1} T_t + \varepsilon_{f1t},$$

$$(2)\ (P_{mt}Y^*_{mt})/\Pi_{mt} = \alpha_{m1} + \beta_{m1}\, ln\, q_{mt} + \gamma_{m1}\, ln\, P_{mt} + \delta_{m1}\, ln\, A_{mt} + \omega_{m1} DTAR_t + \eta_{m1} DMO_t$$

$$+ \theta^J_{m1} DJAN + \theta^M_{m1} DMAR + \theta^A_{m1} DAPR + \phi_{m1} ER_t + \tau_{m1} T_t + \varepsilon_{m1t}, \text{ and}$$

$$(3)\ Y^r_t = \alpha_r + \beta_r\, ln\, P^r_t + \gamma_r\, ln\, I_t + \delta_r\, ln\, W_t + \varepsilon_{rt},$$

where P = wholesale price of tomatoes, Y = supply of tomatoes, Π = profit, q = wage rate, f = Florida, m = Mexico, Y^r = US demand for tomatoes, P^r = retail price of tomatoes, I = US real disposable income, and W = percentage of women employed in the US labour force (the other variables are defined below). Following LaFrance (1985), the demand function *(3)* may be interpreted as an incomplete demand system with only one commodity of interest; i.e., fresh tomatoes.

Due to a paucity of labour supply data, the Florida and Mexican labour markets are modelled only with derived labour demand equations *(4)* and *(5)*, as follows:

$$(4)\ -(q_{ft}X^*_{ft})/\Pi_{ft} = \alpha_{f2} + \beta_{f2}\, ln\, P_{ft} + \gamma_{f2}\, ln\, q_{ft} + \delta_{f2}\, ln\, A_{ft} + \omega_{f2} DUNPH_t + \theta^J_{f2} DJAN$$

$$+ \theta^F_{f2} DFEB + \theta^M_{f2} DMAR + \theta^A_{f2} DAPR + \phi_{f2} FF_t + \tau_{f2} T_t + \varepsilon_{f2t}, \text{ and}$$

$$(5)\ -(q_{mt}X^*_{mt})/\Pi_{mt} = \alpha_{m2} + \beta_{m2}\, ln\, P_{mt} + \gamma_{m2}\, ln\, q_{mt} + \delta_{m2}\, ln\, A_{mt} + \omega_{m2} DTAR_t + \eta_{m2} DMO_t$$

$$+ \theta^J_{m2} DJAN + \theta^M_{m2} DMAR + \theta^A_{m2} DAPR + \phi_{m2} ER_t + \tau_{m2} T_t + \varepsilon_{m2t},$$

where X = hired labour force. The plausible assumption is made that the aggregate wage rates are determined exogenously because Sinaloan minimum daily wages are established by the Mexican federal government and, in southern Florida, minimum hourly wage rates are established by the US government with tomato piece rates set to compete for citrus field labour. The assumption of exogenously determined wage rates is tantamount to assuming an infinitely elastic aggregate labour supply in each region.

Dichotomous variables are included in the empirical model to represent the imposition of the US unit tariff (*DTAR*) and nontariff barriers by Mexico's UNPH (*DUNPH*) and the US federal marketing order (*DMO*). These trade barriers are viewed as exogenously imposed restrictions that increase the fixed costs of production but do not affect the price-taking behaviour of individual producers.[2]

Monthly dummy variables (*DJAN, DFEB, DMAR, DAPR*) are appended to reflect seasonality in production (Torok and Huffman, 1986).[3] In addition to seasonal weather patterns, frosts occur every three years on average in Florida. Thus a dummy variable representing Florida frost shocks (*FF*) is also included.

Although the nature of technical change in both producing regions is distinct, substantial changes in production technology have occurred over the past two decades; e.g., Florida yields have increased due to the adoption of plastic mulch technology (Taylor and Wilkowske, 1984) and Mexican producers have switched from direct seeding to transplanting greenhouse seedlings (Zepp and Simmons, 1979). Because these changes have occurred gradually, a continuous time trend variable (*T*) is included to track temporal changes in both regions.[4]

Exchange rate movements have affected the profitability of Mexican tomatoes. During the 1960s and mid-1970s, the Mexican peso was consistently overvalued in the sense that the real exchange rate, defined as $ER_r = ER_n(WPI_{MEX}/WPI_{US})$, exceeded the nominal exchange rate ER_n (Longmire and Morey, 1983). During those harvest seasons, gross revenue in US dollar terms was unchanged, but variable harvest costs incurred in Mexico were diminished by overvaluation of the Mexican peso. The producer product supply and labour share equations were shifted out by the degree of overvaluation. Thus a measure of overvaluation of the Mexican peso (*ER*) is introduced.

Regional acreage (*A*) is included as a fixed factor because intraseasonal harvest decisions are made on the basis of a given planted area. Although time-series data are used, harvest season data from January to May reflect tomato quantities, prices, and labour quantities used once planting decisions are made and implemented.

Data and Estimation

Monthly observations for all the variables enumerated were used for the winter harvest season from January to May for 1964-81. Because volatility in perishable commodity prices is not adequately reflected in monthly average prices, an expected monthly price was generated using a weighted moving average of the mean, variance, and skewness of weekly f.o.b. price.

Due to nonlinearities in the variables, the identification conditions for the structural model are slightly modified from the usual linear identification conditions (Brown, 1983). The structural model is overidentified using Brown's criteria. The most efficient estimator is two-stage least squares. A systems estimator such as three-stage least squares cannot be used due to singularity of the estimated covariance matrix.[5]

Econometric Results

The parameter estimates of the structural model are not presented because a complete check of the regularity conditions of the "parent" regional profit functions is not possible; the output supply and labour share equations do not contain all the parameters of the "parent" functions. The structural elasticities displayed in Table 1 represent the partial effects on the endogenous variables of changes in the right-hand side structural variables (Chavas, Hassan, and Johnson, 1981). Elasticities for the dichotomous tariff and nontariff variables are not defined.

The structural elasticities conform to prior expectations. Florida tomato supply is more price responsive, probably due to the longer shelf life afforded by mature green tomatoes. Once Mexican vine ripe tomatoes are harvested, they must be marketed rapidly to prevent spoilage. Sinaloan labour demand is more wage and output price responsive. The Sinaloan wage bill accounts for 38 percent of production costs, whereas Florida labour costs represent only 27 percent of production costs (Zepp and Simmons, 1979).

Table 1—Structural Elasticities Evaluated at Sample Means

	Y/P	Y/q	Y/A	X/q	X/P^r	X/A
Florida	0.00136	0.00046	-0.00191*	-2.21603*	1.37511	0.88651*
	(0.00231)	(0.00234)	(0.00061)	(1.08401)	(1.06774)	(0.28268)
Mexico	0.00062	0.02044	-0.01671	-2.52097*	2.09019*	8.11950*
	(0.01986)	(0.01850)	(0.04214)	(0.37844)	(0.40633)	(0.86225)

	Y^r/P^r	Y^r/I	Y^r/W
US Demand	0.81589*	-0.20118	0.24572
	(0.40850)	(0.47917)	(1.66080)

*Significant at the 0.95-percent level.
Note: Asymptotic standard errors are in parentheses.

Reduced-Form Estimates

The reduced form of the structural nonlinear-in-variables model does not yield a closed-form solution (Brown, 1983). The tariff and nontariff effects on tomato production and labour demand can be analyzed, however, through an approximation to the true reduced form. A second-order Taylor series expansion in the logarithms of the exogenous variables was regressed on each of the endogenous variables. For ease of interpretation, only the tariff and nontariff reduced-form estimates are presented in Table 2.

Despite the decreasing ad-valorem equivalent of the unit tariff (Zepp, 1981), the tariff has had a much more significant impact on fresh tomato trade than nontariff barriers. The unit tariff has been in effect throughout all the seasons analyzed; marketing order and UNPH restrictions have been intermittent and varying in degree over the same period. Hence, tariff impacts are more apparent when measured over the past two decades. Although the impacts of marketing order barriers and UNPH restrictions are not all as expected, both US marketing order and Mexican trade restrictions have had effects of comparable magnitude. Many discussions of nontariff barriers in the US fresh winter tomato have mentioned Mexican market interventions, but few have demonstrated the magnitude of UNPH market restrictions.

The tariff and nontariff barrier impacts on the derived demand for labour in each region are mixed. Product heterogeneity may be one cause of an apparently anomalous increase in output and decrease in labour demand associated with UNPH restrictions. When production of less labour-intensive mature green tomatoes substitutes for more labour-intensive vine ripe tomatoes, labour use may decline. However, the tariff impact indicates that Mexican labour demand declines while Florida labour demand increases.

Conclusions

The US unit tariff has had the most significant impact on fresh winter tomato trade in the USA. Marketing order restrictions and Mexico's UNPH short-run interventions had had less effects on tomato prices, quantities, and labour demand in both regions. The unit tariff has affected labour demand most by increasing Florida labour demand and diminishing Mexican labour demand.

Table 2–Reduced-Form Estimates of Tariff and Nontariff Impacts

Exogenous Variables	Endogenous Variables Y_f	Y_m	X_f	X_m	P_f	P_m	P^r
DUNPH	-3.452	3.616	0.174	-3.647	-1.214	-0.773	-1.774
	(6.536)	(3.281)	(5.256)	(12.943)	(0.982)	(1.730)	(1.568)
DMO	-4.656	2.050	2.862	0.065	-1.333	0.462	0.304
	(6.355)	(3.190)	(5.110)	(12.585)	(0.954)	(1.682)	(1.525)
DTAR	31.313*	2.333	8.717*	-6.611	-2.613*	0.170	2.825*
	(5.775)	(2.899)	(4.644)	(11.435)	(0.867)	(1.528)	(1.385)
R^2	0.86	0.95	0.83	0.91	0.55	0.85	0.90
D-W	1.82	1.97	1.14	2.04	1.56	1.72	1.52

*Significant at the 0.95-percent level.
Note: Standard errors are in parentheses.

Product heterogeneity appears to be an important factor in determining the derived demand for labour in tradeable commodities. Tariff and nontariff barriers may have differential effects on labour demand in both countries, depending on the labour intensity of mature green and vine ripe tomatoes. Full assessment of labour migration and trade barrier elimination would require analysis of Mexican labour supply and labour migration linkages with US agricultural labour markets. Qualitative analysis suggests that internal Mexican agricultural migrant labourers would continue migrating to the USA once their seasonal jobs end in May, producing a counterintuitive increase in illegal migration (Thompson, Amon, and Martin, 1986).

Notes

[1]Department of Agricultural Economics, University of Arizona.

[2]Nontariff barriers may not be entirely exogenously determined. Short-run restrictions imposed by UNPH are recommended by a committee that growers may influence. Unfortunately, insufficient data are available for endogenizing nontariff barrier decision rules.

[3]Note that the seasonal dummy *DFEB* is not included in the Mexico share equations because the tariff dichotomous variable (*DTAR*), combined with *DJAN* and *DFEB*, would have been perfectly collinear with the intercept.

[4]Various combinations of dummy variables to represent pre- and postadoption periods were rejected for lack of statistical significance.

[5]With labour as the only variable input, the output and input shares sum to one. Therefore, the corresponding blocks of the estimated variance-covariance matrix are singular.

References

Bliss, C. (1978) *Capital Theory and Distribution of Income*, North Holland, New York, N.Y., USA.

Bredahl, M.E., Schmitz, A., and Hillman, J.S. (1987) "Rent Seeking in International Trade: Great Tomato War," *American Journal of Agricultural Economics*, Vol. 69, pp. 1-10.

Brown, B.W. (1983) "Identification Problem in Systems Nonlinear in the Variables," *Econometrica*, Vol. 51, pp. 175-196.

Chavas, J.P., Hassan, Z.A., and Johnson, S.R. (1981) "Static and Dynamic Elasticities and Flexibilities in Systems of Simultaneous Equations," *Journal of Agricultural Economics*, Vol. 32, pp. 177-187.

Diewert, W.E. (1984) "Applications of Duality Theory," in Intrilligator, M.D., and Kendrick, D.A. (Eds.) *Frontiers of Quantitative Economics*, North Holland, Amsterdam, Netherlands.

Dixon, B.L., Garcia, P., and Anderson, M. (1987) "Usefulness of Pretests for Estimating Underlying Technologies Using Dual Profit Functions," *International Economic Review*, Vol. 28, pp. 623-633.

Emerson, R.D. (1982) "Trade in Products and International Migration in Seasonal Labor Markets," *American Journal of Agricultural Economics*, Vol. 64, pp. 339-346.

Huffman, W.E. (1982) "International Trade in Labor Versus Commodities: U.S.-Mexican Agriculture," *American Journal of Agricultural Economics*, Vol. 64, pp. 989-999.

LaFrance, J.T. (1985) "Linear Demand Functions in Theory and Practice," *Journal of Economic Theory*, Vol. 37, pp. 147-166.

Longmire, J., and Morey, A. (1983) *Strong Dollar Dampens Demand for U.S. Farm Exports*, Foreign Agricultural Economic Report No. 193, Economic Research Service, US Department of Agriculture, Washington, D.C., USA.

Lopez, R. (1985) "Structural Implications of a Class of Flexible Functional Forms for Profit Functions," *International Economic Review*, Vol. 26, pp. 593-601.

Mundell, R.A. (1957) "International Trade and Factor Mobility," *American Economic Review*, Vol. 4, pp. 321-335.

Taylor, T.G., and Wilkowske, G.H. (1984) "Productivity Growth in the Florida Fresh Winter Vegetable Industry," *Southern Journal of Agricultural Economics*, Vol. 16, pp. 55-61.

Thompson, G., Amon, R., and Martin, P. (1986) "Agricultural Development and Emigration: Rhetoric and Reality," *International Migration Review*, Vol. 20, pp. 575-597.

Torok, S.J., and Huffman, W.E. (1986) "U.S.-Mexican Trade in Winter Vegetables and Illegal Migration," *American Journal of Agricultural Economics*, Vol. 68, pp. 246-260.

Zepp, G.A., and Simmons, R.L. (1979) *Producing Fresh Winter Vegetables in Florida and Mexico*, ESCS-72, Economic Research Service, US Department of Agriculture, Washington, D.C., USA.

Zepp, G.A. (1981) *U.S. Winter Fresh Tomato Price and Quantity Projections for 1985*, ESS-4, Economic Research Service, US Department of Agriculture, Washington, D.C., USA.

DISCUSSION OPENING—*Robert W. Dubman* (Economic Research Service, US Department of Agriculture)

The paper presented by Thompson is a significant step towards quantifying the effects of tariff and nontariff barriers on input demands. Most major factors that could influence the fresh winter tomato market have been accounted for in the model. The structure of the model and the econometrics are commendable.

One significant econometric point, however, stands clear. The unit tariff may not be best represented by a dummy variable. The variable *DTAR* is the central variable from which most conclusions were drawn. A dummy variable may not adequately reflect the intensity of the tariff and may be picking up influences other than the tariff. Perhaps including the total tariff revenues or adjusting the prices would lead to more precise and unadulterated estimates.

The IRCA's goal is to eliminate the flow of illegal aliens into the USA. We need to question whether a trade barrier reduction would allow Mexico to export commodities rather than workers. Product substitution may allow Florida farmers to circumvent a tariff by producing nontariff- or nonlabour-intensive crops. Florida farmers may still want to take advantage of relatively inexpensive Mexican labour to grow, for example, other vegetable crops. The wages for farmworkers in Mexico are likely to remain well below wages for farmworkers in the USA. In addition, the Mexican tomato farms are more labour intensive. That nontariff barriers were found insignificant may indicate that product substitution is occurring. Only a general equilibrium analysis can deal with all commodities and inputs at once.

The method may be difficult to duplicate for other commodities. In particular, winter tomatoes are grown in two regions with a common source for labour. The tariff and nontariff barriers are clear. Commodities other than winter tomatoes may be grown in several regions facing a myriad of nontariff barriers. Thus, the data requirement and number of equations may be unmanageable for other commodities.

In conclusion, the economic impacts of legislation restricting the mobility of farmworkers must consider the fairness of the law and the impacts on all parties. The partial equilibrium analysis appears to be lacking in this respect. However, Thompson's paper does give convincing evidence that lowering tariffs may be as effective as immigration control in restricting labour mobility.

[No general discussion of this paper was reported.]

Tariffs, Agricultural Performance, and Regional Disparities within a General Equilibrium Framework: Brazilian Case

Maria da Conceição Sampaio de Sousa[1]

Abstract: The purpose of this study is to assess quantitatively the impact of a tariff cut on agricultural performance and intersectoral and interregional disparities in Brazil. A general equilibrium model was built, nonlinear and dynamic, in which the price mechanism plays an important role. The model is disaggregated in such a way as to permit the analysis of the agricultural sector within the context in which it is inserted. Special attention is given to the effects of urban protection on growth and welfare variables, and strong emphasis is put on the role played by rural-urban interactions. The simulation of the model shows that tariffs constitute a burden to the rural sector as they benefit urban activities. Protection, through rural-urban links, also exacerbates regional disequilibria as they worsen the situation of the poor, agricultural Northeast region.

Introduction

In developing countries, trade policy discriminates heavily against agriculture. Positive urban tariffs together with several price distortions that keep rural domestic prices below world prices reduce rural profitability and imply a transfer of the agricultural surplus to urban areas. In the case of Brazil, if one considers that most of the low income population is concentrated in primary activities, then traditional trade policy can have strong implications for income distribution. Also, the existence in Brazil of two distinct regions—the primary exporter, poor Northeast and the rich, industrialized South—accentuates the impact of urban protection on growth and welfare variables, as the rural-urban duality could be an important determinant of regional disparities. Tariffs, by discriminating against the rural sector, contribute to regional inequalities in Brazil. That could be a serious indirect cost of protection, as Brazil is one of the countries where income is the most concentrated. One thus needs to examine the way protection policies affect rural-urban relations and through them interregional and intersectoral income distribution.

This question has usually been discussed in a partial equilibrium framework, an approach that is restrictive as it does not take into account the complex supply and demand interactions among economic sectors and regions. Nor does it consider that the immediate effects of protection could be different from long-run effects. Those questions can be better answered within a general equilibrium approach.

The purpose of this paper is to assess quantitatively the impact of protection on agricultural performance and intersectoral and interregional income inequalities using a computable general equilibrium model.

Model

The model presented here belongs to the family of computable general equilibrium models developed by Adelman and Robinson (1978). It is formed by two regional models describing the interrelationships between the Northeast and the Centre-South regions in Brazil. The regional models are linked by trade and migrations. In each region, two production sectors are defined: rural and urban sectors. They produce different products and are connected through a regional input-output matrix obtained using Chenery's (1953) method. Each sector was split into two parts according to the regional origin of production.

Three production factors are considered: urban capital, urban labour, and an aggregated rural factor. An important hypothesis in this study is that a good produced in a given region is not a perfect substitute for the same good produced in the other region; i.e., different prices exist in the regions considered.

Producers in the urban sector maximize profits subject to a CES production function of labour and capital. In agriculture, maximizing behaviour applies only to products; for production factors, the model does not imply the classical matching between marginal costs and prices.

Consumers are aggregated into rural and urban groups; they receive all the income generated by production in the different sectors and use an extended linear expenditure system to choose between consumption and saving. Government behaviour does not imply any maximizing behaviour; it receives direct taxes, tariffs, gives subsidies, and saves what remains after subtracting exogenous public consumption. In the urban sector, *ad valorem* tariffs are differentiated by products. In the agricultural sector, implicit tariffs are calculated as the difference between domestic and world prices.

In the agricultural sector, imports are perfect substitutes for domestic production. Hence, a unique price exists for both variables. Net exports/imports is simply the difference between production and domestic demand; any production increase in the short run means higher net exports, as the economy is assumed to be "small" and the elasticity of the foreign demand for rural products infinite. In the urban sector, substitution between domestic production and imports takes place within an Armington system that defines a composite good and its price as a CES function of quantities and prices of domestic and imported goods. Exporters face a foreign demand that is not perfectly elastic.

Although the theoretical framework of this study is the competitive model, it incorporates some rigidities that are supposed to characterize the developing economies. Factorial mobility, for example, is imperfect. Labour does not move instantaneously among sectors and/or regions. Capital mobility is also imperfect within each region, and this factor is specific to the two sectors considered. Savings generated in each sector is locally invested. Capital imports are invested exclusively in each regional urban economy. Nevertheless, the existence of capital transfers between the Northeast and the Centre-South is admitted. In the model, these flows are calculated as the difference between the value of the purchases and sales of intermediate goods for each region. This difference was added (subtracted if the region was a net exporter of intermediate products) to urban investment and constitutes an addition (subtraction) to the existing capital stock. Prices are determined in such a way as to eliminate excess demand in the different markets. In the labour market, the following hypotheses were adopted concerning urban real wage growth: (a) a fixed real wage was imposed, giving rise to unemployment, and (b) wage flexibility ensures full employment if the market real wage is higher than the minimum fixed wage; i.e., the wage constraint becomes inoperative. In the agricultural sector, the income adjusts to eliminate unemployment. This assumption reflects the idea that the subsistence production absorbs the workers who could not find a job in the urban sector or in agricultural formal employment; as a result, productivity and household per capital income are reduced.

Within periods, the model is solved for the endogenous variables, given the values of the exogenous variables and parameters used. Between periods, the dynamic adjustment is done through extrapolation of the production factor values, sectoral productivity growth rates, and labour mobility. The solution is obtained using the Gauss-Seidel algorithm to adjust prices to eliminate demand excess.

The most important equations of the agricultural part of the model are briefly described below. A complete description of the model is provided in Sampaio de Sousa (1987).

Agricultural Sector

The main advantage of the agricultural system developed in this study comes from the fact that it offers a general equilibrium framework in which one can analyze production decisions in agriculture. This approach takes into account the fact that increasing the supply of a given product requires resources that could be used elsewhere, thus reducing the supply of other crops. The agricultural system presented here distinguishes (a) supply functions disaggregated by products and a resource demand function and (b) an aggregated function representing the total availability of rural resources. Those equations are connected through an equilibrium price P_r that assures the equality between the resource demanded with the P_r resources supplied.

Production and resource demand. Agricultural supply function by-products are described by equations (1a) and (1b):

$$(1a)\ X_i = \alpha_i (PP_i / PI_i - c_i)\beta_i, \text{ if } PP_i / PI_i > c_i, \text{ and}$$

$$(1b)\ X_i = 0, \text{ if } PP_i / PI_i \leq c_i.$$

Maximizing profits under competitive conditions requires that:

$$(2)\ PP_i / PI_i = [df_i(X_i)] / dX_i.$$

Rearranging terms in equation *(1)*, combining with equation *(2)*, and integrating over X_i yields:

$$(3)\ R_i = (1/\alpha_i)^{1/\beta i} [\beta_i / (1+\beta_i)] X_i^{\beta i/(1+\beta i)} + c_i X_i.$$

If c_i is zero, this expression corresponds to a Cobb-Douglas production function. R_i represents the aggregated resources required to produce the *i*th crop. It includes intermediate inputs as well as labour and capital inputs. Rearranging the terms in *(3)* and replacing them in equation *(1)*, one can express R_i as a function of the production level and relative prices.

$$(3a)\ R_i = \{[\beta_i / (1+\beta_i)][PP_i / (PI_i - c_i)] + c_i\}\ X_i.$$

Net demand for rural resources *RND* for the whole set of agricultural products is:

$$(4)\ RND = \sum_i R_i - \sum_i \sum_j a_{ji} X_i.$$

Total resource supply. Production capacity in the rural sector is given by equation *(5)*.

$$(5)\ Y_{rr} = [a_0 + a_1(L_r / T_c) + a_2(L_r / T_c)^2 + a_3(FERT/T_c) + a_4(T_i / T_c) + a_5(T_i / T_c)^2$$
$$+ a_6(DST/T_c) + a_7(LSTK/T_c)] T_c.$$

This specification comes from the work of Hellinghausen and Mundlak (1982). It takes into account the traditional agricultural production resources: labour (L_r), cultivated land (T_c), irrigated land (T_i), livestock *(LSTK)*, tractors *(DST)*, and fertilizer *(FERT)*. Resource growth is conditioned by the availability of cultivated land and labour as well as by agricultural savings. Cultivated land grows at an exogenous rate and the labour force depends on demographic growth and intersectoral and interregional income disparities through migration. Finally, agricultural investment in irrigation, livestock, and tractors is related to rural savings.

Price Determination

Equilibrium between total demand of net resources defined by equation *(4)* and production capacity given in equation *(5)* determines P_r, the resource price that relates the supply system by-products to the aggregated supply of resources. All producers face the same resource price.

P_i, the price of the aggregated input R_i, is a weighted average of the intermediate and factor prices:

$$(6)\ PI = (\sum_i \sum_j a_{ji} X_i Pd_j + P_{rr} Y_{rr}) / \sum_i R_i .$$

Finally, equation *(7)* defines agricultural producer prices:

$$(7)\ PP_i = \phi 1_i Pw_i + \phi 2_i PI_i + \phi 3_i P_{GDP}, \text{ with } \sum_j \phi j_i = 1,$$

where Pw_i is the world price of the *i*th good, PI_i is the equivalent input price, and P_{GDP} is the implicit GDP deflator. Parameters ϕ_1, ϕ_2, and ϕ_3 reflect price policies adopted for the different products. They are chosen in such a way as to reconcile the need to obtain foreign exchange through exports with the requirements of the urban economy in terms of food and raw materials. The price of export crops is supposed to be more linked to international prices, while food crops are protected to preserve urban purchasing power and prevent industrial costs from rising.

Simulation Results and Conclusions

The following is a description of the impacts of a 50-percent tariff reduction for all urban products. Special attention is given to the effects on sectoral production, intersectoral terms of trade, and intersectoral and interregional income distribution. The results are shown in Tables 1 and 2 and represent percentage change in relation to the base case for 1976 (initial year) and 1990 (final year).

Table 1 shows that protection has a negative impact on production in both regions. Indeed, in 1990, lower urban tariffs increase GDP by 3.45 percent and 0.52 percent, respectively, for the Northeast and Centre-South regions. As concerns income, the tariff cut reduces regional inequalities. The interregional income differential diminishes by 5.4 percent compared with the base-case level, which could be explained by the fact that the increase in rural real revenue does not offset the reduction of urban income in the Centre-South region, while in the Northeast, real revenue grows in the two sectors. This phenomenon can be better understood if one distinguishes between the short-run and long-run effects of this policy.

Table 1—Impact of a 50-Percent Urban Tariff Cut: Selected Results*

Variables	Northeast 1976	Northeast 1990	Centre-South 1976	Centre-South 1990
	- - - - - *Percent*	- - - - -		
Value added				
Rural	0.16	3.45	0.05	1.94
Urban	-0.77	2.10	-0.70	0.39
Total (GDP)	-0.62	2.27	-0.61	0.52
Disposable real income				
Rural	14.35	7.80	10.37	10.39
Urban	-2.73	7.25	-3.87	-2.97
Rural-urban income differential (per capita)	-15.63	5.21	-14.53	-11.63
Resource prices				
Rural *(P_r)*	22.38	0.31	5.09	-3.72
Urban *(P_u)*	-8.55	3.85	-9.72	-9.50
Rural-urban terms of trade	33.82	-3.41	16.44	6.39
Agricultural prices				
Producer prices *(PP)*	-1.84	1.94	-2.81	-3.12
Input prices *(PI)*	-1.96	-4.70	-2.93	-5.04
PP/PI	0.12	2.89	0.13	2.01
Urban consumer price	-8.53	-0.57	-9.40	-8.69
Urban real wage	0.00	7.95	0.00	0.56

*Percentage change with respect to the base case.

In the short run, lower urban prices caused by lower urban production improve agricultural terms of trade as rural prices are partially linked to fixed world prices and so diminish more slowly. As a result, rural profitability increases, resulting in excess demand

Table 2—Protection and Regional Imbalances: Selected Indicators*

Indicators	1976	1990
	- Percent -	
Regional income differential (per capita)	0.01	-6.40
Interregional migrations	-1.23	-12.73
Interregional capital transfers	-11.76	-31.95

*Percentage change with respect to the base case.

for agricultural resources. Higher rural resource prices accentuate the initial improvement in the agricultural terms of trade. This effect is more important in the Northeast region, as protection discriminates mainly against agricultural export activities that constitute the economic basis of this region.

In the long run, the results are different in each region. In the Centre-South, the initial rural factor price increase is completely absorbed thanks to the fast capital accumulation in agriculture; in 1990, this price is 3.72 percent lower than its level in the base case. But, as urban prices fall more, the terms of trade still benefit the country. In the Northeast, the situation is different. Reduced capital transfers hinder capital accumulation in the urban sector and transform the initial fall in the urban resource prices into a rise of 3.85 percent compared with the base run. In spite of the fact that, in the Northeast, the agricultural sector is relatively more important, the terms of trade turn against agriculture. As they are an important determinant of income distribution, rural-urban disparities are worsened. Such an effect partially offsets the reduction of regional imbalances, as one considers that changes in the income distribution are unfavourable to rural areas and increase income concentration in Brazil as a whole as the rural sector comprises most of the low-income population.

In conclusion, the results show that protection exacerbates regional disequilibria, worsening the situation of the poorest region, the Northeast. Indeed, protectionist policies imply a resource transfer from rural to urban areas. As the urban sector is more developed in the Centre-South, this region benefits from higher tariffs as it comprises most of the import-competing activities. Previous results (Reboucas, 1974) are confirmed, and the role played by rural urban interactions in strengthening the Northeast/Centre-South duality in Brazil is made explicit.

Note

[1]Departamento de Economia, Universidade Federal de Pernambuco.

References

Adelman, I., and Robinson, S. (1978) *Income Distribution Policy in Developing Countries: Case Study of Korea*, Oxford University Press, London, UK.

Chenery, H.B. (1953) "Regional Analysis," in Chenery, H.B., *et al.*, *Structure and Growth of the Italian Economy*, US Mutual Security Agency, Rome, Italy.

Hellinghausen, R., and Mundlak, Y. (1982) "Intercountry Production Function: Another View," *American Journal of Agricultural Economics*, Vol. 64, pp. 664-672.

Reboucas, O.E. (1974) "Interregional Effects of Economic Policies: Multisectoral General Equilibrium Estimates for Brazil," PhD dissertation, Harvard University, Cambridge, Mass., USA.

Sampaio de Sousa, M. da C. (1987) "Políticas Econômicas e Desigualdades Regionais dentro de um Modêlo de Equilíbrio Geral: O Caso do Nordeste e do Centro-Sul Brasileiro," in *Anais do IX Encontro da Sociedade Brasileira de Econometria*, Salvador, Bahia, Brazil, pp. 447-474.

DISCUSSION OPENING—*Monika Hartman* (Frankfurt University)

Sampaio de Sousa has provided us with an interesting paper, which is based on the important and well-known observation that developing country trade policies discriminate heavily against agriculture, thus leading to adverse effects not only on the agricultural sector but on the economy as a whole. Sampaio de Sousa uses a computable general equilibrium model, which she says is also of a dynamic nature, to quantify the effects of a 50-percent industrial tariff reduction on the agricultural sector and on intersectoral as well as on intraregional income parity. Unfortunately not all the promises made in the abstract and introduction are fully met within the text.

First and foremost, no explanation is given of the model used in the paper. I understand that this might be partly due to space limitations since it is nearly impossible to give a complete picture of the model and the results in only six pages. Nevertheless, some clarification would be useful to improve our understanding of the approach. The major questions I have are: What is the data base and what are the data sources? Are the parameters empirically estimated or are they taken from literature? Are the overall results of the model robust with respect to the model parameters? Have sensitivity analyses been conducted and what results did they reveal? With respect to the missing lags, the question arises whether the model is really of a dynamic nature as stated in the abstract and introduction or is it only a sequential dynamic approach, which solves equilibrium models each year separately? Some more information about the absolute values of the results would make it easier to estimate the absolute magnitude of the documented changes of a tariff reduction comparison to the base run.

I agree with Sampaio de Sousa that a general equilibrium approach is needed to capture the complex linkages among sectors and regions. Nevertheless, the results of this model should be compared with other studies even if those studies only use a partial equilibrium approach.

In addition, other ways of discriminating against agriculture in developing countries exist beyond just sector-specific price and tax policies. As has been shown during this conference, discrimination against agriculture also encompasses macroeconomic issues like overvalued currencies and balance-of-payments and budgetary deficits. Their effects might do even more harm to the agricultural sector than the policies mentioned in Sampaio de Sousa's paper. Since the focus of the study is on politically induced intersectoral and interregional income inequality, an interesting extension would be to analyze the effect of protected urban labour markets on income parity—an economic reality in many developing countries that has been incorporated in Sampaio de Sousa's model.

GENERAL DISCUSSION—*Mathew Shane* (Economic Research Service, US Department of Agriculture)

The questions on the CGE model of Brazil related to its structural characteristics; in particular, whether changes in real wages were taken into account. The author replied that they were not, since the framework was set up as a medium-to-long-term equilibrium model.

One participant asked why the Northeast is particularly affected by the tariff reductions. The author replied that the answer was related to the intensity of agricultural activity in that region relative to other regions of the country. Since an import substitution policy tends to be an implicit tax on agriculture, this is the expected result.

Participants in the discussion included R. Ayerza and G.T. Jones.

Politico-Economic Analysis of the US Sugar Programme

Rigoberto A. Lopez and Kay G. Sachtler[1]

Abstract: This paper presents a politico-economic analysis of decision making about the US sugar programme. It analyzes the linkages between the economic surpluses of market participants and the policy response via the level of target prices and import quotas. The legislative decisions of the sugar programme are captured by the target price choices, while the administrative aspects of the programme are captured by the import quota choices. Explanatory variables in the empirical model include domestic sugar producer and consumer surplus, corn sweetener producer surplus, sugar quasi-rents of US quota-holding countries, and US federal budget deficit. Target price decisions were found to be weakly linked to domestic sugar producer surplus but strongly linked to corn sweetener producer surplus. The impact of the federal budget deficit on quota levels is clear. Restrictive quotas reduce Treasury outlays while supporting domestic producers. The influences of various market participants are also examined for both target prices and import quotas.

Introduction

The sugar policies of the US government are one of the best case studies for analyzing politico-economic decision making in agriculture. Since 1789, the US government has involved itself in the sugar industry, setting import and domestic quotas, tariffs, and support prices, singly and in combination. In only four of the last 200 years, 1975-76 and 1980-81, did the government not approve a sugar target price, and, in those years, the abnormally high world sugar prices obviated the need for one. As a result of the US government involvement, the price of sugar has been much higher and more stable domestically than in the world market.

In the late 1980s, the US sugar programme faced challenges on several fronts. Critics contend that high domestic prices have encouraged the development and adoption of sugar substitutes, such as high-fructose corn syrup; that ever more restrictive import quotas increase foreign policy risk (the quota was reduced by 41 percent from 1986 to 1987 alone); and that the programme is highly inefficient. Government officials and all those who make policy and participate in domestic and foreign markets must strive better to understand how policies are formed and what factors affect policy choices. The purpose of this paper is to develop a framework to analyze the determinants of the level of US sugar policy instruments—sugar import quotas and target prices—based on the economic surpluses of market participants. By so doing, the empirical framework incorporates both the economic and political aspects involved in the US sugar case.

Conceptual Framework

Pressure groups and government agencies interact in US sugar policy making. The end product is a sugar programme that consists of policy choices, including price support levels and import quotas. Lobbyists provide a critical input in policy making by representing the special interests of pressure groups trying to influence policies in their favour. The political and economic importance of corn sweeteners cannot be underestimated, especially that of high-fructose corn syrup, which had captured over 35 percent of the US caloric sweetener market by 1986.

As in other public policies, sugar policy involves two strata of decision making: legislating and administering (or implementing) a sugar programme. The first part is done by Congress and the second by executive branches. In the case of sugar policy, the role of Congress has been confined to establishing the price support level for domestic sugar producers. Administering the programme to achieve the price support level starts with an interagency review by a Sugar Working Group composed of representatives of the Departments of Agriculture, State, Treasury, and Commerce; the Office of the US Trade Representative; the National Security Agency; and the Council of Economic Advisers

(Nuttall, 1986). This group develops recommendations on programme administration that then go to the Cabinet and are ultimately approved by the President.

The conceptual framework in this paper follows from the premise that the government authorities form preferences over the welfare of domestic producers and consumers, the Treasury's position (which can be viewed as an income claim to others), and foreign interests. According to Nuttall, administrative decisions in the sugar programme involve four policy areas: domestic farm programmes, domestic budgets, foreign policy ramifications, and implications of trade policy. Modifying the theoretical model presented by Riethmuller and Roe (1986), policy decisions (G_k^*) resulting from the policy-making process can be represented by:

$$(1)\ G_{kt}^* = G_k(PS_{t-\tau k}, CS_{t-\tau k}, FS_{t-\tau k}, BS_{t-\tau k}),$$

where τk is the institutional lag associated with policy instrument k, PS is producer surplus, CS is consumer surplus, FS is foreign country surplus, and BS is the federal budget surplus. The lag is introduced because US sugar policies follow market conditions but lag behind them.

Empirical Framework

Because of the intricacy of the sugar market and the wide variety of policy instrument options, the focus was narrowed to two policy instruments: the government's price-support level (loan rate) and import quota level. The empirical procedures involve the estimation of market parameters, computation of welfare measures based on these parameters, and estimation of policy instruments based on these welfare measures. This paper used the econometric model for the US sugar market presented by Lopez (1989) to estimate PS, CS, and FS.

The levels of policy instruments (G_k^*) chosen by the policy makers are assumed to be effective, and, thus, the observed levels are assumed to correspond to what was chosen. Characterized by a bureaucratic time lag in policy implementation and adjustment, the selected levels of policy instruments are assumed to follow a multiyear distributed lag response. More specifically, an econometric specification of equation *(1)* for government behaviour in setting sugar policy instruments is expressed as:

$$(2)\ G_{kt}^* = \lambda_0^k + \sum_{\tau=1}^{nk} (\delta_{1\tau}^k PS_{t-\tau} + \delta_{2\tau}^k CS_{t-\tau} + \delta_{3\tau}^k FS_{t-\tau} + \delta_{4\tau}^k BS_{t-\tau}) + U_{kt},$$

where τ represents a lagged period. Let $\delta_{j\tau}^k$ be represented by a polynomial of degree n, which is assumed to be a continuous function of τ so that it can be expressed as $\delta_{j\tau}^k = \Sigma_{ki=1}^{n} \lambda_i^k \tau^i$. Substituting this into equation *(2)* yields:

$$(3)\ G_{kt}^* = \lambda_0^k + \sum_{j=1}^{4} \sum_{i=1}^{nk} \lambda_{ji}^k W_{jit}^k + U_{kt},$$

where $W_{jit}^k = \Sigma_{\tau=1}^{nk}\ \tau^i X_{jt-\tau} (i=1,\ ...,\ nk)$, and $X_j = (PS, CS, FS, BS)$. W_{jit}^k represents the "scrambled" terms treated as ordinary regressors that can be unscrambled after estimation to obtain the implied lag coefficients.

Data and Estimation

Most of the data came from various issues of US government publications, including *Sugar and Sweetener Outlook and Situation Report* (US Department of Agriculture, Economic Research Service). The federal budget balance data were obtained from the *Statistical Abstract of the United States* (US Department of Commerce). Annual observations were collected for the 1955-85 period.

The estimated sugar market parameters were used to estimate domestic consumer and producer surpluses in real terms. Following Just, Hueth, and Schmitz (1982), consumer surplus estimation took into account the feedback or multimarket effect of changes in the price of sugar, given that this is a price umbrella for corn sweeteners. Following Just *et al.*, producer surpluses in the production of corn sweeteners (high-fructose corn syrup, glucose, and dextrose) were measured by quasi-rent estimates (returns over variable costs) based on the work of Lopez and on market data. The producer surpluses in the corn sweetener sector were then summed and deflated by the price of maize and entered as an argument of the policy equations.

For the import quota and target price equations, all variables were expressed in logarithms, except for the federal budget surplus. The target price was deflated with the index of prices paid by farmers. Since the aggregate import quota is a policy instrument to implement the target price set by Congress, the real target price (approximated by an instrumental variable estimator) was included as an argument in the quota equation.

The distributed lag models are estimated by assuming a first-degree (import quota) and second-degree (target price) polynomial on the lag coefficients and end-point constraints. Finally, the 1975-76 and 1980-81 observations for the target price and the 1975-81 observations for the import equation equations were excluded from the sample, because these policy instruments were not in effect in those years.

Empirical Results

The empirical results for acreage decisions, corn sweetener prices, and demand parameters are presented in Table 1. In general, the results for the domestic sugar market parameters were reasonable. The results in Table 1 were used along with producer surplus from the corn sweetener market and sample data to compute domestic producer and consumer surpluses.

The polynomial distributed lag results for the target price equation are presented in Table 2. The target price equation was augmented by adding a slope shifter (*D74*). The coefficients associated with sugar producer surplus were the only ones not statistically significant at the 10-percent level. The empirical results fail to show a significant statistical association between sugar producer surpluses (*PS*) and target price level choices. A significant negative statistical association was found between corn sweetener producer surplus (*PSCORN*) and sugar price levels; i.e., Congress tends to set higher sugar target prices when the corn sweetener producers are worse off. Supporting the sugar price partially supports the price of maize to the extent of the corn sweetener share of the maize market.

A statistically significant association was found between consumer surplus (*CS*) and target price levels; i.e., Congress tends to set lower target prices when consumers and sweetener user manufacturers are worse off. Although consumers are not organized to lobby on target prices, sweetener users and manufacturers are. A statistically significant association was found between foreign country surplus (*FS*) and congressional decisions on target price levels; i.e., as sugar export rents of quota-holding countries decline, Congress tends to set lower target prices. Thus, having lower target prices and increased access to the US sugar market coupled with import decisions is in the best interest of foreign countries. The sign associated with the federal budget surplus (*BS*) (deficit if negative) is

Table 1—Estimates of US Sugar Market Parameters

Equation	Parameter	Variable	Coefficient	Standard Error
Cane acreage	α_0	Intercept	1.800**	0.738
	α_1	$ln(P_t^*/D_t)$	0.231*	0.125
	α_2	$ln(S_t^*/D_t)$	-0.204*	0.146
	α_3	$ln(A_{t-1}^c)$	0.601**	0.116
	α_4	Time	0.006*	0.0035
Beet acreage	β_0	Intercept	1.606*	0.874
	β_1	$ln(P_t^*/D_t)$	0.479**	0.150
	β_2	$ln(S_t^*/D_t)$	-0.411**	0.169
	β_3	$ln(A_{t-1}^b)$	0.601**	0.103
	β_4	Time	-0.003	0.002
Corn sweetener prices	π_0	Intercept	-9.282**	2.728
	π_1	P_t	0.671**	0.211
	π_2	$PCORN_t$	0.310	2.166
	π_3	Time	0.628**	0.181
Demand	γ_0	Intercept	58,077.800*	34,650.060
	γ_1	P_t/CPI_t	-1,570.533**	545.661
	γ_2	P_{ot}/CPI_t	1,016.771**	509.463
	γ_3	Q_{t-1}^D	0.814**	0.129
	γ_4	I_t/CPI_t	0.017**	0.062
	γ_5	Time	-1,390.661	2,433.614
Log of likelihood			-304.518	

Notes: D_t is an index of prices paid by farmers (1977=1); S_t^* is an index of expected prices received by farmers (1977=1); CPI_t is the consumers' price index; I_t is consumer disposable personal income; and $PCORN_t$ is the price of maize. All other variables are defined in the text. An asterisk or double asterisks next to the estimated coefficient indicate significance at the 10- and 5-percent levels, respectively.

contrary to expectations. On the other hand, the intercept-shifter coefficient (*D74*) shows that target prices have been generally set lower in real terms after 1974.

The polynomial distributed lag results for the import quota equation are presented in Table 3. The signs of the coefficients associated with sugar producer surplus and consumer surplus are contrary to expectations. A possible explanation of the producer and consumer surplus signs is that the welfare sensitivity by the executive branches in setting import quotas may have been partially captured by the target price. Another possible explanation is that if the amounts of money, time, and effort spent on campaign contributors, lobbying, advertising, and other political activities increase with economic surpluses, then import quota levels may reflect this pressure rather than a pure response to welfare.

The empirical results suggest that the US government has allowed more imports of sugar when quota-holding countries were worse off but has restricted imports when these countries were faring better. This type of response may have changed after 1985 (postsample period), with the implementation of the "no-cost" mandate by which only the

Table 2—Parameter Estimates for the Target Price Equation

Variable	Coefficient (Standard Error) in Lag $\tau = 0$	$\tau = 1$	$\tau = 2$	$\tau = 3$	$\tau = 4$	$\tau = 5$	Sum Lag
$PS_{t-\tau}$		-0.006	-0.009	-0.010	-0.009	-0.006	-0.039
		(0.013)	(0.021)	(0.024)	(0.021)	(0.013)	(0.093)
$PSCORN_{t-\tau}$		-0.020	-0.032	-0.036	-0.032	-0.020	-0.139
		(0.010)	(0.016)	(0.017)	(0.016)	(0.010)	(0.068)
$CS_{t-\tau}$		0.092	0.147	0.166	0.147	0.092	0.645
		(0.020)	(0.032)	(0.036)	(0.032)	(0.020)	(0.139)
$FS_{t-\tau}$		0.019	0.031	0.035	0.031	0.019	0.135
		(0.008)	(0.012)	(0.014)	(0.012)	(0.008)	(0.053)
$BS_{t-\tau}$		-3.079	-4.927	-5.543	-4.927	-3.079	-21.556
		(0.388)	(0.621)	(0.699)	(0.621)	(0.388)	(2.718)
$D74$	-0.315						
	(0.028)						

Notes: $R^2 = 0.948$, $F = 27.132$, and $DW = 2.059$. All variables are expressed in natural logarithms (except $FS_{t-\tau}$ and $D74$) and real terms. The sample includes 1963-85, except 1975-76 and 1980-81, when target prices were not in effect. The parameters were estimated correcting for first-order serial correlation using the Cochrane-Orcutt technique ($\rho = 0.478$).

residual, after unrestricted domestic supply, is imported. Consistent with the conclusions of Leu, Schmitz, and Knutson (1987), Maskus (1987), and the recent no-cost-to-the-Treasury policy, the US government has used import quotas as a substitute for policies requiring Treasury outlays, depending on the federal budget balance. A quota response to the deficit attains two of Nuttall's governmental objectives simultaneously: it protects domestic producer interests and reduces the burden on the Treasury by avoiding the direct use of subsidies.

The results also show that import quotas are effectively used to implement the target price. For an imported commodity, a target price support level can be administered with import quota management as has been true with the implementation of the no-cost-to-the-Treasury mandate. An analogous case is the variable duties imposed by the EC, in which target prices are coordinated with self-adjusting tariffs to support the EC target prices.

Concluding Remarks

An important issue concerns the short-run political horizon of sugar policy makers facing re-election. Although a sugar programme may be effective in attaining the objectives of the policy makers or those of their constituents in the short run, in the long run these policies involve a trade-off because of their inducement of technological and institutional changes. For example, high sugar prices have induced and will continue to induce the

Table 3—Parameter Estimates for the Import Quota Equation

Variable	Coefficient (Standard Error) in Lag $\tau = 0$	$\tau = 1$	$\tau = 2$	$\tau = 3$	Sum Lag
$PS_{t-\tau}$		-0.454 (0.060)	-0.303 (0.040)	-0.151 (0.020)	-0.908 (0.119)
$PSCORN_{t-\tau}$		0.049 (0.040)	0.033 (0.027)	0.016 (0.013)	0.0982 (0.084)
$CS_{t-\tau}$		0.501 (0.076)	0.334 (0.051)	0.167 (0.025)	1.002 (0.152)
$FS_{t-\tau}$		-0.074 (0.026)	-0.049 (0.017)	-0.025 (0.009)	-0.148 (0.052)
$BS_{t-\tau}$		6.689 (1.033)	4.460 (0.689)	2.230 (0.344)	13.379 (2.065)
P_t^{iv}	-4.041 (1.017)				

Notes: R^2 = 0.959, F = 46.77, and DW = 1.540. All variables are expressed in natural logarithms except $FS_{t-\tau}$. The sample includes 1960-85, except 1975-81, because no quotas were in effect in those years.

development and adoption of sugar substitutes, thus decreasing long-term demand for sugar and reducing imports. If the current trend continues, a zero-import situation may be attained in less than a decade. In that event, political choices would involve a direct trade-off among domestic interest groups as well as Treasury outlays. Finally, this paper finds some evidence to reinforce the widespread view that policy decisions are as much a matter of wider political considerations as they are of economics. Attesting to this view are the weak linkage found between domestic sugar producer surpluses and target prices and the strong linkage between federal budget deficits and import quota choices.

Note

[1]Department of Agricultural Economics and Marketing, Rutgers University.

References

Just, R.E., Hueth, D.L., and Schmitz, A. (1982) *Applied Welfare Economics and Public Policy*. Prentice Hall, Englewood Cliffs, N.J., USA.

Leu, G.M., Schmitz, A., and Knutson, R.D. (1987) "Gains and Losses of Sugar Programme Policy Options," *American Journal of Agricultural Economics*, Vol. 69, No. 3, pp. 591-602.

Lopez, R.A. (1989) "Political Economy of U.S. Sugar Policies," *American Journal of Agricultural Economics*, Vol. 71, No. 1, pp. 20-31.

Maskus, K.E. (1987) *International Political Economy of U.S. Sugar Policy in the 1980s*, Planning and Economic Analysis Working Paper No. WP/87/1, US Department of State, Washington, D.C., USA.
Nuttall, J. (1986) "Operation of the U.S. Sugar Programme," in *California Sugar Beet 1986 Annual Report*, California Growers Association, Stockton, Calif., USA.
Riethmuller, P., and Roe, T. (1986) "Government Behavior in Commodity Markets: Case of Japanese Rice and Wheat Policy," *Journal of Policy Modeling*, Vol. 8, pp. 327-349.

DISCUSSION OPENING—*David R. Lee* (Department of Agricultural Economics, Cornell University)

The paper by Lopez and Sachtler makes several contributions to the growing body of research on the political economy of agricultural policy. First, the use of economic surplus measures to assess expected gains and losses of market participants represents a conceptual improvement over simpler proxy measures (e.g., expected prices) that have previously been used in this type of analysis. Second, the paper's simultaneous attention to the politicoeconomic determinants of two major policy interventions brings an element of realism into the treatment of sugar policy. Third, the integration of foreign economic agent gains and losses into what is, after all, fundamentally an international market for sugar is a useful innovation that broadens the scope of the study beyond simply domestic considerations.

A number of limitations also characterize the analysis, however. The empirical results reported in the paper are less than totally compelling. The presence of perverse signs and lack of statistical significance of regression coefficients associated with key hypothesized determinants of sugar policy is troublesome, notwithstanding the possible explanations for these unexpected results cited by the authors. Perhaps other factors were at work; the paper would benefit from a closer examination of these opposite-from-expected results. A second concern is the issue of continuity in policy formulation. For sugar and many other commodities in the USA, the quadrennial nature of farm legislation imparts a source of discontinuity or stepwise behaviour to policy outcomes through a variety of specific mechanisms. Ignoring this factor in time-series estimation may suggest an unrealistic degree of continuity compared to what actually occurs in commodity policy formulation, such as in the setting of target prices. Lastly, while the paper makes a beginning in attempting to specify the international sources of policy determination, we still have a long way to go, especially for a commodity like sugar for which the market is inherently international and which is driven by noneconomic policies as well, including political and security concerns.

At a more fundamental level, the paper also raises a number of questions pertaining to the broader politicoeconomic literature in agricultural policy. What, for example, are the unique uses and attributes of politicoeconomic analysis? Traditional agricultural policy analysis examines the welfare impacts, distortions, and incidence of past and anticipated policy interventions. Policy makers may not always (or even often) listen to the results, but these studies provide a point of reference for political bargaining and compromise. Are the uses of politicoeconomic analysis any different? To what extent does the introduction of explicitly political elements into economic analysis necessitate greater attention to the policy *process* and the political viability of alternative economic proposals? Questions like these inevitably arise once one goes beyond purely economic considerations.

A related issue concerns the inherent nature of the questions that applied economists ask in politicoeconomic research. Political scientists addressing economic policy issues are generally concerned with questions such as the construction and maintenance of political coalitions, the nature of public support for policy interventions, and the internal dynamics of the policy formulation process. While economists may not have a comparative advantage in addressing these issues, we should not avoid them in our haste to force what are often highly complex and subtle political processes into preconceived boxes that may be quantifiable and estimable.

Finally, a further cautionary note is in order concerning what one might call a political "aggregation problem." Generic use of monolithic terms like "government policy" obscures the number of interest groups active in policy formulation and the wide divergence of their interests. In Bill Browne's recent book on the politics surrounding passage of the 1985 Farm Bill, for example, nearly 20 different interest groups active in the formulation of sugar policy in 1985 are mentioned. Sugar "producers" and sugar "consumers" each comprise many different individual parties, with often opposing views and positions. Aggregating these groups to enable empirical analysis to proceed may be a necessary evil but may also be partly responsible for the difficulty in obtaining powerful and robust empirical results in politicoeconomic studies.

GENERAL DISCUSSION—*Thomas C. Pinckney, Rapporteur* (International Food Policy Research Institute)

In his reply to the discussant, Lopez agreed that the econometric results were less than compelling, perhaps because of the lack of any specification for direct lobbying in the model. During the research, the authors had attempted to model direct lobbying in several ways but had not succeeded in finding an effective method. As for the quadrennial nature of changes in US farm legislation, this affects only the sugar target price. The quota is determined annually. As with direct lobbying, an attempt was made to include a dummy variable for the year of a new farm bill, but the variable was insignificant.

Do Nonagricultural Distortions Justify the Protection of US Agriculture?

John C. Beghin and Larry S. Karp[1]

Abstract: Optimal agricultural distortions are calculated, taking as given distortions in the nonagricultural sector. The calculations use a general equilibrium model and assume that the sole criterion is economic efficiency. For most agricultural commodities, existing distortions should be decreased; for cotton and oil-bearing crops, the existing tariff should be increased. Under these optimal distortions, the USA would become an importer of dairy products, poultry, and eggs. Imports of meat, fruit, and vegetables would increase, as would exports of feed grains. The USA would become a major exporter of food and beverage products.

Introduction

Empirical evidence is used to determine whether distortions in the nonagricultural sector of the US economy justify, on efficiency criteria, the current level of distortions in the agricultural sector. Estimates of optimal distortions for the US agricultural sector are provided under the assumption that distortions in other sectors of the economy are fixed. This is a standard problem of choosing second-best policies (the first best being to remove all distortions). In a simple two-good model, the distortion in one sector can be chosen to offset exactly the fixed distortion, so that the economy faces world relative prices. This makes it tempting to compare aggregate distortions in the US manufacturing and agricultural sectors and to argue that, if the former were fixed, economic efficiency would be improved by setting the aggregate agricultural distortions at the same level. This would maintain the domestic relative aggregate price of agricultural to industrial goods at the same level as the world relative aggregate price. This proposal ignores the general equilibrium linkages within and between sectors and can be expected to yield poor results.

A general equilibrium model, which disaggregates the agricultural and manufacturing sectors, is used to calculate optimal distortions within the former, taking as given the distortions within the latter.

The producer distortions (hereafter referred to as tariffs) are defined as the difference between the producer price (adjusted for transport costs and subsidies) and the shadow price of a commodity in *ad valorem* form. Although policy makers should clearly prefer altering both agricultural and nonagricultural tariffs simultaneously, this seldom occurs in practice. A notable example was the 1985 Farm Bill. The debate surrounding this Bill concerned how to modify agricultural policy independently of manufacturing policy. Many reasons exist as to why actual policy choices may not approximate optimal (i.e., economically efficient) decisions, but the extent and direction of the discrepancy are worth understanding. This understanding may provide surprising evidence for or against certain policies.

The current GATT discussions illustrate another potential use of the calculations performed here. The USA is especially interested in reducing international distortions in agricultural trade. Estimating the effects of particular compromises and measuring how changes in one sector make other compromises more or less palatable are, therefore, important. For example, the empirical results indicate that a reduction in the protection of the textile sector has a dramatic effect on the optimal distortion for raw cotton.

The use of computable general equilibrium models provides the most sophisticated method of determining these effects. An alternative developed by Dixit and Newbery (1985) is used in this paper. The advantages of this latter method are its simplicity and more modest demand on data. These features permit one to develop the empirical model quickly and perform relatively transparent sensitivity analysis. Dixit and Newbery (1985), Dixit and Norman (1980), and Dixit (1985) show that the optimum tariff on the sector in which the policy maker intervenes is a weighted average of the existing tariffs in the other sectors of the economy. In the present study, agriculture is disaggregated into seven sectors, and the methodology is extended to determine the vector of optimum tariffs.

Because most of the input-output and final demand data were available for 1982, it was used as a reference year. The existing market distortions have been estimated for the same year. The results suggest that lower tariffs should be applied to the dairy, cattle, pig, sugar, tobacco, and fruits and vegetables sectors. More protection (a higher tariff) should be given to oil-bearing crops and cotton. Optimum tariffs for the food and feed grains sectors are close to zero, exposing those two sectors to international competition.

Model

A Ricardo-Viner-Leontief model and duality theory constitute the core of the methodology. World prices are initially taken to be exogenous, but this assumption is relaxed later. No formal consideration is made of retaliation by US trading partners to changes in US policy. Costs of adjustment are ignored.

Demand is represented by a single consumer having a Cobb-Douglas utility function, u, with an associated expenditure function, e. This assumption is not restrictive since efficiency and not distributional questions is of concern here. Government revenues can be redistributed in a nondistortionary way through lump-sum transfers. Production is characterized by a revenue function, r. The production functions exhibit constant returns to scale, with labour being the only mobile factor, and capital sector specific. The model has m traded goods and l nontraded ones. Domestically produced and foreign-traded goods are assumed to be perfect substitutes. The accounting identity for this economy is given by:

$$(1)\ e(p+t+c,\ q+b,\ u) = r(p+t,\ q) + (t+c)e_p + be_q - tr_p - pg - qg^n,$$

where p is a vector of world prices; t is a vector of tariffs; q is a vector of producer prices for nontraded goods; c and b are vectors of consumer taxes applied on traded and nontraded goods, respectively; e_p and e_q are gradients of the expenditure function with respect to p and q; r_p is a gradient of the revenue function with respect to p; and g and g^n are vectors of government consumption of traded and nontraded goods. The vector of excess supply of nontraded goods must be equal to zero at equilibrium. Differentiating *(1)* and the equilibrium condition of the nontraded goods, holding b, g, g^n constant, yields:

$$(2)\ B\,du = [(t+c)E_{pp} + (b+h)E_{qp} - tR_{pp} - hR_{qp}]dt' + [(t+c)E_{pp} + (b+h)E_{qp}]dc',$$

where B is a positive scalar; h is a vector of the differences between the producer price and shadow price for nontraded goods; E_{pp} is a Hessian submatrix of the expenditure function corresponding to the traded goods ($d^2e/dpdp'$); and E_{qp} is a Hessian submatrix for the cross derivatives of e with respect to q and p. Similarly, R_{pp} and R_{qp} are Hessian submatrices of the revenue function ($d^2r/dpdp'$ and $d^2r/dqdp'$). Assume the policy maker can change taxes and tariffs in the first n traded sectors, holding taxes and tariffs constant in the other sectors. Define t^* and c^* as the vectors of optimum tariffs and taxes that will maximize utility; i.e., $t = [t^*: t(-n)]$ and $c = [c^*: c(-n)]$, where $t(-n)$ and $c(-n)$ give the last $m - n$ elements of t and c, respectively. The optimum t^* is:

$$(3)\ t^* = -[t(-n)R_{mn} + hR_{qn}]R_{nn}^{-1},$$

where R_{mn} is $d^2r/dp_w dp_j$ for, $w = n + 1, ..., m$ and $j = 1, ..., n$; R_{qn} is $d^2r/dq_k dp_j$, for $k = 1, ..., l$ and $j = 1, ..., n$; and R_{nn} is a square matrix $d^2r/dp_i dp_j$ for i and $j = 1, ..., n$. Equation *(3)* expresses the optimum tariffs as a weighted average of the existing distortions, $t(-m)$ and h, in the remaining sectors. The vector c^* is:

$$(4)\ c^* = -t^*\ \{[c(-n) + t(-n)]E_{mn} + (b+h)E_{qn}\}/E_{nn}^{-1},$$

where E_{mn}, E_{qn}, and E_{nn} are the counterparts of R_{mn}, R_{qn}, and R_{nn} for the expenditure function. According to *(4)*, the optimum consumer tax should be the negative of the optimum tariff minus a correction term accounting for the distortions in the other sectors. The values of t^* and c^* are computed after the Hessian matrices R and E have been estimated at a point using current data (1982). The underlying model implies that the Hessian R varies with prices. Therefore, the computed values of t^* and c^* are only approximations to the optimal level.

Data

The estimation of the Hessian matrix of the revenue function requires the knowledge of input-output and value-added data. The data set of Adelman and Robinson (1986) was used. It gives the input-output table and value-added matrix for 1982. Elasticities of substitution between labour and capital are also needed for the estimation of the Hessian R. The estimated elasticities come from Whalley *[reference not provided—eds.]*. The Hessian matrix of the expenditure function is calculated using expenditure shares and total expenditure. The 1982 final demand data of Adelman and Robinson were used. Total expenditure is the sum of private consumption and investment. The shares are the ratio of the expenditure for each sector divided by total expenditure.

The vector of consumption taxes is estimated by the vector of "total indirect business taxes" paid by each sector, which appears in the value-added data of Adelman and Robinson. Consumption taxes are expressed as percentages of the value of total output of each sector. These tax rates underestimate the true consumption tax rates because they do not include sales taxes. The effect of this underestimation is investigated in the sensitivity analysis. The tariffs for the agricultural sectors are computed using weighted averages of tariffs prevailing in the markets within each sector in *ad valorem* form. The tariff in a given market is the difference between the producer price, adjusted for transport costs and direct payments (deficiency, storage, and disaster payments), and the border price, c.i.f. for imports and f.o.b. for exports. The price data come from USDA (1983 and 1985), World Bank *[reference not provided—eds.]*, Commodity Research Bureau (1985), UN Conference on Trade and Development (1985), Duncan (1984), and Finger and Yeats (1976). The tariffs for the manufacturing sectors are based on Morici and Megna (1983); they estimated *ad valorem* equivalents of the different producer subsidies in manufacturing for 1976. Custom duties for 1982 are also available from the US International Trade Commission *[reference not provided—eds.]*. The duties and subsidies, in *ad valorem* form, are aggregated to approximate the tariffs for the manufacturing sectors.

The tariffs in the nontraded sectors are calculated following the Dixit-Norman methodology. The sector nomenclature, existing tariffs, and consumer tax rates are presented in Table 1.

Results

The computed optimum tariffs and consumer taxes for the seven agricultural sectors are shown in Table 1. The results suggest that the price support to the "dairy, poultry, and eggs" sector should be decreased from the existing level of 26.02 percent to the optimum tariff of 2.98 percent. Similarly, the tariff on the "meat and livestock" sector should be lowered to 2.77 percent.

The optimum producer price level of the food and feed grains sector is close to the prevailing level in 1982. The protection of the fifth sector (cotton and oil-bearing crops) should be increased significantly to 49 percent. The opposite conclusions are reached for the last two sectors. For the "fruits and vegetables" sector, the tariff should be reduced to 3.81 percent; the price support to the "tobacco, sugar, and other agriculture" sector should be lowered to 3.33 percent. The aggregation scheme in the Adelman and Robinson data

Table 1—Sector Nomenclature, Existing Tariffs, and Consumer Tax Rates

Sector Nomenclature	Existing Tariff	Distortions of Consumption Tax	Optimum Tariff	Distortions of Consumption Tax	Predicted Net Exports	Existing Net Exports
1. Dairy, poultry, and eggs	26.02	1.41	2.985	5.852	-13,884.46	5.755
2. Meat and livestock	35.26	2.04	2.777	6.060	-40,397.89	-471.406
3. Food grains	0.78	1.94	1.326	7.511	4,608.891	5,420.757
4. Feed grains and grass seeds	7.44	1.96	0.575	8.262	17,048.66	5,771.896
5. Cotton and oil-bearing crops	6.60	1.49	49.009	-40.173	4,520.979	6,142.924
6. Fruits, vegetables, and tree nuts	23.93	1.42	3.811	5.026	-4,563.377	-734.723
7. Tobacco, sugar, and other agriculture	54.04	2.55	3.333	5.504	-16,745.28	-2,082.531
8. Metal, coal, nonmetal, and mining	-17.27	4.88			3,413.338	3,621.865
9. Crude petroleum gas	-25.12	12.80			-48,978.60	-50,117.23
10. Construction*	4.54	1.06			0.016	0.0
11. Munitions	6.03	1.11			3,428.766	3,788.338
12. Food, beverage, and tobacco products	5.57	3.56			70,548.15	-1,631.046
13. Textiles	13.82	0.97			-6,863.791	-566.050
14. Apparel	32.60	0.44			-10,313.36	-10,123.76
15. Wood and wood products	2.54	1.01			13,511.29	-1,096.472
16. Paper, paper products, and publishing	2.33	1.27			-5,697.080	-501.500
17. Chemical and chemical products	6.47	1.52			6,765.098	6,064.629
18. Petroleum and petroleum products	0.45	2.65			-7,955.418	-6,623.216
19. Leather and leather products	9.77	0.49			-6,066.524	-5,938.161
20. Nonmetallic mineral products	9.13	2.00			-2,717.214	-1,348.169
21. Iron and steel	5.82	2.07			-9,785.712	-9,535.274
22. Nonferrous metals	1.20	1.71			-4,486.537	-4,494.346
23. Metal products	5.12	1.03			-1,743.050	1,943.725
24. Farm equipment and motor vehicles	3.46	1.90			-21,536.23	-19,925.71
25. Machinery	5.88	1.10			8,784.966	10,356.95
26. Computing, radio, and TV equipment	5.46	1.03			-2,616.547	-515.754
27. Electrical machinery	5.09	0.69			1,975.568	2,866.238
28. Aircraft and other transport	3.69	0.72			9,781.806	11,271.73
29. Transport and communicaticn*	6.83	4.26			0.0	0.0
30. Electricity, gas, and water*	2.99	4.00			0.004	0.0
31. Wholesale and retail trade	0.00	15.73			16,834.97	2,680.16
32. Banking and insurance*	4.72	3.50			0.0	0.0
33. Real estate*	-10.32	19.06			0.0	0.0
34. Hotel, personal services, and eating	4.38	3.69			0.0	0.0
35. Business services	0.00	0.77			3,113.490	6,427.182
36. Health, education, and social services	4.66	0.24			0.0	0.0
37. Federal, state, and local enterprises	5.57	0.00			0.004	0.0
38. Other industry	6.80	1.52			-10,255.17	-8,341.947

*The distortions for the nontraded sectors are computed with the optimum tariffs and consumption taxes.

does not allow one to determine the optimum protection on a commodity base. No obvious rule exists to translate the optimum tariff of a subsector into a set of optimum tariffs for each commodity within that subsector. The only rigorous way to proceed would be to use a disaggregated data set commodity by commodity.

The findings are quite robust to sensitivity analysis. This analysis is centred on the elasticities of substitution, existing consumer tax rates, and small-country assumption.

The influence of the elasticity of substitution on the value of the Hessian *R* is analytically ambiguous. A series of scenarios is considered within two extreme cases, with all elasticities of substitution equal to 0.05 and 5, respectively. The magnitude of the optimum tariff does not vary substantially except for the fifth sector, for which the optimum tariff drops from 49 percent to 34 percent in the case of very low elasticities (0.05).

The second part of the sensitivity analysis concerns the underestimation of the consumer tax rates. The estimates do not include sales taxes and are biased downwards. The tax rates of Table 1 are scaled up by 20 and 50 percent to determine the impact of their probable underestimation. The optimum consumption taxes are increased by approximately one cent per dollar (20-percent case) and three cents per dollar (50-percent case). The optimum tariffs are almost invariant to the changes in the consumer tax rates.

The small-country assumption is relaxed for three of the agricultural sectors (food, feed grains, and cotton and oil-bearing crops). Dixit's methodology, modified to take into account the nontraded sectors, is used to endogenize prices for these commodities. Several cases are considered. For each scenario, cross-price elasticities are set to zero and all commodities have the same own-price elasticity. Tariffs decrease significantly and become negative as the world demands for the three sectors become less elastic; i.e., exercising market power by means of an export tax becomes optimal. In the extreme case of unit elasticity of world demand, the tariffs on food and feed grains and cotton and oil-bearing crops are -98 percent, -99 percent, and -51 percent, respectively. Gardiner and Dixit (1986) survey the existing estimates of world demand elasticities for US agricultural exports. According to that study, no consensus exists on the real magnitude of the elasticities. One can conclude that the optimum tariffs presented in Table 1 are an upper bound for the "true" optimum tariffs for sectors 3, 4, and 5 (unless cross-price effects dominate).

The persistence of a high optimal tariff for the cotton and oil-bearing crops suggests that the high degree of protection of the textile industry determines the optimum tariff on raw cotton via the input-output coefficients. Similarly, the existing tariff on food and beverages affects the optimal tariff on oil-bearing crops. When the tariff on textiles (sector 13) is decreased by 50 percent, the optimal tariff on cotton and oil-bearing crops drops to 17 percent; conversely, when it is increased by 50 percent, the optimum tariff on cotton rises to 80 percent. The same analysis is performed for sector 12 (food and beverages). When the existing tariff on sector 12 is decreased by 50 percent, the optimum tariff on cotton and oil-bearing crops falls to 41 percent and the optimum tariff on feed grains falls to -11 percent (an export tax); i.e., a fall in the effective rate of protection of sector 12 caused by a decrease in the tariff on that sector should be partially offset by a decrease in the price of inputs. The tariffs on each of the other agricultural sectors are also decreased but to a lesser extent.

An attempt was made to determine the effects on production and trade of changing the current distortions. The Hessian matrix of the revenue function, used to calculate the optimal distortions, was used to construct own- and cross-price elasticities of supply at 1982 prices. These elasticities were used to generate constant elasticity supply curves. The revenue function implied by the model does not lead to constant elasticity supply curves, so the estimates reported here are only tentative. The predicted levels and the existing (1982) levels of net exports are presented in Table 1. The predictions indicate that, under the optimal distortions, the USA would change from being a net exporter to being a net importer of dairy, poultry, and eggs. Meat and livestock imports would increase by a factor of almost 10; exports of feed grains would increase by a factor of 3. Relatively little change would occur in exports of cotton and oil-bearing crops (despite the increased tariff in that sector), but textile imports would increase by a factor of more than 10. This reflects the fact that an increase in the protection of raw cotton decreases the effective protection of the textile industry. A sixfold increase would occur in the imports of fruits and vegetables, and an eightfold increase in tobacco and sugar imports. This would change the USA from an importer to an exporter of food, beverage, and tobacco products (sector 12). These effects are intuitive, given the changes in the distortions.

Conclusion

This study was motivated by asking whether existing (1982) distortions in the nonagricultural sectors justify the current (1982) level of distortions in the agricultural sectors. Since no theoretical basis for answering this question exists, this paper attempted to provide empirical evidence. This evidence must be interpreted cautiously because the model involves several strong assumptions. However, the extensive sensitivity analysis suggests that the results provide at least a rough guide. For four subsectors—dairy, poultry, and eggs; meat and livestock; fruit and vegetables; and tobacco and sugar—the existing distortions cannot be justified on efficiency criteria. For two subsectors—food and feed grains—the existing distortion, which is quite low, is approximately optimal.

For one subsector—cotton and oil-bearing crops—the existing distortion should be greatly increased. Both consumers and producers of these commodities should be subsidized. This result is due to the existing protection of the textile and food and beverage industries. Decreases in the tariff on these industries should be translated into a decrease in the optimal level of protection of the raw cotton sector.

The analysis uses economic efficiency as the sole criteria. The estimates of changes in production and trade induced by changes in the distortions suggest that the distributional issues may be significant. This observation is reinforced by the fact that the analysis ignores adjustment costs that increase the burden and decrease the benefits of proposed changes. Despite these qualifications, an important conclusion remains: levels of protection of the most highly protected agricultural commodities are not justified by efficiency criteria.

Note

[1]Department of Economics and Business, North Carolina State University; and Department of Agricultural and Resource Economics, University of California, Berkeley; respectively. Giannini Foundation Paper No. 876.

References

Adelman, I., and Robinson, S. (1986) "Application of General Equilibrium Models to Analyze U.S. Agriculture," paper presented at the American Agricultural Economics Association annual meeting, Reno, Nev., USA.

Commodity Research Bureau (1985) *Commodity Yearbook*, Jersey City, N.J., USA.

Dixit, A.K. (1985) "Tax Policy in Open Economies," in Auerback, A., and Feldstein, M. (Eds.) *Handbook of Public Economics*, North-Holland Publishing Co., Amsterdam, Netherlands.

Dixit, A.K., and Newbery, D.M.G. (1985) "Setting the Price of Oil in a Distorted Economy," *Economic Journal*, Vol. 95, pp. 71-82.

Dixit, A.K., and Norman, V. (1980) *Theory of International Trade*, Cambridge University Press, Cambridge, UK.

Duncan, R.C. (1984) *Outlook for Primary Commodities, 1984 to 1995*, World Bank Staff Commodity Working Paper No. 11, World Bank, Washington, D.C., USA.

Finger, J.M., and Yeats, A.J. (1976) "Effective Protection by Transportation Cost and Tariffs: Comparison of Magnitudes," *Quarterly Journal of Economics*, Vol. 90, pp. 169-176.

Gardiner, W.H., and Dixit, P.M. (1986) *Price Elasticity of Export Demand: Concepts and Estimates*, Staff Report No. AGES-860408, Economic Research Service, US Department of Agriculture, Washington, D.C., USA.
Morici, P., and Megna, L.L. (1983) "U.S. Economic Policies Affecting Industrial Trade," National Planning Association, Washington, D.C., USA.
UN Conference on Trade and Development (1985) *Monthly Price Bulletin*, New York, N.Y., USA.
USDA (US Department of Agriculture) (1983) "U.S. Foreign Agriculture Trade Statistical Report: Calendar Year 1982," Economic Research Service, Washington, D.C., USA.
USDA (US Department of Agriculture) (1985) *[Various Commodities] Background for the 1985 Farm Legislation*, Agriculture Information Bulletins Nos. 465 to 478, Economic Research Service, Washington, D.C., USA.

DISCUSSION OPENING—*John Fogarty* (University of Melbourne)

An important question has been posed in a challenging fashion and appropriate methodology employed. However, as is often the case with a highly specified model, the tight specification and qualification of results leave little to argue about. On the other hand, the rigorous methodology means that some of the most interesting issues are assumed away.

The object of the paper is to measure the optimum levels of distortions for agricultural production in a second-best situation where the existing distortions in the manufacturing sector remain intact. The conclusions, that those primary products where existing distortions are greatest (i.e., dairy, poultry, and eggs; meat and livestock; sugar; tobacco; and fruits and vegetables) should be subjected to more vigorous competition are hardly surprising. What I find most interesting are the conclusions with respect to other agricultural products such as cereals and cotton.

Estimates of the producer distortions are adjusted for subsidies and, in the case of food grains, found to be neutral. How are programmes like target prices taken into account? How, for instance, would the $2,000 million export assistance programme announced in the 1985 Farm Bill be brought into the calculations? Are we in the Southern Hemisphere mistaken in thinking that our grain is competing against subsidized US wheat in international markets?

I confess to being a little confused by the results for the cotton and oil-bearing crops. The argument is that high tariffs in textile manufacturing should be offset by increased protection for raw cotton in order to reduce the protection afforded to textiles. The model calls for a considerable rise in imports of textiles accompanied by a fall in cotton exports. Presumably raw cotton production declines as both internal and external markets are reduced, which intuitively I find difficult to reconcile with the optimum situation for a crop that suffers from low levels of distortion.

I have no difficulty with the conclusion that "levels of protection of the most highly protected agricultural commodities are not justified by efficiency criteria." I am convinced that efficiency criteria justify protection for agricultural commodities because they happen to be inputs into protected manufacturing industries.

I realize that my comments could be dismissed as lying outside the assumptions of the model. But my final question still must be, "How adequate, for practical purposes, is the second-best assumption that levels of distortions in the manufacturing sector remain intact?"

GENERAL DISCUSSION—*Thomas C. Pinckney, Rapporteur* (International Food Policy Research Institute)

The author was asked to clarify the distinction between tariff and sector-specific subsidies in term of their effects on resource shifts. Karp replied that a tariff raises both the producer and the consumer price of the product, while a sector-specific subsidy is assumed to raise the producer price but not the consumer price. In the latter case, the consumer price is assumed to move to world market levels, with the world price unaffected by domestic production levels. This small-country assumption has been relaxed in some versions of the model not reported in the paper.

One participant pointed out that every policy recommendation assumes an implicit constrained optimization model, with some of the constraints being distortions in other markets. The authors were commended for making the other trade policy distortions explicit, but many other distortions could have been added, including any misalignment of the exchange rate. Although this approach is correct methodologically, one questions whether such second-, third-, or fourth-best results should be used for policy recommendations when we economists frequently cannot even explain and interpret the first-best results.

This paper points to the danger in using PSEs *[producer subsidy equivalents]* or any other scalar representation of subsidies, since, according to the paper, the effects of production from a tariff are quite different from the effects of an equal amount of protection from a subsidy.

Participants in the discussion included D. Colman, D. Kirschke, and D. Orden.

Supply Management: Analyzing the Values of Tradeable Output Quotas

Michele M. Veeman[1]

Abstract: This paper is concerned with the analysis of some economic impacts of supply-management quota schemes based on evidence from some of the Canadian quota programmes. Reasons underlying the wide acceptance of these programmes and the use of cost-increasing methods of quota administration are briefly explored. Some evidence from Canadian quota programmes is presented to illustrate the economic effects of restrictive quota transfer policies. An econometric analysis of economic factors affecting the supply of and demand for transferable output quotas is presented. The results of a single-equation model of the derived demand for quotas are compared to the results of a simultaneous equation model of demand and supply for quotas. Econometric analysis of quota price and transaction data provides useful insights into the behaviour of the market for quotas.

Introduction

This paper is concerned with the analysis of some effects of a particular form of government-authorized intervention in the marketing of agricultural commodities, specifically programmes of supply management involving quota-specified constraints on output levels of individual producers. These programmes are well entrenched in Canada for dairy and poultry products; they are also applied in Australia for similar products and have more recently been introduced for milk in some countries of northern Europe and in the EC. Such programmes are allied with maintenance of price and income levels for farmers at levels higher than would be achieved without intervention.

Supply managing quota programmes have a number of problems and disadvantages. They involve increased levels of consumer expenditures; the increased farm asset values that occur with these programmes lead to increased costs of entry for young producers and higher levels of capital costs for the industry; the programmes can involve appreciable social costs, depending on the ways in which they are administered. Nonetheless, supply control has been given increasing emphasis in the debate on agricultural policy reforms, being seen by many governments as a politically acceptable short-term solution to surplus problems (OECD, 1987, p. 21). A number of people have studied the Canadian supply management programmes (e.g., Forbes, Hughes, and Warley, 1982). Evidence from the relatively long-established Canadian programmes may be useful in evaluating potential merits and problems in wider use of supply-management quota programmes. Appropriate approaches to empirical analysis of quota values also requires exploration. In addressing these issues, this paper gives an analysis of some of the factors affecting the values of quotas, applying evidence from some Canadian supply management programmes. A preliminary econometric analysis of some Canadian quota value and transaction data for Ontario fluid milk is also presented.

Factors Affecting Quota Values

Quota programmes have been a politically favoured method of providing income support to producers of domestically oriented farm products in Canada. The price-inelastic domestic demand schedules for such products as fluid milk and poultry products have enabled producer total revenue to be increased appreciably by supply limitation. The limitation of imports used to support the national supply-management programmes is justified under Article 11 of GATT, to which Canada is a signatory. The programmes have been perceived by some groups of producers as means of achieving "fair" prices and incomes justified on cost-related pricing formulas. Further, the considerable income transfers from consumers to producers are achieved without explicit government expenditures. All these factors have contributed to the popularity of supply management programmes among many producers and to widespread political support for these programmes.

One characteristic feature of programmes that maintain agricultural prices and incomes above competitive levels is the tendency for the benefits of the programmes to become capitalized into the value of farm assets; this feature can be expected as long as the rights of use of quotas lead to net returns greater than alternative uses of producer resources. Specifically, the anticipated stream of net benefits from the use of quota rights becomes capitalized into the present value of these rights. When quotas are attached to inputs such as land or cows, the capital values of these assets inflate, reflecting the benefits of gaining access to the programme through use of these assets. When supply management programmes are administered in the form of negotiable output quotas, the values attached to these assets provide a measure of the capitalized value of the stream of rents associated with use of the quotas.

Social costs of quota programmes can be increased appreciably by their application as input quotas (rather than as output quotas) and by limitations on transferability of quotas among producers. Restrictions on quota transfers may obscure quota values (as when these are reflected in the capital values of farmland or livestock). They also reduce the net benefits of quota use to producers, for example, by increasing the transaction costs of transfers, preventing the achievement of economies of scale, and preventing locational adjustments that would otherwise occur. Producer cost levels rise as restraints on quota transfers and the use of input quotas prevent producers from using the least-cost combinations of resources and limit their use of the most efficient scale of plant and the lowest cost location (Veeman, 1982 and 1987). Thus, some advocate that existing quota programmes be applied through transferable output quotas with minimal restrictions on transferability. Nonetheless, all supply-management quota programmes in Canada restrict quota transfers to some degree.

The extent of restrictions on quota transfers tends to vary by province and commodity. In some instances, this has changed over time. In the Prairie Provinces, broiler chicken, egg, and turkey quotas are not transferred by negotiated sales but are essentially transferred with land and buildings. Although changes have occurred over time, negotiated sale transfer of quota rights is now applied in most other provinces, but limitations on these transfers are widespread. These limitations include restrictions on relocation of production between specified areas, restrictions on the entitlement of those involved in transfers to share in subsequent allocations of expanded quota rights, limitations of the quantity of transferred quotas (e.g., restriction to "whole farm" transfers) and restrictions on the length of time quota purchasers must hold quotas before resale. Renting quotas is often not allowed. Restrictions on allowable quota prices are applied in some provinces in an effort to reduce these values. Restrictions exist on the maximum size of quotas that may be held by individuals in all provinces. No provision exists for negotiated transfer of quotas between provinces, although under the national supply-management programmes a very limited opportunity exists for administrative reallocation of quotas from province to province (Veeman, 1988).

These quota transfer restrictions persist for two apparent reasons, despite their deleterious effects on social costs of the programmes. First, they are used to effect desired structural changes or to limit structural changes considered undesirable by quota programme administrators and supervisors. Thus, quota policies are used to maintain "family" farms, limit purchases by nonfarmers, and limit the extent of vertical integration. Second, transfer limitations are applied to reduce the visibility and level of quota values, to limit adverse publicity on the income transfers to producers under these programmes and to reduce adverse public reaction to the programmes.

Examination of differences among provinces in quota policy for eggs and related features of this sector illustrates the implications of quota policy to producer benefits and social costs of the programmes. Some of these features are summarized in Table 1. Quota allocation and transfer policies, in particular, appear to be major factors underlying both the considerable differences in relative profitability of egg production (as indicated by the reported or imputed quota values) and the wide variation in average size of production units in different provinces outlined in Table 1. Quota values tend to be highest in those provinces with fewer quota transfer restrictions. Contrary to the belief of some producers

Table 1—Quota Transferability and Average Size of Egg Production Units, by Canadian Province

Province	Negotiated Quota Transfer	Maximum Quota Level (1983)	Quota Value Per Layer ($)	Average Size of Producing Unit[1]	No. of Producers
B.C.	Yes	20,000	[2]31	14,937	163
Alta.	No[3]	[4]23,000	[5]2-5	6,426	234
Sask.	No[3]	30,000	[5]2-5	8,248	85
Man.	No[3]	20,000	[5]2-5	9,606	242
Ont.	Yes[6]	30,000	[7]10	9,501	784
Qué.	Yes[8]	50,000	[9]18	18,991	170
N.B.	Yes	25,000	na	16,771	25
N.S.	Yes	50,000	na	19,828	43
P.E.I.	No	15,000	na[10]	4,461	32
Nfld.	No[3]	25,000	na	12,272	36

[1]Average number of laying hens per regulated producer, 1986. For Canada as a whole, this was 10,748 (CEMA, 1987).

[2]Based on $2,400/case for 1983 (Dawson, 1983).

[3]Quota is attached to land and buildings; asset transfer and board reallocation are required.

[4]1.5 percent of provincial entitlement.

[5]Officially, these values are zero; unofficial estimates typically range from $2 to $5 per layer.

[6]Since 1980.

[7]Administered price for board purchases.

[8]Since 1973.

[9]1983 (Dawson, 1983).

[10]Officially zero.

Sources: Arcus (1981); Barichello and Cunningham-Dunlop (1987); CEMA (1987); Dawson (1983); and annual reports of various boards.

and marketing board administrators, this is not due to negotiability of quotas alone. Rather, as was noted previously, it is due primarily to the lower levels of costs that accompany negotiability of quotas when quota transfers are less restricted. This is reflected, for example, in the relatively larger scales of production associated with fewer limitations on transfer (see Table 1). However, even in provinces with fewer restrictions on egg quota transfers, average plant size is considerably less than the 30,000 layers believed to be required for a technically efficient scale of plant, ignoring pecuniary effects (Dawson and Associates, 1983). Other sources of social costs include distortions in resource allocation (such as those arising from input rather than output quotas, or when poultry boards continue to specify such input requirements as floor space allocations or production cycle times) and increased costs from prevention of locational adjustments. In addition, producer costs are increased when restrictions on quota transfers result in underuse of existing productive capacity. Administrative costs, including costs of monitoring and enforcing quota and levy regulations, as well as costs associated with rent seeking by producers, boards, and other bodies, add to the social costs of these programmes. Added risk and uncertainty arising from the possibility of programme changes also appear to contribute to the social costs of these programmes.

Empirical Analysis of Quota Values

Despite the limitations in quota value data implied by the preceding discussion, monitoring and analyzing the levels of available quota value data may provide useful information on the economic effects of supply-management programmes. Quota value data are relatively scanty for most of the regulated commodities. However, some reliable time-series data on quota values are available from organized quota exchanges, specifically for Ontario milk quotas. One purpose of analyzing quota value data is to explore the reasons underlying the tendency for milk quota values to increase over time. In addition, such analyses may shed light on the underlying economic behaviour and characteristics of market behaviour in a regulated industry.

The capital asset pricing model has commonly been used in analyzing the economic effects of quotas in Canada; e.g., in imputing annual net benefits to producers from quota use. This paper follows an alternative analytical procedure involving an econometric analysis of quota price and transaction data. In this preliminary analysis, quotas are treated as an input required for the production of fluid milk. The derived demand for quotas is estimated using the monthly data on quota prices and transactions for Ontario milk and other variables from March 1980 to December 1985.

Following standard microeconomic theory, the derived demand for quotas in time t, QD_t, the monthly volume of quota purchases, is hypothesized to be a function of the price of quotas, P_t; PM_t, the administered and thus exogenously determined price of fluid milk; the price of the major input, feed, PF_t; monthly dummy variables M_i, $i = 2, \ldots, 12$; and the error term ud_t; giving Model 1 as:

$$(1)\ QD_t = D_0 - D_1P_t + D_2PM_t - D_3PF_t + \sum_{i=2}^{12} \alpha_i M_i + ud_t.$$

Model 1 is estimated using OLS. The price variables are deflated and all variables except M_i are expressed in logarithmic form.

Model 2 consists of the previously specified demand function of Model 1 to which is added a supply function for quota transactions and an equilibrium condition, as outlined below:

$$(2)\ P_t = S_0 + S_1QS_t + S_2P_{t-1} + S_3INT_t + \sum_{i=2}^{12} \beta_i M_i + us_t, \text{ and}$$

$$(3)\ QD_t = QS_t,$$

where INT_t denotes chartered bank prime interest rate at time t, and the other variables are as previously defined.

The specification of single-equation demand models, such as Model 1, could be justified on the basis that quotas are a nonproduced factor, administratively fixed in total quantity, and thus not appropriately represented by a supply schedule. However, this argument can be challenged on the grounds that although the total stock of quotas is fixed in quantity, producer willingness to sell quotas will be affected by economic variables and constitutes the supply schedule. Specification of Model 2 thus allows assessment of the appropriateness of a single-equation approach as compared to the simultaneous equation approach of the model. The hypothesized dependent variables for the supply function (which is expressed in price-dependent form) include both quota transactions and quota prices in the previous period, since it is hypothesized that adjustment to equilibrium is not instantaneous but occurs over time. Inclusion of the interest rate variable relates to the opportunity cost of a producer's decision to retain rather than sell a quota. All price variables, including INT, are deflated and are expressed in logarithmic form. The system of

Table 2–Results of Econometric Analysis of Ontario Fluid Milk Quota Values and Transactions, Demand Equation, Model 1*

Independent Variables	Estimated Coefficients
	Dependent Variable: QD
P	0.42 (2.378)
PM	4.96 (3.179)
PF	-0.18 (0.667)
Constant term	13.25 (9.532)
R^2 (adjusted)	0.50
D.W. statistic	2.105

*Due to space constraints, the coefficients and *t*-statistics for M_i are not reported here, but application of an *F*-test to test H_0: $\beta_i = 0, i = 2, \ldots, 12$, gives an *F*-statistic that exceeds the critical value of *F* at the 99-percent level of significance, suggesting that inclusion of the seasonality variables is warranted.

Note: *t*-statistics are in parentheses.

equations involved in Model 2 is overidentified and estimated using 3SLS. The resulting estimates for both models are given in Tables 2 and 3.

Examination of the results of the single-equation model of quota demand of Model 1 indicates that the milk price variable has the appropriate positive sign and is significant. Feed price also has the expected negative sign but is not significantly different from zero. The coefficient on the quota price variable is positive and is significant at the 5-percent level. This sign is not consistent with expectations but can be explained by outward shifts in the demand for quotas over time that may have outweighed any price-associated movement along the demand curve for quotas.[2] Results for the monthly dummy variables included to test for seasonality in quota demand are not reported in Table 2, but a test of the absence of seasonal patterns leads to rejection of the null hypothesis and thus implies that seasonal patterns of quota demand are evident. Demand for quotas in June and July, at the end of the dairy year, is typically lower than in other months.

The inclusion of the supply equation of Model 2 led to a decrease in standard errors of the estimated coefficients, supporting the use of the simultaneous equation approach reported in Table 3.[3] The demand estimates in Table 3 are similar in sign to those of Model 1 but the magnitudes of these estimates, and the associated elasticities, are slightly larger than those from the single-equation demand model. The price of milk, a major factor in the profitability of milk production, appears to have a major influence on the demand for quotas. The results in Table 3 imply that a 1-percent increase in milk price is associated with a 5.4-percent increase in the demand for quotas. An increase of 1 percent in the price

Table 3—Results of Econometric Analysis of Ontario Fluid Milk Quota Values and Transactions, Demand-Supply System, Model 2*

Demand, Dependent Variable: *QD*		Supply, Dependent Variable: *P*	
Independent Variables	Estimated Coefficients	Independent Variables	Estimated Coefficients
P	0.57 (3.141)	*QS*	0.012 (0.239)
PM	5.377 (3.737)	*INT*	-0.19 (-4.256)
PF	-0.04 (-0.178)	P_{t-1}	0.79 (14.964)
Constant term	13.45 (10.627)	Constant term	-0.45 (-0.969)
R^2 (adjusted)	0.60	R^2 (adjusted)	0.97
D.W. statistic	2.095	*D.W.* statistic	1.471

*Due to space constraints, the coefficients and *t*-statistics for M_i are not reported here, but application of an *F*-test to test H_o: $\beta_i = 0, i = 2, ..., 12$, gives an *F*-statistic that exceeds the critical value of *F* at the 99-percent level of significance, suggesting that inclusion of the seasonality variables is warranted.

Note: *t*-statistics are in parentheses.

of quotas has been associated with 0.57-percent increase in quota demand. Interest rates and the previous level of quota prices are both highly significant explanatory variables in the supply equation. The results suggest that a 1-percent increase in real interest rates decreases quota prices by 0.19 percent on average.

Overall, econometric analysis of quota value and transaction data from markets for transferable quotas may provide helpful insights into the functioning of these programmes. A priority for continuing work in the study described here is to further explore the relationships among the administered prices for milk, the demand for quotas, and quota values. Both econometric models and extensions of the capital-asset-pricing model may be useful in this context.

Summary and Conclusions

The relatively long-established Canadian supply management programmes may provide some lessons for such programmes in other regions. Despite the preference of some producers and their associations for quota policies that obscure quota values, a quota policy that emphasizes output quotas that can be freely traded with limited restrictions on negotiability is conducive to higher levels of producer returns, lower levels of social costs, and more visible programme implications than when more restrictive quota transfer policies are applied.

Econometric estimates were derived for a hypothesized single-equation demand function and for a simultaneous equation system of hypothesized supply and demand functions for Ontario fluid milk quotas. The results suggest that outward shifts in the demand for quotas have been related to increasing levels of fluid milk prices, and these higher prices have been associated with appreciation of the real value of fluid milk quotas. The major influence on the demand for quotas appears to arise from changes in the level of the administered prices for fluid milk. Statistical support exists for use of the simultaneous equation approach to the analysis of quota values. Major supply-side influences on quota prices appear to be the real interest rate (which is negatively associated with quota prices) and previous quota prices. A pattern of seasonality is evident in the demand for quotas. The results suggest that any administrative action to moderate quota value increases should focus on the levels of fluid milk prices rather than on limiting transferability of fluid milk quotas. Econometric analyses may provide useful means of analyzing the economic implications of negotiable output quotas.

Notes

[1]Department of Rural Economy, University of Alberta. Research assistance with the econometric estimation by Peter Chen is gratefully acknowledged as is financial assistance for that estimation from an Agriculture Canada EMR grant.

[2]Subsequent substitution of measures of anticipated rather than current quota prices (modelled, for example, as $P_t - P_{t-1}$ or as deviations of current prices from three-year moving averages) yields coefficients with the expected negative sign.

[3]Subsequent application of Wu-Hausman endogeneity tests suggests that both *QD* and *P* are endogenous, supporting the simultaneous equation approach.

References

Arcus, P.L. (1981) *Broilers and Eggs*, Technical Report No. E/13, Economic Council of Canada and Institute for Research on Public Policy, Ottawa, Ont., Canada.

Barichello, R.R., and Cunningham-Dunlop, C. (1987) *Quota Allocation and Transfer Schemes in Canada*, Working Paper No. 8, Policy Branch, Agriculture Canada, Ottawa, Ont., Canada.

CEMA (Canadian Egg Marketing Agency) (1987) *14th Annual Report*, Ottawa, Ont., Canada.

Dawson, D., and Associates (1983) *Management of Quota in Alberta, Parts I, II, and III*, Consultants' Report to the Agricultural Marketing Council, Alberta, Canada.

Forbes, J.D., Hughes, R.D., and Warley, T.K. (1982) *Economic Intervention and Regulation in Canadian Agriculture*, Economic Council of Canada, Ottawa, Ont., Canada.

OECD (Organization for Economic Cooperation and Development) (1987) *National Policies and Agricultural Trade*, Paris, France.

Veeman, M.M. (1982) "Social Costs of Supply-Restricting Marketing Boards," *Canadian Journal of Agricultural Economics*, Vol. 30, pp. 21-36.

Veeman, M.M. (1987) "Marketing Boards: Canadian Experience," *American Journal of Agricultural Economics*, Vol. 69, No. 4, pp. 992-1000.

Veeman, M.M. "Supply Management Systems: Impact on Interprovincial Trade," paper presented at the Symposium on Farm Policy for a Freer Trade World, Canadian Agricultural Economics and Farm Management Society, Département d'Économie Rurale, Université Laval, Sainte-Foy, Qué., Canada, 4-6 May 1988.

DISCUSSION OPENING—*Praveen M. Dixit* (Economic Research Service, US Department of Agriculture)

Supply controls are being introduced as short-term solutions in various proposals being made for the Uruguay Round of the GATT, and a thorough analysis of their effects on the market place is sorely needed.

Veeman's paper is especially informative when it discusses the problems, advantages, and disadvantages of the Canadian supply management system. She rightly points out that producer groups often see this as a means of obtaining "fair" prices and incomes justified on cost-related pricing formulas, and social costs of quota programmes are increased by limitations on transferability of quotas. While agreeing with her argument that gains from transferability are related to the economies of scale that can be achieved, I find her evidence rather inconclusive—weak supportive evidence within the purview of the chosen market. The sample size is rather small and based largely on observations made over one year. Also, how were the quota values calculated? Finally, I believe that the type of quota transfer system has an important bearing on the outcome. Her conclusions about the benefits of transferability depending on size of operation, therefore, may be a bit strong given the narrow purview of the chosen market.

I have more problems accepting the validity of the part of her analysis that examines forces that influence the derived demand for quotas. Her results indicate that the own-price effects on demand are perverse and significant, which she argues "can be explained by outward shifts in the demand for quotas over time that may have outweighed any price-associated movement along the demand curve for quotas." While this may be true, an econometric problem still exists with either a misspecified demand function, a poor proxy for the own-price variable, or an inappropriate estimation system. Curiously, even the price of industrial milk is not included in the demand equation. Moreover, where she tries to remedy the estimation problem by using 3SLS, the issue of demand specification still exists. The structural coefficient still has the wrong sign. Also, decreases in standard errors of the estimated coefficients do not necessarily indicate more reasonable fits but rather an estimation property when moving from OLS to 3SLS. The choice of instruments hence needs to be questioned.

Despite some of these problems, this paper, along with some of Veeman's earlier work on supply management, could be great use to both economists and policy makers alike. The Uruguay Round is expected to focus a great deal on supply management, its implications for aggregate measures of support (producer subsidy equivalents), and its effects on international agricultural trade. Veeman's work on supply management and quota rents provides a good start for Canada; it also paves the way for others to do similar work.

[No general discussion of this paper was reported.]

Transboundary Environmental Degradation and the Growing Demand for Institutional Innovation

Marie L. Livingston and Harald von Witzke[1]

Abstract: Transboundary pollution constitutes an important component of environmental degradation in many countries. The demand for institutional changes that reduce transboundary pollution grows with increasing levels of economic development and accumulation of environmental degradation. Single countries, however, can set up such institutions only in cooperation with other countries. This paper analyzes the strategic game theoretic situation of countries concerned with transboundary pollution under alternative benefit-cost situations. The results suggest that a system of reciprocal obligations of countries can result in supranational agreements if the assurance problem of each signatory can be solved and the distribution of costs and benefits of such agreements are perceived as being fair.

Introduction

The problem of transboundary environmental degradation is global; many nations in Europe, the Americas, and elsewhere have been cited as emitters and/or receivers of polluted air or water (Hart, 1987). Economic analysis of transboundary pollution is in its infancy. Only a few avenues of study have been explored.

One of the aspects that has received little attention is game strategic dimensions of the problem and their implications for institutional innovation. The objective of this paper is to explore the implications of incentive structures associated with pollution of air resources and to discuss potential solutions to the problem.

Particular characteristics of international air resources and the conceptual underpinnings of a game theoretical approach are also be discussed. Under the incentive structures faced by many countries, demand for institutional innovation is growing. The paper concludes with the economic implications of a possible alternative institutional arrangement for dealing with the problem of transboundary pollution.

Incentive Structures Associated with Transboundary Pollution

Much semantic confusion exists among resource economists about the difference between common property, public goods, and externalities. Sketching the physical characteristics of resources and their economic consequences is useful to create meaningful distinctions. Market goods are exclusive, independent with respect to utility and production functions and mobile only with respect to money. In the case of transboundary pollution, none of these characteristics is met completely. Global resources are often nonexclusive, rife with externalities, and fugitive.

An efficient, competitive market in air resources will probably not develop via private contracting by households and firms due to the physical and economic characteristics of air resources. Optimal resource use will probably involve supranational institutional arrangements. Successful institutions must also take into account the specific physical attributes of global air resources and the incentive issues that result.

The incentive structure applicable to a particular transboundary pollution problem depends largely on the size and distribution of benefits and costs under alternative decisions by each country. They define the payoff matrix; i.e., the nature of the game. In the matrices presented here, net benefits are comprised of the profits attributable to production activities minus the external costs due to environmental degradation. The distribution of benefits and costs determines each individual country's incentives and thus the potential for negotiation. As with other externality problems, a separation of private and social costs is crucial. The following paragraphs outline two games that are instructive as general examples of the different degrees of skewness in payoffs and their impact on incentive structures.

Case One

Let us assume that two countries, A and B, are identical with respect to production technology and the imposition of pollution on each other. The existence of transboundary pollution means that social costs exceed private costs. Hence, both countries overproduce from a social point of view. The payoff matrix (Table 1) assumes that at the privately optimal level of production (Q_p), profits (Π) are 90 and external costs (XC) are 60. However, the socially optimal level of production (Q_s) would yield profits of 60 and external costs of 10. For simplicity, let us assume further that the external costs generated by A accrue entirely to B and vice versa.

Table 1—Payoff Matrix

	Country B			
	Q_p	Q_s	Q_p	Q_s
Q_p	(30, 30)	(80, 0)	(70, -30)	(73.5, -29.5)
Q_s	(0, 80)	(50, 50)	(52.5, 7.5)	(56, 8)
	Case One		Case Two	

Case one represents a typical prisoners' dilemma game. If both countries pollute, each realizes benefits of 90 from domestic production but imposes a pollution cost of 60 on the other country. Hence, the net benefits in each country are 30. If only country A pollutes, the production benefits to A are 90 and external costs (imposed by B) are 10, yielding a net of 80. In country B, the benefits are 60 and the damage of transboundary pollution caused by A is 60. Therefore, country B's payoff is zero. The outcome of Q_p in country B and Q_s in country A is symmetric to the above case. Finally, if neither country pollutes, the benefits remain at 60 each but each country has external costs of 10. Hence, the net benefits for each country are 50.

Case Two

The scenario in case two assumes that 75 percent of the externality-producing activity is concentrated in country A. Again, for country A at Q_p, Π = 90 and XC = 60, whereas at Q_s, Π = 60 and XC = 10. However, let us assume that, in country B, Q_p yields profits of 30 and external costs equal to 20, while Q_s results in Π = 20 and XC = 6. This case also assumes that 75 percent of the total external costs generated are suffered by country B and 25 percent by country A. For example, when both countries pollute, total external costs are 80 (60 are generated by country A and 20 by country B). However the damage *accrues* to countries A and B in the amounts 20 and 60, respectively, due to the fugitive nature of the global air resource.

As may be expected, with a skewed incidence of benefits and costs, incentives are also lopsided. In this case, country A continues to pollute and country B has the incentive to abate. Outcome (73.5, -29.5) is the stable equilibrium. The global optimum (56, 8) is achievable only through compensation. Country B could compensate country A in the amount 17.5 and experience an overall gain of 20. However, equity concerns may prevent this solution regardless of its economic efficiency.

Demand for Institutional Change

This section discusses how alternative payoffs translate into a private demand for institutional change; i.e., the practical prospects for attaining an institutional solution in an international context. Categorically, the central determinants of the demand for institutional innovation are efficiency and equity.

Efficiency Considerations

Changing relative factor scarcities and product demands can render existing institutions inefficient. In terms of efficiency, the demand for institutional change results from constraints that inhibit a more profitable use of production factors (Ruttan and Hayami, 1984). In some cases, efficiency gains can be captured via voluntary transfers of existing property rights. In others, formal government changes in the conditions attached to rights may be necessary (Livingston, 1987).

In the case of transboundary pollution, efficiency gains stem from the net gains that can be realized by reducing environmental degradation. Conceptually, net benefits are equal to the reduction in external costs minus the reduction in profits/utility attributable to a change in the level of production and emission. Thus the efficiency demand for institutional change increases whenever the demand for environmental quality increases or supply decreases. As the external costs of pollution increase or abatement technology becomes less costly, the potential net benefits of institutional innovation increase. Many argue that global air quality is better today than it was a few decades ago. Nevertheless, perhaps due to income effects, public awareness of and attention to environmental issues has grown tremendously. The increase in demand for clean air seems to have outstripped the change in supply. The result is an increasing demand for institutional arrangements that effectively reduce pollution.

Equity Issues

When the distribution of costs and/or benefits of an existing institution are perceived as unfair, the impetus for institutional change emerges as well (Runge and von Witzke, 1987). One can reasonably expect that, as global integration continues, attention to international equity will increase. The equity concerns relating to transboundary environmental degradation derive from the skewedness of production benefits and external costs.

Baumol (1982) and others have developed utility-based fairness theory by introducing the notion of symmetry between parties. A fair allocation is defined as one in which neither party envies the other. Obviously egalitarian (strictly equal) allocations are fair. The possibility of unequal but fair allocations arises out of heterogeneous tastes. The possibility of fair distributions that do not actually derive from equal initial endowments rests on the concept of an egalitarian equivalent allocation, which is an allocation that could have, *in principle*, arisen from egalitarian resource endowment.

This is illustrated in Figure 1. This graph is plotted in commodity space where X = industrial production and Y = environmental quality. Assume that B is a lower income country that places a lower value on environmental quality. D_E (equidistant from the two origins) represents an equal and therefore fair allocation of goods, according to Baumol. If tastes were identical, one would expect U_A and U_B to be tangent at D_E. However, given the divergent tastes, other allocations (specifically on the contract curve between D_1 and D_2) are both fair and Pareto optimal. The range of fair, contracted allocations expands as taste diverges.

Unequal initial endowment D_3, although not equal, may yield a negotiated solution of D_2 (if country B captures all gains from trade) and therefore can be deemed fair via the egalitarian equivalence principle; i.e., although the outcome D_2 arose from an unequal initial endowment (D_3), it could have, in principle, arisen out of D_E and is thus fair. At some

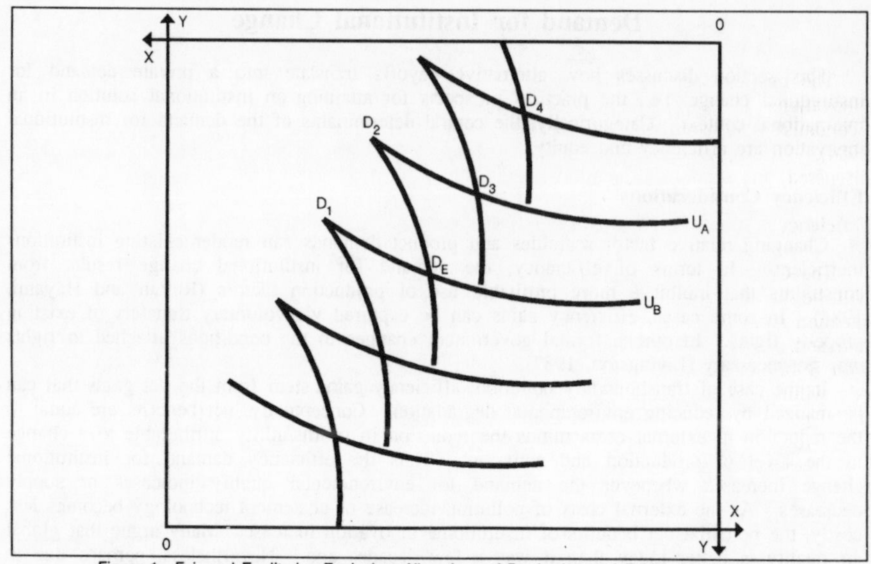

Figure 1—Fair and Egalitarian Equivalent Allocations of Production and Environmental Quality

point, however, the initial allocation is so skewed (like D_4) as to render a fair solution impossible.

The implication of Baumol's theory for the demand for institutional change is that where countries exhibit a very unequal distribution of initial endowments of production and environmental quality (i.e., where certain countries are particularly disadvantaged by virtue of initial conditions), private contracting within the existing institutional structure is unlikely to produce a fair outcome. In these cases, equity issues can be dealt with only through substantial institutional changes that, in effect, alter endowments.

Implications

To a large extent, the incidence of costs and benefits determines the prospects for an institutional solution. In general, the more homogeneous the countries involved in pollution, the greater the private impetus for an institutional solution. As income level and external costs incurred by a nation rise, so does the demand for institutional innovation. If the growing demand for institutional arrangements reduces the reelection chances of a government, policy makers have a growing incentive to seek international agreements over transboundary pollution.

Institutional arrangements are more likely to arise voluntarily when the countries involved are relatively homogeneous in regard to high income, environmental damage, and technology. International agreements on transboundary pollution are therefore more likely to emerge between countries of similar levels of economic development, such as in West Europe or North America. Low income countries, where the domestic political pressure for environmental quality is low, may not be willing to sign an agreement on transboundary pollution that bears the risk that the number of potential signataries is too low to create a critical mass (e.g., Hurwicz, 1951).

As the characteristics of nations diverge, either due to climatic circumstances or income differences, less efficiency and more equity motivation exists for voluntary institutional innovation. As specialization in externality-producing activities increases, one would expect the incidence of benefits and costs to become increasingly skewed. As Sugden (1984) has argued, with increasing heterogeneity of countries, solving the assurance problem becomes more and more difficult unless some outside enforcement mechanism exists.

Design Perspective on Institutional Innovation

The previous section discussed the factors that influence the demand for institutional innovation. The supply of innovation is an endogenous response to the demand for change. Economists can contribute to the debate by providing social science knowledge (Ruttan, 1984). In this section, the efficiency and equity issues that must be considered are discussed, and a potential solution is explored.

Efficiency: Institutional and Transaction Costs

The Coase theorem suggests that in a zero-transaction-costs world, negotiated outcomes will be invariant with respect to the structure of property rights. Let us consider the situation shown in Figure 2 where country A reaps all the benefits from production of acid rain and country B bears the entire cost. With no liability, Q_{NL} will initially be produced with B bribing A back to Q^* (as long as B's willingness to pay to avoid damage exceeds A's willingness to accept to forego production). Similarly, with full liability, Q_L is the initial position with A bribing B to Q^*.

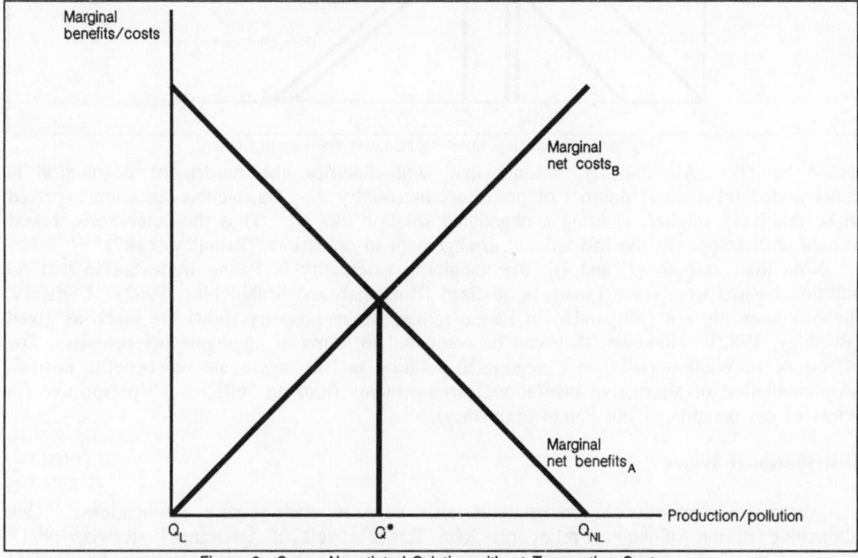

Figure 2—Coase Negotiated Solution without Transaction Costs

With the introduction of transaction costs or nonseparability, the Coase theorem breaks down; i.e., the negotiated outcome will be variant with respect to property rights (Bromley, 1986). In addition to other considerations, transaction costs rise with the number of parties involved (Olson, 1965). Assume that, with no liability, the costs of acid rain are dispersed widely among consumers in country B. The transaction costs associated with organization and negotiation would likely be large and reduce the amount available to bribe country A, as shown in Figure 3 as the net offer curve. Under these conditions, the negotiated solution would be Q_1^*. Alternatively, assume that, with liability, the burden of negotiation is concentrated on a small number of producers in country A. Transaction costs are expected to be relatively smaller, yielding a negotiated solution like Q_2^*. Thus the outcome is indeed variant with respect to the institutional arrangement in operations (Bromley, 1987).

Note that, at both Q_1^* and Q_2^*, the remaining externality is Pareto irrelevant in that no additional gains from trade can to be realized (Buchanan and Stubblebine, 1962). Certainly, the outcomes are not comparable in Pareto terms, where property rights are taken as given

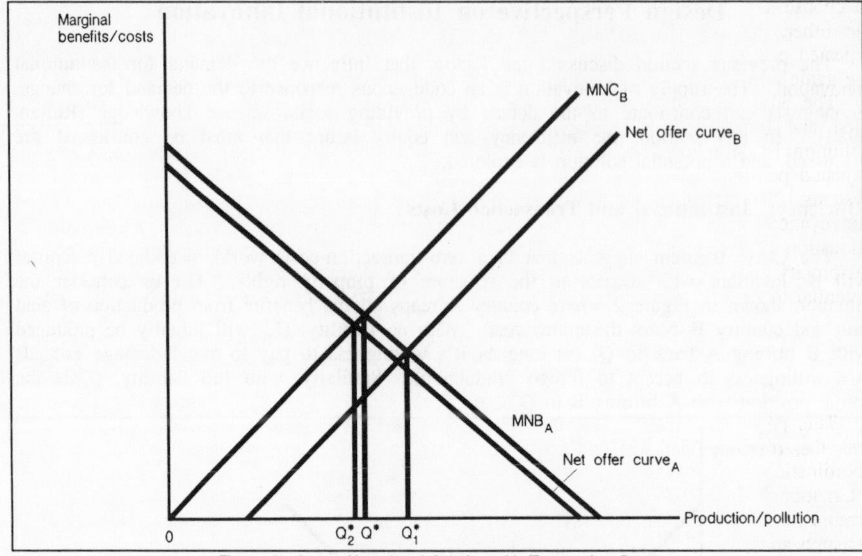

Figure 3—Coase Negotiated Solution with Transaction Costs

would be Q_1^*. Alternatively, assume that, with liability, the burden of negotiation is concentrated on a small number of producers in country A. Transaction costs are expected to be relatively smaller, yielding a negotiated solution like Q_2^*. Thus the outcome is indeed variant with respect to the institutional arrangement in operations (Bromley, 1987).

Note that, at both Q_1^* and Q_2^*, the remaining externality is Pareto irrelevant in that no additional gains from trade can to be realized (Buchanan and Stubblebine, 1962). Certainly, the outcomes are not comparable in Pareto terms, where property rights are taken as given (Bromley, 1982). However, they can be compared in terms of aggregate net benefits. The effects of transaction costs on a negotiated solution and on aggregate net benefits justifies an examination of alternative institutional arrangements from an "efficiency" perspective (in terms of net benefits, if not Pareto optimality).

Distributional Issues

Alternative institutional arrangements also vary in their equity implications. One alternative notion of equity relies on John Rawls' "veil of ignorance" (Rawls, 1971): assuming that individuals are ignorant as to where and/or when they were born, how would one structure the institutions governing pollution of international resources? By tackling the problem in this way, individuals are divested of personal interests and are free to focus on the viability of the whole. The following section suggests one institutional arrangement that may be equitable in the Rawls sense.

Potential Institutional Solution

Based on the efficiency and equity factors discussed above, cooperation among nations according to an institutional arrangement embodying reciprocity may be appropriate. A reciprocal institutional arrangement is a conditional cooperative commitment designed to overcome the "free-rider" problem. In this case, it implies that contributing to reducing a public ill is fair only if others contribute as well (Sugden, 1984). The contribution could be a reduction in domestic emissions proportional to the country's global share of production/pollution. The overall goal would be to meet an agreed "safe" global standard. The to choose a noncooperative strategy because each agent is uncertain about the behaviour of the other. Assurance is necessary to achieve coordinated, optimal solutions. With a repeated prisoners' dilemma game, an incentive exists for all players to change the rules of the game and to agree on a system of conditional commitments (Snidal, 1985).

The advantages of the institutional arrangement set forth above include the following. First and foremost, it recognizes the interdependence between nations facing the global pollution by structuring a set of conditional commitments. Second, a physical standard, adjusted periodically, accommodates long-run concerns about the sustainability of ecological systems. Third, given the difficulty in obtaining accurate information about the source, conveyance, physical impacts, and economic value of international pollution, a proportional allocation of responsibility may be the least-cost approach. And, finally, the principle of reciprocity may be perceived as fair. Overall, such an institutional arrangement has the potential to be both equitable and more efficient.

Summary and Conclusions

This paper examines typical incentive structures associated with transboundary pollution and the resulting demand for institutional innovations. The problem is often one of coordination. In this regard, institutional innovations must reflect explicit recognition of international interdependencies. Thus, the design of efficient and equitable institutional arrangements becomes crucial (Hurwicz, 1987). In designing institutions, social science research and analytical skill are usually socially far less expensive than processes of learning by trial and error (Ruttan, 1984).

In pursuing this approach to understanding institutional design, this paper discusses reciprocity and its potential as a solution under different circumstances. Reciprocal agreements hold significant promise among countries that are homogeneous in terms of income, production, and environmental damage. As heterogeneity increases, institutional innovations may require wider scope for negotiation. Transboundary resource problems are likely to become increasingly important in the global economy. Game theoretical analysis of these problems provides a rich research topic for the future.

Note

[1]Department of Economics, University of Northern Colorado; and Department of Agricultural and Applied Economics, University of Minnesota; respectively.

References

Baumol, W.J. (1982) "Applied Fairness Theory and Rationing Policy," *American Economic Review*, Vol. 72, pp. 639-651.

Bromley, D.W. (1982) "Land and Water Problems: Institutional Perspective," *American Journal of Agricultural Economics*, Vol. 64, pp. 834-844.

Bromley, D.W. (1986) *Natural Resource Economics*, Kluver, Boston, Mass., USA.

Bromley, D.W. (1987) *On Reallocating Economic Opportunity: Rent Seeking Clarified*, Staff Paper No. 274, University of Wisconsin, Madison, Wis., USA.

Buchanan, J.M., and Stubblebine, W.C. (1962) "Externality," *Economica*, Vol. 29, pp. 371-384.

Hart, D. (1987) "Acid Deposition: European Situation," *Forum for Applied Research and Public Policy*, Vol. 2, No. 3, pp. 58-67.

Hurwicz, L. (1951) *Optimality Criteria for Decision Making under Ignorance*, Cowles Commission Discussion Paper No. 370 (Statistics), University of Chicago, Chicago, Ill., USA.

Hurwicz, L. (1987) "Inventing New Institutions: Design Perspective," *American Journal of Agricultural Economics*, Vol. 69, pp. 395-402.

Livingston, M.L. (1987) "Evaluating the Performance of Environmental Policy: Contributions of Neoclassical, Public Choice and Institutionalist Models," *Journal of Economic Issues*, Vol. 21, pp. 281-294.

Olson, M. (1965) *Logic of Collective Action*, Harvard University Press, Cambridge, Mass., USA.

Rawls, J. (1971) *Theory of Justice*, Harvard University Press, Cambridge, Mass., USA.

Runge, C.F., and von Witzke, H. (1987) "Institutional Change in the Common Agricultural Policy of the European Community," *American Journal of Agricultural Economics*, Vol. 69, pp. 213-222.

Ruttan, V.W. (1984) "Social Science Knowledge and Institutional Change," *American Journal of Agricultural Economics*, Vol. 66, pp. 549-559.

Ruttan, V.W., and Hayami, Y. (1984) "Toward a Theory of Induced Innovation," *Journal of Development Studies*, Vol. 20, pp. 203-223.

Snidal, D. (1985) "Coordination vs. Prisoners' Dilemma: Implications for International Cooperation and Régimes," *American Political Science Review*, Vol. 79, pp. 923-942.

Sugden, R. (1984) "Reciprocity: Supply of Public Goods through Voluntary Contributions," *Economic Journal*, Vol. 94, pp. 772-787.

DISCUSSION OPENING—*Terence J. Centner* (Department of Agricultural Economics, University of Georgia)

Livingston and von Witzke advocate reciprocal agreements as a solution to the problem of transboundary air pollution. This conclusion implicates two underlying principles that must be reconciled in any transboundary agreement: territorial sovereignty and external responsibility. Under the first principle, a sovereign state is able to use its environment without interference from other states. However, most countries acknowledge that they do not possess an unqualified right to use their environment to cause harm to another state under the 1972 Declaration of the UN Conference on the Human Environment. Furthermore, the USA and many western European countries have signed the 1979 Convention on Long-Range Transboundary Air Pollution. External responsibilities are embedded in these agreements, but in the absence of effective enforcement mechanisms, countries have few remedies for actual transboundary pollution problems.

Continued acid rain pollution in North America and Europe shows that overcoming territorial sovereignty is difficult. Despite binding international conventions, Canada and the Scandinavian countries have experienced little success in being able to control external pollution. Control of air pollution needs to be founded on agreed rights and obligations that recognize territoriality and external responsibility. Although a clear way to harmonize these two principles may not be obvious, a starting point is to recognize both national and international institutions.

On the national level, centralized authority with enforcement provisions and private rights of action provide an administrative model with considerable merit. Two features of such a model deserve further comment. First, countries may assign property rights to resources, such as the right-to-farm legislation in the USA or legislation establishing standards. If countries are to internalize pollution costs, domestic legislation must refrain from adopting legal provisions that privatize limited aspects of pollution. Second, the right of private citizens to sue polluters for violation of statutes, as is available under numerous federal laws in the USA but is less common in Europe, may diminish the need for alternative transboundary pollution controls.

On the international level, relaxation of jurisdictional prerequisites, diplomacy, and economic and legal sanctions compelling polluters to internalize costs of transboundary pollution may provide for greater pollution control. The impact of the principle of territorial sovereignty on these factors means that pollution controls should be easier in cases where the nations are developed and relatively homogeneous. Such nations would have the financial ability to pay for pollution costs and would be expected to have similar notions of fairness and equity and similar property rights in air resources.

The limited success of past pollution agreements suggests that more than one institution might be pursued simultaneously to maximize pollution control. First, reciprocal agreements may assist in fostering mechanisms to encourage the reduction of pollution activities. Second, various public remedies, such as arbitration, an international environmental protection authority, or commissions to deal with pollution problems may help compel polluting states to take responsibility for external damages caused by internal polluters. Third, private remedies that provide access to foreigners in judicial proceedings and domestic tort doctrines that force polluters to internalize the extraterritorial costs of air pollution are possible additional means of enforcing external responsibility for transboundary pollution.

GENERAL DISCUSSION—*Bill R. Miller, Rapporteur* (Department of Agricultural Economics, University of Georgia)

One participant asked if enough scientific knowledge existed to allow economists to apply the kinds of theoretical devices described by Livingston. Livingston replied that data are not available to estimate loss functions as a basis for taxation. Therefore, developing reciprocal standards seems most appropriate. Reciprocity is the key to the interdependent nature of the problem.

Livingston replied to the discussion opener that the principles of territory and responsible behaviour must be enforceable to ensure fairness. Mutual monitoring and enforcement are important parts of reciprocal agreements.

Participants in the discussion included G.H. Peters.

Consideration of Natural Disasters in the Economic Analysis of Agricultural Development Projects

Randall A. Kramer and Anna Lea Grieco[1]

Abstract: Nearly 90 percent of the world's natural disasters occur in LDCs. Agricultural sectors are particularly prone to economic damage from natural disaster, yet, economic analyses of agricultural development projects seldom recognize the potential impacts of natural disasters on project net benefits. Several methods are available for incorporating natural disaster information into benefit-cost analysis. Using data from a development project in St. Lucia, a stochastic simulation approach is applied to assess the feasibility of the project with and without a disaster mitigation practice. The mitigation practice is the use of nematicides to reduce wind damage to newly established banana plantings. Mitigation is found to lower the project's expected internal rate of return and to lower the riskiness of the project. This type of information could be useful to project planners for evaluating disaster mitigation measures and for selecting among competing projects.

Introduction

Approximately 90 percent of the world's natural disasters occur in LDCs. When the natural disasters strike, they often have short- and long-term effects on economic activity. Agriculture in LDCs is particularly prone to economic damage from natural disasters for two reasons. First, agriculture is frequently a major, if not the dominant, economic activity. Second, agriculture tends to have less institutional and infrastructural protection from natural disasters than is the case in developed countries. Yet, the planning process for agricultural development seldom considers natural disaster information in a systematic manner.

The purpose of this paper is to review methods to incorporate natural disaster information into development plans and to illustrate the use of one of the approaches in an analysis of a development project on the Caribbean island of St. Lucia.

Natural Disasters and Economic Development

Because agriculture is the basic sector in many of the countries most prone to natural disasters, the resulting disruptions can have far-reaching economic consequences. Large shortfalls in agricultural production can have ripple effects throughout the economy, not only reducing food supplies but affecting employment and spending in other sectors of the economy as well.

Let us consider some examples of the economic damages storms have inflicted on agriculture. When hurricanes David and Frederick struck the Dominican Republic in 1979, they caused an estimated $342 million of damage to the agricultural sector. The hurricanes destroyed the entire banana crop (UN, 1980). In a country where agriculture provides employment for 40 percent of the labour force and accounts for 37 percent of the GDP, the storms had a major affect on the economy (USAID, 1982).

In 1984, the worst floods in Colombia in a decade caused an estimated $400 million of damage to crops and livestock, and floods in Ecuador in 1982 and 1983 reduced the value of the banana crop by $4.3 million (UN, 1983). These are only a few examples of the direct effects of natural disasters on agricultural sectors.

In addition to these immediate economic impacts, natural disasters can have long-term impacts on the development process. Earthquakes, floods, and other natural disasters destroy a country's productive assets, including roads, bridges, buildings, port facilities, and agricultural enterprises. Given that natural disasters divert a country's savings into recovery uses rather than the creation of new productive assets, they can slow development. This suggests that the destruction of productive capital by natural disasters can help explain some of the differences in economic well-being around the world (Deaton, undated).

Greater attention should be paid to the potential effects of natural disasters on development projects. One contribution that economists could make would be to conduct benefit-cost analyses of disaster mitigation measures to determine if financial resources could be better spent preventing damage rather than recovering from it.

Natural Disasters and Project Planning

A development project represents an investment of capital to create assets capable of producing a future stream of net benefits. Careful project planning is considered a critical determinant of the success of a project. A variety of ways exist to characterize the project planning cycle. The planning process generally includes these three phases: identification, prefeasibility analysis, and feasibility analysis. The identification phase is finding potential projects in the country of interest. The prefeasibility phase involves a rough determination of project benefits and costs. Some projects can be eliminated from further consideration based on the prefeasibility analysis. The feasibility analysis phase considers the technical and economic viability of a project. Refined estimates are made of evaluation criteria such as internal rates of return or benefit-cost ratios.

Although not widely done, natural disaster information can be used at each planning phase. At the identification phase, risk maps and disaster return frequencies can be consulted to eliminate high-risk project locations. If the location cannot be easily shifted, disaster mitigation measures can be included as part of the project design. In the prefeasibility analysis, probabilities of natural disasters can be estimated and used to adjust project costs and benefits. In the feasibility phase, more precise information on the probabilities and consequences of disasters can be collected and used in a formal benefit-cost analysis.

To incorporate natural disaster information into an agricultural project feasibility analysis, one should ideally have information on the probability of the disaster, intensity of the event, and likely damage to agriculture. To obtain this type of information may not be easy, particularly in LDCs, although the probability or risk of the event often can be determined from weather data. The intensity can also be determined this way. Potential damage is more difficult to assess but can be roughly estimated with the help of agronomists and horticulturalists.

Including Natural Disaster Information in Benefit-Cost Analysis

Benefit-cost analysis is a method used by economists to determine the efficiency of public-sector investments. It can be a part of both the prefeasibility and feasibility analysis phases of project planning. The usual approach consists of enumerating all benefits and costs, evaluating all benefits and costs in monetary terms, and discounting future net benefits.

The problem with this typical approach to benefit-cost analysis in areas affected by natural disasters is that it fails to account for the fact that the future benefits of a project are highly uncertain. For example, the major benefits of a project to provide irrigation water to farmers will be higher yields. However, if these yields were severely curtailed in those years when a tropical storm occurs, the usual benefit-cost study would fail to reflect this.

Several methods exist for incorporating uncertainty into benefit-cost analysis (for a review of such methods, see Kramer and Florey, 1987). Those that demand less data can be conducted with limited information on the effects of natural disasters on project net benefits. More sophisticated approaches require probability distributions of net benefits.

The limited-information approaches include sensitivity analysis, discount rate adjustments, cutoff periods, and minimax and maximin strategies. All these approaches attempt to adjust project net benefits to reflect uncertainty. For example, analysts examining a project for a flood-prone area might use a high discount rate to reflect that the future stream of benefits may be disrupted by floods. These limited-information approaches recognize that natural disasters can influence a project's feasibility, but they are crude in their ability to convey useful information to decision makers.

If information is available to allow the analyst to estimate the probability distribution of the project's net present value (or other economic feasibility measure), one can use the probability distribution to conduct an expected-value analysis, mean-variance analysis, or safety-first analysis (Reutlinger, 1970). The expected-value analysis uses the probability distribution to compute a mean return measure. This approach is inadequate because it ignores useful information about higher moments. A safety-first approach considers the probability of a project earning a rate greater than some critical level. While useful in some contexts, the definition of the critical level is arbitrary. In this study, a mean-variance approach is taken to generate information on the mean and variability of project returns.

Case Study: Agricultural Development Project in St. Lucia

To demonstrate a method for incorporating natural disaster information into agricultural project analysis, a case study was developed. The case study chosen was based on an agricultural development project on the Dennery Estate in St. Lucia. The case study focused on a major component of the Dennery project—increasing banana production.

Bananas are the major crop in St. Lucia, planted on 71 percent of the arable land. Bananas are the largest export earner, but export volume is highly variable. During 1970-84, export volume fluctuated widely between 29,000 and 64,000 tons (World Bank, 1985). One of the reasons for the fluctuations is production shortfalls caused by natural disasters. Banana crops are susceptible to damage from drought, high winds, and hurricanes (Simmonds, 1987; and Hammerton, George, and Pilgrim, 1979). The drought problem is the subject of intensive research and a solution is being sought through irrigation development. Damage caused by high winds and hurricanes cannot be mitigated as easily. Crop damage results from defoliation and stripping of fruit, breaking and bending of stems, uprooting, flooding, and soil erosion. The uprooting problem can be lessened with improved control of nematodes.

The Dennery Estate in the central part of the island was purchased by the government in 1978 to avert an impending bankruptcy. In 1984, the Organization of American States (OAS) began a project to assist the government of St. Lucia to rehabilitate the Dennery Estate, a major employer in an area with high unemployment. Approximately 300 acres were targeted for new plantings of banana trees.

The case study project used to illustrate the incorporation of natural disaster information was development of banana production on 300 acres, half of which will be irrigated. Other activities of the larger project, such as land reform and soil conservation, were not considered in this analysis. Actual project data (OAS, 1985) were used wherever possible, although some assumptions and simplifications were necessary due to incomplete data.

Existing roads were considered adequate to service the additional farm production, so the only new infrastructure needed was an office, temporary storage facilities, a toilet, a workshop, and a garage. Other initial investment costs were the purchase of a jeep, the construction of an irrigation system, and land clearing. Cost data were obtained from the OAS project proposal. These investment costs totalled EC$1,359,450 (East Caribbean dollars).[2] The cost data are summarized in Table 1.

Operating costs for the project include transport, security, and debt-service activities. Operating costs totalled EC$519,275 for the first year and increased slightly in later years due to increased transport costs. Costs for producing the bananas were EC$532,200 in the first year and dropped to EC$476,700 in subsequent years.

The major benefit associated with the project is increased banana production: 1,074 tons in the first year and 1,434 tons in subsequent years. Because of the high unemployment in the area, wages paid to labour were considered a project benefit. In

Table 1–Annual Benefits and Costs for an Agricultural Development Project in St. Lucia

	First Year	Subsequent Years
	East Caribbean dollars	
Benefits:		
Income from banana production	397,595	530,866
Direct employment	621,736	572,896
Off-farm employment	269,016	359,188
Road maintenance	20,000	20,000
Total benefits	1,308,346	1,482,951
Costs:		
Initial capital costs	1,359,450	--
Production costs	532,200	476,700
Other operating costs	519,275	519,914
Total costs	2,410,925	996,614

Source: OAS (1985).

addition to the labour benefits from direct employment, additional labour benefits of EC$259 per ton were associated with processing and handling of the bananas. The project benefits, shown in Table 1, totalled EC$1,308,346 in the first year and EC$1,482,951 in subsequent years.[3]

The data on project benefits and costs in Table 1 are sufficient for conducting a standard benefit-cost analysis. However, this study also required information on the economic impacts of natural disasters on the project. Table 2 shows data on return frequencies for four types of natural events affecting banana production. Estimates of yield declines resulting from the events are also shown. Hurricanes can cause the greatest damage, reducing yields by 90 percent, but have a rather low return frequency of 6 percent. Both droughts and tropical storms have return frequencies of about 14 percent, but the yield damage from tropical storms is much greater. High winds occur rather frequently but have a moderate effect on yields.

Table 2–Disaster Return Frequencies and Estimated Yield Effects

	Return Frequency	Yield Decrease
	- - - *Percent* - - -	
Hurricane	5.95	90
Drought	14.28	15
Tropical storm	14.81	60
Moderate winds (13-24 mph)	34.20	20

Sources: O'Keefe and Shakow (1975), O'Keefe and Westgate (1974), and NOAA (1941-49).

Initially, the effects of these weather events were captured indirectly in the analysis by using historical yield probabilities. Banana yield data for the Dennery Estate were obtained for 1970-84 (OAS, 1985). The yields were highly variable, ranging between 2.77 and 8.15 tons per acre. These data were used to estimate a probability distribution for yields from which random draws were generated.

The randomly drawn yields were then used to adjust the benefits and costs, and an internal rate of return was calculated for each state of nature. In effect, this generated a probability distribution of net benefits. From this, an average internal rate was calculated. In addition, a coefficient of variation was calculated as a measure of the variability in project returns. The random-number generation and benefit-cost calculations were carried out with a stochastic simulation program developed by the authors.

Next, the effects of a disaster mitigation practice were analyzed. A mitigation practice recommended by experts on the island is the use of nematicides. Treatment with nematicides strengthens the roots and reduces the probability of wind storms uprooting the banana plants. However, this practice is ineffective in protecting against the high wind speeds associated with hurricanes. Based on information in Simmonds (1966) and the OAS Dennery project proposal, the use of nematicides was estimated to increase establishment costs by EC$74 per acre and production costs by $EC270 per acre. The major benefit would be higher yields in those years with wind storms. .

To estimate the yield effect of the mitigation practice, the historical yield data were reexamined. The three lowest yields occurred in 1976, 1978, and 1979. These low yield levels were assumed to be due to the effects of high winds, since they occurred in years when neither a hurricane nor a drought affected the island. The yields in those three years were 22, 18, and 23 percent lower than the historical mean. The average yield decline, 21 percent, is close to the 20-percent estimate of wind damage reported in Table 2. Assuming that the mitigation measure would prevent damage from the wind storms, the three lowest yields were dropped and replaced by the average for the remaining years. A new probability distribution was then estimated and used to calculate the probability distribution of rates of returns with the mitigation measure. The decision to replace the three lowest years was admittedly somewhat arbitrary, but should illustrate the mitigation benefits.

Without mitigation, the mean rate of return to the agricultural development project is 29.5 percent, a rather high return. The coefficient of variation is 69 percent. Adding the mitigation practice to the project lowers the expected rate of return to 27.6 percent. However, this reduction in expected return has bought a reduction in risk associated with the project. The coefficient of variation declines to 62 percent, indicating that, as expected, less risk is incurred with the mitigation practice implemented. Depending on their degree of risk aversion, project planners or policy makers might be willing to trade off the reduction in expected return for a lower variation in returns.

Conclusions

Development organizations use feasibility studies to determine the economic potential of agricultural development projects. Little attention is paid to the effects that natural disasters may have on a project's economic viability. Yet, agricultural projects are often affected by natural disasters, particularly in tropical areas.

Several methods are available for considering information on natural disasters when carrying out project feasibility analysis. One such method was illustrated with an application to an agricultural development project in St. Lucia. Using a simulation model, internal rates of return were computed for different states of nature. Altering the original project to include a disaster mitigation measure (treatment of banana trees with nematicides) lowered the expected internal rate of return to the project but also made project returns less risky. If feasibility studies regularly included this type of analysis, project planners could compare the relative riskiness of alternative projects. Furthermore, careful analysis of the risk effects of mitigation measures could help decision makers determine whether or not to include disaster mitigation in their development projects.

Notes

[1]School of Forestry and Environmental Studies, Duke University; and Foreign Agricultural Service, US Department of Agriculture; respectively.

[2]At the time of the study, US$1 was equivalent to EC$2.70.

[3]For more information on the project benefits, see Florey (1986).

References

Deaton, B.J. (undated) "The Economic Consequences of Disaster Mitigation," in *Proceedings of the International Conference on Disaster Mitigation Program Implementation*, Center for International Development Planning and Building, Virginia Polytechnic Institute and State University, Blacksburg, Va., USA.

Florey, A.L. (1986) "Incorporating Natural Disaster Risk Information into Economic Analyses of Agricultural Projects," MS thesis, Department of Agricultural Economics, Virginia Polytechnic Institute and State University, Blacksburg, Va., USA.

Hammerton, J.L., George, C., and Pilgrim, R. (1979) "Hurricanes and Agriculture: Losses and Remedial Actions," *Disasters*, Vol. 8, pp. 231-240.

Kramer, R.A., and Florey, A.L. (1987) "Use of Natural Hazard Information in the Economic Analysis of Agricultural Projects," in *Course on the Use of Natural Hazards Information in the Preparation of Investment Projects*, Vol. 2, Department of Regional Development, Organization of American States, Washington, D.C., USA.

NOAA (National Oceanic and Atmospheric Administration) (1941-49) "Uniform Summary of Surface Weather Observations, St. Lucia," US Department of Commerce, Washington, D.C., USA.

O'Keefe, P., and Shakow, D. (1975) "Environment and Development," CENTED Working Paper, Clark University, Worcester, Mass., USA.

O'Keefe, P., and Westgate, K. (1974) "Hurricane Probability in Windward Islands," Disaster Research Unit, Bradford, UK.

OAS (Organization of American States) (1985) *Report by the Advisory Committee for Dennery Basin Development*, Washington, D.C., USA.

Reutlinger, S. (1970) *Techniques for Project Appraisal under Uncertainty*, World Bank Staff Occasional Paper No. 10, Johns Hopkins University Press, Baltimore, Md., USA.

Simmonds, N.W. (1987) *Bananas*, 3rd Ed., Longman Scientific, Harlow, UK.

UN (United Nations) (1980) "Case Report on Hurricanes David and Frederick in the Dominican Republic," Disaster Relief Organization, Geneva, Switzerland.

UN (United Nations) (1983) "Incidence of Natural Disasters in Island Developing Countries," UN Conference on Trade and Development, New York, N.Y., USA.

USAID (US Agency for International Development) (1982) "Countries of the Caribbean Community," Office of Foreign Disaster Assistance, Washington, D.C., USA.

World Bank (1985) "St. Lucia: Economic Performance and Prospects," World Bank Country Report, Washington, D.C., USA.

DISCUSSION OPENING—*Des Doran* (Agriculture Development Branch, Agriculture Canada)

I agree with the authors that more attention should be paid to the potential effects of natural disasters. I need not cite a long list of such disasters. To quote the well-known Jamaican proverb about hurricanes:

June, too soon
July, stand by
August, come it must
September, remember
October, all over

All over, that is, except the reconstruction; hence, the need for disaster-mitigating activities.

The authors are right to direct attention to the need for more work in the area of evaluating the relative merits of expenditures for measures to prevent damages from disasters versus expenditures for measures to recover from them. Unfortunately, governments of developing countries frequently pose the task to agricultural planning teams in terms of their perception of directly productive activities. Similarly, agricultural economists are frequently called on to evaluate project impacts of technical designs that failed to consider more feasible alternatives.

Nevertheless, current project formulation and evaluation practices are used to deal with disaster-type information. Where an agricultural development project is the work of a team of specialists, including agronomists, soil scientists, animal husbandry specialists, irrigation engineers, etc., then a great deal of "environmental" data will be incorporated into a project. For example, irrigation engineers plan irrigation works with the possible disastrous effects of the 100-year flood clearly in mind. I recall how delighted the hydrologists and hydrogeologists were on one project in Africa to find a store house of climatic data for 60 or more years in the country. Resettlement villages were sited with a host of possible disaster factors in mind. My point here is that current practices include attention to national disaster factors.

The provision of measures of the degree of risk associated with a proposed agricultural development project, by the economic analyst, will affect the decision making of the government or institution that proposes the project and of the agency (national or international) that will provide financing for the project. We shall want to know something about the risk preference frontiers.

A possible outcome of the proposed change in the way projects are evaluated could thus be that projects that have a "lower" rate of return and a "higher" degree of risk will be proposed and funded. What kinds of projects display these characteristics of low expected rates of return and high degrees of risk? Some technology innovation projects probably fall into this category, and further examining the possible effects on a country's agricultural development of selecting more of such projects at the expense of other projects would be useful.

GENERAL DISCUSSION—*Bill R. Miller, Rapporteur* (Department of Agricultural Economics, University of Georgia)

A comment was made that the methodology seemed more appropriate for low risk, high payoff activities. Would it apply to situations where survival might force a high-risk decision? Kramer responded that the methodology presented is appropriate for economic development planning and not necessarily for decision making at the consumer or producer level.

In his response to the discussion opener, Kramer said that disaster prevention was not a popular concept among development planners as it does not focus on positive effects. The positive pay-offs from a project, such as a school, are much more likely to be the subejct of research. However, if the implicit assumption made by engineers with respect to events such as a 100-year storm could be made explicit, then they might be quantified and contribute to economic analysis.

Participants in the discussion included J. McKinsey.

Harmonizing Health and Safety Standards in the GATT: Proposals and Issues

Carol S. Kramer[1]

Abstract: Each of the tabled GATT proposals includes as a major negotiating item the harmonization of phytosanitary regulations, which function as nontariff barriers to trade. These health and safety standards have proliferated since World War II and are problematic because many are technically complex and contain genuine elements of consumer protection. This paper discusses economic aspects of health and safety standards under autarkic and trade conditions, including health and safety benefits. It then reviews elements of current GATT proposals from Canada, the Cairns Group, the EC, and the USA relevant to phytosanitary regulations, concluding that, despite broad agreement on some general principles, few substantive specifics have emerged, and some significant stumbling blocks remain. Tensions between national autonomy and international conformity in establishing regulations and equivalent versus identical standards mean that careful negotiation will be needed to establish enforceable liberalization. Recommendations for negotiating principles conclude the paper.

Introduction

Each of the major proposals thus far in the new GATT round of multilateral trade negotiations includes as a major negotiating item the harmonization of phytosanitary regulations. Many recognize the significant progress made since World War II in reducing tariff barriers to industrial trade; nevertheless, agricultural trading partners have suffered in international markets from nontariff barriers. One important class of these nontariff barriers is health and safety standards set up in the name of consumer protection.

Phytosanitary regulations (referred to hereafter as health and safety standards or HSSs) have proliferated in agricultural and food trade in the last 40 years despite international efforts to subdue their disruptive trade effects. A premise of this paper is that HSSs have gained such a secure and notorious position as nontariff barriers to trade precisely because of their ambivalent and nontransparent nature: they are the only type of trade barrier having any potential benefit to consumers. This is one reason they are difficult to dislodge. Neither tariffs, quotas, nor voluntary export restraints can be claimed to benefit consumers. At most, rather shallow arguments can be made about protection of infant or transitional industries to generate or preserve employment.

However, proponents of HSSs can and do argue that HSSs may offer benefits of a public good nature, reductions in morbidity or mortality or pain and suffering, in cases where product safety or characteristics are not easily knowable or observable in the market. Further, some argue that such standards may legitimately differ between countries due to differences in dietary patterns and agricultural practices and thus cumulative exposure to foodborne hazards. The potential for alliance between interests of consumers and certain producer groups seeking to protect markets should be noted. In the USA, for example, soyabean interests have recently been pressing for mandatory labelling for imported tropical oils. Do these producer groups seek to protect consumer health or markets?

In tackling conflicts over HSSs, negotiators are often quick to agree that protection of human health is desirable, while unnecessary nontariff barriers are not. Discussions of the legitimacy or lack of legitimacy of a given HSS generally tail off fairly rapidly into genuinely arcane technical discussions of sampling methodologies, risk exposure models, acceptable daily intakes, threshold levels, and such *ad infinitum*, so that free-trading economists and well-intentioned politicians soon lose interest. If and when resolved, these discussions are only a preliminary to equally complex deliberations of international lawyers concerning acceptance of international standards into national law.

Reductions in HSSs impeding international trade will therefore depend on development of a different negotiating model than more conventional types of trade barriers, one which: (1) recognizes the potential legitimacy of particular HSSs and provides for effective representation of consumer and producer interests; and (2) integrates specific technocratic and broader political economic perspectives repeatedly over the course of discussions. Because liberalization of phytosanitary regulations is likely to founder in its implementation rather than its initiation, continuous monitoring and feedback to international negotiating bodies must accompany agreed statements of general principles.

Economic Aspects of HSSs in International Trade

Most true HSSs are motivated by domestic considerations. Among other costs and benefits, regulatory benefit-cost analysis identifies and values benefits to consumers consisting of reductions in risk of disease or death from the consumption of safer consumer products, in this case food products. Conceptually, willingness to pay for these reductions in risk is the correct measure of benefits to consumers. Frequently, however, assessing the amount consumers would be willing to pay is the problematic step because consumers do not have perfect knowledge and are not forced to reveal their bids for increased safety.[2] Economists have spent a great deal of time in recent years devising ways in which consumer revealed market bids in one instance may be transferred for valuation purposes to a similar case.

In the absence of market bids, an alternative method of evaluating the benefits of HSSs identifies probable cost savings from the regulation. Thus, medical costs saved and productivity losses avoided are the two main measures in this type of evaluation, generally considered an underestimate of what the consumer would actually be willing to pay.

In the absence of economic measures for value of life or lost productivity, public health analysts can sometimes develop scenarios estimating the incidence of disease or disability attributable to a food safety hazard. In many cases, however, information pertinent to each of these types of benefit determinations is not available, and therefore benefit estimates are not available.

Among the costs of the health and safety regulation in the domestic economy are the increased costs of production required to produce products meeting the specifications of the regulation. Regulations may require particular changes in processing techniques (processing standards) or merely specify the required attributes of the final product (product standards). Finally, regulations may require particular product information on labels or in package inserts or advertising (information standards).

While most regulatory benefit-cost analysis is partial and static in nature, one ought to account for changes in exposure to public health risk resulting from regulatory-induced changes in consumption patterns. Thus, if safety regulations raise the price of red meats relative to poultry meat and consumers substitute poultry meat for red meat, a complete analysis of the benefits and costs of the regulation would take into account the net impact on public health of a partial switch towards consumption of poultry meat and away from red meat as well as the altered quality of the red meat itself. Changes in consumer perceptions of the safety of red meat might also expand red meat demand.

As borders are opened to international trade, the calculus of benefits and costs encompassed in an economic analysis of a HSS expands. Consumer gains from free trade include broader product choice and lower product prices due to well-known benefits from specialization in products for which a country has a comparative advantage.

The impacts of a HSS in this case depend on several factors. If the HSS applies only to products produced in country A but not country B, then producers in country A may be at a cost disadvantage (depending on production technology). Consumer actions in this case and whether consumers will benefit from trade or not depend on: (1) the risk inherent in the unregulated imported goods and (2) whether unregulated imported goods are distinguishable from regulated domestic goods. If informed consumers are free to select either good and if the risks from the unregulated goods are minimal, consumers will benefit from trade.

If the HSS applies to all countries, then impacts on consumers depend on which producers can meet the HSS. If exporting countries do not meet the standard, then the situation reverts to autarky in the regulated nonexporting country. Consumers pay higher prices for safer products, and some consumers substitute other less expensive goods. The impact on world markets depends on whether the regulated country is a significant actor in world markets (Peterson, Paggi, and Henry, 1987). If all countries meet the standards, consumers pay higher prices than before domestic regulations but lower prices than in the regulated autarkic situation.

Consumers in exporting countries benefit from lower prices if exporters are able to sell fewer products in world markets, but exporting producers who do not comply with regulations lose from reduced exports, particularly if the regulating country was a major buyer in world markets. In addition, reductions in trade result in dead-weight losses from loss of economic efficiency.

The critical issues in sorting out the costs and benefits of HSSs that influence international trade are thus the risks of being regulated against and consumer willingness to pay to reduce these risks; efficacy of regulations in accomplishing risk reduction; costs of complying with the regulations; changes in consumption patterns (and exposure to risk) induced by changes in relative prices and by changes in perceived quality of the regulated products.

Potential spillover effects are associated with HSSs if companies seeking to comply with stricter standards in country A no longer produce goods conforming to the less strict standard for countries B and C. This might occur if countries B and C represent smaller markets and country A is less burdened by producing for only one standard. Then, consumers in countries B and C pay for HSSs not chosen by their governments in their behalf.

One problematic aspect of divergent HSSs is the high transaction costs associated with regulatory compliance in international settings. Countries seeking to export to multiple trading partners, each with different HSSs, must invest diverse resources in regulatory affairs, including intelligence, compliance, and legal advice. These transaction costs may be asymmetrically distributed. For example, penetrating the vast US consumer market may be less difficult and more cost effective for an exporter due to its relative regulatory uniformity than attempting to export to the EC or Asia where national standards prevail and individual markets are smaller. This fact means that countries such as the USA may benefit proportionately more from international liberalization of HSSs than the EC.

LDCs are also disadvantaged by HSSs due to their limited resources for regulatory intelligence and compliance. Recognition of this fact lay behind formation of the Codex Alimentarius Group of FAO and WHO.

In view of the difficulties inherent in disentangling consumer protection (public and individual health and safety and economic integrity) and market protection elements of a HSS that serves as a nontariff barrier, analysts can expect difficulty in integrating these into computations of overall producer and consumer subsidy equivalents or overall levels of protection. In the current Uruguay Round of GATT, these or similar measures are recommended as the yardstick by which trade protection and agricultural subsidization can be calibrated for disassembly. For HSS to be analyzed in terms of trade or agricultural protection for purposes of international negotiations, an additional procedure is required to determine the nature and extent of consumer benefits from the regulation in question.

Current GATT Proposals

While those GATT proposals currently tabled (the US, EC, Canadian, and Cairns proposals) suggest some relevant principles for forthcoming negotiations, they supply remarkably few details. Among the general statements are: negotiations related to agricultural products are considered extremely important in this round of the GATT; agricultural negotiations will cover products of first- and second-stage processing as well as primary products; and issues of domestic agricultural support are considered of primary importance because domestic excesses drive many of the distortions in international trade—by implication this pressure fosters use of HSS protective devices as well.

The EC considers that "the [GATT] code on technical barriers to trade is not properly suited to the particular case of animal and plant health regulations and barriers." The EC wants "to negotiate a specific framework of rules which should lay down criteria for the harmonization of regulations at international level. This framework of rules should also cover production methods and processes."

The USA has stated: "On sanitary and phytosanitary regulations and barriers we propose: that regulations be harmonized and be based on internationally agreed standards. In addition, regulations pertaining to processing and production methods should recognize equivalent guarantees as opposed to identical methods. ... We believe rules and procedures governing technical barriers to trade should be expanded: to apply more explicitly to processes and production methods; to give greater recognition to the principle of equivalence of laws and regulations; and to provide procedures for early technical and policy consultations on legal and regulatory changes that have a high potential for disrupting trade." President Reagan stated on July 6, 1987, "... our proposal calls for instituting uniform food health regulations around the world to prevent nontariff barriers to agricultural trade." Negotiations should focus on all agricultural commodities, food, beverages, forest products, and fish and fish products. Insofar as animal, plant, and human health and safety are not affected, he called for harmonized health and sanitary regulations based on international standards and processing and production methods on equivalent guarantees.

The Canadian proposal states: "The three major elements of agricultural trade reform which the Punta del Este declaration identifies (access, subsidies, and technical regulations) are inseparable in the sense that failure to deal effectively with one element is likely to prejudice any gains which may be negotiated in other areas. Past GATT negotiations have revealed clearly the limitations of a commodity specific, request and offer approach. The experience of seven previous rounds suggests that adoption of a request and offer approach would doom the agricultural negotiations in the Uruguay Round to failure." Canada calls for "strengthened commitments to prohibit the use of technical regulations as disguised trade barriers, encouraging the use of international standards where possible, and agreeing to minimize the trade effects where harmonization of technical regulations is not feasible."

The Cairns Group proposal suggests that a long-term framework for sanitary and phytosanitary measures be established "which reflects only strict justification to protect human, animal, or plant life or health. The aim shall be to harmonize sanitary and phytosanitary regulations to remove barriers to international trade: and where full harmonization is not technically feasible adverse trade effects of differing regulations will be minimized to the maximum extent." Specifically the Cairns Group calls for: "establishing a procedure of notification and reverse notification to achieve full transparency concerning the application of such measures, with provision for review under the relevant provisions of the General Agreement, clarified as appropriate: harmonizing sanitary and phytosanitary regulations and standards among countries with the aim of removing barriers to international trade. Even where full harmonization is not feasible, countries would give greater recognition to the principle of equivalency of treatment; developing procedures to require any contracting party so requested by another contracting party to set out the precise terms and timetable of steps required to be undertaken to achieve conformity with its sanitary or phytosanitary regulations; providing technical assistance from countries with regulations in place for exporting developing countries would be given to help them overcome the substantive and administrative problems arising from phytosanitary and sanitary measures."

The Cairns Group also calls for effective procedures for verification and settlement of disputes. "Countries should provide binding commitment to implement agreed schedules including an undertaking not to resort to any measures to circumvent commitment ... [they suggest] need [for a] surveillance mechanism ... No introduction of new sanitary or phytosanitary regulations operating as a disguised barrier to trade and inconsistent with the long term objectives of negotiations."

The common threads that emerge from the four proposals seem to be a recognition of the need to deal with phytosanitary and sanitary regulations in a broad manner; a recognition that full harmonization may not be possible and that, in such cases, trade distorting effects should be minimized; and a general consensus that international standards should provide the basis for agreement. Other common themes are the request for early notification of regulations with trade disrupting effects and agreement that no new regulations should be instituted as other barriers are reduced. Uniquely mentioned by the Cairns Group are provisions for technical assistance in meeting standards.

In addition, whereas a commonality appears in the call for recognition of equivalency of nonequal standards and systems, a point of some difference or ambiguity between the US and EC positions relates to procedures and processes. Reading between the lines, while both parties mention procedures and processes being brought under the aegis of an expanded code of standards applying to technical barriers, the implications as seen by the USA and EC may diverge, if recent experience is any guide. The USA calls for recognition of equivalency of laws and regulations. The EC asks that procedures and processes be dealt with by the standards. In recent months, the USA and EC have disagreed strongly on principles of equivalency as related to safety standards. In the so-called meat wars, the EC has issued two broadsides at the equivalency of US safety standards: one concerning use of hormones in livestock production, the other concerning sanitation within US meat plants. In each case, the EC has chosen to attack a production process through nonequality of production standards rather than the final characteristics of the food product in question.

Thus, tensions between those advocating principles of national flexibility in standards setting versus global conformity will complicate forthcoming negotiations. A corollary is the predictable tension between technical negotiators trained to focus on a particular situation and political negotiators seeking a broader concurrence and therefore prepared to trade off costs and benefits.

Institutional Design and Negotiating Prognosis

An institutional design for progress in future attempts to harmonize phytosanitary regulations was left largely unspecified in the four initial GATT proposals. Equally important are new incentives that must be provided by GATT encouraging national acceptance of international rules. Currently, several international organizations participate to one degree or other in food standardization. The valuable work performed by the 129 member countries of the Codex Alimentarius, particularly, offers substantive analysis from which to begin. Weaknesses, however, include lack of enforceability and the rather slow pace of progress in deliberation and incorporation of Codex standards into national rules. One promising avenue may be to integrate the priorities of GATT (once determined) and Codex to guide preparation of draft standards and to expand GATT rules with respect to integrating these standards into rules of international trade. The Codex is currently organized into 28 subsidiary bodies, 5 that deal with general policy and coordination, 6 with subject matters relevant to work of all commodity committees, and 17 with specific groups of foods. The USA, for example, hosts the Committees on Food Hygiene, Processed Fruits and Vegetables, Cereals, Cereal Products, Pulses and Legumes, and Residues of Veterinary Drugs. The conformation of these groups often reflects trading concerns that are still relevant. Others may be needed when stock is taken of those commodity or product groups with the most burdensome phytosanitary regulations.

The Codex works through the use of technical expert committees, consensus building, and voluntary compliance. Standards developed by the group may be accepted by member nations on one of three levels or not at all. Codex acceptance options are: "full acceptance," "target acceptance," and "acceptance with specified deviations." In the third case, a country may agree to abide by its existing regulations but not limit the entry of goods from another country complying with the Codex standards. Application of this principle may be a negotiating goal.

Other international groups currently set food standards, not necessarily related to the Codex. The most significant of these may be the EC, which issues binding regulations and less binding directives, each of which may pertain to food standards in selected cases.

Once established for the EC, an EC standard is often applied to third countries seeking to export to the EC. Because EC countries are struggling with their own harmonization problems, they may be less likely to accept what they consider noncomplying goods from third countries.

In the end, due to the varying legal, social, economic, and production conditions and traditions among countries, acceptance of essential equivalency of trading partner standards without actual identity is perhaps the most critical requirement for progress in the harmonization of standards. Secondly, the agreement to use product standards rather than process standards whenever possible permits countries the flexibility to produce satisfactory products in distinct, innovative ways. Finally, when consumption risks are minimal, information remedies such as ingredient or process labelling should be used to permit consumer choice and reduce efficiency losses from barriers to trade.

Notes

[1]National Center for Food and Agricultural Policy, Resources for the Future.

[2]Indeed, a theme in the economics of public goods is that consumers actually have an incentive to disguise their willingness to pay in the hope that they may become free riders while others pay.

Reference

Peterson, E.W.F., Paggi, M., and Henry, G. (1987) "Quality Restrictions as Barriers to Trade: Case of European Community Regulations on the Use of Hormones," *Western Journal of Agricultural Economics*, Vol. 13, No. 1, pp. 82-91.

DISCUSSION OPENING—*Ewa Rabinowicz* (Swedish University of Agricultural Sciences)

The paper consists of three parts. The first part discusses welfare economic foundations of HSSs, focusing on market failures, the second part reviews current proposals of various nations in GATT, and the third part formulates proposals for the process of negotiations. My main critical point is that these three parts are not related to each other. In the last part of the paper, the author recommends that product standards rather than process standards should be used. However, the relative merits of the former as compared with the latter are not discussed anywhere in the paper. In the first theoretical part of the paper, HSSs are discussed from a very general point of view.

To continue on this line of lack of correspondence between the parts of the paper, in the second part the author describes positions taken by various countries. This is a positive approach as compared with the basically normative way of reasoning used in parts 1 and 3. This descriptive part of the paper could be related to the rest of the paper in at least two ways. One would be to analyze the political feasibility of the recommendations made by the author in the light of current positions of different countries in GATT. The second, which I find particularly interesting, would be to ask why differences exist between different countries in their opinions on HSSs and whether these can be explained in terms of the market-failure approach used by the author in the first part of the paper. The author mentions that HSSs may legitimately differ between countries. However, the question if, or to which extent, the actual differences are legitimate is not asked. One can otherwise suspect that HSSs are, at least partly, deliberately used as an impediment to trade.

This leads me to my second critical point, namely the lack of the public choice perspective. Pointing out possible market failures as a justification for regulations is only one side of the coin. Government failures should be considered as well. An obvious danger of government failures exists in formulating HSSs. Consumer protection is most vigourously argued by *producers* facing competition; e.g., pesticide residues in imported vegetables are often discussed in Sweden. No controversy exists over the use of pesticides in production of coffee. Another group that is obviously interested in pursuing the regulatory effort beyond the point where it is economically sound is the bureaucracy—lots of people make a living by formulating, applying, and controlling standards. This group is also likely to insist on national rather than international standards.

So where does that leave us? Both market failures and bureaucracy and government failures exist in using HSSs, and we should be aware of that. Our role as economists should be to define the point where the legitimate consumer protection ends and the protectionistic trade policy starts. Hopefully, this point should not be different for different countries, and we should be able to arrive at international standards. In this context, we should distinguish between food safety and food quality, which are often confused, since the case of consumer protection is much stronger for safety reasons. The quality aspects can be left to the market, where the institution of "trade marks" can solve a lot of quality problems. Information is also a way of coping with quality issues, as the author points out in the final part of her paper.

GENERAL DISCUSSION—*Bill R. Miller, Rapporteur* (Department of Agricultural Economics, University of Georgia)

One participant asked for further comments on the need for equivalence of laws and product standards, and whether they will really help. Kramer replied that the conflict between internal autonomy and international standards is a serious obstacle to harmonizing health and safety regulations. Although the benefits are obvious, a great deal of subjectivity is involved in the establishment of each country's standards. Perhaps the best to hope for is the establishment of a common process to determine standards.

Another participant asked if standards to protect safety of the workforce were ever a factor in trade relations. Kramer replied that the subject was beyond the scope of her paper.

Kramer agreed with the discussion opener that protectionism arises from political as well as market failure. Objective data will be needed as the basis of both political and market developments. Although additional testing adds cost, it might provide the information required for least costs of production for those items to be traded.

Participants in the discussion included D. Southgate and S. Thompson.

Terms of Trade of Agriculture and Food Production: Case of Mexico

Antonio Yunez N.[1]

Abstract: This paper presents the main results of a study that proposes a methodology for studying whether or not a heterogeneous agricultural sector, such as that of Mexico, faces unfavourable terms of trade. These results are used to interpret the origins of the basic food production problems experienced by Mexico since the 1960s. The analysis takes classical economics as the theoretical framework; the study's empirical nature makes it one of the few quantitative studies on agricultural terms of trade in this tradition. Agriculture clearly faced unfavourable terms of trade during 1960 and 1970, and the terms of trade of its peasant component explain the phenomenon. This, together with government intervention in setting low basic crop prices, explains the agricultural problems of contemporary Mexico.

Introduction

Several authors have argued that, through unfavourable terms of trade, agriculture supports the process of industrialization. Some have used the labour theory of value to sustain this view; none, however, has proved this empirically.

This paper presents the main results of a study that proposes a methodology for studying whether or not a heterogeneous agricultural sector, such as Mexico's, faces unfavourable terms of trade. These results are used to interpret the origins of the basic food production problems experienced by Mexico since the 1960s.

Agricultural Terms of Trade: 1950, 1960, and 1970

The analysis consists of measuring sectoral values (i.e., the total amount of labour contained in a particular commodity) and comparing them with sectoral, observed prices (i.e., what a productive sector of the economy really receives in the process of buying and selling commodities). If, for example, agriculture's estimated labour value (Z^v_a) happens to be greater than its corresponding price (Z^p_a), it faces unfavourable terms of trade, since the total labour expended in the commodity it produces is lower than the price it receives in the market. The proposed methodology allows for more precise comparisons between agriculture's price-value ratio and the same ratio for the remaining economic sectors; i.e., agricultural terms of trade. So, if one denotes the remaining sectors by *j*, and if, for example, $[(Z^p_a/Z^v_a)/(Z^p_j/Z^v_j)] < 1$ for all *j*, agriculture has unfavourable terms of trade.[2]

The empirical study is based on data for the Mexican economy; the main sources being its input-output tables for 1950, 1960, and 1970 and the population censuses for the same years. Sectoral labour values were estimated using an algorithm worked out by Morishima and Seton (1961), and sectoral gross domestic production, measured in price terms, came from national accounts.

The main results can be summarized as follows:

$(\%Z^p_a/\%Z^v_a)_{1950} = 0.94$,

$(\%Z^p_a/\%Z^v_a)_{1960} = 0.59$, and

$(\%Z^p_a/\%Z^v_a)_{1970} = 0.72$.[3]

Since agriculture's price/value ratios are less than one for the three years under study—particularly for 1960 and 1970—the argument stating that a heterogeneous agricultural sector faces unfavourable terms of trade is not rejected empirically.

The above is confirmed by our more detailed terms-of-trade results. They show that, for 1950, agriculture's unfavourable terms of trade are compensated by its favourable terms

Table 1–Agricultural Terms of Trade, Mexico, 1950–70*

	Sector	1950	1960	1970
1.	Agriculture (a)	1.000	1.000	1.000
2.	Livestock rearing	0.304	0.408	0.670
3.	Forestry, etc.	0.658	0.444	0.829
4.	Mineral products	1.004	0.633	0.655
5.	Oil extraction and refining and coal and by-products	1.048	0.542	0.766
6.	Foods	0.724	0.655	0.676
7.	Drinks and beverages	1.207	0.594	0.642
8.	Tobacco and products	2.645	0.418	0.547
9.	Textile industries	1.154	0.838	0.866
10.	Tailoring	0.974	0.692	0.684
11.	Wood industries	0.765	0.468	0.757
12.	Paper and cardboard	1.027	0.677	0.745
13.	Printing and publishing	1.169	0.807	0.897
14.	Leather and by-products	0.803	0.565	1.033
15.	Rubber products	0.949	0.530	0.675
16.	Chemistry and chemicals	1.033	0.647	0.735
17.	Nonmetalic mineral products	1.181	0.712	0.811
18.	Basic metal industries	1.115	0.660	0.679
19.	Other metal products	0.876	0.761	0.769
20.	Machinery, equipment, and electrodomestics	0.967	0.695	0.651
21.	Motor vehicles, transport, and bodywork	1.023	0.731	0.557
22.	Other manufacturing industries	0.971	0.761	0.757
23.	Construction	1.520	0.845	0.950
24.	Electricity	1.324	0.860	0.793
25.	Commerce	0.675	0.257	0.471
26.	Transport	0.926	0.960	0.818
27.	Communications	8.662	1.095	0.796
28.	Restaurants and hotels	1.907	0.808	0.568
29.	Financial services	1.674	0.921	1.162
30.	Other services	0.993	0.487	0.806

* $(Z^p_a / Z^p_j) / (Z^v_a / Z^v_j)$; $j = 1 \ldots 30$.
Sources: SPP (1980) and the author's own estimations.

of trade. On the other hand, in 1960 and 1970, they were unfavourable with respect to all of the economy's sectors, except for sectors one and two, respectively (Table 1).

So, the outcome for 1950 does not contradict the argument that a heterogeneous agricultural sector faces unfavourable economic terms of trade in the product market, and the findings for 1960 and 1970 provide sound empirical foundations.

Sources of Unfavourable Terms of Trade of Agriculture

In the above analysis, the dual character of Mexico's agrarian structure was considered implicitly; i.e., the fact that family-based producers coexist with commercial farmers. This was taken into account in the agricultural labour value estimation by imputing the ruling minimum wage to the productive members of the peasant economy. This procedure is crucial since, if family labour is ignored, agricultural terms of trade appear to be favourable; furthermore, they become the most favourable when compared with the terms of trade of other sectors.

The sharp contrast between the two sets of results is related to the controversial issue of whether unequal terms of trade are rooted in low productivity or in low remuneration of peasant family labour. One can argue, for example, that since the peasant economy is unproductive, the correct procedure is to dismiss family labour. However, as well as ignoring a component of agriculture's labour value, the outcome of this procedure—agriculture being one of the sectors that benefits most in the process of buying and selling commodities—contrasts with the observed decline of its rates of growth since the mid-1950s. Furthermore, the nature of the adopted methodology makes the results independent of the controversy because the previous analysis shows that, by considering family labour as part of agriculture's value, the fact that the peasant economy uses living labour intensively is taken into account, as well as the incomplete valorization of this component of value. Since intensive use of labour with respect to capital means lower productivity of labour, and nonvalorization of a portion of peasant labour means lower remuneration, both aspects are part of the reason why the peasant economy contributes to making agriculture face unfavourable terms of trade.

This latter conclusion is reinforced by the results relating to terms of trade of the agricultural components when taken separately. The exercise was done for 1970, where agriculture is divided into three sectors: peasant, family-based farms (*p*); commercial, labour-hiring plots (*e*); and intermediate or transitional units (*t*). The main result is that the peasant sector and, to a lesser extent, transitional agriculture, suffered unfavourable terms of trade (i.e., $\%Z^p_p / \%Z^v_p = 0.60$, $\%Z^p_e / \%Z^v_e = 0.93$, and $\%Z^p_t / \%Z^v_t = 0.65$).[4]

In order to complete this study, one must consider the evolution of the other element of the comparisons: prices. The changes in agricultural prices *vis-à-vis* GDP from the mid-1940s to the beginning of the 1970s show that they were not much different (Oliver, 1978, Table 3, p. 717). So, when agriculture is taken as a whole, its conditions of production and not its relative prices explain the terms of trade it faces.

Agricultural Terms of Trade, Prices, and Food Production Problems

The findings can be used to argue that unfavourable terms of trade are one of the factors explaining the reduction of rates of growth that agriculture has experienced since the mid-1950s. After a period of high growth from the 1940s to the mid-1950s, agriculture began to be less dynamic, especially from the mid-1960s up to the end of the 1970s, and this was not true for the other main economic sectors, including livestock rearing (Yunez N., 1988b, Chapter 8). This coincides with the result that, in 1960 and 1970, agriculture clearly faced unfavourable terms of trade with most of the remaining economic sectors.

However, the above is not sufficient to explain why stagnation is found in production of basic crops for human consumption; to establish this, one must study the evolution of the prices of specific peasant and commercial crops and the government influence on them.

From the 1950s, Mexico has established guaranteed prices to regulate the markets for several basic crops: the guaranteed price of beans was first set in 1953, that of maize in 1956, rice and wheat in 1960, sorghum in 1961, safflower and soyabeans in 1965, cotton seed and sesame in 1966, and barley and sunflower in 1971. This control accounted for a general decrease in real prices until 1973, which had a negative influence on production. This was particularly true for maize and, to a lesser extent, for beans—typical peasant crops and the most important grains in the Mexican diet (Santoyo, 1977; Gomez Oliver, 1977; Vera Ferrer, 1987; and Yunez N., 1988b, Chapter 8).

This, together with the observed increases in the production of crops for animal feeding and livestock rearing—typical commercial activities in rural Mexico—leads to the following interpretation being considered plausible. Since the 1960s, Mexico has been experiencing a strong change in the use of land, from crops for human consumption to fodder crops and from crops to livestock rearing. If one considers that the objective of commercial agriculture implies changes in the use of land when profitability of alternative activities change, and that this is not so for the peasant economy, Mexico's basic food production problems are explained by both a reduction in the productive capacity of peasant farms and a change in the use of land by commercial farms.

The historical experience of countries with divergent socioeconomic settings shows that agriculture has played a major role in growth. In not a few cases, this has been implemented by extracting surplus from the agricultural sector.

Mexico, through land reform, created the contemporary peasant economy and, through its agricultural policies, promoted commercial farmers. Both actions contributed to the formation of a heterogeneous agrarian structure. This, together with government intervention to maintain low food prices for urban consumers, created the conditions for agriculture to support urban industrial growth. However, the process has led to contradictions, which have imposed limits on this function: the polarization of agriculture created the conditions for the existence of unfavourable terms of trade, but it also meant increasing productivity and payment differentials between its components as well as the maintenance of low productivity or even the deterioration of the production conditions of those farms facing unequal terms of trade.

The low-productivity, low-reward peasant economy has been incapable of performing the role it had before, and a transformation of agriculture is taking place. The period of prominent agricultural support of growth has come to a halt and one of the consequences has been the erosion of agriculture's capacity to produce enough food for Mexico's population.

Notes

[1]Centro de Estudios Económicos, Colegio de México.

[2]The details are presented in Yunez N. (1986). Also see Yunez N. (1988a) for a theoretical discussion of the conclusions of agricultural terms of trade arising from the labour theory of value.

[3]Note that the price-value ratios are defined in terms of proportions because the nature of the value estimations requires normalization of the elements of the value and price vectors in order to make them comparable. This is not required by the terms of trade (Yunez N., 1986, Part II and Appendices).

[4]Similar results are obtained for the terms of trade of the three agricultural subsectors, and, again, the results on peasant and transitional agriculture's terms of trade become quite favourable when family labour is ignored (Yunez N., 1986, Chapter 6). Agriculture could not be subdivided for the other two years under study due to data restrictions.

References

Gomez Oliver, L. (1977) "Hacia una Fundamentación Analítica para una Nueva Estrategia de Desarrollo Rural," Centro de Investigación del Desarrollo Rural, México, D.F., Mexico.

Gomez Oliver, L. (1978) "Crisis Agrícola, Crisis de los Campesinos," *Comércio Exterior de México*, Vol. 28, pp. 714-727.

Morishima, M., and Seton, F. (1961) "Aggregation of Leontief Matrixes and the Labour Theory of Value," *Econometrica*, Vol. 29, pp. 203-222.

Santoyo, S. (1977) "Política de Precios de Garantía: Situación Actual y Perspectivas," *Demografía y Economía*, Vol. 31, pp. 77-98.

SPP (Secretaria de Programación y Presupuesto) (1980) *Bases Informativas para la Utilización del Modelo de Insumo-Producto*, México, D.F., Mexico.

Vera Ferrer, O.H. (1987) *Caso Conasupo: Evaluación*, Centro de Estudios en Economía y Educación, México, D.F., Mexico.

Yunez N., A. (1986) "Peasantry and Agricultural Exchange Relations: Inquiry Based on Data for the Mexican Economy," PhD Thesis, London School of Economics and Political Science, UK.

Yunez N., A. (1988a) "Theories of the Exploited Peasantry: Critical Review," *Journal of Peasant Studies*, Vol. 15.

Yunez N., A. (1988b) *Crisis de la Agricultura Mexicana: Reflexiones Teóricas y Análisis Empírico*, Colegio de México and Fondo de Cultura Económica, México, D.F., Mexico.

DISCUSSION OPENING—*Dušan Tomić* (Yugoslav Economic Institute)

Yunez's paper is a good stimulus for the exchange of opinions following two directions based on the example of Mexican agriculture: the experience of developing countries concerning agricultural development and what to do to overcome the trend of nonequivalent terms of trade of agricultural products.

The results show that the Mexican agriculture faces, in its local market, unfavourable terms of trade over the long term, which seriously limits its development. That is a common feature of many developing countries. I want to add to this investigation the fact that developing country agriculture also faces unfavourable terms of trade in the world market, resulting in great economic damage for agricultural product exporters. Some data edited by FAO showed that, in the 1960s and 1970s, the losses borne by underdeveloped countries, which arose because of aggravated terms of trade of agricultural products in the world market, were larger than the total economic aid they received.

Past experience based on the example of Mexican agriculture shows that the economic development strategy of the underdeveloped countries was based on agriculture as the source of funds for national industrialization and the maintenance of the average standard of living of the nonagricultural population. In the underdeveloped countries, as also in Mexico, agriculture was in the past in a subordinate economic position, which resulted in the intensification process of agricultural production being retarded, and a serious gap between supply of and demand for food. In that regard, the author's conclusion that agriculture can no longer be the source of funds for nonagricultural development or for carrying out a social function (e.g., to provide cheap food for the nonagricultural population) is correct.

The paper underlines some problems related to food production in Mexico: the agrarian structure, price policy, role of the state, etc. A more complex way of overcoming the unfavourable trend in the terms of trade of agricultural products should be based on the following four points.

1. Increasing labour productivity appears as the central problem in agriculture. Modern agricultural production based on new technology has to replace farmers' own production, which is low on the whole. The technology inflow must be more evenly shared among the agricultural production branches, types of farms, and characteristics of some agricultural regions.

2. Modification of the agrarian structure is a long-term process. Both development and production policies have to stimulate the differentiation of farms more efficiently according to the value of capital owned, types of production, and the scope of commodity production, so as to increase production and labour productivity.

3. A policy of achieving an equal economic position for agriculture in relation to the other sectors must: (a) provide for more efficient use of production factors, since agriculture has many resources in reserve; (b) make new investments and use more and better machines to transform agriculture more quickly into modern and specialized production, to establish larger farms, and to decrease costs of production per production unit; (c) establish an efficient system of economic conditions and stimulate measures that will speed up the development of agriculture. Agricultural producer prices should be formed in accordance with market conditions, with the numerous components of the total agricultural price policy worked out in advance; and (d) integrate modern economic and social developments within the agricultural sector. Integration in food production is an important precondition for achievement of greater production and higher income for farmers.

4. Science and research as well as agricultural policy are important preconditions for more efficient agricultural development. A high degree of interrelationship is needed between long-term and current agricultural policy.

GENERAL DISCUSSION—*Chinkook Lee* (Economic Research Service, US Department of Agriculture)

Yunez was asked if he could explain how the dualistic structure of the Mexican economy, where prices discriminate against agriculture and promote cheaper urban food prices, helps or hinders Mexican agriculture. He was also asked if different rates of technological change on Mexican farms could be segmented in the analysis.

In reply, Yunez said that, in the long-run, Mexico aims to follow world agricultural prices. However, in the short-run the government is using intervention policies to maintain cheaper food prices for consumers. The government is also helping farmers with some support policies that are effective in the short-run.

Only 1970 data were used, which cannot segment commercial (large) and peasant (small) farms in terms of their different rates of technical change.

Participants in the discussion included H.P. Binswanger and F. Homen de Melo.

Determinants of Rural-to-Urban Labour Movements in Mexico: Household Perspective

B. Bravo-Ureta, R.D. Ely, P.J. Pelto,
L. Meneses, L.H. Allen, G.H. Pelto, and A. Chávez[1]

Abstract: The purpose of this paper is to test specific hypotheses about the determinants of temporary rural-to-urban migration (circulation) by male heads of households for the purpose of engaging in wage employment. Data from a sample of 145 rural households located in the central Mexican highlands are used to estimate the model. The circulation equation is formulated as a polychotomous, ordered-response model and is estimated using logistic regression. The results of the model suggest that males' level of education and previous circulation experience have a positive and significant impact on the probability of circulation. By comparison, land has a negative effect, and economic status has a *U*-shaped effect. Age and the number of adults in the household are found to have a statistically weak association with the dependent variable.

Introduction

In recent years, Mexico, like many other developing countries, has experienced considerable rural-to-urban migration. This process became common in the mid-1960s when the 25-year period of prosperity enjoyed by the Mexican agricultural sector came to an end, forcing small-scale farmers to seek seasonal employment in urban areas and/or temporary migration to the USA (Unikel, Chiapetto, and Lazcano, 1973; and Arizpe, 1981).

The economic literature focusing on rural-to-urban migration over the last two decades is heavily influenced by Todaro's (1969) model, which postulates that migration takes place because individuals choose to reside in areas where they can maximize the present value of a discounted net income stream. Tests of the Todaro model have relied almost exclusively on aggregate census data (e.g., state or county) collected in the migrant's destination area. Most of this work has assumed that migration is a one-time or permanent decision (DaVanzo, 1981). Examples of this type of analysis for Mexico are Garrison (1982), Greenwood (1978), and King (1978). In contrast, this paper focuses on the determinants of temporary rural-to-urban migration in Mexico based on household-level data collected at the workers' places of origin.

Migration decisions have been discussed recently in the context of poor household survival strategies (Wood, 1981 and 1982; and Roberts, 1982). According to this view, the behaviour of a household can be seen "as a series of 'sustenance' strategies by which the household actively strives to achieve a fit between its consumption necessities, the labor power at its disposal (both of which are determined by the number, age, sex, and skills of its members), and the alternatives for generating monetary and nonmonetary income" (Wood, 1981, p. 339). Migration is regarded as "an important aspect of the adaptive strategy that the household pursues in response to changing structural constraints" (Wood, 1981, p. 340).

More recently, a growing body of evidence points to the significance of *circulation* (i.e., temporary migration) as an integral component of a household's survival strategy in poor rural areas of many developing countries (e.g., Chapman and Prothero, 1983; Nelson, 1976; and Standing, 1985). Circulation as a component of a complex survival strategy may have significant positive as well as negative effects on household welfare (Nattrass, May, and Peters, 1987).

In the case of Mexico, the growing significance of labour circulation has been attributed to the slowdown in the agricultural sector combined with the *ejido* system. The agricultural recession has pushed small farmers to find income sources outside agriculture, while the *ejido* system has kept them tied to the soil in order to avoid losing their claims to *ejido* lands (Alba and Potter, 1986; and Sanderson, 1986). Some research, primarily descriptive in nature, has analyzed the circulation phenomenon in Mexico (e.g., Arizpe, 1981; DeWalt, 1979; Feindt and Browning, 1972; Roberts, 1982; and Wiest, 1973). This paper goes beyond the existing descriptive literature by formulating a single-equation model to test specific hypotheses concerning the determinants of the decision to circulate by the male household head. Data from a sample of Mexican rural households located in the central highlands are used to estimate the model.

Data

The data used in the analysis are part of a much larger data set collected during the Mexico Collaborative Research and Support Programme on Nutrition and Function, a project conducted jointly, from 1982 to 1987, by researchers from the Instituto Nacional de la Nutrición Salvador Zubirán, División de Nutrición de Comunidad, in Mexico City, and the Department of Nutritional Sciences at the University of Connecticut. The study site included six communities located in the Solis Valley, approximately 75 miles northwest of Mexico City.

A complete survey of the communities was first undertaken to identify potential households for the study. To qualify, the household had to include both a male and a female head. If this was the case, then the couple had to have an infant younger than 8 months, and/or a child 18-30 months of age, and/or a child 7-8 years of age, and/or the woman had to be pregnant. All eligible households identified in the complete survey were invited to become collaborators in the project. Of those eligible, 290 (or 80 percent of those eligible) agreed to participate, which represents about 50 percent of all households located in the site. Of these 290 households, 145 were used to estimate the circulation equation. The latter sample is comprised of households for which extensive socioeconomic data are available. A detailed discussion of the data and sample selection criteria are found in Allen, Pelto, and Chávez (1987).

Model Specification

The broad conceptual framework of this paper, which is common to much of the economic work dealing with migration (or circulation), is that individuals move from one location to another in the expectation that this decision will yield financial rewards (DaVanzo, 1981). An individual's circulation decision is hypothesized to be determined by personal attributes and household characteristics (Bilsborrow, McDevitt, Kossoudji, and Fuller, 1987; and Findley, 1987). For the purposes of this study, circulation is defined as any temporary movement by the male household head away from the community—usually to Mexico City for 5-15 days at a time—in order to engage in wage employment.

In general terms, the circulation model is expressed as:

$$CI_h = f(AGE_h, EDUC_h, CASA_h, LAND_h, ADULT_h, CIEXP_h, COMMUN_h).$$

CI_h is the circulation index of the male head in the *h*th household. This index is a discrete variable set at 0 if the individual did not circulate or at 1, 2, 3, or 4 if he circulated in 1, 2, 3, or 4 quarters during 1984. *AGE* is the age of the male in years. *EDUC* is a binary variable equal to 1 if the male can read and write or 0 otherwise. *CASA* is a continuous index that combines the size and quality of dwellings, including the house and farm buildings, and is assumed to reflect the household's economic status. *LAND* measures the number of hectares controlled by the household and includes privately-owned as well as *ejido* lands. The reliability of the *LAND* variable is difficult to gauge given the intricate land-use arrangements encountered among the farmers in the sample. *ADULT* is the number of people 15 years and older who are members of the household; i.e. who live under the same roof. *COMMUN* is a set of binary variables representing the various communities where the households are located. *CIEXP* is a binary variable equal to 1 if the target male had circulated in more than two quarters between 1978 and 1983 and 0 otherwise.

Table 1 presents descriptive statistics for the variables included in the analysis. Out of the 145 males in the sample, 71 are circulators. Of these 71 individuals, 6 reported circulation in one quarter, 12 in two quarters, 8 in three quarters, and the remaining 45 in four quarters (not shown in Table 1). The data in Table 1 indicate that, on average, circulators are younger, better educated, have a lower *CASA* index, less land, more adults in the household, and considerably more circulation experience than noncirculators.

Table 1–Descriptive Statistics of Variables Used in the Analysis

Variable	All Males Mean	All Males Standard Deviation	Circulators Mean	Circulators Standard Deviation	Noncirculators Mean	Noncirculators Standard Deviation
CI	1.61	1.80	3.30	1.03	0.00	0.00
AGE	37.31	8.14	36.96	7.54	37.65	8.71
EDUC	0.85	0.36	0.90	0.30	0.79	0.40
CASA	24.06	17.60	21.87	15.34	26.17	19.41
LAND	1.38	1.56	1.15	1.43	1.60	1.65
ADULT	3.39	1.68	3.48	1.76	3.31	1.60
CIEXP	0.46	0.50	0.73	0.45	0.20	0.40
Sample size	145		71		74	

The relationship between the probability of circulation and *AGE* is hypothesized to have an inverted *U*-shape (*ceteris paribus*). The rationale for this hypothesis is that income requirements first increase as the family gets larger and the male household head becomes older and then decline as the children get older and start contributing to the household. *EDUC* is hypothesized to have a positive effect on circulation, which is consistent with the notion that better-educated individuals have more and better information about labour markets outside their communities (DaVanzo, 1981; and Sahota, 1968). Also, rural people with higher levels of education are likely to be driven to urban areas to find jobs commensurate with their educational achievements (Carvajal and Geithman, 1974). *CASA*, as a proxy of economic status, is expected to have a *U*-shaped relationship with circulation. This is based on the view that individuals in poor households are forced to circulate in order to survive, while individuals in relatively affluent households circulate to advance the family's economic status (Findley, 1987). *LAND* is hypothesized to have a negative effect on the probability of circulation because the labour absorption capacity and the ability to generate income within the household are directly related to the amount of land available. *ADULT* is expected to be positively related to the probability of circulation because, as the number of adults increases, the day-to-day labour requirements of the household are more easily met (Wiest, 1973). Finally, *CIEXP* is hypothesized to have a positive effect on the dependent variable because circulation experience increases the probability of finding work and also reduces the cost of circulation.

Table 2–Logistic Regression Estimates of Determinants of Rural-to-Urban Circulation for a Sample of Mexican Males

Variable	Regression Coefficient	Asymptotic Standard Error
ALPHA1	-8.6016**	3.5965
ALPHA2	-8.8828**	3.6039
ALPHA3	-9.4721***	3.6145
ALPHA4	-9.8781***	3.6195
AGE	0.1927	0.1687
AGE^2	-0.0022	0.0021
EDUC	1.0367*	0.6360
1/CASA	41.8901***	12.1354
$1/CASA^2$	-144.0836***	45.5450
1/LAND	0.0015***	0.0005
ADULT	0.1282	0.1372
CIEXP	2.5632***	0.4535
COMM1	1.1015	0.7208
COMM2	0.3041	0.7016
COMM3	-0.1043	0.6664
COMM5	0.2061	0.6377
COMM6	0.2179	0.7972

Notes: Number of observations = 145; log-likelihood = 271; model χ^2 = 78.270***; and pseudo-R^2 = 0.225.

*** = parameter significant at 0.01 level.

** = parameter significant at 0.05 level.

* = parameter significant at 0.10 level.

Results

Given the nature of the dependent variable, the circulation equation is formulated as a polychotomous, ordered-response model and is estimated using logistic regression (Maddala, 1983). The model yields four intercepts

(*ALPHA1*, ..., *ALPHA4*) and four probabilities (*P1*, ..., *P4*). *P1*, *P2*, *P3*, and *P4* are defined as the probability that the male household head circulates in one or more quarters, in two or more quarters, in three or more quarters, or in four quarters, respectively.

As shown in Table 2, the pseudo-R^2 statistic indicates that the model explains about 23 percent of the dependent variable's variation, and the model χ^2 provides strong evidence against the hypothesis that all slope parameters are equal to zero. The results reveal that the parameters for *EDUC*, *CASA*, *LAND*, and *CIEXP* are highly significant and that their signs are consistent with the hypotheses. The coefficients for *AGE* and *ADULT* also have the expected sign but are not significantly different from zero at the 10-percent level. In addition, the results suggest that no systematic relationship exists between the male's community of origin, captured by the *COMMUN* binary variables, and his decision to circulate.

Table 3—Marginal Effects of the Explanatory Variables Included in the Rural-to-Urban Circulation Model

Variable	P1	P2	P3	P4
AGE	0.00435	0.00488	0.00552	0.00543
EDUC	0.24022	0.25116	0.24479	0.21941
CASA	-0.11593	-0.12991	-0.14683	-0.14468
LAND	-0.00016	-0.00018	-0.00020	-0.00020
ADULT	0.02520	0.02131	0.01336	0.00877
CIEXP	0.55791	0.53587	0.45179	0.37620

Table 3 shows the change in the probability of circulation with respect to each explanatory variable in the model, holding all continuous variables at their mean value and setting *EDUC* and *CIEXP* at 1 and all *COMMUN* variables at 0. The change in probabilities for the continuous variables is given by the partial derivative of the probability of circulating in 1, 2, 3, or 4 quarters (*P1*, *P2*, *P3*, and *P4*) with respect to the variable in question. By comparison, the change in probability associated with *EDUC* and *CIEXP* is computed by calculating the difference in predicted probabilities when these variables are set first at 1 and then at 0.[2]

The change in probabilities presented in Table 3 shows that the probability of circulating in 1, 2, 3, or 4 quarters increases with previous circulation experience as well as with education. Also, a decline of roughly 11-15 percent in the probability of circulation occurs as *CASA* increases by one unit. By contrast, a one-unit variation in *AGE*, *LAND*, or *ADULT* has a small impact on the probability of circulation.

Concluding Remarks

The results of this paper confirm the notion that individual as well as household characteristics are important determinants in the male household head's decision to circulate for the purpose of engaging in wage employment. Of special significance to policy makers is the fact that the better-educated males from households where land pressure is relatively high tend to rely more heavily on off-farm income. Both of these variables are to some extent subject to policy manipulation and hence can be used to affect circulation.

An important agricultural policy issue that requires further study is the relationship between farm productivity and circulation. Some have suggested that temporary migrants are likely to be exposed to new ideas, which can have a beneficial impact on farm productivity (DeWalt, 1979), and that the earnings realized through wage employment can facilitate the adoption of new techniques (Katz and Stark, 1986). In contrast, Elkan (1982) has argued that circulation by the household decision maker could retard the adoption of technical innovations or otherwise adversely affect productivity, having a detrimental impact on farm profitability. Further study is needed to test these important but competing hypotheses.

Notes

[1]Department of Agricultural Economics and Rural Sociology, University of Connecticut; Department of Nutritional Sciences, University of Connecticut; Department of Medical Anthropology, University of Connecticut; Instituto Nacional de la Nutrición, Mexico; Department of Nutritional Sciences, University of Connecticut; Department of Nutritional Sciences, University of Connecticut; and Instituto Nacional de la Nutrición, Mexico; respectively. Scientific Contribution No. 1258 of the Storrs Agricultural Experiment Station, University of Connecticut. Supported in part by USAID grant #DAN-1309-G-SS-1070-00.

[2]Given the nonlinear nature of the equations involved, the computed changes in probability will vary significantly across individual observations.

References

Alba, F., and Potter, J.E. (1986) "Population and Development in Mexico Since 1940: Interpretation," *Population and Development Review*, Vol. 12, pp. 47-75.

Allen, L.H., Pelto, G.H., and Chávez, A. (1987) "Mexico Collaborative Research and Support Project on Intake and Function," Final Report, University of Connecticut, Storrs, Conn., USA.

Arizpe, L. (1981) "Rural Exodus in Mexico and Mexican Migration to the United States," *International Migration Review*, Vol. 15, pp. 620-649.

Bilsborrow, R.E., McDevitt, T.M., Kossoudji, S., and Fuller, R. (1987) "Impact of Origin Community Characteristics on Rural-Urban Out-Migration in a Developing Country," *Demography*, Vol. 24, pp. 191-210.

Carvajal, M.J., and Geithman, D.T. (1974) "Economic Analysis of Migration in Costa Rica," *Economic Development and Cultural Change*, Vol. 23, pp. 105-122.

Chapman, M., and Prothero, R.M. (1983) "Themes on Circulation in the Third World," *International Migration Review*, Vol. 17, pp. 597-632.

DaVanzo, J. (1981) "Microeconomic Approaches to Studying Migration Decisions," in DeJong, G.F., and Gardner, R.W. (Eds.), *Migration Decision Making: Multidisciplinary Approaches to Microlevel Studies in Developed and Developing Countries*, Pergamon Press, Oxford, UK, pp. 90-129.

DeWalt, B.R. (1979) *Modernization in a Mexican Ejido: Study in Economic Adaption*, Cambridge University Press, Cambridge, UK.

Elkan, W. (1982) "Labor Migration from Botswana, Lesotho and Swaziland," *Economic Development and Cultural Change*, Vol. 28, pp. 583-596.

Feindt, W., and Browning, H.L. (1972) "Return Migration: Its Significance in an Industrial Metropolis and an Agricultural Town in Mexico," *International Migration Review*, Vol. 6, pp. 158-167.

Findley, S.E. (1987) "Interactive Contextual Model of Migration in Ilocos Norte, Philippines," *Demography*, Vol. 24, pp. 163-190.

Garrison, H. (1982) "Internal Migration in Mexico: Test of the Todaro Model," *Food Research Institute Studies*, Vol. 18, pp. 197-214.

Greenwood, M.J. (1978) "Econometric Model of Internal Migration and Regional Economic Growth in Mexico," *Journal of Regional Science*, Vol. 18, pp. 17-31.

Katz, E., and Stark, O. (1986) "Labor Migration and Risk Aversion in Less Developed Countries," *Journal of Labor Economics*, Vol. 4, pp. 134-149.

King, J. (1978) "Interstate Migration in Mexico," *Economic Development and Cultural Change*, Vol. 27, pp. 83-101.

Maddala, G.S. (1983) *Limited Dependent and Qualitative Variables in Econometrics*, Cambridge University Press, London, UK.

Nattrass, J., May, J., and Peters, A. (1987) "Migrant Labour, Subsistence Agriculture, and Rural Poverty in South Africa: Empirical Study of Living Standards in Three Rural Areas of KwaZulu," in Bellamy, M., and Greenshields, B. (Eds.) *Agriculture and*

Economic Instability, IAAE Occasional Paper No. 4, Gower Publishing Co., Aldershot, UK, pp. 245-249.

Nelson, J.M. (1976) "Sojourners versus New Urbanites: Causes and Consequences of Temporary versus Permanent Cityward Migration in Developing Countries," *Economic Development and Cultural Change*, Vol. 24, pp. 721-757.

Roberts, K.D. (1982) "Agrarian Structure and Labor Mobility in Rural Mexico," *Population and Development Review*, Vol. 8, pp. 299-322.

Sahota, G.S. (1968) "Economic Analysis of Internal Migration in Brazil," *Journal of Political Economy*, Vol. 76, pp. 218-245.

Sanderson, S.E. (1986) *Transformation of Mexican Agriculture*, Princeton University Press, Princeton, N.J., USA.

Standing, G. (Ed.) (1985) *Labour Circulation and the Labour Process*, Croom Helm, New York, N.Y., USA.

Todaro, M.P. (1969) "Model of Labor Migration and Urban Unemployment in Less Developed Countries," *American Economic Review*, Vol. 49, pp. 138-148.

Unikel, L., Chiapetto, C.R., and Lazcano, O. (1973) "Factores de Rechazo en la Migración Rural en México, 1950-1960," *Demografía y Economía*, Vol. 7, pp. 24-57.

Wiest, R.E. (1973) "Wage-Labor Migration and the Household in Mexican Town," *Journal of Anthropological Research*, Vol. 29, pp. 180-209.

Wood, C.H. (1981) "Structural Changes and Household Strategies: Conceptual Framework for the Study of Rural Migration," *Human Organization*, Vol. 40, pp. 338-344.

Wood, C.H. (1982) "Equilibrium and Historical-Structural Perspectives on Migration," *International Migration Review*, Vol. 16, pp. 298-319.

DISCUSSION OPENING—*Mohamadreza Arsalanbod* (Urmia University)

While most studies show that migration is selective with respect to the number of adults in the household and especially selective with respect to the age, the insignificant effect of age in this study could be due to the kind of data used. The data comes from six communities located only 75 miles from Mexico City.

For most migrants, both efficiency in production and consumption are the reasons for migration, and the importance of each of these factors depends on the individual case and the personal characteristics and circumstances facing migrants. In this paper, consumption efficiency related factors are totally neglected. In the literature on migration, some elements related to consumption efficiency have been used in explanations of migration, but these factors have not been treated explicitly, either theoretically or empirically. Removing this shortcoming would probably increase the explanatory power of migration models, especially those of permanent migration. The *U*-shaped relationship between economic status and migration found in some studies of migration, including Bravo-Ureta *et al.*'s paper, could, at least to some extent, be due to consumption efficiency behaviour of migrants.

In Bravo-Ureta *et al.*'s paper, the number of hectares of land controlled by the household, including privately owned as well as *ejido* lands, is entered in the model. Using the land-to-labour ratio instead would be more appropriate.

Research on migration has been mostly concerned with identification of differentials between personal and locational characteristics and the extent to which these differentials influence migration, including temporary migration. Bravo-Ureta *et al.*'s paper is one example that confirms that individual as well as household characteristics are important determinants in the decision to circulate.

The impact of migrants on places of origin and destination (origin in particular) are matters of much concern and speculation. Bravo-Ureta *et al.* mention one of these important issues; i.e., the relationship between farm productivity and circulation.

While entering the consumption-efficiency-related variables, both personal and locational, is likely to increase the explanatory power of migration models, the more important area of research on migration would be identification and measurement of impacts of the factors that condition the whole process of migration, factors that are powerful and to a large extent subject to policy manipulation and hence can be used to affect migration and in turn affect the occupational and geographical distributions of population. Factors related to the socioeconomic system of each country include pattern of economic development, government role in the economy, and personal distribution of nonlabour resources and income.

GENERAL DISCUSSION—*Chinkook Lee* (Economic Research Service, US Department of Agriculture)

One participant asked if intertemporal welfare functions could be used in the analysis. For example, labour migration to the USA over time may be an important factor to be considered.

In reply, Bravo-Ureta said that "factors affected by labour migration to the USA are important in analyzing labour movements between urban and rural regions. However, this study is a static analysis and not an intertemporal study. By using a reduced form, intertemporal considerations could probably be included in an empirical study.

Participants in the discussion included S. Larrea and A. Ortega Marquez.

Peasant Exploitation Revisited: Role of Producer Preferences in Red Bean Markets in the Dominican Republic

Kenneth Wiegand and Dwight Steen[1]

Abstract: A 1981 study in the Dominican Republic was replicated in 1987 to analyze the effect of producer preferences on farm prices for red beans and to determine if rural market conditions changed significantly between the two study periods. In contrast to the 1981 study, econometric analysis of the 1987 situation revealed that when adjustments are made for quality, consumer preferences, and transport costs, not even the earlier revealed impact of quantity marketed, habitual sales to the same buyer, or local political power of the farm family significantly affected the farm-wholesale price margin. Again, the lack of any perceptible influence based on the provision of groceries, family relationships, wealth, tied purchase or weight manipulation was substantiated. The analysis once again corroborated that, although farmers may express a sense of obligation to middlemen who are related or who sell them groceries, and where a reservation price may be elicited with respect to sale of their crop to an alternative buyer, farmer actions revealed such expressions to be meaningless. The unabated tendency of producers verbally to exaggerate their social obligations will continue to represent a methodological dilemma for social scientists unwilling or unable to delve quantitatively below such manifestations in order to distinguish between intent and action.

Introduction

In many countries, the shrill cry from politicians and some policy makers to destroy, once and for all, the alleged exploitation practised by rural traders has not diminished. International donors have not remained immune to locally perceived priorities based on such perceptions. During the mid-1970s, an ambitious plan to develop integrated rural service centres was funded by several development agencies in the Dominican Republic, with the primary intent of breaking the power of rural intermediaries by providing nonprofit, locally managed grocery shops, farm supply centres, and warehouse/drying facilities (SEA, 1981).

The effort was directed primarily at small-scale growers of red beans (*Phaseolus vulgaris*), a popular daily food among Dominicans. Evidence of exploitation by rural traders was documented by social scientists using case study interviews. Allusion was made to Wharton's hypothesis that unequal market power could arise based on producer preferences and loyalties for certain rural traders due to social and political power wielded by such middlemen (Wharton, 1962). The $6 million rural service centre project was implemented prior to any rigorous evaluation of whether, in fact, such conditions existed and what impact they had on rural markets.

Four years later, the first attempt was made systematically to measure the frequency and economic impact of such conditions (Wiegand, 1983). The rural service centres already in operation (half the number eventually completed) were failing to make the expected impact on local economies. The farm supply shops were understocked or inoperative; the warehouses were, with rare exception, unused; the food shops operating with government-subsidized basic commodities were in debt and had succeeded only in driving out of business those local rural grocers supplying a full range of items. The 1981 study revealed that many of the hypothesized social conditions that were capable of sustaining a monopsonistic rural market structure were nonexistent, and, equally important, rural producers were often inconsistent between their stated marketing intentions and their subsequent behaviour.

Nevertheless, the concept of rural trader exploitation is a powerful and perhaps convenient theme for policy makers and politicians faced with high rates of inflation, food scarcities, and easily legislated farm price controls. Given these basically unchanged perceptions, a survey was undertaken in precisely the same regions as the 1981 study to determine once again whether conditions exist for a truly imperfectly competitive market among red bean producers and traders, based on producer preferences for particular middlemen (USAID, 1988).

Objectives and Hypothesis

As in the 1981 analysis, this study examined the interface between small-scale farmers and marketing intermediaries to determine the existence, frequency, source, and impact of farmer preferences and opportunity sets with respect to particular buyers or intermediaries. The preferences are hypothesized to be of two types: (1) those created by unique services provided by the intermediary at the time of purchase and directly associated with the transaction, for which no economical close substitutes exist; and (2) those created by the provision of services by those who have unique interpersonal relationships with clients independent of the set of services involved in the particular transaction, but which affect the terms of sale.

The second source of preferences and differentiated opportunity sets (those not directly related to the sale) creates the opportunity for substantial price advantage to the buyer. These immobilities are derived from characteristics unique to the individual buyer-seller relationship, such as social position, political power, family relationships, and other factors that cannot be reproduced by competitors. Preferences derived from these sources may depress sale prices below competitive prices and below the prices available to the farmer from other buyers. Under these circumstances, the *social differentiated price* may be substantially lower than both the competitive price and the service differentiated price.

This study tests the following hypotheses: (1) a hierarchy of prices exists in small farmer agricultural markets; (2) in the presence of such a hierarchy, the small-scale farmer is more likely to receive the social differentiated price (i.e., the lowest price); and (3) a differential exists between the social and service differentiated prices, which, if exceeded, will induce the farmer to seek an alternative, nonpreferred buyer, and this differential (premium) varies inversely with the scale of the farm operation. The study also attempts to determine if the current hierarchy and farmer response is significantly different than conditions uncovered in 1981.

Analytical Procedure

The model may be specified as:

$$P_f = f(M, S, F),$$

where P_f = the farm level price of a given crop in \$/unit at which the farmer sold, M = a set of variables representing the market transaction related services provided by the first buyer of the farmer's product, S = a set of variables representing the preference inducing factors that link the first buyer to a particular farmer, and F = a set of variables representing the wealth of the individual relative to other farmers in the immediate market area.

The hypotheses were tested using multiple regression analysis by fitting the model to empirical data gathered over a three-month period. The dependent variable was specified to reflect the expectations of the buyer for the price received in the central wholesale market. Thus, the dependent variable is the difference between the farm price (converted to a standard measure of \$/cwt) and the average maximum wholesale market price.

The sources of producer preferences based on transaction-related services were suggested in previous research (Nicholls, 1941; Wharton, 1962; Werge, 1975; Murray, 1976; and Sharpe, 1977), and are the same as used in the 1981 study: (1) transfer costs from point of sale to the wholesale market (*TOTLTIME*); (2) provision of production credit by the intermediary to the farmer; (3) only partial payment for the crop at the time of sale, and, where this occurs, deferment of final price determination pending sale of the crop by the middleman in the wholesale market; (4) grading of the product into quality categories at the farm level (*GRADE B, C*); (5) provision of price premiums based on the geographical origin of the crop, reflecting varietal or qualitative consumer preferences (*REGION B, C*); (6) the opportunity for the farmer to sell the crop and receive a price offer using local units of measure (*WEIGHT MANIP*); and (7) the quantity per transaction of beans transacted (*SACK SOLD*).

The sources of additional preference-inducing factors also mentioned in the literature, but which are independent of the particular transaction, are the following, which derive from characteristics unique to the individual buyer-seller relationship (e.g., social position, political power, etc.): (8) the provision of tied purchasing arrangements whereby the sale of the farmer's beans implies additional transactions with the same intermediary for other crops (*TIED PURCHASE*); (9) the provision of productive resources (on credit) to the farmer by the intermediary; (10) the provision of groceries to the farmer by the intermediary who owns a retail establishment (*FOOD CASH, FOOD CREDIT*); (11) the provision of employment to the farmer by the intermediary; (12) the provision of access to political or official influence to the farmer by the intermediary and vice-versa (*FARMPOWR 1, 2*); (13) socially obligatory farmer to buyer linkages through family and/or ritual relationships (*FAMILY/KIN*); (14) indeterminate linkages between buyer and seller that lead the farmer to sell to the same buyer year after year (*HABIT*); (15) ideological, philosophical, or moral commitment to a cooperative outlet; and (16) the wealth of the farmer, measured in terms of land and livestock (*WEALTH*).

For a particular preference-inducing factor substantially to affect the price received by a farmer, it must in fact be operative. Those not found in practice cannot be interpreted as causing widespread exploitation of farmers. Moreover, the impact of practices with low frequencies of occurrence cannot be estimated reliably with multiple regression analysis. Therefore, hypothesized effects of all factors with a frequency of less than five percent were deleted from the regression. Each of the variables included in the regression analysis is reported in Table 1, with a comparison to the 1981 results.

Table 1—Comparison of Variables Included in the Regression Analysis, Red Bean Producer Preferences for Particular Intermediaries

		1981			1987		
Variable	Expected Sign	Coefficient	Standard Error	Level of Significance	Coefficient	Standard Error	Level of Significance
Intercept	+	12.9	3.2	***	46.3	28.2	*
TOTLTIME	+	-0.02	0.005	***	-0.12	0.09	0.16
GRADE B	+	2.5	0.63	***	24.5	11.7	**
GRADE C	+	6.1	0.99	***	30.9	14.5	**
REGION B	-	4.7	3.1	0.13	-20.5	20.8	0.33
REGION C	-	4.3	2.7	0.11	5.93	16.2	0.72
WEIGHT MANIP	+	0.008	0.75		-2.9	12.2	
SACK SOLD	-	-0.02	0.008	**	0.34	0.28	0.23
HABIT	+	1.85	1.00	*	9.1	16.5	0.58
WEALTH	-	-0.0002	0.02		0.04	0.05	
FARMPOWR 1 (regional)	-	-0.04	0.83	*	-3.9	19.1	0.84
FARMPOWR 2 (local)	-	-1.5	0.89		-23.0	21.7	
TIED PURCHASE	+	1.8	1.1		9.1	12.8	
FOOD CASH	+	-1.1	1.4		20.3	31.9	
FOOD CREDIT	+	-0.8	1.5		18.4	21.9	
FAMILY/KIN	?	-1.9	1.3		16.5	18.9	
R^2			0.19			0.18	
Degrees of freedom			722			90	

*** = 0.01 level; ** = 0.05 level; * = 0.10 level.

Source: Agriculture and Rural Development Division, USAID, Santo Domingo, Dominican Republic.

Summary of Results

Little has changed during the six years following the original study of producer preferences that would justify continued policy support for rural interventions to break the alleged market power of rural traders.

Once again, few of the services associated in the literature with the establishment of producer preferences were found to be either frequent or significant in their impacts on the farm-wholesale price margin. The unexpected sign associated with transfer costs is explained by the relatively equal distance among the three regions from the wholesale market. The results confirm the earlier analysis that farm-wholesale price margins are essentially a function of quality distinctions and marketing costs. Designation of product quality by the producer and trader indicated a high level of congruence, again contrary to published reports that purchase by grade differential does not occur at the farm level.

As before, analysis of relative impacts revealed that farmers of small relative wealth (assets owned) confronted farm-wholesale price margins not significantly different from those of greater wealth. The commonly held belief that buyers systematically engage in dishonest weighing or unit measurement practices was again not supported by the evidence.

A few differences between the 1981 and current study reveal subtle but measurable changes in the conduct of rural transactions. The quantity of product transacted, which formerly may have provided a slight advantage to growers selling larger quantities, no longer indicates a significant impact on the farm-wholesale price margin. The number of growers surveyed who sell more than 1,000 cwt of red beans has increased over the years from 39 to 53 percent; the number who sell between 501 to 1,000 cwt per transaction has decreased from 23 percent to 11.

In 1981, 27 percent of the growers had failed to consult other traders prior to the sale of their crop; only 17 percent in this survey had failed to do so. The measure of habitual sale to the same trader over a three-year period, which in 1981 revealed a significant producer-price disadvantage of $1.85/cwt, is apparently no longer operative. Neither does association or familial linkage to regional political or police power now play a significant role in determining a price advantage for the grower.

Again, as in 1981, the preference-inducing factors mentioned most frequently in the literature—provision of groceries and/or inputs on credit—showed no impact on the farm-wholesale price margin. Similarily, family relationships showed no significant impact. The farmer's apparent sense of "weakness" when receiving inputs and/or groceries on credit from the buyer/provider of services increased by 10 to 15 percent since 1981. But, in spite of a stated reservation price 12 percent over the price offered by a relative (i.e., on average, the farmer would have to receive $5.41/cwt more from an alternative buyer to "break" the obligation with the relative, quite similar to $5.50/cwt in 1981), the farmer extracted the stated opportunity cost in only 14 of 30 opportunities where this situation arose. The average opportunity cost of *foregoing* the "obligation" was $3.06/cwt.

Tests of congruency between stated beliefs (implying intentions) and actual behaviour for those producers who confronted a situation of sale to an input/grocery provider or relative indicate little correspondence between action and stated intention. Thus, in spite of increased relative levels of protestations since 1981 of "weakness" when confronting such limitations to free market behaviour, they are apparently as easily disregarded now as they were then.

Given the evidence that little has changed in producer/trader red bean markets at the farm level in the Dominican Republic since 1981, one must question the tenacity with which policy makers and donors cling to the perception that structural interventions in unfair trader practices will improve rural market conditions. On the contrary, this study implies that more efficient investments should have been and could still be made in strengthening institutions that permit increased price transparency based on establishing quality grades and standards, and perhaps in mechanisms to increase higher quality on-farm storage.

Note

[1]Agriculture and Rural Development Division, US Agency for International Development, Santo Domingo.

References

Murray, G.F. (1976) "Dominican Peasants and Rural Traders: Project Oriented Research Methodology," A/D-1/76, Instituto Interamericano de Ciencias Agrícolas, Santo Domingo, Dominican Republic.

Nicholls, W.H. (1941) *Theoretical Analysis of Imperfect Competition with Special Application to the Agricultural Industries*, Iowa State College Press, Ames, Iowa, USA.

SEA (Secretaría de Estado de Agricultura) (1981) "Plan Operativo—1982," Santo Domingo, Dominican Republic, pp. 14, 125.

Sharpe, K.E. (1977) *Peasant Politics: Struggle in a Dominican Village*, Johns Hopkins University Press, Baltimore, Md., USA.

USAID (US Agency for International Development) (1988) "Las Preferencias del Productor en la Comercialización de Habichuelas Rojas," Agricultural and Rural Development Division, Santo Domingo, Dominican Republic.

Werge, R.W. (1975) *Agricultural Development in Clear Creek: Adaptive Strategies and Economic Roles in a Dominican Settlement*, PhD dissertation, University of Florida, Gainesville, Fla., USA.

Wharton, C.R., Jr. (1962) "Merchandising and Moneylending: Note on Middleman Monopsony in Malaya," *Malayan Economic Review*, Vol. 7, No. 2, Oct., pp. 24-44.

Wiegand, K.B. (1983) *Exploitation among Small Scale Farmers: Role of Producers' Preferences for Particular Middlemen*, PhD dissertation, University of Kentucky, University Microfilms International, Ann Arbor, Mich., USA.

DISCUSSION OPENING—*Carlos Seré* (Centro Internacional de Agricultura Tropical)

Wiegand and Steen's paper discusses a topic of great interest in developing countries, and in Latin America in particular: the extent of "exploitation" of small farmers by middlemen. The characteristics of marked dualism and the extent of urbanization in Latin America's rural sector, substantially higher than in other developing regions of the world, have led to a particular sensitivity about this issue. Governments are concerned about food prices for the urban consumers, and wide margins between consumer and producer prices lead policy makers to intervene in the agricultural marketing sector.

It is particularly noteworthy that this is one of the few empirical micro-level studies presented at this meeting. It aims at documenting the absence of a need for public sector intervention to improve competition in rural marketing in the Dominican Republic. But, as Barbara Harriss says in her review of measurements of agricultural market performance, "A competitive market may be necessary, but it clearly is not sufficient for the maximization of productivity. To concentrate attention on the concepts of competition diverts attention from the structural interrelationships between production, exchange, and consumption."

Wiegand and Steen's analysis includes dummy variables for political power, tied purchases, family or kinship relations, etc. and is undertaken during a period of time when, according to the authors, government interventions in the market already were occurring. Is this methodology appropriate to test the hypothesis of the effectiveness of these interventions? Would we not expect the presence of such institutions, acting for example as a buyer of last resort, to make these coefficients nonsignificant?

Can we expect decision makers to accept the analysts' conclusions if the model only explains 18 percent of the marginal variability (and the adjusted R^2 drops to 2 percent if corrected for the number of independent variables included)?

This raises the question of other possible sources of marginal variation. Bean consumers in many countries have distinct preferences for specific bean attributes (size, colour, cooking quality, etc.). Are these differences of varieties captured appropriately by the dummies for regions used by the authority? Another possible source of variation might be the fact that the analysis stretched over three months in a period of high inflation rate, which included the bean harvest and the period thereafter. Were deflated prices or margins used?

Given the low explanatory power of the model, the question remains whether the lack of statistical evidence of distortions is due to their absence or to the model specification. The analysis could probably benefit from putting bean marketing in a wider context. The reader is not informed about the market structure or its functioning. The proxy for transport costs presents the wrong sign, indicating a decreasing margin with increasing distance. This begs for a more detailed analysis of the functioning of the bean market and particularly an analysis of the cost structure of bean marketing. This might document high losses during transport or storage, high labour inputs in reclassification and handling, or it might slow high price volatility on the wholesale market, introducing risk. A better understanding of these aspects might generate additional hypotheses to introduce into the econometric model.

Policy makers are concerned not only with efficiency but also with equity in its various dimensions (income groups, ethnic groups, rural versus urban population, different regions, etc.). This paper stresses efficiency objectives exclusively. But even here, strong statements are made based on weak evidence: a plea for grading is made when existing grading is the only significant variable in the model. Furthermore, additional investments in on-farm storage are suggested even though the model has not included the time factor or variables related to storage.

The Wiegand/Steen paper is a step in the right direction. We do need more empirical studies documenting the impact or lack thereof of the whole range of marketing interventions. Particularly in contemporary Latin America, democratically elected governments will use food marketing policies to achieve their goals. Solidly backed policy advice may, under these circumstances, have a high payoff.

[No general discussion of this paper was reported.]

Rural Poverty and Resource Distribution in Bangladesh: Green Revolution and Beyond

Mohammad Alauddin and Clem Tisdell[1]

Abstract: Recent studies have examined the relationships between agricultural innovations and rural poverty in LDCs, concentrating on either exchange or nonexchange income. However, neither approach is adequate if employed independently. Growing concentration of control of land and the effects of components of new agricultural technology on ancillary resources are documented for Bangladesh. Access to land and other natural resources by the rural poor is gradually diminishing. Increasing landlessness and near landlessness have resulted in greater dependence on wage employment for subsistence. However, agricultural wages, being close to the subsistence level, provide little scope for carry-over into periods of slack agricultural activity. Even though real wages may be trending upwards slightly, much of their effect on rural poverty is neutralized because of seasonality in employment and real wages. The nonexchange component of income is important in slack periods and may become critical in abnormal years when both real wages and employment fall sharply. With rapid population growth and resource depletion and greater penetration of technological and market forces, access to natural resources with a cushioning effect on the rural poor in adverse circumstances has become more limited and income security has been undermined.

Introduction

Evidence is provided in this paper of increasing landlessness in rural areas in Bangladesh and of rising concentration of control over land and other resources essential for the successful application of new technologies associated with the Green Revolution. The new technologies themselves have probably been instrumental in bringing about these changes. The question of whether rural poverty is on the increase is also explored, paying particular attention to the position of the landless or near landless. In doing so, account must be taken of income obtained from exchange such as wages (Ahluwalia, 1985; and Mellor, 1985) and to nonexchange income such as may be obtained from common property (Jodha, 1986; and Conway, 1985).

The impact of technological change in agriculture on income distribution and rural poverty has been examined either by considering variations in exchange income (e.g., Ahluwalia, 1985; and Mellor, 1985) or by focusing primarily on nonexchange income (e.g., Jodha, 1986; Conway, 1985; and Lipton, 1985). Neither of these two approaches taken separately provides a satisfactory explanation of changes that follow population growth and technological change and their impacts on rural poverty. Several studies of Bangladeshi agriculture have examined rural poverty, income distribution, and technological change (Khan, 1984, pp. 192-195; and Ahmed, 1985, p. 126) and found evidence of declining real wages due to slow agricultural productivity growth.

Land-Use Concentration, Landlessness, and Distribution of Ancillary Resources

An analysis of data from various agricultural censuses (ACO, 1962, p. 29; and BBS, 1981, p. 41, and 1986a, p. 81) clearly indicates a substantial degree of inequality in land distribution. The Gini concentration ratio for operational land in the 1960 census (ACO, 1962) was 0.502. The fall in the value of the Gini coefficient (0.419 for operational holdings) in 1977 is due probably not to a trend towards greater equalization but an underreporting of the number of small-farm households (BBS, 1986a, pp. 32-33). If one considers the pattern of land ownership distribution for 1977 and 1983-84, an interesting feature emerges. The 1977 Gini coefficient is estimated to be 0.428, which is higher than that (0.419) for operational holdings in that year. Thus, the operational holdings seem to be slightly more evenly distributed than owner holdings. The 1983-84 data, however, indicate that land distribution on an ownership basis is more evenly distributed than operational holdings (the ownership Gini coefficient is 0.493 versus 0.533 for operational holdings).

This may indicate the emergence of sharecropping of the reverse order, whereby the small farmers as a group are net lessors while the relatively large farmers are net lessees. Thus, access of the rural poor to land resources is gradually becoming more and more limited. This may be: (1) because increased profitability of self-cultivation by large farmers is leading to tenant eviction (Bardhan, 1984, p. 189); (2) because medium and large farmers taken together have attained greater control over land without any formal ownership rights (*khas* land); or (3) because the ownership of irrigation equipment gives large farmers almost absolute control over irrigation water.[2]

Cain (1983, p. 158) reported that an estimated 17 percent of rural households were landless in 1960. Employing 1961 population census data, Abdullah, Hossain, and Nations (1976, pp. 212-213) estimated that 21.9 percent of households had no land. Subsequent surveys and census reports in the 1970s indicate significant increases in landlessness. For instance, the 1977 Land Occupancy Survey reported that about 29 percent of the households owned no land other than homestead land (BBS, 1986a, p. 69; and Cain, 1983, p. 158). However, this figure is likely to be less reliable than the 1961 estimate because of the small sample, which may contain a high sampling error. The 1983-84 census reports that 28.2 percent of the households owned no land other than homestead land (BBS, 1986a, p. 69). However, the census reports a high incidence of farms (more than 70 percent) in the small-farm category (less than 0.40 hectare). As Cain (1983, p. 154) argues, the lower end of the distribution is a sensitive indicator of change. A process of polarization seems to be taking place: the near landless are dispossessed and join the ranks of the landless, while small farmers in turn become near landless.

Considering changes in the use of important components of new technology (i.e., irrigation and HYVs) may give some indication of the changing fortunes of the landless and near landless. Between the two census years, 1977 (BBS, 1981, pp. 42-43 and 45) and 1983-84 (BBS, 1986a, p. 81, and 1986b, p. 111), a significant increase occurred in the percentage of operated area that was irrigated and planted with HYVs for all classes of farmers. The intensity of irrigation (irrigated area as percentage of operated area) and of HYV cultivation (total area under HYVs of different crops of rice and wheat as a percentage of operated area) seem to be inversely related to farm size. These intensities seem to decline with increases in operated area. As of 1983-84, nearly 20 percent of area operated by small farmers was under irrigation, compared to 17 and 16 percent, respectively, for medium and large farmers. However, the overall distribution of area irrigated and area planted with HYVs in 1983-84 produces Gini ratios of 0.506 and 0.439, respectively. An intertemporal comparison suggests a trend towards greater concentration of these elements (0.355 and 0.310 for irrigated and HYV areas in 1977, respectively). Despite underreporting of small-farm households in the 1977 sample census and a likely underestimation of the Gini concentration ratios, an increasing trend towards concentration cannot be ruled out. Irrigated area is more unevenly distributed than the HYV area. The comparatively lower degree of inequality in the distribution of HYVs is because all HYVs are not irrigated. For instance, around a third of total HYV wheat area is irrigated, and the HYVs of *aus* and *aman* (*kharif*) rice are primarily rain fed even though a small percentage of the area under these rice varieties is irrigated.

Degree of access to irrigation is a key determinant of HYV adoption. According to Lipton (1985), in unirrigated and unreliably rain-fed areas, no association exists between amount of land owned and operated (between 0 and 2-4 hectares) and poverty risk. Tiny amounts of well-watered land reduce that risk. Thus, increased inequality in the distribution of irrigated land is likely to increase inequality in the distribution of incremental output. As reported in BBS (1981, pp. 41 and 45, and 1986a, p. 82), a higher percentage of large farms as compared to small and medium farms have access to irrigation. The gap in the access to irrigation has increased over time. For instance, in 1976-77, 32.7 percent of large farms had access to irrigation compared to 31.1 and 29.4 percent, respectively, of the medium and small farms. The corresponding figures for 1983-84 are 57.9, 53.4, and 38.7, respectively. While differences in these percentages are not substantial in the first period, they are in the subsequent period.

Let us now consider the distribution pattern of livestock and poultry resources. Consistent with the pattern of distribution of land and other resources, these resources are also unevenly distributed. In 1983-84 (BBS, 1986a, pp. 83-85), while most of the medium- and large-sized farms reported having bovine animals, only 55 percent of those in the small farm category did so. For sheep and goats and for poultry, the contrast seems to be less striking. Despite difficulties in making intertemporal comparisons, a significant decline in the area under fodder crops and virtual disappearance of pasture land (BBS, 1986b, p. 101) have made maintaining bovine populations more difficult for the small farms. As BPC (1985, pp. ix-45) points out, "fodder supply was adversely affected by food production, partly due to the decline in grazing land but mainly due to the shift from long-stem to short varieties of rice cultivation." The unevenness in the distribution of livestock implies that the shortage seems to affect the small farms more severely than the large ones in terms of cost of cultivation (Gill, 1981, p. 14).

The above trends seem to be supported by farm-level evidence from Ekdala and South Rampur in Bangladesh (Alauddin and Tisdell, 1987).[3]

Market and Nonmarket Income of the Rural Poor and Reasons for Concentration of Resource Control

To some extent, the rural poor, consisting of the landless and near landless, depend on natural resources such as land, which they may hire or have limited access to, to supplement their income. They are primarily wage labourers. The supplementary incomes assume greater significance during the slack months or in depressed economic conditions when only a small residue of work is available and/or wage rates are relatively low.

With the introduction of new technology in rural areas, the rural poor are likely to be relatively disadvantaged because of likely increases in the demand for natural resources. This is further reinforced by persistent population pressure (Repetto and Holmes, 1983). The price of natural resources is forced up, and, therefore, only those capable of adopting the new technology are capable of buying (hiring) the natural resources on any scale. The adoption of new technology may be limited or relatively limited to the wealthier members of the farming community. Consequently, the price of the resource rises and the poor can no longer afford to purchase it and their income falls. But the rich can purchase the resource and their income may increase in absolute terms. In any case, the differential adoption of technology may increase income inequality. The poor may be forced to try to obtain full-time work as labourers. As Bardhan (1984, p. 189) argues, "increased dependence on purchased inputs and privately controlled irrigation is driving some small farmers with limited access to resources and credit out of cultivation and into crowding the agricultural labor market."

Figure 1 illustrates a case where poor farmers are forced out of farming by their failure to adopt new technology, which, however, is adopted by others and causes a rise in the price of a vital natural resource such as irrigation water. The curve *SS* represents the supply of a natural resource at the village or community level and D_1D_1 demand curve for it prior to the introduction of a new technology. It sells for a price of P_1 per unit, and poor farmers, with a marginal value product curve MVP_A, make a profit indicated by the triangle in the middle panel. Suppose that, with the introduction of new technology, the community demand for the natural resource rises to D_2D_2. Its price increases to P_2 per unit. If the poor farmers do not adopt the new technology, they are unable to make any profit by purchasing the natural resource at price P_2 and are forced out of farming. Rich farmers, by adopting the new technology, may find the value of their marginal value product curve rise to MVP'_B, and their profits would also rise (right panel). Even if the price of the natural resource does not rise to such an extent as to force the small farmers out, their surplus will be reduced by a rise in the price of the natural resource if they are unable to adopt the new technology.

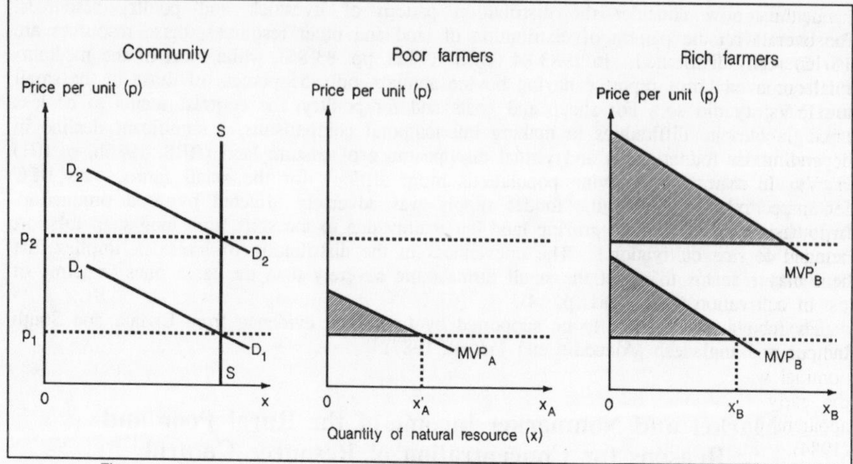

Figure 1—Case in which Technological Progress Increases the Price of a Natural Resource and Leads to Exit of a Small Farmer

One could consider the impact of technological change on common or easy access resources. With technical progress, private property rights would tend to be enforced because the value of doing so is higher (Cornes, Mason, and Sandler, 1986; and Demsetz, 1967). Property that was once common may be enclosed. Or, due to transaction costs, access to property or resources may be denied (Posner, 1980).

Due to technical progress, farmers may increase their profits by clearing land, increasing its drainage, not leaving it fallow for long, and cultivating it more intensively. This may mean the loss of wildlife and wild fruits as food for the poor. Also, adverse spillovers on the fish population, etc., may occur from greater use of pesticides and chemical fertilizers. This may have its greatest impact on the poor, who tend to be gatherers rather than farmers. Also, the poor may lose access to fuel (firewood) and thatching and other housing materials.

Although this may not strictly apply to large parts of Bangladesh, natural environments provide resources to draw on in bad times. They are like a security blanket. Lipton (1985) discusses these issues. Clarke (1971) specifically observes this in relation to New Guinea. In the absence of these cushions, the poor are likely to suffer greatly during times of economic stress.

Income Variation and Real Wages of the Rural Poor

An increase in the number of landless and near landless and the gradual loss of their access to natural resources makes their economic position more dependent on the demand for their labour. However, one needs to ask whether the increased opportunities in the labour market have been able to compensate those who have lost easy access to the natural resources that provide them with supplementary income. To what extent has demand for labour increased following the introduction of new technology? What impact has it had on the functional (family labour and hired labour) and seasonal (*rabi* season and *kharif* season) demand for labour? Does a transition from traditional to modern varieties necessarily imply an increase in the relative share of labour in total output? To what extent have real wages for agricultural labour increased in recent years?

Alauddin and Mujeri (1985), using district-level data, report that significant increases in the demand for labour per cropped hectare occurred during the *rabi* season. On the other hand, the replacement of traditional rice varieties by rain-fed HYVs has had little impact on the overall demand for labour during the *kharif* season. Alauddin and Tisdell (1986, pp. 13-15) reported that: the relative share of labour (as opposed to absolute income) in the total output per hectare seems to be much higher from traditional varieties of rice compared to HYVs; the relative share of family labour in total output is much higher than that of hired labour; and striking differences in the returns to family labour seem to exist, depending on the mode of operation (owner or sharecropper) and technology (local or HYV). In either case, returns to family labour for owners seem to be far in excess of those for sharecroppers. As for the functional demand for labour, evidence seems to support the hypothesis that the new technology has significantly increased employment in terms of demand for family labour and to a lesser extent in terms of hired labour (Ahmed, 1981). This may reduce underemployment rather than unemployment *per se*.

In a recent study, Alauddin and Tisdell (1987) considered trends in daily agricultural wages for the 1969/70–1985/86 period using various price deflators such as cost-of-living indices for industrial workers and rice and food prices. Despite a tenfold increase in nominal wages, little trend in real wages was apparent. Real wages dropped sharply during the early 1970s and remained depressed until the early 1980s. An increasing trend is apparent in the last 2-3 years. These findings seem to be consistent with those of Khan (1984). Furthermore, sudden drops in real wages to drastically low levels occurred in adverse natural and weather conditions (e.g., the flood of 1974 and the drought of 1979).

The landless and small farmers faced problems because of resource depletion and alternative land use due to increased population pressure and following technological change. The households dependent on on-farm employment reported serious economic problems. In abnormal years, when a serious drought or flood occurs, not only do real wages fall drastically but employment becomes more limited. Opportunities for supplementary income through rearing cattle and other animals and poultry become increasingly limited. Furthermore, opportunities for growing vegetables for domestic consumption or for sale at critical times become more limited because of scarcity of water. Landless labourers and small-farm households in the Ekdala area reported having difficulties in getting water from privately owned tanks or ponds for watering vegetables and seasonal fruit plants. This was not because they were charged for it but because its use was restricted, for two reasons: water as a resource is valued more highly by the owners and transaction costs would be incurred in monitoring its sale if it were sold. Bardhan (1984, p. 189), citing Indian experience, points out another mechanism through which the rural poor might have been at a disadvantage. "Some small farmers were being driven out of cultivation as pumpsets enabled rich farmers to appropriate communal ground water, resulting in a possible drop in water tables and making the traditional lift irrigation technology even less effective than before for the poor farmers without pumpsets, hurting the poor farmers who depend on them."

Because of gradual destruction of permanent fruit trees to clear land for food production, fruit gathering in hard times is even more difficult. Also, loss of shrubs and trees results in loss of leaves used as cooking fuel as well as firewood. Thus, opportunities to draw on the reserves of natural resources, especially during difficult times, seem to be disappearing with increased population and greater penetration of market forces following the adoption of new technology. Access to grazing opportunities for livestock was also reported to be dwindling (Alauddin and Tisdell, 1987).

Most farmers surveyed in Ekdala and South Rampur believe that their economic situation is more risky or uncertain compared to the past. For Rampur, most farmers thought that this was so. A χ^2 test indicated that the null hypothesis of independence across farm size could be accepted with a high degree of confidence (χ^2 value significant at a probability level of 0.2670) against an alternative of variation of poverty risk across farms. For Ekdala, however, the alternative hypothesis could not be accepted so confidently (χ^2 value significant at a probability level of 0.0593). This suggests that small-farm households in particular feel they are at greater risk than before. The intervillage difference may be due to differences in density of population, variations in size of small and large farms, and perhaps diversity of cropping patterns. However, farmers in both villages feel that they are at greater economic risk than ever before.

Conclusion

Recent studies have examined the relationship between agricultural innovations and rural poverty in LDCs, concentrating on either exchange or nonexchange income. However, neither approach is adequate if employed independently. Growing concentration of control of land and the effects of components of new agricultural technology on ancillary resources have gradually decreased the access of the rural poor to land and other natural resources. Increasing landlessness and near landlessness have resulted in greater dependence on wage employment for subsistence. However, agricultural wages, being close to the subsistence level, provide little scope for carry-over into periods of slack agricultural activity (Clay, 1981; and Khan, 1984). Even though real wages may show a slight upward trend, much of their effect on rural poverty is neutralized because of seasonality in employment and real wages. The nonexchange component of income is important in slack periods and may become critical in abnormal years when both real wage and employment fall sharply. With rapid population growth and resource depletion and greater penetration of technological and market forces, access to natural resources with a cushioning effect on the rural poor in adverse conditions has become more limited and income security has been undermined.

Notes

[1]Department of Economics, University of Melbourne; and University of Newcastle; respectively.

[2]The traditional sharecroppers (small farmers) who depend on irrigation supplies from large farmers may sometimes be forced to rent out land to large farmers who, with relatively easier access to irrigation water and other complementary inputs, are able to appropriate greater relative gains than the traditional sharecroppers.

[3]Their survey of individual farmers and the landless in these villages was conducted in 1986.

References

Abdullah, A.A., Hossain, M., and Nations, R. (1976) "Agrarian Structure and IRDP: Preliminary Considerations," *Bangladesh Development Studies*, Vol. 4, No. 2, pp. 209-266.

ACO (Agricultural Census Organization) (1962) *Pakistan Census of Agriculture 1960: Final Report—East Pakistan*, Vol. 1, Part 1, Ministry of Food and Agriculture, Government of Pakistan, Karachi, Pakistan.

Ahluwalia, M.S. (1985) "Rural Poverty, Agricultural Production and Prices: Reexamination," in Mellor, J.W., and Desai, G.M. (Eds.) *Agricultural Change and Rural Poverty: Variations on a Theme by Dharm Narain*, Johns Hopkins University Press, Baltimore, Md., USA, pp. 59-75.

Ahmed, I. (1981) *Technological Change and Agrarian Structure: Study of Bangladesh*, International Labour Office, Geneva, Switzerland.

Ahmed, R. (1985) "Growth and Equity in Indian Agriculture and a Few Paradigms from Bangladesh," in Mellor, J.W., and Desai, G.M. (Eds.) *Agricultural Change and Rural Poverty: Variations on a Theme by Dharm Narain*, Johns Hopkins University Press, Baltimore, Md., USA, pp. 124-127.

Alauddin, M., and Mujeri, M.K. (1985) "Employment and Productivity Growth in Bangladesh Agriculture: Inter-District Analysis," *Marga*, Vol. 8, No. 1, pp. 50-72.

Alauddin, M., and Tisdell, C. (1986) "Market Analysis, Technical Change and Income Distribution in Semi-Subsistence Agriculture: Case of Bangladesh," *Agricultural Economics*, Vol. 1, No. 1, pp. 1-18.

Alauddin, M., and Tisdell, C. (1987) "Poverty, Resource Distribution and Security: Impact of New Agricultural Technology in Rural Bangladesh," Department of Economics, University of Newcastle, Newcastle, New South Wales, Australia.

Bardhan, P.K. (1984) *Land, Labor and Rural Poverty: Essays in Development Economics*, Oxford University Press, New Delhi, India.

BBS (Bangladesh Bureau of Statistics) (1981) *Report on the Agricultural Census of Bangladesh 1977*, National Volume, Dacca, Bangladesh.

BBS (Bangladesh Bureau of Statistics) (1986a) *Bangladesh Census of Agriculture and Livestock: 1983-84, Vol. 1—Structure of Agricultural Holdings and Livestock Population*, Dacca, Bangladesh.

BBS (Bangladesh Bureau of Statistics) (1986b) *Bangladesh Census of Agriculture and Livestock: 1983-84, Vol 2, Cropping Patterns*, Dacca, Bangladesh.

BPC (Bangladesh Planning Commission) (1985) *Third Five Year Plan 1985-90*, Dacca, Bangladesh.

Cain, M. (1983) "Landlessness in India and Bangladesh: Critical Review of National Data Sources," *Economic Development and Cultural Change*, Vol. 32, No. 1, pp. 149-168.

Clarke, W.C. (1971) *Place and People: Ecology of a New Guinean Community*, Australian National University Press, Canberra, Australia.

Clay, E.J. (1981) "Seasonal Patterns of Agricultural Employment in Bangladesh," in Chambers, R., Longhurst, R., and Pacey, A. (Eds.) *Seasonal Dimensions of Rural Poverty*, Frances Pinter Publishers, London, UK, pp. 92-101.

Conway, G.R. (1985) "Agricultural Ecology and Farming Systems Research," in Remenyi, J.V. (Ed.) *Agricultural Systems Research for Developing Countries*, ACIAR Proceedings No. 11, Australian Centre for International Agricultural Research, Canberra, Australia.

Cornes, R., Mason, C.F., and Sandler, T. (1986) "Commons and the Optimal Number of Firms," *Quarterly Journal of Economics*, Vol. 101, No. 3, pp. 641-647.

Demsetz, H. (1967) "Toward a Theory of Property Rights," *American Economic Review*, Vol. 57, No. 2, pp. 347-359.

Gill, G.J. (1981) "Is There a 'Draught Power Constraint' on Bangladesh Agriculture," *Bangladesh Development Studies*, Vol. 9, No. 3, pp. 1-20.

Jodha, N.S. (1986) "Common Property Resources and Rural Poor in Dry Regions of India," *Economic and Political Weekly*, Vol. 21, No. 27, pp. 1169-1181.

Khan, A.R. (1984) "Real Wages of Agricultural Workers in Bangladesh," in Khan, A.R., and Lee, E. (Eds.) *Poverty in Rural Asia*, Asian Employment Programme (ARTEP), International Labour Office, Bangkok, Thailand, pp. 185-203.

Lipton, M. (1985) *Land Assets and Rural Poverty*, Staff Working Paper No. 744, World Bank, Washington, D.C., USA.

Mellor, J.W. (1985) "Determinants of Rural Poverty: Dynamics of Production and Prices," in Mellor, J.W., and Desai, G.M. (Eds.) *Agricultural Change and Rural Poverty: Variations on a Theme by Dharm Narain*, Johns Hopkins University Press, Baltimore, Md., USA, pp. 21-40.

Posner, R. (1980) "Theory of Primitive Society with Special Reference to Primitive Law," *Journal of Law and Economics*, Vol. 23, No. 1, pp. 1-55.

Repetto, R., and Holmes, T. (1983) "Role of Population in Resource Depletion in Developing Countries," *Population and Development Review*, Vol. 9, No. 4, pp. 609-632.

DISCUSSION OPENING—*Ibrahim Soliman* (Department of Agricultural Economics, Zagazig University)

The paper presented by Alauddin and Tisdell raises some important development issues. It is a good diagnostic study that identifies, in a descriptive way, the factors that may negatively affect the standards of living of the poor agricultural population in Bangladesh. The authors concluded that among these factors is the technological component, which will not only be effective but will also accelerate these negative impacts. Accordingly, two questions can be raised: Is it a view through a glass, darkly, and, if so, what ought to be done?; *or* is it a signal to choose the proper technology that fits each LDC's rural community? and, if so, what type of technology may fit such conditions? The study did not show explicitly the features of the traditional versus the proposed or existing package of modern technology.

In this context, Japan, for example, started agricultural development under conditions of high population density and small farm size. The Japanese used economic incentives to motivate biological technology. When Japan reached a given plateau, it moved to physical technology. Even though the present paper concluded that technical progress would diminish the demand for human labour, it did not provide any empirical evidence about such substitution elasticity of mechanization vs. human and/or animal labour in Bangladesh. On the other hand, the paper gives the impression that production under risk or uncertainty is the common performance of Bangladeshi agriculture, due to floods, fluctuations in rainfall, etc. However, the study did not consider the limitations imposed by this performance on input intensification and technological progress, which may surpass the limitations imposed by farm size and capital scarcity. Therefore, some further investigations are needed on a zonal base.

I cannot tell from the paper whether land fragmentation is a constraint or not with respect to technology expansion. Whereas the authors showed early in the paper that the intensities of irrigation and HYVs seem to decline with increases in farm size, they showed later in the paper that higher percentages of larger and medium farmers have access to irrigation than the smaller ones. Therefore, they expect that the small farmers will face difficulties in obtaining their water requirements because the water resource is going to be valued more highly by the rich (large) farmers, in addition to the transaction costs. Even if that is right, the problem is probably one of how to find an efficient cooperative system for water management.

Finally, although the paper criticized previous studies that identified rural poverty by farm size only, it did not offer an apparent alternative, except to use the terms "richer farmer" and "larger farmer."

GENERAL DISCUSSION—*Jerome C. Wells, Rapporteur* (University of Pittsburgh)

The general discussion of this paper included comparisons of contemporary technical change and worker displacement with the situations in the UK and Japan in the 18th and 19th centuries as well as consideration of the (graphical) measurement of the gains from improved technologies in the Bangladeshi case. Given the frequency of worker displacement associated with technological improvement, the need for policies to aid displaced workers was also stressed.

Participants in the discussion included E. Asante, S. Ehui, T.E. Gina, R. Herrmann, T.N. Jenkins, D. Kirschke, H. Lee, W. Mukhebi, W. Oluoch-Kosura, and N. Traoré.

Sources of Producer Income Instability in Kenya

James R. Russell, Isaac K. Arap Rop and David M. Henneberry[1]

Abstract: The objective of this paper is to examine the sources of producer income instability for marketed commodities in Kenya. Producer income instability can increase foreign exchange administrative costs, create domestic budgetary problems, lead to inefficiencies in resource use, and even to political upheavals. Using a variance decomposition methodology, demand was identified as the major contributor to export earnings instability for coffee, hides and skins, beans and peas, and canned pineapples. Supply was the major contributor of export earnings instability for tea and pyrethrum extract. With respect to domestic producer income instability, supply was the major culprit for most commodities. Supply was the major source of instability for tea, maize, wheat, and fluid milk, while demand was the major source of instability for coffee. Producer income instability of export crops was relatively constant over the study period (1964-83), whereas income instability of domestic crops, and, hence, the instability-minimizing share of exports, rose over the same period. Limitations of the study include the use of aggregate data, selection of methodologies that ignore structure, and using only marketed commodities for analysis.

Introduction

Agriculture is important to Kenya. It is a major source of employment and foreign exchange earnings. Kenyan agriculture can be divided into two components: those products consumed directly by producers and those marketed in either the domestic or foreign markets. This study concentrates on the marketed products. Major export commodities include coffee, tea, and sisal. Major commodities that enter the domestic marketing system are maize, wheat, and fluid milk.

Most current policies associated with food production in Kenya are embedded within the goals of Kenya's national food policy. Broadly, the major policy goals include: (1) self-sufficiency in the basic foodstuffs, with the surplus being exported profitably; (2) a reasonable degree of food security; and (3) increased availability of nutritionally balanced diets for all citizens. Inherent in these goals is the stabilization of domestic food prices. In attempting to achieve these goals, all major farm commodities are marketed through government controlled agencies. A better understanding of the sources of instability will be beneficial to policy makers. The objective of this paper is to examine the sources of producer income instability for marketed commodities in Kenya.

Instability has been defined as a temporary deviation from some underlying trend (Gelb, 1979). Its effects, in a risky, adverse economic environment, cannot be overemphasized. A number of *a priori* propositions regarding its effects have dominated trade and economic development literature for several years (Knudsen and Parnes, 1975). At the national level, unstable government revenues create budgetary problems. Fluctuating foreign exchange earnings increase foreign exchange administrative costs. Budgetary problems may jeopardize domestic economic planning in developing countries. These problems may culminate in political upheavals. At the farm level, unexpected income shortfalls or surpluses induce inefficiencies in resource use. Income instability then represents a cost to an individual producer as well as society at large.

Export Earnings Instability

Producer earnings are a product of price and quantity. Using variance of earnings as a measure of instability, its decomposition can provide useful information. It has been used in a number of studies (Burt and Finley, 1968; Hazell, 1982 and 1984; Murray, 1978; Offutt and Blandford, 1983; and Piggott, 1978). Using a procedure similar to Murray's, which assumes the variables are log-normally distributed, the proportional contribution of each component to the total variability of Kenya's commodity export earnings are presented in Table 1. The table indicates that, for coffee, tea, and hides and skins, price played a dominant role. The variability of quantity dominates in the case of canned pineapples and

Table 1—Components of Export Earnings Instability in Terms of Kenya Shillings, 1964-83

Commodity	Total Var(ln PQ)	Price Var(lnP)	Quantity Var(lnQ)	Covariance 2Cov(lnP, lnQ)
	Variation			
	Percent*			
Coffee	0.1371	76.59	10.58	12.84
Tea	0.0527	105.69	47.82	-53.51
Hides and skins	0.1124	52.22	31.23	16.55
Pyrethrum extract	0.0454	241.85	197.36	-339.21
Beans and peas	0.4105	8.21	84.24	7.55
Canned pineapples	0.2396	14.27	56.59	29.13

*Percentages indicate the proportional contribution of each component to total variability.
Source: Arap Rop (1986).

of beans and peas. For pyrethrum extract, the covariance term between price and quantity dominates.

The sign of the covariance term is often used as an indicator of the source of instability (Murray, 1978). If supply remains unchanged, movements in demand lead to quantity and price variations in the same direction. Price and quantity vary in opposite directions if demand does not change when shifts in supply occur. For a small, open economy facing no international trade barriers, demand for its exports is perfectly elastic. Similarly, producers who market exportables through the marketing board, which then takes responsibility for marketing abroad, face an infinitely elastic demand at the board's prices. Consequently, price and quantity vary in the same direction whenever shifts in the demand schedule occur. But, any shift in supply results in changes in the quantity exported only. If supply is perfectly inelastic and demand is relatively inelastic, then quantity and price vary in opposite directions for any shifts in supply. In this case, shifts in demand results in price changes only.

A negative covariance term implies that demand changes have been relatively stable while changes have been unstable. In any particular year, if the value of prices and quantities are below or above the trend line, then a positive covariance term is expected. This would occur if supply were to fluctuate in a steady manner while demand changes were relatively erratic.

From Table 1, tea and pyrethrum extract have negative covariance terms, suggesting that the source of instability has been supply. For the rest of the export commodities, the signs of the covariance terms are positive, indicating that, in general, demand fluctuations have been the main source of instability.

The above analysis has centred on Kenya's exports. Except for beans and peas, all the commodities are storable after some processing. In the absence of suitable storage facilities at the farm level, the commodities are generally perishable, so that producers have to sell to marketing agencies immediately after harvesting. The sources of producer income instability can thus be identified by considering the quantity delivered to the marketing boards and the average price to the producer. The sources of instability of the domestically marketed commodities can then be evaluated and compared with export-oriented commodities.

Producer Income Instability

Policy changes on commodity prices occurred in 1975 to reflect the surge of inflation that started after 1972. To obtain more insight into producer income instability, the data are divided into two sets. The first set covers 1964-73, while the second set covers 1974-83. In both cases, instability of the five major market-oriented commodities is considered.

With respect to coffee and tea, the sources of export earnings instability are presented in Table 2. During the 1964-73 period, the variability of quantity exported was dominant. Quantity exported had a low positive correlation with the f.o.b. prices earned. Since the covariance terms are positive, one could conclude that volatility on the demand side was the main source of earnings variability. The importance of price variability as a source of

Table 2—Components of Export Earnings Instability from Coffee and Tea for Selected Periods

Commodity and time period	Total Var(ln PQ)	Price Var(lnP)	Quantity Var(lnQ)	Covariance 2Cov(lnP, lnQ)
		Variation		
		Percent*		
Coffee:				
1964-83	0.1371	76.59	10.58	12.84
1964-73	0.0400	30.50	50.00	19.50
1974-83	0.1940	72.47	4.38	23.19
Tea:				
1964-83	0.0527	105.69	47.82	-53.51
1964-73	0.0199	29.65	69.35	1.01
1974-83	0.0834	52.64	21.94	25.54

*Percentages indicate the proportional contribution of each component to total variability.
Source: Arap Rop (1986).

earnings instability rose significantly in the later period for both commodities. In both cases, the covariance terms contributed more to total fluctuations than quantity terms. Correlation coefficients between the quantities exported and f.o.b. prices improved. Unlike the situation in the former period, earnings and quantities were more highly correlated than earnings and prices.

Of interest to producers is the income instability for the commodities they sell to the marketing agencies. In most cases, quantities exported do not fully reflect quantities sold by farmers to the marketing agencies during the year because of storage by the marketing agencies. Also, commodity taxation by the government and marketing costs, both at the producer and the agency levels, reduce the price paid to producers. Using average producer prices and gross marketed production during the two periods, the decomposition process yields the results presented in Table 3. The striking feature for the export crops is that the stability of f.o.b. prices does not necessarily mean that average producer prices are stable. Considering the 1964-83 period, volatility in price was a major source of income fluctuations in coffee, tea, and wheat, while variability in quantity contributed to most of the instability in income from maize and milk. The covariance terms indicate that, except for coffee, supply fluctuations were the major sources of income instability. The negative correlation coefficients between the prices and quantities of tea, maize, wheat, and milk imply that one of the variables was declining while the other was increasing. The original data indicated that, in the 1960s, prices paid to farmers exhibited a slightly downward trend.

Table 3—Components of Income Instability from Selected Marketed Production

Commodity and time period	Total Var(ln PQ)	Price Var(lnP)	Quantity Var(lnQ)	Covariance 2Cov(lnP, lnQ)
		Variation		
		Percent*		
Coffee:				
1964-83	0.1347	77.13	9.43	13.44
1964-73	0.0286	52.80	54.90	-7.69
1974-83	0.2015	69.03	4.76	26.20
Tea:				
1964-83	0.0754	105.30	23.74	-29.05
1964-73	0.0086	76.74	132.56	-109.30
1974-83	0.1095	51.69	14.06	34.34
Maize:				
1964-83	0.1501	36.24	96.47	-32.71
1964-73	0.0934	22.27	86.51	-8.78
1974-83	0.2324	7.79	73.54	18.67
Wheat:				
1964-83	0.0736	61.68	46.06	-7.74
1964-73	0.0485	11.55	111.08	-27.63
1974-83	0.0087	59.77	55.17	-16.09
Fluid Milk:				
1964-83	0.0603	34.16	151.41	-85.57
1964-73	0.0531	22.60	74.39	3.01
1974-83	0.0309	21.68	53.40	25.24

*Percentages indicate the proportional contribution of each component to total variability.
Source: Arap Rop (1986).

During the 1964-73 period, variability in quantity was dominant (Table 3). The figures for the 1974-83 period suggest that price volatility was important for all commodities except for maize and milk, which had quantity as the major source of variability. The 1964-73 period had variability in supply as an important instrument in total commodity income instability. Except for wheat, the covariance terms suggest that fluctuations in the demand for commodities were sources of income instability during the 1974-83 period. Unlike the former period, the correlation between prices and quantities was positive except in the case of wheat. The correlation between milk prices and quantities marketed remained positive in both sets of data.

Several factors contribute to the negative correlation between prices and quantities during the 1964-73 period. Generally, price trends were declining while production was expanding. Expansion in production was attributed to increased yield per unit area, especially for maize, due to the rapid adoption of the hybrid seed technology. The introduction and subsequent rapid adoption of the new maize variety in the 1960s opened up an alternative price policy that producer prices would be reduced progressively as returns per unit area increased due to yield increases. This policy was implemented in 1966 to obviate unnecessarily large surpluses that could be exported at a loss. The ultimate producer price would be that at which surpluses could be exported profitably and at the same time production be encouraged to match with the domestic market needs. Lobbying by producers, coupled with several periodic droughts, led to a reassessment of the policy that resulted in maize price increases in 1971.

The area under the traditional plantation crops, coffee and tea, expanded as a result of postindependence government policy that encouraged smallholder participation. The subdivision of large-scale farms and absence of appropriate technology for small-scale production led to a decline in the production of wheat. In some cases, limited production activities hampered the diversion of resources away from those commodities whose relative prices were declining. Kenyan producers often exhibit this less "rational" behaviour.

Notwithstanding the perception of some underdevelopment theorists, agricultural production for export and domestic markets in Kenya is interdependent. Domestic exports are vulnerable to international market fluctuations, while production directed to the domestic market is subject to government control. The linkages between these categories, in addition to government attempts to insulate domestic production from the vagaries of world prices, reinforce the need to stabilize total income through balanced production.

Given that the government's primary goal is to secure domestic food supply, the share of export-oriented production that minimizes total income instability is meaningless. The variability in combined income from coffee and tea, the main exports of Kenya, has been relatively constant over the study period (Table 4). As compared with the combined income variability from maize, wheat, and milk, income instability from exports has been higher than from domestic sales. Assuming no correlation between income from exports and domestic sales, then the instability-minimizing percentage of export value has risen from 12.00 in 1964-73 to 25.00 in the period 1974-83. These results imply that the share of exports that leads to minimum income instability is relatively small.

Table 4—Producer Income Instability from Agricultural Sales for Selected Periods

Source	1964-83	1964-73	1974-83
		Percent	
Variability of income index from domestic sales*	20.56	11.22	17.89
Variability of income index from export sales*	29.71	30.88	30.60
Instability-minimizing share of exports	32.00	12.00	25.00

*The index is a corrected coefficient of variation derived from log-linearly detrended data (Cuddy and della Valle, 1978).

Sources: Bautista (undated) and Arap Rop (1986).

Summary and Conclusions

Considering coffee and tea, the two most important export crops, fluctuations in price contributed most to their export earnings instability over the entire study period. However, during the first 10 years, the contribution of quantity to total variability was dominant. The dominance of price variability prevailed during the later decade, so that not only has variability of earnings increased over the 20-year period, but also the source has changed. In consequence, using this criterion, policy makers facing such situations should be more concerned with external demand than domestic production. This requires stronger multilateral cooperation between producers and consumers, as in the case of coffee, or some other cohesive international commodity cartel.

Comparing producer income instability for 1964-73 and 1974-83, the variability in the income from coffee, tea, and maize has increased; that for wheat and milk has declined. In all cases, the proportional contribution of quantity to total variability has decreased. The sources of instability, as indicated by the signs of the covariance terms, have shifted from supply-dominated to demand-dominated fluctuations in the case of coffee, tea, and maize. Wheat and milk face supply- and demand-dominated fluctuations, respectively. In the case of coffee and tea, income instability measures support the findings obtained in terms of export earnings instability. Maize, the staple food crop in Kenya, followed the pattern of those crops produced mainly for export. For wheat, policy should concentrate on domestic production.

Except in the case of wheat, changes in both export and domestic demand are becoming the major source of income variability for the market-oriented commodities. This suggests that a restructuring of the market is essential for increased income stability, irrespective of destination. Furthermore, the increased price-quantity correlations exhibited by most of the commodities studied would suggest that potential gains in terms of increased stability might be obtained through price manipulation by the Kenyan government. On total income instability, the results indicate that the high level of variability in export earnings was accompanied by an increase in the proportion of exports in total income during 1974-83. Income stabilization measures appeared to favour only domestically marketed commodities.

This study is based on time series data for the 1964-83 period. The results are, therefore, period specific and may not be appropriate for other periods. However, the validity of the results within the time span is not expected to change drastically. The analytical procedure is limited by the fact that the underlying production complexities are excluded. A detailed study is required to isolate the causes of production instabilities. Variation in output may be due to changes in yield per unit of area or to changes in area under cultivation. Also, changes in export earnings may be attributable to fluctuations in the effective exchange rate rather than the volatility in the quantities exported.

Limitations and Scope for Further Research

This study suffers from a number of drawbacks. First, decomposition of statistical identities precludes any direct reference to underlying structural relationships. Second, due to data constraints, aggregate data were used. The results may not necessarily extend to the micro level. Kenya produces a wide variety of agricultural commodities, but only the five most important commodities were studied in detail. The selection criterion was the degree to which they influence Kenya's commercial agriculture.

A wide range of problem areas exist for further research. First, the structural relationship between export commodities and those marketed locally deserves further study. Research that considers not only marketed production but total production would provide much needed information for better decisions. Such a study could include changes in the monetary sector and their impact on income variability. The effects of risky production and product market environments on the overall welfare of producers and consumers should be rigorously investigated. Finally, and perhaps of more immediate importance, is the need to analyze the long-run implications of price rigidities for quantities produced and supplied to markets.

Note

[1]Department of Agricultural and Resource Economics, University of Maryland; Department of Agricultural Economics, Oklahoma State University; and Department of Agricultural Economics, Oklahoma State University; respectively. The work was completed while all three authors were at Oklahoma State University.

References

Arap Rop, I.K. (1986) "Economic Analysis of Producers Income Instability in Kenya's Agricultural Sector: Case of Selected Market Commodities." PhD thesis, Oklahoma State University, Stillwater, Okla., USA.

Bautista, R.M. (undated) "Does Increasing Agricultural Exports Raise Income Instability: Empirical Note," International Food Policy Research Institute, Washington, D.C., USA.

Burt, D.M., and Finley, R.M. (1968) "Statistical Analysis of Identities in Random Variables," *American Journal of Agricultural Economics*, Vol. 50, pp. 734-744.

Cuddy, J.D.A., and della Valle, P.A. (1978) "Measuring the Instability of Time Series Data," *Oxford Bulletin of Economics and Statistics*, Vol. 40, pp. 79-85.

Gelb, A.H. (1979) "On the Definition and Measurement of Instability and Costs of Buffering Export Fluctuations," *Review of Economic Studies*, Vol. 46, pp. 149-162.

Hazell, P.B.R. (1982) *Instability in Indian Foodgrain Production*, Research Report No. 30, International Food Policy Research Institute, Washington, D.C., USA.

Hazell, P.B.R. (1984) "Sources of Increased Variability in World Cereal Production Since the 1960's," *Journal of Agricultural Economics*, Vol. 36, pp. 145-159.

Knudsen, O., and Parnes, A. (1975) *Trade Instability and Economic Development*, D.C. Heath and Co., Lexington, Mass., USA.

Murray, D. (1978) "Export Earnings Instability: Price, Quantity, Supply, Demand?" *Economic Development and Cultural Change*, Vol. 27, pp. 61-72.

Offutt, S.E., and Blandford, D. (1983) *Review of Empirical Techniques for the Analysis of Commodity Instability*, Agricultural Experiment Station, Cornell University, Ithaca, N.Y., USA.

Piggott, R.R. (1978) "Decomposing the Variance of Gross Revenue into Demand and Supply Components," *American Journal of Agricultural Economics*, Vol. 60, pp. 145-157.

DISCUSSION OPENING—*Carlos E. Cuevas* (Ohio State University)

The paper discusses an important concern of policy makers in developing countries. As the authors correctly point out, producer income instability may create (or be associated with) inefficiencies and adjustment problems at different levels in the economy.

The approach adopted in the paper is to examine the sources of (gross) income instability for selected marketed commodities in Kenya. Using a variance decomposition method, the authors infer the causes of producer income instability by looking at the sign of the covariance term. They are thus able to determine whether the observed variation in the value of total sales is due to demand fluctuations or can be attributed to supply instability.

The authors acknowledge several drawbacks of the study due primarily to the use of a nonanalytical method and of aggregate data. Hence, this comment will focus on some of these limitations and will suggest possible improvements in the presentation of the paper.

Among the limitations pointed out by the authors, perhaps the most important is the applicability of their results to the micro level. However, this limitation does note arise only from the use of aggregate data; the fluctuation of *gross* revenues from individual commodities may not represent a good proxy for the variations in *net* revenues experienced by Kenyan farmers with some degree of product diversification.

On the one hand, the variance of earnings is only one component of the instability of net surplus at the farm level. Variations on the expenditure side should be taken into account. Furthermore, even though individual producers are not able to affect output prices, they are likely to react to fluctuations in input prices by adjusting the amounts of purchased inputs used in production.

On the other hand, product diversification is one of the most common strategies to reduce production risk at the farm level. Hence, instability of net revenue, at the producer level will certainly be affected by fluctuations in gross revenues from individual commodities, but it is likely to include effects of fluctuations on the expenditure side and the compensating influence of product diversification. In this sense, the paper would benefit from a discussion of the patterns of input use in Kenyan agriculture and a description of the typical output mix of different farm types in Kenya.

Data problems forced the authors to use official prices paid by government-controlled agencies. An implicit, and legitimate, concern in the paper is to what extent fluctuations in these prices are fully transmitted to the farm level. A brief description of the marketing chains associated with the commodities dealt with in the paper would help the reader. Indeed, the observed variability of total sales to marketing agencies might be reflecting, in some cases, the instability of total revenues for market intermediaries, rather than that experienced by the primary producers.

The way in which the results are presented (variance of the logarithm of total sales) prevents one from comparing variability across commodities. The use of the coefficient of variation or other standardized indicator would allow comparisons of the relative instability of revenues among different production activities.

Finally, would "price manipulation by the Kenya government" really be income-stabilizing for Kenyan producers as the authors conclude? In fact, the reported increase in instability for several commodities occurred under sustained government intervention in agricultural marketing.

GENERAL DISCUSSION—*Jerome C. Wells, Rapporteur* (University of Pittsburgh)

In the general discussion of this paper, the problem of relating measures of instability in receipts for crops with instability of farmer income was raised, as was the issue of the conditions under which the covariance of price and quantity fluctuations could appropriately be used to assess whether fluctuations were demand or supply determined. The prospects for government (or international) schemes to stabilize producer income were discussed, as was the appropriateness of measures of instability around a trend line.

Participants in the discussion included E. Asante, S. Ehui, T.E. Gina, R. Herrmann, T.N. Jenkins, D. Kirschke, H. Lee, W. Mukhebi, W. Oluoch-Kosura, and N. Traoré.

Formulating Rural Development Programmes to Aid Low-Income Farm Families

Jill L. Findeis and Venkateshwar K. Reddy[1]

Abstract: Rural development programmes may facilitate the off-farm employment of low-income farm families and provide additional public support beyond traditional US farm income and price support programmes. To examine the implications of alternative rural development strategies for low-income farmers, joint off-farm labour participation models are developed for farm operators and spouses. Univariate and bivariate probit models are estimated, based on 1985 Current Population Survey farm household data. The bivariate model is applied to data on 240 farm families that qualify as low-income families. Study results indicate that age, education, number of young children, and location represent constraints to participation among differentiable segments of the low-income farm population. The implications of these results for the formulation of rural development programmes to aid farm families are examined.

Introduction

Since 1980, US farm families on average have earned over 50 percent of total farm income from off-farm sources. Income from off-farm employment of farm family members represents the principal source of off-farm income, particularly for small- and medium-sized farms. In the USA, as well as in many developed countries, the majority of farm families depend on off-farm employment of family members to provide a significant income supplement (Kada, 1980; OECD, 1977; Ahearn, 1986; Ahearn and Lee, 1988; and Fuller 1988).

Despite the trend towards greater reliance on off-farm income, a significant number of farm families continue to earn low total incomes. These families earn low net farm incomes and are either unable or unwilling to supplement their farm incomes significantly with income from off-farm work. In some cases, family members are unable or unwilling to participate in the off-farm labour market. The option of working off the farm may not be available due to lack of off-farm job opportunities or lack of human capital demand from employers recruiting for jobs geographically accessible to farm families. The time requirements of farming, household work, and child care may also constrain participation. Alternatively, farm family labour resources employed off the farm may be underemployed, due to low hours or low income.[2]

This study examines factors affecting the joint off-farm labour participation decisions of US farm operators and spouses, using 1984 farm household data from the 1985 Current Population Survey (CPS). Univariate and bivariate probit models are developed to assess the influence of selected individual, family, farm, and location characteristics on the probabilities that the farm operator, farm spouse, or both work off the farm. Unlike Reddy and Findeis (1988), the jointness of household decision making is explicitly modelled. Alternative rural development strategies to benefit low-income farm families are assessed on the basis of the study results.

Off-farm Employment Decisions

Farm households are assumed to maximize utility by choosing between purchased goods and leisure, subject to a full-income constraint and constraints imposed by farm production and time.[3] The probability that the individual works off the farm depends on the individual's reservation wage (w_i^*) relative to the market wage rate net of commuting costs (w_i^m). Participation decisions by the farm operator and farm spouse (i.e., D_o and D_s) can be expressed as follows, where jointness between decision rules *(1)* and *(2)* is assumed:

(1) $D_o = 1$ if $w_o^* < w_o^m$ and 0 if $w_o^* \geq w_o^m$; and

(2) $D_s = 1$ if $w_s^* < w_s^r$ and 0 if $w_s^* \geq w_s^r$.

Whether the farm operator, farm spouse, or both participate in off-farm work is assumed to depend on the characteristics of the individual, the farm family, the farm, and the location of the farm relative to off-farm employment opportunities. To measure the influence of these factors on the likelihood of off-farm work, the following models were specified:

(3) participation function of the farm operator—

$$P(D_o=1) = \beta_0 + \beta_1 AGE_o + \beta_2 AGESQ_o + \beta_3 NCHS_o + \beta_4 COLGE_o + \beta_5 GTCOL_o + \beta_6 ED_s + \beta_7 CHL5_f + \beta_8 CHL13_f + \beta_9 SMSA_f + \beta_{10} NE_f + \beta_{11} SOUTH_f + \beta_{12} WEST_f + \beta_{13} Y_f + \beta_{14} OT_f + \varepsilon_o; \text{ and}$$

(4) participation function of the farm spouse—

$$P(D_s=1) = \beta_0 + \beta_1 AGE_s + \beta_2 AGESQ_s + \beta_3 NCHS_s + \beta_4 COLGE_s + \beta_5 GTCOL_s + \beta_6 ED_o + \beta_7 CHL5_f + \beta_8 CHL13_f + \beta_9 SMSA_f + \beta_{10} NE_f + \beta_{11} SOUTH_f + \beta_{12} WEST_f + \beta_{13} Y_f + \beta_{14} OT_f + \varepsilon_s;$$

where, for the operator ($i=o$) and spouse ($i=s$):

$P(\bullet)$ = probability of stated outcome;
AGE_i = age of individual;
$AGESQ_i$ = square of age of individual;
$NCHS_i$ = 1 if operator/spouse has not completed high school, 0 otherwise;
$COLGE_i$ = 1 if operator/spouse has one to four years of college-level education, 0 otherwise;
$GTCOL_i$ = 1 if operator/spouse has more than four years of college level education, 0 otherwise;
ED_i = 1 if spouse of the operator has education beyond high school, 0 otherwise;
$CHL5_f$ = number of children 5 years of age or younger in the household;
$CHL13_f$ = number of children 13 years of age or older in the household;
$SMSA_f$ = 1 if farm is located in a Standard Metropolitan Statistical Area (SMSA), 0 otherwise;
NE_f = 1 if farm is located in the Northeast, 0 otherwise;
$SOUTH_f$ = 1 if farm is located in the South, 0 otherwise;
$WEST_f$ = 1 if farm is located in the West, 0 otherwise;
Y_f = net farm income of farm family in thousands of dollars; and
OT_f = other income (i.e., all income received from sources other than from the farm, off-farm wages and salaries, and self-employment income), in thousands of dollars.

Univariate probit models were first estimated for farm operators and spouses separately. A simultaneous equation bivariate probit model was then estimated using the two-stage method for estimating simultaneous binary equations suggested by Maddala (1983).[4]

Factors Affecting Participation in Off-Farm Work

The results of the univariate and bivariate probit models for farm operators and spouses are presented in Tables 1 and 2. Likelihood-ratio tests were significant for the univariate

Table 1–Estimated Coefficients of Off-Farm Labour Participation Models for US Farm Operators, 1984*

Variable	Univariate Estimate	t-statistic	Derivative†	Bivariate Estimate	t-statistic	Derivative†
Intercept	-0.3466	-0.96	--	1.7221	0.76	--
AGE_o	0.0235	1.21	0.0086	0.0362	2.08	0.0141
$AGESQ_o$	-0.0006	-1.17	-0.0002	-0.0005	-0.63	-0.0002
$NCHS_o$	-0.3274	-4.53	-0.1248	-0.2715	-2.61	-0.1039
$COLGE_o$	0.1422	1.83	0.0563	0.1521	2.20	0.0597
$GTCOL_o$	0.5289	3.07	0.2079	0.5128	6.72	0.2009
ED_s	0.3167	2.92	0.1223	0.3339	7.27	0.1296
$CHL5_f$	-0.0421	-0.85	-0.0159	-0.0382	-1.38	-0.0145
$CHL13_f$	0.0113	0.91	0.0044	0.0329	1.84	0.0127
$SMSA_f$	0.2991	2.65	0.1201	0.3670	4.70	0.1509
NE_f	0.3082	1.89	0.1228	0.2983	2.17	0.1187
$SOUTH_f$	0.3710	3.99	0.1494	0.3728	2.48	0.1496
$WEST_f$	0.0721	1.06	0.2093	0.0906	0.80	0.0369
Y_f	-0.0224	-8.22	-0.0099	-0.0275	-12.66	-0.0120
OT_f	-0.0096	-0.63	-0.0037	-0.0183	-0.92	-0.0072

*n = 1,184.

†The partial derivative measures the change in the probability of off-farm labour participation resulting from a per-unit increase in the exogenous variable.

models at the given χ^2 distribution degrees of freedom, but the correlation between the disturbance terms of the univariate operator and spouse models was statistically significant. The hypothesis of nonjointness of participation decisions by farm operators and spouses was thus rejected.[5] The bivariate model in which the jointness of decision making is implicitly considered was therefore accepted as the truer representation of the relationships between the explanatory variables and participation. This result was in contrast to the jointness tests in Hallberg, Lass, and Findeis (1988) based on 1986 Massachusetts farm household data but consistent with CPS-based models estimated by Tokle (1988) in collaboration with Huffman.

Previous studies of off-farm work participation (e.g., Huffman, 1980; Sumner, 1982; Hallberg, Lass, and Findeis, 1988; and Findeis, 1988) have incorporated age and age-squared exogenous variables to capture the hypothesized curvilinear effects of age on participation. Statistically significant relationships are found between participation and the age of the operator and age-squared of the spouse (Tables 1 and 2). However, the signs of the age and age-squared variables are consistently positive and negative, respectively. The consistency of these results with other studies suggests that age has an important (curvilinear) influence on participation in off-farm work.

Education is also important. The models estimated here measure the effects of the individual attaining alternative levels of education (not a high school graduate, one to four years of college-level training, and postgraduate college education) relative to the effect of attaining a high school degree. The education of the individual's spouse also is incorporated into the models with a variable representing the spouse's education beyond high school (ED_i).

In the bivariate model, the education estimates are (in general) statistically significant. Higher levels of education increase the likelihood that the operator will work off the farm, higher levels of education increase the opportunities for higher wage rates (i.e., w_o and w_s), and attainment of certain levels of education (e.g., graduation from high school) may qualify the individual for a greater diversity of jobs. The education level of the farm spouse also positively affects the operator's probability of off-farm employment.

For the farm spouse, education beyond high school positively affects the probability of off-farm work. However, no significant difference exists between not being a high school graduate and earning a high school degree, in terms of the likelihood of working off the farm. Similarly, education of the farm operator beyond high school is shown to have no

Table 2–Estimated Coefficients of Off-Farm Labour Participation Models for US Farm Spouses, 1984*

Variable	Univariate Estimate	*t*-statistic	Derivative†	Bivariate Estimate	*t*-statistic	Derivative†
Intercept	0.2163	0.54	--	0.5217	0.92	--
AGE_s	0.0309	1.65	0.0118	0.0482	1.49	0.0186
$AGESQ_s$	-0.0007	-3.51	-0.0003	-0.0008	-3.48	-0.0003
$NCHS_s$	-0.2089	-1.65	-0.0842	-0.2104	-1.40	-0.0840
$COLGE_s$	0.1588	2.01	0.0632	0.1575	3.82	0.0632
$GTCOL_s$	0.6533	3.67	0.2583	0.6497	6.08	0.2574
ED_o	-0.1256	-0.89	-0.0497	-0.1652	-1.10	-0.0653
$CHL5_f$	-0.4620	-5.61	-0.1781	-0.4738	-7.89	-0.1833
$CHL13_f$	-0.0763	-0.97	-0.0299	-0.0771	-0.74	-0.0301
$SMSA_f$	-0.0625	-0.70	-0.0250	-0.1088	-0.74	-0.0398
NE_f	-0.2153	-1.09	-0.0843	-0.2180	-1.32	-0.0862
$SOUTH_f$	-0.0043	-0.08	-0.0017	-0.0050	-0.21	-0.0020
$WEST_f$	-0.1284	-1.74	-0.0522	-0.1161	-1.36	-0.0473
Y_f	-0.0049	-2.17	-0.0021	-0.0032	-2.88	-0.0014
OT_f	-0.0182	-1.49	-0.0071	-0.0153	-1.33	-0.0061

*n = 1,184.

†The partial derivative measures the change in the probability of off-farm labour participation resulting from a per-unit increase in the exogenous variable.

significant effect on the probability of off-farm employment of the farm spouse. The coefficient of ED_o is in fact negative.

The number of young children in the farm household significantly influences participation by farm spouses; the estimate measuring the influence of the number of preschool children is negative and highly significant, indicating the constraint of young children on nonfarm work among farm spouses. Previous studies of US farm spouses and farm women have found similar results (e.g., Rosenfeld, 1985; and Thompson, 1985). The estimate for the effect of young children on participation among farm operators is also negative but not significant at the 5-percent level.

The effects of older children on participation in off-farm work among farm operators and spouses are not statistically significant at the 5-percent level, although a statistically weaker relationship for farm operators is demonstrated. On farms with older children in the household, the farm operator is more likely to be employed off the farm. Older children can provide labour resources to substitute for farm operator labour. At the same time, farm operators may be "pushed" into the nonfarm labour market to finance college educations (and assets) to benefit older children.

Tables 1 and 2 confirm that the farm's location has an effect on off-farm work decisions among US farm operators.[6] Operators in the Northeast and South are more likely to be employed off the farm than farmers in the North Central region, the region selected for comparison. No statistically significant difference was found for farm operators in the West, relative to the North Central region. However, the farm's location in an SMSA positively affects participation. These results probably reflect the smaller average size of farms in the Northeast and South and near urban centres and may reflect an increased availability and accessibility to nonfarm jobs in these regions. Multiple job-holding among farm operators is more prevalent in these regions, and the proportion of income earned from off-farm sources is higher. In contrast, neither regional location nor location of the farm in an SMSA appears to have an impact on the likelihood of off-farm work among farm spouses. The location estimates for farm spouses are not statistically significant in either the univariate or bivariate probit models.

Finally, net farm income is an important variable for both farm operators and spouses. The lower the net farm income, the greater the probability that farm family members work off the farm. The amount of income earned from other income sources appears to have no significant impact on work/no work decisions with respect to off-farm employment.

Participation among Low-income Farm Families

Of the 1,184 farm families in the 1985 CPS farm (couple) sample, 240 families were classified as having low income. Low-income farm families were defined as families comprised of four or fewer individuals jointly earning less than the 1980 US Census weighted average poverty threshold for four-person families, and families of five or more individuals earning less than the respective poverty thresholds for larger family sizes.

The off-farm participation models in Tables 1 and 2 showed the importance of age, education, family characteristics, location, and net farm income as factors influencing the off-farm work decisions of farm family members. Families least likely to earn income from off-farm employment are older farm couples, farm operators and spouses with less education, families operating farms in the North Central and West regions of the USA, and farms in nonmetropolitan locations. Families with higher net farm incomes are less likely to be multiple job-holding farm families.

Low-income farmers earn low net farm incomes, a factor shown to be associated with higher off-farm participation rates. Yet among the low-income families, 19 percent of the farm operators were employed off the farm compared to 47 percent for all farm operators in the CPS sample. Among low-income spouses, 41 percent had off-farm jobs, compared to 55 percent for the total sample. Clearly, low-income farm family members are less likely to have off-farm jobs providing supplementary income to the farm household.

Constraints to participation among low-income families suggest potential avenues for policy interventions to aid farm families most in need. When the bivariate participation models in Tables 1 and 2 are applied to data for low-income farm family members, several observations can be made. The low-income farm operators not working off the farm generally can be classified into one of two groups: older farm operators who in many cases had not graduated from high school and younger operators with at least a high school education (and in many cases college-level training or even postgraduate work). Among the former group, none of the farm operators was predicted to work off the farm.

Farm spouses could be similarly categorized: younger spouses who had generally graduated from high school and in many cases had acquired some college-level training, and older farm spouses with a spouse that did not work off the farm. The bivariate probability model generally predicted that spouses in the former group would be less likely to work off the farm, principally due to the presence of young children. Few of the older farm spouses were predicted to work off the farm despite the observation that most of these individuals had graduated from high school. Few older farm spouses lacked a high school degree, an unanticipated observation.

The higher proportion of low-income families in the North Central region (58 percent compared to 50 percent for the entire sample) and the observation that 90 percent of the low-income families operated farms in nonmetropolitan areas of the USA further constrain off-farm work among many low-income households. Off-farm jobs are less accessible, and job opportunities are more limited in nonmetropolitan areas, in the North Central states, and in many states in the West.

Implications for Policy

One option for farm families is to use off-farm employment as a strategy to alleviate farm financial stress, either on a permanent basis or as a temporary means of facilitating movement out of (or even into) agriculture. Low-income farm families are less likely to work off the farm, on average. One reason appears to be the higher proportion of older farm operators and spouses. These individuals are either unable or unwilling to adjust labour resources out of agriculture, even partially, into the off-farm labour market.

The lack of formal education and job-specific off-farm work experience may constrain older farm operators from seeking off-farm jobs. Older farm spouses are less likely to be constrained by education but may be negatively affected by lack of (nonhousehold) work experience. These factors put older operators and spouses at a disadvantage in the rural nonfarm labour market and generally mean lower returns to off-farm work.

Human capital policies have been one focus of rural development policy in the USA. Such policies have typically attempted to enhance educational opportunities available to rural residents. Brown *et al.* (1987) emphasize the need for human capital policies to provide educational opportunities for displaced rural workers. Older farm family members are quasi-displaced, not willing to leave agriculture but either unable or unwilling to commit labour resources off the farm. To the extent that farm family members are willing but unable to find off-farm jobs, programmes that focus on retraining serve farm as well as rural nonfarm families. However, older farm families must be willing to take advantage of such opportunities for such programmes to be beneficial.

Younger low-income farm families are, in general, better educated and less in need of human capital development programmes. A high proportion of these farm families operate full-time farms in the North Central region. Many of these families also have children of preschool age. Thus, even though the farm spouse is generally well-educated, the presence of young children in the household may limit the spouse's participation in the off-farm labour market. Such families could benefit from additional child care programmes being established in rural communities. However, in some low-income farm families in the CPS sample, the farm spouse was employed full-time off the farm, but the family continued to be financially stressed. On these farms, the losses from the farm, probably due to high farm-debt loads, were too substantial to be offset by the off-farm income earned by the farm spouse.

Finally, policies to create, retain, and improve rural job opportunities accessible to farm families, particularly families in the North Central region, are appropriate. To the extent that rural economic development of the North Central region is considered an appropriate policy goal, programmes to create new job opportunities and maintain existing opportunities in this region will facilitate the process of adjustment for a high proportion of those farm families most in need of public aid.

Notes

[1]Pennsylvania State University.

[2]Lichter and Costanzo (1986) document higher rates of underemployment in US nonmetropolitan regions compared to urban areas. Lichter and Costanzo used a labour use framework to measure the prevalence of different types of underemployment, including the inability of workers to work as many hours as preferred (low hours) and the prevalence of the working poor (underemployed by reason of low income).

[3]For a thorough discussion of theoretical issues related to agricultural household models, see Huffman (1988). Also see Bollman (1979), Huffman (1980), and Sumner (1982).

[4]This method (also used in Hallberg, Lass, and Findeis, 1988) involves the estimation of a reduced-form probit in the first stage and use of the fitted values from the first stage as exogenous variables in the second stage. The estimates from the second stage are then used as starting values for the final estimation of the bivariate probit model.

[5]An alternative test is to jointly restrict the estimates for the predicted endogenous variables and the correlation between the models to zero and perform a likelihood-ratio test (Hallberg, Lass, and Findeis, 1988).

[6]See Findeis, Hallberg, and Lass (1987) for a comparison of estimated off-farm participation and off-farm labour supply models for farm operators and spouses. As discussed in Findeis, Hallberg, and Lass (1987), location is recognized as an important determinant but has not been effectively measured by less aggregated measures.

References

Ahearn, M. (1986) *Financial Well-Being of Farm Operators and Their Households*, Agricultural Economic Report No. 563, Economic Research Service, US Department of Agriculture, Washington, D.C., USA.

Ahearn, M., and Lee, J. (1988) "Multiple Job-Holding among Farm Operator Households in the United States: Historical Perspective and Future Prospect," paper presented at the Symposium on Multiple Job-Holding among Farm Families in North America, Arlington, Va., USA, 16-17 May.

Bollman, R.D. (1979) "Off-Farm Work by Farmers: Application of the Kinked Demand Curve for Labor," *Canadian Journal of Agricultural Economics*, Vol. 27, pp. 37-60.

Brown, D., *et al.* (Eds.) (1987) *Rural Economic Development in the 1980's: Preparing for the Future*, Staff Report No. AGES-870724, Economic Research Service, US Department of Agriculture, Washington, D.C., USA.

Findeis, J.L. (1988) "Effects of Location on Off-farm Employment Decisions," paper presented at the Symposium on Multiple Job-Holding among Farm Families in North America, Arlington, Va., USA, 16-17 May.

Findeis, J.L., Hallberg, M.C., and Lass, D. (1987) "Off-Farm Employment: Research and Issues," paper presented at the Off-farm Employment and Labor Adjustments Symposium, American Agricultural Economics Association annual meeting, East Lansing, Mich., USA, 2-5 August.

Fuller, A. (1988) "Multiple Job-Holding among Farm Families in Canada: Historical Perspectives and Future Prospects," paper presented at the Symposium on Multiple Job-Holding among Farm Families in North America, Arlington, Va., USA, 16-17 May.

Hallberg, M.C., Lass, D.A., and Findeis, J.L. (1988) "Off-Farm Labor Decisions by Farm Households," paper presented at the American Agricultural Economics Association annual meeting, Knoxville, Tenn., USA, 31 July–3 August.

Huffman, W. (1988) "Agricultural Household Models: Survey and Critique," paper presented at the Symposium on Multiple Job-Holding among Farm Families in North America, Arlington, Va., USA, 16-17 May.

Huffman, W.E. (1980) "Farm and Off-Farm Work Decisions: Role of Human Capital," *Review of Economics and Statistics*, Vol. 62, pp. 14-23.

Kada, R. (1980) *Part-Time Family Farming: Off-Farm Employment and Farm Adjustments in the United States and Japan*, Centre for Academic Publications, Tokyo, Japan.

Lichter, D., and Costanzo, J. (1986) "Underemployment in Nonmetropolitan America, 1970 to 1982," in *New Dimensions in Rural Policy: Building upon Our Heritage*, a study prepared for the Subcommittee on Agriculture and Transportation, Joint Economic Committee, US Congress, Washington, D.C., USA.

Maddala, G.S. (1983) *Limited Dependent and Qualitative Variables in Econometrics*, Cambridge University Press, Cambridge, UK.

OECD (Organization for Economic Cooperation and Development) (1977) *Part-Time Farming: United States*, Agricultural Policy Reports, Paris, France.

Reddy, V.K., and Findeis, J.L. (1988) "Determinants of Off-Farm Labor Force Participation: Implications for Low Income Farm Families," *North Central Journal of Agricultural Economics*, Vol. 10, No. 1, pp. 91-102.

Rosenfeld, R. (1985) *Farm Women: Work, Farm and Family in the United States*, Institute for Research in Social Science Monograph Series, University of North Carolina Press, Chapel Hill, N.C., USA.

Sumner, D. (1982) "Off-Farm Labor Supply of Farmers," *American Journal of Agricultural Economics*, Vol. 64, pp. 499-509.

Thompson, S. (1985) "Model of Off-Farm Employment," *Forum No. 10*, Kieler Wissenschaftsverlag, Kiel, FRG.

Tokle, J.G. (1988) "Econometric Analysis of Family Labor Supply Decisions and Household Incomes: U.S. Rural Farm and Nonfarm Households, 1978-82, " PhD dissertation, Department of Economics, Iowa State University, Ames, Iowa, USA.

DISCUSSION OPENING—*Judith I. Stallman* (Virginia Polytechnic Institute and State University)

The paper by Findeis and Reddy examines the factors that influence members of a farm family to seek employment off the farm. The model incorporates supply factors, family labour characteristics, and demand factors, particularly the region of the country and location of the farm near an urban area. In addition, the author recognizes that off-farm employment is a joint decision, even though only one member may be employed off the farm.

The model and the results are reasonable. However, two variables that could be expected to affect off-farm employment are not included in the model—wealth and type of farm. I assume that the variables are omitted from the model because they were not available in the data set that the author chose. In the future, these variables (or proxies) should be included.

The type of farming affects the number of hours that the family has available for off-farm employment. Part of this may be picked up in the region variables, but these variables were intended to reflect labour demand, not supply. Certain farm enterprises, particularly those dealing with livestock, require continual attention. Even though farm income is low, family members may not work off the farm because they cannot find a job that complements their on-farm hours. This family dilemma certainly has rural policy implications.

Income from certain types of wealth is included in the "other income" variable. However, farm families tend to have large amounts of wealth tied up in land and equipment, representing potential future income. In particular, members of older farm families may not seek off-farm employment if the low annual income is perceived as temporary and if they have a wealth "cushion." Thus, lack of off-farm work history may not be the only factor represented by the squared-age variable. These two factors have different policy implications.

The negative coefficient on age squared may also be the result of the life cycle of the farm. As a result of age, illness, or injury, some older farm families cut back the farming operation several years before retirement, causing annual income to decrease. These people have no intention of seeking a second job, since they are already unwilling or incapable of handling the original farm operation. Some measure of health might be a reasonable proxy for this life-cycle affect.

In general, discussions of rural policy need clarification. A rural transition policy seeks to ease human adjustments to market forces. A rural development policy seeks to modify market outcomes in favour of other goals valued by society, such as distribution of income. The policy objective has implications both for the model chosen and for the recommendations made as a result of the modelling exercise.

GENERAL DISCUSSION—*Jerome C. Wells, Rapporteur* (University of Pittsburgh)

The general discussion of this paper included consideration of the distinction between the concepts of "rural development" and "rural transition," and whether the definition of "farm family income" included earnings from items such as tourism, investments, and pensions. Also raised was the question of the *level* as well as the *presence* of off-farm labour-force participation, the subject of a new study by one of the authors of the paper.

Participants in the discussion included E. Asante, S. Ehui, T.E. Gina, R. Herrmann, T.N. Jenkins, D. Kirschke, H. Lee, W. Mukhebi, W. Oluoch-Kosura, and N. Traoré.

Role of Agricultural Marketing in Transforming Subsistence Agriculture: African Case Study

G.C.G. Fraser and G.G. Antrobus[1]

Abstract: A lack of agricultural marketing facilities is generally seen as one of the major obstacles to agricultural development. However, subsistence producers in southern Africa are influenced by certain exogenous factors, such as competition from commercial production, the well-developed marketing system, and off-farm employment opportunities in South Africa. This paper studies the effect of the institution of an organized marketing system in Ciskei on the level of agricultural production. This is found to have had no significant effect because the majority of the able-bodied males are working in the metropolitan areas of South Africa. This has resulted in agriculture becoming a part-time supplementary activity for the women, old men, and children in the rural areas.

Introduction

Researchers in the field of agricultural development (Abbott, 1962; Heyer, 1976; Lele, 1975; and Mellor, 1966) generally agree that marketing is one of the main ingredients in agricultural development, and that inadequate marketing facilities will have a detrimental effect on rural development. With improvements in productivity and greater specialization, a demand for services provided by the marketing situation is created.

Developing countries are generally characterized by the inefficiency of their marketing systems, so that if farmers do not receive an economic return from the sale of their marketable surplus production, they will tend to produce at the subsistence level only (Arnon, 1981). On the other hand, a shortage in the supply of a marketable surplus makes the development of an efficient marketing system extremely difficult. The production of a marketable surplus and the concomitant specialization in agricultural production are only possible if people are willing to buy the added output (Anthony *et al.*, 1979). Abercrombie (1967) makes the point that "... the transition from a predominantly subsistence agriculture must depend mainly on the growth of domestic markets. This, in turn, is largely tied to industrialization and the growth of nonagricultural, generally urban, occupations."

Several problems peculiar to the situation in southern Africa further complicate the role of marketing in development. In the first place, subsistence production often takes place in close geographic proximity to commercial production. Thus, although a developed marketing system also exists in close proximity to subsistence producers, they nevertheless find themselves separated from markets. Second, most urban consumers are well supplied with high quality products, thus providing little stimulus to subsistence producers. Third, off-farm employment opportunities, both at regional and national levels, tend to make agricultural production an unattractive alternative. Low (1986) has argued persuasively that householders with the greatest comparative disadvantage in wage employment will be allocated first to agriculture.

The present study reports on the effect of the institution of agricultural marketing facilities in Ciskei on the level of production in rural areas, which face the additional constraints of lack of off-farm employment opportunities and strong competition from commercial production and marketing channels.

Study Area

Ciskei, which covers an area of about 7,800 km^2, is situated in the southeastern part of southern Africa. The entire area, from the coast to the farthest inland point, about 170 km, falls within the Republic of South Africa (RSA). Historically, much of the area was demarcated in the time of the British occupation of the Cape in the early 1800s and remained relatively underdeveloped in terms of infrastructure, industry, and agriculture until 1981, when Ciskei was created as an independent "homeland."

Within the immediate geographical context, Ciskei's economy has been inextricably linked with that of the Eastern Cape-Border region, which itself has been recognized as one of the most economically disadvantaged regions within the RSA's so-called Regional Development Plan. Ciskei, like Botswana, Lesotho, and Swaziland, is heavily dominated by the larger South African economy. Nevertheless, such development as did take place occurred mostly in towns such as East London and King William's Town in the RSA and, to a very much lesser extent, in Mdantsane (50 km from East London) and Zwelitsha (30 km from King William's Town) in Ciskei. Major expansion of urban and industrial areas has occurred at Bisho and Dimbaza, which both border King William's Town.

Agricultural production for the market predominates in the RSA, while, in Ciskei, production is generally for own consumption, with some notable exceptions. The Ciskei Agricultural Corporation, while exercising wide powers of control (such as pricing, import-export control, and production control), is effectively limited by the statutory South African Control Boards. Several commodities produced in Ciskei are marketed in cooperation with South African institutions; e.g., milk is supplied to the Model Dairies Co-operative in East London, and wool is ultimately marketed through the SA Wool Board, which acts as a single channel marketing scheme. In the case of livestock, the SA Meat Board, through its pricing and supply limitation policies in its controlled areas such as East London and Port Elizabeth, effectively sets prices in Ciskei, since the controlled market floor prices are used as floor prices on Ciskei auctions. The Ciskei Agricultural Corporation, to encourage the marketing of local produce, has established subregional offices, which operate as agencies for the purchase of products such as wool, grain, and fresh vegetables, but these operations still reach a relatively small proportion of subsistence producers. Fresh produce markets are to be found in both East London and nearby Mdantsane and in King William's Town and nearby Zwelitsha, with those in East London and King William's Town being substantially larger and better developed and thus exercising a dominate role.

Methodology

A sample survey was conducted in two typical rural villages, Majwareni and Roxeni. The villages were selected from different areas based on their suitability for rainfed cropping, so as to provide a basis for comparison of the level of production and marketing of agricultural products.

Orthophotographs and aerial photographs were used to draw a sample, and houses were used as the sampling units. The number of houses identified in Majwareni and Roxeni was 151 and 131, respectively, and a random sample of 60 was drawn from each village. In some cases, houses drawn in the sample were occupied by the same household or the houses were vacant. This resulted in only 51 interviews being conducted in Majwareni and 43 in Roxeni, approximately one third of the total identified houses in each of the villages.

Survey Results

The socioeconomic factors prevailing in the rural areas play an important role in the level of agricultural production. The majority of the respondents in each of the villages were female (75 percent). In a number of cases, however, the male head of the household did reside in the village but was not available at the time of the interview. Despite this, 65 percent and 63 percent of the *de facto* heads of the households in Majwareni and Roxeni, respectively, were female. The survey also revealed that approximately 40 percent of the *de jure* heads of households in each of the villages were female. Of the heads of households in Majwareni and Roxeni, 36 percent and 40 percent, respectively, were not permanently resident in the villages. A large percentage (76 percent) of the 17 absentee heads of households in each of the villages are males working in the metropolitan areas of the RSA.

The age distribution shows that the majority of the heads of households fall into the upper age groups. Of the 51 heads of households interviewed, 75 percent were 60 years of age or older and an additional 15 percent were between 50 and 59 years of age. None of the heads of households interviewed was under 40 years of age. The majority (58 percent) of the wives of heads of households were 50 years of age or older. The husbands of the remaining 42 percent of the wives interviewed are among those employed elsewhere in the RSA or engaged in occupations other than farming.

Although nine of the residents in Majwareni regard their present employment as farming, only one stated that farming was the main source of income. This gives an indication of the relative lack of importance of agriculture as a source of income in the villages. Farming was not regarded by any of the respondents in Roxeni as an avenue of employment or their chief source of income. More than half (54 percent) the households surveyed in the two villages derived their income either entirely or in part from government old-age pensions. In eight households in Roxeni, pensions were supplemented by either wage employment or migrant remittances, which form the next single most important source of income. This is the case in about 30 percent of the households surveyed. The remainder of the respondents stated that their main source of income was nonfarm employment, either in the village or in the nearby town. Two of these respondents, however, also had this income supplemented by remittances.

Crop production in the two villages did not enjoy a very high priority. The survey revealed that 30 percent of the respondents had no arable land holdings, and respondents with land had an average of 2.8 hectares. This compares with an estimated 4 hectares under dryland cropping needed for subsistence-level farming (Bembridge, 1984). Only 11 percent of the respondents had 4 hectares or more of land. However, a number of the respondents in Majwareni with no land holdings do use garden plots next to their homestead. Despite the shortage of land, only 58 percent and 46 percent of the land holdings in Majwareni and Roxeni, respectively, were ploughed in the season studied.

Approximately 60 percent of respondents in both villages produced no crops during the preceding 12 months. Only six of the respondents in Majwareni and three in Roxeni stated that they planted crops with the intention of producing enough to be able to market the surplus. Of the remaining 24 and 23 respondents who planted crops in Majwareni and Roxeni, respectively, 79.2 percent in Majwareni and all in Roxeni planted solely as a source of food. The main reasons given for not attempting to produce a surplus for sale in Majwareni were that the land holdings were too small and a combination of no markets and low rainfall. In Roxeni, the main reasons given were low rainfall and poor soils. Other reasons put forward were that production of crops was not necessary as other sources of income were enough and that, traditionally, food produced was not sold. In Majwareni and Roxeni, 47 percent and 77 percent, respectively, did not produce enough to meet their own food needs. This problem was overcome by buying food, which indicated that the availability of money was not a major constraint in the production decision.

Livestock is the major component of farming enterprises in Ciskei (Steyn, 1982), and most of Ciskei is suited to livestock production off natural veld (rangeland). The turnover of livestock, especially cattle, however, is very low (van Rooyen *et al.*, 1981). Only nine of the respondents stated that they sold livestock on a regular basis, and, of these, seven were in Roxeni. Of the remaining respondents, the main reason given for not selling was not enough animals.

The survey revealed that more than of half the respondents (66 percent and 54 percent in Majwareni and Roxeni, respectively) did not own cattle and that the average herd size of those with cattle was 5.1 animals in both the villages.[2] The herd sizes varied between 1 and 12, but less than 30 percent of the cattle owners had 8 or more cattle. Van Rooyen *et al.* (1981) came to the conclusion that the marketing system in Ciskei was therefore directed only at a minority group of wealthier farmers and would not necessarily increase sales. One of the three main reasons for keeping cattle given by approximately half the cattle owners was that, by selling them, they were a source of income. During the 12 months prior to the survey, a total of 5 cattle were sold, all in Majwareni. This constitutes a 2.6 percent turnover of cattle held by the respondents in the two villages, which would seem to imply that, although the cattle are seen as a potential source of income, cattle are sold only when a definite need exists for money, rather than on a regular basis.

A greater proportion of the respondents in Roxeni (72 percent) than in Majwareni (51 percent) did not own sheep but the average flock size in Roxeni (19.7 animals) was greater than in Majwareni (15.3). The sales of sheep were also very small, only 1.7 percent of the total number of sheep owned. This is not surprising considering that two thirds of the sheep owners in Roxeni and 88 percent in Majwareni regard the sale of wool as the main reason for keeping sheep.

The turnover of goats in the villages is even lower than that of sheep, only 1 percent, despite the fact that 71 percent of the goat owners in Majwareni maintained that they kept goats as a source of income. In Roxeni, which had a larger proportion of goat owners and a larger average flock size, the reasons given for keeping goats were somewhat different; i.e., that they were kept for customary purposes (37.9 percent) and for meat (27.6 percent), or as a source of income (20.7 percent).

The only marketing channel used by the respondents to any great extent, albeit for relatively small quantities, was that for wool and hides and skins. All the sheep owners sold wool during the 12 months prior to the survey, and 40 percent of the respondents sold hides and skins. These products were marketed more readily as they were generally of little use to the people in their raw state.

Conclusion

Evidence from two villages showed that the institution of an organized marketing system in Ciskei has not had the expected effect of encouraging rural households to produce a marketable surplus. The less-developed areas of southern Africa, such as Ciskei, are exposed to certain exogenous influences not experienced in other areas of Africa. The off-farm employment opportunities in the RSA, with their relatively high wages, attract the abler people away from the rural areas. Remittances to family members remaining in the rural areas largely negate their need to produce enough to meet their own food needs as well as to provide income for the purchase of consumer goods. In order to attract more rural people to farming, certain other sensitive issues like land tenure will have to be tackled. Possibly the land holdings could become a marketable asset, which would enable people wishing to farm to obtain an economically viable unit. Farming will have to provide an income equivalent to that obtainable in off-farm employment before better use will be made of the agricultural resources and a marketable surplus be produced.

Notes

[1]Department of Agricultural Economics, University of Fort Hare.

[2]Bembridge (1979) estimated that, in traditional subsistence-oriented agriculture, a requirement of up to eight animals was needed to meet the many primary and social needs.

References

Abbott, J.C. (1962) *Marketing—Its Role in Increasing Productivity*, Food and Agriculture Organization of the United Nations, Rome, Italy.

Abercrombie, K.C. (1967) "Transition from Subsistence to Market Agriculture in Africa South of the Sahara," in Whetham, E.H., and Currie, J.I. (Eds.) *Readings in the Applied Economics of Africa, Vol. 1: Microeconomics*, Cambridge University Press, Cambridge, UK.

Anthony, K.R.M., Johnston, B.F., Jones, W.O., and Uchendu, V.C. (1979) *Agricultural Change in Tropical Africa*, Cornell University Press, Ithaca, N.Y., USA.

Arnon, I. (1981) *Modernization of Agriculture in Developing Countries*, John Wiley and Sons, Chichester, UK.

Bembridge, T.J. (1984) "Systems Approach Study of Agricultural Development Problems in Transkei," PhD thesis, University of Stellenbosch, Stellenbosch, RSA.

Bembridge, T.J. (1979) "Problems of Livestock Production in the Black States and Future Strategy," paper presented at the annual conference of the South African Society of Animal Production.

Heyer, J. (1976) "Marketing System," in Heyer, J., Maitha, J.K., and Senga, W.M. (Eds.) *Agricultural Development in Kenya: Economic Assessment*, Oxford University Press, Nairobi, Kenya.

Lele, U.J. (1975) *Design of Rural Development*, Johns Hopkins University Press, Baltimore, Md., USA.

Low, A. (1986) *Agricultural Development in Southern Africa*, James Currey, London, UK.

Mellor, J.W. (1966) *Economics of Agricultural Development*, Cornell University Press, Ithaca, N.Y., USA.

Steyn, G.J. (1982) "Livestock Production in the Amatola Basin," MSc thesis, University of Fort Hare, Alice, Ciskei.

van Rooyen, C.J., de Swardt, S.J., and Fraser, G.C.G. (1981) "Economic Evaluation of Cattle Marketing in Less Developed Agriculture with Special Reference to Ciskei, *Development Studies Southern Africa*, Vol. 3, No. 3, pp. 294-306.

DISCUSSION OPENING—*Brian D'Silva* (Economic Research Service, U.S. Department of Agriculture)

The paper's title states that this is a paper on the "Role of Agricultural Marketing in Transforming Subsistence Agriculture: African Case Study." The title promises more than it provides. While this may be a case study of two villages in Ciskei, we are not told about how representative these villages are of agriculture in Ciskei. In fact, little information is provided on the role of agriculture at an aggregate level in Ciskei. Secondly, I question whether a major institutional marketing development has occurred in Ciskei and if that is what the paper really tries to analyze.

The paper mentions the establishment of a Ciskei Agricultural Corporation (CAC), but also states that it is "effectively limited by the statutory South African Control Boards." We are also told that the CAC has established subregional offices, "but these operations still reach a relatively small proportion of subsistence producers." Finally, we are told that, due to historical factors, Ciskei is largely a rural residential settlement and that agriculture is a part-time supplementary activity of women, old men, and children. All of this suggests that we are not being told about anything major or substantial, as the title promises.

We are talking of a situation that is unrepresentative of the situation in southern Africa, let alone Africa. As the authors themselves conclude, Ciskei is exposed to certain exogenous influences not experienced in other areas of Africa. We could debate the political economy of the region, but that will not lead us anywhere. But the authors have not specified how they view Ciskei within the Southern African region, especially within the agricultural economy of the region.

The reader has the impression that the conclusions are predetermined. For example, the points I mentioned earlier on the role and extent of the Ciskei Agricultural Corporation and historical factors (such as agriculture in Ciskei being a part-time supplementary activity) all appear before the methodology and data are presented. This gives the reader the feeling that the conclusions are already known. One can rationalize that if we have a minimal agricultural labour force and hence minimal agricultural activity, the introduction of marketing institutions will not have an impact.

The main conclusion of the paper is that the introduction of a marketing institution has not led to an increase in marketed surplus among rural households. The reason for this is clear: not much being produced. Farming is not considered a major occupation by most surveyed. Over 50 percent of the respondents produced no crops; over 50 percent owned no cattle or sheep. So, the reasons for the conclusions are clear: this is not a representative African environment. To go further, other countries in Southern Africa have made major marketing infrastructural changes and have seen an increase in marketed surplus. Of specific interest is Zimbabwe, where total marketed surplus of maize from the traditional "communal" sector has now reached nearly 50 percent of the country's total marketed output. It was close to zero at independence in 1980. We find no references to this or other recent findings reported in the literature from other parts of Africa.

GENERAL DISCUSSION—*Gopal Naik, Rapporteur* (Indian Institute of Management)

Questions from the participants were: Whether adequate marketing institutions could raise livestock production in Ciskei, to what extent the collective action can assist small farmers in Ciskei, concern about the study area not having a strong farming background, what kind of tenancy system exists, and whether farmers can avail themselves of subsidies from the government.

In reply, Fraser agreed that while collective actions could be taken in the study area, only a few such actions exist at present. On the question of importance of farming in the area, he said that maize is the main crop and the yields are low. Farmers have access to land which they cannot sell. Share cropping also exists in the study area. Farmers can participate in the Ciskei Agricultural Corporation packages (mainly for input supply) to avail themselves of subsidies. Organized credit facilities exist in the study area.

Fraser agreed that the title is misleading. But he stressed his conclusion that improvements in marketing facilities will not increase production because off-farm employment opportunities exist.

Participants in the discussion included T. Gina, G.T. Jones, and J. van Rooyen.

Marketing, Markets, and Price Policy in China's Grain Economy

Wen Simei[1]

Abstract: The grain sector plays a crucial role in China's agriculture. The government has intervened heavily in grain marketing, markets, and price formation. The objectives of market and price intervention are to secure farmer incomes and ensure consumer food supply at low prices. The economic reform started in 1979 has provided farmers with more freedom to take advantage of free markets, but consumers are still heavily subsidized in food consumption. Grain marketing will be further liberalized, but the government will be in a dilemma, given its unwillingness to raise consumer prices of food grains in the short run.

The government has actively intervened in grain marketing, markets, and price formation in China since the early 1950s. The state procurement of grains, which began in 1953, set the stage for government monopoly of food grains by state or parastatal agencies. This policy was based on the well-accepted perception in China's development strategy that food grains should be treated as "the first class of vital commodities," so that they must be controlled directly by the state in order to secure farmer income and ensure consumer food security as well as stability of the society. The practical mechanisms implementing this policy were that grain producers must sell their grain surpluses to the state-run food agency at state-set prices according to preset procurement quotas, and that the state-run food agency resells food grains through its local fair-price food shops to urban consumers at low prices (usually lower than prices farmers receive), using rationing. Before 1979, grain sales to free markets by producers were prohibited, so that the state actually monopolized all grain markets and marketing activities, including transport, storage, and processing of grains. Grain price formation took place in the planning office of the Ministry of Commerce rather than in the real marketplace.

With the relaxation of controls over the private sector and the reopening of free markets in both rural and urban areas in 1979, farmers have been allowed to enter the free market with their surplus grains, but only after the procurement quota being delivered to the state has been fulfilled. The quota delivery scheme, however, was not changed until the beginning of the 1985 crop year, when the central government introduced a new arrangement of contracting for the purchase of grains in place of the quota procurement system. In principle, the contract purchase system gives grain producers more freedom to decide the volume of their surplus grains being sold to the state. The mechanisms implementing this new system are that, at the beginning of a crop year, the state food agency, in its local offices, reaches a contract with the grain producer about the volume and varieties of grain delivery at the state-set prices during the coming harvest time, and that, by the time the harvest comes, the local state food agency (located in each township even in some villages) is responsible for collecting and paying farmers. The state food agency is also ready to purchase overcontract delivery at a higher price, which is also set by the state but linked to the corresponding free market price to some extent. Farmer decisions on how much of the overcontract surpluses are sold to the state will be influenced mainly by the price offered by the state in relation to the free market price and some benefits that may be associated with overcontract deliveries to the state. Under these dual arrangements, therefore, the state food agency forms the major market for China's food grains, and the rural and urban free market constitute the residual.

Both theoretically and practically, producers are more willing to deliver their grain surplus to free markets where the government exerts little direct influence on prices and where prices are in general 30-50 percent higher than average contract prices. This raises a question about whether the previous quota procurement system differs from the current contract purchase system in terms of the bargaining position of both sides. It does, for farmers saw the share of surplus grains delivered to the state decline, on average, from over 90 percent a few years ago to around 50-60 percent in 1985-86 (Figure 1), which implies that farmers have more freedom to decide for themselves the volume of grains delivered to the state, although the contract purchase system still has, in some sense, the nature of a compulsory arrangement (Wen, 1987).

Grain trade in free markets has taken place primarily in the traditional rural and urban food and other local produce markets, such as local town fairs and urban street-side agricultural product markets, with some exceptions, such as Changsha and Wuxi, two major grain trading centres. The primary function of these traditional markets is to provide an opportunity to exchange locally produced agricultural products and handicrafts, and a substantial amount of the activity is barter. Grain traders in these markets include local grain producers; part-time farmers who may bring grains from surplus to deficit areas for resale or those who must buy grain for their own and their family's consumption; or those "urban" consumers who formally work in cities, but without access to food rationing because their legal residence is still in rural areas (for various reasons). Participants in these markets also include the private "specialized" marketing agents from both urban and rural areas who have emerged in recent years. Moreover, some local government-administered food agencies or companies have also been participating in interregional or interprovincial grain trade, because the regional allocation of grains directly by the central government has been recently reduced and the local governments in grain-deficit regions have to buy grains from other regions in order to avoid grain shortage.

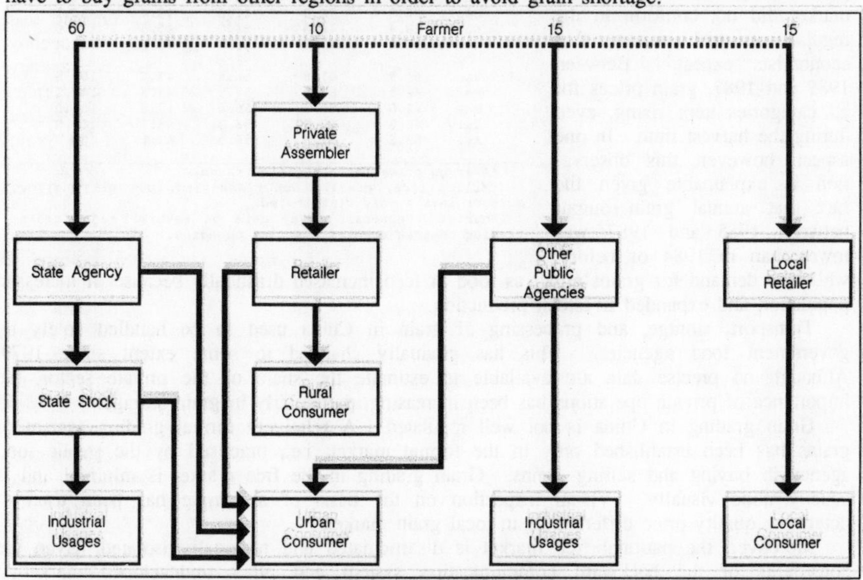

Figure 1—Grain Marketing Chain

Figure 1 illustrates the marketing chain for grains currently operating in China. The numbers above the arrow lines represent the percentage of total grain marketed by farmers, based on a very rough estimation of the situation observed in Changsha and Wuxi, the grain trading centres. In this example, farmers sold 60 percent of their marketed grain to state food agencies (according to contracts reached between the farmer and the state), 40 percent to local free markets (of which 10 percent was sold to private assemblers, both local and visiting), 15 percent to other public food agencies (such as neighbouring provincial government-administered food companies), and 15 percent directly to local consumers (both rural and urban). The numbers have not been broken down further since detailed data are not available. Figure 1 is constructed to identify the main actors in China's grain marketing rather than the quantitative results.

With respect to the price formation of grains in free markets, one can argue that the general principles of supply and demand determinants apply. However, in addition to the normal determinants of supply, grain supply in these free markets is also influenced by the cash obligations of the smallholders and market accessibility to nonfarm traders and part-time farmers who may bring grains from surplus to deficit areas, as well as the effect of the central government's grain allocations on local governments.

Data on free market prices of grains in total and by major commodity between January 1985 and July 1987 are presented in Table 1. These markets appear to be fairly competitive in the sense that prices for all commodities followed similar movements, which implies that substitution effects between commodities are at work. However, as Table 1 shows, the price movements for all grain categories in the free market did not conform to the regular seasonal pattern that economists expect. Between 1985 and 1987, grain prices for all categories kept rising, even during the harvest time. In one aspect, however, this observation is explainable given the fact that annual grain output between 1985 and 1987 was lower than in 1984 or before, while the demand for grains either as food or feed increased drastically because of increased population and expanded livestock production.

Table 1—Free Market Price of Grain

		Grain*	Rice†	Wheat	Maize	Soyabeans
		- - - - - - -	Yuan/100 kg	- - - - - - -		
1985	Jan.	46.3	61.0	46.8	32.7	74.8
	Mar.	47.1	61.6	46.8	33.5	76.9
	May	47.5	61.4	46.2	33.8	79.6
	July	47.6	61.6	45.1	34.3	79.8
	Sept.	48.4	62.6	46.0	34.8	82.0
	Nov.	49.4	63.5	47.8	36.0	82.7
	Av.	48.0	62.2	46.6	34.4	79.6
1986	Jan.	51.1	66.1	49.5	37.5	85.4
	Mar.	53.3	68.5	50.8	39.6	89.2
	May	54.9	69.6	50.9	41.2	92.0
	July	55.5	70.0	50.5	42.6	93.5
	Sept.	56.8	72.0	51.5	43.4	96.1
	Nov.	59.4	76.3	54.0	45.5	100.0
	Av.	55.8	71.5	51.7	42.2	93.4
1987	Jan.	61.9	81.5	56.6	47.4	102.0
	Mar.	62.5	83.0	57.0	47.5	103.0
	May	62.0	83.0	56.0	47.0	104.0
	July	62.3	83.6	56.3	46.3	104.0
	Av.	62.2	82.8	56.5	47.1	103.3

*Average price for all grain traded.
†Milled rice, quality not classified, but all quality more or less evenly distributed.
Source: Personal survey data on several major grain trading centres such as Wuxi and Changsha.

Transport, storage, and processing of grain in China used to be handled solely by government food agencies. This has gradually changed to some extent since 1979. Although no precise data are available to estimate the share of the private sector, the importance of private operations has been increasing, particularly in grain storage.

Grain grading in China is not well regulated. A relatively formal grading system of grains has been established only in the formal market; i.e., practised by the public food agency in buying and selling grains. Grain grading in the free market is minimal and is usually done visually. Visual inspection on the basis of a sample has been used to determine quality price differentials in local grain markets.

Moreover, the national free market is disarticulated and regionally isolated, given the constraints of the backward communication system and other undeveloped marketing infrastructure. Interregional bulk flows of grain are handled mainly by the state food agency under the guidelines of the Commerce Ministry and by local government food companies. Few private traders are engaged in interregional grain transactions. However, buyers and sellers in the local free markets are equally well informed. Prices are determined largely by the forces of supply and demand, actual or anticipated. Although the flow of information in these markets is intricate, both buyers and sellers appear to have perfect knowledge of market conditions.

On the government side, active policies have been designed and implemented to intervene in price formation of grains so as to achieve the objective of grain (food) self-sufficiency. In summarizing the price policy implemented before 1978-79, Barker *et al.* (1982) end with the following observations: "...China maintained low food grain prices and rationed basic necessities so as to ensure a more equitable distribution of supply. Although the government subsidized grain prices to consumers, producer prices remained well below international levels and low relative to prices of noncrops."

However, this policy, to keep food grain prices low (Lardy, 1984) and to ensure that a food grain supply at low prices was at the expense of other crops, was expensive and led to severe distortions of resource allocation (Wen, 1986). In late 1978, the Chinese government, after a series of heated debates on the consequences of previous policies, adopted new policies that have given agriculture high priority, including price incentives to farmers and reduced quota deliveries to the state. In 1979, the first year of the new policy implementation, quota prices for grains were raised 20 percent and overquota prices were set at 50 percent above that. By 1985, the state purchasing price for grain as a category was, on average, 67 percent higher than in 1978. Prices rose, however, not only for grain crops, but for nongrain crops as well. Table 2 shows that, between 1978 and 1985, prices for major grain crops relative to nongrain crops remained almost unchanged. Inputs such as chemical fertilizer have been rationed according to acreage. However, rationed fertilizer at state-subsidized prices constitutes a small proportion (perhaps only 10-30 percent) of total fertilizer used by farmers. Most chemical fertilizers as well as other important inputs are purchased on the parallel market at about double the rationed prices. Hence, the grain-fertilizer price ratio does not say much about farmer responsiveness, even if it was favourable.

Table 2—Relative Price Ratios between Commodities*

Commodity	1952	1957	1978	1985
Grain† to:				
Fertilizer‡	0.37	0.51	1.14	1.13
Other chemicals‡	0.06	0.08	0.19	0.11
Wheat§ to:				
Rice	1.63	1.55	1.20	1.24
Maize	1.84	1.59	1.44	1.47
Soyabeans	1.11	1.02	0.67	0.66
Groundnuts	0.85	0.67	0.54	0.44
Rapeseed	1.09	0.67	0.50	0.46
Cured tobacco	0.20	0.19	0.20	0.28

*The same unit is used for commodity comparisons, such as kilograms or tons. The price ratios are calculated using grain and wheat as numerators and the other commodities as denominators.

†The price used is for grain as a category; i.e., the weighted average of all grain procurement prices.

‡The prices used here are the average state-set retail prices. Fertilizer and chemical prices are based on standard nutrient weights; e.g., ammonium sulfate with 20 percent nitrogen.

§The ratios are computed on the same basis, using the relationship between salt and the individual commodity concerned; e.g., 100 kg of wheat in 1952 were valued at 70 kg of salt, while the same unit of rice could exchange 43 kg of salt, so the wheat/rice price ratio in 1952 is 1.63.

Source: SSB (1986, pp. 637-640).

On the consumption side, absolute prices of major foodstuffs have remained almost unchanged since the middle 1950s. The government has, for both political and economic reasons, committed itself to ensuring a food supply to urban consumers at low prices through rationing and by subsidy from the state budget. Rationed retail prices of food grains have not changed visibly, while the state budget allocations for food price subsidies increased from 1,900 million yuan in 1960 to over 20,000 million yuan in 1985 (Carter, 1987).

In conclusion, the Chinese government is not likely to make radical changes in food grain price policy. However, the government will certainly use more market mechanisms to provide producers and consumers with economic signals. Recent developments show that, in several provinces, rationed grain prices to urban consumers increased by 50-100 percent on average, which moved the state retail price of food grains close to the free market price (*People's Daily*,

Table 3—Grain Price and Price Relations between Markets

Year	Actual Procured Price (1)	Free Market Price (2)	Ration Retail Price (3)	Price Relation (1)/(2)	Price Relation (1)/(3)	Price Relation (2)/(3)
	- - - Yuan/100 kg - - -			- - - Percent - - -		
1980	31.56	55.40	28.34	57	111	195
1981	33.02	54.60	28.10	61	118	194
1982	33.92	56.00	28.34	61	120	198
1983	35.44	53.80	28.88	66	123	187
1984	36.24	48.60	29.04	75	125	169
1985	37.28	47.90	28.18	78	132	170

Sources: Table 1 for free market prices and SSB (1986, pp. 639-640).

July 11, 1988, p. 2). Table 3 indicates that both the procurement prices and rationed retail prices of grains by the state moved towards free market prices between 1980 and 1985. This may facilitate the price reform of food grains in the future. In the short run, however, grain prices for both producers and consumers are unlikely to reflect the relative scarcity of the commodity, although the private sector may play an increasing role in price formation of grains. In addition, neither the state budget being allocated to agriculture nor grain imports are likely to exceed the current levels. This poses a dilemma in terms of concern about producer incentives and consumer welfare.

Note

[1]Department of Agricultural Economics, South China Agricultural University.

References

Barker, R., Sisler, D.G., and Rose, B. (1982) "Prospects for Growth in Grain Production," in Barker, R., Sinha, R., and Rose, B. (Eds.) *Chinese Agricultural Economy*, Westview Press, Boulder, Colo., USA, pp. 65-79.

Carter, C.A. (1987) "Profile of China's Grain Trade," paper presented in the Workshop on North-South Grain Policy and International Trade, Cornell University, Ithaca, N.Y., USA, 14-21 September.

Lardy, N.R. (1984) "Prices, Markets and the Chinese Peasants," in Eicher, C.K., and Staatz, J.M. (Eds.) *Agricultural Development in the Third World*, Johns Hopkins University Press, Baltimore, Md., USA, pp. 420-435.

SSB (1986) *Statistical Yearbook 1986*, China Statistical Publishing House, Beijing, China.

Wen, S.M. (1986) *National and Regional Trends in Production and Productivity for Post-1978 Chinese Agriculture*, International Agriculture No. 111, Cornell University, Ithaca, N.Y., USA.

Wen, S.M. (1987) "China's Grain Economy: Production, Marketing, and Government Policy," paper presented in the Workshop on North-South Grain Policy and International Trade, Cornell University, Ithaca, N.Y., USA, 14-21 September.

DISCUSSION OPENING—*Catherine Halbrendt* (University of Delaware)

The purpose of Wen's paper was to describe China's food (grain) policy and price reform. He did an excellent job in describing the past and current intervention mechanisms of the Chinese government in the food production-marketing-consumption chain. This paper is essential reading for those who want a short but comprehensive overview of China's current price reform and its impact on the grain sector.

The objectives of the Maoist and post-Mao food policies are basically the same, but the means to achieve the objectives are quite different. The objectives, according to Wen, are to: "secure farmer incomes and ensure consumer food security as well as stability of the society." With regard to the means of achieving the objectives, the Maoist and post-Maoist régimes pose a stark contrast. The Maoist régime did not allow for selling on the free market, and the procurement prices paid to farmers and consumer prices did not change much during the period. In contrast, the post-Maoist régime allows surplus quantities to be sold on the free market after the individual household has fulfilled its contractual agreement and government prices are responsive to market forces. The post-Maoist strategy, in essence, concentrates on motivating higher productivity through household efforts and price signals. As stated by Wen, with the current means, the percent of grain contracted to the government has been declining from 90 percent in the late 1970s to the current 60 percent. Wen did not examine how the government can acquire enough grains to meet its obligations to consumers at subsidized prices. The government appears to have the following alternatives to offset the shortages: (1) buy on the international market, (2) increase procurement prices to ensure an adequate amount, or (3) buy on the free market. The first and third alternatives are less than desirable for they are subject to price uncertainties and fluctuations caused by world and domestic supply and demand factors. The most desirable alternative to the government appears to be alternative (2), which is to increase the procurement prices to ensure sufficient amount of grain grown and contracted to the government. We can actually observe this strategy occurring, as indicated by the author, as the gap between the government and market prices is narrowing. The question that then needs to be raised is, if the government intervenes in the grain market, so that most of the sales are going back to government agencies (state and provincial), then what role does the free market play in the future?

The second issue that I would like to raise pertains to the differential impacts of the post-Maoist policies at a more disaggregate level, the provincial level in the case of China. As I understand it, the procurement prices are uniform across provinces. If this is true, they are neither efficient nor equitable, since production costs vary among provinces. Moreover, the market prices among provinces exhibit huge differences, due to the limited interprovincial trade due to emphasis on self-sufficiency and inadequate and inefficient marketing infrastructure. Perhaps Wen can elaborate on whether the government is considering (1) adjusting procurement prices across provinces and (2) embracing the theory of comparative advantage to promote more regional specialization and trade.

A third issue is the continuous upward trend of real grain prices since 1985. The reason given by the author was that demand growth has been outpacing supply growth. Will this upward trend be sustained uniformly across all grains? Currently, close to 80 percent of the Chinese diet is food grain based. Further improvement in income levels is unlikely to lead to further increases in per capita consumption of food grains but rather to increases in feed grain consumption via livestock consumption. I would like Wen to comment on whether he sees different demand growth between direct and indirect grain consumption.

Finally, the paper ends by speculating that the government will not intervene as much in the future. Currently, the transmission of world grain prices to domestic prices is zero. Does the author imply that the government will allow for some price transmission to occur?

GENERAL DISCUSSION—*Gopal Naik, Rapporteur* (Indian Institute of Management)

A suggestion was made that, given the provincial imbalances in supply and demand situations, the question of grain imports by the provinces should be examined.

Wen replied that the government provides funds to grain-deficit areas to import grain from outside the country. In his reply to the discussion opener, Wen said that world food price transmission in China will not be significant in the future.

Participants in the discussion included K.-E. Wädekin.

Price Transmission for Agricultural Products in Brazil

Geraldo S.A.C. Barros and João G. Martines[1]

Abstract: This paper analyzes the farm, wholesale, and retail price series of nine agricultural products (rice, beans, maize, soyabeans, potatoes, onions, bananas, tomatoes, and oranges). Causality analysis is carried out to determine the possible existence of a market level that systematically tends to lead price changes. Immediate and total elasticities of price transmission are estimated to provide evidence regarding the relative size of price variations at different market levels. All results relate to the city of São Paulo, as a consumption centre, and the relevant supplying wholesale firms and production regions. For most of the products analyzed (those traded predominantly in the domestic market), wholesale was detected to be the market level at which price changes were initiated. For products traded internationally—like soyabeans and oranges—the farm level was apparently the point from which price changes are transmitted to the domestic market. Price transmission may also originate at the retail level for products with high income elasticity of demand or with a consumption pattern affected by weather conditions, like oranges and tomatoes. In general, a price change initiated at the wholesale level is reasonably reduced when it reaches the retail level. Almost all other price changes tend to be transmitted approximately proportionally between market levels. Price transmission is distributed over time, but most of the variation tends to be transmitted within three months of the initial shock.

Introduction

In Brazil, as in many other Latin America countries, people are concerned with the inflationary effects of agricultural price shocks as well as with their transmission along the marketing system. At the same time, people believe that marketing agents, at both wholesale and retail levels, are always able to increase their selling price more than proportionally to the increase in costs, resulting in ever increasing marketing spreads and profits. As a consequence, agricultural market intervention—such as price and marketing margin ceilings, import subsidies, and export taxes and quotas—have been common practices in Brazil.

In order to better understand the behaviour of prices along the marketing channels, this paper analyzes farm, wholesale, and retail price series of nine agricultural products (rice, beans, maize, soyabeans, potatoes, onions, bananas, tomatoes, and oranges). Special interest is directed towards both the direction and intensity of price transmission.

The analytical procedure to be used includes two phases. First, causality analysis is used to determine the direction of price transmission. Second, elasticities of price transmission are estimated to provide evidence regarding the relative size of price variations at different market levels.

Theoretical Aspects

Market structure has been considered the most important factor associated with the direction and intensity of price variations. Gardner (1975) provided a comparative-static model explaining farm-retail price spread formation and the price transmission process. Competitive equilibrium price variations may originate at any market level—farm, wholesale, or retail. With respect to price transmission, Gardner shows that its elasticity, as measured from the farm-to-retail level, will be less than or at most equal to unity if constant returns to scale prevail in the marketing process and if the elasticity of supply of marketing inputs is higher than both the elasticity of supply of the farm product and the elasticity of demand at the retail level.

Heien (1980) formulated a dynamic model in which competitive disequilibrium is allowed at the retail level. In this model, only farm-to-retail price transmission is possible, since markup pricing is assumed. Although markup pricing is compatible with market competition, as illustrated by Heien's model, this type of behaviour is usually associated with noncompetitive markets. Indeed, in many situations, the assumption of competition in the marketing sector may be seen as rather unrealistic.

Access to information as well as abilities to assimilate and respond to it are not uniformly distributed along the several levels of the marketing system. In addition, structural differences and the degree of specialization can affect how quickly prices change in response to available information regarding market conditions. These characteristics may favour wholesale agents both in terms of access to information and ability to lead price changes.

Ward (1982) presented evidence for fresh vegetables in the USA that wholesale prices tend to lead both retail and shipping-point prices. Results indicating that wholesale prices lead retail prices are also presented by Heien (1980) for several food products in the USA. Kinnucan and Forker (1987) decided to assume a unidirectional upward causal relationship between farm level and retail prices. In general, estimates of the elasticities of price transmission, as measured from farm or wholesale levels to retail, are less than one.

Data and Methods

The city of São Paulo was selected as the consumption centre, and relevant marketing channels and production regions were defined for each food product analyzed—rice, beans, maize, soyabeans, potatoes, onions, bananas, tomatoes, and oranges. In the cases of maize and soyabeans, prices at wholesale and retail levels refer to the most relevant form for human consumption; maize flour and soyabean oil, respectively. For rice, beans, maize flour, and soyabean oil, the supermarket was chosen as the relevant retail unit. The "feira livre"—a popular street market where many small traders operate—was selected as the retail unit for fruits and vegetables. For these products, the wholesale level considered was the Central de Abastecimento de São Paulo, a state promoted and controlled wholesale market. Products sold at the supermarket were supplied at wholesale by the industries (in the case of maize and soyabean products) and by traditional wholesale units (in the case of rice and beans). Monthly price data from 1972 to 1985 were obtained from the Instituto de Economia Agricola (State of São Paulo) and Fundação Getúlio Vargas.

The method for testing the direction of causality among prices at the three market levels was devised by SIMS (1972). Jacobs, Leamer, and Ward (1979) discuss the several meanings of causality tests. The procedure suggested by SIMS detects causality in Granger's sense.

The test proceeds by first filtering the series. Absence of autoregressive residuals was confirmed by the Box-Pierce test Q (Box and Pierce, 1970). Two basic regressions are run:

$$(1)\ Y_t = a_0 + a_1X_t + \sum_{i=1}^{4} a_{2i}X_{t+i} + \sum_{k=1}^{8} a_{3k}X_{t-k} + \sum_{j=1}^{11} a_{4j}D_j + a_5t = e_{1t}, \text{ and}$$

$$(2)\ X_t = b_0 + b_1Y_t + \sum_{i=1}^{4} b_{2i}Y_{t+i} + \sum_{k=1}^{8} b_{3k}Y_{t-k} + \sum_{j=1}^{11} b_{4j}D_j + b_5t + e_{2t},$$

where X and Y are two price series, say wholesale and retail prices, D represents monthly seasonal dummy variables. Two hypotheses regarding coefficients of future variables are tested by means of an F-statistic (Bishop, 1979).

Elasticities of price transmission are estimated according to the direction of causality previously determined. For example, if causality runs from X and Y, then, following Ward (1982), the following regression is run:

$$(3)\ \ln Y_t = B_0 + \sum_{i=0}^{h} B_i \ln X_{t-i} + \mu_t,$$

where the B_i are the elasticities of price transmission. The total response of Y (say retail prices) to changes in X (say wholesale prices) is assumed to be distributed over time (Kinnucan and Forker, 1987). The number of lags to be considered is determined by a F-test of exclusion of variables form an "unrestricted" model with $h = 12$.

When causality is bidirectional, a simultaneous model is run. Another equation analogous to *(3)* is included, with X being the dependent variable and Y the explanatory variable. In this case, the restriction $h \leq 2$ was imposed. Two-stage least squares was the estimation method used.

Table 1–Effects of a 10-Percent Variation in the Wholesale Price on the Retail Price, São Paulo, 1972-85

Product	Immediate Effect	Total Effect	Lags
	- - *Percent* - -		*Months*
Bananas	1.06	5.02	4
Potatoes	3.96	6.30	1
Onions	5.39	8.18	1
Beans	5.39	8.89	1
Maize flour	5.55	5.55	0
Soyabean oil	4.68	10.65	6
Tomatoes	0.00	6.02	2

Results

The results from the analysis of causality may be summarized as follows: (a) causality is from wholesale to both farm and retail levels for rice, bananas, potatoes, onions, and beans; (b) causality is from farm level to wholesale and from retail to wholesale for oranges; (c) unidirectional causality is from wholesale to farm level and bidirectional causality is between wholesale and retail for tomatoes; and (d) bidirectional causality is between farm and wholesale and unidirectional is from wholesale to retail for soyabeans and maize.

Estimates of the elasticities of price transmission are presented in Tables 1 to 4 only for those marketing linkages in which causality was detected. Three characteristics of the price transmission mechanism are reported: immediate (current month) and total (given by summation of significant coefficients) effects of a 10-percent price change at one level on the other level and the number of lags associated with the total effects. A substantial part of the total effect takes place within three months of the initial price shock.

In general, a price change initiated at the wholesale level is reasonably reduced when it reach-

Table 2–Effects of a 10-Percent Variation in the Farm Price on the Wholesale Price, São Paulo, 1972-85

Product	Region	Immediate Effect	Total Effect	Lags
		- - *Percent* - -		*Months*
Potatoes	Minas Gerais	24.38	9.71	2
Onions	Campinas	14.48	9.99	2
Beans	Sorocaba	8.09	8.09	0
Oranges	São Paulo	4.88	4.88	0
Maize flour	São Paulo	64.89	18.31	2
Maize flour	Paraná	15.80	10.01	2
Soyabean oil	São Paulo	5.73	5.73	0
Soyabean oil	Mato Grosso	4.60	4.91	1

Table 3–Effects of a 10-Percent Variation in the Wholesale Price on the Farm Price, São Paulo, 1972-85

Product	Region	Immediate Effect	Total Effect	Lags
		- - *Percent* - -		*Months*
Bananas	São Paulo	4.31	8.51	1
Potatoes	Campinas	5.99	9.26	4
Potatoes	Sorocaba	5.51	9.04	4
Potatoes	Paraná	2.82	9.83	2
Potatoes	Minas Gerais	0.00	7.70	2
Onions	Santa Catarina	2.30	9.95	3
Onions	Sorocaba	6.55	9.92	9
Onions	Campinas	1.98	14.74	2
Beans	Paraná	3.65	7.42	3
Beans	Campinas	6.79	9.49	3
Maize flour	Minas Gerais	2.14	7.20	1
Maize flour	São Paulo	8.92	9.12	2
Maize flour	Paraná	10.83	9.94	2
Tomatoes	Minas Gerais	23.56	11.50	2
Tomatoes	Sorocaba	6.93	9.11	8
Tomatoes	Campinas	7.70	9.41	8

es retail level. Almost all price transmissions involving wholesale and farm levels as well as those originating at the retail level tend to be approximately proportional to the initial shock; i.e., given enough time, a 10 percent change at one level of the market tends to result in a change of about 10 percent at the other level.

Table 4—Effects of a 10-Percent Variation on the Retail Price on the Wholesale Price, São Paulo, 1972-85

Product	Immediate Effect	Total Effect	Lags
	- - *Percent* - -		*Months*
Oranges	6.51	10.37	12
Tomatoes	12.28	8.01	2

Conclusions

For many products—bananas, potatoes, onions, maize flour, and beans—wholesale was detected to be the market level at which price changes tended to initiate. All those products are traded predominantly in the domestic market.

Products traded internationally, like soyabeans and oranges, present price changes originating at the farm level. Apparently what happens is that, when the orange juice price changes in the external market, the national juice industry transmits the variation to orange growers. In the sequence, the domestic price would change at the wholesale level. An analogous linkage could be established between soyabeans or meal and soyabean oil.

Price variations may also begin at the retail level. Apparently this is the case for products presenting high income elasticity of demand or a consumption pattern significantly affected by weather conditions, like oranges and tomatoes. In other cases, like those of rice, maize flour, beans, and soyabean oil, retail agents play a passive role in the price transmission mechanism.

An important conclusion of the paper is that no evidence exists that the marketing sector tends to widen the initial price shocks. Since, in most cases, price transmission is at most proportional, the current opinion of unstabilizing behaviour in the marketing system is not justified. Therefore, price controls are not needed for this purpose and may indeed be a source of great distortions in the market.

Note

[1]Escola Superior de Agricultura "Luiz de Queiroz," Universidade de São Paulo.

References

Box, G.E.P., and Pierce, D.A. (1970) "Distribution of Residual Autocorrelations in Autoregressive Integrated Moving Average Time Series Models," *Journal of American Statistical Association*, Vol. 65, No. 332, pp. 1509-1526.

Bishop, R.V. (1979) "The Construction and Use of Causality Tests," *Agricultural Economics Research*, Vol. 31, No. 4, pp. 1-6.

Gardner, B.C. (1975) "The Farm-Retail Price Spread in a Competitive Food Industry," *American Journal of Agricultural Economics*, Vol. 57, No. 3, pp. 399-409.

Heien, D.M. (1980) "Markup Pricing in a Dynamic Model of the Food Industry," *American Journal of Agricultural Economics*, Vol. 61, No. 1, pp. 10-18.

Jacobs, R.L., Leamer, E.E., and Ward, M.P. (1979) "Difficulties with Testing for Causation," *Economic Inquiry*, Vol. 17, No. 3, pp. 401-413.

Kinnucan, H.W., and Forker, O.D. (1987) "Asymmetry in Farm-Retail Price Transmission for Major Dairy Products," *American Journal of Agricultural Economics*, Vol. 69, No. 2, pp. 285-292.

Sims, C. (1972) "Money, Income and Causality," *American Economic Review*, Vol. 62, No. 4, pp. 540-552.

Ward, R.W. (1982) "Asymmetry in Retail, Wholesale and Shipping Point Pricing for Fresh Vegetable," *American Journal of Agricultural Economics*, Vol. 64, No. 2, pp. 205-212.

DISCUSSION OPENING—*Lilian Barros* (University of Exeter)

This paper covers an important subject and uses an appropriate approach for high-inflation countries. Critical policy intervention points (farm price supports, wholesale margin regulations, and consumer prices controls) and critical product groups are covered.

My questions pertain to the size of the coefficients and to "how to" issues; i.e., causality of price changes is difficult to determine in quantitative terms only and *a priori* assumptions for product groups might be useful, perhaps based on price elasticities of supply (ε_S^P) and income elasticities of demand (ε_D^Y).

I suggest grouping the products based on the reported results, as follows:

High ε_S^P → High Tech → Oligopoly (e.g., oranges)
+ΔP: *Farm* → Wholesale

Low ε_S^P → Low Tech → Price takers (e.g., rice and beans)
+ΔP: Farm ← *Wholesale*

High ε_D^Y → "Luxury" or expensive foods (e.g., tomatoes and oranges)
+ΔP: Wholesale ← *Retail* or Wholesale ↔ Retail

Low ε_D^Y → staple foods, steady demand for exports (e.g., soyabean oil)
+ΔP: *Wholesale* → Retail

Combining the assumptions yields:

ε_S^P	ε_D^Y	Source of +ΔP	Product
High	High	*Farm* → Wholesale Wholesale ← *Retail*	Oranges
High	Low	*Farm* → Wholesale *Wholesale* → Retail	Soyabeans
Low	Low	Farm ← *Wholesale* *Wholesale* → Retail	Beans
Low	High	Farm ← *Wholesale* Wholesale ← *Retail*	Tomatoes

The reported coefficients on retail price changes seem more "dangerous" than those on the other price levels. The sizes of the coefficients reported for the 6-month lagged wholesale-to-retail price transmission for soyabean oil (11 percent) and the immediate farm-to-wholesale price transmissions for potatoes (24 percent), maize flour (65 percent), and onions (14 percent) seem large. Finally, why do the price effects vary by location (e.g., the wholesale-to-farm price transmission for onions, which varied from 9 to 15 percent)?

GENERAL DISCUSSION—*Gopal Naik* (Indian Institute of Management)

Several questions were raised by the participants: whether the upper limit of the elasticity of price transmission be 1, even in the long run, and whether this will hold when one analyzes retail-to-farm level prices. Even if the causation is correct, errors of measurement will tend to depress the coefficients unless diagonal regression is used. The reasons for different results of causality for different commodities need to be explained.

In reply, Barros noted that price controls have undesirable effects on commodity supply. In the past, due to such price controls, many products disappeared from the market. He noted the suggestion by the discussion opener to classify commodities according to elasticities as an interesting one. Barros clarified that he did not mean the upper limit of the elasticity of price transmission should be 1. He said that he is aware of the problems of the causality method used, but he is comfortable with it in his study. He used the single-equation method to test unidirectional causality.

Participants in the discussion included G.T. Jones, W. Martin, and F. Rosa.

Trade Policy, Self-Sufficiency, and Liberalization in the Indonesian Food Economy

Sjarifudin Baharsjah, Soetatwo Hadiwigeno, H.S. Dillon, Douglas D. Hedley, and Steven R. Tabor[1]

Abstract: International trade in food crops has historically played a residual, supply-augmenting role in the Indonesian food economy. Indonesia was able to transform its rice economy technologically and stimulate rapid growth in rural income and consumption levels while protecting the domestic economy over the 15-year period ending in 1985. A slowdown in economic growth, combined with a deteriorating external payments situation, has led Indonesian planners to adopt a more open and outward-oriented approach to economic management. For agriculture, trade liberalization is understood as being a part of this new, outward-oriented, development approach. The costs of shifting the agricultural economy to a more liberalized trade régime were simulated using a multimarket agricultural sector econometric model. The results of the static simulation show that the transition costs, in terms of higher import demand, lower farm income, and lower employment absorption, will be high. This argues that, particularly in a depressed world primary commodities market, a sound economic case can be made for special and differential treatment of protectionism in the developing economies. The extent to which labour wages are flexible will also have a significant influence on the economic gains from trade liberalization. In the Indonesian agricultural economy, where a high degree of rural underemployment is evident, complete trade liberalization will not be a first-best development policy choice.

Trade and Protection in Indonesian Agricultural Development

In Indonesia, the historical role of international trade in food crops has been to balance domestic demand and supply at target, or politically sanctioned, levels. The international market has been treated as a residual market, to be used by the government or appointed traders to clear markets, rather than as a catalyst to allocate domestic resources. The lack of reliance in the international market as an allocative device is related to the role of agriculture and, more broadly, agricultural development in the national economy. This role is changing, and, consequently, the agricultural economy must now place greater reliance on the international market to improve domestic competitiveness.

The main role of the Indonesian agricultural sector is to provide an adequate diet to consumers and a sufficient supply of raw materials to industry and to generate adequate incomes for crop producers. Generating foreign exchange has traditionally been accorded a low priority in the food sector. Over the past decade, the main aim of agriculture has been import substitution, first in rice and then in all other foodstuffs.

Although near-autarky in food and in other strategic commodities remains official policy, downturn in economic performance of the mid-1980s has led to a rethinking of the role of trade in economic development. Economic policy makers have adopted a more outward-looking orientation in order to diversify export earnings, increase domestic competitiveness, and encourage new sources of growth. This new direction is reflected in recent trade reforms in industry and services. Trade in agricultural commodities, by comparison, has not been directly affected by the trade liberalization measures of 1986 and 1987. Still, calls for agricultural trade reform continue to mount, through GATT, in reports of the government's major creditors (World Bank, 1987b), in key bilateral government meetings, and from technocrats within the government's own ministries (IFPRI, 1987; and Deptan, 1988). The limits to which trade liberalization can be accommodated and the problems involved in adjusting to a more liberalized trade régime require an understanding of the historical linkage between trade, protectionism, and agricultural development in Indonesia.

Trends in Food Crop Trade and Agricultural Development

Before 1975, Indonesia was an occasional exporter of small quantities of food crops. Import demand was held in check by foreign exchange constraints, low income growth, and low urbanization. Between 1976 and 1985, high growth rates in income and population created an excess food and feed demand that could not be satisfied by domestic production. A rise in petroleum earnings, available foreign assistance (which eased foreign exchange constraints), concessional food imports, and rapid infrastructural growth allowed imports to escalate quickly. By 1983, Indonesian imports of foodstuffs had risen to $950 million, with foodstuff exports of only $45 million. The food crop sector was, in effect, running a negative trade balance of $905 million annually. The largest imports by volume and value in 1983 were rice, followed by wheat, soyabeans, and soyabean meal. Cassava chips and pellets were the largest export items. Because of the very rapid growth in rice production after 1979, rice imports had ceased by 1984; small surpluses of rice were exported in 1985 and 1986 at distressed prices to relieve pressure on domestic stockholding. However, imports of soyabeans, soyabean meal, and wheat for human consumption had increased considerably. Spurred by demand increases for animal products, maize imports for animal feeds also expanded in the 1980s. With the fall in world prices for Indonesia's food crop imports and an increase in unit values for cassava exports, the Indonesian net food import balance declined from the earlier level of $905 million in 1983 to about $400 million in 1986 (Deptan, 1988).

These trade figures mask the degree to which the government has actively intervened to constrain growth in import demand. On average, between 1984 and 1986, medium-quality rice in the Jakarta market was selling at 125 percent of the import parity price for "Thai 25 percent brokens" rice. Wheat flour was selling at 30 percent over the comparable price of Australian wheat flour, soyabeans at twice the border price of China-origin beans, and maize at 22 percent over the border price of Thai yellow maize (Deptan, 1988). These differences between domestic and international prices are maintained primarily through the use of nontariff barriers. Government is the sole importer and exporter for rice, soyabeans, soyabean meal, and wheat. Import licencing is used to control trade in maize, cassava flour, groundnuts, and mung beans.

The comparison of border and domestic prices does not take into account the public subsidies for irrigation, fertilizers, and pesticides. About 70 percent of the total value of domestic food production is derived from irrigated areas, primarily wetland rice. On irrigated lands, water is delivered at less than five percent of the capital, operations, and maintenance costs for the irrigation (World Bank, 1987b; and IFPRI, 1987). During 1986, fertilizers were selling at half the equivalent import parity price, on average, with a financial subsidy to domestic fertilizer consumption estimated at $520 million in 1986 (Hedley, 1987). To this can be added the smaller, direct subsidies for pesticides and improved seeds.

In the food sector, Indonesia has relied on nontariff barriers and input subsidies as a wedge between the world market and the domestic economy. Historically, these means were used to provide some stability in domestic markets and to develop an "infant" staple food economy. Between 1976 and 1982, real private per capita expenditures grew by 52 percent and population by 21 million. Domestic demand for foodstuffs outstripped the growth in production, and imports were used in a controlled manner to balance supply and demand. In Figure 1, this is represented by an outward shift of the demand curve from the D_{1976} to the D_{1986} position. Demand became more inelastic as incomes rose, and prices became increasingly unstable in the face of supply disturbances. Supply was unable to meet this demand growth because of the continued dependence on traditional (largely nonprice responsive) technologies in the nonrice crops and due to a lack of complementary production and marketing infrastructure. Domestic prices rose quickly; imports were one means of easing the upward price pressure, even though world prices were high at the time. In order to ensure that the bulk of the benefits from the demand growth did not leak to the world market, Indonesia intensified trade controls, expanded production subsidies, and strengthened public-sector investment in irrigation, new rice technologies, input subsidies, and infrastructure. This led to an outward shift in the supply curve for foodstuffs (S_{1986} in Figure 1).

Behind such protectionist barriers, Indonesia was successful in raising consumption levels while stimulating the technological transformation of the rice sector. Between 1976 and 1984, wetland rough rice yields increased from 2.9 t to 4.2 t per hectare, while per capita domestic availability increased from 110 kg to 125 kg per year. Other commodities, for which little new technology was available, did not perform nearly so well under trade protection (Deptan, 1988).

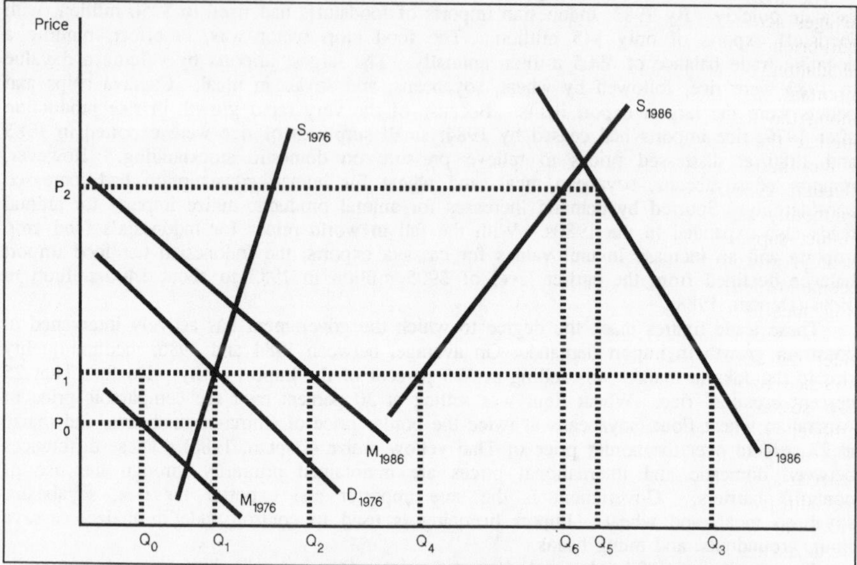

Figure 1—Changes in Supply and Demand in the Indonesian Food and Agricultural Sector

Q_0 = 1976 food imports (under subsidy)
Q_1 = 1976 domestic consumption
Q_2 = 1986 food imports (under free trade) (Q_3-Q_4)
Q_3 = 1986 food consumption (under free trade)
Q_4 = 1986 potential food supply (under free trade)
Q_5 = 1986 food consumption (under protection)
Q_6 = 1986 food production (under protection)
P_0 = 1976 prices for food to consumers
P_1 = world food prices
P_2 = 1986 domestic food prices

Trade Liberalism as a Source of Growth

By the mid-1980s, Indonesian economic growth had slowed considerably. The causes were a rising debt service ratio, an abrupt fall in petroleum prices, the secular decline in primary commodity prices generally, and the weakening of the US dollar. Within food crop agriculture, the usual Green Revolution rice technology had been nearly fully exploited, since more than 97 percent of the rice on Java was coming from HYV rice under high fertilizer and pesticide applications. For the nonrice crops, little technology was available to foster a growth pattern similar to the rice success. Trade reform and the reduction in direct and indirect public sector subsidies have been used as a part of a broader economic reform package to stimulate growth and diversify export earnings.

As part of the overall economic reform movement, Indonesia has been called upon to liberalize trade in the agricultural sector (World Bank, 1987b). The positive gains from agricultural trade liberalization would be to reduce domestic food costs, improve efficiency in the allocation of production resources, and stimulate growth and technological transformation in markets where Indonesia may have a comparative advantage (World Bank, 1987b; and Ministry of Agriculture Round Table, 1987). The efficiency gains from a more outward-oriented trade strategy has been proposed as, in effect, an important new source of growth for the sector.

Multimarket Simulation of a Liberalized Food Economy

The Indonesian economy has become increasingly complex, with rapidly strengthening linkages across sectors and within the food crop subsector. Because single market, partial equilibrium approaches can lead to bias in domestic resource cost estimates and the calculation of economic surplus when the cross-commodity and cross-factor effects are important, the methodology selected for this study takes into account these interactions among the food crop production and demand systems. A multimarket model was used to simulate the effects of trade liberalization on the Indonesian food economy. The structure of the Indonesian agricultural sector model has been described in more detail elsewhere (Deptan, 1988). In brief, the model is an econometrically estimated, seven food crop commodity sector model using a profit function and adaptive response approach to derive product supply. On the demand side, a variant of an "almost ideal demand system" is used. Agricultural production is linked to a three sector macromodel to generate national income, which is then linked, through a consumption function, to food demand. Prices are exogenous in the model, and trade is used to clear domestic markets.

The sector model is used to test the static equilibrium effects of trade liberalization, under the assumption that Indonesia is a large country (and hence exerts an important influence on price) in the rice market but a small country in other commodity markets. Two scenarios are tried. In the first, domestic prices of rice, soyabeans, maize, and fertilizer, with minor adjustments, are set equal to world market parity price forecasts for 1988 using World Bank (1987a) commodity price forecasts. The model is used to forecast the near-term effects of trade liberalization. In the second scenario, domestic prices (with rice adjusted for large-country effects) are set equal to 1984 and then 1985 border parity prices for the major traded foodstuffs. This can be interpreted as a "backcast" of a liberalized trade régime. Two variants of each scenario are tested. In the first, farm labour wages are completely flexible and adjust to reflect rice prices; in the second, wages do not adjust downwards but instead follow the rate of growth in aggregate expenditures.

In the first scenario, future liberalization, under 1988 World Bank price forecasts, would result in a 4.1-percent decline in farm income, an increase in import demand to $1,300 million and a decline in agricultural employment of 6.3 percent, or 1.2 million full-time jobs, compared to 1987 base conditions. GDP would increase by 3.1 percent in 1988 under liberalization, slightly slower than the 3.7-percent growth rate projected under a more protected trade régime.

If only product prices were liberalized and input subsidies remained in place, then the farm sector would still lose income and employment, but at a marginally slower rate than in the more complete liberalization scenario. Furthermore, if wages adjust downwards to the lower output price régime, then the effects on farm income and national growth are the same for a protected and a liberalized trade régime. Under flexible rural wage rates (without fertilizer subsidy removal), trade liberalization would lead to an increase in sector net imports from $450 million to slightly under $1,000 million per year. Imports of about 1.1 to 2.6 million t of rice, 680,000 t of soyabeans (for direct human consumption), and 1.5 million t of wheat would be required under a more liberalized trade régime for 1988.

In the 1984 and 1985 "backcast" scenario, trade liberalization in inputs and outputs, with flexible rural wages, would have resulted in an increase in imports of $750 million per year. This included average rice imports of 1.6 million t, maize imports of 410,000 t, and soyabean imports of 1.5 million t.

Under protection, farm incomes would have increased by 1.8 percent in 1984 and by 10.9 percent in 1985. Under the case of liberalization of input subsidies and trade, with flexible wages, farm income would have risen by 4.6 percent in 1984 and would have been constant in 1985. Slower growth in farm sector income would have been partly offset by the effect of lower food prices on nonagricultural growth. The net effect of liberalization would have been growth in national product of 0.1 percent below historical rates of growth.

Under the 1984 and 1985 "backcast" scenario, trade liberalization of key outputs, with rural wages indexed to inflation, would have resulted in a 2-percent decline in labour absorption in 1984 and a 7-percent decline in labour absorption in 1985, compared to the actual level. This would be the equivalent of a loss of 800,000 full-time jobs in 1985 alone. In the "backcast" scenario, with wages falling proportional to the fall in rice prices along with liberalization in fertilizer and some product prices, labour demand would rise slightly in 1984 but would then fall sharply in 1985. The net result would be an aggregate loss of 100,000 jobs over the 1983 base case, with much greater instability in year-to-year farm labour demand.

Economics of Special and Differential Treatment

The results of the static simulation show that the transition costs of liberalization, in terms of higher import demand, lower farm incomes, and lower employment absorption, will be high in the Indonesian economy. This argues that, particularly in a depressed world primary commodities market, a sound economic case can be made for special and differential treatment for some trade insulation in the developing economies. The extent to which labour wages are flexible will also have a significant influence on the efficiency gains from trade liberalization. In the Indonesian agricultural economy, where a high degree of rural underemployment is evident, complete trade liberalization will not be the first-best trade policy choice. The model results suggest that the best trade policy choice would be a variant of the "staple theory" approach to trade and growth, in which the mainstay of the rural economy, in this case the rice market, is protected and transformed gradually, while the balance of the sector is gradually liberalized.

For a large developing economy, trade liberalization adds many risks as well as the high frictional costs of initial adjustment. Uncertainties about likely movements in international prices, the ability of the smallholder peasants to move resources in a more competitive economy, and the ability of the market to communicate trade information efficiently and equitably complicate the issue of liberalizing the trade régime. To this should be added the political risks involved in promoting greater trade openness when heavy investments of political capital have been made in legitimizing the goal of self-sufficiency in basic goods. These economic and political risks are significant for the Indonesian agricultural economy and should be explicitly considered to provide a balanced assessment of the effects of trade liberalization.

Note

[1]Indonesian Ministry of Agriculture; except Hedley, Winrock International.

References

Deptan (Department of Agriculture) (1988) "Supply and Demand Prospects for Indonesian Foodcrops," report prepared for the SFCDP-USAID Project, Jakarta, Indonesia.

Hedley, D.D., and Tabor, S.R. (1987) "Fertilizer in Indonesian Agriculture: Subsidy Issue," report prepared for the Bureau of Planning, Ministry of Agriculture, Jakarta, Indonesia.

IFPRI (International Food Policy Research Institute) and Centre for Agro-Economic Research (1987) "Price and Investment Policies in the Indonesian Food Crop Sector," report submitted to the Asian Development Bank, Washington, D.C., USA.

Ministry of Agriculture Roundtable (1987) "Report of the Workshop on Indonesian Agricultural Development for Repelita V Preparation," Bureau of Planning, Jakarta, Indonesia.

World Bank (1987a) *Commodity Prices and Price Projections*, Washington, D.C., USA.

World Bank (1987b) *Indonesia: Agricultural Incentive Policies—Issues and Options*, Vols. I and II, Projects Department, East Asia and Pacific Region, Washington, D.C., USA.

DISCUSSION OPENING—*Don Kanel* (University of Wisconsin)

The paper distinguishes three distinct periods in Indonesia's situation. In the first, before 1976, slow economic growth and scarcity of foreign exchange limited agricultural imports. In the second, high petroleum prices facilitated imports, but also in this period improvements in rice technology, prices above world levels, and input subsidies achieved self-sufficiency in rice and decreased the total cost of food imports. The 1980s are different. Lower petroleum prices and lower prospects for further productivity increases in agriculture mean that nontraditional exports will need to grow and that liberalization of trade policies may be the key to economic growth and the growth of such nontraditional exports.

To analyze the impacts of trade liberalization, the authors present the results of a simulation study. In this study, prices are set at levels that can be expected from trade liberalization, and an econometrically estimated model is used to calculate the consequences of the prices for different rates of growth of GDP, agricultural employment and income, and the value of food imports.

The results are given in only five paragraphs of text. This is too condensed to be clear. Possibly a table could have been used to make the results clearer.

What does the analysis indicate about the growth of nontraditional exports? Does the model indicate growth of exports from any of the seven food crop commodities in the model? Even more important, is liberalization of agricultural trade an important factor in lowering Indonesian costs and improving the competitiveness of the Indonesian exports? The authors conclude that, compared to liberalization of agricultural trade, a better policy would be protection of the rice market and only a gradual transformation of the rest of the agricultural sector. But this conclusion would be stronger if the policy proposed by the authors were to have minimal impacts on Indonesian costs.

The model measures impacts of liberalization on both agricultural income and employment. How is the impact on employment measured? Is it an aggregate estimate or does it distinguish family labour of cultivators from that of agricultural workers?

GENERAL DISCUSSION—*Philippe Burny, Rapporteur* (Faculté des Sciences Agronomiques de l'État, Belgium)

A question was raised whether Indonesia is considered a small or large country in the model. When a country is considered large, it has a nonnegligible influence on world prices. In reply, Dillon said that Indonesia was not considered a large country in the model.

One of the most important points discussed was the effect of trade liberalization on agricultural employment and rural wages. Would the wages rates decrease as well as the output prices? Would people leave the agricultural sector? What about the disparity between rural and urban areas? What would be the impact on nonagricultural investments on exchange rates?

In reply, Hedley said that, in his model, two hypotheses were related to this point: rural wages remain stable or decrease with prices. The impact on employment would be negative though, in Indonesia, if the labour force continues to increase in absolute terms but decreases in relative terms. And the consequence of trade liberalization would be the appearance of different wages and prices in different parts of the country (i.e., regional adjustments would be a problem). He agreed that exchange rates would be changed. He noted that income increases and then the elasticity decreases; other products would reajust.

Another speaker wondered if the problem treated in this paper could be dealt with better. Is it really appropriate to assume trade liberalization and then try to identify its consequences for the Indonesian economy? In fact, the Indonesian government has always proceeded differently: it fixes the desired price. So, would evaluating the consequences after the government fixes a domestic price have been preferable?

In reply, Hedley said that, indeed, that was historically so. But, since the mid-1980s, Indonesia has experienced less economic growth and problems have arisen concerning external debts. So, the government changed its policy and the industrial sector was liberalized to a certain extent. So far the agricultural sector has not been liberalized, but trade liberalization must be considered in the future.

Participants in the discussion included R.R. Barichello, A. Siamwalla, and A. Valdés.

Impact of Trade Liberalization on Indonesian Food Crops

Mark W. Rosegrant[1]

Abstract: This paper presents a multimarket food crop supply/demand model for Indonesia and assesses the impact of food crop trade liberalization using the model. The results indicate that a trade liberalization policy would generate substantial net benefits to society because gains to consumers from reduced food expenditures are larger than losses in farm revenues. The net import bill for food commodities increases with trade liberalization due to increased demand for the liberalized commodities. However, because of the strong cross effects from price changes on the production and consumption of other crops, increases in the import bill are moderated. Increases in import expenditures for food due to liberalization are small relative to total export earnings. The results suggest that Indonesia should reduce protective trade barriers for food crops and move towards trade liberalization. Given government concerns with farm income and with potential adjustment problems in the process of liberalization, a possible alternative to full trade liberalization would be to permit free trade in food crops but to institute a moderate import tariff on the most highly protected commodities: soyabeans, sugar, and wheat. Full trade liberalization generates larger net welfare gains than free trade with moderate tariffs. However, a moderate tariff on soyabeans, wheat, and sugar combined with free trade would reduce the degree of distortion of incentives to producers relative to current policies and would rationalize the current system of import controls and regulated transfer pricing that encourages inefficient rent seeking in the distribution of these commodities.

Introduction

Government policy has been a key factor in the rapid growth of the Indonesian agricultural sector over the past decade. Since 1978, the agricultural sector has grown at the rate of 4.3 percent in real terms, while the food crop sector has grown at 5.4 percent over the same period. The largest contribution has been from growth in rice production, which has been achieved in significant part due to government policies, including investment in irrigation and research, extension programmes for new technologies and inputs, favourable input pricing policies, and stabilization of rice prices.

The government has also heavily influenced prices of the other important food crops, particularly soyabeans, sugar, and wheat, through control of imports and intervention in domestic markets. Intervention in maize and cassava markets has been less pronounced. Control of imports of soyabeans and sugar has been used to maintain domestic prices of these commodities far above world prices. For many years, domestic wheat prices were subsidized by the government, but, in recent years, domestic prices of wheat have also moved above world prices. Government objectives in exercising control over prices have included price stabilization, provision of incentives to boost domestic production and farm income, and reduction in foreign exchange costs of food imports.

However, trade protectionism to maintain domestic prices above world prices may entail large costs to the economy. Trade policies that protect some commodities at the expense of others may cause resources to shift from more efficient production activities to less efficient ones. Protective trade policies also penalize consumers through increased domestic prices. Removal of trade restrictions may result in more efficient allocation of resources in production and may increase consumer welfare to a greater degree than producer income is reduced, resulting in net welfare gains to society.

In this paper, the impact of food commodity trade liberalization policies on crop production, farm revenues, consumer food expenditures, and import expenditures is analyzed using a multimarket food crop supply/demand model. The model is briefly outlined, government price policies for major food crops are described, and key impacts of liberalization are presented. General conclusions are then discussed.

MARK W. ROSEGRANT

Multimarket Supply/Demand Model of the Indonesian Food Crop Sector

In this section, the multimarket food crop demand/supply model is briefly presented. A detailed description of the structure and operation of the model is given in Rosegrant *et al.* (1987, chap. 5). The simplified structure of the food crop supply/demand model is presented in Figure 1. The key components of the model are supply, demand, and government policy.

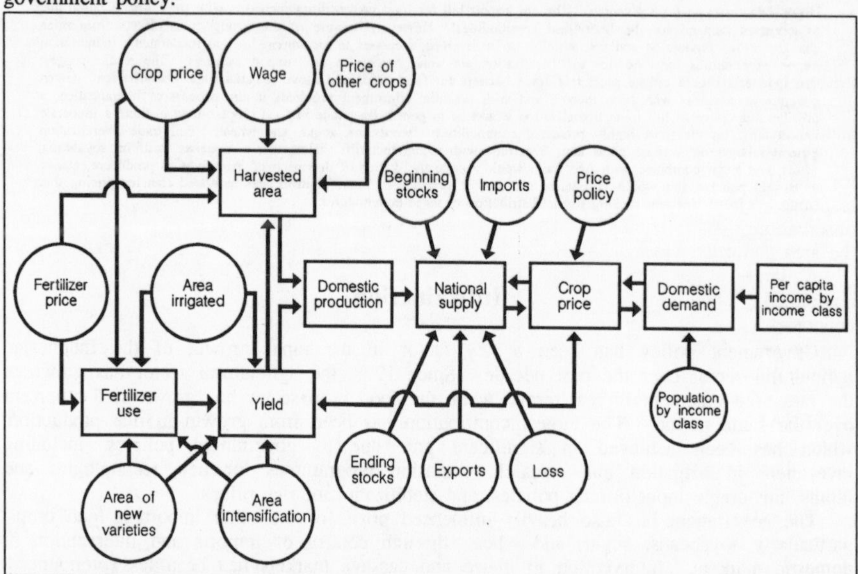

Figure 1—Simplified Structure of the Food Crop Supply/Demand Model

Supply. Total production of five food crops—rice, maize, cassava, soyabeans, and sugar—is determined by fertilizer demand functions, yield response functions, and area response functions estimated for Java and off Java. Fertilizer demand for each crop is estimated as a function of expected crop price, fertilizer price, technology shift variables (such as percentage use of modern varieties, percentage of area irrigated, and percentage of area under intensification programmes) and trend (which represents the effect of unmeasurable technological shift variables). Crop yields are estimated as a function of fertilizer use, technology shift variables, and lagged yield. Area harvested is estimated as a function of expected crop revenues, expected revenues of competing crops, and lagged area. The specification and estimation of the response functions are discussed below.

Demand. Per capita demand for six food crops (including wheat, which is not produced domestically) is estimated as a function of per capita consumption expenditures, own prices of the crops, and prices of complementary and substitute food commodities. Demand functions are estimated for different income classes and regions. Demand functions for maize and soyabean for feed and a demand function for consumption of home maize production are also specified.

Government policy. The impacts of government pricing and investment policies are assessed by specifying the level of investment in irrigation, market intervention policies in support of food crop prices, and government fertilizer subsidies. Under any specified set of policies, area, yield, production, consumption, supply/demand balances, farm revenue, food expenditures, and import expenditures can be projected to the year 2000.

The model can be simulated by fixing import levels and generating market-clearing domestic prices or by fixing domestic prices and generating market-clearing import levels. In determining market clearing prices or imports, Indonesia is treated in the model as a large country in the world rice trade. The world price is, therefore, a function of net Indonesian imports, with the world price increasing as imports increase.

Data and Estimation Procedures

Provincial area, yield, technology, and price data from the Central Bureau of Statistics for 1969-85 were aggregated on a regional basis, including East, Central, and West Java, North Sumatera, other Sumatera, South Sulawesi, other Sulawesi, and other Indonesia. Provincial fertilizer use for total food crops was taken from PUSRI *[reference not provided—eds.]*. Allocation of total fertilizer use to individual crops was based on the annual Survey of Agriculture.

The time series data for the three regions on Java were then pooled, as were the data for the five regions off Java. This procedure permitted estimation of separate supply response relationships on and off Java, while providing for an adequate number of observations for estimation of the functions. Regional dummy variables were included in the area and yield functions, and the functions were estimated using ordinary least squares.

A large number of studies of food demand parameters in Indonesia have been completed. This study, therefore, did not undertake a full-fledged attempt to econometrically estimate a complete set of demand parameters. Instead, the model relies largely on a synthesis of existing studies to develop a set of own- and cross-price and income elasticities for rice, maize, soyabean, cassava, sugar, and wheat.

The elasticities of demand for rice are based on econometric estimates using 1981 SUSENAS *[reference not provided—eds.]* data. These estimates of rice demand parameters from cross-sectional data represent long-run elasticities. The estimated elasticities for rice were thus adjusted downwards to obtain short-run elasticities appropriate for use in the model.

For other crops, already completed demand studies were reviewed (Teklu and Johnson, 1986; and Dixon, 1982). The relationships between rice demand parameters and nonrice demand parameters from these studies were then used to make proportional adjustments from the rice demand parameters to develop estimates of the demand parameters for the other crops. Demand elasticities for all crops are disaggregated by region and income class.

Price Policy for Food Crops

The government has actively intervened in domestic rice markets, maintaining ceiling prices for consumers and farm level floor prices for producers. These have generally been successfully defended through control of imports and domestic open market operations. Rice price policy has resulted in stabilization of domestic prices relative to volatile world prices but has not been highly protective. Between 1972 and 1986, the nominal protection rate was negative in 8 years and positive in 7 years. In 1986, despite historically low world rice prices, the nominal protection rate was only 14 percent.

Intervention in maize and cassava markets has been minimal. Although the government guarantees a floor price for maize, actual farm prices are usually above it. The government occasionally sells domestic or imported maize to dampen seasonal price rises and reduce feed costs. Nominal protection of maize has generally been slightly negative, with domestic prices below world prices. Cassava is essentially freely traded, with domestic prices formed relative to the f.o.b. price to the EC.

Soyabeans have historically enjoyed a high rate of price protection in Indonesia in order to encourage domestic production. From 1984 to 1986, the average nominal protection rate for soyabeans was 40 percent. This policy has tended to shift land from more efficiently produced crops, such as maize and cassava, to soyabeans. Wheat imports and distribution are under the control of BULOG, the national logistics agency, which sells wheat grain to the three existing flour mills at a government-determined "surrender" price and regulates sale of the flour at wholesale to licenced distributors at a fixed price. In addition to controlling the prices of grain to the mills and wholesale prices of flour, BULOG determines the fee structure of mills. The fee structure permits the mills to recover handling and processing costs plus a "reasonable" profit.

In the 1970s and early 1980s, the government's wheat pricing policy generally entailed a substantial subsidy, with BULOG surrendering wheat to the mills at less than the c.i.f. cost of the wheat. In recent years, with the rapid decline in world wheat prices, domestic prices have moved above the world price. In 1985 and 1986, the domestic price of wheat averaged about 20-30 percent above world prices.

The government uses control of domestic production and marketing of sugar and control of imports to fix domestic sugar prices. In addition to area quotas at the farm level, the government has a monopoly on procurement, marketing, and distribution of sugar. BULOG purchases all sugar from mills at government-determined prices, and sets wholesale and retail prices based on the ex-mill price, marketing costs, and "reasonable profit margins" at wholesale and retail levels. This pricing system has been used to protect the sugar industry at rates as high as 200 percent in 1985, and, in 1986, the nominal protection rate was still at 75 percent following devaluation.

Impact of Trade Liberalization

The multimarket food crop demand/supply model was used to examine the impact of trade liberalization for food crops. Key results are presented here for three scenarios: a base run with domestic prices fixed at average 1984-86 levels, so that the structure of protection is maintained; full trade liberalization for the six crops, with prices phased over a five-year period to World Bank projected 1995 world prices; and trade liberalization combined with a 20 percent import tariff on soyabeans, wheat, and sugar. Summary results of the trade liberalization scenarios are compared in Table 1 to base run results. In addition to the effects of liberalization on farm revenue, consumer food expenditures, and net import expenditures for food, the table summarizes the impact on rice production, prices, and imports, because of the importance of these to Indonesian policy makers. Detailed results for the alternative trade liberalization scenarios are presented in Rosegrant *et al.* (1987, chap. 7).

The results summarized in Table 1 show that trade liberalization and the reduction in the domestic price of importable commodities to world price levels generate large gains for consumers, while causing smaller losses for producers. For example, under full trade liberalization for the three crops, consumer expenditures are projected to decline by *Rp*813,000 million in 1995, while farm revenues decline by *Rp*577,000 million. Farm revenues decline because of the drop in farm prices of the importable commodities that are domestically produced. However, these price changes also induce a shift into other crops, particularly maize and cassava, partially offsetting the loss in farm revenue. Production of nonrice crops actually increases due to trade liberalization. Beneficial adjustments in cropping patterns to changes in prices are probably somewhat understated because not all crops are covered in the model. Therefore, the degree to which farm revenues decline due to liberalization may be overstated. Despite this possible overestimation of farm revenue losses, benefits to consumers from trade liberalization are substantially larger than estimated farm revenue losses.

The net import bill for food commodities increases as demand for wheat, sugar, and soyabeans increases and production, particularly of soyabeans, declines. However, because of the substantial cross effects in production and consumption, the increase in the net import trade bill is moderated. The drop in the price of soyabeans, wheat, and sugar, combined with stable cassava prices and slightly increasing maize prices, causes a decline in domestic demand for maize and cassava and boosts their production, generating increased exports,

Table 1—Summary of Key Results from Trade Liberalization Scenarios

	Base Run: Fixed Domestic Prices	Trade Liberalization for Food Crops	Trade Liberalization with 20-percent Import Tariff on Soyabeans, Wheat, and Sugar
1990:			
Domestic wholesale rice price (*Rp*/kg)	348	338	344
Paddy production (1,000 t)	42,543	42,503	42,644
Other crop production (1,000 t)	22,839	23,099	22,938
Rice imports (1,000 t)	125	-44	25
Cost of food imports (*Rp*1,000 million)	930	1,051	972
Net farm revenue (*Rp*1,000 million)	8,655	8,104	8,424
Consumer food expenditures (*Rp*1,000 million)	12,578	11,827	12,303
1995:			
Domestic wholesale rice price (*Rp*/kg)	348	344	349
Paddy production (1,000 t)	47,657	47,331	47,608
Other crop production(1,000 t)	25,951	26,264	26,078
Rice imports (1,000 t)	91	-79	-26
Cost of food imports (*Rp*1,000 million)	1,157	1,363	1,219
Net farm revenue (*Rp*1,000 million)	9,874	9,369	9,724
Consumer food expenditures (*Rp*1,000 million)	14,146	13,390	13,943

which partially offset the direct impact on the import bill. The projected increase in import expenditures for food commodities, at most *Rp*234,000 million in 1995 under full trade liberalization, is less than 1 percent of total Indonesian export earnings.

The impact of trade liberalization on the rice sector is small. The slight initial decline in the price of rice (about 5 percent) due to liberalization, together with the more rapid decline in prices of the other commodities, induces a shift in demand from rice to these commodities, particularly wheat. This causes a slight drop in rice imports, prices, and production, causing, in turn, a partially offsetting recovery in demand for rice. A new equilibrium in the rice market is reached at slightly lower levels of rice prices, production, and consumption.

Conclusions

This paper has briefly presented a multimarket food crop supply/demand model for Indonesia and assessed the impact of food crop trade liberalization using the model. The results indicate that a trade liberalization policy would generate substantial net benefits to society. The government of Indonesia should reduce protective trade barriers for food crops and move towards trade liberalization.

Given government concerns with farm income and with potential adjustment problems in the process of liberalization, a possible alternative to full trade liberalization would be to permit free trade in food crops but to institute a moderate import tariff on soyabeans, wheat, and sugar, which are currently the most highly protected food commodities. As shown in Table 1, a moderate tariff policy results in smaller net gains from trade liberalization, but the negative impact on net farm revenues is also reduced, and the increase in the import bill is slowed. Import tariffs on these commodities also generate significant government revenues through a relatively progressive tax, since consumption of soyabeans, wheat, and sugar is higher among high income groups.

Full trade liberalization generates larger net welfare gains than a policy of free trade with moderate tariffs. However, a moderate tariff on soyabeans, wheat, and sugar, combined with free trade, would reduce the degree of distortion of incentives to producers relative to current policies and would rationalize the current system of import controls and regulated transfer pricing that encourages inefficient rent seeking in the distribution of these commodities.

Note

[1]International Food Policy Research Institute.

References

Dixon, J.A. (1982) *Food Consumption Parameters and Related Demand Parameters in Indonesia: Review of Available Evidence*, Working Paper No. 6, Rice Policies in Southeast Asia Project, International Food Policy Research Institute, Washington, D.C., USA.

Rosegrant, M.W., Kasryno, F., Gonzales, L.A., Rasahan, C., and Saefudin, Y. (1987) "Price and Investment Policies in the Indonesian Food Crop Sector," report submitted to the Asian Development Bank, International Food Policy Research Institute and CAER, Washington, D.C., USA.

Teklu, T., and Johnson, S. (1986) "Preliminary Analysis of Demand Parameters for Indonesia," Iowa State University, Ames, Iowa, USA.

DISCUSSION OPENING—*David W. Skully* (Economic Research Service, US Department of Agriculture)

The secondary effects of liberalizing wheat, soyabean, and sugar trade in Indonesia—substitution in production and consumption—can be significant, as the paper demonstrates with respect to Indonesian rice production and use. Clearly, our understanding of the possible consequences of liberalization is enhanced by models that incorporate off-diagonals.

All of us who are involved in measuring government intervention in agriculture and assessing the impacts of liberalization face some yet unresolved issues. Two of these are tangential to Rosegrant's paper. The first problem is, how does one know if a policy is protectionist? At its inception, Indonesia's wheat policy subsidized millers and consumers; during the base run of this paper, however, world prices were low and millers were paying above the world price for wheat. Does this mean that the policy is protectionist?

Any policy that attenuates variations in world prices could be alternatively protectionist and subsidizing, depending on the border price. If a policy is rule governed (no discretion), one can calculate a mathematical expectation of the producer or consumer bias of the rule for a given distribution of world prices. Such a technique would allow us to distinguish ephemeral protection from essential protection.

A second issue concerns the often favourable terms of payment developing countries face when importing agricultural commodities. Indonesia imports much of its wheat from the USA at below-market credit rates. The foreign exchange opportunity cost of such imports is exceptionally low, and, by this opportunity cost criterion, the Indonesian government would not have difficulty pricing "protectively" in the domestic market (and capturing rent). This issue is pervasive when trying to identify the bias of LDC intervention. If full liberalization occurs among the OECD nations, will such exports still be available?

GENERAL DISCUSSION—*Philippe Burny, Rapporteur* (Faculté des Sciences Agronomiques de l'État, Belgium)

GENERAL DISCUSSION—*Philippe Burny, Rapporteur* (Faculté des Sciences Agronomiques de l'État, Belgium)

The first remark from the floor concerned the projection results. The differences between the three scenarios—fixed domestic prices, trade liberalization, and 20 percent import tariff—were much less important than expected, or so the verbal presentation indicated (effects on domestic prices, on farm income, on consumer expenditures, etc.). In reply, Rosegrant said that was so because the projection results included the cross-commodity effects (e.g., when the price of rice falls, farmers produce more other crops and exports increase, so rice exports decline but other exports increase). Another point concerned the possible regional implications of that trade liberalization. Rosegrant answered that the main shifts could be seen in the production of sugar and cassava.

On the impact of trade liberalization on rural employment, Rosegrant said that it was not a point of particular interest in his study, but that he will attempt to work on it more thoroughly because it is an important consequence. Concerning the way he dealt with the problem (of assuming trade liberalization instead of the fixation of domestic prices) Rosegrant answered that Indonesia has succeeded in achieving self-sufficiency for rice and so a change in policy can occur. One can take agricultural products one by one to see what happens when the usual policy is removed. Rosegrant also added that trade liberalization would avoid high costs within the Ministry of Agriculture (complicated import control).

Participants in the discussion included R.R. Barichello, A. Siamwalla, F. Tarrett, and A. Valdés.

Food Cost and Nutrient Availability in Urban Indonesia: Estimates for Food Policy Analysis

Tesfaye Teklu and Helen H. Jensen[1]

Abstract: Evaluating the effects of economic growth and the effectiveness of targeted government intervention requires identification of target groups and information on food and nutrient consumption patterns. A model of nutrient consumption linked to food choice behaviour is used to evaluate nutrient availability in urban Indonesia. Nutrient demand responses varied significantly across income levels.

Introduction

A recent World Bank (1986) report highlights the problem of undernourishment in low-income countries, where three quarters of the calorie undernourished people live. The report calls for sustained economic growth as a long-term solution, coupled with government intervention to guarantee food security to the most undernourished groups. Yet, several studies show that increases in income in the short run may not be effective ways of improving nutrition of the poor (e.g., Gray, 1982; and Wolfe and Behrman, 1983). Furthermore, the effectiveness of targeted government intervention requires proper identification of the target group and information on food and nutrient consumption patterns, dietary practices, and measures assessing nutritional health. The present study applies a model of nutrient consumption linked to food choice behaviour to evaluate nutrient availability in urban Indonesia and to illustrate the use of estimated nutrient demand parameters in food and nutrition policy analysis.

Several recent studies have analyzed food consumption and dietary practices in Indonesia (e.g., Timmer and Alderman, 1979; Chernichovsky and Meesook, 1984; and Johnson, Teklu, and Jensen, 1987). In these studies, expenditures on food constituted a major component of total household expenditures. Starchy staples, particularly rice, accounted for at least one third of the average food budget. While the diets of the poor were diversified, particularly among staples, the diets of those with more income contained relatively more rice. As income increased, food budget shares decreased and households shifted from consumption of starchy staples to animal products and processed foods. However, shortages of calories, protein, iron, and thiamine were evident for all income groups and regions in Indonesia, especially those in large families and the urban poor.

Chernichovsky and Meesook (1984) estimated income and region-specific nutrient demand elasticities for 11 dietary components specific to nutrient risk groups, using a single-equation, log-linear form. Their study and the earlier work by Timmer and Alderman (1979) showed that nutrient demands were responsive to changes in income, food prices, and demographic variables. The present study builds on this earlier work, with two notable differences. First, the effects of selected variables are estimated in a simultaneous framework, assuming that allocation decisions within households with respect to nutrients are made simultaneously with food choices. Second, the dietary sources of nutrients are more broadly defined: the estimation of food components are neither restricted to those derived from rice, cassava, and maize (Timmer and Alderman, 1979) nor limited to the population at nutritional risk (Chernichovsky and Meesook, 1984). The results are intended to provide additional knowledge on the linkages between socioeconomic variables, food cost, and nutrient consumption. They also provide additional information for anticipating the effects of policy changes across different socioeconomic groups.

Model

The behavioural model that governs the dietary choice problem of a household is based on a direct utility maximization process (Basiotis *et al.*, 1983). A utility function, modified to account for differences in household demographic characteristics, is defined over separable food and nonfood groups. The household maximizes the utility function subject to an income constraint. The optimal food consumption is determined in two stages. In stage one, the household determines its optimal food budget (C_f):

$$(1)\ C_f = C(P, I, Z1),$$

dependent on a vector of commodity prices (*P*), household income (*I*), and household-specific demographic variables (*Z1*). In the second stage, the household allocates the food budget, maximizing the food utility branch within the limits set by the optimal food budget. The solution in stage two gives the demand functions for food commodity *i* (F_i):

$$(2)\ F_i = F_i(P_f, C_f, Z2),\ i = 1, 2, ..., n,$$

conditioned on the vector of food prices (P_f), food cost (C_f), and a vector of demographic variables (Z2).

The optimal bundle of food commodities can be translated into nutrient equivalents using a linear transformation:

$$(3)\ N_j = \Sigma_i\ b_{ji}F_i,\ j = 1, 2, ..., m,$$

where N_j is the level of nutrient type *j* and b_{ji} is the quantity of the *j*th nutrient per unit of commodity *i*. The resulting derived demand functions for nutrients are dependent on food prices, food cost, and household-specific variables that influence the choice of nutrients:

$$(4)\ N_j = N_j(P_f, C_f, Z3).$$

In the empirical application of this model, joint estimation of food cost *(1)* and nutrient demands *(4)* accounts for the presence of the endogenous food cost in the nutrient demand equations. Thus, a two-stage household decision process is hypothesized: first, a choice between food and nonfood groups and, second, choices across foods that are consumed primarily for their nutrient content. An alternative approach would be to estimate food cost and food demand equations *(1)* and *(2)* and translate the estimates into nutrient equivalents using the relationship defined in equation *(3)*.

Data

Data from the 1980 nationwide household survey for Indonesia (SURGASAR) provided demographic characteristics, household expenditures, and food consumption to estimate the model. The data on consumption contained quantities of foods consumed in a household in the week prior to the taking of the survey.

Household consumption of food energy, protein, iron, and thiamine was computed from 96 food items. Results for food energy and protein are reported here.[2] Food cost was measured as the money value of food used from purchases, the household's own inventory, and transfers. The value of total household expenditures, a proxy for income, was set equal to an aggregate of food and nonfood expenditures. Prices for food (rice, vegetables and fruits, and fish and meat) were obtained from constructing geometrically weighted implicit prices at the district level, with households in a district assumed to face similar district level prices. Household composition variables included decomposition of family size into three age-sex categories: number of children under 10, number of adult males, and number of adult females. Other conditioning variables included main occupation and education of household heads.

Results

The parameters of equations *(1)* and *(4)* were estimated using a three-stage least squares procedure, and results are reported in Table 1. First, the food cost equation *(1)* was estimated, conditional on group-specific food prices, total expenditures, and household composition variables. Then, the structural coefficients of the nutrient equations were estimated to measure the marginal effect of the exogenous variables holding food cost fixed. The low values of the standard errors indicate that variables explaining food cost had significant influence on household food budgets. Prices of rice and vegetables and fruits had positive marginal effects; the price of fish and meat had a negative effect. Food cost increased with income but at a decreasing rate. Family size also had a positive effect on food allocation, but the effects varied depending on age and sex of members. Compared with adult females and children under 10 years of age, the marginal effect of additional adult males was relatively stronger.

Table 1—Parameter Estimates of Food Cost and Nutrient Availability for Urban Indonesian Households

Variable	Structural Equation Estimates: Food Cost (1)	Food Energy (2)	Protein (gm) (3)	Derived Reduced Form Estimates: Food Energy (kgal) (4)	Protein (gm) (5)
Intercept	-1,848.71 (731.88)	5,208.49 (736.23)	178.56 (20.72)	4,383.85 (879.44)	149.36 (26.03)
Rice price	9.16 (3.48)	-13.88 (3.46)	-0.44 (0.10)	-9.81 (4.11)	-0.30 (0.12)
Vegetable/ fruit price	1.42 (0.51)	-0.31 (0.51)	-0.05 (0.01)	-0.32 (0.60)	-0.03 (0.02)
Fish/meat price	-0.42 (0.17)	-1.47 (0.17)	-0.6 (0.1)	-1.66 (0.20)	-0.7 (0.1)
Food cost		0.44 (0.01)	0.02 (0.001)		
Income	0.48 (0.01)			0.21 (0.01)	0.01 (0.003)
Income squared	-0.00 (0.00)			-0.00 (0.00)	-0.00 (0.00)
Children under 10	297.37 (41.53)	759.53 (41.68)	14.83 (1.17)	891.59 (48.11)	19.52 (1.47)
Adult males	372.37 (40.81)	1,039.39 (42.01)	19.00 (1.18)	1,204.76 (46.10)	24.88 (1.47)
Adult females	301.02 (41.53)	857.03 (42.44)	17.47 (1.19)	990.71 (46.10)	22.22 (1.49)
Head's occupation		187.91 (92.66)	7.20 (2.60)	187.91 (93.08)	7.20 (2.60)
Education		-143.02 (141.30)	0.72 (3.96)	-143.02 (141.30)	0.72 (3.96)

Note: Standard errors are in parentheses.
Source: 1980 SURGASAR Data.

For the structural coefficients of the nutrient equations (Table 1, columns 2 and 3), food prices had negative marginal effects on the availability of calories and protein, with the rice price having the largest marginal effect. Food cost and family composition variables had a positive effect on consumption of nutrients. Those with at least an elementary school education consumed lower levels of available nutrients, while households in production or related physical occupations had higher levels of available nutrients.

The derived reduced-form coefficients, shown in columns 4 and 5, capture the direct and indirect (via food cost) effects of nutrient conditioning variables. For example, with family composition, both the direct and indirect effects of the respective variables reinforced each other: the marginal effects were larger for each in the long run. Indeed, variations in nutrient consumption due to household composition (age and sex) differences provide an empirical basis for the need for composition-augmented measures of household size.

Elasticity Estimates

Food cost and selected nutrient demand elasticities evaluated at sample means are given in Table 2. The absolute values of all the food cost elasticities were less than one, indicating that aggregate food demands were inelastic with respect to food prices, total expenditures, and family composition variables. Food cost was most sensitive to change in household total expenditures. Among the food prices, food cost was most sensitive to changes in the rice price, reflecting the relative insensitivity of rice demand to its own price. In short, total expenditures (as a proxy for income) followed by the rice price had the most impact on food cost.

Table 2–Food and Selected Nutrient Demand Elasticities under Fixed and Variable Food Cost Hypotheses, Urban Indonesia

Elasticities with Respect to:	Food Cost	Fixed Food Cost: Food Energy	Fixed Food Cost: Protein	Variable Food Cost: Food Energy	Variable Food Cost: Protein
All households:					
Prices:					
Rice price	0.23	-0.32	-0.40	-0.23	-0.24
Vegetable/fruit price	0.05		-0.06		-0.02
Fish/meat price	-0.05	-0.16	-0.25	-0.18	-0.29
Income:					
Income	0.81			0.32	0.58
Food cost		0.40	0.71		
Household size groups:					
Children under 10	0.05	0.12	0.09	0.14	0.13
Adult males	0.09	0.22	0.16	0.26	0.22
Adult females	0.07	0.19	0.15	0.21	0.20
Lowest 40 percent income households:					
Prices:					
Rice price		-0.35	-0.47	-0.25	-0.32
Vegetable/fruit price			-0.06		-0.033
Fish/meat price		-0.17	-0.30	-0.19	-0.33
Expenditures:					
Income				0.19	0.29
Food cost		0.28	0.42		
Household size groups:					
Children under 10		0.17	0.14	0.20	0.18
Adult males		0.26	0.20	0.31	0.27
Adult females		0.22	0.19	0.25	0.24
Highest 20 percent income households:					
Prices:					
Rice price		-0.31	-0.35	-0.22	-0.24
Vegetable/fruit price			-0.05		-0.03
Fish/meat price		-0.15	-0.23	-0.17	-0.26
Expenditures:					
Income				0.48	0.65
Food cost		0.53	0.69		
Household size groups:					
Children under 10		0.07	0.06	0.09	0.07
Adult males		0.19	0.13	0.22	0.17
Adult females		0.17	0.12	0.19	0.16

Source: 1980 SURGASAR Data.

No *a priori* basis exists for predicting the signs of the nutrient demand elasticities. The short-run elasticities, which are based on the structural coefficients holding food cost fixed, are weighted sums of demand elasticities of nutrient-contributing food items; i.e.,

(5) $\varepsilon_{NjX} = \Sigma \alpha_{ji} \varepsilon_{QiX}$,

where ε_{NjX} is the observed elasticity of the *j*th nutrient with respect to a variable *X*, α_{ji} is the share contributed by the *i*th food to total availability of the *j*th nutrient, and ε_{QiX} is the demand elasticity of the *i*th food with respect to the variable *X*. The elasticities based on equation *(5)* are given in Table 2 under the fixed food cost hypothesis. When the simultaneity of food cost and nutrient demands is taken into account, the elasticities are expressed as:

(6) $\eta_{NjX} = \varepsilon_{NjX} + \varepsilon_{NjC}\varepsilon_{CX}$,

where η_{NjX} is the long-run elasticity of the *j*th nutrient with respect to a variable *X*, ε_{NjX} is the elasticity of *j*th nutrient with respect to a variable *X* under the constant food cost assumption *(5)*, ε_{NjC} is the demand elasticity of the *j*th nutrient with respect to food cost, and ε_{CX} is the food cost elasticity with respect to a variable *X*. These elasticities are presented in Table 2 when food costs were allowed to vary. The expressions of equations *(5)* and *(6)* show that nutrient elasticities reflect the combined effects of demand responses of the nutrient-source food items. Food items that are relatively important in contributing to the nutrient availability and have large demand elasticities have a significant influence on levels and signs of nutrient demand elasticities.

Both when food costs were held fixed and otherwise, the price elasticities for calories and protein were negative and less than one; i.e., changes in food prices brought about inverse changes in the quantities of calories and protein and had less than proportionate effects on nutrient consumption. The rice price was relatively more important. The negative price effects of rice and vegetables and fruits on demand for nutrients diminished when households could adjust their food budgets in response to price changes. This is true because the positive effect of these prices on food costs partially offset the negative price effect on nutrient demands.

The estimated expenditure elasticities of calories and protein were all positive and less than one (Table 2). The relatively low calorie elasticity reflects the large share of rice contributing to calories. Rice itself was the least expenditure-responsive food item. Similar to expenditure elasticities, household composition elasticities for nutrients were positive and less than one, with nutrient demands being most sensitive to an addition of adult male members to a household. Calories were more sensitive to changes in household composition than was protein. This partly reflected a shift in food consumption towards basic staple food items for large households. Nutrients derived from these staple foods are likely to show more sensitivity to change in family size and composition.

In order better to understand the income effects and to interpret the results with respect to programme targeting, the elasticities for calories and protein were evaluated at sample means for the lowest 40 and top 20 percent of households in the income distribution (Table 2). Price elasticities showed a decline in absolute value at higher income levels. Even though the differences were small, households at lower income levels appeared to be more sensitive to price effects. Calorie and protein expenditure elasticities also varied significantly at different income levels. High-income households were more sensitive to income change, as indicated by the higher expenditure elasticities, than low-income households. Similar patterns have been observed in studies on Bangladesh (Pitt, 1983) and rural Sierra Leone (Strauss, 1986). Such variations in elasticities reflected a systematic shift in the diet structure, which embodied variations in relative nutrient shares, expenditure elasticities of food components, and costs associated with these nutrient sources. A possible explanation for the Indonesian case may be a shift to income-sensitive calorie and protein sources as households experience improved income levels. These households moved to more nutritious foods.

Implications

The dietary practices of the urban Indonesian households revealed important variations across socioeconomic groups. Dietary components varied in quantity and kind, depending on income, family size, location, and occupation of the household. Increased income was associated with increased levels of consumption and a shift in composition of diets; the variations were conditioned by age and sex composition of the households. Households with low income and/or large families often account for a large proportion of nutrient-risk households.

Evaluation of calorie and protein elasticities by income groups for Indonesia using a simultaneous food decision model indicates several important implications. First, demand responses varied significantly across income levels; low-income consumers were, for example, more sensitive to changes in the rice price than high-income consumers. Food policies based on price parameters can be effectively targeted to income groups.

Contrary to previous findings on Indonesia (Chernichovsky and Meesook, 1984; and Timmer and Alderman, 1979), a positive relationship was evident between nutrient expenditure elasticities and income levels. Income as well as prices had a significant impact on household nutrient consumption; increases in income had a greater impact on available nutrients for those with higher incomes. This implies that programmes designed to change selected commodity prices may be more effective at achieving increased calorie and protein consumption by low-income households than programmes designed to change income. While changing rice prices would have the largest relative impact on available calories and protein, rice pricing policies are less effectively targeted to low-income households because rice is a preferred staple crop across all income groups. Price changes for other commodities may be better pricing policy instruments.

Notes

[1]International Food Policy Research Institute and Iowa State University, respectively. This research was conducted at the Center for Agricultural and Rural Development, Iowa State University, and supported by the Office of Nutrition, US Agency for International Development through the Office of International Cooperation and Development, US Department of Agriculture.

[2]Food items without reported nutrient values and standard quantity measures were excluded, as were foods or meals consumed away from the home.

References

Basiotis, P.P., Brown, M., Johnson, S.R., and Morgan, K.J. (1983) "Nutrient Availability, Food Costs, and Food Stamps," *American Journal of Agricultural Economics*, Vol. 65, pp. 685-693.

Chernichovsky, D., and Meesook, D.A. (1984) *Patterns of Food Consumption and Nutrition in Indonesia*, Staff Working Paper No. 670, World Bank, Washington, D.C., USA.

Gray, C.W. (1982) *Food Consumption Parameters for Brazil and their Application to Food Policy*, Research Report No. 32, International Food Policy Research Institute, Washington, D.C., USA.

Johnson, S.R., Teklu, T., and Jensen, H.H. (1987) "Evaluating Food Policy in Indonesia Using Full Demand Systems," final report submitted to the US Agency for International Development, Center for Agricultural and Rural Development, Iowa State University, Ames, Iowa, USA.

Pitt, M. (1983) "Food Preferences and Nutrition in Rural Bangladesh," *Review of Economics and Statistics*, Vol. 65, pp. 105-114.

Strauss, J. (1986) "Estimating the Determinants of Food Consumption and Caloric Availability in Rural Sierra Leone," in Singh, I., Squire, L., and Strauss, J. (Eds.) *Agricultural Household Models: Extensions, Applications, and Policy*, Johns Hopkins University Press, Baltimore, Md., USA.

Timmer, C.P., and Alderman, H. (1979) "Estimating Consumption Parameters for Food Policy Analysis," *American Journal of Agricultural Economics*, Vol. 61, pp. 982-987.

Wolfe, B.L., and Behrman, J.R. (1983) "Is Income Overrated in Determining Adequate Nutrition?," *Economic Development and Cultural Change*, Vol. 31, pp. 525-549.

World Bank (1986) *Poverty and Hunger...Issues and Options for Food Security in Developing Countries*, Washington, D.C., USA.

DISCUSSION OPENING—*Stephen J. Hiemstra* (Purdue University)

I would like to know more about the type and quality of the data analyzed. We were not given the size of the sample nor an indication of its representativeness. We were told that it was a national survey and that the data came from seven-day recall of household expenditures on food in the previous week. This type of data can be quite reliable, in my experience, but I would like to know more about the way it was collected and the time period spanned in collection. For example, is potential seasonality a problem with the data?

We were told, in a footnote to the paper, that food items without reported nutrient values and standard quantity measures were excluded from the analysis. How many foods were eliminated for these reasons? Rice is not a problem, but the data for starchy vegetables and some fruits may contain serious omissions. We found, for example, in our own study in Liberia, that many foods—vegetables, fruits, cassava, fish, and some meats—were sold in piles or by count rather than by units of weight simply because the villages had no scales. Deriving prices and implied quantities in a meaningful manner for purposes of measuring nutrient content thus becomes difficult. (Further, some of the foods we found did not have known nutrient composition.)

Since prices were derived from cross-sectional expenditure data grouped at the district level, some aggregation problems can be expected. I am surprised that the model avoided a high degree of multicollinearity. Was this problem dealt with? Cross-sectional data yield value weights rather than true prices specified in the theoretical model. Perhaps that is why the three groups selected were significant—they probably had quite different values per pound. How does one interpret the results of a price elasticity of a single commodity, such as rice, for example, on the consumption of total calories. One needs to reorient ones thinking to take account of the importance of the commodity in question in relation to the total consumption of all foods. I would prefer to see price elasticities of a commodity measured with respect to the quantities of that same commodity.

In terms of the findings, I was surprised at the low levels of the elasticities with respect to the household size groups. As I understand them, they should average near 1.0 over the three groups of people, rather than around 0.2, if people at the margin are going to eat anywhere near the average amounts of food.

Finally, I find it hard to rationalize the positive relationships between expenditure elasticities with respect to food energy and protein between the two.

GENERAL DISCUSSION—*Philippe Burny, Rapporteur* (Faculté des Sciences Agronomiques de l'État, Belgium)

In reply to the discussion opener, Jensen said that we can be confident in the data because the sample is large and the representativeness is good. The interviews were seriously undertaken and the questions were clear. However, the problem of seasonality still remains. The prices are aggregated ones.

One participant asked about the decision to study nutrient consumption instead of consumption of the different products. Jensen replied that it is a way to aggregate many commodities. What is important is to know quantities of calories and proteins consumed, whatever commodities they come from.

In conclusion, Jensen pointed out the following findings of the study: (1) low-income households are more sensitive to rice prices than higher income households, and (2) expenditure elasticities increase when income goes up (in fact, a shift from traditional staple foods towards animal products—meat, dairy products—occurs).

Participants in the discussion included I. Soliman.

Computing the Socially Optimal Forest Stock for the Ivory Coast

Simeon K. Ehui and Thomas W. Hertel[1]

Abstract: A two-sector dynamic model is used to determine the optimal steady-state forest stock for the Ivory Coast. The optimal steady-state forest stock is shown to be most sensitive to changes in the discount rate and the expected technological change. When agricultural technology is assumed to be stagnant, the forest stock is not completely exhausted in the optimal steady-state situation. However, with continual technological change, eventually clearing all the forest lands is optimal.

Introduction

In spite of widespread concern about deforestation in the tropics, little formal analysis of the socially optimal allocation of land between forest and agricultural use is available. This is compounded by a lack of knowledge about the relationship between deforestation, erosion, and productivity in tropical soils. This paper uses an optimal control model to estimate the optimal steady-state forest stock for the Ivory Coast, which currently has the highest rate of deforestation in the world (300,000 ha or 6.5 percent per year) (Bertrand, 1983; OTA, 1984; Allen and Barnes, 1985; and Bene *et al.*, 1977). By "mining" its forest resources, the Ivory Coast has achieved the fastest agricultural growth rate (5 percent per year) in sub-Saharan Africa (Spears, 1986).

The theoretical framework for this paper is outlined in the next section. It is followed by the specification of a quadratic agricultural yield function. The optimal steady-state forest stock is derived, and comparative static results regarding the impacts of prices, the social rate of discount, and technology are developed. This is followed by numerical estimates of optimal steady-state forest stocks for the Ivory Coast under a variety of scenarios. The paper closes with a summary and some concluding qualifications and comments.

Analytical Framework

This section presents a theoretical model for optimal control of forest lands in the tropics. The social objective is assumed to be to maximize the utility derived from aggregate profit, subject to changes in forest stocks over time. Both forested and deforested lands are considered as a source of future profits, and this relationship is a nonlinear one that highlights the interplay between deforestation and agricultural productivity.

Formally, the control problem, over an infinite horizon, is stated as follows:

(1) $\max_{F_t, D_t} W = \int_0^\infty e^{-\delta t}[V(\pi_t)]dt$, subject to:

(2) $\pi_t = P_{Ft}F_t + (L-F_t)(P_{At})Z(D_t, F_0-F_t, X_t) - P_{Xt}X_t,$

(3) $\dot{F}_t = -D_t = 0$, if $F_t = 0$,

(4) $F_t, D_t, X_t \geq 0$, and

(5) $F_0 = \bar{F}_0, L = \bar{L}.$

Here, W is a measure of the present value of society's welfare; δ is the social rate of discount and thus provides an indication of how future-generation welfare is discounted; $V(\cdot)$ is a twice differentiable instantaneous utility function depending on aggregate profit, π_t;

profit is equal to the sum of net returns in both agriculture and forestry [equation *(2)*]; L represents total arable land; and F_t represents the land area covered by forest at time t (i.e., the forest "stock," in hectares). Thus L-F_t represents total land area devoted to agriculture at time t.

$Z(\cdot)$ is a concave aggregate agricultural yield function and is assumed to depend on current period purchased inputs, X_t, the current rate of deforestation, D_t, and the cumulative amount of deforested lands, F_0-F_t. Average yield is assumed to be increasing in purchased inputs and current period deforestation. The latter effect is attributable to the nutrient content of the ash left after burning the forests (Cordero, 1984; and Sanchez, 1981). Yield is assumed to decline with increases in cumulative deforestation. This is because of productivity losses due to increased erosion and leaching of nutrients (Sanchez, 1981; and Lal, 1981 and 1985).

The variables P_{At} and P_{Ft} are used to denote per-kilogram returns to agriculture and per-hectare returns to forestry at time t. P_{Xt} is the per-kilogram cost of purchased inputs. These are assumed to be exogenously determined in the international marketplace. Constraint *(3)* describes the changes in forest "stock" over time. It also dictates that if, over some interval, F_t equals zero, then the rate of deforestation must be constrained so that $\dot{F}_t$ equals zero over that interval as well.[2] Constraint *(4)* is the nonnegativity conditions on D_t, F_t, and X_t. Finally, constraint *(5)* defines the initial endowment of forest lands and the total arable land available at time equals zero.

Defining $V[\pi(X, D, F)]$ as equal to $U(X, D, F)$, the current value Hamiltonian associated with the control problem described by *(1)*-*(5)* is given by:[3]

$$(6)\ H(D, F, X, 4) = U(D, F, X) - \psi D,$$

where ψ is the current value costate variable associated with the equation of motion *(3)*. Assuming an interior solution the maximum principle requires that the following hold:

$$(7)\ 0 = U_X = U_\pi(L\text{-}F)(P_AZ_X\text{-}P_X),$$

$$(8)\ \psi = U_D = U_\pi[P_AZ_D(L\text{-}F)],$$

$$(9)\ \delta\psi - \dot{\psi} = U_F = U_\pi[P_F + P_AZ_F(L\text{-}F)\text{-}P_AZ + P_XX], \text{ and}$$

$$(10)\ \lim_{t\to\infty} e^{-\delta t}\,\psi_tF_t = 0.$$

Equation *(7)* indicates that, at the optimum, purchased inputs are applied up to the point where their marginal utility (or profitability) is zero. Equation *(8)* indicates that, at any point in time, the rate of deforestation should be chosen so that the marginal utility of deforestation (U_D) is equal to the efficiency price of the forest stock (ψ). Here, ψ measures the future benefit foregone by a decision to deforest today.

Equation *(9)* implies that forest stock services should be employed up to the point where the marginal utility of forest capital is equal to the social cost of this capital. The right-hand side of *(9)* represents the marginal utility of forest stock. It is composed of two parts, the direct marginal contribution of forestry ($U_\pi P_F$) and the indirect marginal contribution of the forest stock through its effect on agricultural productivity. The latter has two components. The first, $U_\pi P_AZ_F(L\text{-}F)$, captures enhanced agricultural yields due to increased forest cover. The second component, $U_\pi(\text{-}P_AZ + P_XX)$, measures the net cost of not having an additional unit of land in agriculture. The left-hand side of *(9)* measures the cost of employing the services of one unit of the forest capital at any point in time. It includes both an interest charge ($\delta\psi$) and a capital gains term ($-\dot{\psi}$). Finally, equation *(10)* is the transversality condition.

Totally differentiating *(8)* with respect to time and combining this result with *(9)* and *(7)* yields an expression for the time rate of change in the rate of deforestation along the optimal path:

$$(11)\ \dot{D} = [(U_{XX})/(U_{XX}U_{DD}-U_{DX}^2)]\{-\delta U_D+[U_F-D(U_{DF}-\alpha U_{XF})]\},$$

where α equals U_{DX}/U_{XX}. The sign of $\dot{D}$ along the optimal path is determined by the following condition:

$$(12)\ \dot{D} \gtreqless 0,\ as\ \delta^{-1}[U_F-D(U_{DF}-\alpha U_{XF})] \gtreqless U_D.$$

Recall that U_D is the marginal utility of deforestation in current periods. A large value of U_D indicates a large agricultural yield response from current period deforestation. This in turn translates into a higher marginal utility due to increased profit. This is a one-time only effect and may be identified as the deforestation motive.

The term in brackets ($[\cdot]$) represents the difference between the marginal contribution of forest area to utility and any indirect interactions between the forest stock, the productivity of purchased inputs, and the rate of deforestation. Along the optimal path, this may be defined as the *net* marginal utility of forests. The latter lingers into perpetuity and has a present value equal to $\delta^{-1}[\cdot]$. This term can be described as the conservation motive. This stems from valuing forest lands not only for their potential agricultural productivity but also as a source of future income (increased income from forestry plus increased agricultural yields from preventing erosion). Thus, condition *(12)* states that the rate of deforestation falls over time[4] if the conservation motive is weaker than the preference for current deforestation.

In the steady state, the net deforestation rate is necessarily zero. Setting $\dot{F}$ equal to $\dot{D}$ equal to zero in equation *(11)*, a steady-state forest stock (F^*) exists that is uniquely defined by:

$$(13)\ (1/\delta)[U_F(D^*, F^*, X^*)] = U_D(D^*, F^*, X^*),\ \text{and}$$

$$(14)\ D^* = 0.$$

The left-hand side of equation *(13)* can be described as the present value of the stream of marginal utility derived from sustainable economic rents. The right-hand side is the marginal utility of current deforestation. Thus, equation *(13)* asserts that, in the steady state, the marginal utility of further deforestation (U_D) must equal the present value of the foregone marginal future benefit $[(1/\delta)/U_F]$.

Specification of the Yield Function and Steady-State Implications

Equation *(13)* is implicit in F^*. In order actually to solve for the steady-state forest stock, a parametric form for the aggregate yield function is necessary. Since second-order derivatives of the yield function are key to the analysis, a quadratic functional form was chosen:

$$(15)\ Z_t = \beta_0 + \beta_1 X_t + \beta_2 D_t + \beta_3(F_0-F_t) + \beta_4 TR + (\beta_{11}X_t^2)/2 + (\beta_{22}D_t^2)/2 + \beta_{12}D_tX_t.$$

Note that *(15)* is not a complete second-order approximation to $Z(X,D,F)$. Important interaction terms are chosen based on agronomic evidence. A fairly short time series of data is also a constraint. As a result, measurement of the interaction effects between forest stock and the variables X_t and D_t was not attempted. Also, the squared term $(F_0-F_t)^2$ was omitted.[5] The interaction term between X_t and D_t is included because the current period deforestation is analogous to a good dose of fertilizer (Sanchez, 1981).

Based on assumptions about the yield function, the following signs are expected for the parameters in *(15)*: β_0, β_1, $\beta_2 \geq 0$; β_3, β_{11}, β_{22}, and $\beta_{12} \leq 0$. In addition, for nonzero values of D_t and X_t, the following are expected: $(\beta_1+\beta_{11}X_t+\beta_{12}D_t) \geq 0$ and $(\beta_2+\beta_{12}X_t+\beta_{22}D_t) \geq 0$. A time trend, TR, is used as a proxy for technological change. The associated coefficient (β_4) is expected to be positive.

Steady-State Comparative Statics

Using equations *(13)*, *(14)*, and *(15)*, one can now solve analytically for the optimal steady-state forest stock level. Assuming that the discount rate is positive and bounded, the expression for the steady-state forest stock is given by the following:

(16) $F^* = \bar{F}_0 + \Delta/\mu + (\mu-\beta_3)A/\mu$, where:

(17) $\Delta = \{[\beta_0+\beta_1X^*+(\beta_{11}X^{*2}/2)+\beta_4TR^*]-\bar{P}_XX^*\} - \bar{P}_F$, and

(18) $\mu = \delta(\beta_2+\beta_{12}X^*) + 2\beta_3$.

The level of X^* is determined by equation *(7)*, and is a function of the price of fertilizer relative to food: X^* equals $\beta^{\prime}_{11}(P_X-\beta_1)$. TR^* represents the level of technology expected in steady state. The parameter A in *(16)* equals $\bar{L}$ minus $\bar{F}_0$, and this denotes the amount of arable land not under forest cover at time t equals zero. $\bar{P}_X$ and $\bar{P}_F$ are the price of purchased inputs and per-hectare forest returns, relative to the price of agricultural output; i.e., $\bar{P}_X$ equals P_X/P_A, and $\bar{P}_F$ equals P_X/P_A.

The partial derivatives of F^* with respect to P_X and P_F are positive:

(19) $\partial F^*/\partial\bar{P}_X = -X^*/\mu > 0$, and $\partial F^*/\partial\bar{P}_F = -1/\mu > 0$.

That is, an increase in the relative profitability of forestry, brought about either by an increase in agricultural costs or by an increase in forestry returns, leads to an increase in F^*.[6]

Steady-state comparative static results may also be obtained for changes in the social discount rate:

(20) $\partial F^*/\partial\delta = [(\beta_3A-\Delta)/\mu^2](\beta_2+\beta_{12}X^*) < 0$, *for* $\beta_3A - \Delta < 0$.

Equation *(20)* indicates that a higher social discount rate lowers F^* as long as modified agricultural returns exceed per-hectare returns for forestry by less than the value of the stock effect on arable land available at t equals zero.[7]

Finally, the effect of the expected level of technology on steady-state forest stock level can be assessed. Partial differentiation of F^* with respect to TR^* yields:

(21) $\partial F^*/\partial TR^* = \beta_4/\mu < 0$.

This result indicates that the higher the expected level of technology, the lower the steady-state forest stock. This is because technological progress raises returns to agriculture. In other words, improved technology can offset the loss in productivity due to leaching of nutrients and erosion associated with diminished forest cover.

Empirical Results

Ehui (1987) reports results from estimation of an aggregate agricultural yield function for the Ivory Coast. His estimated equation is repeated here (t-statistics in parentheses):

$$(22)\quad Z_t = \underset{(2.863)}{109.713} + \underset{(3.952)}{9.92\, X_t} + \underset{(2.606)}{0.36\, D_t} - \underset{(-3.202)}{0.03\, (F_0 - F_t)} - \underset{(-4.024)}{0.322\, (X_t^2/2)} - \underset{(-2.826)}{0.00074\, (D_t^2/2)}$$

$$- \underset{(-1.358)}{0.0037\, X_t D_t} + \underset{(3.57)}{9.12\, TR} + \underset{(2.381)}{9.96\, DUM}$$

$$[R^2 = 0.87,\ F = 9.192,\ \text{and } DW = 1.063]$$

In equation *(22)*, *DUM* designates a (weather-related) dummy variable that takes the value of 1 in 1975 and 1976 and 0 otherwise. Other variables are defined as in the previous manner. As anticipated above, increases in current period deforestation and fertilizer applications both raise yields, but at a decreasing rate. The coefficient on the interaction term between X_t and D_t is also negative, which follows from both serving to increase nutrient availability. The stock effect associated with cumulative deforestation is negative, as expected. This is offset by an exogenous increase in productivity, as measured by the coefficient on the time trend.

Based on 1984 prices and the estimated yield function given by equation *(22)*, the socially optimal steady-state forest stock, F^*, may be computed. Rows 1-8 in Table 1 report the outcomes of a series of simulations where the discount rate and the expected level of technology are each varied. Four discount rates and two different technology "scenarios" are considered. In the first, TR^* is set equal to 20, reflecting the 1985 technology as estimated by equation *(22)*. The alternative scenario is generated by assuming a constant rate of technical change over the next 30 years equal to the rate observed over the last 20 years. Thus, TR^* equals 50, and F^* is based on "predicted" 2015 technology. Neither of these scenarios is likely to be correct. However, they serve to demonstrate the dramatic impact of exogenous technical change on the optimal steady-state forest stock.

Table 1—Optimal Steady-State Forest Stock Levels in the Ivory Coast (in 1,000 ha)*

Row	Discount Rate δ (%)	State of Technology†	Steady-State Forest Stock Levels‡
1	[δ = 3%]	*A*	5553.99
2		*B*	332.57
3	[δ = 7%]	*A*	4278.13
4		*B*	negative
5	[δ = 9%]	*A*	3380.88
6		*B*	negative
7	[δ = 11%]	*A*	2202.38
8		*B*	negative

*The technical parameters used to determine the optimal steady-state forest stock level include total, nonurban arable land (L) (10,900,000 ha) and initial (1985) forest stock level (F_0) (3,400,000 ha). The biological coefficients used are the estimated parameters of equation *(27)*. The optimal fertilizer rate used is X^* (30.68 kg/ha).

†*A* represents the case where technology is constant and set at its 1985 level (TR^* equals 20). *B* represents the case where technology is *expected* to increase steadily between 1985 and 2015 at the rate estimated in equation *(27)*. Thus, TR^* equals 50.

‡All prices are set at their 1984 levels. Gross agricultural returns (P_A) are *CFAF*786.87/kg. This is the ratio of 1984 per-hectare agricultural returns (*CFAF*93,975/ha) divided by the 1984 aggregate yield index. Returns to forestry (P_F) are *CFAF*17,839/ha. All returns are expressed in 1975 *CFA* francs. In 1975, $1 equalled *CFAF*214.

When technology is expected to remain constant at the 1985 level (case *A*), steady-state forest stocks are all positive. When the discount rate (δ) is less than 7 percent, all F^* are greater than $\bar{F}_0$ (3,400,000 ha, the observed 1985 forest stock). In these cases, further deforestation is not optimal. This stands in sharp contrast to the case where technology is set at the projected 2015 level. In this case, *B*, three of the four F^* in Table 1 fall below zero, suggesting that complete exhaustion of the forest stock is optimal.

The sensitivity of F^* to relative prices may be illustrated by employing the steady-state comparative static results *(19)* to calculate the elasticities of F^* with respect to $\bar{P}_F$ and $\bar{P}_X$. Assuming constant (1985) technology and δ equal to 0.05, these elasticities equal 0.09 and 0.005. Thus, F^* is quite insensitive to changes in the prices of fertilizer and net forestry returns, relative to food prices. By contrast, the elasticity of F^* with respect to δ is equal to -0.32.

Summary and Conclusions

This paper has used a two-sector dynamic model to determine the impacts of the social rate of discount, relative agricultural and forestry returns, and expected technology on the optimal steady-state forest stock (F^*) in the Ivory Coast. F^* was shown to be most sensitive to changes in the discount rate (δ) and the rate of expected technological change. Assuming current (1985) technology, F^* exceeds the 1985 forest stock for all values of δ less than 9 percent. Only when δ reaches 9 percent does some further deforestation appear socially optimal. If future technological change in food production can be expected to proceed (exogenously) at the same rate observed in the Ivory Coast over the 1965-85 period, then a very different set of conclusions is reached. For example, if F^* is computed based on expected technology projected for the year 2015 (based on historical rates of technical change), then F^* is less than zero for discount rates above 3 percent. This suggests that complete deforestation may be optimal. This conclusion is based on the assumption that forthcoming technological change is costless. Furthermore, while the model takes into account the external benefits that the forest stock confers on agriculture, it does not include any other positive externalities, such as preservation of genetic diversity and climatic benefits.

Notes

[1]International Institute of Tropical Agriculture; and Department of Agricultural Economics, Purdue University; respectively. The authors wish to acknowledge the funding of this research by the US Department of Agriculture and the Ivory Coast Research Center for Economic and Social Sciences (CIRES, Abidjan). Jim Binkley, Wade Brorsen, and Sheng Hu provided valuable comments on an earlier draft of this paper.

[2]See Arrow and Kurz (1977, p. 41) for more details.

[3]Time subscripts have been omitted in order to simplify notation.

[4]$\dot{D}$ is less than zero so that the deforestation rate is higher in current periods relative to the future.

[5]Ehui (1987) explores the theoretical implications of incorporating these variables in the aggregate yield function.

[6]μ *must* be negative to be assured of finding a point of maximum welfare (Ehui, 1987).

[7]This must always be the case when F^* is less than $\bar{F}_0$.

References

Allen, J.C., and Barnes, D.F. (1985) "Causes of Deforestation in Developing Countries," *Annals of the Association of American Geographers*, Vol. 75, No. 2, pp. 163-184.

Arrow, K., and Kurz, M. (1977) *Public Investment, Rate of Return, and Optimal Fiscal Policy*, Johns Hopkins University Press, Baltimore, Md., USA.

Bene, J.G., Beall, H.W., and Cote, A. (1977) "Trees, Food and People: Land Management in the Tropics," International Development Research Centre, Ottawa, Canada.

Bertrand, A. (1983) "Déforestation en Zone de Forêt en Côte d'Ivoire," *Revue Bois et Forêts des Tropiques*, No. 202, pp. 3-17.

Cordero, A. (1984) "Effects of Land Clearing on Soil Fertility in the Tropical Region of Santa Cruz, Bolivia," MS thesis, University of Florida, Gainesville, Fla., USA.

Ehui, S.K. (1987) "Deforestation, Soil Dynamics, and Agricultural Development in the Tropics," PhD dissertation, Purdue University, West Lafayette, Ind., USA.

Lal, R. (1981) "Clearing a Tropical Forest II: Effects on Crop Performance," *Field Crops Research*, Vol. 4, pp. 345-354.

Lal, R. (1985) "Soil Erosion and Its Relation to Productivity in Tropical Soils," *Soil Erosion and Conservation*, pp. 237-247.

OTA (Office of Technology Assessment) (1984) *Technologies to Sustain Tropical Forest Resources*, US Congress, Washington, D.C., USA.

Sanchez, P. (1981) "Soils of the Humid Tropics," in *Blowing in the Wind: Deforestation and Long-Range Implications*, Studies in Third World Societies, Publication No. 14, Department of Anthropology, College of William and Mary, Williamsburg, Va., USA.

Spears, J. (1986) "Côte d'Ivoire," Forest Subsector Discussion Paper, Key Forest Policy Issues for the Coming Decade in the Rain Forest Zone, World Bank, Washington, D.C., USA.

DISCUSSION OPENING—*Ernst-August Nuppenau* (Department of Agricultural Economics, University of Kiel)

These two authors are concerned with the interesting and broadly discussed question of deforestation in developing countries. They have presented us with a good introduction to the formal analysis of the complex problem of an intertemporal forest stock reduction policy. Of course, the socially optimal forest stock policy could, under certain conditions, involve negative deforestation (reforestation), as the authors compute. As is often the case, though, the formal and systematic treatment of this problem and the development of a preliminary solution also give rise to a range of further questions and possible modifications to the analysis that deserve consideration. However, before I discuss some of these issues, I would like to mention two shortcomings. First, I believe that there should be a δ in front of F_t in equation *(10)*. Second, the authors do not state which time period they used in their estimation. The empirical investigation needs some more attention in general. The authors estimate a linear relationship between yield per hectare and various variables, especially deforestation embodied in $F_0 - F_t$. This relationship may hold for a certain period and range of existing deforestation. This raises the question of whether it is equally valid in more extreme situations; e.g., given nearly total deforestation. Similarly, is the functional relationship correctly specified? I suspect that deforestation might have a long-term effect on soil fertility. Perhaps a long-term decrease in soil fertility could be considered by introduction of a lagged yield variable in the model. This would, however, make the analysis more complicated.

The part of the model that deals with forestation could also be made more complex and perhaps more realistic. The existing model seems biased towards agriculture. First, in contrast to agriculture, forest production is a multiperiod biological process of an addition to stocks in biomass, which requires an adequate formulation. Second, how can one model an increase in forest if an optimal forest policy needs time for implementation. Perhaps a well-designed forest policy could provide better yields when cropping on tropical soils.

At least one further factor could be integrated in the model: population growth. This problem and its consequences for a policy recommendation concerning deforestation have been neglected in the model, which assumes constant prices for agricultural products.

Despite these suggestions, the approach chosen can incorporate all these points at the cost of increased complexity. This reduced mathematical simplicity might in turn make dialogue between researchers and public authorities more difficult. On the other hand, this increased complexity would allow the model to include factors that are important to policy makers.

GENERAL DISCUSSION—*T. Haque* (Indian Agricultural Research Institute)

The main issues raised on this paper concerned: (1) specification of variables selecting yield and other independent variables, (2) the use of the adopted linear model as a policy tool, (3) the time period required to implement the optimal forest policy, and (4) given the use of so many (immeasurable) utility functions, the practical applicability of the model used in policy decision making.

The authors felt that they were analyzing the policy implications of their model through a further study, which may be more revealing. They also mentioned that the time needed to implement the optimal forest policy may be infinite. The authors were of the opinion that, instead of a linear model, a quadratic model could give better results.

Participants in the discussion included M. Schiff and P. Thompson.

International Risk Management: Optimal Hedging for the Government Export Agency in the Ivory Coast

Gboroton F. Sarassoro and Raymond M. Leuthold[1]

Abstract: A risk management model based on portfolio theory, which accounts jointly for price, quantity, interest rate, and exchange rate risks, is developed and applied to cocoa and coffee production and exports in the Ivory Coast. Using commodity and financial futures markets jointly, the results show that a government export agency can reduce risks from 27 to 86 percent by following a multicommodity hedging programme. The model and technique developed are applicable to many international risk management situations.

Introduction

Economic development in a number of countries depends heavily on the export sector. This is particularly true for developing countries where the export sector usually represents a substantial part of the economy. Fluctuations in the export revenues of these countries may cause adverse effects on the economy as the whole. To guard against these effects, most developing countries have taken steps to stabilize their export proceeds by acting at two levels. First, at the domestic level, these countries have isolated farmers from fluctuations in the world markets by guaranteeing them fixed prices for their products. Second, these countries have acted at the international level in concert with other countries to reduce world price fluctuations. This second effort has consisted mainly of managing buffer stocks and/or allocating export quotas to maintain world prices within agreed on ranges.

The stabilization efforts at the domestic level have been, for the most part, effective (Denis, 1982; and Blandford, 1974), but, at the international level, they have been less successful. Factors cited as difficulties encountered by many international stabilization schemes range from the inability of the producing and consuming countries to reach agreements on export quotas and price ranges (MacBean, 1966; and Ernst, 1982) to more fundamental economic ones. For example, Newbery and Stiglitz (1981) argue that the effectiveness of these schemes is limited because they do not take into account existing stabilization tools such as the futures markets. In addition, these schemes fail to incorporate two major sources of export revenue fluctuations, exchange rate and interest rate variations.

The objective of this paper is to present a risk management model, based on modern risk management concepts, which takes into account not only price and quantity risks but also interest rate and exchange rate risks. Specifically, this paper uses portfolio theory to demonstrate how the futures markets can be used to manage simultaneously quantity, price, interest rate, and exchange rate risks associated with the marketing of cocoa and coffee by the Ivory Coast. The approach developed here can be applied to many international trading situations.

Revenue Risks from Ivory Coast Exports

In the Ivory Coast, cocoa and coffee are the two major export crops, despite the diversification policy promoted by the government since the 1960s. About 60 percent of the total export revenue is generated by the sale of these two commodities. Fluctuations in cocoa and coffee export proceeds can be detrimental to Ivory Coast's economy. To protect farmers against world price fluctuations, the government, through its marketing agency (Caisse), guarantees farmers a fixed price at the start of each season. Caisse, which does not take physical possession of the products, regulates the actions of private exporters who buy the commodities from the farmers at the guaranteed price and sells them in the world market. These private exporters are also guaranteed a fixed price, which reflects the cost of transporting and handling the commodities from the farm gate to the ports. Any positive margin between the world price and the exporter fixed price is collected by Caisse. When the margin is negative, Caisse pays the difference to the exporters. Over the years, the typical situation has been for the world price to be higher than the domestic price (Delaporte, 1976). The margin collected by Caisse can be invested in the international financial market or used to finance development projects. In the 1985 government investment budget, the receipts from Caisse represented about 19 percent of total receipts and 30 percent of total domestic receipts. The revenue generated by Caisse depends on the quantity of cocoa and coffee produced, the world cocoa and coffee prices, the interest rate in international financial markets, and the exchange rate between the US dollar and the CFA franc. Most of the world cocoa and coffee transactions are in US dollars or dollar-related currencies.

Over the years, cocoa and coffee production in the Ivory Coast have fluctuated widely. For example, from 1975 to 1986, their coefficients of variation were 36 and 26 percent, respectively. During the same period, world cocoa and coffee prices varied an average of 54 and 53 percent around their respective means. Similarly, the US dollar/CFA franc exchange rate and US interest rate had coefficients of variation of 30 and 36 percent, respectively.

Hedging Model

Portfolio theory, as developed by Markowitz (1952) and applied to hedging in the futures market by Johnson (1960) and Stein (1961), is the basis of the risk management model presented here. The Johnson-Stein minimum variance hedge ratio model was expanded by Rolfo (1980) to an optimal hedge ratio based on utility maximization, which includes a speculative component along with the minimum variance ratio. Rolfo applied this framework to cocoa exporting countries, including the Ivory Coast. Anderson and Danthine (1980) expanded the framework to multiple risks and showed specifically the speculative and the pure hedge components of optimal hedges. A model similar to the Anderson and Danthine paradigm is outlined here, with the goal to apply it empirically.

Using the mean-variance framework, the objective of Caisse is assumed to be to maximize expected revenue subject to a certain level of risk, where risk is measured by the variance of the revenue. The objective function to be maximized can be formalized as follows:

$$(1)\ \Omega = E_t(Y_{t-1}) - \delta V_t(Y),$$

where, Y_{t+1} is the revenue in period $t + 1$, E_t is the expectation operator, V_t is the variance operator, and δ is the risk aversion parameter ($\delta \geq 0$).

The revenue in $t + 1$ is a function of the action undertaken by Caisse before harvest and at harvest, both in the cash and the futures markets. At harvest, Caisse, through private exporters, buys quantities Q_{cc} and Q_{co} of cocoa and coffee at fixed domestic prices P^d_{cc} and P^d_{co}, respectively. These quantities are sold in the world markets at prices $P_{cc}X$ and $P_{co}X$, respectively (the dollar prices are converted back to CFA francs by exchange rate X). The proceeds are then invested at a one-period rate of interest r. The total revenue of the cash cocoa and coffee activities are designated as R_{cc} and R_{co}, respectively.

Before harvest, Caisse sells a quantity H_{cc} and H_{co} of cocoa and coffee forward in the futures market at price f^t_{cc} and f^t_{co}, respectively. At harvest, Caisse buys back these quantities at price f^{t+1}_{cc} and f^{t+1}_{co}, respectively. In local currency, the returns from these activities in the cocoa and coffee futures markets are R^f_{cc} and R^f_{co}, respectively.

Before harvest, Caisse also sells quantity C of foreign currency futures at price X^t_f to be bought back at time $t + 1$ at price X^{t+1}_f. The return from this action is R^f_c.

Before harvest, Caisse buys quantity I of futures contracts at futures interest rates paying a rate r^t_f to be sold back at harvest $t + 1$ at rate r^{t+1}_f. The return from this investment is R^f_r.

In the risk management context, the unknowns to be solved by Caisse are the levels of the commodity hedges, H_{cc} and H_{co}, the amount of currency hedge, C, and the level of interest rate hedge, I.

The net income generated by Caisse is:

$$(2)\ Y_{t+1} = K'R,$$

where K is a (6×1) vector of ones and futures positions, $K' = [1\ 1\ H_{cc}\ H_{co}\ C\ I]$; and R is a (6×1) vector of cash and futures returns, $R' = [R_{cc}\ R_{co}\ R^f_{cc}\ R^f_{co}\ R^f_c\ R^f_r]$.

The objective function (1) becomes:

$$(3)\ \Omega = K'E(R) - \delta[K'RR'K].$$

The above function is concave; consequently, the maximum is obtained at point where the first derivatives with respect to H_{cc}, H_{co}, C, and I are equal to zero. Following the derivatives in Sarassoro (1988), the optimal hedges are given by the following equation:

$$(4)\ K_1 = P^{-1}[(1/\delta E)(R_1)-S],$$

where $K_1' = [H_{cc}\ H_{co}\ C\ I]$; $P = [a_{ij}]$ $(i=3,\ 6$ and $j=3,\ 6)$ is a (4×4) matrix of simple regression coefficients of i on j, where $i = j = 1,\ 6$ represent R_{cc}, R_{co}, R^f_{cc}, R^f_{co}, R^f_c, and R^f_r, respectively; $R_1' = [R^f_{cc}\ R^f_{co}\ R^f_c\ R^f_r]$; and $S = [a_{i1} + a_{i2}],\ i = 3,\ 6$.

Equation (4) will be used to estimate the optimal hedges for H_{cc}, H_{co}, C, and I for selected values of the risk parameter δ in the interval 10^{-5} to 10^5, where 10^{-5} indicates very low risk aversion and 10^5 signifies high risk aversion. For highly risk averse decision makers or when δ is large, the optimal hedge coincides with the risk minimization strategy. Consequently, the proportion of risk reduction, $e = [1\text{-}var(Y_h)]/[var(Y_u)]$, due to hedging can be used to evaluate the hedging strategy. $Var(Y_h)$ and $var(Y_u)$ are the variance of the hedged and the unhedged portfolios, respectively.

Empirical Findings

Cocoa and coffee are harvested continuously from October to September of the following year, with the bulk of the harvested occurring from December to March. In this paper, the cocoa and coffee seasons are divided into the four periods: October-December, January-March, April-June, and July-September.

The optimal hedging strategy proposed here assumes that just before each period (in September, December, March, and June), Caisse take a position in the cocoa, coffee, currency, and interest rate futures markets, to be reversed at the end of the period (December, March, June, and September) when the cash commodities are sold in the spot markets and the proceeds invested. No futures market exists for the CFA franc, and the French franc, to which the CFA franc is tied, has no active futures market. Consequently, an alternative futures currency, the pound sterling, is used to cross hedge the CFA franc.

The basic data needed to calculate the commodity and financial optimal hedges are the monthly average futures prices for those months futures contracts are bought and sold and the total quantities of cocoa and coffee exported by the Ivory Coast during the quarter. The US 90-day Treasury bill futures is used to hedge the interest rate risk. The proceeds are invested in three-month Treasury bills. Finally, the domestic prices for cocoa and coffee are fixed for each year. This analysis covers the period from 1976 to 1986.

Table 1 gives the ratios of the futures returns to their respective variances for the four periods being studied. In most cases (except for the currency futures returns), these ratios are close to zero, suggesting that little speculative opportunity exists.

Actual estimation of the optimal hedge for values of δ varying from 10^{-5} to 10^5 show that the optimal hedges do not vary significantly. Consequently, only the results corresponding to the risk minimization strategy ($\delta = 10^{-5}$) are reported. The hedging model can then be evaluated using the hedging efficiency criteria, $e = [1\text{-}var(Y_h)]/[var(Y_u)]$.

Table 1–Ratios of the Expected Futures Returns to Variances for the Cocoa, Coffee, Currency, and Interest Rate Futures Markets

	Cocoa	Coffee	Currency	Interest Rate
Dec.-Mar.	1.86×10^{-6}	-2.94×10^{-6}	5.39	-0.007
Mar.-June	-0.16×10^{-6}	2.02×10^{-7}	1.23	-0.28
June-Sept.	-1.25×10^{-7}	1.53×10^{-7}	-1.18	0.09
Sept.-Dec.	1×10^{-6}	-11×10^{-7}	-1.18	-0.0039

Table 2 reports the optimal cocoa, coffee, currency, and interest rate hedge ratios and the proportion of total risk eliminated by the hedging strategy. The hedge ratios range from buying futures contracts larger than the cash position (currency in September-December) to small futures positions (coffee in September-December) to selling more futures positions (coffee in September-December) to selling more futures contracts than the size of the cash position (cocoa in June-September). Most importantly, the hedging effectiveness column indicates that the commodity and financial futures markets are useful risk management tools, since Caisse can reduce between 27 and 87 percent of the risk associated with cocoa and coffee export revenue. These represent substantial reductions in risks.

Table 2–Optimal Commodity and Financial Hedge Ratios and Hedging Effectiveness (in percent)

	- - - - -	Optimal Hedges	- - - - -		
	Cocoa	Coffee	Currency	Interest Rate	Hedging Effectiveness
Sept.-Dec.	111	8	-491	127	67
Dec.-Mar.	68	-54	275	-147	26
Mar.-June	17	-234	75	135	85
June-Sept.	301	17	51	-10	47

Several observations can be drawn from the above results. First, across the four quarters, the average risk reduction is 56 percent, which is noteworthy. The results obtained in this analysis also suggest that, contrary to traditional hedging theory, taking futures positions greater and smaller than the cash position may be consistent with optimal hedging decisions. Sometimes these results show the futures position to be on the same side rather than the opposite side of the cash position. Gemmill (1980) found that long positions in futures were consistent with risk minimization. Also, Rolfo (1980) found that, for low risk aversion, long positions in the futures were optimal.

Second, considerable variability exists in the hedge positions from quarter to quarter. This means that a government agency needs to be flexible in establishing futures positions and willing to alter them in the next quarter. This need for flexibility may suggest why many stabilization schemes fail where countries are locked into specific trading scenarios for a whole year.

Third, some of the results of this paper may be difficult to implement because political leaders in many developing countries believe that participation in futures markets is speculation. Therefore, one may have difficulty convincing the decision makers at Caisse to take futures positions at all, let alone futures positions that are greater than the cash positions. Consequently, upper and lower bounds corresponding to the expected cash position and zero, respectively, can be put on the different hedges. For example, when the hedge is found to be negative, set it equal to zero. Similarly, a futures position greater than the corresponding expected cash position is set to that expected cash position. Experimentation with this constrained risk minimization strategy reduced the hedging effectiveness for all four periods on average from 56 percent to 28 percent, making these results, based on constrained trading positions, less interesting and less appealing.

Conclusion

This paper demonstrates how a marketing agency faced with multiple (quantity, price exchange rate, and interest rate) international risks may use commodity and futures markets jointly as management tools. In particular, this paper develops a multicommodity hedging model based on portfolio theory and applies it to Ivory Coast cocoa and coffee exports.

When the average of past returns is used as an expectation model, the cocoa, coffee, pound sterling, and three-month US Treasury bill futures markets offer little speculative opportunity. However, when the objective of the decision maker is to minimize risk, the cocoa, coffee, exchange rate, and interest rate futures markets provide substantial risk reduction opportunity. In particular, Ivory Coast's government export agency may reduce 27 to 86 percent of the risk it faces in marketing cocoa and coffee. The futures positions have considerable range, and, on occasion, risk minimization would require futures positions greater than the expected cash positions and on the same side as the cash positions. A policy using such trading strategies may be politically difficult to implement in many developing countries; however, this study demonstrates the potential for substantial risk reduction when managing several risks simultaneously.

Note

[1]Department of Agricultural Economics, University of Illinois, Urbana-Champaign.

References

Anderson, R.W., and Danthine, J.P. (1980) "Hedging and Joint Production: Theory and Illustration," *Journal of Finance*, Vol. 35, pp. 487-498.

Blandford, D. (1974) "Analysis of Buffer Fund Price Stabilization by Export Monopoly Marketing Agencies in Developing Countries," *Journal of Agricultural Economics*, Vol. 25, pp. 37-62.

Delaporte, G. (1976) "Caisse de Stabilization et de Soutien des Prix des Produits Agricoles: Vingt Années au Service du Planteur et de l'État," *Marchés Tropicaux*, 9 April, pp. 959-978.

Denis, J.E. (1982) "Export Performance of the Marketing Boards in LDC's—Case of Cocoa and Coffee in West Africa," in Kostecki, M.M. (Ed.) *State Trading in International Markets*, Saint Martin's Press, New York, N.Y., USA.

Ernst, E. (1982) *International Commodity Agreements*, Martinus Nijhoff Publishers, The Hague, Netherlands.

Gemmill, G. (1980) "Optimal Hedging on Futures Markets for Commodity-Exporting Nations," City University Business School, London, UK.

Johnson, L.L. (1960) "Theory of Hedging and Speculation in Commodity Futures," *Review of Economic Studies*, Vol. 27, pp. 139-151.

MacBean, A. (1966) *Export Instability and Economic Development*, Harvard University Press, Cambridge, Mass., USA.

Markowitz, H. (1952) "Portfolio Selection," *Journal of Finance*, Vol. 7, pp. 77-91.

Newbery, D.M. and Stiglitz, J.E. (1981) *Theory of Commodity Price Stabilization*, Oxford University Press, Oxford, UK.

Rolfo, J. (1980) "Optimal Hedging under Price and Quantity Uncertainty: Case of a Cocoa Producer," *Journal of Political Economy*, Vol. 88, pp. 100-116.

Sarassoro, G.F. (1988) "International Risk Management: Case of Cocoa and Coffee in the Ivory Coast," PhD dissertation, University of Illinois, Urbana, Ill., USA.

Stein, J. (1961) "Simultaneous Determination of Spot and Futures Prices," *American Economic Review*, Vol. 51, pp. 1012-1025.

DISCUSSION OPENING—*Parr Rosson* (Clemson University)

The effects of export-led economic development on GDP growth are well documented by Krueger and others. Little doubt exists that the export sector and agriculture are both critical if successful economic development is to occur in most developing nations. The paper by Sarassoro and Leuthold makes a solid contribution towards enhancing the research base in such a critical area. Further, the authors treat a difficult topic with a useful model that provides strong evidence of the benefits to effective management of export risk. Therefore, this brief comment is designed to stimulate discussion about the implications of the results and to explore one possible caveat to the theoretical base on which this research is built.

First, as the authors point out, the ratio of currency futures returns to variance were relatively high, suggesting some degree of speculative market opportunity. How might this research be extended to include the use of currency options? Although historical data on options are limited, they afford a viable alternative for risk management. In concept, a currency option would allow the exporter to hedge against an appreciating currency yet take full advantage of a decline in currency values. The use of currency options seems an important alternative, which deserves further attention.

Second, Sarassoro and Leuthold's study assumes that export revenue stability and economic growth are positively correlated. However, as Newbery and Stiglitz point out, this need not always occur. Economic signals sent via the international market to producers would be distorted under this scheme. Alternatives that appear logical in a static framework can have severe economic consequences as adjustment occurs. Linkages to employment, capital markets, and investment are crucial. Artificial stability may lead to resource misalignment, overinvestment, and higher input prices. Further, spillover effects into the rest of the economy from reduced domestic investment in critical sectors could adversely affect economic growth patterns. From a policy perspective, these questions are crucial for the Ivory Coast or any other developing nation seeking effectively to manage economic development and are worthy of further discussion.

GENERAL DISCUSSION—*T. Haque, Rapporteur* (Indian Agricultural Research Institute)

One participant asked that, assuming that high risk was involved in the export of coffee and cocoa due to price fluctuations and exchange rate variations, could we explore the possibility of farmers and government sharing the risk? The authors replied that exploring such a possibility was needed.

Another participant asked if the inclusion of transaction costs would influence the results of the study in a significant manner? The authors felt that transaction costs could be included in the optimal hedging plan and the implications studied.

Participants in the discussion included G.C.W. Ames and S.K. Ehui.

New Land Valuation System for an Economy without a Land Market

Aladár Sipos[1]

Abstract: A new land valuation system was developed, consisting of two elements: the *ecological* valuation of land, based on the fact that the natural factors (soil, climate, land relief, and hydrological factors) can be separately valued and the result expressed by a single value, and the *economic* valuation of land, based on the principle of returns to land as a factor of production. The basis for the economic valuation of land is the earning of rent-like income on farms with better than marginal land. On the basis of differences in land rent, 23 such economic districts could be formed, taking in major areas of the country. The new land valuation system accounts for more of the variation in land rents than does the old system, or a system that only uses ecological factors.

Introduction

Economic competition, intensifying both internationally and at home in the intensive stage of economic growth, increasingly demands exploration of the reserves of economic efficiency. A major opportunity to do so is inherent in a more rational use of natural resources, particularly land, where the costs of production are lower than average (or than the international market price) and thus allow the realization of lasting economic advantages, rent-like income.

Questions related to the rational use of natural resources also include the system of measures (standards) of land valuation. In Hungary, the land valuation system in use today was established more than 100 years ago. Its substance is that the net income per hectare of different land uses was determined in the then-prevailing unit of currency, the gold crown. This was a complex indicator that took into account, besides quality and fertility of the land, economic factors relevant at that time (inputs and sales opportunities). But this mode of valuation has now become obsolete. Most criticisms of it concentrate on the fact that the economic factors on the basis of which it was developed have completely changed.

Those values of income and yield (returns) that were true in the last century or in the first decades of the present one no longer hold. The management system in Hungary's agriculture has changed. Cultivation with draught animals has been replaced by modern, mechanized production. Yields have multiplied and former market relationships have completely changed. The structure of production inputs, price system, and relative prices are quite different. Profitability relations have been rearranged.

Soil fertility has changed, frequently even at the regional level, as a result of the large-scale improvements carried out over the last 20 years.

Also, development of soil science has facilitated a more up-to-date system of land valuation. In the old land valuation system, the soil could not be analyzed with modern instruments.

The fact that land has always been and always will be at the centre of economic processes also supports the need for developing and introducing a new land valuation system. The appropriation of land as a means of production is of vital interest to the various classes and groups of society. This is why, even today, several economic and sociopolitical tasks are related to land (e.g., economic regulation, withdrawal of land, expropriation, etc.). In view of the fact that Hungary does not have a land market, these issues can only be tackled by relying on a scientifically founded valuation system.

According priority to efficiency, the relative scarcity of land could be mitigated by increasing the commodity nature of land; e.g., turnover of land among the various sectors (state, cooperatives, and private individuals) and among enterprises could be accelerated and land could be ceded to such productive firms that can better use it. In spite of this, precisely because the land market has to be regulated by the state, one cannot imagine, even in the long run, that the calculated price of land can be replaced by one emerging from market turnover.

Examining the importance of up-to-date land valuation requires referring to that aspect of economic regulation that is related to the system of taxes and subsidies, as well as to the formation of agricultural prices. In Hungary, taxes levied and subsidies granted depend, first, on the quality of land. Belonging to the taxed or the subsidized category may, for some state farm or cooperative, result in additional income or loss amounting to several million forints, essentially independently of management, simply because the state purchase prices of agricultural products have not been set on the basis of individual inputs on the marginal lands. The responsibility of macrolevel managers is great; they decide the criteria on the basis of which individual farms are ranked as to whether to be subsidized or not. This ranking cannot be objectively arrived at if the system of land valuation applied was established more than 100 years ago and has become distorted since then.

New System of Complex Land Valuation

The economic valuation of land means the consideration and qualification—in the framework of a unified system—of a complex system of ecological and economic criteria. Under the new system reported on here, ecological conditions and the economic environment in which economic organizations carry out their productive activities are valued separately. This is the standard (the system of measures) that provides the basis for various economic policy measures related to land. The ecological and economic characteristics of the land are expressed by a complex land-value figure, in points. Thus, the new system of complex land valuation in Hungary rests on two pillars: ecological and economic.

As regards ecological valuation, its end product is the value characterizing the place of production. The theoretical basis of the ecological valuation is that natural factors (soil, climate, relief, and hydrological factors) can be valued separately and the final result of the valuation can be summed up in a single figure into the "value"[2] characteristic of the place of production. This figure expresses the fertility of a given land area as determined by the natural conditions with a number between 1 and 100. The ecological valuation does not comprise any economic elements.

Between 1981 and 1985, first of all because of financial considerations, instead of introducing a valuation system based on the genetic mapping of the soil, the new kind of valuation was applied to the old sample areas, using a system of values of relatively more modest content, but nationally uniform. The value figure for the place of production was adapted to the areas with reference to the limits of quality classes established in the soil classification system.

The land valuation system based on sample areas has to be gradually raised to the level of soil maps, as the soil maps gradually become available. This work has already begun. Nevertheless, until the valuation based on soil maps is performed by establishments, in the new complex land valuation system, the ecological conditions are expressed by value figures of productive areas established with the aid of valuation based on sample areas. According to control computations, they are a more realistic measure of value than the gold crown, and the economic valuation is based on them.

The system and method of the complex valuation of productive land has been established by taking into account several theoretical and methodological ideas.

As regards arable land, the computations were based on 14 crops, while with respect to other land uses the computations were based on seven kinds of fruit and two kinds of grapes, as well as grass and forest. The average cost and income data for 1980-84 were considered.

Taking into account the lessons of related discussions, a system of land valuation based on the principle of yields/returns was worked out. This system uses net returns to land as a factor of production; i.e., how much is the net income from crop production on different lands and how much of it may be attributed to the land itself. The values of output and income were worked out in variants based on basic prices, factual prices, and ideal prices.[3]

At basic and factual prices, a negative land rent was arrived at on the areas of poorer land quality. With a negative or zero land rent, the task of establishing a uniform land valuation system cannot be solved. This is why the solution chosen was to attempt to work out rent-like income produced on farms with the aid of an ideal (calculated) price.

In these computations, the basis for the ideal price was the individual inputs established with average production technology on the worst lands still being drawn into cultivation, in view of the fact that the better quality lands are only available in restricted quantity. The inputs (costs) on the worst quality (marginal) lands were complemented by an income proportionate to costs, corresponding to the national economic average.

The economic valuation of land is based on that rent-like part of income that accrues in farms with better than average land, owing to the quality and situation of the land. When quantifying the rent-like income, the normative demand for fixed and variable assets used in production was deducted from the total income from crop production and the remaining income was attributed to land as a factor of production.

Economic Regions of the New Complex Land Valuation

The delimitation of regions was approximated by analyzing the spatial differences in the rent-like income of farms. The deviation from average income was assumed to be partly traceable back to general economic factors that are not locally characteristic of one farm but are of a more general nature, based on a region comprising several farms.

Methodologically, the delimitation of regions was approached indirectly; i.e., no spatial projections of individual factors were made (this was not possible because of the information base), but the final result of the effects, the income of the farms (more exactly, the spatial situation of differences in rent-like income) was sought.

From the national average land rent belonging to the values of individual productive units, the own land rent of farms with the same ecological value deviates in such a manner that these deviations show definite geographical differences. Based on these differences, 23 such economic regions could be distinguished, which cover major areas of the country. The numbering of the regions does not involve ordering either by size or quality.

By mapping the differences, regular and unambiguous limits of regions were obtained. Delimitation was based on the agricultural area of large socialist farms.

The analyses performed provided a good starting point for judging the differentiation among regions and for assessing the differences among and within regions. The differences are significant in some regions and indicate that the impacts of economic environments are directly observable in the development of enterprise incomes.

According to the logic of computations, the economic (complex) value of productive land within the region is equal to the average land rent belonging to the values of the individual productive units. The rent of lands with the same ecological endowments but belonging to a different economic region is different. The deviation may be traced back to the modifying effect of economic conditions. Several such variants were computed where the impact of the economic environment was restricted (±30 and ±50 percent). The analyses have proved that the new economic values have a greater reallocative effect on farms than the old point system based on the gold crown. Therefore, the effects of economic factors should not be restricted in the new valuation system.

Several such factors were omitted from the system for determining the values of productive units, which, by their nature, cannot be unambiguously classified as ecological or economic, but which still have to be reckoned with when the number of complex figures is determined.

Corrections to values for individual units/farms to be considered include damage due to inland water, air and soil pollution, and outside factors on the land (electricity pylons, oil wells, gas pipelines, railways, etc.) hindering cultivation.

The first three groups of factors causing damage or improving conditions have been nationally assessed by the Land and Mapping Office. Five categories of damage were distinguished: (1) areas under inland water for 1-4 weeks (during the growing season), (2) areas under inland water for longer than 4 weeks (during the growing season), (3) polluted areas, (4) at most one outside factor per 10 ha that hinders production (oil well, electric grid), and (5) more than one hindering factor per 10 ha.

The extent of damage caused by the correcting factors was determined at the enterprise level according to the kind of damage and its extent.

Determination of the Complex Point Values of Productive Land

The number of complex points of productive land is composed in all large-scale farms of three parts: (1) the values of productive land expressing the combined effect of ecological conditions, (2) the impact of economic factors modifying the values of productive land, quantified by forming economic regions, and (3) accounting for the local correction factors hindering production, which are established at the enterprise level.

The system comprises arable land, vineyards, fruit orchards, as well as forests (the latter displaying particular features from the aspect of valuation). The economic valuation was carried out uniformly on the basis of the system developed for arable land, and also for the other land uses.

Main Characteristics of the New System of Valuation

The potential income-producing ability of productive units farmed under different ecological and economic conditions is expressed by the new order of values in a way better corresponding to reality. Analyzing the system of relations between the factors, the correlations in Table 1 have to be stressed.

Table 1—Correlation Coefficients

Factors	Land rent (*Ft*/hectare)	Plant receipts from plant production per *Ft*100 of direct costs
Gold crown	0.66	0.67
Value of productive place	0.69	0.65
Complex points	0.83	0.71

The correlation coefficients prove that the complex points expressing the combined impacts of ecological and economic factors determine the income-producing ability of land areas to a highly significant extent. The difference between 0.83 and 1.0 may be ascribed to the differences in individual management levels (leadership and work organization) of farms.

Notes

[1]Hungarian Academy of Sciences.

[2]In this system, "value" is not an economic term but a category expressing quality.

[3]Basic price means net price receipt per unit (one ton) attained by the farms. Thus, it does not comprise the factors modifying the price receipts under various titles. The actual average sales price comprises, in addition to the net price receipts from the main product, also the items modifying the price receipts.

DISCUSSION OPENING—*Gene Wunderlich* (Economic Research Service, US Department of Agriculture)

In the paper by Sipos, we are challenged to design a system for valuing land without the aid of market prices of land. Prices for both land and the products of land are administered, so decisions concerning allocation of resources must be based on criteria other than decisions of individual users of the land.

The stated purpose of the new system proposed in the paper is to improve efficiency; i.e., to better allocate nonland resources to land. Other purposes such as regulation and expropriation are mentioned, but the primary purpose is apparently resource allocation.

The proposed system of evaluation is presented as a replacement for a 100-year old procedure. However, the author fails to describe the original purpose of the ancient system. Can we assume that it was for taxation? Some additional information on the history and function of the old system would have been helpful.

The proposed valuation scheme has two components: (1) an assessment of the physical characteristics of the land and (2) an economic feature for converting physical yields into economic returns. The function of the "returns" is to provide a numeraire or index to the many diverse physical measures. It performs one of the functions of price in a market-oriented system; i.e., to provide a common basis for comparing different commodities or resources.

The values are determined by calculating net returns on various classes of land. The procedure resembles budgeting by enterprise and by environmental group (soils, slope, etc.). The land classes are apparently determined by no-rent land; i.e., land for which, after all other costs are paid, no residual remains. At this point, the idea of an "ideal price" for the land arises as the difference between average quality and quality of a particular location. The economic valuation of land, according to Sipos, is based on "rent-like" income associated with farms having better than average land. It appears to emulate Ricardian rent. The pattern of these "rent-like income differences" becomes the basis of regions. The 23 regions become the aggregative planning regions for state or cooperative management.

Are the values simply net revenue figures from budgets based on physical yield estimates? If yes, then I must ask why we assume that actual performance of a farm will be the same as its theoretical norm? What in the scheme will induce managers to neither exceed nor fail to achieve the norm? The issue is not the prescription of some calculated optimum or some abstract value of "rent-like" income, but performance of the various production units. In other words, we have here a theoretical measure of capacity, not necessarily an indicator of performance.

For the objective of achieving efficiency, why not supply the technical parameters such as soil, slope, and moisture to the managers of various production units or the state or cooperative farms and allow them to bid for the land? They would quickly create a market-like demand for land and generate rental payments to the state-owned lands. Rentals would perform the allocative function directly.

Open bid rentals would perform an additional function. They would return to the economy the value inherent in land. As Hawtrey told us a generation ago, the production value of land is its "cost-saving efficacy"; i.e., the value of labour and capital for which it substitutes. Therefore, all return to land above that necessary for transfer and information is economic rent and may be returned to society or economy that created its value.

Finally, the problems of valuation and administered prices are not unique to Hungary or other centrally planned economies. Even in market-oriented economies such as the USA, empirically specifying a land value is problematic; e.g., (1) not all transfers are under market conditions (in the USA less than 40 percent of the land is transferred by market sales), (2) observed prices may reflect special credit terms, (3) some land is purchased as a final good, not a productive resource, and (4) taxes and subsidies affect values.

GENERAL DISCUSSION—*T. Haque, Rapporteur* (Indian Agricultural Research Institute)

The points raised on this paper were: (1) what procedures are followed in evaluating the land prices when factor prices are administered in a country like Hungary?, and (2) would the results vary significantly as a result of any change in the procedure?

Sipos replied that his economic valuation of land was based on "rent-like income." Since the question of land valuation has not gained much importance in Hungary, looking into its economics is not really needed. He also agreed that adoption of different procedures could lead to different results.

Participants in the discussion included S. Gabor.

Author Index

IAAE *Occasional Papers* Nos. 1-5